Pokémon
EMERALD VERSION

PRIMA OFFICIAL GAME GUIDE

LEVI BUCHANAN

Prima Games
A Division of Random House, Inc.

3000 Lava Ridge Court, Suite 100
Roseville, CA 95661
1-800-733-3000
www.primagames.com

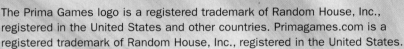

PRIMA OFFICIAL GAME GUIDE

Product Manager: Jill Hinckley
Editor: Kate Abbott
Design and Layout: Keating Design
Copyeditor: Asha Johnson

ISBN: 0-7615-5107-7
Library of Congress Catalog Card Number: 2005920955
Printed in the United States of America

05 06 07 08 LL 10 9 8 7 6 5 4 3 2 1

Acknowledgments:
Prima would like to thank Cammy Budd, Amanda Bowes, and Tom Herzog at Nintendo, and Lawrence Neves, Maya Nakamura, and Kristina Naudus at Pokémon USA, Inc.

Table of Contents

Welcome to Pokémon Emerald

Pokémon Emerald is the third jewel in the line of Game Boy Advance *Pokémon* games—the companion to the best-selling *Pokémon Ruby* and *Pokémon Sapphire*. As part of that series, *Emerald* bears some similarities to the previous games. The adventure unfolds in Hoenn, where you can collect all of the 200 Pokémon from *Ruby* and *Sapphire* in your Pokédex.

You are again cast as a young adventurer, arriving fresh-faced in Hoenn without a single Pokémon to your name. Your goal is to change that. As you wander the map, you catch Pokémon and train them into the ultimate team. With these Pokémon, you enter a series of battles with other Trainers. The biggest battles take place in Gyms, where the winner receives Gym badges. After you have conquered all of the Gyms, it's time to head to Ever Grande City and take on the Elite Four, the most tremendous Pokémon Masters in the world.

Pokémon Emerald also offers some big differences that make it an entirely new game. Rather than face either Team Magma or Team Aqua, the two rival Pokémon Trainer clans, *Emerald* casts you as a third party attempting to make peace between the two warring groups. You must track down both Team Magma and Team Aqua, stopping them before they can further their plots to forever change the face of Hoenn. You may visit some of the same locations, but your goals are often different.

Some of the Pokémon that were readily available or rare in *Pokémon Ruby* and *Sapphire* have been switched around. Some Pokémon don't appear in *Emerald* and you must trade them from the other games. A new Safari Zone offers Pokémon that were previously unavailable.

The biggest addition to *Pokémon Emerald* is the Battle Frontier. This new region is like a theme park for Pokémon Trainers. There are seven arenas to battle through, and each successful Trainer offers a greater challenge than the last. If you like to battle, you'll love this new area.

In addition to these new areas, *Pokémon Emerald* also offers a new level of connectivity. The game takes full advantage of the Wireless Adapter for connecting to other players to engage in battles or trade Pokémon. *Emerald* also links up with the GameCube game *Pokémon Colosseum*, so you can exchange Pokémon between the two games. Plus, you can link up with *Pokémon Box* and use its organizational tools to put your Pokémon in order.

A word of warning for any Trainer who thought *Pokémon Ruby* and *Sapphire* weren't enough of a challenge—wait until you play *Emerald*. The game is a lot tougher, requiring you to really hone your battle tactics. Many more Trainers walk the routes. The Gym Leaders have newer, stronger Pokémon. And if you want to become the Pokémon Champion, you'd better bring your best, because the Elite Four are like no one you've ever battled before.

Using the Guide

This book contains a wealth of information that enhances your *Pokémon Emerald* experience. The next section takes you through the basics of Pokémon catching and battling. Two walkthrough chapters help you complete your adventure in Hoenn. Check out the full Pokédex for detailed statistics and move lists on the more than 200 Pokémon you can collect in Hoenn.

Pokémon 101

The essence of *Pokémon* is battling—encountering other Pokémon Trainers in the field and engaging them in skill contests. But there's more to raising and battling Pokémon than mastering powerful move sets. To succeed as a Trainer, you must assemble the best Pokémon team you can—which doesn't necessarily mean stacking it with the strongest Pokémon in all of Hoenn. You must choose a well-rounded team, of which there are thousands of possible combinations. The following section is a primer for budding Pokémon Trainers who hope to achieve the title of Pokémon Champion. It details how to catch, raise, train, and breed Pokémon. In *Pokémon Emerald*, as with the other *Pokémon* games, you get out of it what you put in. The harder you work to build a great team, the more fun you'll have touring Hoenn and battling against both its Trainers and your friends.

Gotta Catch 'Em All

At the beginning of *Pokémon Emerald*, you receive your starter Pokémon. You can carry up to six in your team, as well as fill an entire Pokédex with more than 200 Pokémon. To round out not only your team, but also the Pokédex, search Hoenn to catch wild Pokémon. Wild Pokémon are not visible on the world map. They love to hide and jump out, surprising adventurers. If you know where to look, you'll find more Pokémon than you know what to do with!

To complete your Pokédex and get strong Pokémon, trade with friends. If you have two Game Boy Advances and a Game Boy Advance Wireless Adapter, you can trade Pokémon between the following games:

Pokémon Emerald
Pokémon Ruby and *Pokémon Sapphire*
Pokémon LeafGreen and *Pokémon FireRed*

If you have a GameCube, you can also connect and trade/manage your Pokémon with these two titles:

Pokémon Colosseum
(Game Boy Advance Game Link® cable)
Pokémon Box
(Game Boy Advance Game Link® cable)

In the Wild

Hoenn is teeming with wild Pokémon. Behind every rustling leaf or shifting blade of grass there may be a new friend. You may also reel in a new member of your Pokémon team from below the waves. Here's how to best situate yourself for a new wild Pokémon encounter in Hoenn's environments.

Grass

To encounter wild Pokémon, run through tall grass. Walk around these leafier areas, and you'll meet a wild Pokémon every few steps. There are  times when you will not want to encounter wild Pokémon. Maybe your Pokémon are weak from a tough battle. If that's the case, either stay off the grass or use an Item such as Repel to keep wild Pokémon from interrupting your journey.

Surfing/Diving

Many Pokémon live in Hoenn's waters. To encounter these Pokémon, take to the open blue by either surfing on a Pokémon's back, after finding HM03 (Surf), or slipping beneath the waves, after finding HM08 (Dive). As you skim across the surface, wild

Pokémon jump up to greet you. While under the water, look in the seaweed patches to find wild Pokémon.

Fishing

The only way to catch some Water-type Pokémon is by fishing. In order to cast your line, you must first find a Fishing Rod. There are

three types of Fishing Rods in Hoenn: Old Rod, Good Rod, and Super Rod, and each Rod offers different results. Some wild Pokémon turn up their noses at an Old Rod, preferring to wait for a Super Rod's bait. Some Pokémon nibble at the Rods, but the frequency changes depending on which Rod you use. For example, a rare Pokémon caught with the Good Rod may be common when you upgrade to the Super Rod.

Find the three different Fishing Rods here:

Dewford Town (Old Rod)

Route 118 (Good Rod)

Mossdeep City (Super Rod)

Caves

Some Pokémon linger in Hoenn's caves. They are hard to see in the dark, so even if you're not looking behind boulders, they can surprise you. If you're trying to get to a Pokémon Center with weak Pokémon, tramping through a cave is not the best route.

Rock Smash

After you learn Rock Smash (HM06), you can smash small boulders. This sometimes releases hiding Pokémon, such as Geodude. Not every rock unveils a Pokémon, but if you're going to reduce boulders to gravel, be ready for the occasional surprise.

Poké Balls

You cannot catch wild Pokémon unless you have a Poké Ball. The more Poké Balls you have, the better. There are many types of Poké Balls, some better suited for certain situations and Pokémon than others. Some Poké Balls are more expensive, and while the expensive Ultra Balls may have a higher success rate than a regular Poké Ball, your results may vary. If you have the cash, feel free to load up on expensive Poké Balls, but be aware that sometimes the best tools for the job are the cheapest.

Use this table to track the many specialty types of Poké Balls created by the Devon Corporation, Hoenn's biggest manufacturer of Poké Balls.

Name	Description	Location	Price
Dive Ball	A special Poké Ball that makes it easier to catch a Pokémon underwater.	Pokémart in Mossdeep City; Abandoned Ship	₽1,000
Luxury Ball	A super luxurious Poké Ball that makes the Pokémon caught with it like you more.	Abandoned Ship	—
Master Ball	The ultimate Poké Ball that allows you to catch a Pokémon regardless of strength, level, power, etc.	Pokémon Lottery at at the Lilycove Dept. Store; Team Magma/Aqua Hideout	—
Nest Ball	A special Poké Ball that makes it easier to capture weaker Pokémon.	Pokémart in Verdanturf Town; Route 120; Team Magma/Aqua Hideout	₽1,000

Name	Description	Location	Price
Net Ball	A special Poké Ball that makes it easier to capture Bug- and Water-type Pokémon.	Pokémart in Mossdeep City	₽1,000
Premier Ball	A special Poké Ball commemorating an event at the Devon Corporation. It's a pretty Poké Ball that Pokémon like.	After purchase of 10th Poké Ball; Rustboro City	—
Repeat Ball	A special Poké Ball that makes it easier to capture Pokémon you've caught before.	Rustboro City; Route 116	₽1,000
Timer Ball	A special Poké Ball that makes it easier to capture a Pokémon the longer your battle with it lasts.	Rustboro City; Trick House	₽1,000

Trading Pokémon

Pokémon Emerald links up to several other Game Boy Advance *Pokémon* titles. To link, report to a Pokémon Center and head upstairs. Use the Union Room to initiate a link with another Pokémon Trainer.

You can swap Pokémon back and forth, trading one of your friend's favorites for a Pokémon you want or need. In fact, some Pokémon are not available in *Pokémon Emerald* and you can only add them to the Pokédex by trading with a player of *Pokémon Ruby* or *Pokémon Sapphire*.

Some Pokémon cannot evolve to their final form unless you trade them with friends. For example, Graveler will not evolve into Golem no matter what level it is unless you trade it to a friend.

NOTE

You cannot trade Pokémon from *Pokémon LeafGreen* and *FireRed* until you complete the game and earn the National Pokédex, which encompasses all Pokémon released in North American *Pokémon* games.

CAUTION

It would be too easy to just trade high-level Pokémon from another game to *Pokémon Emerald* and start the story mode. What Gym Leader could stand up against a newcomer that magically has a team full of Legendary Pokémon, such as Groudon and Latias? You must wait until you have earned the Gym badges required for Pokémon of specific levels to obey your commands. Otherwise, that LV85 Rayquaza on your team will ignore your requests in a battle.

Evolution and Breeding

After you catch a Pokémon, you must raise it and teach it new moves. The natural result of raising a Pokémon is Evolution, the process of strengthening a Pokémon so it can take on its advanced forms. However, for some Pokémon, there is more to Evolution than gaining enough experience points to trigger a shape change. Certain Items and conditions also affect the Evolution process.

Normal Evolution Tactics

As you battle wild Pokémon and Pokémon Trainers, your Pokémon gain experience. The more experience a Pokémon gains, the more it levels up. When a Pokémon reaches a pre-determined level, it attempts to evolve into its next form, if it has one.

The more battles a Pokémon participates in, the quicker it will gain levels. Every level requires more experience than the last to achieve. When your Pokémon are at low levels, they rapidly gain levels. At a higher level, gaining levels takes longer—but the results are greater. And besides, the further you are in your adventure, the more experience you earn from Trainer battles or wild Pokémon encounters.

There are ways to share experience among your Pokémon and spread out the level gains. (It's not a good team tactic to have a couple of Pokémon at LV35 while the rest of your team is sitting idle at LV13.) Any Pokémon that participates in a battle

gains experience after a victory. So, you can set a Pokémon you want to gain levels in the "lead" position (it's the first Pokémon put into a battle) and when the battle starts, switch it out for a stronger Pokémon or one that is a better fit for the battle conditions. When the battle ends, the Pokémon you switched out in the beginning receives some of the experience earned. The more Pokémon who participate in a battle, even if they are switched in and out for just a single turn, the more the experience is spread out. This slows level gains, but it's a good way to help a team evenly level up.

You can also equip one of your Pokémon with an Exp. Share, a Held Item that automatically diverts earned experience to the bearer, even if it does not participate in a battle. This is a great tool for leveling up a new Pokémon or a weaker Pokémon. Share the Exp. Share with the team and watch those level counts creep up.

Preventing Evolution

When a Pokémon reaches the required level for Evolution, the process automatically begins. You cannot reverse it. However, you can stop the Evolution process before it is complete. This keeps the Pokémon in its current form, but it gains the extra level and whatever benefits that brings.

Why would you want to halt Evolution? For one thing, the evolved form of a Pokémon may learn new moves at a decreased pace. The move a Pokémon learns at LV39 in current form may not be learned until LV44 in its evolved form. You give up the increased stats of the evolved form to get that move sooner—there is a trade-off for everything.

You can also equip a Pokémon with the Everstone to automatically prevent Evolution. Every level gain after the required number for Evolution triggers the Evolution process. An Everstone prevents this process from starting until you un-equip it.

Special Condition Evolutions

Evolution Stones

A handful of Pokémon will not evolve unless they hold an Evolution Stone. These special Items are linked to the Pokémon's type and are in areas that match up with the Evolution Stone's namesake. For example, the Fire Stone is found in the Fiery Path. A Treasure Hunter near Mossdeep City will make you Evolution Stones if you bring him some booty from beneath the sea.

Vulpix + Fire Stone = **Ninetales**

Pikachu + Thunderstone = **Raichu**

Staryu + Water Stone = **Starmie**

Lombre + Water Stone = **Ludicolo**

Nuzleaf + Leaf Stone = **Shiftry**

Gloom + Leaf Stone = **Vileplume**

Gloom + Sun Stone = **Bellossom**

Skitty

+ Moon Stone =

Delcatty

Jigglypuff

+ Moon Stone =

Wigglytuff

Evolution via Trading

A small group of Pokémon refuses to evolve, no matter if you are at the appropriate level to trigger the process, unless you trade them with a friend. You must also equip some of these Pokémon with special Held Items before trading to trigger an Evolution.

Kadabra

+ Trade =

Alakazam

Machoke

+ Trade =

Machamp

Graveler

+ Trade =

Golem

Seadra

+ Trade w/
Dragon Scale =

Kingdra

Clamperl

+ Trade w/
Deepseascale =

Gorebyss

Clamperl

+ Trade w/
Deepseatooth =

Huntail

Taming Evolutions

Some Pokémon will not evolve unless they like their Trainer. Every Pokémon has a Friendship rating associated with their Trainer, but it cannot be checked as easily as other stats. To find out if your Pokémon likes you, stop by the Friendship rater in Verdanturf Town. This woman has a special gift for "reading" a Pokémon's pleasure, and she'll reward you with more than information, depending on whether or not your Pokémon likes you.

To increase a Pokémon's Friendship rating, spend time with it. Use the Pokémon in battles or at least keep it on your team while on an adventure. The more time it spends with you, the more it will like you. You can also give the Pokémon special treats it likes the taste of, such as Iron and Zinc. Keep your Pokémon happy by healing it when it is injured. If your Pokémon has been Poisoned, for example, the quicker you reverse the damage, the more the Pokémon will like you.

It's also possible to make a Pokémon dislike you. If you feed the Pokémon bitter-tasting herbs instead of yummy recovery Items, it will become upset. If you use a Pokémon in battle until it faints, the Pokémon will dislike you. And while leaving a Pokémon at a Day Care Center or in storage will not make it dislike you, the longer it is out of sight, the easier it is for the Pokémon to forget how much it liked you.

It is possible to curry a Pokémon's favor again should it grow indifferent or dislike you. Spend more time with it and feed it treats, and soon you will be best friends again. You can only evolve certain baby Pokémon this way. Examples include:

Azurill

+ Level Up/
Friendship =

Marill

Golbat

+ Level Up/
Friendship =

Crobat

Igglybuff

+ Level Up/
Friendship =

Jigglypuff

Pichu

+ Level Up/
Friendship =

Pikachu

7

Unique Evolutions

Wurmple evolves into one of two species when it enters its cocoon state. The time of day affects this Evolution.

Wurmple **+ Evolution at LV7 =** **Silcoon or Cascoon**

Feebas is not the prettiest Pokémon in Hoenn, but it has potential. Increase Feebas's Beauty Condition with PokéBlocks, and it evolves into a beautiful Milotic!

Feebas **+ Maxed Beauty Condition =** **Milotic**

Nincadas have a most unusual Evolutionary chain. When a Nincada evolves into Ninjask, it leaves behind a shell. If you have an empty Poké Ball in your Bag and an empty space in your team line-up when the Evolution occurs, you will discover an extra Pokémon: Shedinja.

Nincada **+ Evolution at LV20 =** **Ninjask**

Nincada **+ Evolution at LV20 + empty Poké Ball and space in belt =** **Ninjask/Shedinja**

Breeding Pokémon

You can get more Pokémon through breeding, which you can do only at the Day Care Center on Route 119. The Day Care Center's function is to "baby-sit" Pokémon while you are on an adventure. While you battle Trainers, the Pokémon left at the Day Care Center gain levels—for a price.

Sometimes magical things happen while you are gone. If you leave two Pokémon at the Day Care Center, there is a chance that when you retrieve them, there will be a surprise waiting for you: an Egg! From this Egg, you can hatch a new Pokémon, albeit one at LV5.

Certain conditions must be met to create an Egg. Most important, the two Pokémon left at the Day Care Center must be opposite genders and they must like each other. To find out if the two Pokémon are compatible, chat with the man in front of the Day Care Center. He has a sense about these things and will tell you if the two Pokémon have a spark. When an Egg is created, the resulting Pokémon is the most basic form of the female parent Pokémon.

NOTE

Pokémon keep track of family trees. You cannot mate the offspring of a Pokémon with its parent, even if they are compatible.

Some Pokémon cannot produce Eggs, no matter what. Usually these are Legendary Pokémon, such as Kyogre, so don't try to use the Day Care Center as a breeding ground for Legendary Pokémon. Use these tables to determine which Pokémon are compatible. Pokémon are compatible with other Pokémon in the same group. Some Pokémon belong to multiple groups, meaning they can breed with more Pokémon.

Rule 1: Pokémon belonging to Group 0 cannot produce Eggs.

Rule 2: The Pokémon in Groups 1–13 are compatible only with other Pokémon in their respective group(s).

GROUP 0: NO EGGS-GROUP POKÉMON

Azurill	Groudon	Magnemite	Regirock	Voltorb
Baltoy	Kyogre	Magneton	Registeel	Wynaut
Beldum	Latias	Metagross	Shedinja	
Claydol	Latios	Metang	Solrock	
Electrode	Lunatone	Rayquaza	Starmie	
Igglybuff	Pichu	Regice	Staryu	

GROUP 1: PLANT-GROUP POKÉMON

Bellossom	Gloom	Ludicolo	Roselia	Shroomish
Breloom	Lombre	Nuzleaf	Seedot	Tropius
Cacnea	Lotad	Oddish	Shiftry	Vileplume
Cacturne				

GROUP 2: BUG-GROUP POKÉMON

Beautifly	Heracross	Nincada	Silcoon	Vibrava
Cascoon	Illumise	Ninjask	Surskit	Volbeat
Dustox	Masquerain	Pinsir	Trapinch	Wurmple
Flygon				

GROUP 3: FLYING-GROUP POKÉMON

Altaria	Doduo	Pelipper	Swellow	Xatu
Crobat	Golbat	Skarmory	Taillow	Zubat
Dodrio	Natu	Swablu	Wingull	

GROUP 4: HUMANSHAPE-GROUP POKÉMON

Abra	Hariyama	Machamp	Makuhita	Sableye
Alakazam	Illumise	Machoke	Medicham	Spinda
Cacnea	Kadabra	Machop	Meditite	Volbeat
Cacturne				

GROUP 5: MINERAL-GROUP POKÉMON

Geodude	Golem	Graveler	Nosepass	Snorunt
Glalie				

GROUP 6: INDETERMINATE-GROUP POKÉMON

Banette	Duskull	Kirlia	Ralts	Weezing
Castform	Gardevoir	Koffing	Shuppet	Wobbuffet
Chimecho	Grimer	Magcargo	Slugma	
Dusclops	Gulpin	Muk	Swalot	

GROUP 7: GROUND-GROUP POKÉMON

Absol	Grumpig	Phanpy	Seedot	Torkoal
Blaziken	Kecleon	Pikachu	Seviper	Vigoroth
Camerupt	Linoone	Poochyena	Shiftry	Vulpix
Combusken	Loudred	Psyduck	Skitty	Wailmer
Delcatty	Manectric	Raichu	Slaking	Wailord
Donphan	Mawile	Rhydon	Slakoth	Walrein
Electrike	Mightyena	Rhyhorn	Spheal	Whismur
Exploud	Ninetales	Sandshrew	Spinda	Zangoose
Girafarig	Numel	Sandslash	Spoink	Zigzagoon
Golduck	Nuzleaf	Sealeo	Torchic	

GROUP 8: WATER 1-GROUP POKÉMON

Azumarill	Golduck	Lotad	Mudkip	Surskit
Clamperl	Gorebyss	Ludicolo	Pelipper	Swampert
Corphish	Horsea	Marill	Psyduck	Walrein
Corsola	Huntail	Marshtomp	Seaking	Wingull
Crawdaunt	Kingdra	Masquerain	Sealeo	
Feebas	Lombre	Milotic	Spheal	

GROUP 9: WATER 2-GROUP POKÉMON

Barboach	Goldeen	Luvdisc	Seaking	Wailord
Carvanha	Gyarados	Magikarp	Sharpedo	Whiscash
Chinchou	Lanturn	Relicanth	Wailmer	

GROUP 10: WATER 3-GROUP POKÉMON

Anorith	Corphish	Cradily	Lileep	Tentacruel
Armaldo	Corsola	Crawdaunt	Tentacool	

GROUP 11: MONSTER-GROUP POKÉMON

Aggron	Grovyle	Marshtomp	Rhyhorn	Treecko
Aron	Lairon	Mudkip	Sceptile	Tropius
Exploud	Loudred	Rhydon	Swampert	Whismur

GROUP 12: FAIRY-GROUP POKÉMON

Azumarill	Glalie	Minun	Raichu	Skitty
Breloom	Jigglypuff	Pikachu	Roselia	Snorunt
Castform	Marill	Plusle	Shroomish	Wigglytuff
Delcatty	Mawile			

GROUP 13: DRAGON-GROUP POKÉMON

Altaria	Gyarados	Magikarp	Sceptile	Shelgon
Bagon	Horsea	Milotic	Seadra	Swablu
Feebas	Kingdra	Salamence	Seviper	Treecko
Grovyle				

Breeding Moves and Stats

Breeding does more than create new Pokémon. Be clever about which Pokémon you breed so you're sure to create new Pokémon that have greater talents than their parents did at their early stages, such as moves and increased stats.

Newborn Pokémon inherit stats from the parent of the opposite gender. If the baby Pokémon is male, it enjoys the stat increases of the female parent Pokémon. If the baby Pokémon is female, it earns the stat upgrades of the male parent Pokémon. You can use this to your advantage if you have two compatible Pokémon of opposite genders and both have excellent skills and stats. The offspring will be LV5, but loaded with power.

Your new Pokémon can also be on the receiving end of the high-level moves its parents took a long time to learn. Three types of moves can be taught through this strategy: Learned Moves, Inherited Moves, and Egg Moves.

Learned Moves: Moves any Pokémon caught in the wild would know at LV5.

Inherited Moves: Moves learned through the Evolutionary process or via a TM can be passed from the male parent Pokémon, even if the move cannot be learned or used until after LV5.

Egg Moves: Egg Moves are learned from the male parent Pokémon, but these are different than Inherited Moves. Egg Moves are moves the Pokémon would not normally be able to learn.

When a Pokémon hatches, it has the moves a wild Pokémon at LV5 would know. For example, a new Treecko will know Pound and Leer. The Pokémon has enough room to learn two more moves; these spots can be filled with Inherited Moves. Inherited Moves and Egg Moves take greater precedence over Learned Moves, so if the Pokémon has access to more moves than you have empty space for, it will replace the Learned Moves with the Inherited and Egg Moves.

There are ways to breed a Pokémon with impressive move sets. If both parents know the same high-level move, the baby Pokémon will also know it, even though it is LV5. Plus, TM moves you would normally have one shot at using can be "re-used" by breeding the move down from the male parent Pokémon.

The included Pokédex details which Egg Moves the newborn Pokémon can learn, so check the entries before you breed to make the "ultimate" Pokémon. Play your cards right to have a really amazing Pokémon on your team. It takes a little time, but the results are worth it.

Hatching Eggs

When the Day Care Center alerts you of a new Egg, you must work at hatching it. First, you must have an empty space on your team to accept the Egg. Without it, the Day Care Center will keep the Egg. After you have the Egg, leave it in your Active Pokémon list to hatch it. Every Egg has a special number of steps required to hatch it, so tramp around Hoenn and you'll soon have a bouncing baby Pokémon.

TIP

Breed two of the same Pokémon to hatch the resulting Egg faster.

Pokémon Battles

There are two types of battles in *Pokémon Emerald*: battles against wild Pokémon and those against Pokémon Trainers. To succeed at a battle, you must have a basic understanding of the battle system, from selecting moves to pitting Pokémon against weaker types. Battles with wild Pokémon are always 1-on-1 Battles. Battles with Pokémon Trainers can be either 1-on-1 or 2-on-2.

Course of Action

When the battle starts, the first Pokémon on your team enters the field. This Pokémon is called your lead Pokémon. You can switch out your lead Pokémon when you're not in a battle. After your lead Pokémon is outside of battle, it's time to choose a course of action. You have four choices:

Fight: The Fight command allows you to tell the Pokémon which move to use in the battle, whether it is offensive or defensive. Each move has a limited number of uses, which is detailed by its Power Point (PP) level. You can replenish PP between battles at a Pokémon Center, or in battle with a recovery Item.

Pokémon: This command allows you to shift Pokémon in and out of battle. Is your Pokémon not doing so well against its opponent? Do you have a Pokémon in reserve who is better suited for a particular battle? Call back the Pokémon in the battle and replace it with another Pokémon from the team.

Bag: Your Bag is full of Items, such as Potions and berries. You can use these Items in battle to recover HP or increase your fighting abilities. If you are battling a wild Pokémon, dip into your Bag to get a Poké Ball with which to catch it. Using an Item from your Bag completes your turn. You cannot complete a battle move and use an Item in the same turn.

Run: You cannot flee from a Trainer Battle, but if you are battling against a wild Pokémon, use this command to exit the fight. This is not always successful. Some opponent Pokémon have special abilities or moves that can prevent you from running.

Affect Random Opponents: You cannot direct certain moves at an individual opponent during 2-on-2 Battles. Rayquaza's Outrage, for example, randomly attacks either of the opponent Pokémon during the course of attack.

Affect All Pokémon: Some attack moves affect your own Pokémon during battle. When you cast a move that affects every Pokémon outside of battle, be sure that your Pokémon will not be eliminated because of it. Make sure you either have enough HP, or that it will finish the battle in your favor, even if it causes your Pokémon to faint.

Trainer Battles

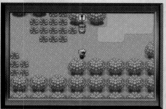

Hoenn's fields are full of Pokémon Trainers looking for battles. If you walk into their line of sight, the Trainer challenges you to a battle. You cannot refuse, and you must battle until all of one Trainer's Pokémon have fainted (lost all HP).

There are a few different battle types in *Pokémon Emerald*. In addition to regular 1-on-1 Battles, there are 2-on-2 Battles where two Trainers send out a single Pokémon each. In these battles, you must respond with two Pokémon. Your lead Pokémon and the second Pokémon are automatically sent into the battle. There are also some rare four-Trainer battles where you have an ally. During these battles, you and your ally each send out your lead Pokémon.

Using Moves

Offensive moves can dish out different kinds of damage. Some moves direct damage at a single opponent. Other moves affect every Pokémon in the battle.

Affect One Opponent: In 1-on-1 Battles, this is a given. However, during 2-on-2 Battles, you must select which opponent Pokémon you want to target with a move.

Affect Two Opponents: Some moves in 2-on-2 Battles affect both of your opponent Pokémon. HM03 (Surf) is a good example of this. It brings a wave of water crashing on both opponents.

Pokémon Types and Battle Strategies

The true essence of a Pokémon battle is the art of matching up your opponent Pokémon's type with a move type that will send it reeling. Every Pokémon is assigned a specific type, such as Fire or Steel. Every type has at least one type against which it is weak. For example, Water-type Pokémon are weak against Electric-type moves.

Because of this system, you must have a well-rounded Pokémon team that spans several types. It's a good idea to have Water-, Fire-, and Electric-type Pokémon on your team. Beyond those three types, you may wish to concentrate on raising strong Rock- and Ground-type Pokémon, as well as Psychic- and Flying-type Pokémon. However you assemble your team, though, is up to you.

This chart details the strengths and weakness of Pokémon types and move types. Use the legend to determine which kinds of moves you should use against opponent Pokémon, as well as to identify when you should switch out your Pokémon should an opponent Trainer send in something that exploits your weaknesses.

NOTE

In *Pokémon Emerald*, many Pokémon are dual-type, meaning they have two types, such as Grass and Water. In some situations, the second type can work against what would normally be a power move. The Fire-type attack that would damage a Grass-type Pokémon is negated by the secondary Water-type.

SINGLE-TYPE POKÉMON-MOVE TYPE COMPATIBILITY

	NORMAL	FIRE	WATER	GRASS	ELECTRIC	ICE	FIGHTING	POISON	GROUND	FLYING	PSYCHIC	BUG	ROCK	GHOST	DRAGON	DARK	STEEL
NORMAL													▲	■			▲
FIRE		▲	▲	●		●						●	▲		▲		●
WATER		●	▲	▲					●				●		▲		
GRASS		▲	●	▲				▲	●	▲		▲	●		▲		▲
ELECTRIC			●	▲	▲				■	●					▲		
ICE		▲	▲	●		▲			●	●					●		▲
FIGHTING	●					●		▲		▲	▲	▲	●	■		●	●
POISON				●				▲	▲				▲	▲			■
GROUND		●		▲	●			●		■		▲	●				●
FLYING				●	▲		●					●	▲				▲
PSYCHIC							●	●			▲					■	▲
BUG		▲		●			▲	▲		▲	●			▲		●	▲
ROCK		●				●	▲		▲	●		●					▲
GHOST	■										●			●		▲	▲
DRAGON															●		▲
DARK							▲				●			●		▲	▲
STEEL		▲	▲		▲	●							●				▲

● = 2x damage ▲ = 1/2 damage ■ = It has no effect

Damage Multipliers

To be a successful Trainer, you must master damage multipliers. Depending on what type of move you use against an opponent Pokémon, you can see a variety of effects. You can also affect the amount of damage done by holding Items that affect a Pokémon's strength (such as giving Charcoal to a Fire-type Pokémon) or scoring the occasional Critical Hit. Certain moves, such as TM18 (Rain Dance), affect a Pokémon's attacks, depending on the type of Pokémon in the battle.

MULTIPLIERS

CONDITION	MULTIPLIER
Move is the same type as Pokémon	1.5x
Move is effective against opponent's type	2–4x
Move scores a Critical Hit	2x
Pokémon has an Item that raises the move's Strength	1.1x
TM18 (Rain Dance) or TM11 (Sunny Day) effects (depending on move)	1.5x or .5x

Battle Messages

During a battle's course, you may see messages at the screen's bottom. These messages let you know if the attacks you are using (or the attacks being used against you) are working, if an attack is not effective, or if your Pokémon has scored a Critical Hit.

BATTLE MESSAGES

MESSAGE	DAMAGE MULTIPLIER
"It's super-effective!"	x2
No message	x1
"It's not very effective."	x0.5
"It has no effect."	x0
"A Critical Hit!"	x2

TIP

If a Pokémon uses a move that is the same type as itself (for example, a Water-type Pokémon uses a Water-type Move), the damage is 1.5x greater.

Status Anomalies

Some moves are Special Attacks that cause additional effects beyond damage. These attacks cause status changes, such as Poison and Sleep, which have lasting effects beyond the single turn. You can cure many of these status changes with healing Items, such as Antidote or Awakening. A trip to the Pokémon Center can also reverse these effects.

STATUS ANOMALIES AND THEIR CURES

Status Problem	Effect	Recovery Moves	Recovery Items
Attraction	Pokémon is Attracted to its opponent, and will not attack it 50% of the time.	Switch Pokémon with another Pokémon.	Red Flute, Mental Herb
Burned	Pokémon takes burn damage every round. This status anomaly also lowers the Pokémon's Attack.	Refresh, TM44 (Rest)	Burn Heal, Full Heal, Full Restore, Heal Powder, Lava Cookie, Rawst Berry, Lum Berry
Confusion	Pokémon is Confused and may attack itself.	Switch Pokémon with another. Recovers automatically after a number of turns.	Yellow Flute, Full Heal, Heal Powder, Full Restore, Persim Berry
Fainted	Pokémon cannot participate in battle.	Revive and recover at Pokémon Center.	Revive, Max Revive, Revival Herb
Flinch	Pokémon flinches and cannot attack that round.	This condition lasts only one turn.	N/A
Frozen	Pokémon cannot move from the frostbite.	Recovers when attacked by Fire-type moves or automatically over time.	Ice Heal, Full Heal, Full Restore, Heal Powder, Lava Cookie, Aspear Berry, Lum Berry
Paralysis	25% of time your Pokémon tries to attack, it can't move because of Paralysis. This status anomaly also lowers your Pokémon's Speed.	Refresh, TM44 (Rest)	Parlyz Heal, Lava Cookie, Full Heal, Full Restore, Heal Powder, Cheri Berry, Lum Berry
Poison	Pokémon takes damage every round. Depending upon the type of Poisoning, the damage amount inflicted may increase every round.	Refresh, TM44 (Rest)	Antidote, Full Heal, Full Restore, Heal Powder, Lava Cookie, Pecha Berry, Lum Berry
Sleep	Pokémon is unable to move while it remains asleep.	Awakens automatically after a number of battle rounds.	Awakening, Full Heal, Full Restore, Heal Powder, Lava Cookie, Chesto Berry, Lum Berry, Blue Flute

Trainer Knowledge

Pokémon Natures

Your Pokémon have Natures, things that add to their individual personalities. Natures affect the stat increases your Pokémon enjoys while leveling up. Use this table to judge how your Pokémon will change and grow with each level.

POKÉMON NATURES

Stat	Hardy	Lonely	Adamant	Naughty	Brave	Bold	Docile	Impish	Lax	Relaxed	Modest	Mild	Bashful	Rash	Quiet	Calm	Gentle	Careful	Quirky	Sassy	Timid	Hasty	Jolly	Naïve	Serious
Attack	—	0	0	0	0	X	—	—	—	—	X	—	—	—	—	X	—	—	—	—	X	—	—	—	—
Defense	—	X	—	—	—	0	—	0	0	0	—	X	—	—	—	—	X	—	—	—	—	X	—	—	—
Sp. Attack	—	—	X	—	—	—	—	X	—	—	0	0	—	0	0	—	—	X	—	—	—	—	X	—	—
Sp. Defense	—	—	—	X	—	—	—	—	X	—	—	—	—	X	—	0	0	0	—	0	—	—	—	X	—
Speed	—	—	—	—	X	—	—	—	—	X	—	—	—	—	X	—	—	—	—	X	0	0	0	0	—

0 = Easy to raise the stat   X = Hard to raise the stat

Manually Raising Stats

You can also increase your Pokémon's stats manually by feeding it special Items between battles. These Items affect stats in a positive way.

Calcium: Raises the base number of the Pokémon's Special Attack and Special Defense

Carbos: Raises base Speed points

HP Up: Raises the base number of Hit Points

Iron: Raises the base amount of the Pokémon's Defense

Protein: Raises the base sum of the Pokémon's Attack

In-Field Moves

While exploring Hoenn, you find eight Hidden Machines (HM) that teach your Pokémon new moves it can use both in and out of battle. These special moves help you negotiate Hoenn's landscapes, from the salty seas to the dark caves.

HM FIELD ABILITIES

MOVE	ABILITY
HM01 (Cut)	Slice through shrubbery to create a path.
HM02 (Fly)	Take to the skies and instantly travel to any city you've previously visited.
HM03 (Surf)	Travel across water on a Pokémon's back.
HM04 (Strength)	Move boulders.
HM05 (Flash)	Light up caves.
HM06 (Rock Smash)	Reduce large cracked boulders to rubble (and find something underneath).
HM07 (Dive)	Swim deep beneath the ocean's surface.
HM08 (Waterfall)	Scale waterfalls.

OTHER MOVES WITH FIELD ABILITIES

MOVE	ABILITY
Sweet Scent	Attracts wild Pokémon, increasing the random battle frequency.
Teleport	Teleport automatically to the last Pokémon Center visited.
TM28 (Dig)	Tunnel out of caves.
TM43 (Secret Power)	Create a Secret Base from holes in mountains, large trees, and blades of tall grass.

A Quick Walkthrough

If time is of the essence, check out this walkthrough first. Follow the chart from the beginning of your adventure in tiny Littleroot Town all the way to your showdown with the Elite Four. This chart details the places you must visit in the right order to unlock all the pivotal events. However, we recommend you use the next chapter, the full guide to the world of Hoenn, to plan your adventure, and use this chart for reference.

Littleroot Town Pg. 18
- Set the clock in your bedroom on the second floor.
- Talk to Prof. Birch's kid next door.

Route 101 Pg. 20
- Rescue Prof. Birch from the Zigzagoon. Choose a Pokémon (Mudkip, Torchic, or Treecko) with which to battle.

Littleroot Town Pg. 18
- Get the Pokémon you chose earlier from Prof. Birch.

Route 101 Pg. 20

Oldale Town Pg. 21

Route 103 Pg. 22
- "Rival" Battle #1 against Prof. Birch's kid (Brendan or May).

Oldale Town Pg. 21

Route 101 Pg. 20

Littleroot Town Pg. 18
- Go to Prof. Birch's lab. Get the Pokédex and first set of Poké Balls.
- Get the Running Shoes from Mom.

Route 101 Pg. 20

Oldale Town Pg. 21

Route 102 Pg. 23
- Encounter your first Pokémon Trainers on the road.

Petalburg City Pg. 24
- Speak to Dad at the Petalburg Gym.
- Help Wally catch his first Pokémon.

Route 104 Pg. 26

Petalburg Woods Pg. 28
- Protect the Devon researcher from an attack by Team Aqua.

Rustboro City Pg. 29
- Get HM01 (Cut) from the Cutter's House.
- **Take on Roxanne at the Rustboro Gym and win the Stone Badge.**
- Help the Devon Corporation get the Devon Goods back from Team Aqua.

Route 116 Pg. 32

Map of Hoenn

LILYCOVE CITY

MOSSDEEP CITY

MT. PYRE

SOOTOPOLIS CITY

EVER GRANDE CITY

SKY PILLAR

PACIFIDLOG TOWN

The Keys to Hoenn
Maps and Events

The streamlined walkthrough was designed to give you a basic sense of what maps need to be visited and what events need to be completed to play through the main story. However, there is so much more to Pokémon Emerald than walking from route to route, catching Pokémon. This section contains detailed maps, shop and move lists, and the many things you can do in each area. Each map is accompanied by the Pokémon you will encounter on that specific route—so stock up on Poké Balls in town before heading into a region with a specific Pokémon you truly want.

NOTE

Many routes have areas that can be accessed only after you receive a Hidden Machine (HM) and teach the new move, such as HM03 (Surf) or HM06 (Rock Smash), to one of your Pokémon.

Littleroot Town

Moves Needed: *None*

ITEMS

- Amulet Coin
- Pokédex
- Poké Ball x5
- Potion
- Running Shoes
- S.S. Ticket

POKÉMON APPEARANCES

POKÉMON	CONDITIONS
Mudkip	Awarded to you after rescuing Prof. Birch
Torchic	Awarded to you after rescuing Prof. Birch
Treecko	Awarded to you after rescuing Prof. Birch

Welcome to your new home: Littleroot Town. The small township is located in the southern region of Hoenn, surrounded on all sides by thick forest. Though you will stray far from home while exploring Hoenn and becoming a Pokémon Master, this place will always remain special.

Event 1: New Neighborhood

Pokémon Emerald begins with you making your new home in Littleroot Town. Your father is already away at work, so you and your mother must take care of getting everything put away. Thankfully, the moving company's Pokémon are doing most of

the heavy lifting. Your mother suggests you go upstairs and check out your new room. Set the clock on the wall to the correct time to get things started.

Which house you live in depends on whether you decided to play as a boy or girl. If you chose to be a girl, you live in the house on the right. If you chose to be a boy, you live in the house on the left. When it comes time to visit your neighbor, which is soon, visit the house just opposite of yours.

Event 2: Get Neighborly

Now that you are all settled in to your new home, it's time to meet your neighbors. Littleroot Town is a quiet place, but the people next door seem inter-

esting. Head to the house next to yours and introduce yourself to the Birch family. Prof. Birch is away doing research, but both his wife and your new friend (May or Brendan, depending on whether you chose a boy or girl—your new friend will be the opposite gender) are still home. Head upstairs to meet Prof. Birch's kid.

Event 3: Rescue Prof. Birch

After meeting the Birch family, it's time to head out into Hoenn. As you head north to Route 101, though, you run into Prof. Birch—and he's not alone. The professor is being chased by a wild Zigzagoon and he needs your help. Fortunately, Prof. Birch left his knapsack full of Poké Balls nearby.

To help him, Prof. Birch allows you to select one of the three Poké Balls in his bag. This will be your first Pokémon. You can choose either Water-type Mudkip, Grass-type Torchic, or Fire-type Treecko. After selecting the Pokémon you like the most, battle the Zigzagoon and save Prof. Birch.

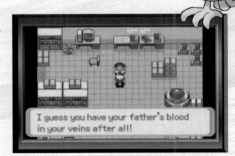

Prof. Birch is grateful for your assistance. Back at his Lab in town, he allows you to keep the Pokémon you selected. With your first Pokémon, you can now head out of town and start battling.

NOTE

There is no "correct" Pokémon to choose when Prof. Birch allows you to pick from his three Poké Balls. Choose the one with the look and moves you like the most. As you play, you can catch other Pokémon to complement your first choice.

Event 4: After Rival Battle #1

That's great! Just like me!
I've got something for you, too!

Words reaches Prof. Birch quickly that you successfully battled his kid. He is impressed with your natural talent and gives you a Pokédex so you can catalog your finds. His kid also gives you five Poké Balls, essential for catching wild Pokémon.

Before you leave Littleroot Town again, though, stop at home. Your mother has a present for you: Running Shoes. These speedy sneakers

Here, honey! If you're going out on an adventure, wear these RUNNING SHOES. ♥

help you cover ground quickly. Manners matter, though, and you cannot run while inside other people's homes or most buildings. But outside of battles? Run free!

Event 5: After Getting HM03 (Surf)

After you receive the Balance Badge from your father at Petalburg Gym, return to your home. Show the Badge to your mother and she

absolutely beams—and gives you an Amulet Coin. This helpful Item can double the amount of money won in a battle.

Event 6: After Defeating The Elite Four

Defeating the Elite Four is quite an achievement. Head home and share the news with your parents. They proudly give you

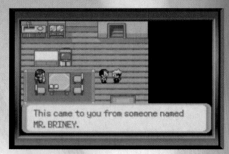

This came to you from someone named MR. BRINEY.

a ticket for the S.S. *Tidal*, Capt. Stern's new ferry. The ferry, which is finally ready to set to sea, can be found in both Lilycove City and Slateport City.

Route 101

Moves Needed: None

ITEMS
None

To Oldale Town

To Littleroot Town

POKÉMON APPEARANCES

POKÉMON	CONDITIONS
Poochyena	Very Common
Wurmple	Very Common
Zigzagoon	Common

Event 1: Catch 'Em

This route has three different Pokémon. However, until you receive the five Poké Balls from Prof. Birch's child, you

can only battle the wild Pokémon you encounter. Return to this route once you get those Poké Balls and start padding your new Pokédex.

Oldale Town

Moves Needed: None

Oldale Town is a small township near Littleroot Town. It's the first place you encounter both a Pokémart and a Pokémon Center. Chat with everybody in town—not only do they have interesting things to say, but you may be surprised by their generosity.

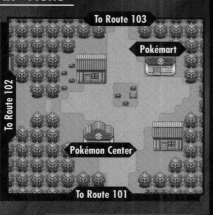

POKÉMART MERCHANDISE	
ITEM	**PRICE**
Poké Ball	₽200
Potion	₽300
Antidote	₽100
Parlyz Heal	₽200
Awakening	₽250

Event 1: Speak to Pokémart Representative

When you first arrive in Oldale, visit the Pokémart representative standing near the front door of the Pokémart. The representative is happy to tell you about the shop and she even hands out free samples of the wares.

Event 2: West is a No-Go

The way to Route 102 is blocked by a researcher. The scientist is sketching what he believes are footprints from rare Pokémon. You can access Route 102 only after heading up through Route 103 and finding Prof. Birch's child. When you come back, the researcher sheepishly stands aside.

Event 3: The Pokémon Center

You definitely want to stop by the Pokémon Center while visiting Oldale Town. Every city in Hoenn hosts a Pokémon Center, which is the most useful place for a budding Trainer. The woman at the main counter on the first floor is always happy to heal your Pokémon for free. The PC next to the counter lets you access your storage to switch out Pokémon and access stored Items. Because your pockets

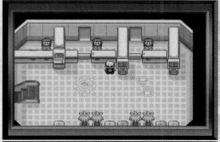

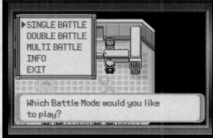

aren't bottomless, you'll find yourself stopping by the PC often, especially if you're a shopper.

Head upstairs to find the connectivity center, where you can link up with other *Pokémon* players. You can trade Pokémon, exchange Secret Base information, and enjoy some fun battles. If you have the Wireless Adapter, you can do even more stuff up here!

NOTE

The prices for Items at the Pokémarts are consistent at every shop across Hoenn. A Poké Ball costs the same in Oldale Town as it does in Slateport City.

Route 103

Moves Needed: _HM01 (Cut), HM03 (Surf)_

To Oldale Town

To Route 110

POKÉMON APPEARANCES ON LAND

POKÉMON	CONDITIONS
Poochyena	Very Common
Wingull	Common
Zigzagoon	Common

POKÉMON APPEARANCES IN WATER

POKÉMON	CONDITIONS
Magikarp	Very Common (Old Rod, Good Rod)
Pelipper	Rare
Sharpedo	Very Common (Super Rod)
Tentacool	Very Common; Common (Old Rod, Good Rod)
Wailmer	Common (Good Rod); Very Common (Super Rod)
Wingull	Common

ITEMS

- Cheri Berries x4
- Leppa Berries x2
- Guard Spec.
- PP Up

SHORTCUT ALERT

Once you have HM03 (Surf), you can cross the water to the east in Route 103 and easily access both Mauville City and Slateport City via Route 110.

Prof. Birch's child is waiting for a battle in Route 103. In fact, this is the first of a series of battles with the kid. With each battle, Prof. Birch's child gets better and better, coming at you with more experienced Pokémon and smarter battle strategies. Enjoy this first battle while you can, because he or she will not be so easy later in your adventure.

Prof. Birch's child uses a different Pokémon in the battle depending on which Pokémon you selected from the Professor after the rescue in Littleroot Town. If you chose Torchic, look out for Mudkip. If you chose Mudkip, look out for Treecko. And if you chose Treecko, expect to face Torchic.

Event 1: Battle with Prof. Birch's Child

TIP

The battle may seem mismatched because Prof. Birch's child brings out a Pokémon that offsets yours, but keep at it and you will emerge victorious.

Route 102

Move Needed: *HM03 (Surf)*

To Petalburg City

To Oldale Town

ITEMS
- Oran Berries x2
- Pecha Berries x2
- Potion

POKÉMON APPEARANCES ON LAND

POKÉMON	CONDITIONS
Lotad	Common
Poochyena	Common
Ralts	Rare
Seedot	Rare
Wurmple	Common
Zigzagoon	Common

POKÉMON APPEARANCES IN WATER

POKÉMON	CONDITIONS
Corphish	Common (Good Rod); Very Common (Super Rod)
Goldeen	Common (Good Rod); Rare (Old Rod)
Magikarp	Very Common (Old Rod, Good Rod)
Marill	Very Common
Surskit	Rare

Event 1: Trainer Battles

You encounter your first Trainer battles while walking through Route 102. However, Trainers will not challenge you unless you either speak to them or they catch your eye. Trainers sometimes look around. If you want to avoid a battle, wait to see if the Trainer looks elsewhere and then slip out of sight. However, avoiding Trainer battles is not the way to become the best Trainer in Hoenn. Every successful battle results in experience points for your Pokémon, plus you receive cash. You'll need as much cash as you can get to shop for needed Items.

Event 2: Berry Picking

There are berry trees all over Hoenn, and the first ones you find are along Route 102. Berries have many uses—they negate status changes, they heal Pokémon, and they can also be used to create PokéBlocks.

When you pick the berries, the tree crumbles back to the dirt. You could pocket the berries and keep walking, but that's hardly the neighborly thing to do. You are encouraged to plant berries in the vacant soil so they can grow new trees. All it takes is one berry to sprout a new tree, so keep one

berry from your harvest and plant the other. If there are particular berries that you are fond of or use more than others, plant those whenever possible. The berries may take time to grow, but you'll soon have a bumper crop all over Hoenn of your favorite berries.

Petalburg City

Move Needed: *HM03 (Surf)*

Petalburg City is the biggest township you have visited yet. The city has its own Gym, which is where you must go to prove yourself as a Pokémon Trainer. Although you cannot compete in the Petalburg Gym just yet (patience, young Trainer) stop in and say hello to the very familiar (and familial) Gym Leader.

ITEMS

- Balance Badge
- Ether
- HM03 (Surf)
- Max Revive
- TM42 (Facade)

To Route 102

POKÉMON APPEARANCES IN WATER

POKÉMON	CONDITIONS
Marill	Very Common

POKÉMART MERCHANDISE

ITEM	PRICE
Poké Ball	P200
Potion	P300
Antidote	P100
Parlyz Heal	P200
Awakening	P250
Escape Rope	P550
Repel	P350
X Speed	P350
X Attack	P500
X Defend	P550
Orange Mail	P50
Great Ball	P600
Super Potion	P700

Event 1: Visit the Gym

Your father runs the Gym in Petalburg City, so be sure to stop there as soon as you visit town. You need to compete at every Gym in Hoenn, but your father will not battle you until you have four Gym badges. However, he offers some words of encouragement and sends you on your way. Your father has a Gym badge that is essential to your adventure, though, so come back to him as soon as you have the required four Gym badges.

Event 2: Meet Wally

Much like Prof. Birch's child (and a certain gentleman in sunglasses), Wally is somebody you encounter throughout your adventures in Hoenn. Wally is about to head to Verdanturf Town for an extended stay, but your father thinks he should have a Pokémon to keep him company. Accompany Wally to the grassy Route 102 and help him catch his first Pokémon, Ralts. Perhaps having a Pokémon will be enough to turn Wally's health situation around?

Event 3: Gym Leader Battle #5— Norman

Norman, Petalburg Gym Leader

Pokémon Type:

NORMAL

Recommended Move Type:

FIGHTING

GYM LEADER'S POKÉMON

POKÉMON	LV	TYPE
Vigoroth	LV27	NORMAL
Slaking	LV31	NORMAL
Spinda	LV27	NORMAL
Linoone	LV29	NORMAL

Once you have earned four Gym badges, it's time to return to Petalburg and battle your father, Norman. But before you can challenge your father, you must battle at least three Trainers first. The Petalburg Gym is set up as a series of rooms. Each room contains a Trainer who specializes in a way of battling, such as causing Confusion or using HP recovery. A sign on each door explains what kind of tactics to expect from the Trainer just beyond.

Your father has set up the Gym this way to test your various methods for reacting to different battling tactics. But when it finally comes time to battle your father, you're going to need more than just a strong Pokémon. Your father has several Potions, so have Pokémon with good moves that can counter his Pokémon types. If you can keep on top of his Pokémon with super effective moves, he won't have a chance to break out his Potions.

ITEMS WON

Balance Badge: Increases your Pokémon's Defense and allows you to use HM03 (Surf) on the field.

TM42 (Facade)

TIP

You only need to battle three Trainers to reach Norman, but why not take on all seven and earn the extra experience points?

Event 4: Post-Gym Pick-Up

Obtained the HM03!

After you win the Balance Badge at the Petalburg Gym, visit Wally's House just next door. His father, so pleased with the help you've given Wally, rewards you with HM03 (Surf). This Hidden Machine is pivotal for exploring the waterways and seas of Hoenn.

25

Pokémon EMERALD VERSION

NOTE

There's more to do in town than just visit the Gym and see Wally. When you visit the Pokémon Center, look for a gentleman standing near the PC in the corner. The fellow is interested in your exploits and would love to hear all about them. From a collection of available words, assemble a brief profile of yourself and tell it to gentleman.

Don't forget to explore the two small ponds in Petalburg once you receive HM03 (Surf). There are some goodies near the shores that you shouldn't be without!

Route 104

Moves Needed: *HM01 (Cut), HM03 (Surf)*

ITEMS

- Cheri Berries x2
- Leppa Berries x2
- Oran Berries x2
- Pecha Berries x2
- Poké Ball x2
- Potion
- PP Up x2
- TM09 (Bullet Seed)
- Wailmer Pail
- White Herb
- X Accuracy

FLOWER SHOP MERCHANDISE

ITEM	PRICE
Big Plant	₽5,000
Colorful Plant	₽5,000
Gorgeous Plant	₽5,000
Pretty Flower	₽3,000
Red Plant	₽3,000
Tropical Plant	₽3,000

POKÉMON APPEARANCES ON LAND

POKÉMON	CONDITIONS
Marill	Common
Poochyena	Very Common
Taillow	Common
Wingull	Common
Wurmple	Common

POKÉMON APPEARANCES IN WATER

POKÉMON	CONDITIONS
Magikarp	Very Common (Old Rod, Good Rod, Super Rod)
Pelipper	Rare
Wingull	Common

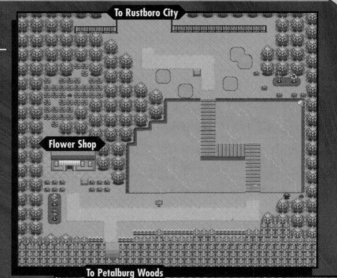

To Rustboro City

Flower Shop

To Petalburg Woods

To Petalburg Woods

Mr. Briney's House

To Petalburg City

To Route 105

Event 1: Visit Mr. Briney's House

On your way to the Petalburg Woods to the north of this route, look for a small cottage near the shore with a dock next to it. The owner, Mr. Briney, isn't home right now. However, you return later in your adventure for some help from Mr. Briney—after you've helped him.

Event 2: Get a Green Thumb

After passing through Petalburg Woods, you come upon a small flower shop. It's hard to miss it as the front of the building is decorated with lots of pretty petals. The women running the flower shop aren't selling their wares just yet. They're too busy tending the plants. Talk to them to get the Wailmer Pail, a helpful tool for growing berries in Hoenn.

Check back with the shop after you've completed more of your adventure. As soon as you can start decorating your Secret Base, these women will sell you some plants to liven up the place.

TIP

After you receive the Wailmer Pail from the flower shop, return to your previous berry seedlings and water them. This helps them grow faster. Water them often and you'll be pleasantly surprised with the results.

TIP

Be Friendly!

Talk to everybody in Hoenn. Almost everybody you meet is gracious and willing to chat, but some of them also share their possessions with you. For example, the young man outside of the flower shop has TM09 (Bullet Seed). He's merrily spitting seeds and would love to share the talent with your Pokémon for absolutely free.

Event 3: 2-on-2 Battle

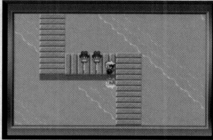 

After passing through Petalburg Woods, you must cross a bridge. However, there is no way to get past a pair of twins named Mia and Gia. These girls offer you your first 2-on-2 Battle. The battle setup is simple. The first two Pokémon in your pack are brought out. So, before reaching the twins, move the Pokémon you want to use in battle up to the first and second slots.

When you enter a 2-on-2 Battle, you can choose a specific recipient of each of your Pokémon's moves. That includes support moves in addition to offensive moves. For example, if you have a move that raises Attack, you can use it on your other Pokémon. This also raises a challenge. If you have a move that affects all of the Pokémon in the battle, such as Selfdestruct, your other Pokémon will be affected negatively, too.

Event 4: After Visiting Devon Corporation President

Once you have helped the Devon Corporation in Rustboro City and accepted the request of the President, return to Mr. Briney's seaside cottage. The man is so grateful that you helped him retrieve his pet Pokémon that he will ferry you across the sea in his boat. This is the only way to get to Dewford Town right now.

Petalburg Woods

Move Needed: *HM01 (Cut)*

The Petalburg Woods connects the northern and southern halves of Route 104. The thick forest setting is home to several wild Pokémon, so make sure you have a Poké Ball or two before heading in—especially if you can access the right half of the woods via HM01 (Cut).

To Route 104

To Route 104   To Route 104

ITEMS

- Ether
- Great Ball x2
- Miracle Seed
- Parlyz Heal
- Tinymushroom x2
- X Attack

POKÉMON APPEARANCES

POKÉMON	CONDITIONS
Cascoon	Common
Shroomish	Common
Silcoon	Common
Slakoth	Rare
Taillow	Rare
Wurmple	Common

Event 1: Aqua Encounter

Your first encounter with the enemy groups in Hoenn, Team Aqua and Team Magma, happens in Petalburg Woods. Unlike the previous games, *Pokémon Ruby* and *Pokémon Sapphire*, you are caught in the middle of a conflict between the two teams, rather than just taking one side over the other.

Hand over those papers!

And, hey, we of TEAM AQUA are also after something in RUSTBORO. ♥

In the woods here, you meet Team Aqua. They are attempting to steal something from a researcher from Devon Corporation. Battle the Team Aqua Grunt to prevent him from accomplishing his mission. After the battle, the researcher shows his appreciation by handing over a Great Ball.

Event 2: Into the Woods

Once you have HM01 (Cut), you can access the right half of Petalburg Woods, including a passage leading back to a previously inaccessible area in Route 104. Explore the woods completely to pick up some great Items and add to your Pokémon collection.

NOTE

None of the three starting Pokémon (Torchic, Treecko, or Mudkip) can use HM01 (Cut). You must catch a wild Pokémon, such as a Zigzagoon, to be able to use the Hidden Machine's new move.

Rustboro City

Moves Needed: *None*

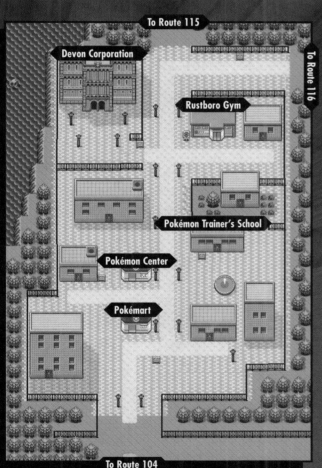

To Route 115

Devon Corporation

Rustboro Gym

To Route 116

Pokémon Trainer's School

Pokémon Center

Pokémart

To Route 104

ITEMS

- Exp. Share
- Great Ball
- HM01 (Cut)
- Letter
- PokéNav
- Premier Ball
- Quick Claw
- Stone Badge
- TM39 (Rock Tomb)
- X Defend

POKÉMART MERCHANDISE

ITEM	PRICE
Poké Ball	P200
Repeat Ball*	P1,000
Timer Ball*	P1,000
Potion	P300
Super Potion	P700
Antidote	P100
Parlyz Heal	P200
Escape Rope	P550
Repel	P350
X Speed	P350
X Attack	P500
X Defend	P500

* These two Balls appear in the catalog only after you smash the rocks blocking Rusturf Tunnel.

POKÉMON APPEARANCES

POKÉMON	CONDITIONS
Anorith	Take Claw Fossil to Devon Corporation
Lileep	Take Root Fossil to Devon Corporation
Seedot	Trade with townsperson

Rustboro City is home to the first Gym you can compete in—against Gym Leader Roxanne. After touring this pleasant little burg, head for the Gym and prove yourself against this accomplished Trainer. Emerge victorious and you are well on your way to becoming a Pokémon Master.

FANCY A TRADE?

If you want a
Grass-type
Pokémon on
your team, talk
to the towns-
person in the
house to the
right of the Gym.
The townsperson

wants to trade a Seedot for a Ralts. If you did not
choose Treecko at the beginning of the adventure,
this is a good opportunity to get a Grass-type
Pokémon and start leveling it up.

Event 1: Visit Cutter's House

After stopping by
the Pokémon
Center to rest up
your Pokémon,
head into
Cutter's House.
This is where you
receive your first
Hidden Machine,

HM01 (Cut). This new move allows you to cut down
trees, such as the ones blocking your path in
Petalburg Woods. There's a slight catch, though. You
cannot use the Hidden Machine until you possess
the Stone Badge—which is granted only to a Trainer
who beats the local Gym Leader.

Event 2: Pokémon Trainer's School

You may have
the new Hidden
Machine, but
don't rush to the
Gym just yet.
Stop at the
Pokémon
Trainer's School
and meet a

group of budding Trainers under the tutelage of a
wise teacher. Of course, none of the kids are paying

much attention, but if you listen to the teacher, he
rewards you with a special Item: Quick Claw. This
Item proves quite useful during your first Gym battle.

Event 3: Gym Leader Battle #1– Roxanne

**Roxanne, Rustboro
Gym Leader**

Pokémon Type:

ROCK

**Recommended
Move Type:**

WATER

GRASS

GYM LEADER'S POKÉMON			
POKÉMON	**LV**	**TYPE**	
Geodude	LV12	ROCK	GROUND
Geodude	LV12	ROCK	GROUND
Nosepass	LV15	ROCK	

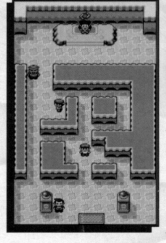 

While many of the later
Gyms are set up as
puzzles, the Rustboro Gym
is fairly straightforward.
Head through the hallways
until you reach Roxanne at
the very end. It's recom-
mended that you engage the Trainers along the way.
You can always exit the Gym to rest up before the
showdown with the Gym Leader.

Once you do reach Roxanne, don't send out a
Fire-type Pokémon. (If you chose Torchic as your first
Pokémon, you better have other Pokémon in your
menagerie to bring out.) However, if you caught a
Water-type Pokémon (or traded for the Seedot), you
have a good shot at beating Roxanne. Just keep on

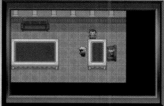

volleying Water- and Grass-type Moves at her Rock-type Pokémon and the Gym badge (specifically, the Stone Badge) will be yours.

ITEMS WON

Stone Badge: Raises your Pokémon Attack strength and allows you to use HM01 (Cut).

TM39 (Rock Tomb)

Event 4: Devon Corporation Gets Robbed

Beating the Gym Leader is hardly the end of the excitement in Rustboro City. Team Aqua apparently regrouped while you were busy and successfully robbed the Devon Corporation. You are led to the same researcher that you met before. He's staring in disbelief that Team Aqua was able to steal his Devon Goods. The thief is hiding in Rusturf Tunnel, so if you can catch up with him and defeat him, the Devon Corporation will be extremely grateful. This gratefulness translates into a handsome reward.

TIP

Explore all of the buildings in this city. A boy in the apartment complex south of the Devon Corporation is giving away a Premier Ball, a very special type of Poké Ball. Once you get it, hold on to the Premier Ball. Don't use it right away. Save this strong Poké Ball for later in your adventures when you discover a truly rare Pokémon.

Event 5: Returning the Devon Goods

After defeating the Team Aqua Grunt in the Rusturf Tunnel and recovering the Devon Goods, return to the Devon Corporation. Give the Devon Goods to the researcher and he takes you upstairs to the top floor office of the President of the company. You've proved your reliability, and the President has a couple of tasks for you. You need to take a Letter to a Trainer named Steven in Dewford Town and deliver a package to Capt. Stern in Slateport City. Both of these cities are reached by water, so you need to find a boat first.

The President doesn't ask you to run these errands for free. He gives you a new Item called the PokéNav. This communication and information tool is invaluable to Trainers. The PokéNav allows you to receive messages from Trainers you've met and battled. It also holds a map of Hoenn that proves extremely useful when you are outside of battle.

TIP

After you deliver the Letter to Steven, return to see the President. He gives you the Exp. Share, a Held Item that that helps you level up your newer Pokémon faster—even without them having to set foot in a battle.

Event 6: Archaeology Hunt

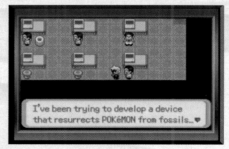

The second floor of the Devon Corporation is entirely dedicated to developing new Pokémon technologies. Some of the gadgets in the works are a little silly, but make sure to chat with the scientist in the room's far corner.

He's making serious progress on an invention that will restore Pokémon from their fossils.

Return to this fellow after you find either the Root Fossil or the Claw Fossil from the Mirage Tower. He'll take the fossil and get to work on restoring the Pokémon. This process takes time, though, so leave the scientist to his work after giving him the fossil. The reward is well worth the time.

NOTE

Two special Poké Balls go on sale in the Pokémart only after you open the path in the Rusturf Tunnel. The Timer Ball is a handy Poké Ball that becomes more and more effective the longer the battle rages. So if you are in for a long battle against a wild Pokémon, having a Timer Ball in your Bag makes the effort worth it. The Repeat Ball has a higher capture rate for Pokémon you have already caught. For example, if you have caught a Marill that has already evolved into Azumarill, you can use a Repeat Ball to easily catch a new Marill.

Route 116

Move Needed: *HM01 (Cut)*

ITEMS

- Blackglasses
- Chesto Berries x2
- Ether
- HP Up
- Pinap Berries x3
- Repeat Ball
- Repel
- X Special

POKÉMON APPEARANCES

POKÉMON	CONDITIONS
Nincada	Common
Poochyena	Common
Skitty	Rare
Taillow	Common
Whismur	Common

To Rustboro City

To Rusturf Tunnel

To Rusturf Tunnel

Event 1: Rescue Mr. Briney's Pet

Team Aqua is doing more than stealing Devon Goods—they're harassing poor Mr. Briney. The Grunt has abducted Mr.

We were on our walk, PEEKO and I, when we were jumped by an odd thug...♥

Briney's pet Pokémon, Peeko, and is holding it in the Rusturf Tunnel. Get in there and rescue Peeko. Not only is it the right thing to do, but Mr. Briney will then agree to ferry you across the seas to Dewford Town and Slateport City—both places you need to go for the President of Devon Corporation.

Event 2: Opening Rusturf Tunnel

After you open up the tunnel from the other side (via Verdanturf Town), you can check out the small area on the east side of Route 116. A man there is frantically searching for his glasses. Use the Itemfinder to help him locate the specs and receive the Blackglasses, a good Item for Dark-type Pokémon to have.

NOTE

Turn up the sound on your Game Boy Advance or Nintendo DS (or plug in the headphones) when using the Itemfinder. The gadget beeps loudly when you are near a special Item.

Rusturf Tunnel

Move Needed: HM06 (Rock Smash)

To Route 116

To Verdanturf Town

To Route 116

ITEMS
- Devon Goods
- HM04 (Strength)
- Max Ether
- Poké Ball

POKÉMON APPEARANCES
POKÉMON	CONDITIONS
Whismur	Very Common

Event 1: Get the Goods

What, are you coming? Come and get some, then!

The Team Aqua Grunt that's causing so much trouble for everyone has holed up in the Rusturf Tunnel. Enter the tunnel to battle him. If you win, the Team Aqua Grunt willingly (but reluctantly) hands over the Devon Goods and releases Peeko. Return the Devon Goods and Peeko to their rightful owners for your rewards.

TIP

While the wild Whismur in Rusturf Tunnel aren't that formidable, you may wish to use a Repel to prevent them from engaging you on the way to the Team Aqua Grunt. That way, you can approach the battle with Pokémon with full HP and PP for their moves.

Event 2: Clearing Rusturf Tunnel

This rock appears to be breakable. Would you like to use ROCK SMASH?

HM06 (Rock Smash) allows you to smash the boulders in Rusturf Tunnel, but only after you have received the Dynamo Badge. Smashing those rocks not only reunites the two love-struck kids in the tunnel, but you also open up a clever shortcut between Rustboro City and Verdanturf Town.

33

Route 105, Route 106, and Dewford Town

Move Needed: *HM03 (Surf)*

Your next stop, Dewford Town, lies along the sea route of southern Hoenn. After passing through the rocky straits, you come to this quiet island community, complete with its own Gym.

ITEMS

- Full Heal
- Iron
- Knuckle Badge
- Old Rod
- Protein
- Silk Scarf
- TM08 (Bulk Up)
- TM36 (Sludge Bomb)

To Route 104

Island Cave

To Route 105

To Route 106

Granite Cave

Pokémon Center

Dewford Gym

To Route 107

Dewford Town

POKÉMON APPEARANCES ON LAND (ROUTE 105)

POKÉMON	CONDITIONS
Regice	Island Cave, after Sealed Chamber mystery is solved

POKÉMON APPEARANCES IN WATER (ROUTE 105)

POKÉMON	CONDITIONS
Magikarp	Very Common (Old Rod, Good Rod)
Pelipper	Rare
Tentacool	Very Common; Common (Old Rod, Good Rod)
Wailmer	Common (Good Rod); Very Common (Super Rod)
Wingull	Very Common

POKÉMON APPEARANCES IN WATER (ROUTE 106)

POKÉMON	CONDITIONS
Magikarp	Very Common (Old Rod, Good Rod)
Pelipper	Rare
Tentacool	Very Common; Common (Old Rod, Good Rod)
Wailmer	Common (Good Rod); Very Common (Super Rod)
Wingull	Very Common

POKÉMON APPEARANCES IN WATER (DEWFORD TOWN)

POKÉMON	CONDITIONS
Pelipper	Rare
Tentacool	Very Common; Common (Old Rod, Good Rod)
Wingull	Very Common

USING SURF

Without the Balance Badge or HM03 (Surf), you must rely on Mr. Briney and his boat to get across the water to Dewford Town and Slateport City. Because you are riding in a vessel, you pass the swimming Trainers without a battle invitation. You also don't encounter any wild Pokémon. However, as soon as you can use HM03 (Surf), you can tackle the sea routes yourself and challenge the many Trainers in the water. This is a great way to pick up additional experience for your Pokémon.

NOTE

You pass an Island Cave on the way between Route 104 and Dewford Town. Until you learn HM03 (Surf) and have the Balance Badge, you cannot visit this mysterious locale. And even when you can, there is still another puzzle to solve before a door magically opens. Could this be the resting place of the Legendary Ice-type Pokémon, Regice?

Event 1: Learn to Fish

After stepping off Mr. Briney's boat, see the fisherman on the beach. Share your love of the sea with him and he gives you the Old Rod as a sign of friendship. Now you can start fishing for wild Pokémon in Hoenn's waters.

TIP

Even though you have a Rod now, you cannot just start catching every wild Pokémon in the water. Some Pokémon will not bite on a line from the Old Rod—and some are so picky they will wait for the Super Rod before getting interested.

Event 2: Trendy Folks

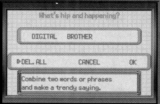

The good people of Dewford Town are into the latest trends, whatever those may be. You can have a big effect on the local scene at Dewford with a few choice words. Talk to the boy just north of the Pokémon Center. He tries to impress you with how cool he is, but you can teach him what cool truly means. Come up with a two-word phrase and teach it to the boy. Before you know it, everybody in town is gabbing about your new catchphrase.

There is a tiny house by the dock where Mr. Briney drops you off. Pop inside and chat with the people there. They bestow upon you the latest in trendy duds, the Silk Scarf.

Event 4: Gym Leader Battle #2— Brawly

Brawly, Dewford Gym Leader

Pokémon Type:
FLYING

Recommended Move Type:
FIGHTING
PSYCHIC

GYM LEADER'S POKÉMON

POKÉMON	LV	TYPE
Machop	LV16	FIGHTING
Makuhita	LV19	FIGHTING
Meditite	LV19	FIGHTING

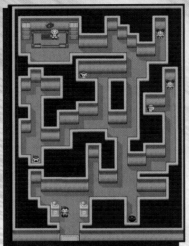

The Dewford Gym is dark—and it stays that way unless you challenge the multitude of Trainers that line the path to Gym Leader Brawly. Every time you complete a battle, a little more light is shed on the Gym. Once the path to Brawly has been fitfully illuminated,

challenge the Gym Leader's Fighting-type Pokémon with Flying- or Psychic-type Moves. You'll do even better if these moves come from same-type Pokémon. Keep countering his moves with powerful attacks and the Knuckle Badge will be yours.

ITEMS WON

Knuckle Badge: Pokémon up to LV30 will obey your commands. Also allows you to use HM05 (Flash) outside of battle.

TM08 (Bulk Up)

Granite Cave

Moves Needed: *HM05 (Flash), HM06 (Rock Smash), Mach Bike*

To Route 106

ITEMS

- Escape Rope
- Everstone
- HM05 (Flash)
- Poké Ball
- Rare Candy
- Repel
- TM47 (Steel Wing)

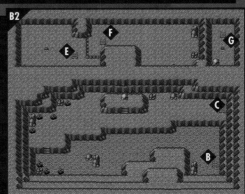

Granite Cave is a pretty dark place, unless you have Flash, which allows you to light up the cavern. Granite Cave is definitely worth exploring. You'll find many good items inside, as well as a few new wild Pokémon that you should definitely try to capture with Poké Balls.

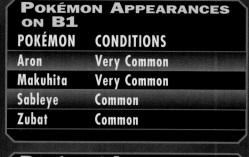

Pokémon Appearances on 1F

POKÉMON	CONDITIONS
Geodude	Common
Makuhita	Very Common
Zubat	Common

Pokémon Appearances on 1F (Small Chamber)

POKÉMON	CONDITIONS
Aron	Common
Makuhita	Very Common
Zubat	Common

Pokémon Appearances on B1

POKÉMON	CONDITIONS
Aron	Very Common
Makuhita	Very Common
Sableye	Common
Zubat	Common

Pokémon Appearances on B2

POKÉMON	CONDITIONS
Abra	Common
Aron	Very Common
Geodude	Very Common (Rock Smash boulders)
Nosepass	Common (Rock Smash boulders)
Sableye	Common
Zubat	Common

Event 1: Grab the Everstone

Fletchr put away the EVERSTONE in the ITEMS POCKET.

While searching for Steven, you come across the special boulder, raised on a small ledge. Examine the boulder to receive the Everstone, a special Held Item that affects a Pokémon's Evolution process. If you have a Pokémon that you do not want to evolve, pass it the Everstone and it will not try to evolve after each level up past the Evolution requirement.

Event 2: Speedy Delivery

After trekking through the Granite Cave all the way to the small outside section of 1F (the route takes you through the other two floors of the cave), you come to Steven. Hand off the Letter to Steven and he gives you TM47 (Steel Wing) in appreciation. Place this powerful TM in your Bag and exit Granite Cave with the Escape Rope, or weave back through the passages and keep encountering wild Pokémon.

TIP

Return to Granite Cave after you have picked up the Mach Bike from Rydel in Mauville City. This lets you zoom up the steep slope on B1 and cross the fragile floor. You have to be swift, though. Stop too long to make a turn and the floor will crumble beneath your wheels. Explore the rest of the cave on the Mach Bike to pick up some rare Items.

Routes 107, 108, 109, and Slateport City

Move Needed: *HM03 (Surf)*

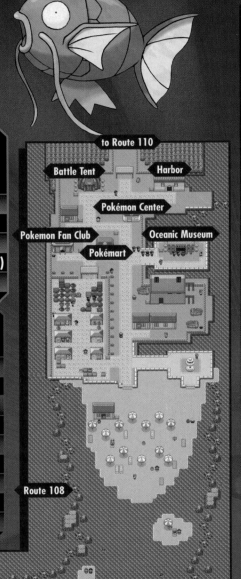

At the end of what might have been a long voyage—Mr. Briney sure steers fast—you come to Slateport City, a coastal community built on a beautiful beach. Slateport City is one of the few major Hoenn metropolises that doesn't have its own Gym. Instead, the city hosts a Battle Tent.

POKÉMON APPEARANCES IN WATER (ROUTE 107, 108, 109, AND SLATEPORT CITY)

POKÉMON	CONDITIONS
Magikarp	Very Common (Old Rod, Good Rod)
Pelipper	Rare
Tentacool	Very Common; Common (Old Rod, Good Rod)
Wailmer	Common (Good Rod); Very Common (Super Rod)
Wingull	Very Common

ITEMS

- Deepseascale or Deepseatooth
- Powder Jar
- PP Up
- Soda Pop x6
- Soft Sand
- Soothe Bell
- TM41 (Torment)
- TM46 (Thief)

POKÉMART MERCHANDISE

ITEM	PRICE
Poké Ball	₽200
Great Ball	₽600
Potion	₽300
Super Potion	₽700
Antidote	₽100
Parlyz Heal	₽200
Escape Rope	₽550
Repel	₽350
Harbor Mail	₽50

to Route 110

Battle Tent

Harbor

Pokémon Center

Pokemon Fan Club

Oceanic Museum

Pokémart

Route 108

Route 107

Route 108

SLATEPORT MARKET

Slateport City has more commerce opportunities than most Hoenn towns. Regular citizens sell special wares at an open-air market to the beach's north. After you receive TM43 (Secret Power) on Route 111, the two kids at the top edge of the market start selling some slick decorations for your Secret Base.

Doll Shop	
ITEM	PRICE
Azurill Doll	₽3,000
Marill Doll	₽3,000
Skitty Doll	₽3,000

Energy Guru	
ITEM	PRICE
Protein	₽9,800
Iron	₽9,800
Carbos	₽9,800
Zinc	₽9,800
Calcium	₽9,800
HP Up	₽9,800

Secret Power Club Shop	
ITEM	PRICE
Red Brick	₽500
Blue Brick	₽500
Yellow Brick	₽500
Red Balloon	₽500
Blue Balloon	₽500
Yellow Balloon	₽500
C Low Note Mat	₽500
D Note Mat	₽500
E Note Mat	₽500
F Note Mat	₽500
G Note Mat	₽500
A Note Mat	₽500
B Note Mat	₽500
C High Note Mat	₽500

NOTE

The trip to Slateport City on Mr. Briney's Vessel is fast—blink and you might miss the Abandoned Ship on the way to the city. Once you have HM03 (Surf) and HM08 (Dive), return to this vessel and seek out a special Item that Capt. Stern of Slateport City has been looking for. He will reward your efforts.

Event 1: Fizzy Drinks

There is a small beach house on the sand in front of Slateport City. The joint is full of Trainers, but if you win every battle, the owner gives you a six-pack of Soda Pop. This fizzy drink restores your Pokémon's HP.

Event 2: Shipyard

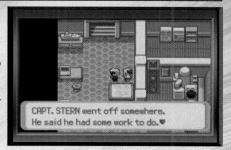

The President asked you to deliver a package to Capt. Stern, so visit the Shipyard to make the drop. Unfortunately, Capt. Stern isn't there. He's away right now doing some important work.

Event 3: Oceanic Museum

On your first visit to the Oceanic Museum, you cannot get in. Out front, there is a huge line of people with very familiar-looking uniforms. But after you find out that Capt. Stern is absent, the line has vanished. Head into the Oceanic Museum, pay the entrance fee, and then start talking to everybody inside. You'll run into a Team Aqua Grunt you had a previous encounter with, and his ego is still bruised. However, he gives you a gift.

Find Capt. Stern upstairs among the ship models. When you try to give the Devon Goods to Capt. Stern, though, the Team Aqua Grunts attempt to steal the package again. Battle the Grunts to keep them from getting the Goods.

NOTE

After you leave the Oceanic Museum, you're visited by a stranger who is currently chronicling talented Trainers. And it seems he has his eye on you. Who is this fellow?

Event 4: See the City

Explore the entirety of Slateport City after dropping the Devon Goods off with Capt. Stern. The open-air market has lots of fantastic goods. And visit the Pokémon Fan Club to learn valuable insights on how to condition Pokémon for Pokémon Contests. You receive an essential Item, the PokéBlock Case, inside this clubhouse.

The Chairman of the Pokémon Fun Club awards you a specific colored scarf if you have completely maxed out your lead Pokémon's Condition with PokéBlocks.

If your Pokémon has a high Beauty rating, he awards a Blue Scarf.

If your Pokémon has a high Cool rating, he awards a Red Scarf.

If your Pokémon has a high Cute rating, he awards a Pink Scarf.

If your Pokémon has a high Smart rating, he awards a Green Scarf.

If your Pokémon has a high Tough rating, he awards a Yellow Scarf.

Speak to two more people inside the clubhouse. A club member gives you a Soothe Bell if your Pokémon truly likes you.

And a Move Tutor in the clubhouse teaches Swagger.

NOTE

For a complete list of all the Move Tutors and their locations, see the Lists chapter of this guide.

Event 5: After Defeating Team Magma

After you defeat Team Magma at their Hideout on Jagged Pass, return to Slateport City to catch up with Team Aqua. They successfully

steal Capt. Stern's submersible, but the chase to find it leads you to the feet of a very impressive Pokémon.

Event 6: After Exploring the Abandoned Ship

Once you finish exploring the Abandoned Ship, return the Scanner to Capt. Stern at the Shipyard. As a reward, Capt. Stern gives you one of two Held Items that help a Clamperl evolve. If you choose the Deepseatooth and then trade the Clamperl to another Trainer, it evolves into a Huntail. If you choose the Deepseascale and perform the trade, the Evolution results in a Gorebyss.

SLATEPORT CITY BATTLE TENT

Slateport hosts the first of three Battle Tents you encounter during your travels through Hoenn. These contests test your skills as a Trainer by providing highly individual challenges. At the Slateport Battle Tent, you must complete a series of battles—but not with your own Pokémon. You must choose three of five randomly selected rental Pokémon and battle Trainers with their own randomly selected Pokémon. If you can win three battles in a row, you will win a Full Heal.

You don't have to do all three battles in a row. You can save between each round in case the battle goes awry. But if you go from one victory into another round without saving your game, you must start all over again if you lose.

Route 110

Moves Needed: *HM03 (Surf), Mach Bike or Acro Bike*

POKÉMON APPEARANCES ON LAND

POKÉMON	CONDITIONS
Electrike	Common
Gulpin	Common
Minun	Common
Oddish	Common
Plusle	Rare
Poochyena	Common
Wingull	Rare

POKÉMON APPEARANCES IN WATER

POKÉMON	CONDITIONS
Pelipper	Rare
Tentacool	Very Common; Common (Old Rod, Good Rod)
Wailmer	Common (Good Rod); Very Common (Super Rod)
Wingull	Very Common

ITEMS

- Dire Hit
- Itemfinder
- Nanab Berries x9
- Rare Candy

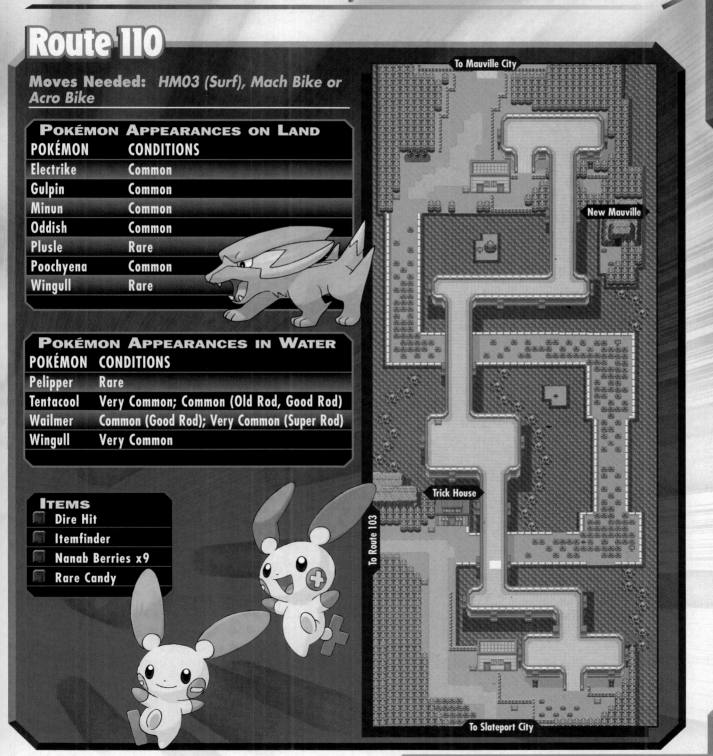

To Mauville City

New Mauville

Trick House

To Route 103

To Slateport City

Event 1: Trick House

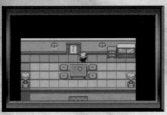

When you walk up the path through Route 110, you come across a small house with a pink roof: Trick House. This is the home of the Trick Master, a mischievous man who arranges his house differently after every one of your badge battles. If you manage to find the Trick Master when you enter the home (and he moves with every visit), he lets you attempt to weave your way through his back room.

There are two goals inside the Trick House. First, you must find the password that allows you through the exit, and then you must find the exit itself. The Trick House is full of Trainers who have lost their way inside. There are eight different variations on the Trick House, but the Trick Master needs time to re-do the labyrinth after you successfully complete one, so stop back later to see what surprises he has in store for you.

TRICK MASTER		
VISIT	**HIDING PLACE**	**PRIZE**
1	Under Table	Rare Candy
2	Right Tree	Timer Ball
3	Chest of Drawers	Hard Stone
4	Left Window	Smoke Ball
5	Left Tree	TM12 (Taunt)
6	Cupboard	Magnet
7	Right Window	PP Max
8	SW Cushion	Tent

Event 2: Cycling Road

A bicycle highway above Route 110 offers a quick route to Mauville City. However, you don't have a Bike just yet, so the high road is off-limits. After you get either the Mach Bike or the Acro Bike from Mauville City, you can use the Cycling Road to quickly zip between Mauville City and Slateport City.

A race sheet on the road chronicles the fastest times from one end to the other, but it also counts the number of collisions you have, so watch the road!

Event 3: Battle with Prof. Birch's Child

Prof. Birch's kid is waiting for you on Route 110. He or she has been practicing battle tactics and has assembled some strong Pokémon. You cannot pass into Mauville City without battling this budding Trainer, so make sure your Pokémon are in top condition before the challenge. If you win the battle, you receive the Itemfinder. The Itemfinder helps you discover dropped or buried Items in Hoenn. The Itemfinder beeps when you are near a secret Item, so prick up your ears and keep your eyes on the ground.

Event 4: New Mauville

After you receive HM03 (Surf), there is a quest to undertake south of Mauville City. Talk with a man in Mauville City, and he asks you to visit an underground electrical plant called New Mauville, in the northeast corner of Route 110. Access the island by using HM03 (Surf) at the water's edge near the Cycling Road's northern exit and head to the east, ducking under the highway itself.

Mauville City

Moves Needed: *None*

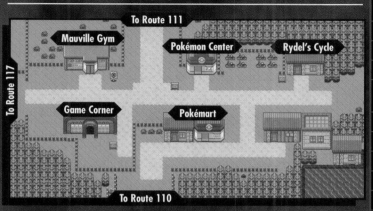

ITEMS
Basement Key
Coin Case
Dynamo Badge
HM06 (Rock Smash)
Mach Bike or Acro Bike
TM24 (Thunderbolt)
TM32 (Double Team)
TM34 (Shock Wave)
Coins x20
X Speed

POKÉMART MERCHANDISE	
ITEM	PRICE
Poké Ball	₽200
Great Ball	₽600
Super Potion	₽700
Antidote	₽100
Parlyz Heal	₽200
Awakening	₽250
X Speed	₽350
X Attack	₽500
X Defend	₽550
Guard Spec.	₽700
Dire Hit	₽650
X Accuracy	₽950

Mauville City is situated at the north end of the bicycle highway that sits high above Route 110. The city hosts its own Gym, in which you must compete if you want to earn the necessary talents to progress deep into Hoenn. Check out all of the town's features, as there is a lot to do in Mauville that you cannot do elsewhere, such as get a Bike or try out some parlor games for prizes.

Event 1: Find HM06 (Rock Smash)

The first thing to do in Mauville is to head into the house to the Pokémart's right. The person inside thinks your Pokémon look strong enough to handle a new Hidden Machine, HM06 (Rock Smash). You now can dispose of the boulders that impede your progress. All you need now is the Dynamo Badge to unlock its strength.

Event 2: Get a Bike

You cannot use the highway along Route 110 without a Bike, so stop by the pink-roofed house on the city's right side. The owner of the bicycle shop, Rydel, sells two styles of bicycles: a speed Bike (Mach Bike) and a trick Bike (Acro Bike). Rydel is kind enough to give you one for free, but even better, he lets you bring it back and trade it for the other Bike style whenever you want.

Use the Mach Bike to cover distance quickly, or zip across fragile floors and head up steep slopes. The Acro Bike is slick enough to let you hop across special trick routes and access previously unreachable areas.

Event 3: Battle with Wally

Before you can enter the Mauville Gym, you must battle against Wally. The little fella has been practicing his battling skills since you first saw him and would like to challenge you. Wally has a Ralts at LV16.

![Pokémon Emerald Version logo]

Event 4: Gym Leader Battle #3— Wattson

Wattson, Mauville Gym Leader

Pokémon Type:

ELECTRIC

Recommended Move Type:

GROUND
FIGHTING
FIRE

GYM LEADER'S POKÉMON

POKÉMON	LV	TYPE	
Electrike	LV20	ELECTRIC	
Magneton	LV22	ELECTRIC	STEEL
Manectric	LV24	ELECTRIC	
Voltorb	LV20	ELECTRIC	STEEL

The path to Wattson is blocked by a series of electric fences. The fences are controlled by switches on the Gym's floor, so carefully step on the switches to open up the route to Wattson. Battle the Trainers on the way for valuable experience. Remember, you can always step outside the Gym and visit the Pokémon Center before going in for the final challenge.

Wattson's line-up is primarily Electric-type Pokémon, but two of them also have Steel-type traits, so in addition to using reliable Ground-type Moves, you can also use Fire- and Fighting-type Moves to wrest the Dynamo Badge from Wattson.

ITEMS WON

Dynamo Badge: Increases your Pokémon's Speed and grants use of HM06 (Rock Smash) outside of battle.TM34 (Shock Wave)

Event 5: New Mauville Quest

Here, this is the KEY to get into NEW MAUVILLE.

After you can use HM03 (Surf), seek out Wattson standing at the crossroads in Mauville City. He asks you to perform a quest to help Mauville City. Apparently the electric generation in the underground New Mauville is malfunctioning. Wattson gives you the Basement Key that grants access to New Mauville. If you complete his task, he gives you the TM24 (Thunderbolt).

MAUVILLE CITY GAME CORNER

Check out the Game Corner in the southwest corner of Mauville City where you can exchange some ₽ for Coins and play a couple of minigames. However, before you can play, you must get a Coin Case from the woman who lives next to the Pokémart. (She requests the Harbor Mail in return.) Once you have the Coin Case, return to the Game Corner and buy some Coins to get started. You can exchange the Coins you win for great prizes at the main counter.

GAME CORNER PRIZES

ITEM	PRICE IN COINS
TM32 (Double Team)	1,500
TM29 (Psychic)	3,500
TM35 (Flamethrower)	4,000
TM24 (Thunderbolt)	4,000
TM13 (Ice Beam)	4,000
Treecko Doll	1,000
Torchic Doll	1,000
Mudkip Doll	1,000

The Slot Machines let you bet Coins on a series of lines. If you line up certain icons, you win more Coins. The more Coins you play in a turn, the more Coins you might win. Of course, there's always a chance you'll lose, too.

The Roulette Tables allow you to bet on which symbol the metal ball will drop on after spinning around the wheel. There are multiple ways to bet on this game, such as picking individual spaces or choosing all symbols of a like-color.

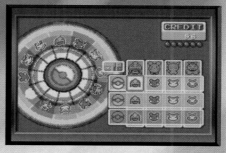

Before leaving, talk to the girl in the corner. She won an extra Doll and is happy to share it with you.

Route 117

Moves Needed: HM01 (Cut), HM03 (Surf)

ITEMS
- Great Ball
- Revive
- Wepear Berries x9

POKÉMON APPEARANCES ON LAND

POKÉMON	CONDITIONS
Illumise	Common
Marill	Common
Oddish	Very Common
Poochyena	Common
Volbeat	Very Rare

POKÉMON APPEARANCES IN WATER

POKÉMON	CONDITIONS
Corphish	Common (Good Rod); Very Common (Super Rod)
Goldeen	Very Rare (Old Rod); Common (Good Rod)
Magikarp	Very Common (Old Rod, Good Rod)
Marill	Very Common

Event 1: Visit the Day Care Center

The Day Care Center is an incredibly important location in Hoenn. This is where you can drop off your Pokémon, two at a time, to level up while you are away on your adventures. It only costs ₽100 to drop them off and another ₽100 for every level they gain while in the Day Care Center's custody.

The Day Care Center is also where breeding happens. If you drop two compatible Pokémon off at the center, you may find a surprise when you return: an Egg. Carry the Egg with you and it will soon hatch into a new Pokémon.

Pokémon EMERALD VERSION

TIP

There are a lot of Trainers on the west route to Verdanturf Town. If you want to gain more experience and cash, this is an excellent place to do so.

Verdanturf Town

Moves Needed: *None*

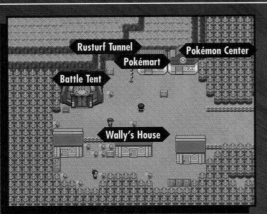

ITEM
☐ TM45 (Attract)

POKÉMART MERCHANDISE

ITEM	PRICE
Great Ball	₽600
Nest Ball	₽1,000
Super Potion	₽700
Antidote	₽100
Parlyz Heal	₽200
Awakening	₽250
Ice Heal	₽250
Burn Heal	₽250
Repel	₽350
X Special	₽350
Fluffy Tail	₽1,000

Verdanturf Town is a smaller township in Hoenn, located near the center of the main landmass. The other entrance to the Rusturf Tunnel is here, which is almost complete. Perhaps you can help the final stage of construction and maybe earn something cool in the process?

Event 1: Check in on Wally

Verdanturf was where Wally was headed the last time you saw him, so stop by his house and say "hello." Wally feels good about his loss to you in

Mauville City. You've actually inspired him to try even harder next time. And he will, so be ready.

Event 2: Visit Rusturf Tunnel

Enter the cave between the Battle Tent and the Pokémart. This is Rusturf Tunnel, and you've been here before—but on the other side of the boulders that block

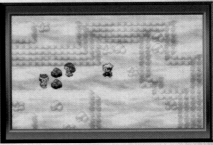

the tunnel. Use HM06 (Rock Smash) to eliminate the obstruction and unite Verdanturf Town citizen Wanda with her boyfriend. In return for your assistance, you receive TM45 (Attract). You now have a great shortcut between Rustboro City and Verdanturf Town.

▶ VERDANTURF TOWN BATTLE TENT

The Battle Tent here is especially difficult—in fact, it's recommended you don't try it until your Pokémon are at LV30 or higher. The contest allows

you to select which three Pokémon you want to use in your battle—and you have no warning of what random Pokémon your opponent will use. On top of this, you also do not choose which moves your Pokémon use in the battle. It's all up to the Pokémon's instinct.

This doesn't mean you cannot switch out Pokémon or use Items from your Bag to help out. You'll likely need to switch out your Pokémon a few times in an attempt to match up the right moves for the battle. Like the previous Battle Tent, you can save between battles.

Routes 111 and 112

Moves Needed: HM03 (Surf), HM06 (Rock Smash), Mach Bike, Go-Goggles

Mt. Chimney

To Fiery Path

To Lavaridge Town

Desert Ruins

Winstrate House

Trainer Hill

ITEMS

- Claw Fossil
- HP Up
- Macho Brace
- Nugget
- Oran Berries x4
- Pecha Berries x4
- Rawst Berries x4
- Razz Berries x6
- Root Fossil
- Stardust
- TM37 (Sandstorm)
- TM43 (Secret Power)

TRAINER HILL MERCHANDISE

ITEM	PRICE
Super Potion	₽700
Antidote	₽100
Parlyz Heal	₽200
Awakening	₽250
X Speed	₽350
X Special	₽350
X Attack	₽500
X Defend	₽550
Dire Hit	₽650
Guard Spec.	₽700
X Accuracy	₽950

To Route 113

To Fiery Path

Rest Stop

To Mauville City

47

Pokémon Appearances on Land (Route 111)

POKÉMON	CONDITIONS
Baltoy	Common
Cacnea	Common
Geodude	Very Common (Rock Smash)
Sandshrew	Very Common
Trapinch	Very Common
Regirock	After Sealed Chamber mystery is solved

Pokémon Appearances in Mirage Tower

POKÉMON	CONDITIONS
Sandshrew	Very Common
Trapinch	Very Common

Pokémon Appearances (Route 112)

POKÉMON	CONDITIONS
Numel	Very Common

Pokémon Appearances in Water (Route 111)

POKÉMON	CONDITIONS
Barboach	Common (Good Rod); Very Common (Super Rod)
Goldeen	Very Rare (Old Rod); Common (Good Rod)
Magikarp	Very Common (Old Rod, Good Rod)
Marill	Very Common

Event 1: Winstrates

The first house you see as you head up Route 111 is the home of the Winstrates, an entire family of Trainers. You must challenge every member of the family, from the youngest to the oldest in succession to win the prized Item: Macho Brace.

That's the spirit! I like you!

NOTE

Unless you have HM06 (Rock Smash) and the Dynamo Badge, you cannot head very far into Route 111. Two boulders block the way. Complete the necessary challenges to earn these moves and Items, then come back.

Event 2: TV Interview

Television is a big part of daily life in Hoenn. So many televisions means a constant need for new pro-gramming, so a reporter/camera-man team is seeking out notable Trainers in Hoenn to interview.

TV: Hey, lookie here! A tough-looking TRAINER here, of all places!♥

You meet them along Route 111. The media people aren't just looking for a few words, though. You must battle them before the interview, and then select a choice comment to describe the battle. The next time you are in a house with a television, check it out. Your interview may be the lead story.

Event 3: Sandstorm

You cannot access the desert on Route 111, due to a massive sandstorm blanketing the desert region to the north. Instead, you must head east in hopes of finding an Item that allows you to see through the storm: Go-Goggles. Once you have the Go-Goggles, you can brave the storm and check out that large stone pillar just beyond the edge of the sand.

Event 4: Cable Car

The Cable Car at the top of Route 111 is currently unavailable thanks to a couple of Team Magma Grunts standing guard over the area.

Sounds like it, yeah. But I heard we need a METEORITE to do it.

You overhear the Grunts talking about Fallarbor Town, so that's the best lead to follow at this point.

NOTE

After you deal with Team Magma at Meteor Falls, the Cable Car is back in commission. Use it to ride up to the top of Mt. Chimney.

Event 5: TM43 (Secret Power)

In addition to creating your own team of Pokémon, decorating a Secret Base is a way to completely personalize your *Pokémon Emerald*

experience. But until you visit the young man standing next to a large tree in Route 112, you have no way to access a Secret Base. He gives you TM43 (Secret Power), which, when taught to one of your Pokémon, allows you to get a Secret Base of your own. Find Secret Bases in large trees, tall grass, and mountain indentations.

Rest Stop

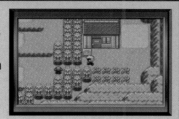

The Old Lady's Rest Stop, on Route 112, is a great place to stop and rest your Pokémon before continuing your adventure. The woman running the house provides a bed for free, so stop by anytime and recharge.

MIRAGE TOWER

Rising out of the sand in Route 112, the Mirage Tower can be accessed only after you receive the Go-Goggles. As soon as you can make your way through the sandstorm, head for this towering pillar and duck inside to find some Pokémon relics.

Head up the Mirage Tower using the ladders. There are several wild Pokémon in the Tower, so use Repel if you are in a hurry, or have a Water-type Pokémon in your party to offset the Ground-type Pokémon.

You need HM06 (Rock Smash) and the Mach Bike to access the top floor. Use HM06 (Rock Smash) to bash the boulders blocking the route upstairs. Patches of fragile flooring crumble away if you linger on them, so speed across with the Mach Bike.

Two fossils are on the top floor. The Claw Fossil is on the right and the Root Fossil is on the left. You can only select one of these fossils,

though. As soon as you pick up one of them, the entire Mirage Tower disappears into the sand and the other fossil is lost.

Once you have the fossil, take it back to the scientist at the Devon Corporation working on a resurrection process. Leave the fossil with him and return later to receive the resurrected Pokémon.

Event 6: Desert Ruins

After you have solved the mystery of the Sealed Chamber, come back to Route 111 and trek into the Desert Ruins, which now has

an open door. (On your first visit, there is no such opening.) This is the resting place of Regirock, so make sure you are well-stocked on Ultra Balls or Timer Balls before heading into the ruins.

Trainer Hill

There is a Trainer Hill to the right of the Winstrate House in Route 111. Trainer Hill is open for battles throughout the game— and there are plenty of

them, making it a great place to hone your tactics and gain coveted experience.

However, even if the place is closed, you can still shop at the counter or rest your Pokémon at the make-shift Pokémon Center in the lobby.

Fiery Path

Move Needed: HM04 (Strength)

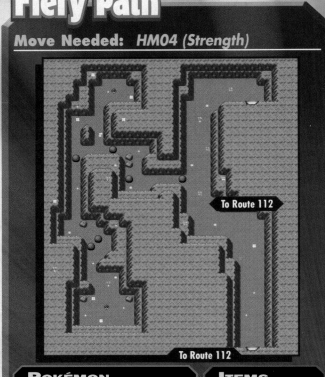

To Route 112

To Route 112

POKÉMON APPEARANCES	
POKÉMON	**CONDITIONS**
Grimer	Rare
Koffing	Common
Machop	Common
Numel	Common
Slugma	Common
Torkoal	Common

ITEMS	
🔲	Fire Stone
🔲	TM06 (Toxic)

Event 1: Using HM04 (Strength)

Almost half of the Fiery Path is blocked off by some large boulders that are too big to use HM06 (Rock Smash) on. Instead, you

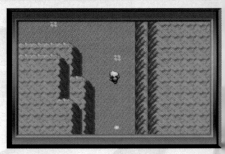

must come back after learning HM04 (Strength) and roll them out of the way. Now you can see the other half of this area and not only pick up some great Items, but also encounter some new wild Pokémon to add to your Pokédex.

Route 113

Moves Needed: *None*

To Fallarbor Town

Glass Workshop

To Route 111

ITEMS

- ☐ Max Ether
- ☐ Soot Sack
- ☐ Super Repel

GLASS WORKSHOP MERCHANDISE

ITEM	NUMBER OF STEPS
Blue Flute	250
Yellow Flute	500
Red Flute	500
White Flute	1,000
Black Flute	1,000
Pretty Chair	6,000
Pretty Desk	8,000

POKÉMON APPEARANCES

POKÉMON	CONDITIONS
Skarmory	Rare
Slugma	Common
Spinda	Very Common

Event 1: Glass Workshop

Route 113 is located at the base of volcanic Mt. Chimney, so almost everything is covered with a layer of ash. As you walk through the grass, you knock the ash loose and restore the grass to its original green.

The ash is actually good for something, though. The owner of the Glass Workshop can turn the ash into beautiful Items, but he doesn't have time to collect ash right now. He gives you a Soot Sack, which collects ash with every step. Different Items require different amounts of ash. You get a little ash with every step, so check out the table here to see how much tromping through the ashen route is required for each piece of work.

CAUTION

Look out for Trainers hiding in the ash. They attempt to surprise you, but if you keep your eyes open for any small bumps in the ash, you can spot the sneaky Trainers well in advance. If you step close to them, they will challenge you to a battle.

Fallarbor Town

Moves Needed: *None*

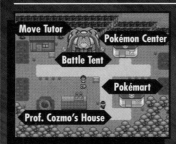

Move Tutor
Pokémon Center
Battle Tent
Pokémart
Prof. Cozmo's House

Fallarbor, a small town near the foot of Mt. Chimney, is home to one of the three Battle Tents in Hoenn. This small town has a lot of big-city features, including a Pokémart and Pokémon Center. It's also where Prof. Cozmo (a famous researcher) lives. As you continue into the heart of Hoenn, Fallarbor is a great place to replenish supplies and rest your Pokémon before getting back to your adventure.

POKÉMART MERCHANDISE

ITEM	PRICE
Great Ball	₽600
Super Potion	₽700
Antidote	₽100
Parlyz Heal	₽200
Escape Rope	₽550
Super Repel	₽500
X Special	₽350
X Speed	₽350
X Attack	₽500
X Defend	₽550
Dire Hit	₽650
Guard Spec.	₽600

Event 1: Team Magma Trouble

Team Magma has been causing trouble for Prof. Cozmo, a leading citizen of Fallarbor Town. Team Magma's latest antic? They've

kidnapped Prof. Cozmo and taken him to Meteor Falls—and only you can rescue him.

Event 2: Lanette

Inside the Pokémon Center, you meet Lanette. She is the programmer who devised the PC Pokémon Storage System. Lanette lives nearby on Route 114 and invites you to stop by when you have a chance. Take her up on the offer as soon as possible.

Event 3: Visit the Move Tutor

The Move Tutor helps Pokémon remember moves they have forgotten in order to make room for newer talents. If you have a Pokémon that has forgotten a move you want access to again, return to the Move Tutor with a Heart Scale. In exchange for this precious Item, the Move Tutor will coax your Pokémon's forgotten move out of its memory, putting it back into play. This is a good service if you ever need to recover a move you had to forget to use an HM move, such as HM03 (Surf) or HM04 (Strength).

Event 4: Prof. Cozmo's Reward

After you get the Meteorite back from Team Magma on Mt. Chimney, return to Prof. Cozmo's house and hand it over. The pleased professor gives you TM27 (Return) in, well, return.

FALLARBOR TOWN BATTLE TENT

The third Battle Tent is in Fallarbor Town. This offers another three-battle challenge, but with a different set of rules than the previous Battle Tents. You challenge a series of Trainers who match your Pokémon levels, but these battles are short-lived. Each battle lasts only three turns. The goal is to knock the other Pokémon out as fast as possible.

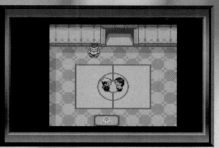

If you can knock a Pokémon out with a single move, you're off to a good start.

If the battle is not over after three moves, it goes to judging. You are judged on three categories: Mind, Skill, and Body. Aggressive use of offensive moves helps you earn Mind points. The effectiveness of your moves earns you Skill points. The amount of HP remaining at the battle's end determines your Body points. The Trainer with the most points (the most points you can earn in a single category is two) is declared the winner.

Route 114

Moves Needed: HM03 (Surf), HM06 (Rock Smash), HM07 (Waterfall)

ITEMS

- Energypowder
- Lotad Doll
- Persim Berries x6
- Protein
- Rare Candy
- TM05 (Roar)
- TM28 (Dig)

POKÉMON APPEARANCES ON LAND

POKÉMON	CONDITIONS
Geodude	Very Common (Rock Smash)
Lombre	Common
Lotad	Common
Nuzleaf	Very Rare
Seviper	Rare
Swablu	Very Common

POKÉMON APPEARANCES IN WATER

POKÉMON	CONDITIONS
Barboach	Common (Good Rod); Very Common (Super Rod)
Goldeen	Common (Old Rod, Good Rod)
Magikarp	Very Common (Old Rod, Good Rod)
Marill	Very Common

Fossil Maniac's House

Lanette's House

To Meteor Falls

Event 1: Fossil Maniac

I'm the FOSSIL MANIAC...
I'm a nice guy who loves FOSSILS...

You can access Meteor Falls, where Magma is holding Prof. Cozmo, only via the rocky paths of Route 114. However, before you head for Meteor Falls, swing by the Fossil Maniac's house, which is just beyond the route's starting point.

The Fossil Maniac isn't willing to share any of his fossils, but he does offer a tip on where you could possibly find some: the desert in Route 111. Remember that tower you saw peeking out of the sandstorm?

Event 2: Get TM05 (Roar) for Free

Another example of the generosity abounding in Hoenn is found on the path to Meteor Falls. A man on the road has some noisy Pokémon, and  he's willing to give up the TM that taught them how to Roar.

Event 3: Lanette's Doll Collection

Don't run straight to Meteor Falls just yet. Lanette lives along this route; you should definitely visit her. She is embarrassed  about the state of her house—things are a wee bit messy—but she seems to function just fine in the

chaos. But that doesn't mean she wants everybody to know about the state of her house. In exchange for being hush-hush, Lanette gives you a Lotad Doll. That will certainly look nice in your Secret Base. (You have a Secret Base, don't you?)

TIP

There are several new wild Pokémon on Route 114, so be sure you start exploring with plenty of Poké Balls.

Meteor Falls

Moves Needed: HM03 (Surf), HM07 (Waterfall)

Meteor Falls is an area you only touch upon during your initial adventure, but once you have the moves needed to fully explore the cave system, return and explore the cave to its fullest. There are some good surprises in here, including a couple of finds that will help you in your quest to defeat the Elite Four.

POKÉMON APPEARANCES ON LAND (ROOM 1)

POKÉMON	CONDITIONS
Solrock	Common
Zubat	Very Common

POKÉMON APPEARANCES ON LAND (ROOM 2, ROOM 3 AND ROOM 4)

POKÉMON	CONDITIONS
Bagon	Common
Golbat	Very Common
Solrock	Very Common

POKÉMON APPEARANCES IN WATER (ROOM 1)

POKÉMON	CONDITIONS
Barboach	Common (Good Rod); Very Common (Super Rod)
Goldeen	Common (Old Rod); Very Common (Good Rod)
Magikarp	Very Common (Old Rod, Super Rod)
Solrock	Common
Zubat	Very Common

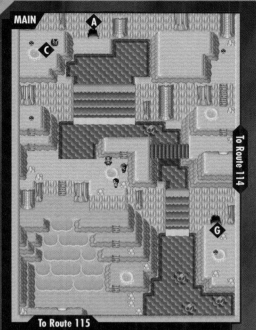

MAIN

To Route 114

To Route 115

POKÉMON APPEARANCES IN WATER (ROOM 2)

POKÉMON	CONDITIONS
Barboach	Common (Good Rod); Very Common (Super Rod)
Golbat	Very Common
Goldeen	Common (Old Rod, Good Rod)
Magikarp	Very Common (Old Rod, Super Rod)
Solrock	Common
Whiscash	Common (Super Rod)

POKÉMON APPEARANCES IN WATER (ROOM 3 AND ROOM 4)

POKÉMON	CONDITIONS
Barboach	Common (Good Rod); Very Common (Super Rod)
Golbat	Very Common
Goldeen	Common (Old Rod, Good Rod)
Magikarp	Very Common (Old Rod, Super Rod)
Solrock	Common

ROOM 2

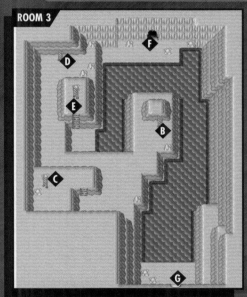

ROOM 3

ROOM 4

ITEMS

- Full Heal
- Moon Stone
- PP Up
- TM02 (Dragon Claw)
- TM23 (Iron Tail)

Event 1: Thwart Team Magma

As you enter Meteor Falls, Team Magma is about to abscond with a priceless Meteorite— something you know is going to nefarious purposes. After the Magma villains run off to Mt. Chimney with their stolen prize, head down and speak to Prof. Cozmo to get more information on Team Magma's plotting. After the conversation, head up to Mt. Chimney via the now-available Cable Car.

But they tricked me.
They even took my METEORITE away...

TIP

Meteor Falls deserves some serious exploration—but you cannot do it just yet. Return to this place after you receive HM07 (Waterfall) and you can access the lower levels where you find some good Items and rare Pokémon, such as Bagon. This Dragon Pokémon, if properly cared for, can grow into a very formidable Pokémon.

Route 115

Moves and Items Needed: *HM03 (Surf), HM06 (Rock Smash), Mach Bike*

ITEMS
- Bluk Berries x6
- Great Ball
- Iron
- Kelpsy Berries x6
- Super Potion
- TM01 (Focus Punch)

POKÉMON APPEARANCES ON LAND

POKÉMON	CONDITIONS
Jigglypuff	Common
Swablu	Common
Swellow	Common
Taillow	Very Common
Wingull	Common

POKÉMON APPEARANCES IN WATER

POKÉMON	CONDITIONS
Magikarp	Very Common (Old Rod, Good Rod)
Pelipper	Rare
Tentacool	Very Common; Common (Old Rod, Good Rod)
Wailmer	Common (Good Rod); Very Common (Super Rod)
Wingull	Common

To Meteor Falls

To Rustboro Town

Event 1: Exploration

Route 115 is a big area and it's almost impossible to see on a single visit unless you have HM03 (Surf). If you do have it, you can use the water lane just off the coast to move up and down the route.

From the beaches, you can explore the northernmost region of the route and pick up some Items.

Once you get either the Good Rod or the Super Rod, return to Route 115 to catch a wild Wailmer. That Pokémon is absolutely pivotal to solving a puzzle much later in your adventure, so be good to it.

Mt. Chimney

Moves Needed: None

ITEM
🎒 Meteorite

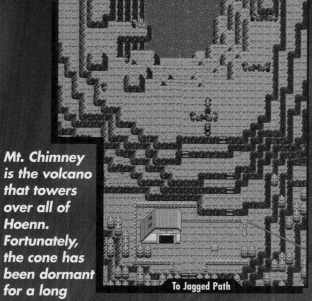

To Jagged Path

Mt. Chimney is the volcano that towers over all of Hoenn. Fortunately, the cone has been dormant for a long time. However, Team Magma is interested in the volcano, and that's bad news. While you are unsure of what they are trying to accomplish on the summit, it's definitely something that must be stopped. But the only way to reach the summit from the bottom (at least, for now) is the Cable Car.

Event 1: Ride the Cable Car

Now that Team Magma has acquired the Meteorite, no guards are posted at the Cable Car station. Ride the Cable Car to the

summit of Mt. Chimney to catch up with Team Magma as well as get an update on what Team Aqua has been up to.

Event 2: Team Magma and Team Aqua Locked in Battle

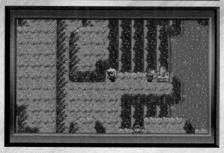

When you arrive at the summit, you see Team Magma and Team Aqua battling each other. That Meteorite causes concern among Team Aqua. Pass the battles and head north along the summit until you catch up with Team Magma Leader Maxie. Maxie is about to dump the

Meteorite into the volcano, so battle the leader to pause this plan. Maxie has powerful Pokémon, but by now, you should have a solid team yourself.

Don't forget to grab that Meteorite from the edge of the volcano and return it to Prof. Cozmo for your reward.

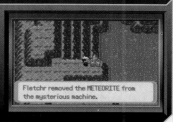

Fletchr removed the METEORITE from the mysterious machine.

Event 3: After Riding Team Magma Out

Things settle back into their normal routine once Team Magma has been run off of the summit. There will be a new batch of Trainers

on the mountaintop you can challenge in battles. Make sure you also stop by the Lava Cookie Lady who is selling Lava Cookies for only ₽200 each next to the Cable Car station. These are a local delicacy and your Pokémon are sure to love them.

Jagged Pass

Item Needed: *Acro Bike*

Jagged Pass leads down the side of Mt. Chimney. Unless you have the tools to get back up the face, it's a one-way trip down. There's something fishy about Jagged Pass, too. Team Magma seems to be concentrated in the area. Are they hiding something in the pass?

To Mt. Chimney

To Route 112

ITEMS

None

POKÉMON APPEARANCES

POKÉMON	CONDITIONS
Machop	Common
Numel	Very Common
Spoink	Common

Event 1: Explore the Pass

As mentioned, Jagged Pass is a one-way trip—unless you have the Acro Bike. (If you have the Mach Bike, switch it out at Rydel's shop in

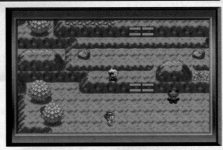

Mauville City.) The Acro Bike can pull wheelies that let you "hop" up the small stones on the side of the pass.

CAUTION

Carefully step down the side of Mt. Chimney. Unless you have the Acro Bike, there is no way back up the Jagged Pass. You have to go all the way around to the Cable Car again, ride it up to the summit, and then walk back down Jagged Pass.

Event 2: Access Team Magma Hideout

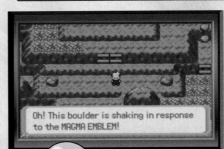

Oh! This boulder is shaking in response to the MAGMA EMBLEM!

After you get the Magma Emblem, you can access the Team Magma Hideout. Just walk down the face of the pass until you hear a low rumble. The presence of the Magma Emblem causes the doorway to the Hideout to reveal itself. Slip inside to take care of some unfinished business with Team Magma.

NOTE

Just because a Pokémon appears commonly, that doesn't mean it's any less of an asset. Commonly caught Pokémon, if taken care of properly, can evolve into wonderful new forms that are quite effective in battles.

Lavaridge Town

Moves Needed: None

Because it's located at the foot of Mt. Chimney, Lavaridge Town has a Hot Springs and hot sand resort where people come from all around to soak it up and unwind. The waters are known for their healing powers—perhaps you should slip in yourself and see what happens?

POKÉMART MERCHANDISE

ITEM	PRICE
Great Ball	₽600
Super Potion	₽700
Antidote	₽100
Parlyz Heal	₽200
Awakening	₽250
Burn Heal	₽250
Revive	₽1,500
Super Repel	₽500
X Speed	₽350

ITEMS
- Charcoal
- Go-Goggles
- Heat Badge
- Mystery Egg
- TM50 (Overheat)

POKÉMON HERB SHOP MERCHANDISE

ITEM	PRICE
Energypowder	₽500
Energy Root	₽800
Heal Powder	₽450
Revival Herb	₽2,800

POKÉMON APPEARANCES

POKÉMON	CONDITIONS
Wynaut	Hatch from Egg given by townsperson

Event 1: Hot Springs

I'd hoped to hatch it by covering it in hot sand by the hot springs. ♥

Stop by the Hot Springs when you first arrive in Lavaridge Town. Not just because of the reputation of the waters, but also to

receive a Mystery Egg from one of the townspeople. She has tried nurturing the Egg in the warm sand, but apparently it needs a little more personal care than that.

Event 2: Visit the Pokémon Herb Shop

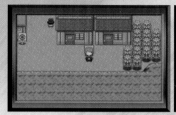

Welcome to the HERB SHOP, home of effective and inexpensive medicine!

The Pokémon Herb Shop is unique to Lavaridge Town—you won't find this little shop anywhere else in Hoenn. This store sells a small variety of Herbs that affect your Pokémon, such as restoring HP or reviving a fainted Pokémon. But there's a catch to these Herbs, which are noticeably less expensive than their equivalents: Pokémon loathe their bitter taste. Giving these Herbs to your Pokémon may cause them to dislike you, and that can affect battle performance, so use with care.

Event 3: Gym Leader Battle #4— Flannery

Flannery, Lavaridge Gym Leader

Pokémon Type:

FIRE

Recommended Move Type:

WATER
GROUND
ROCK

GYM LEADER'S POKÉMON

POKÉMON	LV	TYPE
Slugma	LV24	FIRE
Camerupt	LV26	FIRE
Torkoal	LV29	FIRE
Numel	LV24	FIRE

The Lavaridge Gym is full of haze, probably from all the Fire-type Pokémon within its walls. The Gym is separated into two levels, a ground floor and a basement. Flannery is on the ground floor, but there is no direct route from the front door to her. You must move from room to room, using the holes in the floor and ceiling to eventually reach her seat. Along the way, you have ample opportunity to practice battling Fire-type Pokémon with the Trainers guarding the holes. Once you reach Flannery herself, use your Water-type Moves to douse her Fire-type Pokémon. If you don't have a Water-type Pokémon at a high enough level to match Flannery's Pokémon, fall back on Ground- and Rock-type Moves, which also exploit a Fire-type Pokémon's weakness.

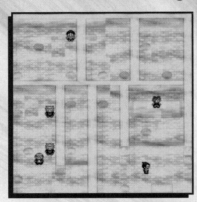

Items Won

Heat Badge: Pokémon up to LV50 now obey your commands. Also allows you to use HM04 (Strength) outside of battle.

TM50 (Overheat)

Event 4: Getting to Go-Goggles

After you defeat Flannery and earn the Heat Badge, Prof. Birch's child approaches you outside the Gym. So impressed with your Badges,

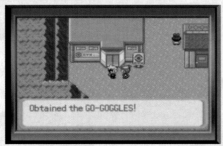

Obtained the GO-GOGGLES!

he/she gives you the Go-Goggles. These special specs allow you to see in a thick sandstorm, which means you can now explore the desert area of Route 111.

TIP

Receiving the Go-Goggles means you can now search for fossils in Mirage Tower and some new Pokémon in the desert. But don't forget that you now have the required number of Gym badges to challenge your father, Norman, back at the Petalburg Gym. Return to Petalburg Gym and face off against your father to earn one of the most useful Badges in the game. It allows you to use HM03 (Surf).

New Mauville

Moves and Items Needed:
HM03 (Surf); Basement Key

Items
- [ ] Escape Rope
- [ ] Full Heal
- [ ] Parlyz Heal
- [ ] Thunderstone
- [ ] Ultra Ball

Pokémon Appearances

POKÉMON	CONDITIONS
Electrode	Very Rare
Magnemite	Very Common
Magneton	Very Rare
Voltorb	Very Common (sometimes disguised as Poké Balls on ground)

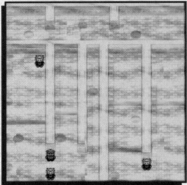

Event 1: Color-Coded Doors

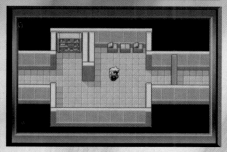

The route to the New Mauville electric generator is not a direct path. The hallways are locked down with a system of color-coded doors, and the doors swing open only if you step on like-colored floor switches. But beware, stepping on one switch either opens or shuts every door of that color. Put your foot down on the wrong switch and you may find yourself using an Escape Rope and starting all over again.

Event 2: Shut Down Generator

After slipping through the system of doors and battling wild Electric-type Pokémon, you finally reach the malfunctioning generator. Step on the small red switch in front of it to shut it down.

TIP

With four potentially new wild Pokémon to catch inside New Mauville, why not bring along some Poké Balls and expand your Pokédex?

Route 118

Moves and Items Needed: *HM03 (Surf), HM01 (Cut)*

To Mauville City · To Route 119 · To Route 123

POKÉMON APPEARANCES IN WATER	
POKÉMON	**CONDITIONS**
Carvanha	Common (Good Rod); Very Common (Super Rod)
Magikarp	Very Common (Old Rod, Good Rod)
Pelipper	Rare
Sharpedo	Very Common (Super Rod)
Tentacool	Very Common; Common (Old Rod, Good Rod)
Wingull	Very Common

POKÉMON APPEARANCES ON LAND	
POKÉMON	**CONDITIONS**
Electrike	Common
Kecleon	Very Rare
Linoone	Common
Manectric	Common
Wingull	Common
Zigzagoon	Common

ITEMS

- Good Rod
- Hyper Potion
- Sitrus Berries x4

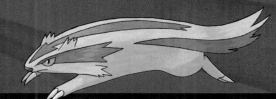

Event 1: Find the Good Rod

Hmm!
Take this GOOD ROD!

Cross the channel in the center of Route 118 to reach a Fisherman on the far shore. The avid angler is wild about his sport of choice and will give you a Good Rod for showing interest in it, too. The Good Rod is a significant upgrade over the Old Rod.

NOTE

Now that you have the Good Rod, consider returning to previous watery routes to fish for wild Pokémon that would not respond to the Old Rod.

Event 2: TV Idol

The media await you on the opposite shore. Gabby and Ty are ready with more than just cameras and microphones. They will engage you in another battle just so they can report on it. Take them on and then have a choice word ready for the after-battle interview.

Route 119

Moves and Items Needed: *HM03 (Surf), HM07 (Waterfall), Acro Bike*

To Fortree City

Weather Institute

To Route 118

ITEMS

- Elixir
- HM02 (Fly)
- Hondew Berries x4
- Hyper Potion
- Leaf Stone
- Leppa Berries x2
- Pomeg Berries x6
- Rare Candy
- Sitrus Berries x2
- Super Repel
- Zinc

POKÉMON APPEARANCES IN WATER

POKÉMON	CONDITIONS
Carvanha	Common (Good Rod); Very Common (Super Rod)
Feebas	Very Rare
Magikarp	Very Common (Old Rod, Good Rod)
Pelipper	Rare
Tentacool	Very Common; Common (Old Rod, Good Rod)
Wingull	Very Common

POKÉMON APPEARANCES

POKÉMON	CONDITIONS
Kecleon	Very Rare
Linoone	Common
Oddish	Common
Tropius	Rare
Zigzagoon	Common

NOTE

Without a doubt, you have by now noticed the proliferation of wild Magikarp in the waters of Hoenn. These wild Pokémon are not especially effective battlers—so why collect one? A little care and experience will reveal the Magikarp's evolved form, the Gyarados.

Event 1: Tall Grass

The short grass of Hoenn gives way to tall grass in Route 119. This thick, tall foliage is much harder to wade through—in fact, it's so thick you can't even ride a bike through it. The tall grass hides a lot, too. Trainers, Items, and wild Pokémon are all waiting for you in the thick of it.

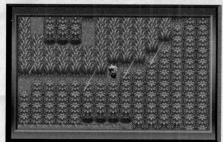

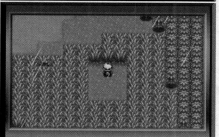

However, you don't have to use Repel to slink through the grass without encountering wild Pokémon. Use HM01 (Cut) to trim the green around you, creating a clear path through the tall grass. However, this will not stop Trainers from engaging you.

CAUTION

Notice the occasional tree or rock that doesn't quite match those around it? Watch out—that's a Ninja Boy. These Trainers attempt to hide behind painted cut-outs of nature and then jump out when unsuspecting adventurers wander by.

Event 2: Weather Institute

The Weather Institute studies climate patterns across Hoenn, but right now the researchers inside are staving off the unwanted interests of Team Aqua. Is there something you can do to help?

Event 3: Battle with Prof. Birch's Kid

After you run Team Aqua out of the Weather Institute, you encounter Prof. Birch's child on the way to Fortree City. He or she has had plenty of time to raise Pokémon and wants to battle you to test their progress. If you win the battle, you receive more than just admiration—you get HM02 (Fly). The HM allows you to teach Fly to one of your Pokémon, a move that's not only handy in battle, but also allows you to flit from town to town through the air, as long as you have the Feather Badge to use it. You can get the Feather Badge in the Fortree Gym.

TIP

After you have HM07 (Waterfall), you can explore this route's northernmost tip. Use the Acro Bike to cross the tiny bridge and pick up a rare Item as well as access a hard-to-reach Secret Base.

Secret Base Real Estate

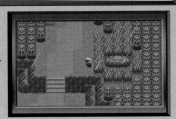

Potential Secret Bases are hidden in the tall grass along Route 119. Look for bushes like this and then unleash Secret Power to unlock them.

Weather Institute

Moves Needed: *None*

ITEM
☐ Mystic Water

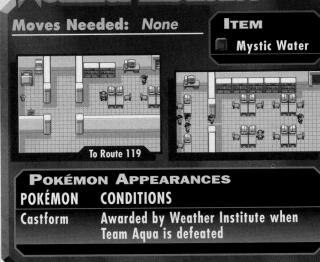

To Route 119

POKéMON APPEARANCES

POKéMON	CONDITIONS
Castform	Awarded by Weather Institute when Team Aqua is defeated

Event 1: Rest Your Weary Head

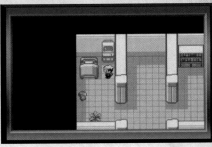

There is a comfy bed on the first floor of the Weather Institute where you can rest up before taking on the string of Team Aqua Grunts inside the Weather Institute. You can sleep in the bed as often as you like.

Event 2: Defeat Team Aqua

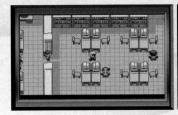

It might be an odd way of thanking you, but take this POKéMON.

Team Aqua has taken over the Weather Institute, desperately in search of a special Pokémon that it believes could affect the climate and rainfall in Hoenn: Castform. Battle all of the Team Aqua Grunts to rid the Institute of them, and then speak to the scientists. They reward you with a Castform of your own.

NOTE

On the way out of the Weather Institute, you overhear that Team Magma was last spotted heading to Mt. Pyre.

Legendary Spoiler Alert

After you defeat the Elite Four, return to the Weather Institute and speak to the same man who gave you the Castform. He has been tracking some strange weather patterns in Hoenn lately and his observations will have a very positive effect on your Pokédex.

Presently, a drought has been recorded in ROUTE 114. ♥

Fortree City

Moves Needed: None

ITEMS
- Feather Badge
- Mental Herb
- TM10 (Hidden Power)
- TM40 (Aerial Ace)

Fortree City is a small town nestled in tree groves. The houses are connected by a system of rope bridges that hang high above the ground. But even though the town is one with nature, it still boasts many modern conveniences, such as a Pokémart and Pokémon Center, as well as a Gym in the town's center. Now, if there were just a way to actually get to it....

POKÉMON APPEARANCES
POKÉMON	CONDITIONS
Plusle	Trade for a Volbeat in town

POKÉMART MERCHANDISE
ITEM	PRICE
Great Ball	₽600
Ultra Ball	₽1,200
Super Potion	₽700
Hyper Potion	₽1,200
Antidote	₽100
Parlyz Heal	₽200
Awakening	₽250
Revive	₽1,500
Super Repel	₽500
Wood Mail	₽50

DESK STORE MERCHANDISE
ITEM	PRICE
Small Desk	₽3,000
Pokémon Desk	₽3,000
Heavy Desk	₽6,000
Ragged Desk	₽6,000
Comfort Desk	₽6,000
Brick Desk	₽9,000
Camp Desk	₽9,000
Hard Desk	₽9,000

CHAIR STORE MERCHANDISE
ITEM	PRICE
Small Chair	₽2,000
Pokémon Chair	₽2,000
Heavy Chair	₽2,000
Ragged Chair	₽2,000
Comfort Chair	₽2,000
Brick Chair	₽2,000
Camp Chair	₽2,000

Event 1: Secret Base Shopping

Two counters in Fortree City sell furniture for your Secret Base. You can buy a variety of Desks and Chairs from these counters, an excellent way to spruce up your home away from home.

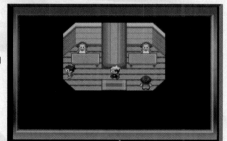

Event 2: Hidden Power

A woman in Fortree City believes you can deduce whether or not you have hidden powers of your own. If you can guess which hand she is hiding a coin in three times in a row, she will gift you the TM10 (Hidden Power).

Now, tell me, have I palmed it in the right hand? Or in the left?

▶Right
　Left

Event 3: Lonely Minun?

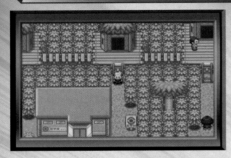

A little girl in the northwest corner of Fortree City would like to get her hands on a Volbeat and is willing to trade a rare Plusle for it.

Event 4: Hit the Gym

Unfortunately, you cannot access the Fortree Gym on your first visit to Fortree City. The path is blocked by an invisible force. The answer to this puzzle lies on Route 120 with a familiar face.

TIP

After you receive the special Item, Devon Scope, which lets you see these invisible barriers, return to the Gym to challenge the Gym Leader.

Event 5: Gym Leader Battle #6— Winona

Winona, Fortree Gym Leader

Pokémon Type:

| FLYING |

Recommended Move Types:

| ELECTRIC |
| ICE |
| ROCK |

GYM LEADER'S POKÉMON

POKÉMON	LV	TYPE	
Swablu	LV29	FLYING	NORMAL
Altaria	LV33	DRAGON	FLYING
Tropius	LV29	GRASS	FLYING
Pelipper	LV30	WATER	FLYING
Skarmory	LV31	STEEL	FLYING

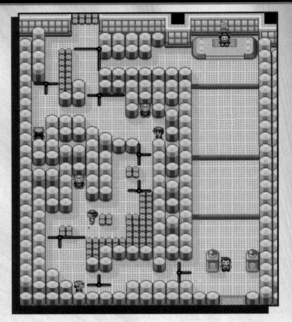

The path to Winona, Fortree Gym Leader, is a bit tricky. You must navigate a system of revolving gates, but sometimes the gates aren't as user-friendly as you may hope. Some gates revolve only once or twice, meaning you must sometimes cross back through a gate multiple times to finally get it in the correct position to pass. Add some pretty powerful Trainers to the route, and you may need to rest before battling Winona.

Winona uses Flying Pokémon, but all of her Pokémon have secondary types, too, such as Steel and Dragon. Keep these dual-types in mind when sending your Pokémon into battle. If you have a strong Electric-type Pokémon, though, you can tap into the weakness that they all share and earn the Gym badge.

ITEMS WON

Feather Badge: Pokémon up to LV70 will obey your commands; grants use of HM02 (Fly) in the field.

TM40 (Aerial Ace)

Route 120

Moves Needed: HM01 (Cut), HM03 (Surf)

ITEMS

- Aspear Berries x6
- Devon Scope
- Full Heal
- Hyper Potion
- Nanab Berries x3
- Nest Ball
- Nugget
- Pecha Berries x6
- Pinap Berries x3
- Razz Berries x2
- TM11 (Sunny Day)
- Wepear Berries x3

POKÉMON APPEARANCES ON LAND

POKÉMON	CONDITIONS
Absol	Rare
Kecleon	Very Rare; find two with Devon Scope
Marill	Common
Mightyena	Common
Oddish	Common
Poochyena	Common
Registeel	After unlocking Sealed Chamber
Seedot	Very Rare

POKÉMON APPEARANCES IN WATER

POKÉMON	CONDITIONS
Barboach	Common (Good Rod); Very Common (Super Rod)
Goldeen	Very Rare (Old Rod); Common (Gold Rod)
Magikarp	Very Common (Old Rod, Good Rod)
Marill	Very Common

To Fortree City

To Route 121

Event 1: Devon Scope

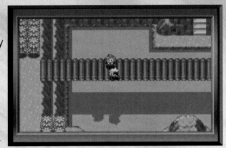

Something invisible is blocking your way to the Fortree Gym, but Steven is waiting on the bridge with just the thing you need to see your way through: the Devon Scope. The Devon Scope flushes out invisible Pokémon, like the Kecleon, so take it back to the Gym and use it to make your way through.

Event 2: Invisible Pokémon

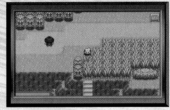 

Use the Devon Scope to spy a Kecleon blocking the way to the cave at the top of Route 120. After the battle, head into the cave and pick up TM11 (Sunny Day), the perfect complement to your Fire-type Pokémon.

Event 3: Ancient Cave?

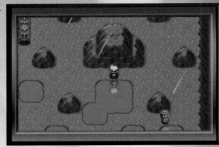

It is rumored that Route 120 is host to an Ancient Cave, but nobody can find the entrance to the ruins. There is an explorer in the correct spot, but without the Sealed Chamber to guide him, he will never spot the entrance. When you complete the mystery for yourself, return here to seek out one of the mystic Legendary Pokémon, Registeel.

Event 4: Fresh Berries

A girl in Route 120's southern region will present you with a very rare berry if you talk to her. Take the berry and use the soft soil nearby to plant it. Try to grow a few trees' worth of this berry so its special powers can flourish in Hoenn.

NOTE

Gabby and Ty are in the area, searching for a good interview. If you want to be on TV again, engage them in battle.

Route 121

Moves and Items Needed: *HM01 (Cut), HM03 (Surf)*

POKÉMON APPEARANCES ON LAND

POKÉMON	CONDITIONS
Gloom	Rare
Kecleon	Very Rare
Mightyena	Common
Oddish	Common
Poochyena	Common
Shuppet	Common
Wingull	Rare

ITEMS

- Aspear Berries x2
- Carbos
- Chesto Berries x2
- Nanab Berries x6
- Persim Berries x2
- Rawst Berries x2

POKÉMON APPEARANCES IN WATER

POKÉMON	CONDITIONS
Magikarp	Very Common (Old Rod, Good Rod)
Pelipper	Rare
Tentacool	Very Common; Common (Old Rod, Good Rod)
Wailmer	Common (Good Rod); Very Common (Super Rod)
Wingull	Very Common

Event 1: Team Aqua's Up to Something

As you head west through Route 121, you catch up with Team Aqua. They are on their way to Mt. Pyre. Follow them to find out what their plans are.

Event 2: Safari Zone

Route 121 hosts the entrance to the Safari Zone, a special game area where you can collect Pokémon not found elsewhere in the Hoenn region, such as Psyduck and Pikachu. It costs only ₽500 to test your skills in the Safari Zone, and in a feature exclusive to *Pokémon Emerald*, a new area opens in the Safari Zone after you defeat the Elite Four. This new area offers even more wild Pokémon.

Safari Zone

Moves and Items Needed: *HM03 (Surf), Acro Bike, Mach Bike*

ITEMS

- Calcium
- Max Revive
- TM22 (Solarbeam)

The Safari Zone is a special area in Hoenn where Trainers and Pokémon Masters can come and test their skills at catching Pokémon without traditional battling methods. Many of the Pokémon in the Safari Zone cannot be found anywhere else in Hoenn, so if there is one particular Pokémon you really want in your collection, you must visit Safari Zone at least once. But because there is a timer on your visit (only 500 steps), you'll likely need to visit at least a few times to see everything and catch all of the Pokémon you want.

POKÉMON APPEARANCES ON LAND (NE)

POKÉMON	CONDITIONS
Geodude	Very Common (Rock Smash)
Gloom	Common
Heracross	Rare
Natu	Common
Oddish	Common
Phanpy	Common
Xatu	Rare

POKÉMON APPEARANCES ON LAND (NW) AND (SE)

POKÉMON	CONDITIONS
Dodrio	Rare
Doduo	Common
Girafarig	Common
Gloom	Rare
Natu	Common
Oddish	Very Common
Pikachu	Rare
Pinsir	Rare
Rhyhorn	Common
Wobbuffet	Common

POKÉMON APPEARANCES ON LAND (SW)

POKÉMON	CONDITIONS
Doduo	Common
Girafarig	Common
Gloom	Rare
Natu	Common
Oddish	Very Common
Pikachu	Rare
Wobbuffet	Common

POKÉMON APPEARANCES IN WATER (SW)

POKÉMON	CONDITIONS
Goldeen	Common (Old Rod); Very Common (Good Rod, Super Rod)
Magikarp	Very Common (Old Rod, Good Rod)
Psyduck	Very Common
Seaking	Common (Super Rod)

POKÉMON APPEARANCES IN WATER (NW)

POKÉMON	CONDITIONS
Goldeen	Common (Old Rod); Very Common (Good Rod, Super Rod)
Golduck	Rare
Magikarp	Very Common (Old Rod, Good Rod)
Psyduck	Very Common
Seaking	Common (Super Rod)

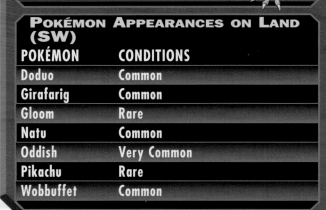

The Safari Zone entrance fee is ₽500. For this small amount, you receive 30 Safari Balls and the keys to the kingdom. Your movement is restricted only by whether or not you bring Pokémon that can use HM03 (Surf) or which Bike you have in your Bag. You cannot take any Safari Balls outside of the Safari Zone, though.

Once you enter the Safari Zone, start seeking out wild Pokémon in the grass and water. When you happen upon a Pokémon, you have four choices:

Throw a Safari Ball and try to catch it.

Get closer to the wild Pokémon.

Offer the Pokémon a PokéBlock.

Back away and look for another Pokémon.

The wild Pokémon of the Safari Zone can be pretty cagey. Almost anything can spook them enough to run away. You can throw as many Safari Balls as you have at the Pokémon in an effort to catch it, but you may cause it to flee. You can also attempt to ingratiate yourself to the Pokémon by either sidling up to it carefully (Go Near) or offering it a tasty PokéBlock.

The PokéBlock is sometimes your best bet for capturing a rare Pokémon in the Safari Zone. You can try to encourage rare Pokémon out of hiding by placing a PokéBlock in one of several feeders throughout the Safari Zone. If you match up the PokéBlock with the nature of the Pokémon, there's a good chance you'll lure a desired wild Pokémon close enough to catch.

TIP

A couple areas in the Safari Zone can be accessed only with the Acro Bike or the Mach Bike, such as the small area on the other side of the trick rail in the northeast corner.

NOTE

Check back with the Safari Zone after you defeat the Elite Four. A new area opens up directly above the Safari Zone entrance. This area is home to many more wild Pokémon not available in the original Safari Zone. For additional details on the additional Safari Zone, please see this guide's Bonuses and Extra Content section.

Lilycove City

Move Needed: HM03 (Surf)

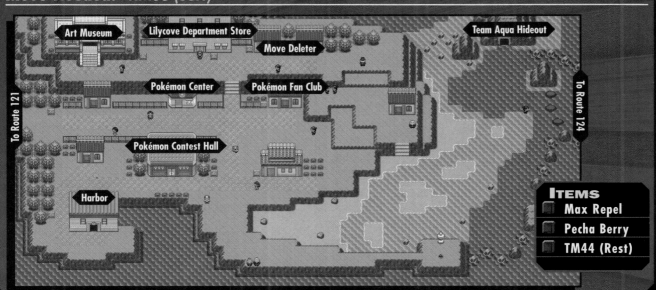

Art Museum
Lilycove Department Store
Move Deleter
Team Aqua Hideout
Pokémon Center
Pokémon Fan Club
To Route 121
To Route 124
Pokémon Contest Hall
Harbor

ITEMS
- Max Repel
- Pecha Berry
- TM44 (Rest)

If Lilycove City isn't one of the biggest metro centers in Hoenn, it's at least the biggest hub of commerce in the land. The Lilycove Department Store is a multi-story monument to the fine art of shopping. However, there's certainly more to do in town than just spend your hard-won cash. Stop by the Pokémon Contest Hall to enter your Pokémon in move-based challenges or visit the Art Museum for a dose of culture. Maybe one day you'll help cover the halls with beautiful artwork.

POKÉMON APPEARANCES IN WATER

POKÉMON	CONDITIONS
Pelipper	Rare
Staryu	Common (Super Rod)
Tentacool	Very Common; Common (Old Rod, Good Rod)
Wingull	Very Common

LILYCOVE DEPARTMENT STORE MERCHANDISE

There are 11 shopping opportunities at the Lilycove Department Store, the largest shopping experience in Hoenn. You can buy everything from recovery Items to Secret Base decor from the counters in this five-story mall.

LEFT COUNTER, 2F

ITEM	PRICE
Poké Ball	₽200
Great Ball	₽600
Ultra Ball	₽1,200
Escape Rope	₽550
Full Heal	₽600
Antidote	₽100
Parlyz Heal	₽200
Burn Heal	₽250
Ice Heal	₽250
Awakening	₽250
Fluffy Tail	₽1,000

RIGHT COUNTER, 2F

ITEM	PRICE
Potion	₽300
Super Potion	₽700
Hyper Potion	₽1,200
Max Potion	₽2,500
Revive	₽1,500
Repel	₽350
Super Repel	₽500
Max Repel	₽700
Wave Mail	₽50
Mech Mail	₽50

LEFT COUNTER, 3F

ITEM	PRICE
Protein	₽9,800
Calcium	₽9,800
Iron	₽9,800
Zinc	₽9,800
Carbos	₽9,800
HP Up	₽9,800

RIGHT COUNTER, 3F

ITEM	PRICE
X Speed	₽350
X Special	₽350
X Attack	₽500
X Defend	₽550
Dire Hit	₽650
Guard Spec.	₽700
X Accuracy	₽950

LEFT COUNTER, 4F

ITEM	PRICE
TM38 (Fire Blast)	₽5,500
TM25 (Thunder)	₽5,500
TM14 (Blizzard)	₽5,500
TM15 (Hyper Beam)	₽7,500

RIGHT COUNTER, 4F

ITEM	PRICE
TM17 (Protect)	₽3,000
TM20 (Safeguard)	₽3,000
TM33 (Reflect)	₽3,000
TM16 (Light Screen)	₽3,000

LEFT BOTTOM COUNTER, 5F

ITEM	PRICE
Ball Poster	₽1,000
Green Poster	₽1,000
Red Poster	₽1,000
Blue Poster	₽1,000
Cute Poster	₽1,000
Pika Poster	₽1,500
Long Poster	₽1,500
Sea Poster	₽1,500
Sky Poster	₽1,500

RIGHT BOTTOM COUNTER, 5F

ITEM	PRICE
Surf Mat	₽4,000
Thunder Mat	₽4,000
Fire Blast Mat	₽4,000
Powder Snow Mat	₽4,000
Attract Mat	₽4,000
Fissure Mat	₽4,000
Spikes Mat	₽4,000
Glitter Mat	₽2,000
Jump Mat	₽2,000
Spin Mat	₽2,000

LEFT TOP COUNTER, 5F

ITEM	PRICE
Pichu Doll	₽3,000
Pikachu Doll	₽3,000
Marill Doll	₽3,000
Jigglypuff Doll	₽3,000
Duskull Doll	₽3,000
Wynaut Doll	₽3,000
Baltoy Doll	₽3,000
Kecleon Doll	₽3,000
Azurill Doll	₽3,000
Skitty Doll	₽3,000
Swablu Doll	₽3,000
Gulpin Doll	₽3,000

RIGHT TOP COUNTER, 5F

ITEM	PRICE
Pika Cushion	₽2,000
Round Cushion	₽2,000
Zigzag Cushion	₽2,000
Spin Cushion	₽2,000
Diamond Cushion	₽2,000
Ball Cushion	₽2,000
Grass Cushion	₽2,000
Fire Cushion	₽2,000
Water Cushion	₽2,000

ROOFTOP VENDING MACHINE

ITEM	PRICE
Fresh Water	₽200
Soda Pop	₽300
Lemonade	₽350

ROOFTOP CLEAR-OUT SALE*

ITEM	PRICE
Breakable Door	₽3,000
Cute TV	₽15,000
Fence Length	₽500
Fence Width	₽500
Mud Ball	₽200
Rhydon Doll	₽10,000
Round TV	₽15,000
Sand Ornament	₽3,000
Slide	₽8,000
Solid Board	₽3,000
Stand	₽7,000
Tire	₽800
TV	₽12,000
Wailmer Doll	₽10,000

* The Sale isn't available until after the game is completed (after you become the Pokémon League Champion).

Event 1: Battle at the Department Store

When you first enter Lilycove City, head up to the Department Store and face off against Prof. Birch's child again. As promised, he or she has been practicing and offers a greater challenge this time—especially since the team has grown to four members. If you've been leveling up your Pokémon evenly, you should be able to emerge from this battle victorious.

Event 2: Shopping Spree

Now hit the Department Store and start spending all that cash you've won from your Trainer battles. There are five floors of commerce in this single building, including a rooftop complete with a Vending Machine. (Score a few drinks from the Vending Machine before you leave—Pokémon love the sweet recovery Items.)

After you've shopped a little, head back down to the first floor and get your Lottery Ticket from the front desk. The clerk will compare your Lottery Ticket's numbers to the winning set of numbers. If you match at least two of the numbers, you win a prize. The more numbers you match, the better your prize. if you're really lucky, you could win an awesome Master Ball—one of the most coveted Poké Balls in all of Hoenn.

In addition to the Lottery, the Department Store also holds special sales. Check the televisions in other towns to find out when these deals will be offered. Return to the store when a sale is on and you'll be able to decorate your Secret Base on the cheap.

Event 3: Pokémon Contest Hall

The Pokémon Contest Hall is where Trainers from across Hoenn gather to enter their Pokémon in special Pokémon Contests. These aren't like regular battles. Instead, your Pokémon's traits and moves are judged on various merits. Is your Pokémon cool? Beautiful? The best way to improve your chances in these contests is to use the Berry Blenders in the lobby to create tasty PokéBlocks.

TIP

Visit the house to the left of the Pokémon Contest Hall to receive PokéBlock-making tips from the PokéBlock Master. Listen to her carefully and you'll be a better PokéBlock-maker for it.

Event 4: Pokémon Trainer Fan Club

This club loves to gather and talk about all things Trainer-related. They always recognize the best talent in Hoenn, and if you manage to beat all of the Gym Leaders or even defeat the Elite Four, they are sure to sing your praises.

Event 5: Museum Visit

The Art Museum next to the Department Store is full of priceless works of art, but there is always room for more. The Curator takes you upstairs to show you the new display space and asks you to help him cover the walls with new

paintings. If you ever happen across a cool painting while exploring Hoenn, mention the Art Museum and perhaps the work will soon hang in its hallowed halls.

Event 6: Move Deleter

The Move Deleter offers a very valuable service to Trainers—he helps your Pokémon un-learn HM moves you no longer need or want. By freeing up space for a new move, you can teach your Pokémon newer skills that will help them in the tougher battles ahead, or perhaps a slick move that will go over huge at the Pokémon Contest Hall.

Event 7: Team Aqua Hideout

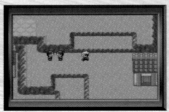 

Team Aqua has settled down in Lilycove City and is using the sea cave to the east as their Hideout. Team Aqua Grunts are currently teaching a legion of Wailmer new moves in the east bay, effectively cutting off access to the town from Route 124. Unfortunately, there isn't much you can do to displace Team Aqua right now, but as soon as you have the tools to evict them, come back and help the people of Lilycove City.

Route 122 and Mt. Pyre

Move Needed: HM03 (Surf)

POKÉMON APPEARANCES IN MT. PYRE (FLOORS 1–3)	
POKÉMON	CONDITIONS
Shuppet	Very Common

POKÉMON APPEARANCES IN MT. PYRE (FLOORS 4–6)	
POKÉMON	CONDITIONS
Shuppet	Very Common
Duskull	Common

POKÉMON APPEARANCES ON LAND (MOUNTAIN WALL)	
POKÉMON	CONDITIONS
Shuppet	Very Common
Vulpix	Common
Wingull	Common

POKÉMON APPEARANCES ON LAND (MOUNTAIN SUMMIT)	
POKÉMON	CONDITIONS
Chimecho	Rare
Duskull	Common
Shuppet	Very Common

POKÉMON APPEARANCES IN WATER (ROUTE 122)	
POKÉMON	CONDITIONS
Magikarp	Very Common (Old Rod, Good Rod)
Pelipper	Rare
Sharpedo	Very Common (Super Rod)
Tentacool	Very Common; Common (Old Rod, Good Rod)
Wailmer	Common (Good Rod); Very Common (Super Rod)
Wingull	Very Common

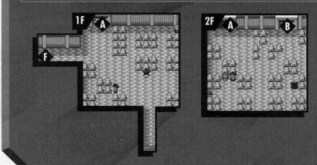

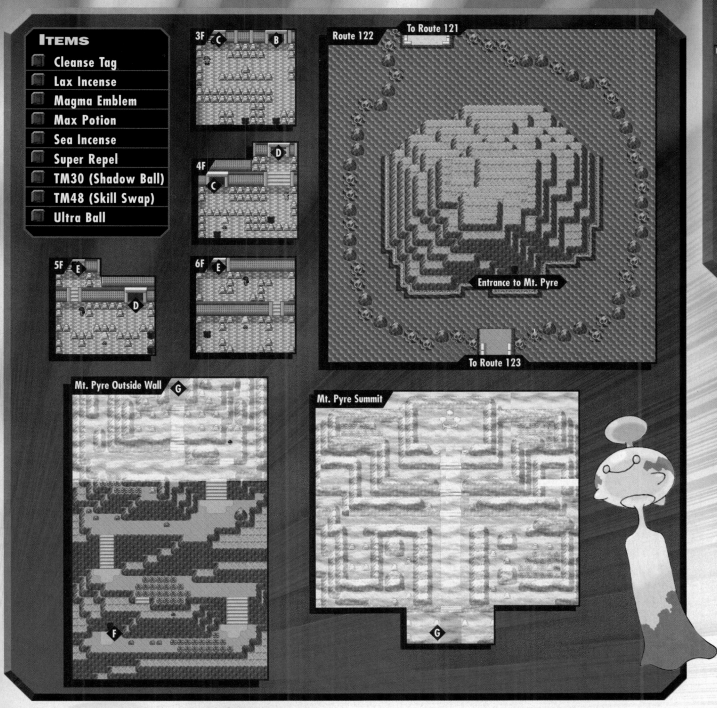

ITEMS

- Cleanse Tag
- Lax Incense
- Magma Emblem
- Max Potion
- Sea Incense
- Super Repel
- TM30 (Shadow Ball)
- TM48 (Skill Swap)
- Ultra Ball

3F

4F

5F

6F

Route 122

To Route 121

Entrance to Mt. Pyre

To Route 123

Mt. Pyre Outside Wall

Mt. Pyre Summit

Event 1: Enter the Mausoleum

There are two routes you can take at Mt. Pyre. From the first floor, you have two choices. You can immediately head outside and scale the face of the mountain to challenge Team Aqua at the summit. Or, you can explore the six floors of the mausoleum inside and collect both some very good Items and some rare Pokémon.

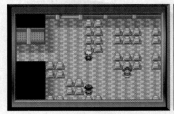

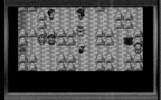

Event 2: Summit Challenge

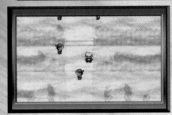 

Obtained the MAGMA EMBLEM!

When you're finished exploring the interior of the mountain, start ascending the outer mountain wall. A mist settles over the path the closer you get to the top. You must challenge Team Aqua at the summit, eventually coming into contact with Team Aqua Leader Archie. It seems he has stolen a precious Red Orb from a summit shrine and Team Magma Leader Maxie has absconded with a Blue Orb.

Only trouble can come from these two Leaders having the Orbs, so it's up to you to stop them. But where? The old couple at the top of the mountain gives you an Item they found dropped after the scene, the Magma Emblem. With this token, you can enter the Team Magma Hideout on the Jagged Pass.

Route 123

Moves Needed: *HM01 (Cut), HM03 (Surf)*

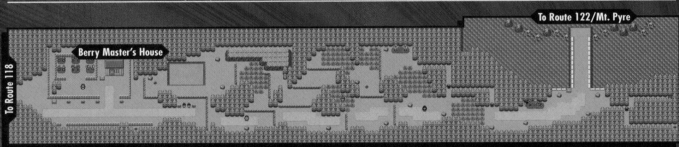

To Route 122/Mt. Pyre

Berry Master's House

To Route 118

ITEMS

- Calcium
- Elixir
- Grepa Berries x8
- Lum Berry
- Pecha Berries x2
- Pomeg Berries x8
- PP Up
- Qualot Berries x8
- Rawst Berries x2
- Revival Herb
- Sitrus Berries x2
- Tamato Berries x2
- TM19 (Giga Drain)
- Ultra Ball

POKÉMON APPEARANCES ON LAND

POKÉMON	CONDITIONS
Gloom	Rare
Kecleon	Rare
Mightyena	Common
Oddish	Common
Shuppet	Common
Wingull	Rare

POKÉMON APPEARANCES IN WATER

POKÉMON	CONDITIONS
Magikarp	Very Common (Old Rod, Good Rod)
Pelipper	Rare
Tentacool	Very Common; Common (Old Rod, Good Rod)
Wailmer	Common (Good Rod), Very Common (Super Rod)
Wingull	Very Common

Event 1: See the Berry Master

The chief feature of Route 123 is the Berry Master's House, the destination in Hoenn for the discerning berry fan. You can find some very rare

berries at the house. The place is also rich with fertile soil, so consider turning this into your own private orchard. Be sure to step inside and chat for a spell.

Event 2: Getting TM19 (Giga Drain)

Be sure you chat with this young woman on Route 123. She's crazy about Grass-type Pokémon and if you happen to have one in your party, she gives

you TM19 (Giga Drain). This is a great move to teach your Grass-type Pokémon.

Magma Hideout

Move Needed: HM04 (Strength)

Buried deep in Mt. Chimney, the Team Magma Hideout is where the land-loving crew stores its drilling equipment and plots its deeds.

POKÉMON APPEARANCES

POKÉMON	CONDITIONS
Geodude	Very Common
Graveler	Common
Torkoal	Common

ITEMS

- Escape Rope
- Full Restore
- Max Elixir
- Max Revive
- Nugget
- PP Max
- Rare Candy

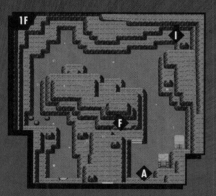

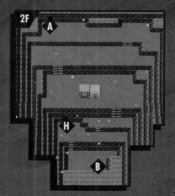

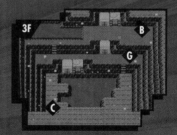

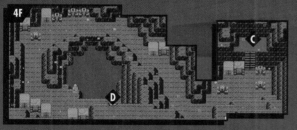

Route 124

Moves Needed: HM03 (Surf), HM08 (Dive)

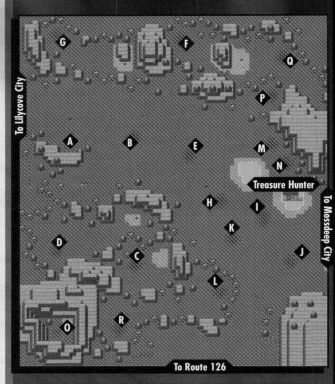

To Lilycove City

Treasure Hunter

To Mossdeep City

To Route 126

Underwater

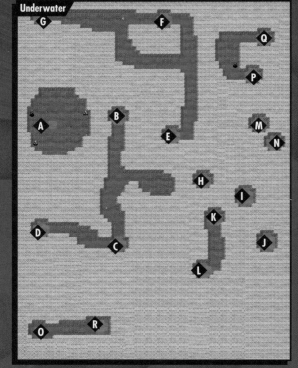

NOTE

You cannot visit the Team Aqua Hideout unless you first stop at Slateport City and see the press conference at the Harbor where Team Aqua steals Capt. Stern's submersible.

Event 1: Stop, Thief!

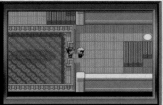

Team Aqua's Hideout has only a few rooms, but they are connected through a clever system of warps that send you to almost every corner of the place before you can finally catch up with the stolen submersible. Unfortunately, a battle delays you just long enough for Team Aqua to escape with the sub.

Event 2: Grab the Master Ball

Before you leave the Team Aqua Hideout, warp all the way to the Team Leader's room in the facility. The room contains a much-coveted

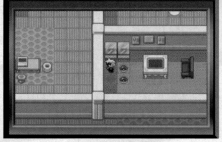

Master Ball, but also a Voltorb disguised as a Poké Ball. You want that Master Ball, so battle the Voltorb and don't leave until the Master Ball is safely in your Bag.

ITEMS
- ☐ Blue Shard
- ☐ Red Shard
- ☐ Yellow Shard

POKÉMON APPEARANCES IN WATER

POKÉMON	CONDITIONS
Magikarp	Very Common (Old Rod, Good Rod)
Pelipper	Rare
Sharpedo	Very Common (Super Rod)
Tentacool	Very Common; Common (Old Rod, Good Rod)
Wailmer	Common (Good Rod); Very Common (Super Rod)
Wingull	Very Common

POKÉMON APPEARANCES UNDERWATER

POKÉMON	CONDITIONS
Chinchou	Common
Clamperl	Very Common
Relicanth	Rare

Event 1: Treasure Hunter

There lives a solitary man on a small island in Route 124, the Treasure Hunter. Stop by the Hunter's House to strike a deal with him. If you bring him special, colored Shards from deep beneath the surface, he will give you some of the treasures he's uncovered over the years. Just bring your booty back to the house for the trade.

SHARD ITEMS

SHARD	EXCHANGE ITEM
Blue Shard	Water Stone
Green Shard	Leaf Stone
Red Shard	Fire Stone
Yellow Shard	Thunderstone

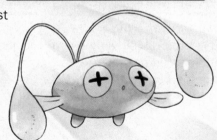

Event 2: Dive Deep

You cannot dive for sunken treasure just yet, though. Not until you get HM08 (Dive) in Mossdeep City can you sink beneath the waves for a look into the briny blue. When you can Dive, look for dark patches of water on the surface. Activate HM08 (Dive) and your Pokémon slips below the surface. When you want to rise to the surface, seek out a light patch of water that indicates light coming from above.

Mossdeep City

Move Needed: *HM03 (Surf)*

Mossdeep City is another island metropolis to the east of Hoenn's main landmass. The island is home to Hoenn's Space Center, the rocket science facility that furthers space exploration. A rocket launch is scheduled to take place soon, but somebody desires the rocket fuel needed to put the vehicle into orbit. Better head to the Space Center and check it out.

ITEMS
- ☐ HM08 (Dive)
- ☐ King's Rock
- ☐ Mind Badge
- ☐ Net Ball
- ☐ Sun Stone
- ☐ Super Rod
- ☐ TM04 (Calm Mind)

POKÉMART MERCHANDISE

ITEM	PRICE
Ultra Ball	₽1,200
Net Ball	₽1,000
Dive Ball	₽1,000
Hyper Potion	₽1,200
Full Heal	₽600
Revive	₽1,500
Max Repel	₽700
X Attack	₽500
X Defend	₽550

POKÉMON APPEARANCES IN TOWN

POKÉMON	CONDITIONS
Beldum	Find this in Steven's House after defeating him at Meteor Falls (after becoming Pokémon League Champion).

Steven's House

Mossdeep Gym

Space Center

Pokémon Center

Pokémart

To Route 124

To Route 127

POKÉMON APPEARANCES	
POKÉMON	**CONDITIONS**
Magikarp	Very Common (Old Rod, Good Rod)
Pelipper	Rare
Sharpedo	Very Common (Super Rod)
Tentacool	Very Common; Common (Old Rod, Good Rod)
Wailmer	Common (Good Rod); Very Common (Super Rod)
Wingull	Very Common

Event 1: Get the Super Rod

Stop by the Fisherman's House next to the Space Center, the large green building on the east side of the island town. He gives you the Super Rod, the best fishing pole in all of Hoenn. Now you can head back to the blue and catch some potent Water-type Pokémon.

Hey there, TRAINER!
A SUPER ROD really is super! ♥

Event 2: Tour Mossdeep City

Mossdeep's citizens are extremely chatty and generous. Visit with everybody, and stop by as many homes as possible to get all of the free Items being handed out, such as the King's Rock.

Also stop by the Wireless House near the town's center. If you have a Wireless Adapter, you can play a pair of fun mini-games at the

Wireless House with other *Pokémon* players. Pokémon Jump is a jump-rope game that only miniature Pokémon (no higher than 28") can enter. If you have a Dodrio, you can try out the Dodrio Berry Picker.

Event 3: Gym Leader Battle #7 — Liza and Tate

Liza and Tate, Mossdeep Gym Leaders

Pokémon Type:

| PSYCHIC |

Recommended Move Type:

| WATER |
| DARK |

GYM LEADERS' POKÉMON

POKÉMON	LV	TYPE	
Xatu	LV41	PSYCHIC	FLYING
Lunatone	LV42	ROCK	PSYCHIC
Solrock	LV42	ROCK	PSYCHIC
Claydol	LV41	PSYCHIC	GROUND

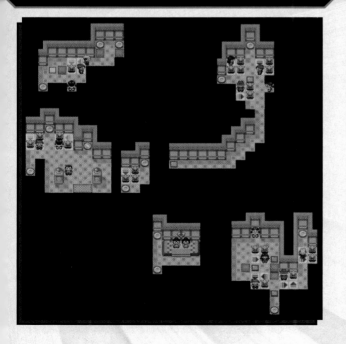

The Mossdeep Gym is made up of a system of rooms connected by small warp pads. But figuring out which warp pad gets you to the Gym Leader isn't the hard part. Rather, navigating the system of button-activated conveyor belts is the bigger headache. Not only do you need to clear obstructions such as statues via the belts, but you may also accidentally move a Trainer into your eye-line if you aren't careful.

Once you reach the twin Gym Leaders, Liza and Tate, you need to have either a very strong Dark- or Water-type Pokémon to undo the potency of their Psychic-type Pokémon. Especially watch out for the Lunatone and Solrock duo. They complement each other perfectly and can keep you at bay for a long time.

Event 4: Battle Team Magma at Space Center

The Space Center in Mossdeep City was about to launch a rocket into space, but Team Magma is trying to thwart the countdown. Apparently, Team Magma Leader Maxie has serious designs on the rocket fuel and will stop at nothing to get it. You must clear out the Space Center's ground floor before heading upstairs.

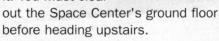

On the second floor, you meet up with Steven. Steven decides to team up with you to stop a pair of Team Magma Grunts from taking the rocket fuel. This is your first real 2-on-2 Battle with another Trainer. You must learn to rely on Steven's judgment during the battle while minding your own three Pokémon. When the battle is over, Team Magma retreats and Steven asks you to meet him at his house.

81

Event 5: Get HM08 (Dive) from Steven

Impressed with your dueling skills at the Space Center, Steven hands over HM08 (Dive). This isn't the last of Steven's generosity, either.

After you defeat the Elite Four and beat Steven at Meteor Falls, check back here to find a rare Pokémon as a present for you. It's Beldum, which if trained correctly, evolves into the fantastically powerful Metagross.

Route 125

Move Needed: *HM03 (Surf)*

Shoal Cave

To Mossdeep City

POKÉMON APPEARANCES

POKÉMON	CONDITIONS
Magikarp	Very Common (Old Rod, Good Rod)
Pelipper	Rare
Sharpedo	Very Common (Super Rod)
Tentacool	Very Common; Common (Old Rod, Good Rod)
Wailmer	Common (Good Rod); Very Common (Super Rod)
Wingull	Very Common

ITEMS

☐ Big Pearl	☐ Nevermeltice	☐ Shoal Salt
☐ Blue Shard	☐ Rare Candy	☐ Shoal Shell
☐ Focus Band	☐ Red Shard	☐ TM07 (Hail)
☐ Ice Heal	☐ Shell Bell	☐ Yellow Shard

Event 1: Shoal Cave

North of Mossdeep City, you find Route 125 and the Shoal Cave. This cave is seriously affected by the tides. At high tide, a good deal

of the cave is hard to explore, but low tide exposes almost everything. A man inside the cave can make a Shell Bell. He is happy to craft one for you, but first he needs the materials.

NOTE

For more on what to do in the Shoal Cave, see this guide's Bonuses and Extra Content section.

Route 126

Moves Needed: *HM03 (Surf), HM08 (Dive)*

ITEMS

☐	Big Pearl
☐	Heart Scale
☐	Green Shard

POKÉMON APPEARANCES IN WATER

POKÉMON	CONDITIONS
Magikarp	Very Common (Old Rod, Good Rod)
Pelipper	Rare
Sharpedo	Very Common (Super Rod)
Tentacool	Very Common; Common (Old Rod, Good Rod)
Wailmer	Common (Good Rod); Very Common (Super Rod)
Wingull	Very Common

POKÉMON APPEARANCES UNDERWATER

POKÉMON	CONDITIONS
Chinchou	Common
Clamperl	Very Common
Relicanth	Rare

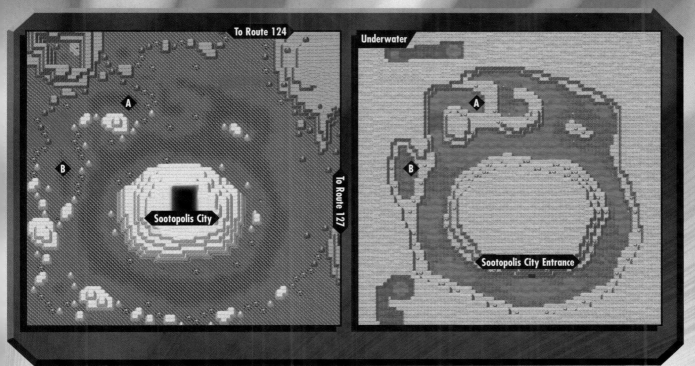

To Route 124

To Route 127

Sootopolis City

A

B

Underwater

A

B

Sootopolis City Entrance

Event 1: Deepsea Diving

The ocean floor beneath Route 126 is littered with sunken treasures. Either use the Itemfinder to locate them or look for shallow indentations in the sand to spot a possible treasure location.

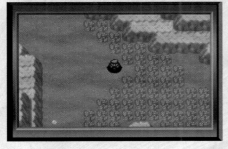

Event 2: Sootopolis Entry

The underwater entrance to Sootopolis is below the waves of Route 126, but you don't need to drop down here yet. (However, there is a Pokémart and Pokémon Center in the city if you need them now.) Most of the city is shut down, so concentrate your attention on Route 127 for now. However, when you are asked to report to Sootopolis City, this is where you will dive to find it.

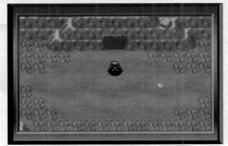

Route 127 and Route 128

Moves Needed: *HM03 (Surf), HM08 (Dive)*

ITEMS
- Carbos
- Rare Candy
- Zinc

POKÉMON APPEARANCES IN WATER (ROUTE 127)	
POKÉMON	**CONDITIONS**
Magikarp	Very Common (Old Rod, Good Rod)
Pelipper	Rare
Sharpedo	Very Common (Super Rod)
Tentacool	Very Common; Common (Old Rod, Good Rod)
Wailmer	Common (Good Rod); Very Common (Super Rod)
Wingull	Very Common

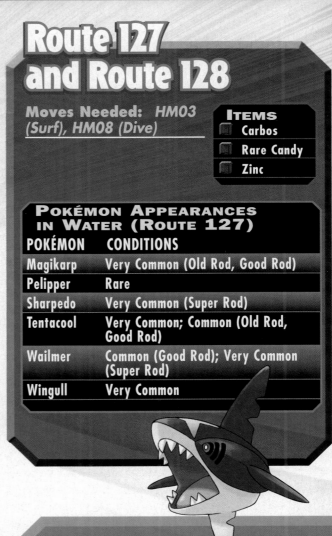

83

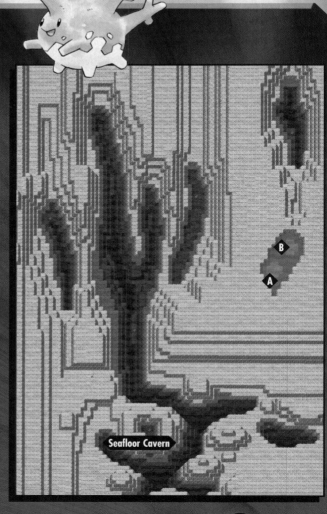

POKÉMON APPEARANCES IN WATER (ROUTE 128)	
POKÉMON	CONDITIONS
Corsola	Common (Super Rod)
Luvdisc	Common (Good Rod); Very Common (Super Rod)
Magikarp	Very Common (Old Rod, Good Rod)
Pelipper	Rare
Tentacool	Very Common; Common (Old Rod, Good Rod)
Wailmer	Common (Good Rod), Very Common (Super Rod)
Wingull	Very Common

Seafloor Cavern

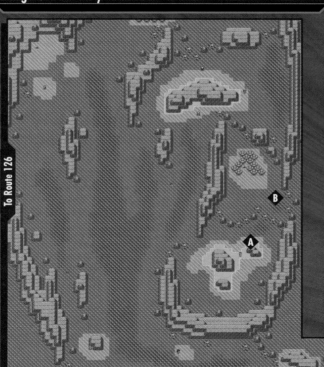

To Route 126

To Route 129

To Ever Grande City

Event 1: Chase Down the Submersible

Deep beneath the waves of Routes 127 and Route 128, the seafloor is a carved-up canvas full of deep trenches. But you must brave the depths to catch up with Team Aqua, as the submersible was last seen in these parts. After you are done fishing and battling wild Pokémon on the surface of the water, use HM08 (Dive) to slip below and follow the troughs south to the entrance of the Seafloor Cavern.

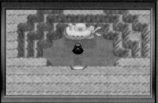

Seafloor Cavern

Moves Needed: HM03 (Swim), HM04 (Strength), HM06 (Rock Smash), HM08 (Dive)

Entrance

ITEM

📦 TM26 (Earthquake)

Entrance Underwater

To Route 128

POKÉMON APPEARANCES ON LAND

POKÉMON	CONDITIONS
Golbat	Common
Zubat	Very Common

POKÉMON APPEARANCES IN WATER

POKÉMON	CONDITIONS
Golbat	Rare
Magikarp	Very Common (Old Rod, Good Rod)
Tentacool	Very Common; Common (Old Rod); Very Common (Good Rod)
Wailmer	Common (Good Rod); Very Common (Super Rod)
Zubat	Very Common

Room 1

Room 2

Room 3

Room 4

Room 5

Room 6

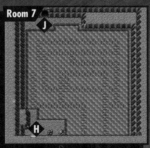

Room 7

Room 9

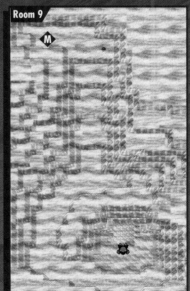

Room 8

Event 1: Strength Is the Key

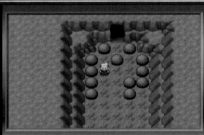

Several rooms lead to the deepest section of the Seafloor Cavern—many of them, however, are blocked by huge boulders that only a Pokémon with great HM04 (Strength) can move out of the way. Some of the rooms require you to move the boulders in specific patterns to clear a path to the exit. Should you accidentally block the doorway with a missed move, leave the room the way in which you came. The boulders will reset to their original position and you can try again.

Event 2: Battle Team Aqua Leader Archie

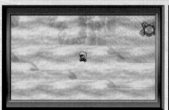

You catch up with Team Aqua Leader Archie at the bottom of the Seafloor Cavern—but he is hardly alone. He stands before a slumbering Kyogre, the Legendary Water-type Pokémon. You must battle Archie before he can awaken Kyogre. The battle will be tough. Archie has some powerful Water-type Pokémon, such as Sharpedo, but an Electric-type Pokémon will go far in this challenge.

Even if you defeat Archie, it's too late to stop him from using the Red Orb. But as Team Magma Leader Maxie discovered, the Orb has an unintended effect. Kyogre stirs, but then it flies away. Now both Kyogre and Groudon are loose—what have these two Leaders done to Hoenn?

TIP

When you return to the surface (an Escape Rope is handy for this), you discover that the climate has gone haywire. The sky is split with fierce bolts of lightning and a horrible torrent of rain pelts the land. Head to Sootopolis City to see if you can make sense of this disaster.

Sootopolis City

Move Needed: HM03 (Surf)

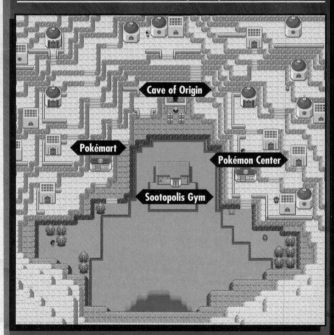

POKÉMON APPEARANCES IN WATER	
POKÉMON	**CONDITIONS**
Gyarados	Common (Super Rod)
Magikarp	Very Common; Very Common (Old Rod, Good Rod, Super Rod)
Tentacool	Common (Old Rod)

Deep underwater to the east of Hoenn's mainland is Sootopolis City. Accessible only by diving beneath the waves, the city is host to the Cave of Origin, a mystical place where the secrets of Legendary Pokémon await a talented Trainer. Are you that Trainer?

ITEMS

- [ ] Rain Badge
- [ ] TM03 (Water Pulse)
- [ ] TM31 (Brick Break)
- [ ] Wailmer Doll

POKÉMART MERCHANDISE

ITEM	PRICE
Ultra Ball	₽1,200
Hyper Potion	₽1,200
Max Potion	₽2,500
Full Heal	₽600
Revive	₽1,500
Max Repel	₽700
X Attack	₽500
X Defend	₽550
Shadow Mail	₽50

Event 1: Legendary Battle

After Kyogre has been released, return to Sootopolis City to see what Team Magma and Team Aqua have done. Kyogre and Groudon are in

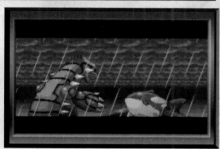

the center of the city, engaged in a ferocious battle that threatens to tear the world asunder. The foul weather is a direct result of their conflict. Is there perhaps a third Legendary Pokémon that can calm the waters and break these two apart?

After you calm the battle, tour the city and speak to the kind citizens. They give you a powerful TM as well a great Secret Base knick-knack.

Event 2: See the Cave of Origin

 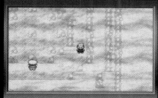

After witnessing the terrible battle in the bay, head for Steven and speak to him. He leads you to the entrance of the Cave of Origin. Inside, you are to speak with Wallace, the former Gym Leader of Sootopolis City and an expert on Legendary Pokémon.

Wallace will ask you a question about what could possibly be done about the great conflict between Groudon and Kyogre. Perhaps there is something at the Sky Pillar that could end their fight?

Event 3: Visit the Gym

After the crisis in the bay has subsided, be sure to head for the Sootopolis Gym. The Gym was previously closed, but now that Kyogre and

Groudon have been dispersed, you can challenge the Gym Leader for the eighth and final Gym badge.

Event 4: Gym Leader Battle #8— Juan

Juan, Sootopolis Gym Leader

Pokémon Type:

WATER

Recommended Move Type:

ELECTRIC

GRASS

GYM LEADER'S POKÉMON

POKÉMON	LV	TYPE	
Luvdisc	LV41	WATER	
Whiscash	LV41	WATER	GROUND
Sealeo	LV43	WATER	ICE
Crawdaunt	LV43	WATER	DARK
Kingdra	LV46	WATER	

Wallace has abdicated his Gym to a new Gym Leader, Juan. The former Gym Leader has left the facility in capable hands, as Juan is a master of Water-type Pokémon. He has assembled a strong team, but if you have a powerful Electric- or Grass-type Pokémon in your ranks, you should be able to dismantle Juan in a matter of several turns.

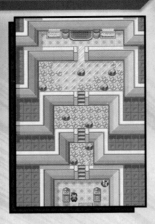
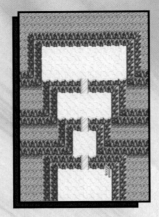

The big catch is getting to Juan, though. The Gym floor is made of ice and all it takes is two steps on the same space to fall through to the basement level, which is full of Trainers. The key to reaching Juan at the top of the Gym is to step on each tile only once—but you must step on every tile at least once to open the staircase leading to the next area.

NOTE

After defeating Juan and earning the eighth Gym badge you are ready to take on the Elite Four!

Routes 129, 130, and 131

Move Needed: *HM03 (Surf)*

To Sky Pillar

To Pacifidlog Town

To Route 128

POKÉMON APPEARANCES IN WATER (ROUTE 129)	
POKÉMON	**CONDITIONS**
Magikarp	Very Common (Old Rod, Good Rod)
Pelipper	Rare
Sharpedo	Very Common (Super Rod)
Tentacool	Very Common; Common (Old Rod, Good Rod)
Wailmer	Common (Good Rod); Very Common (Super Rod)
Wailord	Very Rare
Wingull	Very Common

POKÉMON APPEARANCES IN WATER (ROUTE 130 AND ROUTE 131)	
POKÉMON	**CONDITIONS**
Magikarp	Very Common (Old Rod, Good Rod)
Pelipper	Rare
Sharpedo	Very Common (Super Rod)
Tentacool	Very Common; Common (Old Rod, Good Rod)
Wailmer	Common (Good Rod); Very Common (Super Rod)
Wingull	Very Common

Event 1: Water Route

Use the water along Route 129, 130, and 131 to reach two pivotal locations in Hoenn, the Sky Pillar and Pacifidlog Town. The waters are full of swimming Trainers, so this is an excellent place to gain valuable experience and cash.

Pacifidlog Town

Move Needed: *HM03 (Surf)*

Pacifidlog Town is a tiny city built above a Corsola colony. The floating township is the travel hub between Sootopolis City and the Hoenn mainland. Several rumors in town tell of powerful Pokémon lying in wait for the perfect Trainer to wake them and a mysterious island somewhere off the coast of Hoenn.

ITEMS

- TM21 (Frustration)
- TM27 (Return)
- Wave Mail

POKÉMON APPEARANCES IN TOWN

POKÉMON	CONDITIONS
Horsea	Trade for a Bagon

POKÉMON APPEARANCES IN WATER

POKÉMON	CONDITIONS
Magikarp	Very Common (Old Rod, Good Rod)
Pelipper	Rare
Sharpedo	Very Common (Super Rod)
Tentacool	Very Common; Common (Old Rod, Good Rod)
Wailmer	Common (Good Rod); Very Common (Super Rod)
Wingull	Very Common

NOTE

Pacifidlog Town is small, so it doesn't have its own Pokémart. If you need to restock on Items, use HM02 (Fly) to return to one of the other cities, such as Lilycove City.

Event 1: Seeing Mirages?

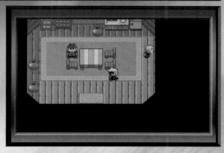

A man who lives on the east end of Pacifidlog has a special gift. Only he can see the elusive Mirage Island off of Route 130. However, the island appears only if the conditions are right—and the gentleman is tight-lipped about exact details. However, when he mentions he can see the island, use HM03 (Surf) to Route 130 and explore.

Event 2: Trade for a Horsea?

If you have a Bagon you are willing to part with, talk to the girl in the small house south of the Pokémon Center. She has a Horsea she would love to trade for a Bagon, which is not an easy Pokémon for her to find.

Event 3: Extended Family

The Pokémon Fan Club Chairman's younger sibling is touring Pacifidlog Town and has a couple TMs he may be willing to part with. Show him your lead Pokémon. If the Pokémon likes you, he will give you TM27 (Return). However, if the Pokémon isn't fond of you, he will award you TM21 (Frustration).

TIP

The Pokémon Fan Club Chairman's little brother will only give you one TM at a time, so don't try to switch out your Pokémon to get the other TM. Wait several days before returning to receive the other TM.

NOTE

The town is abuzz with a new rumor. There are three Legendary Pokémon made of steel, rock, and ice in Hoenn—and the key to discovering these Pokémon is nearby.

Sky Pillar

Moves and Items Needed: *HM03 (Surf), Mach Bike*

The Sky Pillar is a mysterious tower jutting above the sea. The foreboding place is home of the most powerful Legendary Pokémon in Hoenn. Perhaps this slumbering creature is the key to saving the world?

ITEMS
None

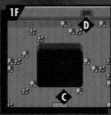

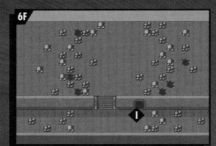
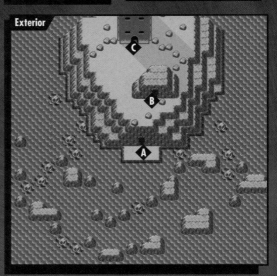

POKÉMON APPEARANCES ON 1F–3F	
POKÉMON	CONDITIONS
Banette	Common
Claydol	Common
Golbat	Common
Sableye	Common

POKÉMON APPEARANCES ON 5F	
POKÉMON	CONDITIONS
Altaria	Rare
Banette	Common
Claydol	Common
Golbat	Common
Sableye	Common

SPECIAL POKÉMON APPEARANCE	
POKÉMON	CONDITIONS
Rayquaza	On second trip to Sky Pillar after Rayquaza leaves Sootopolis City

Ascend Sky Pillar

Wallace is waiting for you at the Sky Pillar. He directs you inside, where you are charged with finding—and waking—the mighty Rayquaza. Hopefully the Legendary Pokémon can stop Groudon and Kyogre.

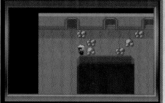 

During this first visit to the Sky Pillar, the ground is clear. There are no fragile floor tiles. You need to get past the wild Pokémon (and there are a lot) and reach Rayquaza on the top floor. When you reach the top, Rayquaza slumbers. Approach Rayquaza, and it will rise up and fly away, off to confront the other two warring Legendary Pokémon.

CAUTION

The first time you ascend the Sky Pillar to wake Rayquaza, you cannot catch it. On your second visit to the Sky Pillar, you can attempt to catch the Legendary Pokémon. However, you have only one chance to do this. If you defeat Rayquaza, it vanishes. If your Pokémon faint, it disappears. Save your game before you enter the 5th floor of the Sky Pillar—and bring all of the Ultra Balls you can afford.

Routes 132, 133, and 134

Moves Needed: *HM03 (Surf), HM08 (Dive)*

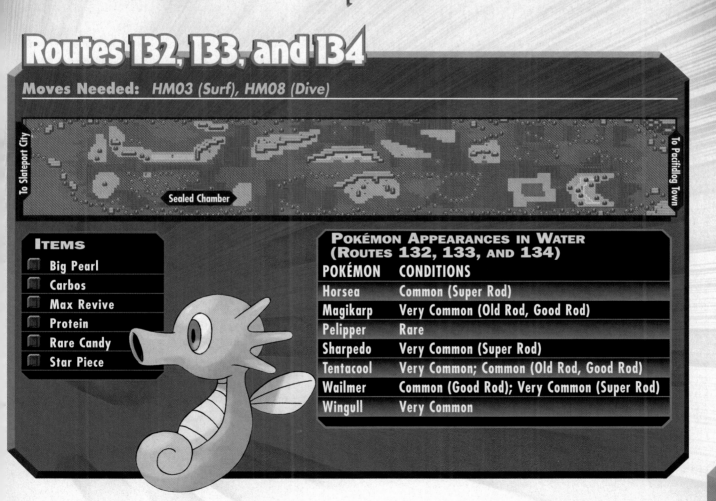

To Slateport City

Sealed Chamber

To Pacifidlog Town

ITEMS

- Big Pearl
- Carbos
- Max Revive
- Protein
- Rare Candy
- Star Piece

POKÉMON APPEARANCES IN WATER (ROUTES 132, 133, AND 134)

POKÉMON	CONDITIONS
Horsea	Common (Super Rod)
Magikarp	Very Common (Old Rod, Good Rod)
Pelipper	Rare
Sharpedo	Very Common (Super Rod)
Tentacool	Very Common; Common (Old Rod, Good Rod)
Wailmer	Common (Good Rod); Very Common (Super Rod)
Wingull	Very Common

Event 1: Watch Out for the Currents

The waterway along Routes 132–134 is full of fast-moving water that can carry you from one side to the other in moments if you're caught in the rush. After you start west on these routes, it's impossible to get to Pacifidlog Town without using HM02 (Fly) or heading back around Hoenn. The routes are full of Trainers, too, so it's easy to be swept from battle to battle.

Event 2: The Sealed Chamber

Route 134 hosts the Sealed Chamber, a mysterious set of ruins deep beneath the waves. To reach it, stay south along the routes or else you will be swept right by the diving spot. When you do reach the special patch of dark water, use HM08 (Dive) to slip beneath the waves and solve the riddles.

TIP

For more information on the Sealed Chamber and the secrets within, see the Bonus Quests, Legendary Pokémon, and the Battle Frontier section.

Ever Grande City

Moves Needed: HM03 (Surf), HM07 (Waterfall)

Pokémon League

To Victory Road

To Victory Road

Pokémon Center

To Route 128

Ever Grande City is home to the Pokémon League, where Pokémon Trainers aspire to take on the Elite Four. The Elite Four are the greatest Pokémon Trainers in Hoenn—do you have the skill and talent to take them on and prove yourself to be a true champion?

POKÉMART MERCHANDISE	
ITEM	**PRICE**
Ultra Ball	₽1,200
Hyper Potion	₽1,200
Max Potion	₽2,500
Full Restore	₽3,000
Full Heal	₽600
Revive	₽1,500
Max Repel	₽700

POKÉMON APPEARANCES IN WATER	
POKÉMON	**CONDITIONS**
Corsola	Common (Super Rod)
Luvdisc	Common (Good Rod); Very Common (Super Rod)
Magikarp	Very Common (Old Rod, Good Rod)
Pelipper	Rare
Tentacool	Common (Old Rod)
Wailmer	Common (Good Rod); Very Common (Super Rod)
Wingull	Very Common

Event 1: Up the Waterfall

The entrance to Ever Grande City and the Pokémon League is up the waterfall, so use HM07 (Waterfall) to ascend the rushing water. Without the HM, there is no way to access the Elite Four challenge.

Event 2: Last-Chance Shopping

Before heading down Victory Road, en route to challenge the Elite Four, stop at the Pokémon Center outside of the Pokémon League and rest up. Do any last-minute Pokémon shifting necessary for the battles ahead. And if you need to stock up on some Items, such as Full Heal, use this final storefront to do so. Victory Road may be the road less traveled, but that's because it's full of wild Pokémon.

Victory Road

Moves Needed: *HM03 (Surf), HM04 (Strength), HM05 (Flash), HM06 (Rock Smash), HM07 (Waterfall)*

ITEMS
- Full Heal
- Full Restore
- Max Elixir
- PP Up
- TM29 (Psychic)

POKÉMON APPEARANCES ON 1F

POKÉMON	CONDITIONS
Aron	Rare
Golbat	Common
Hariyama	Common
Lairon	Common
Makuhita	Common
Whismur	Rare
Zubat	Common

POKÉMON APPEARANCES ON B1F

POKÉMON	CONDITIONS
Geodude	Common (Rock Smash)
Golbat	Very Common
Graveler	Very Common (Rock Smash)
Hariyama	Very Common
Lairon	Common
Mawile	Rare

POKÉMON APPEARANCES ON B2F

POKÉMON	CONDITIONS
Golbat	Very Common
Lairon	Common
Mawile	Rare
Sableye	Very Common

POKÉMON APPEARANCES IN WATER

POKÉMON	CONDITIONS
Barboach	Common (Good Rod); Very Common (Super Rod)
Golbat	Very Common
Goldeen	Common (Old Rod, Good Rod)
Magikarp	Very Common (Old Rod, Good Rod)
Whiscash	Common (Super Rod)

CAUTION

You don't need to use HM05 (Flash) to make it through Victory Road, but it makes seeing your way easier. The dark cave has limited visibility without it.

Event 1: Battle Wally

Wally challenges you one last time, but he has grown as a Trainer. The little guy has five Pokémon under his tutelage, many above LV40! This battle

Fletchr, losing to you that time made me stronger! ♥

is the perfect warm-up before heading into the Pokémon League and challenging the Elite Four.

The Elite Four

Welcome to the big challenge: Defeating the Elite Four at the Pokémon League. This is what Trainers dream of doing, and now you have your chance to stand beside some of the greatest Pokémon Masters in history and prove yourself worthy of keeping their company. The Elite Four are talented Trainers, but they have different Pokémon in their teams, and they use different tactics. Some play aggressively, others are defensive—hoping to draw out your aggressive moves and expose a weakness.

The Pokémon of the Elite Four represent several types, from Ice to Dragon, from Dark to Water. It takes a well-balanced team to work your way up the ranks, as the move you use to exploit one Elite Four's weaknesses stands to do nothing in the next battle. You also need to have a team of significantly leveled up Pokémon. The lowest level Pokémon in the Elite Four challenge is LV46. You should be at least in the high 40s. The higher your levels, the better chance you have at withstanding the contest. Don't be afraid to turn back, level up some more, then return.

There are a few recommendations before taking on the Elite Four. It is good to have many Pokémon in your party that represent these types:

ELECTRIC	FIRE	FIGHTING
ICE	GROUND	WATER

Also give your Pokémon any advantageous Held Items, such as Quick Claw, Charcoal, or a Chesto Berry. And fill your Bag with recovery Items, such as Max Potions and Full Heals. Never enter this challenge without at least a few Revives, especially if you plan on relying on a couple of choice Pokémon to bear the brunt of the work. After you assemble the team you think best stands a chance against the Elite Four, step inside the inner sanctum of the Pokémon League and take the challenge of a lifetime.

Elite Four Battle #1: Sidney

POKÉMON		
NAME	LV	TYPE
Mightyena	LV46	DARK
Shiftry	LV48	GRASS / DARK
Cacturne	LV46	GRASS / DARK
Crawdaunt	LV48	WATER / DARK
Absol	LV49	DARK

RECOMMENDED TYPES:

FIGHTING	ICE	ELECTRIC

Sidney's Dark-type Pokémon present a formidable challenge unless you have the right kind of Pokémon to offset the onslaught. Fighting-type Moves work best against this team, but if you have no solid Fighting-type Moves to use, use Electric- and Ice-type Moves to at least counteract the secondary type of Sidney's Pokémon. For example, a good shot of TM34 (Thunderbolt) will do heavy damage to Sharpedo's ample HP. Considering that Sidney's team is the lowest level you will encounter in the Elite Four challenge, use it as a measuring stick of your abilities. If you struggle during this contest, you may need to forfeit the competition for now and head into Hoenn to gain more experience.

Elite Four Battle #2: Phoebe

POKÉMON		
NAME	LV	TYPE
Dusclops	LV49	GHOST
Dusclops	LV51	GHOST
Banette	LV49	GHOST
Banette	LV49	GHOST
Sableye	LV50	GHOST / DARK

RECOMMENDED TYPES:

GHOST	DARK

Ghost-type Pokémon are a challenge if you do not have a high-level Ghost-type Pokémon to counteract their spooky moves. Dark-type Moves also work well against the majority of this group, save for Sableye. At LV50, this Sableye bears none of the weakness of the other Pokémon in this tier. The contest may turn into a battle of attrition, where you keep laying on same-type moves and using recovery Items, hoping that you can pull off a Critical Hit that turns the tables in your favor.

Elite Four Battle #3: Glacia

POKÉMON		
NAME	LV	TYPE
Glalie	LV50	ICE
Sealeo	LV50	ICE / WATER
Sealeo	LV52	ICE / WATER
Glalie	LV52	ICE / WATER
Walrein	LV53	ICE / WATER

RECOMMENDED TYPES:

FIRE	ELECTRIC
FIGHTING	ROCK

Fire-type Moves would normally ruin an Ice-oriented team, but four of Glacia's five Pokémon have secondary Water types, which undo the effectiveness of the attack. If you have strong Fighting- or Rock-type Moves, use them, but your best weapon in this contest is an Electric-type Pokémon, such as Minun.

Elite Four Battle #4: Drake

POKÉMON		
NAME	LV	TYPE
Shelgon	LV52	DRAGON
Altaria	LV54	DRAGON / FLYING
Flygon	LV53	GROUND / DRAGON
Kingdra	LV53	WATER / DRAGON
Salamence	LV55	DRAGON / FLYING

RECOMMENDED TYPE: ICE

The contest is made up of Dragon-type Pokémon, which are difficult to beat unless you have some strong Ice-type Moves. Heavy Ice attacks do double the damage on Flygon, because its secondary type is Ground. Electric-type Moves also help bring down the Flying Dragon-type Pokémon, such as Salamence and Altaria.

Champion Battle: Wallace

POKÉMON		
NAME	LV	TYPE
Tentacruel	LV55	WATER
Wailord	LV57	WATER
Gyarados	LV56	WATER / FLYING
Whiscash	LV56	WATER / GROUND
Ludicolo	LV56	WATER / GRASS
Milotic	LV58	WATER

RECOMMENDED TYPE: ELECTRIC

Wallace has some high-level Pokémon, but they all share a common weakness: Electric-type Moves. If you have at least one Pokémon with some strong Electric-type Moves, it will be easy to undo this team. However, if your Electric-type Moves are out of PP, you will have difficulty. Keep an Elixir on hand to restore PP in case you run out mid-battle.

Congratulations, Pokémon Master!

After you defeat the Elite Four, you are recognized at the greatest Pokémon Trainer in all of Hoenn, the true Pokémon Master. However, this is not the end of the game. After the end credits roll and you save your game, you end up home in Littleroot Town. Your family gives you a ticket to the S.S. *Tidal*, which will take you to the Battle Frontier—an island where Pokémon Trainers do nothing but battle and prove their mastery. Surely you'll do well here, Pokémon Master. In addition to the Battle Frontier, there are still many things you can do in Hoenn. There are seven Legendary Pokémon you can catch, so stock up on Ultra Balls and get out there.

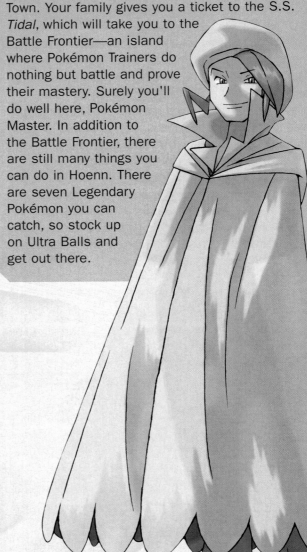

Legendary Pokémon, Bonus Quests, and the Battle Frontier

There are lots of adventures and battle challenges left in Hoenn after you defeat the Elite Four at the Pokémon League. There are additional locations to visit, Pokémon Contests to enter, and Legendary Pokémon to find and catch. And if that wasn't enough, there is the brand-new Battle Frontier—an island off Hoenn's coast where Trainers go to compete in a series of challenges. Imagine a whole theme park dedicated to the art of Pokémon battles, and you have a good idea of what's in store for you at the Battle Frontier.

Legendary Pokémon

A host of Legendary Pokémon are still hiding in Hoenn after you settle the great battle between Kyogre and Groudon. Sometimes, finding these Pokémon is the easy part. It takes a strong, talented, and patient Trainer to battle these Legendary Pokémon long enough to wear them down to the point that they succumb to a Poké Ball. Here are sound tactics for finding and catching these Legendary Pokémon—it's worth the work, because they are a blast to use in battles on your behalf when playing with friends!

Getting Groudon

After the game restarts, Groudon crawls back into hiding. But the effects of its presence on Hoenn linger—and that's the key to finding it. After the game restarts, visit the Weather Institute and talk to the researcher on the second floor, all the way to the right.

Presently, a drought has been recorded in ROUTE 114. ♥

He tells you that a particular region in Hoenn is experiencing a severe drought. It must be due to an incredible heat source. While the weatherman doesn't come right out and say it, you know what's causing it—Groudon. The researcher tells you which route is experiencing the dry weather.

NOTE

Groudon can appear in four different routes. If you dawdle while heading to that route, you risk the Legendary Pokémon relocating somewhere else. You must then go back to the Weather Institute and talk to the researcher again to discover the new route affected by the climate change.

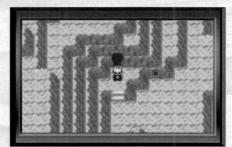

Groudon appears in the Terra Cave, a small, misty, subterranean chamber that consists of an antechamber, then a sleeping room. Terra Cave appears on Routes 114–116, and 118. The trick is to find the entrance to the Terra Cave in time. The entrance can appear in several places, but here's a hint: It always appears in the rocky face of a mountain or cliffside.

97

After you find the Terra Cave, dig in and approach the sleeping Pokémon. Challenge the Legendary Pokémon and

let the battle begin. Make sure you have lots of Ultra Balls, as you will expend a great deal of them while trying to catch this top-tier Pokémon. Groudon is at LV70.

CAUTION

You have only one shot each to catch Groudon, Kyogre, and Rayquaza. Save right before you battle them because if you mistakenly make them faint or lose the battle, they vanish from Hoenn forever. If you lose the battle (or inadvertently win), turn off your Game Boy Advance without saving and battle again.

Finding Kyogre

After you capture Groudon, report to the Weather Institute. The researcher reports heavy rainfall in one of four routes in Hoenn. This is the sign of Kyogre, so hurry to the affected route.

Kyogre is slumbering beneath the waves in the Marine Cave. Marine Cave appears on Routes 105, 125, and 127.

The Marine Cave only appears beneath the waves, so make sure you have a Pokémon that knows both HM03 (Surf) and HM08 (Dive). Look for a patch of dark water in the rainy region and Dive down.

Like Groudon, Kyogre sleeps in a simple two-room chamber. Slip into the mist-filled cave to spy Kyogre resting at the end. Approach

the Legendary Pokémon and challenge it. Kyogre is at LV70.

Catching Rayquaza

You know where Rayquaza sleeps—you've woken the Legendary Pokémon once. However, to catch Rayquaza you must return to the Sky Pillar. The catch is, the place is tougher to ascend than the first time. Path-obstructing rocks and fragile tiles litter the clean, clear floors. Use the Mach Bike to zip across the crumbling floors before you fall through.

Rayquaza rests on the top level of the Sky Pillar. Make sure you have lots of Ultra Balls and recovery Items, because this is going to be a difficult battle. Rayquaza is at LV70.

Chasing Latias and Latios

The Legendary Latias and Latios appear after you have undertaken the Elite Four challenge and emerged victorious. When you begin the game after the credits roll, your mother calls you to the television to watch a snippet of a news story about strange Pokémon seen flying overhead. She asks you if you caught the color of the Flying-type Pokémon.

Depending on the color you choose—red or blue—you will have a chance to catch either Latias or Latios.

What color did the announcer say that POKéMON was?

It is tough to catch Latias and Latios. The trick is to find them. They give no warning as to where they frequent, other than they only appear outdoors and while you are walking through grass. Latias and Latios never appear while you are indoors, whether it is a cave or a building. And every time you enter a structure, they move to another spot on the map. It's a matter of luck and timing to have that first pivotal encounter.

NOTE

If you have the **P**, you can save a lot of time by buying as many Max Repels as you can afford. This keeps away basic wild Pokémon, but you can still encounter the Legendary Pokémon.

After you manage to encounter one of these Pokémon, though, you can track it. The Latias or Latios will run from your first battle. That's OK, because you can then refer to the map in your PokéNav to see where it went. Head for that route and tromp through the grass to flush it out.

Buy a good number of Great and Ultra Balls before you stalk these Pokémon. Also, adjust your team so the lead Pokémon is at LV40 or below. Make sure this Pokémon has a good Speed rating, and if you have the Quick Claw, give it to the Pokémon for a Held Item. This increases your chances of getting the first move, and if you have a Sleep-inducing move, that makes this difficult hunt easier.

Latias and Latios move around the map with great regularity, but they have a small pattern. They stick with connected routes. So, find a series of connected routes, preferably one with a cabin or small house, and start your hunt there. Pop in and out of the small building until the Legendary Pokémon is in your region. Run through the grass to catch up with the elusive Pokémon.

When you encounter Latias or Latios, cast that Sleep-inducing move. If it is successful, your chances of catching the Pokémon skyrocket. If the move fails, though, the Pokémon will flee and you will have to start the process all over again.

After you do get the Legendary Pokémon in a battle, work the HP down to a manageable level. Don't throw Poké Balls until the HP gauge is red. When the gauge is red, go for a Sleep move, then throw a powerful Poké Ball. If the Pokémon is asleep, you have a good chance of catching it. Should the Poké Ball fail, don't worry. Latias and Latios retain whatever damage you did to them into the next battle. Go for the Sleep-inducing move again and throw Poké Balls.

Regice, Regirock, and Registeel Await!

There are three Legendary Rock Pokémon in Hoenn, but they hid before going into a deep sleep. The key to locating these Pokémon—Regice, Regirock, and Registeel—is to solve the Sealed Chamber mystery, which is in Route 134.

The currents are quick in this route, so stay close to the bottom of the water or you may end up watching the entrance to the Sealed Chamber breeze by.

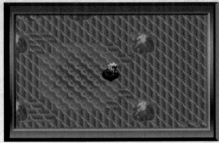

The entrance to the Sealed Chamber is surrounded by six rocks in the southern area of Route 134.

After you reach the entrance, use HM08 (Dive) to slip below the surface and swim through a narrow channel. You soon reach a tablet on the channel's wall. The glyphs on the tablet are the Braille alphabet. We have included a chart on page 100 of Braille which you can use to decipher the tablet's instructions. (Here's a hint: Light shines from above the tablet.)

Inside the Sealed Chamber, you must navigate two rooms. The first room features a series of rocks with the Braille alphabet inscribed on them—a key for deciphering the clues in the next room. Head to the keystone at the top of the first chamber, read the instructions, and follow them. This opens another chamber.

The second chamber includes the instructions for opening the way to all three Legendary Rock Pokémon. Read these inscriptions and take notes so when you head to the surface, you can go to the location of each Legendary Pokémon and open their secret doors.

Route 105: Island Cave, cave of Regice

Route 111: Desert Ruins, cave of Regirock

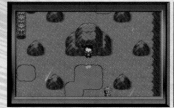

Route 120: Ancient Tomb, tomb of Registeel

BRAILLE ALPHABET

Braille Alphabet

The six dots of the braille cell are arranged and numbered:

```
1 ○ ○ 4
2 ○ ○ 5
3 ○ ○ 6
```

The capital sign, dot 6, placed before a letter makes a capital letter.

```
1   4
2   5
3 ○ 6
```

The number sign, dots 3, 4, 5, 6 placed before the characters a through j, makes the numbers 1 through 0. For example a preceded by the number sign is 1, b is 2, etc.

```
1 ○ 4
2   5
3 ○ ○ 6
```

a b c d e f

g h i j k l

m n o p q r

s t u v w x

y z Capital sign Number sign Period Comma

Question Mark Semi-colon Exclamation point Opening quote Closing quote

Bonus Quests

Five extra locations in Hoenn are worth exploring after you complete the main adventure. Even though these missions are not required to finish the game, you can earn valuable experience points, **P**, and cool Items for completing them.

The Abandoned Ship

Moves Needed: *HM03 (Surf), HM08 (Dive)*

When you zoomed through Route 108 on Mr. Briney's boat, you may have noticed the beached ferry along the waterway's north side. That's the Abandoned Ship. When you have both HM03 (Surf) and HM08 (Dive), you can explore this half-sunken vessel. Capt. Stern wants a Scanner that was onboard the ship before it sank. Perhaps if you wind through the ship's rooms and uncover the Scanner, he will give you a worthy reward?

ITEMS

- Dive Ball
- Escape Rope
- Harbor Mail
- Luxury Ball
- Revive
- Rm. 1 Key
- Rm. 2 Key
- Rm. 4 Key
- Rm. 6 Key
- Scanner
- Storage Key
- TM13 (Ice Beam)
- TM18 (Rain Dance)

POKÉMON APPEARANCES IN WATER

POKÉMON	CONDITIONS
Magikarp	Very Common (Old Rod, Good Rod)
Tentacool	Very Common; Common (Old Rod); Very Common (Good Rod, Super Rod)
Tentacruel	Very Rare; Common (Super Rod)

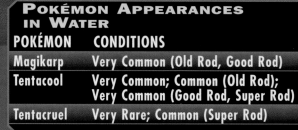

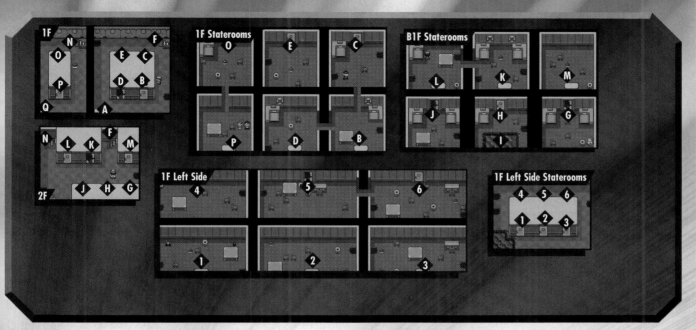

S.S. Tidal

Item Needed:
S.S. Ticket

ITEMS
- TM49 (Snatch)
- Leftovers

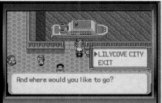

After you defeat the Elite Four, your family rewards you with a ticket for the S.S. *Tidal*, Capt. Stern's sea-faring ferry. This ferry is a quick way to get between Slateport City and Lilycove City—and it is the only way to reach the new Battle Frontier. Board the vessel, and while you wait for it to make its crossing, explore the staterooms for rare Items (especially those Leftovers) and challenge on-board Trainers.

NOTE

Battle Frontier is not an available destination the first time you board the ship. Scott, the man in the sunglasses, is on the ship, and he invites you to Battle Frontier. After he leaves, the choice is available on your next voyage.

Shoal Cave

Moves Needed: *HM03 (Surf), HM04 (Strength)*

Shoal Cave is north of Mossdeep City, carved into the side of a rocky mount rising from the ocean. The tides affect the cave. During high tide, you cannot explore most of the cave because it is full of water. But during the two low tides each day, you can fully inspect the multiple chambers of the cave.

ITEMS
- Big Pearl
- Ice Heal
- Focus Band
- Nevermeltice
- Rare Candy
- Shell Bell
- Shoal Salt x4
- Shoal Shell x4
- TM07 (Hail)

POKÉMON APPEARANCES IN WATER (ENTRANCE AT HIGH TIDE)

POKÉMON	CONDITIONS
Golbat	Rare
Magikarp	Very Common (Old Rod, Good Rod)
Spheal	Common
Tentacool	Very Common; Common (Old Rod, Good Rod)
Wailmer	Common (Good Rod); Very Common (Super Rod)
Zubat	Common

POKÉMON APPEARANCES IN WATER (1F AT HIGH TIDE)

POKÉMON	CONDITIONS
Magikarp	Very Common (Old Rod, Good Rod)
Spheal	Common
Tentacool	Very Common; Common (Old Rod, Good Rod)
Wailmer	Common (Good Rod); Very Common (Super Rod)
Zubat	Common

POKÉMON APPEARANCES ON LAND (ENTRANCE AT LOW TIDE)

POKÉMON	CONDITIONS
Golbat	Rare
Spheal	Very Common
Zubat	Very Common

POKÉMON APPEARANCES ON LAND (1F, B1F AT LOW TIDE)

POKÉMON	CONDITIONS
Golbat	Rare
Spheal	Very Common
Zubat	Very Common

POKÉMON APPEARANCES ON LAND (B2F AT LOW TIDE)

POKÉMON	CONDITIONS
Golbat	Rare
Snorunt	Common
Spheal	Very Common
Zubat	Very Common

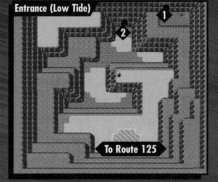

Entrance (Low Tide)

To Route 125

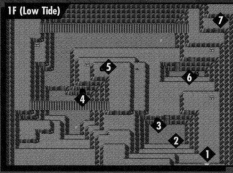

1F (Low Tide)

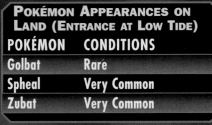

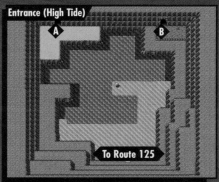

Entrance (High Tide)

To Route 125

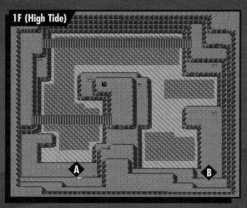

1F (High Tide)

B2F (Low Tide)

TIDE WATCH

TIME OF DAY	TIDE
9 a.m.–3 p.m.	High Tide
3 a.m.–9 p.m.	Low Tide
9 p.m.–3 a.m.	High Tide
3 a.m.–9 a.m.	Low Tide

B1F-1 (Low Tide)

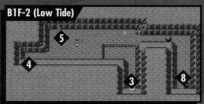

B1F-2 (Low Tide)

The man inside the cave on the first floor is willing to make Shell Bells for you, but only if you can collect four Shoal Salts or four Shoal Shells from the cave. You can recover one or the other during the different tides, so you must visit the cave at least twice if you want to collect the materials for more than one Shell Bell.

Mirage Island

Move Needed: *HM03 (Surf)*

A man in Pacifidlog Town can see a faraway island—but is it real? This place, Mirage Island, is invisible to the naked eye under most conditions, but from time to time, the man reports seeing it. If he tells you Mirage Island is visible, you can Surf to it from Route 130. The best way to coax this island into view is to have a special Pokémon in your party, but the gentleman refuses to disclose which Pokémon this is!

Mirage Island is a great place to catch a Wynaut—the only wild Pokémon that roams the island—and pick Kelpsy Berries.

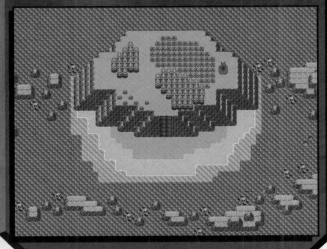

Trainer Hill

Trainer Hill is on Route 111's right side, and it's open for battle throughout the game. When you prove yourself to be a true Pokémon Master, the doors to Trainer Hill open.

Trainer Hill offers a special time-attack battle mode. When you enter the contest, a timer starts keeping track of how long it takes you to battle to the top of the building. There are four types of contests: Normal, Variety, Unique, and Expert—each with escalating difficulty. You can save a different record for each category and measure this time versus friends you link with via the Game Boy Wireless Adapter.

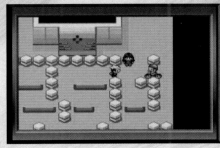

The Pokémon used by Trainers within match your highest level Pokémon. Enter with a LV48 in your team and every Trainer you battle will challenge you with LV48 Pokémon of his/her own. There is no experience or cash awarded in this contest, so enter for the fun of battling and see how your time stacks up against your friends!

Battle with Steven

In *Pokémon Ruby* and *Pokémon Sapphire*, Steven was the final challenger in the Elite Four contest. However, in *Emerald*, it's Wallace at the top of the Pokémon league. What happened to Steven?

The impressive Trainer is in Meteor Falls, in a new cave that opens in the northwest corner after you defeat the Elite Four. However, if you thought the Elite Four were tough, wait until you battle Steven. Follow this new cave to the end to find Steven in the corner. He's friendly to you, but don't expect that friendliness to translate to the battlefield. He's merciless, and if you want to win, you must be, too.

STEVEN'S POKÉMON		
NAME	LV	TYPE
Skarmory	LV77	STEEL / FLYING
Claydol	LV75	GROUND / PSYCHIC
Cradily	LV76	ROCK / GRASS
Armaldo	LV76	ROCK / BUG
Aggron	LV76	STEEL / ROCK
Metagross	LV58	STEEL / PSYCHIC
RECOMMENDED TYPES:		
FIGHTING	ELECTRIC	WATER

Safari Zone

After you defeat the Elite Four, two new areas open in the Safari Zone. You can find additional Pokémon in this new area that aren't in the original Safari Zone, so return to this park to round out your collection. Access the new areas via a small pathway above the entrance to the Safari Zone after passing through the gates and paying the admission fee.

POKÉMON APPEARANCES ON LAND (SOUTH)	
POKÉMON	CONDITIONS
Aipom	Common
Gligar	Rare
Hoothoot	Rare
Mareep	Common
Snubbull	Rare
Spinarak	Common
Stantler	Rare
Sunkern	Common

POKÉMON APPEARANCES IN WATER (SOUTH)	
POKÉMON	CONDITIONS
Goldeen	Common (Old Rod, Good Rod); Very Common (Super Rod)
Magikarp	Very Common (Old Rood, Good Rod)
Marill	Very Common
Octillery	Very Rare (Super Rod)
Quagsire	VeryRare
Remoraid	Common (Good Rod); Very Common (Super Rod)
Wooper	Very Common

POKÉMON APPEARANCES ON LAND (NORTH)	
POKÉMON	CONDITIONS
Aipom	Common
Hoothoot	Rare
Houndour	Rare
Ledyba	Common
Miltank	Rare
Pineco	Rare
Shuckle	Very Common (Rock Smash)
Sunkern	Common
Teddiursa	Common

DESERT UNDERPASS FOSSIL HUNT

Remember when you had to choose between the two fossils in the Mirage Tower? In *Pokémon Emerald*, you can recover the fossil that disappeared into the sand. Head to Route 115 after defeating the Elite Four and slide into the small tunnel opening. Follow the underground tunnel all the way to the end (it's a long walk) and you will find the fossil you did not collect. Take it to the Devon Corporation!

Battle Frontier

Welcome to the Battle Frontier, a new area in Hoenn exclusive to *Pokémon Emerald*. The Battle Frontier is an island off the coast of the mainland dedicated to the fine art of Pokémon battles. Seven contests in the Battle Frontier test your skills as a Trainer. The Battle Tents in Hoenn have acquainted you with some of the battles you can expect in the Battle Frontier, but only a full tour of the park reveals what's in store for you when the S.S. *Tidal* docks at its harbor.

The seven battle areas at the Battle Frontier are:

Battle Tower

Battle Dome

Battle Palace

Battle Arena

Battle Factory

Battle Pike

Battle Pyramid

The following section details the kind of battles you can expect at each of these areas, as well as what kind of challenge you can expect from the champions of each of these areas.

Beginning the Challenge

When you first enter the Battle Frontier, you walk through a corridor full of information desks. Your questions about the island can be answered here.

You are issued a Frontier Pass. This card grants you full access to the park. This is also where you can display your Symbols, the 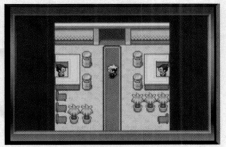 Battle Frontier equivalents of Gym badges. There are seven Symbols, each awarded only after you defeat each Frontier Battle area's leader. These powerful Trainers are known as the Frontier Brains, and they offer you a challenge more intense than the Elite Four. Your Frontier Pass has room to store a single battle, except for battles at the Battle Pike and Battle Pyramid.

Each area has two entry categories: LV50 and Open Level. LV50 matches are open only to Pokémon LV50 or below. All Pokémon you face in LV50 matches, however, are LV50 Pokémon themselves. Open level matches are open to any of your Pokémon over LV60, and your opponent matches the highest level Pokémon you enter. So, if you enter two Pokémon at LV61 and one at LV64, your opponent's Pokémon will be LV64.

Winning battles in the Battle Frontier will not award any cash or experience. You cannot level up your Pokémon at the Battle Frontier. Instead, winners receive Battle Points (BP). You can exchange BP for prizes at the Exchange Service Corner in the Battle Frontier. After you acquaint yourself with the basics of the Battle Frontier, head inside and make a name for yourself.

NOTE

There are two kinds of Symbols you can win at each Battle Frontier area. The first is the Silver Symbol. After you have the Silver Symbol in an area, you can try for the Gold.

NOTE

Many battle areas have two entry options: Single 1-on-1 Battles and Double, which are 2-on-2 Battles.

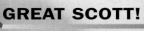

A girl in a small house along the east coast would love to trade you a Skitty for a Meowth, if you have one.

GREAT SCOTT!

Remember that man in the sunglasses that was trailing you throughout your adventure? That's Scott, the proprietor of Battle Frontier, the island paradise where Trainers are treated like royalty. Scott invites only the best of the best to Battle Frontier, and because you proved yourself so worthy of admiration in Hoenn, he extends an invitation to his island to you.

Scott's personal residence is along Battle Frontier's north shore. When you get a chance, stop in and talk to Scott. He will give you 3 BP for the little chat.

Exchange Service Corner

Here is the full catalog from the four sales counters inside the Exchange Service Counter, where you can trade BP for rare Items and Secret Base decorations.

FAR-LEFT COUNTER MERCHANDISE	
ITEM	PRICE (IN BP)
Kiss Poster	16
Kiss Cushion	32
Smoochum Doll	32
Meowth Doll	48
Togepi Doll	48
Ditto Doll	48
Clefairy Doll	48
Totodile Doll	80
Chikorita Doll	80
Cyndaquil Doll	80

FAR-RIGHT COUNTER MERCHANDISE	
ITEM	PRICE (IN BP)
White Herb	48
Leftovers	48
Quick Claw	48
Mental Herb	48
Bright Powder	64
King's Rock	64
Focus Band	64
Choice Band	64
Scope Lens	64

In-Town Amenities

While you cannot earn P in the Battle Frontier, you are welcome to spend it. There is a Pokémart beyond the park's entrance gate, just next to a Pokémon Center. You can use the Pokémon Center to rest your Pokémon, access stored Items, and switch out your team. However, each battle area has a PC in its lobby where you can also perform the same functions.

POKÉMART MERCHANDISE	
ITEM	PRICE
Ultra Ball	P1,200
Hyper Potion	P1,200
Max Potion	P2,500
Full Restore	P3,000
Full Heal	P600
Revive	P1,500
Max Repel	P700
Protein	P9,800
Calcium	P9,800
Iron	P9,800
Zinc	P9,800
Carbos	P9,800
HP Up	P9,800

LEFT MERCHANDISE	
ITEM	PRICE (IN BP)
Blastoise Doll	256
Charizard Doll	256
Lapras Doll	128
Snorlax Doll	128
Venusaur Doll	256

RIGHT MERCHANDISE	
ITEM	PRICE (IN BP)
Protein	1
Calcium	1
Iron	1
Carbos	1
Zinc	1
HP Up	1

Ranking Hall

You can chart your performance at the Ranking Hall's Battle Frontier. Inside, several slates are dedicated to tracking the best Trainers on the island. Maybe your records will be posted here someday?

NOTE

See page 113 for Battle Frontier Move Tutors and prices.

Battle Factory

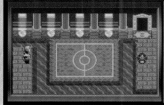

Remember the Battle Tent where you had to choose randomly selected Pokémon and compete against Trainers with their own random Pokémon? That was a warm-up exercise for the Battle Factory, which holds battles in groups of seven. After seven wins, you can take a breather before heading into the next stretch of seven battles.

When you enter the Battle Factory challenge, you must relinquish your Pokémon for a sack of six Poké Balls. Choose three Pokémon from the random collection. Think about what kinds of moves these Pokémon will have available to them—choose Pokémon that can take out multiple types, such as Electric-type Pokémon, which can dish out serious damage to both Water- and Flying-type Pokémon.

Factory Head Noland

After you win 21 consecutive battles in the Battle Factory, you have a shot at Noland, the champion. If you can defeat Noland, you win the Knowledge Symbol for your Frontier Pass. Noland must play by the same rules as you—he must choose random Pokémon, so if you face Noland multiple times, you will encounter different Pokémon at each battle.

FACTORY HEAD NOLAND'S POKÉMON

Noland uses random Pokémon with each battle.

Battle Dome

The Battle Dome is set up tournament-style, where new entrants join 16 Trainers challenges. There are Quarter-Finals, Semi-Finals, and Finals in each tournament—by the end of a single tournament, you will have had four battles. A tournament tree charts your progress through each tournament.

When you enter a tournament, you must choose three of your Pokémon. (However, you cannot select any Legendary Pokémon, so put Rayquaza away for now.) Before every round in the tournament, you are allowed a glimpse at the generalities of your opponent's team. This will help you form a strategy based on your own Pokémon selections before the next battle.

Dome Ace Tucker

After you win five consecutive tournaments, Dome Ace Tucker challenges you. The Frontier Brain is a tough champion, but if you win the battle, you win the Tactics Symbol for your Frontier Pass. Because of Tucker's team, it is difficult to rely on a single Pokémon. For example, an Electric-type Pokémon will help against the Flying-type natures of Charizard and Salamence, but Swampert's Ground-type negates the extra power of Electric-type Moves. Choose Pokémon with moves that straddle at least two of your opponent's Pokémon weaknesses.

Recommended Move Type:

ELECTRIC

DOME ACE TUCKER'S POKÉMON	
NAME	TYPE
Swampert	WATER / GROUND
Salamence	DRAGON / FLYING
Charizard	FIRE / FLYING

Battle Pike

The entrance of the Battle Pike is shaped like a giant Seviper—and the tricky nature of that Pokémon betrays the challenges you will find within. The nature of the Battle Pike is Battle Choice, a contest where you must walk down a hall of rooms. Each room has three doors. There are four possibilities of what is beyond.

Some rooms have Trainers in them, wishing to battle.

I GET TO BEAT UP ON YOU

Other rooms are winding walkways (they all look the same) where you encounter one or two wild Pokémon.

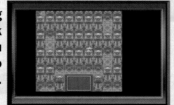

When you enter some rooms, you startle a Pokémon inside. The scared Pokémon will damage your lead Pokémon.

I must apologize to you...♥

If you are lucky, the room will have a healer inside that restores your Pokémon's HP and PP, as well as curing any Status irregularities.

I urge you to enjoy the rest of your Battle Choice challenge...

If you are unsure of which door to try, ask the lady standing in front of them for a hint on what is behind only one of them. You try your luck if you try the other two doors. Each run through the Battle Pike lasts 14 rooms, which includes the three-door corridors between each surprise room.

Pike Queen Lucy

After completing 28 consecutive rooms, you can challenge Pike Queen Lucy. Lucy holds the Luck Symbol. Her team is deceptive—it will be easy for you to defeat the Milotic and Seviper. But the Shuckle will give you a headache. The Pokémon can heal itself with TM44 (Rest) multiple times in an effort to drain the PP of your Attack moves. If you can outlast Shuckle's TM44 (Rest), use your remaining attack moves to defeat it. Because you may run low (or out) of PP, use a Pokémon that can poison Shuckle. Save one use of that move until Shuckle's tenth and final TM44 (Rest) has been used, then use the move to start the countdown.

Recommended Move Types:

ELECTRIC
POISON

PIKE QUEEN LUCY'S POKÉMON	
NAME	TYPE
Seviper	POISON
Milotic	WATER
Shuckle	BUG / ROCK

Battle Arena

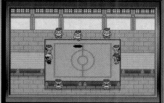

The Battle Arena is a continuation of the Fallarbor Town Battle Tent challenge, where you have only three moves to knock out your opponent's Pokémon. This is called a Set KO Tourney. You have three moves to make your opponent faint. If you cannot accomplish this, the battle results go to the judges. The battle is judged on three categories: Mind, Skill, and Body. You can earn between zero and two points in each category. The Pokémon with the most points after judging wins. You must choose three Pokémon from your team when you enter this contest, so choose those with the most powerful moves that affect the greatest number of Pokémon types.

Arena Tycoon Greta

After your 27th win, you must battle Arena Tycoon Greta for the Guts Symbol. Greta attacks with three powerful Pokémon, but two of them are Bug-type, so exploit that. Enter the challenge with a good Bug-type to use against Umbreon, then have a Flying-type move or two to neutralize Heracross and Shedinja.

Recommended Move Types:

BUG
FLYING

ARENA TYCOON GRETA'S POKÉMON	
NAME	**TYPE**
Heracross	BUG / FIGHTING
Umbreon	DARK
Shedinja	BUG / GHOST

Battle Palace

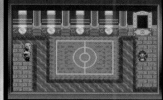

The Battle Palace presents a unique challenge—you can choose which Pokémon you want to enter in the competition, but you cannot choose which moves they make in battle. You must rely on the Pokémon's instincts. However, that doesn't mean you don't have any control over the battle. Consider which are your strongest Pokémon—which have moves that served you well during the adventure in Hoenn? If you choose a double challenge, there's an added wrinkle: You cannot select which one of your opponent's Pokémon your Pokémon will attack.

Palace Maven Spenser

Palace Maven Spenser challenges you after 21 battles. You must beat him to win the Spirits Symbol. This is easier said than done because Spenser anchors his team with the Normal-type Pokémon Slaking. This Pokémon has high HP and can take a bit of damage before getting in trouble. However, an Electric-type Pokémon with a powerful move set can dismantle Slaking's teammates, Crobat and Lapras.

Recommended Move Types:

ELECTRIC
FIGHTING

PALACE MAVEN SPENSER'S POKÉMON	
NAME	**TYPE**
Crobat	POISON / FLYING
Slaking	NORMAL
Lapras	WATER / ICE

Battle Pyramid

The Battle Pyramid hosts the Battle Quest, a challenge that drops you into a dark, randomly generated maze without your regular Items. Instead, you are given a special Bag that holds any Items you find while exploring the dark labyrinth, such as Potions. The maze is full of wild Pokémon and Trainers. You cannot see the first few Trainers, thanks to your limited view, but with every successful battle, you can see a little farther. Your goal is to find the warp square that sends you to the next maze. There are seven mazes to complete every time you enter the Battle Pyramid.

Pyramid King Brandon

Pyramid King Brandon confronts you after you clear your 21st consecutive maze. In order to win the Brave Symbol, you must defeat his team of Legendary Pokémon: Regice, Registeel, and Regirock. Fortunately, Regice and Regirock are weak against Steel-type Moves, but no such luck when battling Registeel. Instead, make sure you have a strong Fire-type Pokémon on your team. A good Fire-type Move is strong against Regice, too.

Recommended Move Types:

| STEEL |
| FIRE |

PYRAMID KING BRANDON'S POKÉMON	
NAME	TYPE
Regirock	ROCK
Regice	ICE
Registeel	STEEL

Battle Tower

The Battle Tower offers a multitude of Trainer Battles where you can hone your skill until you challenge the Battle Tower champion. You can enjoy four kinds of battles in the Battle Tower:

Single: After picking three Pokémon, you engage Trainers in one-on-one matches.

Double: After picking four Pokémon, you engage Trainers in two-on-two matches.

Multi: After picking two Pokémon, you choose another Trainer (controlled by the game) to team up with. Then you challenge teams of two Trainers.

Link Multi: If you have a Wireless Adapter, you and a friend (also with a Wireless Adapter) can play Multi challenges together.

No matter which challenge you select, you must earn seven consecutive wins to complete the round.

Salon Maiden Anabel

You cannot challenge Anabel unless you selected the Single option. After 35 consecutive wins, you battle against Anabel for the Ability Symbol. Anabel's three Pokémon work together, with one Pokémon's weakness being another's strength. For example, a Fighting-type Pokémon will do well against Snorlax, but Alakazam can exploit Snorlax with its Psychic nature. Choose Pokémon that target these types, but be ready to switch them out constantly during the battle.

Recommended Move Types:
- WATER
- BUG
- FIGHTING

SALON MAIDEN ANABEL'S POKÉMON

NAME	TYPE
Alakazam	PSYCHIC
Entei	FIRE
Snorlax	NORMAL

Catching New Pokémon

There are two Pokémon you can catch in the Battle Frontier that do not appear anywhere else in Hoenn: Sudowoodo and Smeargle.

SUDOWOODO

Look next to the waterfall near the center of the Battle Frontier. There is a tree that looks a little different than all of the others. Approach the tree and attempt to water it with the Wailmer Pail. The tree springs to life, revealing that it's no ordinary foliage. Battle the Sudowoodo to capture it.

SMEARGLE

Surf down the waterfall in the middle of the Battle Frontier and follow the river to the left. You will find a small cave entrance carved into the side of the riverbank. This is the entrance to the Artisan Cave, a shortcut route beneath the Battle Frontier that

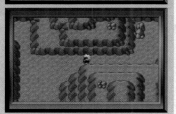

drops you off next to the Battle Tower. Only one kind of wild Pokémon inhabits the cave: Smeargle. And the place is crawling with them.

The Artisan Cave also contains several Items, but you can only recover them if you examine the stones sitting along the cave floor. Inside the cave, you will find these Items:

ITEMS
- Calcium
- Carbos
- HP Up
- Iron
- Protein
- Zinc

Pokémon Contests

Pokémon Contests, pioneered in *Pokémon Ruby* and *Pokémon Sapphire* return in *Pokémon Emerald*. These contests allow Pokémon to strut their stuff for judges and an attending audience. They use battle moves to prove how well-Conditioned they are. The better the move, the more the audience and judges like it. Make your Pokémon put their best feet forward to win prizes, such as special Ribbons.

However, unlike *Pokémon Ruby* and *Pokémon Sapphire*, there is only one Pokémon Contest Hall in Hoenn: Lilycove City. All four levels of the Pokémon Contest are held at this single facility: Normal Rank, Super Rank, Hyper Rank, and Master Rank. You must win Normal Rank before competing in Super Rank, and so forth.

Picking Proper Contests

The most important thing in a Pokémon Contest is to choose the correct contest for your Pokémon. There are five Pokémon Conditions: Cool, Beauty, Cute, Smart, and Tough. Every Pokémon has a particular strength in at least one of these categories. Use your PokéNav to determine the

Condition of your collected Pokémon. After you review your Pokémon's Condition, you can examine this table to determine if your Pokémon is strong in the supplementary Conditions judged in the different contests. For example, if your Pokémon is well-Conditioned in Cool, make sure it also has sufficient moves for Beauty and Toughness. If you attempt to use a Smart move in the contest, you will be penalized for using an inappropriate move.

Use timed button presses on the Berry Blender to create a delicious PokéBlock. The more rhythmic your responses are in the blending process, the more potent your PokéBlock will be.

PokéBlocks affect your Pokémon's Condition. Give the appropriate PokéBlock to a Pokémon to increase the desired Condition. But don't overfeed it. Pokémon can get full and refuse further PokéBlocks. Use this table to determine which PokéBlocks to give to your Pokémon:

CONTEST TYPE AND COMPLEMENTARY CONDITIONS

CONTEST TYPE	CONDITIONS				
	Cool	Beauty	Cute	Smart	Tough
Cool	O	X	—	—	X
Beauty	X	O	X	—	—
Cute	—	X	O	X	—
Smart	—	—	X	O	X
Tough	X	—	—	X	O

O = Greatly Influences   X = Somewhat Influences   — = No Influence

Before the Contest

When you catch a wild Pokémon, its Condition stats are zeroed out. Don't enter a Pokémon in a Pokémon Contest right after its initial capture, because it will fare poorly. You must increase its Conditions before attempting a contest, and the best way to do this is by feeding it PokéBlocks.

PokéBlocks are delicacies for Pokémon. They are created from crushed berries, which are made in Berry Blenders. There are Berry Blenders at the Pokémon Contest pavilion, so when you reach the grand hall, get to work. It takes more than one person to create a PokéBlock, but if you cannot link up with a friend to create one, work with the computer-controlled people standing in the lobby. PokéBlocks are judged on Feel and Level. The higher each number rating for these categories, the better the PokéBlock.

POKÉBLOCKS AND THEIR EFFECTS

COLOR	EFFECTS
Black	Make this thin-flavored, low-level PokéBlock by putting two or more of the same type of berry in the Berry Blender.
Blue	This dry PokéBlock increases a Pokémon's Beauty.
Brown	The strong sweet flavor increases a Pokémon's Cute Condition.
Gold	This PokéBlock is LV50 or above and made of one or two tastes. As a result, it raises one or two Conditions.
Gray	Blended of three tastes, this PokéBlock raises three Conditions.
Green	This bitter PokéBlock raises a Pokémon's Smart Condition.
Indigo	The strong dry taste increases a Pokémon's Beauty.
LiteBlue	The strong bitter taste increases a Pokémon's Smart Condition.
Olive	The strong sour taste increases a Pokémon's Tough Condition.
Pink	This sweet PokéBlock raises a Pokémon's Cute Condition.
Purple	The strong spicy taste increases a Pokémon's Cool Condition.
Red	This spicy PokéBlock raises a Pokémon's Cool Condition.
White	This PokéBlock is made up of four tastes and increases four Conditions.
Yellow	This sour PokéBlock increases a Pokémon's Tough Condition.

There is another factor is determining the effectiveness of a PokéBlock: Your Pokémon's nature. Every Pokémon has a nature, so check this chart against your collection of Pokémon before you start feeding them PokéBlocks.

THE EFFECT OF A POKÉMON'S NATURE ON POKÉBLOCK LIKES

Favorite PokéBlock	Hardy	Lonely	Adamant	Naughty	Brave	Bold	Docile	Impish	Lax	Relaxed	Modest	Mild	Bashful	Rash	Quiet	Calm	Gentle	Careful	Quirky	Sassy	Timid	Hasty	Jolly	Naive	Serious
Spicy (Red)	—	0	0	0	0	X	—	—	—	—	X	—	—	—	—	X	—	—	—	—	X	—	—	—	—
Sour (Yellow)	—	X	—	—	—	0	—	0	0	0	—	X	—	—	—	—	X	—	—	—	—	X	—	—	—
Dry (Blue)	—	—	X	—	—	—	—	X	—	—	0	0	—	0	0	—	—	X	—	—	—	—	X	—	—
Bitter (Green)	—	—	—	X	—	—	—	—	X	—	—	—	—	X	—	0	0	0	—	0	—	—	—	X	—
Sweet (Pink)	—	—	—	—	X	—	—	—	—	X	—	—	—	—	X	—	—	—	—	X	0	0	0	0	—

0 = Easy to raise the stat. Likes the taste of the PokéBlock.   X = Hard to raise the stat. Dislikes the taste of the PokéBlock.

Pokémon Contest Strategy

Pokémon Contests are broken up into two different rounds. During the first round, your Pokémon is judged by the primary Condition of the contest and the two secondary Conditions. The more prepared your Pokémon is for this round of judging, the more approval you will receive. The second round is the appeals of special moves performed for the judge and audience.

The appeals round is further broken down into five sub-rounds, where you can perform moves and special combinations of moves to win

further approval. Use moves that are best suited for the particular contest, such as Cool moves in a Cool contest. Consider using Beauty and Tough moves in this contest, too, because those are the secondary Conditions. If you select a move that applies to the specific contest, you will lose favor. Never use the same move twice in a row. Predictability also loses favor with the audience.

TIP

Check the Lists section of this guide for a complete list of moves and their effects in a Pokémon Contest.

The best way to win a contest is to use moves that make sense considering the situation. For example, if you have a move that penalizes the Pokémon who have already performed appeals, don't use that move in the first sub-round of the appeals portion—since there have been no appeals yet, the move will be completely ineffective. If you have a move that affects all of the Pokémon that appeal after you, don't use it if you are second to last in the order of appeals.

After all of the competing Pokémon have made their appeals, the judge tabulates the score and announces a winner. If you win a Pokémon Contest, you are awarded a special Ribbon, and an artist will paint a portrait of your Pokémon. This portrait may appear in the museum next door in Lilycove City.

Battle Frontier Move Tutors

There are additional Move Tutors to visit in the Battle Frontier that teach your Pokémon different moves than the ones they could learn while exploring Hoenn. However, these Move Tutors request payment for the skills, so you must accumulate Battle Points in order to learn the new moves.

MOVE TUTOR MOVES AND PRICES

MOVE	PRICE (IN BATTLE POINTS)
Defense Curl	16
Softboiled	16
Icy Wind	24
Mud-Slap	24
Snore	24
Swift	24
Seismic Toss	24
Dream Eater	24
Mega Kick	24
Mega Punch	24
Endure	48
Ice Punch	48
Thunder Punch	48
Fire Punch	48
Psych Up	48
Body Slam	48
Rock Slide	48
Thunderwave	48
Swords Dance	48
Counter	48

001 Treecko™
GRASS

GENERAL INFO
SPECIES: Wood Gecko Pokémon
HEIGHT: 1'8"
WEIGHT: 11 lbs.
ABILITY: *Overgrow*—When the Pokémon's HP falls below 1/3, the power of Grass-type Moves increases 1.5x.

STATS

Stat	Value
HP	25
ATTACK	50
DEFENSE	25
SP. ATTACK	50
SP. DEFENSE	50
SPEED	50

EVOLUTIONS
LV16 / LV36

WHERE/HOW TO CATCH
Given by Prof. Birch on Route 101

STRONG AGAINST:
WATER
ELECTRIC
GRASS
GROUND

WEAK AGAINST:
FIRE
ICE
POISON
FLYING
BUG

MOVES LIST

LV	Move Name	Type	ST	ACC	PP
S	Pound	Normal	40	100	35
S	Leer	Normal	—	100	30
06	Absorb	Grass	20	100	20
11	Quick Attack	Normal	40	100	30
16	Pursuit	Dark	40	100	20
21	Screech	—	—	85	40
26	Mega Drain	Grass	40	100	10
31	Agility	Psychic	—	—	30
36	Slam	Normal	80	75	20
41	Detect	Fighting	—	—	5
46	Giga Drain	Grass	60	100	5

TM/HM LIST

TM/HM #	Move Name	Type	ST	ACC	PP
HM01	Cut	Normal	50	95	30
HM04	Strength	Normal	80	100	15
HM05	Flash	Normal	—	70	20
HM06	Rock Smash	Fighting	20	100	15
TM01	Focus Punch	Fighting	150	100	20
TM06	Toxic	Poison	—	85	10
TM09	Bullet Seed	Grass	10	100	30
TM10	Hidden Power	Normal	—	100	15
TM11	Sunny Day	Fire	—	—	5
TM17	Protect	Normal	—	—	10
TM19	Giga Drain	Grass	60	100	5
TM20	Safeguard	Normal	—	—	25
TM21	Frustration	Normal	—	100	20
TM22	Solarbeam	Grass	120	100	10
TM23	Iron Tail	Steel	100	75	15
TM27	Return	Normal	—	100	20
TM28	Dig	Ground	60	100	10
TM31	Brick Break	Fighting	75	100	15
TM32	Double Team	Normal	—	—	15
TM39	Rock Tomb	Rock	50	80	10
TM40	Aerial Ace	Flying	60	—	20
TM42	Façade	Normal	70	100	20
TM43	Secret Power	Normal	70	100	20
TM44	Rest	Psychic	—	—	10
TM45	Attract	Normal	—	100	15

EGG MOVES

Move Name	Type	ST	ACC	PP
Crunch	Dark	80	100	15
Mud Sport	Ground	—	100	15
Endeavor	Normal	—	100	5
Leech Seed	Grass	—	90	10
Dragonbreath	Dragon	60	100	20
Crush Claw	Normal	75	95	10

MOVE TUTOR LIST

Move Name	Type	ST	ACC	PP
Body Slam*	Normal	85	100	15
Counter*	Fighting	—	100	20
Double-Edge	Normal	120	100	15
Dynamicpunch	Fighting	100	50	5
Endure*	Normal	—	—	10
Fury Cutter	Bug	10	95	20
Mimic	Normal	—	100	10
Mega Kick*	Normal	120	85	5
Mega Punch*	Normal	80	75	20
Mud-Slap*	Ground	20	100	10
Rock Slide*	Rock	75	90	10
Seismic Toss*	Fighting	—	100	20
Sleep Talk	Normal	—	—	10
Snore*	Normal	40	100	15
Substitute	Normal	—	—	10
Swagger	Normal	—	90	10
Swift*	Normal	60	—	20
Swords Dance*	Normal	—	—	30
Thunderpunch*	Electric	75	100	15

*Battle Frontier tutor move

002 Grovyle™
GRASS

GENERAL INFO
SPECIES: Wood Gecko Pokémon
HEIGHT: 2'11"
WEIGHT: 48 lbs.
ABILITY: *Overgrow*—When the Pokémon's HP falls below 1/3, the power of Grass-type Moves increases 1.5x.

STATS

Stat	Value
HP	25
ATTACK	50
DEFENSE	50
SP. ATTACK	75
SP. DEFENSE	50
SPEED	50

EVOLUTIONS
LV16 / LV36

WHERE/HOW TO CATCH
Evolve from Treecko

STRONG AGAINST:
WATER
ELECTRIC
GRASS
GROUND

WEAK AGAINST:
FIRE
ICE
POISON
FLYING
BUG

MOVES LIST

LV	Move Name	Type	ST	ACC	PP
S	Pound	Normal	40	100	35
S	Leer	Normal	—	100	30
S	Absorb	Grass	20	100	20
S	Quick Attack	Normal	40	100	30
06	Absorb	Grass	20	100	20
11	Quick Attack	Normal	40	100	30
16	Fury Cutter	Bug	10	95	20
17	Pursuit	Dark	40	100	20
23	Screech	Normal	—	85	40
29	Leaf Blade	Grass	70	100	15
35	Agility	Psychic	—	—	30
41	Slam	Normal	80	75	20
47	Detect	Fighting	—	—	5
53	False Swipe	Normal	40	100	40

TM/HM LIST

TM/HM #	Move Name	Type	ST	ACC	PP
HM01	Cut	Normal	50	95	30
HM04	Strength	Normal	80	100	15
HM05	Flash	Normal	—	70	20
HM06	Rock Smash	Fighting	20	100	15
TM01	Focus Punch	Fighting	150	100	20
TM06	Toxic	Poison	—	85	10
TM09	Bullet Seed	Grass	10	100	30
TM10	Hidden Power	Normal	—	100	15
TM11	Sunny Day	Fire	—	—	5
TM17	Protect	Normal	—	—	10
TM19	Giga Drain	Grass	60	100	5
TM20	Safeguard	Normal	—	—	25
TM21	Frustration	Normal	—	100	20
TM22	Solarbeam	Grass	120	100	10
TM23	Iron Tail	Steel	100	75	15
TM27	Return	Normal	—	100	20
TM28	Dig	Ground	60	100	10
TM31	Brick Break	Fighting	75	100	15
TM32	Double Team	Normal	—	—	15
TM39	Rock Tomb	Rock	50	80	10
TM40	Aerial Ace	Flying	60	—	20
TM42	Façade	Normal	70	100	20
TM43	Secret Power	Normal	70	100	20
TM44	Rest	Psychic	—	—	10
TM45	Attract	Normal	—	100	15

MOVE TUTOR LIST

Move Name	Type	ST	ACC	PP
Body Slam*	Normal	85	100	15
Counter*	Fighting	—	100	20
Double-Edge	Normal	120	100	15
Dynamicpunch	Fighting	100	50	5
Endure*	Normal	—	—	10
Fury Cutter	Bug	10	95	20
Mimic	Normal	—	100	10
Mega Kick*	Normal	120	85	5
Mega Punch*	Normal	80	75	20
Mud-Slap*	Ground	20	100	10
Seismic Toss*	Fighting	—	100	20
Sleep Talk	Normal	—	—	10
Snore*	Normal	40	100	15
Substitute	Normal	—	—	10
Swagger	Normal	—	90	15
Swift*	Normal	60	—	20
Swords Dance*	Normal	—	—	30
Thunderpunch*	Electric	75	100	15

*Battle Frontier tutor move

003 Sceptile™

GRASS

GENERAL INFO
SPECIES: Forest Pokémon
HEIGHT: 5'7"
WEIGHT: 115 lbs.
ABILITY: *Overgrow* — When the Pokémon's HP falls below 1/3, the power of Grass-type Moves increases 1.5x.

STATS
Stat	Value
HP	25
ATTACK	50
DEFENSE	50
SP. ATTACK	75
SP. DEFENSE	50
SPEED	75

EVOLUTIONS

LV16
LV36

WHERE/HOW TO CATCH
Evolve from Grovyle

STRONG AGAINST:
- WATER
- ELECTRIC
- GRASS
- GROUND

WEAK AGAINST:
- FIRE
- ICE
- POISON
- FLYING
- BUG

MOVES LIST
LV	Move Name	Type	ST	ACC	PP
S	Pound	Normal	40	100	35
S	Leer	Normal	—	100	30
S	Absorb	Grass	20	100	20
S	Quick Attack	Normal	40	100	30
06	Absorb	Grass	20	100	20
11	Quick Attack	Normal	40	100	30
16	Fury Cutter	Bug	10	95	20
17	Pursuit	Dark	40	100	20
23	Screech	Normal	—	85	40
29	Leaf Blade	Grass	70	100	15
35	Agility	Psychic	—	—	30
43	Slam	Normal	80	75	20
51	Detect	Fighting	—	—	5
59	False Swipe	Normal	40	100	40

TM/HM LIST
TM/HM #	Move Name	Type	ST	ACC	PP
HM01	Cut	Normal	50	95	30
HM04	Strength	Normal	80	100	15
HM05	Flash	Normal	—	70	20
HM06	Rock Smash	Fighting	20	100	15
TM01	Focus Punch	Fighting	150	100	20
TM02	Dragon Claw	Dragon	80	100	15
TM05	Roar	Normal	—	100	20
TM06	Toxic	Poison	—	85	10
TM09	Bullet Seed	Grass	10	100	30
TM10	Hidden Power	Normal	—	100	15
TM11	Sunny Day	Fire	—	—	5
TM15	Hyper Beam	Normal	150	90	5
TM17	Protect	Normal	—	—	10
TM19	Giga Drain	Grass	60	100	5
TM20	Safeguard	Normal	—	—	25
TM21	Frustration	Normal	—	100	20
TM22	Solarbeam	Grass	120	100	10
TM23	Iron Tail	Steel	100	75	15
TM26	Earthquake	Ground	100	100	10
TM27	Return	Normal	—	100	20
TM28	Dig	Ground	60	100	15
TM31	Brick Break	Fighting	75	100	15
TM32	Double Team	Normal	—	—	15
TM39	Rock Tomb	Rock	50	80	10
TM40	Aerial Ace	Flying	60	—	20
TM42	Façade	Normal	70	100	20
TM43	Secret Power	Normal	70	100	20
TM44	Rest	Psychic	—	—	10
TM45	Attract	Normal	—	100	15

MOVE TUTOR LIST
Move Name	Type	ST	ACC	PP
Body Slam*	Normal	85	100	15
Counter*	Fighting	—	100	20
Double-Edge	Normal	120	100	15
Dynamicpunch	Fighting	100	50	5
Endure*	Normal	—	—	10
Fury Cutter	Bug	10	95	20
Mimic	Normal	—	100	10
Mega Kick*	Normal	120	85	5
Mega Punch*	Normal	80	75	20
Mud-Slap*	Ground	20	100	10
Seismic Toss*	Fighting	—	100	20
Sleep Talk	Normal	—	—	10
Snore*	Normal	40	100	15
Substitute	Normal	—	—	10
Swagger	Normal	—	90	15
Swift*	Normal	60	—	20
Swords Dance*	Normal	—	—	30
Thunderpunch*	Electric	75	100	15

*Battle Frontier tutor move

---

004 Torchic™

FIRE

GENERAL INFO
SPECIES: Chick Pokémon
HEIGHT: 1'4"
WEIGHT: 6 lbs.
ABILITY: *Blaze* — When the Pokémon's HP falls below 1/3, the power of Fire-type Moves increases 1.5x.

STATS
Stat	Value
HP	25
ATTACK	50
DEFENSE	25
SP. ATTACK	50
SP. DEFENSE	50
SPEED	50

EVOLUTIONS

LV16
LV36

WHERE/HOW TO CATCH
Given by Prof. Birch on Route 101

STRONG AGAINST:
- FIRE
- GRASS
- ICE
- BUG
- STEEL

WEAK AGAINST:
- WATER
- GROUND
- ROCK

MOVES LIST
LV	Move Name	Type	ST	ACC	PP
S	Scratch	Normal	40	100	35
S	Growl	Normal	—	100	40
07	Focus Energy	Normal	—	—	30
10	Ember	Fire	40	100	25
16	Peck	Flying	35	100	35
19	Sand-Attack	Ground	—	100	15
25	Fire Spin	Fire	15	70	15
28	Quick Attack	Normal	40	100	30
34	Slash	Normal	70	100	20
37	Mirror Move	Flying	—	—	20
43	Flamethrower	Fire	95	100	15

TM/HM LIST
TM/HM #	Move Name	Type	ST	ACC	PP
HM01	Cut	Normal	50	95	30
HM04	Strength	Normal	80	100	15
HM06	Rock Smash	Fighting	20	100	15
TM06	Toxic	Poison	—	85	10
TM10	Hidden Power	Normal	—	100	15
TM11	Sunny Day	Fire	—	—	5
TM17	Protect	Normal	—	—	10
TM21	Frustration	Normal	—	100	20
TM27	Return	Normal	—	100	20
TM28	Dig	Ground	60	100	10
TM32	Double Team	Normal	—	—	15
TM35	Flamethrower	Fire	95	100	15
TM38	Fire Blast	Fire	120	85	5
TM39	Rock Tomb	Rock	50	80	10
TM40	Aerial Ace	Flying	60	—	20
TM42	Façade	Normal	70	100	20
TM43	Secret Power	Normal	70	100	20
TM44	Rest	Psychic	—	—	10
TM45	Attract	Normal	—	100	15
TM50	Overheat	Fire	140	90	5

EGG MOVES
Move Name	Type	ST	ACC	PP
Counter	Fighting	—	100	20
Reversal	Fighting	—	100	15
Endure	Normal	—	—	10
Swagger	Normal	—	90	15
Rock Slide	Rock	75	90	10
Smellingsalt	Normal	60	100	10

MOVE TUTOR LIST
Move Name	Type	ST	ACC	PP
Body Slam*	Normal	85	100	15
Counter*	Fighting	—	100	20
Double-Edge	Normal	120	100	15
Endure*	Normal	—	—	10
Mega Kick*	Normal	120	85	5
Mega Punch*	Normal	80	75	20
Mimic	Normal	—	100	10
Mud-Slap*	Ground	20	100	10
Rock Slide*	Rock	75	90	10
Seismic Toss*	Fighting	—	100	20
Sleep Talk	Normal	—	—	10
Snore*	Normal	40	100	15
Substitute	Normal	—	—	10
Swagger	Normal	—	90	15
Swift*	Normal	60	—	20
Swords Dance*	Normal	—	—	30

*Battle Frontier tutor move

005 Combusken™

FIRE
FIGHTING

GENERAL INFO
SPECIES: Young Fowl Pokémon
HEIGHT: 2'11"
WEIGHT: 43 lbs.
ABILITY: *Blaze*—When the Pokémon's HP falls below 1/3, the power of Fire-type Moves increases 1.5x.

STATS

HP		50
ATTACK		75
DEFENSE		50
SP. ATTACK		75
SP. DEFENSE		50
SPEED		50

EVOLUTIONS

LV16
LV36

WHERE/HOW TO CATCH
Evolve from Torchic

STRONG AGAINST:
FIRE
GRASS
ICE
BUG
DARK
STEEL

WEAK AGAINST:
WATER
GROUND
FLYING
PSYCHIC

MOVES LIST

LV	Move Name	Type	ST	ACC	PP
S	Scratch	Normal	40	100	35
S	Growl	Normal	—	100	40
S	Focus Energy	Normal	—	—	30
S	Ember	Fire	40	100	25
07	Focus Energy	Normal	—	—	30
13	Ember	Fire	40	100	25
16	Double Kick	Fighting	30	100	30

LV	Move Name	Type	ST	ACC	PP
17	Peck	Flying	35	100	35
21	Sand-Attack	Ground	—	100	15
28	Bulk Up	Fighting	—	—	20
32	Quick Attack	Normal	40	100	30
39	Slash	Normal	70	100	20
43	Mirror Move	Flying	—	—	20
50	Sky Uppercut	Fighting	85	90	15

TM/HM LIST

TM/HM #	Move Name	Type	ST	ACC	PP
HM01	Cut	Normal	50	95	30
HM04	Strength	Normal	80	100	15
HM06	Rock Smash	Fighting	20	100	15
TM01	Focus Punch	Fighting	150	100	20
TM06	Toxic	Poison	—	85	10
TM08	Bulk Up	Fighting	—	—	20
TM10	Hidden Power	Normal	—	100	15
TM11	Sunny Day	Fire	—	—	5
TM17	Protect	Normal	—	—	10
TM21	Frustration	Normal	—	100	20
TM27	Return	Normal	—	100	20
TM28	Dig	Ground	60	100	10

TM/HM #	Move Name	Type	ST	ACC	PP
TM31	Brick Break	Fighting	75	100	15
TM32	Double Team	Normal	—	—	15
TM35	Flamethrower	Fire	95	100	15
TM38	Fire Blast	Fire	120	85	5
TM39	Rock Tomb	Rock	50	80	10
TM40	Aerial Ace	Flying	60	—	20
TM42	Facade	Normal	70	100	20
TM43	Secret Power	Normal	70	100	20
TM44	Rest	Psychic	—	—	10
TM45	Attract	Normal	—	100	15
TM50	Overheat	Fire	140	90	5

MOVE TUTOR LIST

Move Name	Type	ST	ACC	PP
Body Slam*	Normal	85	100	15
Counter*	Fighting	—	100	20
Double-Edge	Normal	120	100	15
Dynamicpunch	Fighting	100	50	5
Endure*	Normal	—	—	10
Fire Punch*	Fire	75	100	15
Fury Cutter	Bug	10	95	20
Mega Kick*	Normal	120	85	5
Mega Punch*	Normal	80	75	20
Mimic	Normal	—	100	10
Mud-Slap*	Ground	20	100	10
Rock Slide*	Rock	75	90	10
Seismic Toss*	Fighting	—	100	20
Sleep Talk	Normal	—	—	10
Snore*	Normal	40	100	15
Substitute	Normal	—	—	10
Swagger	Normal	—	90	15
Swift*	Normal	60	—	20
Swords Dance*	Normal	—	—	30
Thunderpunch*	Electric	75	100	15

*Battle Frontier tutor move

---

006 Blaziken™

FIRE
FIGHTING

GENERAL INFO
SPECIES: Blaze Pokémon
HEIGHT: 6'3"
WEIGHT: 115 lbs.
ABILITY: *Blaze*—When the Pokémon's HP falls below 1/3, the power of Fire-type Moves increases 1.5x.

STATS

HP		50
ATTACK		100
DEFENSE		50
SP. ATTACK		75
SP. DEFENSE		50
SPEED		75

EVOLUTIONS

LV16
LV36

WHERE/HOW TO CATCH
Evolve from Combusken

STRONG AGAINST:
FIRE
GRASS
ICE
BUG
DARK
STEEL

WEAK AGAINST:
WATER
GROUND
FLYING
PSYCHIC

MOVES LIST

LV	Move Name	Type	ST	ACC	PP
S	Fire Punch	Fire	75	100	15
S	Scratch	Normal	40	100	35
S	Growl	Normal	—	100	40
S	Focus Energy	Normal	—	—	30
S	Ember	Fire	40	100	25
07	Focus Energy	Normal	—	—	30
13	Ember	Fire	40	100	25
16	Double Kick	Fighting	30	100	30

LV	Move Name	Type	ST	ACC	PP
17	Peck	Flying	35	100	35
21	Sand-Attack	Ground	—	100	15
28	Bulk Up	Fighting	—	—	20
32	Quick Attack	Normal	40	100	30
36	Blaze Kick	Fire	85	90	10
42	Slash	Normal	70	100	20
49	Mirror Move	Flying	—	—	20
59	Sky Uppercut	Fighting	85	90	15

TM/HM LIST

TM/HM #	Move Name	Type	ST	ACC	PP
HM01	Cut	Normal	50	95	30
HM04	Strength	Normal	80	100	15
HM06	Rock Smash	Fighting	20	100	15
TM01	Focus Punch	Fighting	150	100	20
TM05	Roar	Normal	—	100	20
TM06	Toxic	Poison	—	85	10
TM08	Bulk Up	Fighting	—	—	20
TM10	Hidden Power	Normal	—	100	15
TM11	Sunny Day	Fire	—	—	5
TM15	Hyper Beam	Normal	150	90	5
TM17	Protect	Normal	—	—	10
TM21	Frustration	Normal	—	100	20
TM26	Earthquake	Ground	100	100	10

TM/HM #	Move Name	Type	ST	ACC	PP
TM27	Return	Normal	—	100	20
TM28	Dig	Ground	60	100	10
TM31	Brick Break	Fighting	75	100	15
TM32	Double Team	Normal	—	—	15
TM35	Flamethrower	Fire	95	100	15
TM38	Fire Blast	Fire	120	85	5
TM39	Rock Tomb	Rock	50	80	10
TM40	Aerial Ace	Flying	60	—	20
TM42	Facade	Normal	70	100	20
TM43	Secret Power	Normal	70	100	20
TM44	Rest	Psychic	—	—	10
TM45	Attract	Normal	—	100	15
TM50	Overheat	Fire	140	90	5

MOVE TUTOR LIST

Move Name	Type	ST	ACC	PP
Body Slam*	Normal	85	100	15
Counter*	Fighting	—	100	20
Double-Edge	Normal	120	100	15
Dynamicpunch	Fighting	100	50	5
Endure*	Normal	—	—	10
Fire Punch*	Fire	75	100	15
Fury Cutter	Bug	10	95	20
Mega Kick*	Normal	120	85	5
Mega Punch*	Normal	80	75	20
Mimic	Normal	—	100	10
Mud-Slap*	Ground	20	100	10
Rock Slide*	Rock	75	90	10
Seismic Toss*	Fighting	—	100	20
Sleep Talk	Normal	—	—	10
Snore*	Normal	40	100	15
Substitute	Normal	—	—	10
Swagger	Normal	—	90	15
Swift*	Normal	60	—	20
Swords Dance*	Normal	—	—	30
Thunderpunch*	Electric	75	100	15

*Battle Frontier tutor move

007 Mudkip™

WATER
GROUND

GENERAL INFO
SPECIES: **Mud Fish Pokémon**
HEIGHT: **1'4"**
WEIGHT: **17 lbs.**
ABILITY: **Torrent** — *When the Pokémon's HP falls below 1/3, the power of Water-type Moves increases 1.5x.*

STATS
HP — 17
ATTACK — 25
DEFENSE — 50
SP. ATTACK — 50
SP. DEFENSE — 50
SPEED — 50

EVOLUTIONS

LV16
LV36

WHERE/HOW TO CATCH
Given by Prof. Birch on Route 101

STRONG AGAINST:
FIRE
WATER
ICE
STEEL

WEAK AGAINST:
ELECTRIC
GRASS

MOVES LIST

LV	Move Name	Type	ST	ACC	PP	LV	Move Name	Type	ST	ACC	PP
S	Tackle	Normal	35	95	35	24	Mud Sport	Ground	—	100	15
S	Growl	Normal	—	100	40	28	Take Down	Normal	90	85	20
06	Mud-Slap	Ground	20	100	10	33	Whirlpool	Water	15	70	15
10	Water Gun	Water	40	100	25	37	Protect	Normal	—	—	10
15	Bide	Normal	—	100	10	42	Hydro Pump	Water	120	80	5
19	Foresight	Normal	—	100	40	46	Endeavor	Normal	—	100	5

TM/HM LIST

TM/HM #	Move Name	Type	ST	ACC	PP	TM/HM #	Move Name	Type	ST	ACC	PP
HM03	Surf	Water	95	100	15	TM18	Rain Dance	Water	—	—	5
HM04	Strength	Normal	80	100	15	TM21	Frustration	Normal	—	100	20
HM06	Rock Smash	Fighting	20	100	15	TM23	Iron Tail	Steel	100	75	15
HM07	Waterfall	Water	80	100	15	TM27	Return	Normal	—	100	20
HM08	Dive	Water	60	100	10	TM28	Dig	Ground	60	100	10
TM03	Water Pulse	Water	60	100	20	TM32	Double Team	Normal	—	—	15
TM06	Toxic	Poison	—	85	10	TM39	Rock Tomb	Rock	50	80	10
TM07	Hail	Ice	—	—	10	TM42	Facade	Normal	70	100	20
TM10	Hidden Power	Normal	—	100	15	TM43	Secret Power	Normal	70	100	20
TM13	Ice Beam	Ice	95	100	10	TM44	Rest	Psychic	—	—	10
TM14	Blizzard	Ice	120	70	5	TM45	Attract	Normal	—	100	15
TM17	Protect	Normal	—	—	10						

EGG MOVES

Move Name	Type	ST	ACC	PP
Refresh	Normal	—	100	20
Uproar	Normal	50	100	10
Curse	—	—	—	10
Stomp	Normal	65	100	20
Ice Ball	Ice	30	90	20
Mirror Coat	Psychic	—	100	20

MOVE TUTOR LIST

Move Name	Type	ST	ACC	PP
Body Slam*	Normal	85	100	15
Defense Curl*	Normal	—	—	40
Double-Edge	Normal	120	100	15
Endure*	Normal	—	—	10
Icy Wind*	Ice	55	95	15
Mimic	Normal	—	100	10
Mud-Slap*	Ground	20	100	10
Rollout	Rock	30	90	20
Sleep Talk	Normal	—	—	10
Snore*	Normal	40	100	15
Substitute	Normal	—	—	10
Swagger	Normal	—	90	15

*Battle Frontier tutor move

---

008 Marshtomp™

WATER
GROUND

GENERAL INFO
SPECIES: **Mud Fish Pokémon**
HEIGHT: **2'4"**
WEIGHT: **63 lbs.**
ABILITY: **Torrent** — *When the Pokémon's HP falls below 1/3, the power of Water-type Moves increases 1.5x.*

STATS
HP — 50
ATTACK — 75
DEFENSE — 50
SP. ATTACK — 50
SP. DEFENSE — 50
SPEED — 50

EVOLUTIONS
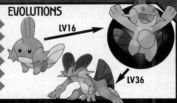
LV16
LV36

WHERE/HOW TO CATCH
Evolve from Mudkip

STRONG AGAINST:
FIRE
WATER
ICE
STEEL

WEAK AGAINST:
ELECTRIC
GRASS

MOVES LIST

LV	Move Name	Type	ST	ACC	PP	LV	Move Name	Type	ST	ACC	PP
S	Tackle	Normal	35	95	35	20	Foresight	Normal	—	100	40
S	Growl	Normal	—	100	40	25	Mud Sport	Ground	—	100	15
S	Mud-Slap	Ground	20	100	10	31	Take Down	Normal	90	85	20
S	Water Gun	Water	40	100	25	37	Muddy Water	Water	95	85	10
06	Mud-Slap	Ground	20	100	10	42	Protect	Normal	—	—	10
10	Water Gun	Water	40	100	25	46	Earthquake	Ground	100	100	10
15	Bide	Normal	—	100	10	53	Endeavor	Normal	—	100	5
16	Mud Shot	Ground	55	95	15						

TM/HM LIST

TM/HM #	Move Name	Type	ST	ACC	PP	TM/HM #	Move Name	Type	ST	ACC	PP
HM03	Surf	Water	95	100	15	TM18	Rain Dance	Water	—	—	5
HM04	Strength	Normal	80	100	15	TM21	Frustration	Normal	—	100	20
HM06	Rock Smash	Fighting	20	100	15	TM23	Iron Tail	Steel	100	75	15
HM07	Waterfall	Water	80	100	15	TM26	Earthquake	Ground	100	100	10
HM08	Dive	Water	60	100	10	TM27	Return	Normal	—	100	20
TM03	Water Pulse	Water	60	100	20	TM28	Dig	Ground	60	100	10
TM06	Toxic	Poison	—	85	10	TM32	Double Team	Normal	—	—	15
TM07	Hail	Ice	—	—	10	TM39	Rock Tomb	Rock	50	80	10
TM10	Hidden Power	Normal	—	100	15	TM42	Facade	Normal	70	100	20
TM13	Ice Beam	Ice	95	100	10	TM43	Secret Power	Normal	70	100	20
TM14	Blizzard	Ice	120	70	5	TM44	Rest	Psychic	—	—	10
TM17	Protect	Normal	—	—	10	TM45	Attract	Normal	—	100	15

MOVE TUTOR LIST

Move Name	Type	ST	ACC	PP
Body Slam*	Normal	85	100	15
Counter*	Fighting	—	100	20
Defense Curl*	Normal	—	—	40
Double-Edge	Normal	120	100	15
Dynamicpunch*	Fighting	100	50	5
Endure*	Normal	—	—	10
Ice Punch*	Ice	75	100	15
Icy Wind*	Ice	55	95	15
Mega Kick*	Normal	120	85	5
Mega Punch*	Normal	80	75	20
Mimic	Normal	—	100	10
Mud-Slap*	Ground	20	100	10
Rock Slide*	Rock	75	90	10
Rollout	Rock	30	90	20
Seismic Toss*	Fighting	—	100	10
Sleep Talk	Normal	—	—	10
Snore*	Normal	40	100	15
Substitute	Normal	—	—	10
Swagger	Normal	—	90	15

*Battle Frontier tutor move

009 Swampert™

WATER
GROUND

GENERAL INFO
SPECIES: Mud Fish Pokémon
HEIGHT: 4'11"
WEIGHT: 181 lbs.
ABILITY: *Torrent* — When the Pokémon's HP falls below 1/3, the power of Water-type Moves increases 1.5x.

STATS
HP	50
ATTACK	75
DEFENSE	50
SP. ATTACK	75
SP. DEFENSE	50
SPEED	50

EVOLUTIONS

LV16 → LV36

WHERE/HOW TO CATCH
Evolve from Marshtomp

STRONG AGAINST:
FIRE
WATER
ICE
STEEL

WEAK AGAINST:
ELECTRIC
GRASS

MOVES LIST
LV	Move Name	Type	ST	ACC	PP
S	Tackle	Normal	35	95	35
S	Growl	Normal	—	100	40
S	Mud-Slap	Ground	20	100	10
S	Water Gun	Water	40	100	25
06	Mud-Slap	Ground	20	100	10
10	Water Gun	Water	40	100	25
15	Bide	Normal	—	100	10
16	Mud Shot	Ground	55	95	15
20	Foresight	Normal	—	100	40
25	Mud Sport	Ground	—	100	15
31	Take Down	Normal	90	85	20
39	Muddy Water	Water	95	85	10
46	Protect	Normal	—	—	10
52	Earthquake	Ground	100	100	10
61	Endeavor	Normal	—	100	5

TM/HM LIST
TM/HM #	Move Name	Type	ST	ACC	PP
HM03	Surf	Water	95	100	15
HM04	Strength	Normal	80	100	15
HM06	Rock Smash	Fighting	20	100	15
HM07	Waterfall	Water	80	100	15
HM08	Dive	Water	60	100	10
TM01	Focus Punch	Fighting	150	100	20
TM03	Water Pulse	Water	60	100	20
TM05	Roar	Normal	—	100	20
TM06	Toxic	Poison	—	85	10
TM07	Hail	Ice	—	—	10
TM10	Hidden Power	Normal	—	100	15
TM13	Ice Beam	Ice	95	100	10
TM14	Blizzard	Ice	120	70	5
TM15	Hyper Beam	Normal	150	90	5
TM17	Protect	Normal	—	—	10
TM18	Rain Dance	Water	—	—	5
TM21	Frustration	Normal	—	100	20
TM23	Iron Tail	Steel	100	75	15
TM26	Earthquake	Ground	100	100	10
TM27	Return	Normal	—	100	20
TM28	Dig	Ground	60	100	10
TM31	Brick Break	Fighting	75	100	15
TM32	Double Team	Normal	—	—	15
TM39	Rock Tomb	Rock	50	80	10
TM42	Façade	Normal	70	100	20
TM43	Secret Power	Normal	70	100	20
TM44	Rest	Psychic	—	—	10
TM45	Attract	Normal	—	100	15

MOVE TUTOR LIST
Move Name	Type	ST	ACC	PP
Body Slam*	Normal	85	100	15
Counter*	Fighting	—	100	20
Defense Curl*	Normal	—	—	40
Double-Edge	Normal	120	100	15
Dynamicpunch	Fighting	100	50	5
Endure*	Normal	—	—	10
Icy Wind*	Ice	55	95	15
Mega Kick*	Normal	120	75	5
Mega Punch*	Normal	80	85	20
Mimic	Normal	—	100	10
Mud-Slap*	Ground	20	100	10
Rock Slide*	Rock	75	90	10
Rollout	Rock	30	90	20
Seismic Toss*	Fighting	—	100	20
Sleep Talk	Normal	—	—	10
Snore*	Normal	40	100	15
Substitute	Normal	—	—	10
Swagger	Normal	—	90	15

*Battle Frontier tutor move

010 Poochyena™

DARK

GENERAL INFO
SPECIES: Bite Pokémon
HEIGHT: 1'8"
WEIGHT: 30 lbs.
ABILITY: *Run Away* — Pokémon can flee from battle (except Trainer battles).

STATS
HP	25
ATTACK	50
DEFENSE	25
SP. ATTACK	25
SP. DEFENSE	25
SPEED	25

EVOLUTIONS

LV18 →

WHERE/HOW TO CATCH
Routes 101, 102, 103, 104, 110, 116, 117, 120, 121, and 123; Petalburg Woods

STRONG AGAINST:
PSYCHIC
GHOST
DARK

WEAK AGAINST:
FIGHTING
BUG

MOVES LIST
LV	Move Name	Type	ST	ACC	PP
S	Tackle	Normal	35	95	35
05	Howl	Normal	—	—	40
09	Sand-Attack	Ground	—	100	15
13	Bite	Dark	60	100	25
17	Odor Sleuth	Normal	—	100	40
21	Roar	Normal	—	100	20
25	Swagger	Normal	—	90	15
29	Scary Face	Normal	—	90	10
33	Take Down	Normal	90	85	20
37	Taunt	Dark	—	100	20
41	Crunch	Dark	80	100	15
45	Thief	Dark	40	100	10

TM/HM LIST
TM/HM #	Move Name	Type	ST	ACC	PP
HM06	Rock Smash	Fighting	20	100	15
TM05	Roar	Normal	—	100	20
TM06	Toxic	Poison	—	85	10
TM10	Hidden Power	Normal	—	100	15
TM11	Sunny Day	Fire	—	—	5
TM12	Taunt	Dark	—	100	20
TM17	Protect	Normal	—	—	10
TM18	Rain Dance	Water	—	—	5
TM21	Frustration	Normal	—	100	20
TM23	Iron Tail	Steel	100	75	15
TM27	Return	Normal	—	100	20
TM28	Dig	Ground	60	100	10
TM30	Shadow Ball	Ghost	60	—	20
TM32	Double Team	Normal	—	—	15
TM41	Torment	Dark	—	100	15
TM42	Façade	Normal	70	100	20
TM43	Secret Power	Normal	70	100	20
TM44	Rest	Psychic	—	—	10
TM45	Attract	Normal	—	100	15
TM46	Thief	Dark	40	100	10
TM49	Snatch	Dark	—	100	10

EGG MOVES
Move Name	Type	ST	ACC	PP
Astonish	Ghost	30	100	15
Poison Fang	Poison	50	100	15
Covet	Normal	40	100	40
Leer	Normal	—	100	30
Yawn	Normal	—	100	10

MOVE TUTOR LIST
Move Name	Type	ST	ACC	PP
Body Slam*	Normal	85	100	15
Counter*	Fighting	—	100	20
Double-Edge	Normal	120	100	15
Endure*	Normal	—	—	10
Mimic	Normal	—	100	10
Mud-Slap*	Ground	20	100	10
Psych Up*	Normal	—	—	10
Sleep Talk	Normal	—	—	10
Snore*	Normal	40	100	15
Substitute	Normal	—	—	10
Swagger	Normal	—	90	15

*Battle Frontier tutor move

011

Mightyena™

DARK

GENERAL INFO
SPECIES: Bite Pokémon
HEIGHT: 3'3"
WEIGHT: 82 lbs.
ABILITY: *Intimidate*—
Lowers the opponent's Attack by one point at the start of a battle.

STATS

Stat	Value
HP	50
ATTACK	75
DEFENSE	50
SP. ATTACK	50
SP. DEFENSE	50
SPEED	50

EVOLUTIONS

LV18

WHERE/HOW TO CATCH
Evolve from Poochyena; Routes 120, 121, and 123

STRONG AGAINST:
PSYCHIC
GHOST
DARK

WEAK AGAINST:
FIGHTING
BUG

MOVES LIST

LV	Move Name	Type	ST	ACC	PP	LV	Move Name	Type	ST	ACC	PP
S	Tackle	Normal	35	95	35	22	Roar	Normal	—	100	20
S	Howl	Normal	—	—	40	27	Swagger	Normal	—	90	15
S	Sand-Attack	Ground	—	100	15	32	Scary Face	Normal	—	90	10
S	Bite	Dark	60	100	25	37	Take Down	Normal	90	85	20
05	Howl	Normal	—	—	40	42	Taunt	Dark	—	100	20
09	Sand-Attack	Ground	—	100	15	47	Crunch	Dark	80	100	15
13	Bite	Dark	60	100	25	52	Thief	Dark	40	100	10
17	Odor Sleuth	Normal	—	100	40						

TM/HM LIST

TM/HM #	Move Name	Type	ST	ACC	PP	TM/HM #	Move Name	Type	ST	ACC	PP
HM04	Strength	Normal	80	100	15	TM27	Return	Normal	—	100	20
HM06	Rock Smash	Fighting	20	100	15	TM28	Dig	Ground	60	100	10
TM05	Roar	Normal	—	100	20	TM30	Shadow Ball	Ghost	60	—	20
TM06	Toxic	Poison	—	85	10	TM32	Double Team	Normal	—	—	15
TM10	Hidden Power	Normal	—	100	15	TM41	Torment	Dark	—	100	15
TM11	Sunny Day	Fire	—	—	5	TM42	Façade	Normal	70	100	20
TM12	Taunt	Dark	—	100	20	TM43	Secret Power	Normal	70	100	20
TM15	Hyper Beam	Normal	150	90	5	TM44	Rest	Psychic	—	—	10
TM17	Protect	Normal	—	—	10	TM45	Attract	Normal	—	100	15
TM18	Rain Dance	Water	—	—	5	TM46	Thief	Dark	40	100	10
TM21	Frustration	Normal	—	100	20	TM49	Snatch	Dark	—	100	10
TM23	Iron Tail	Steel	100	75	15						

MOVE TUTOR LIST

Move Name	Type	ST	ACC	PP
Body Slam*	Normal	85	100	15
Counter*	Fighting	—	100	20
Double-Edge*	Normal	120	100	15
Endure*	Normal	—	—	10
Mimic	Normal	—	100	10
Mud-Slap*	Ground	20	100	10
Psych Up*	Normal	—	—	10
Sleep Talk	Normal	—	—	10
Snore*	Normal	40	100	15
Substitute	Normal	—	—	10
Swagger	Normal	—	90	15

*Battle Frontier tutor move

012

Zigzagoon™

NORMAL

GENERAL INFO
SPECIES: Tinyraccoon Pokémon
HEIGHT: 1'4"
WEIGHT: 39 lbs.
ABILITY: *Pickup*—
Pokémon may find an Item at the end of the battle.

STATS

Stat	Value
HP	25
ATTACK	25
DEFENSE	50
SP. ATTACK	25
SP. DEFENSE	25
SPEED	50

EVOLUTIONS

LV20

WHERE/HOW TO CATCH
Routes 101, 102, 103, 118, and 119

STRONG AGAINST:
GHOST

WEAK AGAINST:
FIGHTING

MOVES LIST

LV	Move Name	Type	ST	ACC	PP	LV	Move Name	Type	ST	ACC	PP
S	Tackle	Normal	35	95	35	21	Mud Sport	Ground	—	100	15
S	Growl	Normal	—	100	40	25	Pin Missile	Bug	14	85	20
05	Tail Whip	Normal	—	100	30	29	Covet	Normal	40	100	40
09	Headbutt	Normal	70	100	15	33	Flail	Normal	—	100	15
13	Sand-Attack	Ground	—	100	15	37	Rest	Psychic	—	—	10
17	Odor Sleuth	Normal	—	100	40	41	Belly Drum	Normal	—	—	10

TM/HM LIST

TM/HM #	Move Name	Type	ST	ACC	PP	TM/HM #	Move Name	Type	ST	ACC	PP
HM01	Cut	Normal	50	95	30	TM24	Thunderbolt	Electric	95	100	15
HM03	Surf	Water	95	100	15	TM25	Thunder	Electric	120	70	10
HM06	Rock Smash	Fighting	20	100	15	TM27	Return	Normal	—	100	20
TM03	Water Pulse	Water	60	100	20	TM28	Dig	Ground	60	100	10
TM06	Toxic	Poison	—	85	10	TM30	Shadow Ball	Ghost	60	—	20
TM10	Hidden Power	Normal	—	100	15	TM32	Double Team	Normal	—	—	15
TM11	Sunny Day	Fire	—	—	5	TM34	Shock Wave	Electric	60	—	20
TM13	Ice Beam	Ice	95	100	10	TM42	Façade	Normal	70	100	20
TM14	Blizzard	Ice	120	70	5	TM43	Secret Power	Normal	70	100	20
TM17	Protect	Normal	—	—	10	TM44	Rest	Psychic	—	—	10
TM18	Rain Dance	Water	—	—	5	TM45	Attract	Normal	—	100	15
TM21	Frustration	Normal	—	100	20	TM46	Thief	Dark	40	100	10
TM23	Iron Tail	Steel	100	75	15						

EGG MOVES

Move Name	Type	ST	ACC	PP
Charm	Normal	—	100	20
Pursuit	Dark	40	100	20
Substitute	Normal	—	—	10
Tickle	Normal	—	100	20
Trick	Psychic	—	100	10

MOVE TUTOR LIST

Move Name	Type	ST	ACC	PP
Body Slam*	Normal	85	100	15
Defense Curl*	Normal	—	—	40
Double-Edge*	Normal	120	100	15
Endure*	Normal	—	—	10
Fury Cutter*	Bug	10	95	20
Icy Wind*	Ice	55	95	15
Mimic	Normal	—	100	10
Mud-Slap*	Ground	20	100	10
Psych Up*	Normal	—	—	10
Rollout	Rock	30	90	20
Sleep Talk	Normal	—	—	10
Snore*	Normal	40	100	15
Substitute	Normal	—	—	10
Swagger	Normal	—	90	15
Swift*	Normal	60	—	20
Thunder Wave*	Electric	—	100	20

*Battle Frontier tutor move

013 Linoone™

NORMAL

GENERAL INFO
SPECIES: Rushing Pokémon
HEIGHT: 1'8"
WEIGHT: 72 lbs.
ABILITY: *Pickup* — Pokémon may find an Item at the end of the battle.

STATS
HP	50
ATTACK	50
DEFENSE	50
SP. ATTACK	50
SP. DEFENSE	50
SPEED	75

EVOLUTIONS

LV20

WHERE/HOW TO CATCH
Evolve from Zigzagoon; Routes 118 and 119

STRONG AGAINST:
GHOST

WEAK AGAINST:
FIGHTING

MOVES LIST

LV	Move Name	Type	ST	ACC	PP	LV	Move Name	Type	ST	ACC	PP
S	Tackle	Normal	35	95	35	17	Odor Sleuth	Normal	—	100	40
S	Growl	Normal	—	100	40	23	Mud Sport	Ground	—	100	15
S	Tail Whip	Normal	—	100	30	29	Fury Swipes	Normal	18	80	15
S	Headbutt	Normal	70	100	15	35	Covet	Normal	40	100	40
05	Tail Whip	Normal	—	100	30	41	Slash	Normal	70	100	20
09	Headbutt	Normal	70	100	15	47	Rest	Psychic	—	—	10
13	Sand-Attack	Ground	—	100	15	53	Belly Drum	Normal	—	—	10

TM/HM LIST

TM/HM #	Move Name	Type	ST	ACC	PP	TM/HM #	Move Name	Type	ST	ACC	PP
HM01	Cut	Normal	50	95	30	TM21	Frustration	Normal	—	100	20
HM03	Surf	Water	95	100	15	TM23	Iron Tail	Steel	100	75	15
HM04	Strength	Normal	80	100	15	TM24	Thunderbolt	Electric	95	100	15
HM06	Rock Smash	Fighting	20	100	15	TM25	Thunder	Electric	120	70	10
TM03	Water Pulse	Water	60	100	20	TM27	Return	Normal	—	100	20
TM05	Roar	Normal	—	100	20	TM28	Dig	Ground	60	100	10
TM06	Toxic	Poison	—	85	10	TM30	Shadow Ball	Ghost	60	—	20
TM10	Hidden Power	Normal	—	100	15	TM32	Double Team	Normal	—	—	15
TM11	Sunny Day	Fire	—	—	5	TM34	Shock Wave	Electric	60	—	20
TM13	Ice Beam	Ice	95	100	10	TM42	Façade	Normal	70	100	20
TM14	Blizzard	Ice	120	70	5	TM43	Secret Power	Normal	70	100	20
TM15	Hyper Beam	Normal	150	90	5	TM44	Rest	Psychic	—	—	10
TM17	Protect	Normal	—	—	10	TM45	Attract	Normal	—	100	15
TM18	Rain Dance	Water	—	—	5	TM46	Thief	Dark	40	100	10

MOVE TUTOR LIST

Move Name	Type	ST	ACC	PP
Body Slam*	Normal	85	100	15
Defense Curl*	Normal	—	—	40
Double-Edge	Normal	120	100	15
Endure*	Normal	—	—	10
Fury Cutter	Bug	10	95	20
Icy Wind*	Ice	55	95	15
Mimic	Normal	—	100	10
Mud-Slap*	Ground	20	100	10
Rollout	Rock	30	90	20
Sleep Talk	Normal	—	—	10
Snore*	Normal	40	100	15
Substitute	Normal	—	—	10
Swagger	Normal	—	90	15
Swift*	Normal	60	—	20
Thunder Wave*	Electric	—	100	20

*Battle Frontier tutor move

---

014 Wurmple™

BUG

GENERAL INFO
SPECIES: Worm Pokémon
HEIGHT: 1'0"
WEIGHT: 8 lbs.
ABILITY: *Shield Dust* — Moves that possess any additional Effects (such as Paralysis) do not affect the Pokémon.

STATS
HP	25
ATTACK	50
DEFENSE	25
SP. ATTACK	25
SP. DEFENSE	25
SPEED	25

EVOLUTIONS

NOTE

The first Pokémon randomly evolves into one of two Pokémon. Each of the two second forms then evolves into a single type of Pokémon.

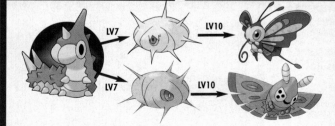
LV7 · LV10 · LV7 · LV10

WHERE/HOW TO CATCH
Routes 101, 102, and 104; Petalburg Woods

STRONG AGAINST:
GRASS
FIGHTING
GROUND

WEAK AGAINST:
FIRE
FLYING
ROCK

MOVES LIST

LV	Move Name	Type	ST	ACC	PP
S	Tackle	Normal	35	95	35
S	String Shot	Bug	—	95	40
05	Poison Sting	Poison	15	100	35

TM/HM LIST

TM/HM #	Move Name	Type	ST	ACC	PP
None					

EGG MOVES

Move Name	Type	ST	ACC	PP
None				

MOVE TUTOR LIST

Move Name	Type	ST	ACC	PP
None				

015

Silcoon™

BUG

GENERAL INFO
SPECIES: Cocoon Pokémon
HEIGHT: 2'0"
WEIGHT: 22 lbs.
ABILITY: *Shed Skin — Every turn, the Pokémon has a 1/3 chance of recovering from a Status condition.*

STATS

HP	→	25
ATTACK	→	25
DEFENSE	→	50
SP. ATTACK	→	25
SP. DEFENSE	→	25
SPEED	→	25

EVOLUTIONS

NOTE
The first Pokémon randomly evolves into one of two Pokémon. Each of the two second forms then evolves into a single type of Pokémon.

WHERE/HOW TO CATCH
Evolve from Wurmple; Petalburg Woods

MOVES LIST

LV	Move Name	Type	ST	ACC	PP
S	Harden	Normal	—	—	30
07	Harden	Normal	—	—	30

TM/HM LIST

TM/HM #	Move Name	Type	ST	ACC	PP
None					

MOVE TUTOR LIST

Move Name	Type	ST	ACC	PP
None				

STRONG AGAINST:
GRASS
FIGHTING
GROUND

WEAK AGAINST:
FIRE
FLYING
ROCK

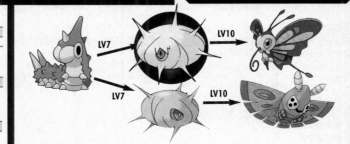

LV7 — LV10
LV7 — LV10

016

Beautifly™

BUG
FLYING

GENERAL INFO
SPECIES: Butterfly Pokémon
HEIGHT: 3'3"
WEIGHT: 63 lbs.
ABILITY: *Swarm — When the Pokémon's HP falls below 1/3, the power of Bug-type Moves increases 1.5x.*

STATS

HP	→	50
ATTACK	→	50
DEFENSE	→	50
SP. ATTACK	→	75
SP. DEFENSE	→	50
SPEED	→	50

EVOLUTIONS

NOTE
The first Pokémon randomly evolves into one of two Pokémon. Each of the two second forms then evolves into a single type of Pokémon.

WHERE/HOW TO CATCH
Evolve from Silcoon

STRONG AGAINST:
BUG
FLYING
GROUND
GRASS

WEAK AGAINST:
FIRE
ELECTRIC
FLYING
ROCK
ICE

MOVES LIST

LV	Move Name	Type	ST	ACC	PP
S	Absorb	Grass	20	100	20
10	Absorb	Grass	20	100	20
13	Gust	Flying	40	100	35
17	Stun Spore	Grass	—	75	30
20	Morning Sun	Normal	—	—	5
24	Mega Drain	Grass	40	100	10
27	Whirlwind	Normal	—	100	20
31	Attract	Normal	—	100	15
34	Silver Wind	Bug	60	100	5
38	Giga Drain	Grass	60	100	5

LV7 — LV10
LV7 — LV16

TM/HM LIST

TM/HM #	Move Name	Type	ST	ACC	PP	TM/HM #	Move Name	Type	ST	ACC	PP
HM05	Flash	Normal	—	70	20	TM27	Return	Normal	—	100	20
TM06	Toxic	Poison	—	85	10	TM29	Psychic	Psychic	90	100	10
TM10	Hidden Power	Normal	—	100	15	TM30	Shadow Ball	Ghost	60	—	20
TM11	Sunny Day	Fire	—	—	5	TM32	Double Team	Normal	—	—	15
TM15	Hyper Beam	Normal	150	90	5	TM40	Aerial Ace	Flying	60	—	20
TM17	Protect	Normal	—	—	10	TM42	Façade	Normal	70	100	20
TM19	Giga Drain	Grass	60	100	5	TM43	Secret Power	Normal	70	100	20
TM20	Safeguard	Normal	—	—	25	TM44	Rest	Psychic	—	—	10
TM21	Frustration	Normal	—	100	20	TM45	Attract	Normal	—	100	15
TM22	Solarbeam	Grass	120	100	10	TM46	Thief	Dark	40	100	10

MOVE TUTOR LIST

Move Name	Type	ST	ACC	PP
Double-Edge	Normal	120	100	15
Endure*	Normal	—	—	10
Mimic	Normal	—	100	10
Sleep Talk	Normal	—	—	10
Snore*	Normal	40	100	15
Substitute	Normal	—	—	10
Swagger	Normal	—	90	15
Swift*	Normal	60	—	20

*Battle Frontier tutor move

121

017

Cascoon™

BUG

GENERAL INFO
SPECIES: Cocoon Pokémon
HEIGHT: 2'4"
WEIGHT: 25 lbs.
ABILITY: *Shed Skin*—Every turn, the Pokémon has a 1/3 chance of recovering from a Status condition.

STATS
HP	25
ATTACK	25
DEFENSE	50
SP. ATTACK	25
SP. DEFENSE	25
SPEED	25

EVOLUTIONS

NOTE

The first Pokémon randomly evolves into one of two Pokémon. Each of the two second forms then evolves into a single type of Pokémon.

WHERE/HOW TO CATCH
Evolve from Wurmple; Petalburg Woods

MOVES LIST
LV	Move Name	Type	ST	ACC	PP
S	Harden	Normal	—	—	30
07	Harden	Normal	—	—	30

TM/HM LIST
TM/HM #	Move Name	Type	ST	ACC	PP
None					

MOVE TUTOR LIST
Move Name	Type	ST	ACC	PP
None				

STRONG AGAINST:
GRASS
FIGHTING
GROUND

WEAK AGAINST:
FIRE
FLYING
ROCK

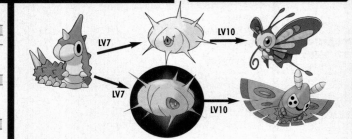

LV7 LV10
LV7 LV10

018

Dustox™

BUG
POISON

GENERAL INFO
SPECIES: Poison Moth Pokémon
HEIGHT: 3'11"
WEIGHT: 70 lbs.
ABILITY: *Shield Dust*—Moves that possess any additional Effects (such as Paralysis) do not affect the Pokémon.

STATS
HP	50
ATTACK	50
DEFENSE	50
SP. ATTACK	50
SP. DEFENSE	50
SPEED	50

EVOLUTIONS

NOTE

The first Pokémon randomly evolves into one of two Pokémon. Each of the two second forms then evolves into a single type of Pokémon.

WHERE/HOW TO CATCH
Evolve from Cascoon

MOVES LIST
LV	Move Name	Type	ST	ACC	PP
S	Confusion	Psychic	50	100	25
10	Confusion	Psychic	50	100	25
13	Gust	Flying	40	100	35
17	Protect	Normal	—	—	10
20	Moonlight	Normal	—	—	5
24	Psybeam	Psychic	65	100	20
27	Whirlwind	Normal	—	100	20
31	Light Screen	Psychic	—	—	30
34	Silver Wind	Bug	60	100	5
38	Toxic	Poison	—	85	10

STRONG AGAINST:
GRASS
FIGHTING
PSYCHIC
BUG

WEAK AGAINST:
FIRE
FLYING
PSYCHIC
ROCK

LV7 LV10
LV7 LV16

TM/HM LIST
TM/HM #	Move Name	Type	ST	ACC	PP	TM/HM #	Move Name	Type	ST	ACC	PP
HM05	Flash	Normal	—	70	20	TM29	Psychic	Psychic	90	100	10
TM06	Toxic	Poison	—	85	10	TM30	Shadow Ball	Ghost	60	—	20
TM10	Hidden Power	Normal	—	100	15	TM32	Double Team	Normal	—	—	15
TM11	Sunny Day	Fire	—	—	5	TM36	Sludge Bomb	Poison	90	100	10
TM15	Hyper Beam	Normal	150	90	5	TM40	Aerial Ace	Flying	60	—	20
TM16	Light Screen	Psychic	—	—	30	TM42	Façade	Normal	70	100	20
TM17	Protect	Normal	—	—	10	TM43	Secret Power	Normal	70	100	20
TM19	Giga Drain	Grass	60	100	5	TM44	Rest	Psychic	—	—	10
TM21	Frustration	Normal	—	100	20	TM45	Attract	Normal	—	100	15
TM22	Solarbeam	Grass	120	100	10	TM46	Thief	Dark	40	100	10
TM27	Return	Normal	—	100	20						

MOVE TUTOR LIST
Move Name	Type	ST	ACC	PP
Double-Edge	Normal	120	100	15
Endure*	Normal	—	—	10
Mimic	Normal	—	100	10
Sleep Talk	Normal	—	—	10
Snore*	Normal	40	100	15
Substitute	Normal	—	—	10
Swagger	Normal	—	90	15
Swift*	Normal	60	—	20

*Battle Frontier tutor move

019

Lotad™

| WATER |
| GRASS |

GENERAL INFO
SPECIES: Water Weed Pokémon
HEIGHT: 1'8"
WEIGHT: 6 lbs.
ABILITIES: *Swift Swim*—*Doubles the Pokémon's Speed when it is raining.*
Rain Dish—*Restores a little HP every turn that it is raining.*

STATS
HP	25
ATTACK	25
DEFENSE	25
SP. ATTACK	50
SP. DEFENSE	50
SPEED	25

EVOLUTIONS

LV14 → WATER STONE

WHERE/HOW TO CATCH
Routes 102 and 114

STRONG AGAINST:
| WATER |
| GROUND |
| STEEL |

WEAK AGAINST:
| POISON |
| FLYING |
| BUG |

MOVES LIST
LV	Move Name	Type	ST	ACC	PP	LV	Move Name	Type	ST	ACC	PP
S	Astonish	Ghost	30	100	15	21	Mist	Ice	—	—	30
03	Growl	Normal	—	100	40	31	Rain Dance	Water	—	—	5
07	Absorb	Grass	20	100	20	43	Mega Drain	Grass	40	100	10
13	Nature Power	Normal	—	95	20						

TM/HM LIST
TM/HM #	Move Name	Type	ST	ACC	PP	TM/HM #	Move Name	Type	ST	ACC	PP
HM03	Surf	Water	95	100	15	TM18	Rain Dance	Water	—	—	5
HM05	Flash	Normal	—	70	20	TM19	Giga Drain	Grass	60	100	5
TM03	Water Pulse	Water	60	100	20	TM21	Frustration	Normal	—	100	20
TM06	Toxic	Poison	—	85	10	TM22	Solarbeam	Grass	120	100	10
TM07	Hail	Ice	—	—	10	TM27	Return	Normal	—	100	20
TM09	Bullet Seed	Grass	10	100	30	TM32	Double Team	Normal	—	—	15
TM10	Hidden Power	Normal	—	100	15	TM42	Façade	Normal	70	100	20
TM11	Sunny Day	Fire	—	—	5	TM43	Secret Power	Normal	70	100	20
TM13	Ice Beam	Ice	95	100	10	TM44	Rest	Psychic	—	—	10
TM14	Blizzard	Ice	120	70	5	TM45	Attract	Normal	—	100	15
TM17	Protect	Normal	—	—	10	TM46	Thief	Dark	40	100	10

EGG MOVES
Move Name	Type	ST	ACC	PP
Synthesis	Grass	—	—	5
Razor Leaf	Grass	55	95	25
Sweet Scent	Normal	—	100	20
Leech Seed	Grass	—	90	10
Flail	Normal	—	100	15
Water Gun	Water	40	100	25

MOVE TUTOR LIST
Move Name	Type	ST	ACC	PP
Body Slam*	Normal	85	100	15
Double-Edge	Normal	120	100	15
Endure*	Normal	—	—	10
Icy Wind*	Ice	55	95	15
Mimic	Normal	—	100	10
Sleep Talk	Normal	—	—	10
Snore*	Normal	40	100	15
Substitute	Normal	—	—	10
Swagger	Normal	—	90	15
Swords Dance*	Normal	—	—	30

*Battle Frontier tutor move

020

Lombre™

| WATER |
| GRASS |

GENERAL INFO
SPECIES: Jolly Pokémon
HEIGHT: 3'11"
WEIGHT: 72 lbs.
ABILITIES: *Swift Swim*—*Doubles the Pokémon's Speed when it is raining.*
Rain Dish—*Restores a little HP every turn that it is raining.*

STATS
HP	50
ATTACK	50
DEFENSE	50
SP. ATTACK	50
SP. DEFENSE	50
SPEED	50

EVOLUTIONS

LV14 → WATER STONE

WHERE/HOW TO CATCH
Evolve from Lotad; Route 114

STRONG AGAINST:
| WATER |
| GROUND |
| STEEL |

WEAK AGAINST:
| POISON |
| FLYING |
| BUG |

MOVES LIST
LV	Move Name	Type	ST	ACC	PP	LV	Move Name	Type	ST	ACC	PP
S	Astonish	Ghost	30	100	15	25	Fury Swipes	Normal	18	80	15
03	Growl	Normal	—	100	40	31	Water Sport	Water	—	100	15
07	Absorb	Grass	20	100	20	37	Thief	Dark	40	100	10
13	Nature Power	Normal	—	95	20	43	Uproar	Normal	50	100	10
19	Fake Out	Normal	40	100	10	49	Hydro Pump	Water	120	80	5

TM/HM LIST
TM/HM #	Move Name	Type	ST	ACC	PP	TM/HM #	Move Name	Type	ST	ACC	PP
HM03	Surf	Water	95	100	15	TM17	Protect	Normal	—	—	10
HM04	Strength	Normal	80	100	15	TM18	Rain Dance	Water	—	—	5
HM05	Flash	Normal	—	70	20	TM19	Giga Drain	Grass	60	100	5
HM06	Rock Smash	Fighting	20	100	15	TM21	Frustration	Normal	—	100	20
HM07	Waterfall	Water	80	100	15	TM22	Solarbeam	Grass	120	100	10
HM08	Dive	Water	60	100	10	TM27	Return	Normal	—	100	20
TM03	Water Pulse	Water	60	100	20	TM31	Brick Break	Fighting	75	100	15
TM06	Toxic	Poison	—	85	10	TM32	Double Team	Normal	—	—	15
TM07	Hail	Ice	—	—	10	TM42	Façade	Normal	70	100	20
TM09	Bullet Seed	Grass	10	100	30	TM43	Secret Power	Normal	70	100	20
TM10	Hidden Power	Normal	—	100	15	TM44	Rest	Psychic	—	—	10
TM11	Sunny Day	Fire	—	—	5	TM45	Attract	Normal	—	100	15
TM13	Ice Beam	Ice	95	100	10	TM46	Thief	Dark	40	100	10
TM14	Blizzard	Ice	120	70	5						

MOVE TUTOR LIST
Move Name	Type	ST	ACC	PP
Body Slam*	Normal	85	100	15
Double-Edge	Normal	120	100	15
Dynamicpunch	Fighting	100	50	5
Endure*	Normal	—	—	10
Fire Punch*	Fire	75	100	15
Ice Punch*	Ice	75	100	15
Icy Wind*	Ice	55	95	15
Mimic	Normal	—	100	10
Mud-Slap*	Ground	20	100	10
Sleep Talk	Normal	—	—	10
Snore*	Normal	40	100	15
Substitute	Normal	—	—	10
Swagger	Normal	—	90	15
Swords Dance*	Normal	—	—	30
Thunderpunch*	Electric	75	100	15

*Battle Frontier tutor move

021 Ludicolo™

WATER
GRASS

GENERAL INFO
SPECIES: Carefree Pokémon
HEIGHT: 4'11"
WEIGHT: 121 lbs.
ABILITIES: *Swift Swim*—Doubles the Pokémon's Speed when it is raining.
Rain Dish—Restores a little HP every turn that it is raining.

STATS
HP	50
ATTACK	50
DEFENSE	50
SP. ATTACK	75
SP. DEFENSE	75
SPEED	50

EVOLUTIONS

LV14 → WATER STONE

WHERE/HOW TO CATCH
Evolve from Lombre with Water Stone

STRONG AGAINST:
WATER
GROUND
STEEL

WEAK AGAINST:
POISON
FLYING
BUG

MOVES LIST
LV	Move Name	Type	ST	ACC	PP
S	Astonish	Ghost	30	100	15
S	Growl	Normal	—	100	40
S	Absorb	Grass	20	100	20
S	Nature Power	Normal	—	95	20

TM/HM LIST
TM/HM #	Move Name	Type	ST	ACC	PP	TM/HM #	Move Name	Type	ST	ACC	PP
HM03	Surf	Water	95	100	15	TM15	Hyper Beam	Normal	150	90	5
HM04	Strength	Normal	80	100	15	TM17	Protect	Normal	—	—	10
HM05	Flash	Normal	—	70	20	TM18	Rain Dance	Water	—	—	5
HM06	Rock Smash	Fighting	20	100	15	TM19	Giga Drain	Grass	60	100	5
HM07	Waterfall	Water	80	100	15	TM21	Frustration	Normal	—	100	20
HM08	Dive	Water	60	100	10	TM27	Return	Normal	—	100	20
TM01	Focus Punch	Fighting	150	100	20	TM31	Brick Break	Fighting	75	100	15
TM03	Water Pulse	Water	60	100	20	TM32	Double Team	Normal	—	—	15
TM06	Toxic	Poison	—	85	10	TM42	Façade	Normal	70	100	20
TM07	Hail	Ice	—	—	10	TM43	Secret Power	Normal	70	100	20
TM09	Bullet Seed	Grass	10	100	30	TM44	Rest	Psychic	—	—	10
TM10	Hidden Power	Normal	—	100	15	TM45	Attract	Normal	—	100	15
TM11	Sunny Day	Fire	—	—	5	TM46	Thief	Dark	40	100	10
TM13	Ice Beam	Ice	95	100	10						
TM14	Blizzard	Ice	120	70	5						

MOVE TUTOR LIST
Move Name	Type	ST	ACC	PP
Body Slam*	Normal	85	100	15
Counter*	Fighting	—	100	20
Double-Edge	Normal	120	100	15
Dynamicpunch	Fighting	100	50	5
Endure*	Normal	—	—	10
Fire Punch*	Fire	75	100	15
Ice Punch*	Ice	75	100	15
Icy Wind*	Ice	55	95	15
Mega Kick*	Normal	120	85	5
Mega Punch*	Normal	80	75	20
Metronome	Normal	—	100	10
Mimic	Normal	—	100	10
Mud-Slap*	Ground	20	100	10
Seismic Toss*	Fighting	—	100	20
Sleep Talk	Normal	—	—	10
Snore*	Normal	40	100	15
Substitute	Normal	—	—	10
Swagger	Normal	—	90	15
Swords Dance*	Normal	—	—	30
Thunderpunch*	Electric	75	100	15

*Battle Frontier tutor move

022 Seedot™

GRASS

GENERAL INFO
SPECIES: Acorn Pokémon
HEIGHT: 1'8"
WEIGHT: 9 lbs.
ABILITIES: *Chlorophyll*—Doubles the Pokémon's Speed when it is sunny.
Early Bird—The Pokémon recovers from Sleep earlier.

STATS
HP	25
ATTACK	50
DEFENSE	50
SP. ATTACK	25
SP. DEFENSE	25
SPEED	25

EVOLUTIONS

LV14 → LEAF STONE

WHERE/HOW TO CATCH
Routes 102, 117, and 120

STRONG AGAINST:
WATER
ELECTRIC
GRASS
GROUND

WEAK AGAINST:
FIRE
ICE
POISON
FLYING
BUG

MOVES LIST
LV	Move Name	Type	ST	ACC	PP	LV	Move Name	Type	ST	ACC	PP
S	Bide	Normal	—	100	10	13	Nature Power	Normal	—	95	20
S	Pound	Normal	40	100	35	21	Synthesis	Grass	—	—	5
03	Harden	Normal	—	—	30	31	Sunny Day	Fire	—	—	5
07	Growth	Normal	—	—	40	43	Explosion	Normal	250	100	5

TM/HM LIST
TM/HM #	Move Name	Type	ST	ACC	PP	TM/HM #	Move Name	Type	ST	ACC	PP
HM05	Flash	Normal	—	70	20	TM22	Solarbeam	Grass	120	100	10
HM06	Rock Smash	Fighting	20	100	15	TM27	Return	Normal	—	100	20
TM06	Toxic	Poison	—	85	10	TM28	Dig	Ground	60	100	10
TM09	Bullet Seed	Grass	10	100	30	TM30	Shadow Ball	Ghost	60	—	20
TM10	Hidden Power	Normal	—	100	15	TM32	Double Team	Normal	—	—	15
TM11	Sunny Day	Fire	—	—	5	TM42	Façade	Normal	70	100	20
TM17	Protect	Normal	—	—	10	TM43	Secret Power	Normal	70	100	20
TM19	Giga Drain	Grass	60	100	5	TM44	Rest	Psychic	—	—	10
TM21	Frustration	Normal	—	100	20	TM45	Attract	Normal	—	100	15

EGG MOVES
Move Name	Type	ST	ACC	PP
Leech Seed	Grass	—	90	10
Amnesia	Psychic	—	—	20
Quick Attack	Normal	40	100	30
Razor Wind	Normal	80	100	10
Take Down	Normal	90	85	20
False Swipe	Normal	40	100	40

MOVE TUTOR LIST
Move Name	Type	ST	ACC	PP
Body Slam*	Normal	85	100	15
Defense Curl*	Normal	—	—	40
Double-Edge	Normal	120	100	15
Endure*	Normal	—	—	10
Explosion	Normal	250	100	5
Mimic	Normal	—	—	10
Rollout	Rock	30	90	20
Sleep Talk	Normal	—	—	10
Snore*	Normal	40	100	15
Substitute	Normal	—	—	10
Swagger	Normal	—	90	15
Swords Dance*	Normal	—	—	30

*Battle Frontier tutor move

023 Nuzleaf™

GRASS
DARK

GENERAL INFO
SPECIES: Wily Pokémon
HEIGHT: 3'3"
WEIGHT: 62 lbs.
ABILITIES: *Chlorophyll* — *Doubles the Pokémon's Speed when it is sunny.*
Early Bird — *The Pokémon recovers from Sleep earlier.*

STATS
HP	50
ATTACK	50
DEFENSE	25
SP. ATTACK	50
SP. DEFENSE	25
SPEED	50

EVOLUTIONS

LV14 → LEAF STONE

WHERE/HOW TO CATCH
Evolve from Seedot; Route 114

STRONG AGAINST:
WATER
ELECTRIC
GRASS
GROUND
PSYCHIC
GHOST
DARK

WEAK AGAINST:
FIRE
ICE
FIGHTING
POISON
FLYING
BUG

MOVES LIST
LV	Move Name	Type	ST	ACC	PP
S	Pound	Normal	40	100	35
03	Harden	Normal	—	—	30
07	Growth	Normal	—	—	40
13	Nature Power	Normal	—	95	20
19	Fake Out	Normal	40	100	10
25	Torment	Dark	—	100	15
31	Faint Attack	Dark	60	—	20
37	Razor Wind	Normal	80	100	10
43	Swagger	Normal	—	90	15
49	Extrasensory	Psychic	80	100	30

TM/HM LIST
TM/HM #	Move Name	Type	ST	ACC	PP
HM01	Cut	Normal	50	95	30
HM04	Strength	Normal	80	100	15
HM05	Flash	Normal	—	70	20
HM06	Rock Smash	Fighting	20	100	15
TM06	Toxic	Poison	—	85	10
TM09	Bullet Seed	Grass	10	100	30
TM10	Hidden Power	Normal	—	100	15
TM11	Sunny Day	Fire	—	—	5
TM15	Hyper Beam	Normal	150	90	5
TM17	Protect	Normal	—	—	10
TM19	Giga Drain	Grass	60	100	5
TM21	Frustration	Normal	—	100	20
TM22	Solarbeam	Grass	120	100	10
TM27	Return	Normal	—	100	20
TM28	Dig	Ground	60	100	10
TM30	Shadow Ball	Ghost	60	—	20
TM31	Brick Break	Fighting	75	100	15
TM32	Double Team	Normal	—	—	15
TM39	Rock Tomb	Rock	50	80	10
TM41	Torment	Dark	—	100	15
TM42	Façade	Normal	70	100	20
TM43	Secret Power	Normal	70	100	20
TM44	Rest	Psychic	—	—	10
TM45	Attract	Normal	—	100	15
TM46	Thief	Dark	40	100	10

MOVE TUTOR LIST
Move Name	Type	ST	ACC	PP
Body Slam*	Normal	85	100	15
Defense Curl*	Normal	—	—	40
Double-Edge	Normal	120	100	15
Endure*	Normal	—	—	10
Explosion	Normal	250	100	5
Fury Cutter	Bug	10	95	20
Mega Kick*	Normal	120	85	5
Mimic	Normal	—	100	10
Mud-Slap*	Ground	20	100	10
Psych Up*	Normal	—	—	10
Rollout	Rock	30	90	20
Sleep Talk	Normal	—	—	10
Snore*	Normal	40	100	15
Substitute	Normal	—	—	10
Swagger	Normal	—	90	15
Swift*	Normal	60	—	20
Swords Dance*	Normal	—	—	30

*Battle Frontier tutor move

---

024 Shiftry™

GRASS
DARK

GENERAL INFO
SPECIES: Wicked Pokémon
HEIGHT: 4'3"
WEIGHT: 131 lbs.
ABILITIES: *Chlorophyll* — *Doubles the Pokémon's Speed when it is sunny.*
Early Bird — *The Pokémon recovers from Sleep earlier.*

STATS
HP	50
ATTACK	75
DEFENSE	50
SP. ATTACK	75
SP. DEFENSE	50
SPEED	75

EVOLUTIONS

LV14 → LEAF STONE

WHERE/HOW TO CATCH
Evolve from Nuzleaf with Leaf Stone

STRONG AGAINST:
WATER
ELECTRIC
GRASS
GROUND
PSYCHIC
GHOST
DARK

WEAK AGAINST:
FIRE
ICE
FIGHTING
POISON
FLYING
BUG

MOVES LIST
LV	Move Name	Type	ST	ACC	PP
S	Pound	Normal	40	100	35
S	Harden	Normal	—	—	30
S	Growth	Normal	—	—	40
S	Nature Power	Normal	—	95	20

TM/HM LIST
TM/HM #	Move Name	Type	ST	ACC	PP
HM01	Cut	Normal	50	95	30
HM04	Strength	Normal	80	100	15
HM05	Flash	Normal	—	70	20
HM06	Rock Smash	Fighting	20	100	15
TM06	Toxic	Poison	—	85	10
TM09	Bullet Seed	Grass	10	100	30
TM10	Hidden Power	Normal	—	100	15
TM11	Sunny Day	Fire	—	—	5
TM15	Hyper Beam	Normal	150	90	5
TM17	Protect	Normal	—	—	10
TM19	Giga Drain	Grass	60	100	5
TM21	Frustration	Normal	—	100	20
TM22	Solarbeam	Grass	120	100	10
TM27	Return	Normal	—	100	20
TM28	Dig	Ground	60	100	10
TM30	Shadow Ball	Ghost	60	—	20
TM31	Brick Break	Fighting	75	100	15
TM32	Double Team	Normal	—	—	15
TM39	Rock Tomb	Rock	50	80	10
TM40	Aerial Ace	Flying	60	—	20
TM41	Torment	Dark	—	100	15
TM42	Façade	Normal	70	100	20
TM43	Secret Power	Normal	70	100	20
TM44	Rest	Psychic	—	—	10
TM45	Attract	Normal	—	100	15
TM46	Thief	Dark	40	100	10

MOVE TUTOR LIST
Move Name	Type	ST	ACC	PP
Body Slam*	Normal	85	100	15
Defense Curl*	Normal	—	—	40
Double-Edge	Normal	120	100	15
Endure*	Normal	—	—	10
Explosion	Normal	250	100	5
Fury Cutter	Bug	10	95	20
Mega Kick*	Normal	120	85	5
Mimic	Normal	—	100	10
Mud-Slap*	Ground	20	100	10
Psych Up*	Normal	—	—	10
Rollout	Rock	30	90	20
Sleep Talk	Normal	—	—	10
Snore*	Normal	40	100	15
Substitute	Normal	—	—	10
Swagger	Normal	—	90	15
Swift*	Normal	60	—	20
Swords Dance*	Normal	—	—	30

*Battle Frontier tutor move

025

Taillow™

NORMAL
FLYING

GENERAL INFO
SPECIES: Tinyswallow Pokémon
HEIGHT: 1'0"
WEIGHT: 5 lbs.
ABILITY: *Guts — The Pokémon's Attack Power rises 1.5x when inflicted with a Status condition.*

STATS
HP	25
ATTACK	50
DEFENSE	25
SP. ATTACK	25
SP. DEFENSE	25
SPEED	75

EVOLUTIONS

LV22

WHERE/HOW TO CATCH
Routes 104, 115, and 116; Petalburg Woods

STRONG AGAINST:
GRASS
GROUND
BUG
GHOST

WEAK AGAINST:
ELECTRIC
ICE
ROCK

MOVES LIST

LV	Move Name	Type	ST	ACC	PP	LV	Move Name	Type	ST	ACC	PP
S	Peck	Flying	35	100	35	19	Double Team	Normal	—	—	15
S	Growl	Normal	—	100	40	26	Endeavor	Normal	—	100	5
04	Focus Energy	Normal	—	—	30	34	Aerial Ace	Flying	60	—	20
08	Quick Attack	Normal	40	100	30	43	Agility	Psychic	—	—	30
13	Wing Attack	Flying	60	100	35						

TM/HM LIST

TM/HM #	Move Name	Type	ST	ACC	PP	TM/HM #	Move Name	Type	ST	ACC	PP
HM02	Fly	Flying	70	95	15	TM32	Double Team	Normal	—	—	15
TM06	Toxic	Poison	—	85	10	TM40	Aerial Ace	Flying	60	—	20
TM10	Hidden Power	Normal	—	100	15	TM42	Façade	Normal	70	100	20
TM11	Sunny Day	Fire	—	—	5	TM43	Secret Power	Normal	70	100	20
TM17	Protect	Normal	—	—	10	TM44	Rest	Psychic	—	—	10
TM18	Rain Dance	Water	—	—	5	TM45	Attract	Normal	—	100	15
TM21	Frustration	Normal	—	100	20	TM46	Thief	Dark	40	100	10
TM27	Return	Normal	—	100	20	TM47	Steel Wing	Steel	70	90	25

EGG MOVES

Move Name	Type	ST	ACC	PP
Pursuit	Dark	40	100	20
Supersonic	Normal	—	55	20
Refresh	Normal	—	100	20
Mirror Move	Flying	—	—	20
Rage	Normal	20	100	20
Sky Attack	Flying	140	90	5

MOVE TUTOR LIST

Move Name	Type	ST	ACC	PP
Counter*	Fighting	—	100	20
Double-Edge	Normal	120	100	15
Endure*	Normal	—	—	10
Mimic	Normal	—	100	10
Mud-Slap*	Ground	20	100	10
Sleep Talk	Normal	—	—	10
Snore*	Normal	40	100	15
Substitute	Normal	—	—	10
Swagger	Normal	—	90	15
Swift*	Normal	60	—	20

*Battle Frontier tutor move

026

Swellow™

NORMAL
FLYING

GENERAL INFO
SPECIES: Swallow Pokémon
HEIGHT: 2'4"
WEIGHT: 44 lbs.
ABILITY: *Guts — The Pokémon's Attack Power rises 1.5x when inflicted with a Status condition.*

STATS
HP	25
ATTACK	75
DEFENSE	50
SP. ATTACK	50
SP. DEFENSE	50
SPEED	100

EVOLUTIONS

LV22

WHERE/HOW TO CATCH
Evolve from Taillow; Route 115

STRONG AGAINST:
GRASS
GROUND
BUG
GHOST

WEAK AGAINST:
ELECTRIC
ICE
ROCK

MOVES LIST

LV	Move Name	Type	ST	ACC	PP	LV	Move Name	Type	ST	ACC	PP
S	Peck	Flying	35	100	35	13	Wing Attack	Flying	60	100	35
S	Growl	Normal	—	100	40	19	Double Team	Normal	—	—	15
S	Focus Energy	Normal	—	—	30	28	Endeavor	Normal	—	100	5
S	Quick Attack	Normal	40	100	30	38	Aerial Ace	Flying	60	—	20
04	Focus Energy	Normal	—	—	30	49	Agility	Psychic	—	—	30
08	Quick Attack	Normal	40	100	30						

TM/HM LIST

TM/HM #	Move Name	Type	ST	ACC	PP	TM/HM #	Move Name	Type	ST	ACC	PP
HM02	Fly	Flying	70	95	15	TM32	Double Team	Normal	—	—	15
TM06	Toxic	Poison	—	85	10	TM40	Aerial Ace	Flying	60	—	20
TM10	Hidden Power	Normal	—	100	15	TM42	Façade	Normal	70	100	20
TM11	Sunny Day	Fire	—	—	5	TM43	Secret Power	Normal	70	100	20
TM15	Hyper Beam	Normal	150	90	5	TM44	Rest	Psychic	—	—	10
TM17	Protect	Normal	—	—	10	TM45	Attract	Normal	—	100	15
TM18	Rain Dance	Water	—	—	5	TM46	Thief	Dark	40	100	10
TM21	Frustration	Normal	—	100	20	TM47	Steel Wing	Steel	70	90	25
TM27	Return	Normal	—	100	20						

MOVE TUTOR LIST

Move Name	Type	ST	ACC	PP
Counter*	Fighting	—	100	20
Double-Edge	Normal	120	100	15
Endure*	Normal	—	—	10
Mimic	Normal	—	100	10
Mud-Slap*	Ground	20	100	10
Sleep Talk	Normal	—	—	10
Snore*	Normal	40	100	15
Substitute	Normal	—	—	10
Swagger	Normal	—	90	15
Swift*	Normal	60	—	20

*Battle Frontier tutor move

027 Wingull™

WATER
FLYING

GENERAL INFO
SPECIES: Seagull Pokémon
HEIGHT: 2'0"
WEIGHT: 21 lbs.
ABILITY: *Keen Eye—Pokémon is not affected by moves that lower Accuracy.*

STATS
HP	25
ATTACK	25
DEFENSE	25
SP. ATTACK	50
SP. DEFENSE	25
SPEED	75

EVOLUTIONS
LV25

WHERE/HOW TO CATCH
Routes 103, 104, 105, 106, 109, 110, 115, 118, 119, 121, 122, 123, 124, 125, 126, 127, 128, 129, 130, 131, 132, and 133; Ever Grande, Mossdeep City, Lilycove City, Slateport City, and Mt. Pyre

STRONG AGAINST:
FIRE
WATER
FIGHTING
GROUND
BUG
STEEL

WEAK AGAINST:
ELECTRIC
ROCK

MOVES LIST
LV	Move Name	Type	ST	ACC	PP
S	Growl	Normal	—	100	40
S	Water Gun	Water	40	100	25
07	Supersonic	Normal	—	55	20
13	Wing Attack	Flying	60	100	35
21	Mist	Ice	—	—	30
31	Quick Attack	Normal	40	100	30
43	Pursuit	Dark	40	100	20
55	Agility	Psychic	—	—	30

TM/HM LIST
TM/HM #	Move Name	Type	ST	ACC	PP
HM02	Fly	Flying	70	95	15
TM03	Water Pulse	Water	60	100	20
TM06	Toxic	Poison	—	85	10
TM07	Hail	Ice	—	—	10
TM10	Hidden Power	Normal	—	100	15
TM13	Ice Beam	Ice	95	100	10
TM14	Blizzard	Ice	120	70	5
TM17	Protect	Normal	—	—	10
TM18	Rain Dance	Water	—	—	5
TM21	Frustration	Normal	—	100	20
TM27	Return	Normal	—	100	20
TM32	Double Team	Normal	—	—	15
TM34	Shock Wave	Electric	60	—	20
TM40	Aerial Ace	Flying	60	—	20
TM42	Façade	Normal	70	100	20
TM43	Secret Power	Normal	70	100	20
TM44	Rest	Psychic	—	—	10
TM45	Attract	Normal	—	100	15
TM46	Thief	Dark	40	100	10
TM47	Steel Wing	Steel	70	90	25

EGG MOVES
Move Name	Type	ST	ACC	PP
Agility	Psychic	—	—	30
Mist	Ice	—	—	30
Twister	Dragon	40	100	20
Gust	Flying	40	100	35
Water Sport	Water	—	100	15
Whirlwind	Normal	—	100	20

MOVE TUTOR LIST
Move Name	Type	ST	ACC	PP
Double-Edge	Normal	120	100	15
Endure*	Normal	—	—	10
Icy Wind*	Ice	55	95	15
Mimic	Normal	—	100	10
Mud-Slap*	Ground	20	100	10
Sleep Talk	Normal	—	—	10
Snore*	Normal	40	100	15
Substitute	Normal	—	—	10
Swagger	Normal	—	90	15
Swift*	Normal	60	—	20

*Battle Frontier tutor move

---

028 Pelipper™

WATER
FLYING

GENERAL INFO
SPECIES: Water Bird Pokémon
HEIGHT: 3'11"
WEIGHT: 62 lbs.
ABILITY: *Keen Eye—Pokémon is not affected by moves that lower Accuracy.*

STATS
HP	50
ATTACK	50
DEFENSE	75
SP. ATTACK	75
SP. DEFENSE	50
SPEED	50

EVOLUTIONS
LV25

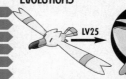

WHERE/HOW TO CATCH
Evolve from Wingull; Routes 103, 104, 105, 106, 109, 110, 115, 118, 119, 121, 122, 123, 124, 125, 126, 127, 128, 129, 130, 131, 132, and 133; Ever Grande City, Mossdeep City, Lilycove City, Slateport City, and Mt. Pyre

STRONG AGAINST:
FIRE
WATER
FIGHTING
GROUND
BUG
STEEL

WEAK AGAINST:
ELECTRIC
ROCK

MOVES LIST
LV	Move Name	Type	ST	ACC	PP
S	Growl	Normal	—	100	40
S	Water Gun	Water	40	100	25
S	Water Sport	Water	—	100	15
S	Supersonic	Normal	—	55	20
S	Wing Attack	Flying	60	100	35
03	Water Gun	Water	40	100	25
07	Supersonic	Normal	—	55	20
13	Wing Attack	Flying	60	100	35
21	Mist	Ice	—	—	30
25	Protect	Normal	—	—	10
33	Stockpile	Normal	—	—	10
33	Swallow	Normal	—	—	10
47	Spit Up	Normal	100	100	10
61	Hydro Pump	Water	120	80	5

TM/HM LIST
TM/HM #	Move Name	Type	ST	ACC	PP
HM02	Fly	Flying	70	95	15
HM03	Surf	Water	95	100	15
TM03	Water Pulse	Water	60	100	20
TM06	Toxic	Poison	—	85	10
TM07	Hail	Ice	—	—	10
TM10	Hidden Power	Normal	—	100	15
TM13	Ice Beam	Ice	95	100	10
TM14	Blizzard	Ice	120	70	5
TM15	Hyper Beam	Normal	150	90	5
TM17	Protect	Normal	—	—	10
TM18	Rain Dance	Water	—	—	5
TM21	Frustration	Normal	—	100	20
TM27	Return	Normal	—	100	20
TM32	Double Team	Normal	—	—	15
TM34	Shock Wave	Electric	60	—	20
TM40	Aerial Ace	Flying	60	—	20
TM42	Façade	Normal	70	100	20
TM43	Secret Power	Normal	70	100	20
TM44	Rest	Psychic	—	—	10
TM45	Attract	Normal	—	100	15
TM46	Thief	Dark	40	100	10
TM47	Steel Wing	Steel	70	90	25

MOVE TUTOR LIST
Move Name	Type	ST	ACC	PP
Double-Edge	Normal	120	100	15
Endure*	Normal	—	—	10
Icy Wind*	Ice	55	95	15
Mimic	Normal	—	100	10
Mud-Slap*	Ground	20	100	10
Sleep Talk	Normal	—	—	10
Snore*	Normal	40	100	15
Substitute	Normal	—	—	10
Swagger	Normal	—	90	15
Swift*	Normal	60	—	20

*Battle Frontier tutor move

029 Ralts™

PSYCHIC

GENERAL INFO
SPECIES: Feeling Pokémon
HEIGHT: 1'4"
WEIGHT: 15 lbs.
ABILITIES: *Synchronize*—Shares the Pokémon's Poison, Paralysis, or Burn condition with the opponent Pokémon.
Trace—Pokémon's Ability becomes the same as the opponent's.

STATS
HP	25
ATTACK	25
DEFENSE	25
SP. ATTACK	50
SP. DEFENSE	25
SPEED	50

EVOLUTIONS
  LV20 LV30

WHERE/HOW TO CATCH
Route 102

STRONG AGAINST:
FIGHTING
PSYCHIC

WEAK AGAINST:
BUG
GHOST
DARK

MOVES LIST
LV	Move Name	Type	ST	ACC	PP		LV	Move Name	Type	ST	ACC	PP
S	Growl	Normal	—	100	40		26	Psychic	Psychic	90	100	10
06	Confusion	Psychic	50	100	25		31	Imprison	Psychic	—	100	15
11	Double Team	Normal	—	—	15		36	Future Sight	Psychic	80	90	15
16	Teleport	Psychic	—	—	20		41	Hypnosis	Psychic	—	60	20
21	Calm Mind	Psychic	—	—	20		46	Dream Eater	Psychic	100	100	15

TM/HM LIST
TM/HM #	Move Name	Type	ST	ACC	PP		TM/HM #	Move Name	Type	ST	ACC	PP
HM05	Flash	Normal	—	70	20		TM29	Psychic	Psychic	90	100	10
TM04	Calm Mind	Psychic	—	—	20		TM30	Shadow Ball	Ghost	60	—	20
TM06	Toxic	Poison	—	85	10		TM32	Double Team	Normal	—	—	15
TM10	Hidden Power	Normal	—	100	15		TM33	Reflect	Psychic	—	—	20
TM11	Sunny Day	Fire	—	—	5		TM34	Shock Wave	Electric	60	—	20
TM12	Taunt	Dark	—	100	20		TM41	Torment	Dark	—	100	15
TM16	Light Screen	Psychic	—	—	30		TM42	Façade	Normal	70	100	20
TM17	Protect	Normal	—	—	10		TM43	Secret Power	Normal	70	100	20
TM18	Rain Dance	Water	—	—	5		TM44	Rest	Psychic	—	—	10
TM20	Safeguard	Normal	—	—	25		TM45	Attract	Normal	—	100	15
TM21	Frustration	Normal	—	100	20		TM46	Thief	Dark	40	100	10
TM24	Thunderbolt	Electric	95	100	15		TM48	Skill Swap	Psychic	—	100	10
TM27	Return	Normal	—	100	20		TM49	Snatch	Dark	—	100	10

EGG MOVES
Move Name	Type	ST	ACC	PP
Disable	Normal	—	55	20
Will-O-Wisp	Fire	—	75	15
Mean Look	Normal	—	100	5
Memento	Dark	—	100	10
Destiny Bond	Ghost	—	—	5

MOVE TUTOR LIST
Move Name	Type	ST	ACC	PP
Body Slam*	Normal	85	100	15
Defense Curl*	Normal	—	—	40
Double-Edge*	Normal	120	100	15
Dream Eater*	Psychic	100	100	15
Endure*	Normal	—	—	10
Fire Punch*	Fire	75	100	15
Ice Punch*	Ice	75	100	15
Icy Wind*	Ice	55	95	15
Mimic	Normal	—	100	10
Mud-Slap*	Ground	20	100	10
Psych Up*	Normal	—	—	10
Sleep Talk	Normal	—	—	10
Snore*	Normal	40	100	15
Substitute	Normal	—	—	10
Swagger	Normal	—	90	15
Thunderpunch*	Electric	75	100	15
Thunder Wave*	Electric	—	100	20

*Battle Frontier tutor move

030 Kirlia™

PSYCHIC

GENERAL INFO
SPECIES: Emotion Pokémon
HEIGHT: 2'7"
WEIGHT: 45 lbs.
ABILITIES: *Synchronize*—Shares the Pokémon's Poison, Paralysis, or Burn condition with the opponent Pokémon.
Trace—Pokémon's Ability becomes the same as the opponent's.

STATS
HP	25
ATTACK	25
DEFENSE	25
SP. ATTACK	50
SP. DEFENSE	50
SPEED	50

EVOLUTIONS
 LV20  LV30

WHERE/HOW TO CATCH
Evolve from Ralts

STRONG AGAINST:
FIGHTING
PSYCHIC

WEAK AGAINST:
BUG
GHOST
DARK

MOVES LIST
LV	Move Name	Type	ST	ACC	PP		LV	Move Name	Type	ST	ACC	PP
S	Growl	Normal	—	100	40		16	Teleport	Psychic	—	—	20
S	Confusion	Psychic	50	100	25		21	Calm Mind	Psychic	—	—	20
S	Double Team	Normal	—	—	15		26	Psychic	Psychic	90	100	10
S	Teleport	Psychic	—	—	20		33	Imprison	Psychic	—	100	15
S	Magical Leaf	Grass	60	—	20		40	Future Sight	Psychic	80	90	15
06	Confusion	Psychic	50	100	25		47	Hypnosis	Psychic	—	60	20
11	Double Team	Normal	—	—	15		54	Dream Eater	Psychic	100	100	15

TM/HM LIST
TM/HM #	Move Name	Type	ST	ACC	PP		TM/HM #	Move Name	Type	ST	ACC	PP
HM05	Flash	Normal	—	70	20		TM29	Psychic	Psychic	90	100	10
TM04	Calm Mind	Psychic	—	—	20		TM30	Shadow Ball	Ghost	60	—	20
TM06	Toxic	Poison	—	85	10		TM32	Double Team	Normal	—	—	15
TM10	Hidden Power	Normal	—	100	15		TM33	Reflect	Psychic	—	—	20
TM11	Sunny Day	Fire	—	—	5		TM34	Shock Wave	Electric	60	—	20
TM12	Taunt	Dark	—	100	20		TM41	Torment	Dark	—	100	15
TM16	Light Screen	Psychic	—	—	30		TM42	Façade	Normal	70	100	20
TM17	Protect	Normal	—	—	10		TM43	Secret Power	Normal	70	100	20
TM18	Rain Dance	Water	—	—	5		TM44	Rest	Psychic	—	—	10
TM20	Safeguard	Normal	—	—	25		TM45	Attract	Normal	—	100	15
TM21	Frustration	Normal	—	100	20		TM46	Thief	Dark	40	100	10
TM24	Thunderbolt	Electric	95	100	15		TM48	Skill Swap	Psychic	—	100	10
TM27	Return	Normal	—	100	20		TM49	Snatch	Dark	—	100	10

MOVE TUTOR LIST
Move Name	Type	ST	ACC	PP
Body Slam*	Normal	85	100	15
Defense Curl*	Normal	—	—	40
Double-Edge*	Normal	120	100	15
Dream Eater*	Psychic	100	100	15
Endure*	Normal	—	—	10
Fire Punch*	Fire	75	100	15
Ice Punch*	Ice	75	100	15
Icy Wind*	Ice	55	95	15
Mimic	Normal	—	100	10
Mud-Slap*	Ground	20	100	10
Psych Up*	Normal	—	—	10
Sleep Talk	Normal	—	—	10
Snore*	Normal	40	100	15
Substitute	Normal	—	—	10
Swagger	Normal	—	90	15
Thunderpunch*	Electric	75	100	15
Thunder Wave*	Electric	—	100	20

*Battle Frontier tutor move

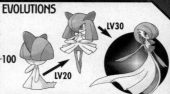

031 Gardevoir™

PSYCHIC

GENERAL INFO
SPECIES: Embrace Pokémon
HEIGHT: 5'3"
WEIGHT: 107 lbs.
ABILITIES: **Synchronize**—*Shares the Pokémon's Poison, Paralysis, or Burn condition with the opponent Pokémon.*
Trace—*Pokémon's Ability becomes the same as the opponent's.*

STATS

HP	50
ATTACK	50
DEFENSE	50
SP. ATTACK	100
SP. DEFENSE	75
SPEED	75

EVOLUTIONS

LV20 / LV30

WHERE/HOW TO CATCH
Evolve from Kirlia

STRONG AGAINST:
FIGHTING
PSYCHIC

WEAK AGAINST:
BUG
GHOST
DARK

MOVES LIST

LV	Move Name	Type	ST	ACC	PP
S	Growl	Normal	—	100	40
S	Confusion	Psychic	50	100	25
S	Double Team	Normal	—	—	15
S	Teleport	Psychic	—	—	20
06	Confusion	Psychic	50	100	25
11	Double Team	Normal	—	—	15
16	Teleport	Psychic	—	—	20

LV	Move Name	Type	ST	ACC	PP
21	Calm Mind	Psychic	—	—	20
26	Psychic	Psychic	90	100	10
33	Imprison	Psychic	—	100	15
42	Future Sight	Psychic	80	90	15
51	Hypnosis	Psychic	—	60	20
60	Dream Eater	Psychic	100	100	15

TM/HM LIST

TM/HM #	Move Name	Type	ST	ACC	PP
HM05	Flash	Normal	—	70	20
TM04	Calm Mind	Psychic	—	—	20
TM06	Toxic	Poison	—	85	10
TM10	Hidden Power	Normal	—	100	15
TM11	Sunny Day	Fire	—	—	5
TM12	Taunt	Dark	—	100	20
TM15	Hyper Beam	Normal	150	90	5
TM16	Light Screen	Psychic	—	—	30
TM17	Protect	Normal	—	—	10
TM18	Rain Dance	Water	—	—	5
TM20	Safeguard	Normal	—	—	25
TM21	Frustration	Normal	—	100	20
TM24	Thunderbolt	Electric	95	100	15
TM27	Return	Normal	—	100	20

TM/HM #	Move Name	Type	ST	ACC	PP
TM29	Psychic	Psychic	90	100	10
TM30	Shadow Ball	Ghost	60	—	20
TM32	Double Team	Normal	—	—	15
TM33	Reflect	Psychic	—	—	20
TM34	Shock Wave	Electric	60	—	20
TM41	Torment	Dark	—	100	15
TM42	Façade	Normal	70	100	20
TM43	Secret Power	Normal	70	100	20
TM44	Rest	Psychic	—	—	10
TM45	Attract	Normal	—	100	15
TM46	Thief	Dark	40	100	10
TM48	Skill Swap	Psychic	—	100	10
TM49	Snatch	Dark	—	100	10

MOVE TUTOR LIST

Move Name	Type	ST	ACC	PP
Body Slam*	Normal	85	100	15
Defense Curl*	Normal	—	—	40
Double-Edge*	Normal	120	100	15
Dream Eater*	Psychic	100	100	15
Endure*	Normal	—	—	10
Fire Punch*	Fire	75	100	15
Ice Punch*	Ice	75	100	15
Icy Wind*	Ice	55	95	15
Mimic	Normal	—	100	10
Mud-Slap*	Ground	20	100	10
Psych Up*	Normal	—	—	10
Sleep Talk*	Normal	—	—	10
Snore*	Normal	40	100	15
Substitute	Normal	—	—	10
Swagger	Normal	—	90	15
Thunderpunch*	Electric	75	100	15
Thunder Wave*	Electric	—	100	20

*Battle Frontier tutor move

032 Surskit™

BUG
WATER

GENERAL INFO
SPECIES: Pond Skater Pokémon
HEIGHT: 1'8"
WEIGHT: 4 lbs.
ABILITY: **Swift Swim**—*Doubles the Pokémon's Speed when it is raining.*

STATS

HP	25
ATTACK	25
DEFENSE	25
SP. ATTACK	50
SP. DEFENSE	50
SPEED	50

EVOLUTIONS

LV22

WHERE/HOW TO CATCH
Must trade from *Pokémon Ruby* and *Pokémon Sapphire*

STRONG AGAINST:
WATER
ICE
FIGHTING
GROUND
STEEL

WEAK AGAINST:
ELECTRIC
FLYING
ROCK

MOVES LIST

LV	Move Name	Type	ST	ACC	PP
S	Bubble	Water	20	100	30
07	Quick Attack	Normal	40	100	30
13	Sweet Scent	Normal	—	100	20
19	Water Sport	Water	—	100	15

LV	Move Name	Type	ST	ACC	PP
25	Bubblebeam	Water	65	100	20
31	Agility	Psychic	—	—	30
37	Mist	Ice	—	—	30
37	Haze	Ice	—	—	30

TM/HM LIST

TM/HM #	Move Name	Type	ST	ACC	PP
HM05	Flash	Normal	—	70	20
TM03	Water Pulse	Water	60	100	20
TM06	Toxic	Poison	—	85	10
TM10	Hidden Power	Normal	—	100	15
TM11	Sunny Day	Fire	—	—	5
TM13	Ice Beam	Ice	95	100	10
TM14	Blizzard	Ice	120	70	5
TM17	Protect	Normal	—	—	10
TM18	Rain Dance	Water	—	—	5
TM19	Giga Drain	Grass	60	100	5

TM/HM #	Move Name	Type	ST	ACC	PP
TM21	Frustration	Normal	—	100	20
TM22	Solarbeam	Grass	120	100	10
TM27	Return	Normal	—	100	20
TM30	Shadow Ball	Ghost	60	—	20
TM32	Double Team	Normal	—	—	15
TM42	Façade	Normal	70	100	20
TM43	Secret Power	Normal	70	100	20
TM44	Rest	Psychic	—	—	10
TM45	Attract	Normal	—	100	15
TM46	Thief	Dark	40	100	10

EGG MOVES

Move Name	Type	ST	ACC	PP
Foresight	Normal	—	100	40
Mud Shot	Ground	55	95	15
Psybeam	Psychic	65	100	20
Hydro Pump	Water	120	80	5
Mind Reader	Normal	—	100	5

MOVE TUTOR LIST

Move Name	Type	ST	ACC	PP
Double-Edge	Normal	120	100	15
Endure*	Normal	—	—	10
Icy Wind*	Ice	55	95	15
Mimic	Normal	—	100	10
Psych Up*	Normal	—	—	10
Sleep Talk	Normal	—	—	10
Snore*	Normal	40	100	15
Substitute	Normal	—	—	10
Swagger	Normal	—	90	15
Swift*	Normal	60	—	20

*Battle Frontier tutor move

033 Masquerain™

BUG
FLYING

GENERAL INFO
SPECIES: Eyeball Pokémon
HEIGHT: 2'7"
WEIGHT: 8 lbs.
ABILITY: *Intimidate — Lowers the opponent's Attack by one point at the start of a battle.*

STATS
HP	50
ATTACK	50
DEFENSE	50
SP. ATTACK	75
SP. DEFENSE	50
SPEED	50

EVOLUTIONS
 LV22

WHERE/HOW TO CATCH
Must trade from *Pokémon Ruby* or trade for Surskit, then evolve

STRONG AGAINST:
BUG
FIGHTING
GROUND
GRASS

WEAK AGAINST:
FIRE
ELECTRIC
FLYING
ROCK
ICE

MOVES LIST
LV	Move Name	Type	ST	ACC	PP
S	Bubble	Water	20	100	30
S	Quick Attack	Normal	40	100	30
S	Sweet Scent	Normal	—	100	20
S	Water Sport	Water	—	100	15
07	Quick Attack	Normal	40	100	30
13	Sweet Scent	Normal	—	100	20
19	Water Sport	Water	—	100	15
26	Gust	Flying	40	100	35
33	Scary Face	Normal	—	90	10
40	Stun Spore	Grass	—	75	30
47	Silver Wind	Bug	60	100	5
53	Whirlwind	Normal	—	100	20

TM/HM LIST
TM/HM #	Move Name	Type	ST	ACC	PP
HM05	Flash	Normal	—	70	20
TM03	Water Pulse	Water	60	100	20
TM06	Toxic	Poison	—	85	10
TM10	Hidden Power	Normal	—	100	15
TM11	Sunny Day	Fire	—	—	5
TM13	Ice Beam	Ice	95	100	10
TM14	Blizzard	Ice	120	70	5
TM15	Hyper Beam	Normal	150	90	5
TM17	Protect	Normal	—	—	10
TM18	Rain Dance	Water	—	—	5
TM19	Giga Drain	Grass	60	100	5
TM21	Frustration	Normal	—	100	20
TM22	Solarbeam	Grass	120	100	10
TM27	Return	Normal	—	100	20
TM30	Shadow Ball	Ghost	60	—	20
TM32	Double Team	Normal	—	—	15
TM40	Aerial Ace	Flying	60	—	20
TM42	Façade	Normal	70	100	20
TM43	Secret Power	Normal	70	100	20
TM44	Rest	Psychic	—	—	10
TM45	Attract	Normal	—	100	15
TM46	Thief	Dark	40	100	10

MOVE TUTOR LIST
Move Name	Type	ST	ACC	PP
Double-Edge	Normal	120	100	15
Endure*	Normal	—	—	10
Icy Wind*	Ice	55	95	15
Mimic	Normal	—	100	10
Psych Up*	Normal	—	—	10
Sleep Talk*	Normal	—	—	10
Snore*	Normal	40	100	15
Substitute	Normal	—	—	10
Swagger	Normal	—	90	15
Swift*	Normal	60	—	20

*Battle Frontier tutor move

---

034 Shroomish™

GRASS

GENERAL INFO
SPECIES: Mushroom Pokémon
HEIGHT: 1'4"
WEIGHT: 10 lbs.
ABILITY: *Effect Spore — Gives the Pokémon's Physical Attacks a 10 percent chance of inflicting Paralysis, Poison, or Sleep on the opponent.*

STATS
HP	50
ATTACK	50
DEFENSE	50
SP. ATTACK	50
SP. DEFENSE	50
SPEED	25

EVOLUTIONS
 LV23

WHERE/HOW TO CATCH
Petalburg Woods

STRONG AGAINST:
WATER
ELECTRIC
GRASS
GROUND

WEAK AGAINST:
FIRE
ICE
POISON
FLYING
BUG

MOVES LIST
LV	Move Name	Type	ST	ACC	PP
S	Absorb	Grass	20	100	20
04	Tackle	Normal	35	95	35
07	Stun Spore	Grass	—	75	30
10	Leech Seed	Grass	—	90	10
16	Mega Drain	Grass	40	100	10
22	Headbutt	Normal	70	100	15
28	Poisonpowder	Poison	—	75	35
36	Growth	Normal	—	—	40
45	Giga Drain	Grass	60	100	5
54	Spore	Grass	—	100	15

TM/HM LIST
TM/HM #	Move Name	Type	ST	ACC	PP
HM05	Flash	Normal	—	70	20
TM06	Toxic	Poison	—	85	10
TM09	Bullet Seed	Grass	10	100	30
TM10	Hidden Power	Normal	—	100	15
TM11	Sunny Day	Fire	—	—	5
TM17	Protect	Normal	—	—	10
TM19	Giga Drain	Grass	60	100	5
TM20	Safeguard	Normal	—	—	25
TM21	Frustration	Normal	—	100	20
TM22	Solarbeam	Grass	120	100	10
TM27	Return	Normal	—	100	20
TM32	Double Team	Normal	—	—	15
TM36	Sludge Bomb	Poison	90	100	10
TM42	Façade	Normal	70	100	20
TM43	Secret Power	Normal	70	100	20
TM44	Rest	Psychic	—	—	10
TM45	Attract	Normal	—	100	15
TM49	Snatch	Dark	—	100	10

EGG MOVES
Move Name	Type	ST	ACC	PP
Fake Tears	Dark	—	100	20
Swagger	Normal	—	90	15
Charm	Normal	—	100	20
False Swipe	Normal	40	100	40
Helping Hand	Normal	—	100	20

MOVE TUTOR LIST
Move Name	Type	ST	ACC	PP
Body Slam*	Normal	85	100	15
Double-Edge	Normal	120	100	15
Endure*	Normal	—	—	10
Mimic	Normal	—	100	10
Sleep Talk*	Normal	—	—	10
Snore*	Normal	40	100	15
Substitute	Normal	—	—	10
Swagger	Normal	—	90	15
Swords Dance*	Normal	—	—	30

*Battle Frontier tutor move

035

Breloom™

| GRASS |
| FIGHTING |

GENERAL INFO
SPECIES: Mushroom Pokémon
HEIGHT: 3'11"
WEIGHT: 86 lbs.
ABILITY: *Effect Spore* — Gives the Pokémon's Physical Attacks a 10 percent chance of inflicting Paralysis, Poison, or Sleep on the opponent.

STATS
HP		50
ATTACK		100
DEFENSE		50
SP. ATTACK		50
SP. DEFENSE		50
SPEED		50

EVOLUTIONS

LV23

WHERE/HOW TO CATCH
Evolve from Shroomish

STRONG AGAINST:
| WATER |
| ELECTRIC |
| GRASS |
| GROUND |
| DARK |
| ROCK |

WEAK AGAINST:
| FIRE |
| ICE |
| POISON |
| FLYING |
| PSYCHIC |

MOVES LIST

LV	Move Name	Type	ST	ACC	PP	LV	Move Name	Type	ST	ACC	PP
S	Absorb	Grass	20	100	20	16	Mega Drain	Grass	40	100	10
S	Tackle	Normal	35	95	35	22	Headbutt	Normal	70	100	15
S	Stun Spore	Grass	—	75	30	23	Mach Punch	Fighting	40	100	30
S	Leech Seed	Grass	—	90	10	28	Counter	Fighting	—	100	20
04	Tackle	Normal	35	95	35	36	Sky Uppercut	Fighting	85	90	15
07	Stun Spore	Grass	—	75	30	45	Mind Reader	Normal	—	100	5
10	Leech Seed	Grass	—	90	10	54	Dynamicpunch	Fighting	100	50	5

TM/HM LIST

TM/HM #	Move Name	Type	ST	ACC	PP	TM/HM #	Move Name	Type	ST	ACC	PP
HM01	Cut	Normal	50	95	30	TM20	Safeguard	Normal	—	—	25
HM04	Strength	Normal	80	100	15	TM21	Frustration	Normal	—	100	20
HM05	Flash	Normal	—	70	20	TM22	Solarbeam	Grass	120	100	10
HM06	Rock Smash	Fighting	20	100	15	TM23	Iron Tail	Steel	100	75	15
TM01	Focus Punch	Fighting	150	100	20	TM27	Return	Normal	—	100	20
TM06	Toxic	Poison	—	85	10	TM31	Brick Break	Fighting	75	100	15
TM08	Bulk Up	Fighting	—	—	20	TM32	Double Team	Normal	—	—	15
TM09	Bullet Seed	Grass	10	100	30	TM36	Sludge Bomb	Poison	90	100	10
TM10	Hidden Power	Normal	—	100	15	TM42	Façade	Normal	70	100	20
TM11	Sunny Day	Fire	—	—	5	TM43	Secret Power	Normal	70	100	20
TM15	Hyper Beam	Normal	150	90	5	TM44	Rest	Psychic	—	—	10
TM17	Protect	Normal	—	—	10	TM45	Attract	Normal	—	100	15
TM19	Giga Drain	Grass	60	100	5	TM49	Snatch	Dark	—	100	10

MOVE TUTOR LIST

Move Name	Type	ST	ACC	PP
Body Slam*	Normal	85	100	15
Counter*	Fighting	—	100	20
Double-Edge	Normal	120	100	15
Dynamicpunch	Fighting	100	50	5
Endure*	Normal	—	—	10
Fury Cutter	Bug	10	95	20
Mega Kick*	Normal	120	85	5
Mega Punch*	Normal	80	75	20
Mimic	Normal	—	100	10
Mud-Slap*	Ground	20	100	10
Seismic Toss*	Fighting	—	100	20
Sleep Talk	Normal	—	—	10
Snore	Normal	40	100	15
Substitute	Normal	—	—	10
Swagger	Normal	—	90	15
Swords Dance*	Normal	—	—	30
Thunderpunch*	Electric	75	100	15

*Battle Frontier tutor move

036

Slakoth™

| NORMAL |

GENERAL INFO
SPECIES: Slacker Pokémon
HEIGHT: 2'7"
WEIGHT: 53 lbs.
ABILITY: *Truant* — Can attack only one or two times.

STATS
HP		50
ATTACK		50
DEFENSE		50
SP. ATTACK		50
SP. DEFENSE		25
SPEED		25

EVOLUTIONS

LV18 LV36

WHERE/HOW TO CATCH
Petalburg Woods

STRONG AGAINST:
| GHOST |

WEAK AGAINST:
| FIGHTING |

MOVES LIST

LV	Move Name	Type	ST	ACC	PP	LV	Move Name	Type	ST	ACC	PP
S	Scratch	Normal	40	100	35	25	Amnesia	Psychic	—	—	20
S	Yawn	Normal	—	100	10	31	Covet	Normal	40	100	40
07	Encore	Normal	—	100	5	37	Counter	Fighting	—	100	20
13	Slack Off	Normal	—	100	10	43	Flail	Normal	—	100	15
19	Faint Attack	Dark	60	—	20						

TM/HM LIST

TM/HM #	Move Name	Type	ST	ACC	PP	TM/HM #	Move Name	Type	ST	ACC	PP
HM01	Cut	Normal	50	95	30	TM24	Thunderbolt	Electric	95	100	15
HM04	Strength	Normal	80	100	15	TM25	Thunder	Electric	120	70	10
HM06	Rock Smash	Fighting	20	100	15	TM27	Return	Normal	—	100	20
TM01	Focus Punch	Fighting	150	100	20	TM30	Shadow Ball	Ghost	60	—	20
TM03	Water Pulse	Water	60	100	20	TM31	Brick Break	Fighting	75	100	15
TM06	Toxic	Poison	—	85	10	TM32	Double Team	Normal	—	—	15
TM08	Bulk Up	Fighting	—	—	20	TM34	Shock Wave	Electric	60	—	20
TM10	Hidden Power	Normal	—	100	15	TM35	Flamethrower	Fire	95	100	15
TM11	Sunny Day	Fire	—	—	5	TM38	Fire Blast	Fire	120	85	5
TM13	Ice Beam	Ice	95	100	10	TM40	Aerial Ace	Flying	60	—	20
TM14	Blizzard	Ice	120	70	5	TM42	Façade	Normal	70	100	20
TM17	Protect	Normal	—	—	10	TM43	Secret Power	Normal	70	100	20
TM18	Rain Dance	Water	—	—	5	TM44	Rest	Psychic	—	—	10
TM21	Frustration	Normal	—	100	20	TM45	Attract	Normal	—	100	15
TM22	Solarbeam	Grass	120	100	10						

EGG MOVES

Move Name	Type	ST	ACC	PP
Pursuit	Dark	40	100	20
Slash	Normal	70	100	20
Body Slam	Normal	85	100	15
Snore	Normal	40	100	15
Crush Claw	Normal	75	95	10
Curse	—	—	—	10
Sleep Talk	Normal	—	—	10

MOVE TUTOR LIST

Move Name	Type	ST	ACC	PP
Body Slam*	Normal	85	100	15
Counter*	Fighting	—	100	20
Double-Edge	Normal	120	100	15
Dynamicpunch	Fighting	100	50	5
Endure*	Normal	—	—	10
Fire Punch*	Fire	75	100	15
Fury Cutter*	Bug	10	95	20
Ice Punch*	Ice	75	100	15
Icy Wind*	Ice	55	95	15
Mega Kick*	Normal	120	85	5
Mega Punch*	Normal	80	75	20
Mimic	Normal	—	100	10
Mud-Slap*	Ground	20	100	10
Rock Slide*	Rock	75	90	10
Seismic Toss*	Fighting	—	100	20
Sleep Talk	Normal	—	—	10
Snore*	Normal	40	100	15
Substitute	Normal	—	—	10
Swagger	Normal	—	90	15
Thunderpunch*	Electric	75	100	15

*Battle Frontier tutor move

037 Vigoroth™

NORMAL

GENERAL INFO
SPECIES: Wild Monkey Pokémon
HEIGHT: 4'7"
WEIGHT: 103 lbs.
ABILITY: *Vital Spirit* —
Pokémon cannot be put to Sleep.

STATS
HP	50
ATTACK	75
DEFENSE	50
SP. ATTACK	50
SP. DEFENSE	50
SPEED	75

EVOLUTIONS

LV18 — LV36

WHERE/HOW TO CATCH
Evolve from Slakoth

STRONG AGAINST:
GHOST

WEAK AGAINST:
FIGHTING

MOVES LIST
LV	Move Name	Type	ST	ACC	PP		LV	Move Name	Type	ST	ACC	PP
S	Scratch	Normal	40	100	35		19	Fury Swipes	Normal	18	80	15
S	Focus Energy	Normal	—		30		25	Endure	Normal	—		10
S	Encore	Normal	—	100	5		31	Slash	Normal	70	100	20
S	Uproar	Normal	50	100	10		37	Counter	Fighting	—	100	20
07	Encore	Normal	—	100	5		43	Focus Punch	Fighting	150	100	20
13	Uproar	Normal	50	100	10		49	Reversal	Fighting	—	100	15

TM/HM LIST
TM/HM #	Move Name	Type	ST	ACC	PP		TM/HM #	Move Name	Type	ST	ACC	PP
HM01	Cut	Normal	50	95	30		TM22	Solarbeam	Grass	120	100	10
HM04	Strength	Normal	80	100	15		TM24	Thunderbolt	Electric	95	100	15
HM06	Rock Smash	Fighting	20	100	15		TM25	Thunder	Electric	120	70	10
TM01	Focus Punch	Fighting	150	100	20		TM26	Earthquake	Ground	100	100	10
TM03	Water Pulse	Water	60	100	20		TM27	Return	Normal	—	100	20
TM05	Roar	Normal	—	100	20		TM30	Shadow Ball	Ghost	60		20
TM06	Toxic	Poison	—	85	10		TM31	Brick Break	Fighting	75	100	15
TM08	Bulk Up	Fighting	—		20		TM32	Double Team	Normal	—		15
TM10	Hidden Power	Normal	—	100	15		TM34	Shock Wave	Electric	60	—	20
TM11	Sunny Day	Fire	—	—	5		TM35	Flamethrower	Fire	95	100	15
TM12	Taunt	Dark	—	100	20		TM38	Fire Blast	Fire	120	85	5
TM13	Ice Beam	Ice	95	100	10		TM40	Aerial Ace	Flying	60	—	20
TM14	Blizzard	Ice	120	70	5		TM42	Façade	Normal	70	100	20
TM17	Protect	Normal	—	—	10		TM43	Secret Power	Normal	70	100	20
TM18	Rain Dance	Water	—	—	5		TM44	Rest	Psychic	—	—	10
TM21	Frustration	Normal	—	100	20		TM45	Attract	Normal	—	100	15

MOVE TUTOR LIST
Move Name	Type	ST	ACC	PP
Body Slam*	Normal	85	100	15
Counter*	Fighting	—	100	20
Double-Edge	Normal	120	100	15
Dynamicpunch	Fighting	100	50	5
Endure*	Normal	—	—	10
Fire Punch*	Fire	75	100	15
Fury Cutter*	Bug	10	95	20
Ice Punch*	Ice	75	100	15
Icy Wind*	Ice	55	95	15
Mega Kick*	Normal	120	85	5
Mega Punch*	Normal	80	75	20
Mimic	Normal	—	100	10
Mud-Slap*	Ground	20	100	10
Rock Slide*	Rock	75	90	10
Seismic Toss*	Fighting	—	100	20
Sleep Talk	Normal	—	—	10
Snore*	Normal	40	100	15
Substitute	Normal	—	—	10
Swagger	Normal	—	90	15
Thunderpunch*	Electric	75	100	15

*Battle Frontier tutor move

---

038 Slaking™

NORMAL

GENERAL INFO
SPECIES: Lazy Pokémon
HEIGHT: 6'7"
WEIGHT: 288 lbs.
ABILITY: *Truant* —
Can attack only one or two times.

STATS
HP	75
ATTACK	100
DEFENSE	75
SP. ATTACK	75
SP. DEFENSE	50
SPEED	75

EVOLUTIONS

LV18 — LV36

WHERE/HOW TO CATCH
Evolve from Vigoroth

STRONG AGAINST:
GHOST

WEAK AGAINST:
FIGHTING

MOVES LIST
LV	Move Name	Type	ST	ACC	PP		LV	Move Name	Type	ST	ACC	PP
S	Scratch	Normal	40	100	35		19	Faint Attack	Dark	60	—	20
S	Yawn	Normal	—	100	10		25	Amnesia	Psychic	—	—	20
S	Encore	Normal	—	100	5		31	Covet	Normal	40	100	40
S	Slack Off	Normal	—	100	10		36	Swagger	Normal	—	90	15
07	Encore	Normal	—	100	5		37	Counter	Fighting	—	100	20
13	Slack Off	Normal	—	100	10		43	Flail	Normal	—	100	15

TM/HM LIST
TM/HM #	Move Name	Type	ST	ACC	PP		TM/HM #	Move Name	Type	ST	ACC	PP
HM01	Cut	Normal	50	95	30		TM22	Solarbeam	Grass	120	100	10
HM04	Strength	Normal	80	100	15		TM24	Thunderbolt	Electric	95	100	15
HM06	Rock Smash	Fighting	20	100	15		TM25	Thunder	Electric	120	70	10
TM01	Focus Punch	Fighting	150	100	20		TM26	Earthquake	Ground	100	100	10
TM03	Water Pulse	Water	60	100	20		TM27	Return	Normal	—	100	20
TM05	Roar	Normal	—	100	20		TM30	Shadow Ball	Ghost	60		20
TM06	Toxic	Poison	—	85	10		TM31	Brick Break	Fighting	75	100	15
TM08	Bulk Up	Fighting	—		20		TM32	Double Team	Normal	—		15
TM10	Hidden Power	Normal	—	100	15		TM34	Shock Wave	Electric	60	—	20
TM11	Sunny Day	Fire	—	—	5		TM35	Flamethrower	Fire	95	100	15
TM12	Taunt	Dark	—	100	20		TM38	Fire Blast	Fire	120	85	5
TM13	Ice Beam	Ice	95	100	10		TM40	Aerial Ace	Flying	60	—	20
TM14	Blizzard	Ice	120	70	5		TM42	Façade	Normal	70	100	20
TM15	Hyper Beam	Normal	150	90	5		TM43	Secret Power	Normal	70	100	20
TM17	Protect	Normal	—	—	10		TM44	Rest	Psychic	—	—	10
TM18	Rain Dance	Water	—	—	5		TM45	Attract	Normal	—	100	15
TM21	Frustration	Normal	—	100	20							

MOVE TUTOR LIST
Move Name	Type	ST	ACC	PP
Body Slam*	Normal	85	100	15
Counter*	Fighting	—	100	20
Double-Edge	Normal	120	100	15
Dynamicpunch	Fighting	100	50	5
Endure*	Normal	—	—	10
Fire Punch*	Fire	75	100	15
Fury Cutter*	Bug	10	95	20
Ice Punch*	Ice	75	100	15
Icy Wind*	Ice	55	95	15
Mega Kick*	Normal	120	85	5
Mega Punch*	Normal	80	75	20
Mimic	Normal	—	100	10
Mud-Slap*	Ground	20	100	10
Rock Slide*	Rock	75	90	10
Seismic Toss*	Fighting	—	100	20
Sleep Talk	Normal	—	—	10
Snore*	Normal	40	100	15
Substitute	Normal	—	—	10
Swagger	Normal	—	90	15
Thunderpunch*	Electric	75	100	15

*Battle Frontier tutor move

039

Abra™

PSYCHIC

GENERAL INFO
SPECIES: Psi Pokémon
HEIGHT: 2'11"
WEIGHT: 43 lbs.
ABILITIES: *Synchronize* — *Shares the Pokémon's Poison, Paralysis, or Burn condition with the opponent Pokémon.*
Inner Focus — *Prevents the Pokémon from Flinching.*

STATS

HP	33
ATTACK	30
DEFENSE	33
SP. ATTACK	66
SP. DEFENSE	30
SPEED	66

EVOLUTIONS

LV16 → TRADE OVER THE GAME BOY WIRELESS ADAPTER

WHERE/HOW TO CATCH
Route 116, Granite Cave

STRONG AGAINST:
FIGHTING
PSYCHIC

WEAK AGAINST:
GHOST
BUG
DARK

MOVES LIST

LV	Move Name	Type	ST	ACC	PP
S	Teleport	Psychic	—	—	20

TM/HM LIST

TM/HM #	Move Name	Type	ST	ACC	PP
HM05	Flash	Normal	—	70	20
TM01	Focus Punch	Fighting	150	100	20
TM04	Calm Mind	Psychic	—	—	20
TM06	Toxic	Poison	—	85	10
TM10	Hidden Power	Normal	—	100	15
TM11	Sunny Day	Fire	—	—	5
TM12	Taunt	Dark	—	100	20
TM16	Light Screen	Psychic	—	—	30
TM17	Protect	Normal	—	—	10
TM18	Rain Dance	Water	—	—	5
TM20	Safeguard	Normal	—	—	25
TM21	Frustration	Normal	—	100	20
TM23	Iron Tail	Steel	100	75	15
TM27	Return	Normal	—	100	20

TM/HM #	Move Name	Type	ST	ACC	PP
TM29	Psychic	Psychic	90	100	10
TM30	Shadow Ball	Ghost	60	—	20
TM32	Double Team	Normal	—	—	15
TM33	Reflect	Psychic	—	—	20
TM34	Shock Wave	Electric	60	—	20
TM41	Torment	Dark	—	100	15
TM42	Façade	Normal	70	100	20
TM43	Secret Power	Normal	70	100	20
TM44	Rest	Psychic	—	—	10
TM45	Attract	Normal	—	100	15
TM46	Thief	Dark	40	100	10
TM48	Skill Swap	Psychic	—	100	10
TM49	Snatch	Dark	—	100	10

EGG MOVES

Move Name	Type	ST	ACC	PP
Barrier	Psychic	—	—	30
Encore	Normal	—	100	5
Knock Off	Dark	20	100	20
Fire Punch	Fire	75	100	15
Thunderpunch	Electric	75	100	15
Ice Punch	Ice	75	100	15

MOVE TUTOR LIST

Move Name	Type	ST	ACC	PP
Body Slam*	Normal	85	100	15
Counter*	Fighting	—	100	20
Double-Edge	Normal	120	100	15
Dream Eater*	Psychic	100	100	15
Dynamicpunch	Fighting	100	50	5
Endure*	Normal	—	—	10
Fire Punch*	Fire	75	100	15
Ice Punch*	Ice	75	100	15
Mega Kick*	Normal	120	85	5
Mega Punch*	Normal	80	75	20
Metronome	Normal	—	100	10
Mimic	Normal	—	100	10
Psych Up*	Normal	—	—	10
Seismic Toss*	Fighting	—	100	20
Sleep Talk	Normal	—	—	10
Snore*	Normal	40	100	15
Substitute	Normal	—	—	10
Swagger	Normal	—	90	15
Thunderpunch*	Electric	75	100	15
Thunder Wave*	Electric	—	100	20

*Battle Frontier tutor move

040

Kadabra™

PSYCHIC

GENERAL INFO
SPECIES: Psi Pokémon
HEIGHT: 4'3"
WEIGHT: 125 lbs.
ABILITIES: *Synchronize* — *Shares the Pokémon's Poison, Paralysis, or Burn condition with the opponent Pokémon.*
Inner Focus — *Prevents the Pokémon from Flinching.*

STATS

HP	33
ATTACK	30
DEFENSE	33
SP. ATTACK	100
SP. DEFENSE	66
SPEED	100

EVOLUTIONS

LV16 → TRADE OVER THE GAME BOY WIRELESS ADAPTER

WHERE/HOW TO CATCH
Evolve from Abra

STRONG AGAINST:
FIGHTING
PSYCHIC

WEAK AGAINST:
GHOST
BUG
DARK

MOVES LIST

LV	Move Name	Type	ST	ACC	PP
S	Teleport	Psychic	—	—	20
S	Kinesis	Psychic	—	80	15
S	Confusion	Psychic	50	100	25
16	Confusion	Psychic	50	100	25
18	Disable	Normal	—	55	20
21	Psybeam	Psychic	65	100	20

LV	Move Name	Type	ST	ACC	PP
23	Reflect	Psychic	—	—	20
25	Recover	Normal	—	—	20
30	Future Sight	Psychic	80	90	15
33	Role Play	Psychic	—	100	10
36	Psychic	Psychic	90	100	10
43	Trick	Psychic	—	100	10

TM/HM LIST

TM/HM #	Move Name	Type	ST	ACC	PP
HM05	Flash	Normal	—	70	20
TM01	Focus Punch	Fighting	150	100	20
TM04	Calm Mind	Psychic	—	—	20
TM06	Toxic	Poison	—	85	10
TM10	Hidden Power	Normal	—	100	15
TM11	Sunny Day	Fire	—	—	5
TM12	Taunt	Dark	—	100	20
TM16	Light Screen	Psychic	—	—	30
TM17	Protect	Normal	—	—	10
TM18	Rain Dance	Water	—	—	5
TM20	Safeguard	Normal	—	—	25
TM21	Frustration	Normal	—	100	20
TM23	Iron Tail	Steel	100	75	15
TM27	Return	Normal	—	100	20

TM/HM #	Move Name	Type	ST	ACC	PP
TM29	Psychic	Psychic	90	100	10
TM30	Shadow Ball	Ghost	60	—	20
TM32	Double Team	Normal	—	—	15
TM33	Reflect	Psychic	—	—	20
TM34	Shock Wave	Electric	60	—	20
TM41	Torment	Dark	—	100	15
TM42	Façade	Normal	70	100	20
TM43	Secret Power	Normal	70	100	20
TM44	Rest	Psychic	—	—	10
TM45	Attract	Normal	—	100	15
TM46	Thief	Dark	40	100	10
TM48	Skill Swap	Psychic	—	100	10
TM49	Snatch	Dark	—	100	10

MOVE TUTOR LIST

Move Name	Type	ST	ACC	PP
Body Slam*	Normal	85	100	15
Counter*	Fighting	—	100	20
Double-Edge	Normal	120	100	15
Dream Eater*	Psychic	100	100	15
Dynamicpunch	Fighting	100	50	5
Endure*	Normal	—	—	10
Fire Punch*	Fire	75	100	15
Ice Punch*	Ice	75	100	15
Mega Kick*	Normal	120	85	5
Mega Punch*	Normal	80	75	20
Metronome	Normal	—	100	10
Mimic	Normal	—	100	10
Psych Up*	Normal	—	—	10
Seismic Toss*	Fighting	—	100	20
Sleep Talk	Normal	—	—	10
Snore*	Normal	40	100	15
Substitute	Normal	—	—	10
Swagger	Normal	—	90	15
Thunderpunch*	Electric	75	100	15
Thunder Wave*	Electric	—	100	20

*Battle Frontier tutor move

041 Alakazam™

PSYCHIC

GENERAL INFO
SPECIES: Psi Pokémon
HEIGHT: 4'11"
WEIGHT: 106 lbs.
ABILITIES: *Synchronize* — *Shares the Pokémon's Poison, Paralysis, or Burn condition with the opponent Pokémon.*

Inner Focus — *Prevents the Pokémon from Flinching.*

STATS
HP	33
ATTACK	33
DEFENSE	33
SP. ATTACK	100
SP. DEFENSE	66
SPEED	100

EVOLUTIONS

LV16

TRADE OVER THE GAME BOY WIRELESS ADAPTER

WHERE/HOW TO CATCH
Trade Kadabra over Game Boy Wireless Adapter

STRONG AGAINST:
FIGHTING
PSYCHIC

WEAK AGAINST:
GHOST
BUG
DARK

MOVES LIST

LV	Move Name	Type	ST	ACC	PP		LV	Move Name	Type	ST	ACC	PP
S	Teleport	Psychic	—	—	20		23	Reflect	Psychic	—	—	20
S	Kinesis	Psychic	—	80	15		25	Recover	Normal	—	—	20
S	Confusion	Psychic	50	100	25		30	Future Sight	Psychic	80	90	15
16	Confusion	Psychic	50	100	25		33	Calm Mind	Psychic	—	—	20
18	Disable	Normal	—	55	20		36	Psychic	Psychic	90	100	10
21	Psybeam	Psychic	65	100	20		43	Trick	Psychic	—	100	10

TM/HM LIST

TM/HM #	Move Name	Type	ST	ACC	PP		TM/HM #	Move Name	Type	ST	ACC	PP
HM05	Flash	Normal	—	70	20		TM27	Return	Normal	—	100	20
TM01	Focus Punch	Fighting	150	100	20		TM29	Psychic	Psychic	90	100	10
TM04	Calm Mind	Psychic	—	—	20		TM30	Shadow Ball	Ghost	60	—	20
TM06	Toxic	Poison	—	85	10		TM32	Double Team	Normal	—	—	15
TM10	Hidden Power	Normal	—	100	15		TM33	Reflect	Psychic	—	—	20
TM11	Sunny Day	Fire	—	—	5		TM34	Shock Wave	Electric	60	—	20
TM12	Taunt	Dark	—	100	20		TM41	Torment	Dark	—	100	15
TM15	Hyper Beam	Normal	150	90	5		TM42	Façade	Normal	70	100	20
TM16	Light Screen	Psychic	—	—	30		TM43	Secret Power	Normal	70	100	20
TM17	Protect	Normal	—	—	10		TM44	Rest	Psychic	—	—	10
TM18	Rain Dance	Water	—	—	5		TM45	Attract	Normal	—	100	15
TM20	Safeguard	Normal	—	—	25		TM46	Thief	Dark	40	100	10
TM21	Frustration	Normal	—	100	20		TM48	Skill Swap	Psychic	—	100	10
TM23	Iron Tail	Steel	100	75	15		TM49	Snatch	Dark	—	100	10

MOVE TUTOR LIST

Move Name	Type	ST	ACC	PP
Body Slam*	Normal	85	100	15
Counter*	Fighting	—	100	20
Double-Edge	Normal	120	100	15
Dream Eater*	Psychic	100	100	15
Dynamicpunch	Fighting	100	50	5
Endure*	Normal	—	—	10
Fire Punch*	Fire	75	100	15
Ice Punch*	Ice	75	100	15
Mimic	Normal	—	100	10
Mega Kick*	Normal	120	85	5
Mega Punch*	Normal	80	75	20
Metronome	Normal	—	100	10
Psych Up*	Normal	—	—	10
Seismic Toss*	Fighting	—	100	20
Sleep Talk	Normal	—	—	10
Snore*	Normal	40	100	15
Substitute	Normal	—	—	10
Swagger	Normal	—	90	15
Thunderpunch*	Electric	75	100	15
Thunder Wave*	Electric	—	100	20

*Battle Frontier tutor move

042 Nincada™

BUG
GROUND

GENERAL INFO
SPECIES: Trainee Pokémon
HEIGHT: 1'8"
WEIGHT: 12 lbs.
ABILITY: *Compoundeyes* — *Raises the Pokémon's Accuracy 30 percent in battle.*

STATS
HP	25
ATTACK	50
DEFENSE	50
SP. ATTACK	25
SP. DEFENSE	25
SPEED	50

EVOLUTIONS

LV20

+ EMPTY POKÉ BALL AND SPACE IN BELT

WHERE/HOW TO CATCH
Route 116

STRONG AGAINST:
ELECTRIC
FIGHTING
POISON
GROUND

WEAK AGAINST:
FIRE
WATER
ICE
FLYING

MOVES LIST

LV	Move Name	Type	ST	ACC	PP		LV	Move Name	Type	ST	ACC	PP
S	Scratch	Normal	40	100	35		19	Mind Reader	Normal	—	100	5
S	Harden	Normal	—	—	30		25	False Swipe	Normal	40	100	40
05	Leech Life	Bug	20	100	15		31	Mud-Slap	Ground	20	100	10
09	Sand-Attack	Ground	—	100	15		38	Metal Claw	Steel	50	95	35
14	Fury Swipes	Normal	18	80	15		45	Dig	Ground	60	100	10

TM/HM LIST

TM/HM #	Move Name	Type	ST	ACC	PP		TM/HM #	Move Name	Type	ST	ACC	PP
HM01	Cut	Normal	50	95	30		TM27	Return	Normal	—	100	20
HM05	Flash	Normal	—	70	20		TM28	Dig	Ground	60	100	10
TM06	Toxic	Poison	—	85	10		TM30	Shadow Ball	Ghost	60	—	20
TM10	Hidden Power	Normal	—	100	15		TM32	Double Team	Normal	—	—	15
TM11	Sunny Day	Fire	—	—	5		TM37	Sandstorm	Rock	—	—	10
TM17	Protect	Normal	—	—	10		TM40	Aerial Ace	Flying	60	—	20
TM19	Giga Drain	Grass	60	100	5		TM42	Façade	Normal	70	100	20
TM21	Frustration	Normal	—	100	20		TM43	Secret Power	Normal	70	100	20
TM22	Solarbeam	Grass	120	100	10		TM44	Rest	Psychic	—	—	10

EGG MOVES

Move Name	Type	ST	ACC	PP
Endure	Normal	—	—	10
Faint Attack	Dark	60	—	20
Gust	Flying	40	100	35
Silver Wind	Bug	60	100	5

MOVE TUTOR LIST

Move Name	Type	ST	ACC	PP
Double-Edge	Normal	120	100	15
Endure*	Normal	—	—	10
Fury Cutter	Bug	10	95	20
Mimic	Normal	—	100	10
Mud-Slap*	Ground	20	100	10
Sleep Talk	Normal	—	—	10
Snore*	Normal	40	100	15
Swagger	Normal	—	90	15
Substitute	Normal	—	—	10

*Battle Frontier tutor move

043

Ninjask™

| BUG |
| FLYING |

GENERAL INFO
SPECIES: Ninja Pokémon
HEIGHT: 2'7"
WEIGHT: 26 lbs.
ABILITY: *Speed Boost—*
Increases the Pokémon's Speed by one point each turn.

STATS

HP	50
ATTACK	75
DEFENSE	50
SP. ATTACK	50
SP. DEFENSE	50
SPEED	100

EVOLUTIONS

LV20

+ EMPTY POKÉ BALL AND SPACE IN BELT

WHERE/HOW TO CATCH
Evolve from Nincada

STRONG AGAINST:

| BUG |
| FIGHTING |
| GROUND |
| GRASS |

WEAK AGAINST:

| FIRE |
| ELECTRIC |
| FLYING |
| ROCK |
| ICE |

MOVES LIST

LV	Move Name	Type	ST	ACC	PP
S	Scratch	Normal	40	100	35
S	Harden	Normal	—	—	30
S	Leech Life	Bug	20	100	15
S	Sand-Attack	Ground	—	100	15
05	Leech Life	Bug	20	100	15
09	Sand-Attack	Ground	—	100	15
14	Fury Swipes	Normal	18	80	15
19	Mind Reader	Normal	—	100	5
20	Double Team	Normal	—	—	15
20	Fury Cutter	Bug	10	95	20
20	Screech	Normal	—	85	40
25	Swords Dance	Normal	—	—	30
31	Slash	Normal	70	100	20
38	Agility	Psychic	—	—	30
45	Baton Pass	Normal	—	—	40

TM/HM LIST

TM/HM #	Move Name	Type	ST	ACC	PP
HM01	Cut	Normal	50	95	30
HM05	Flash	Normal	—	70	20
TM06	Toxic	Poison	—	85	10
TM10	Hidden Power	Normal	—	100	15
TM11	Sunny Day	Fire	—	—	5
TM15	Hyper Beam	Normal	150	90	5
TM17	Protect	Normal	—	—	10
TM19	Giga Drain	Grass	60	100	5
TM21	Frustration	Normal	—	100	20
TM22	Solarbeam	Grass	120	100	10
TM27	Return	Normal	—	100	20
TM28	Dig	Ground	60	100	10
TM30	Shadow Ball	Ghost	60	—	20
TM32	Double Team	Normal	—	—	15
TM37	Sandstorm	Rock	—	—	10
TM40	Aerial Ace	Flying	60	—	20
TM42	Façade	Normal	70	100	20
TM43	Secret Power	Normal	70	100	20
TM44	Rest	Psychic	—	—	10
TM45	Attract	Normal	—	100	15
TM46	Thief	Dark	40	100	10

MOVE TUTOR LIST

Move Name	Type	ST	ACC	PP
Double-Edge	Normal	120	100	15
Endure*	Normal	—	—	10
Fury Cutter	Bug	10	95	20
Mimic	Normal	—	100	10
Mud-Slap*	Ground	20	100	10
Sleep Talk	Normal	—	—	10
Snore*	Normal	40	100	15
Substitute	Normal	—	—	10
Swagger	Normal	—	90	15
Swift*	Normal	60	—	20
Swords Dance*	Normal	—	—	30

*Battle Frontier tutor move

044

Shedinja™

| BUG |
| GHOST |

GENERAL INFO
SPECIES: Shed Pokémon
HEIGHT: 2'7"
WEIGHT: 3 lbs.
ABILITY: *Wonder Guard—*
The Pokémon is harmed only by moves that cause "Super Effective" damage.

STATS

HP	25
ATTACK	75
DEFENSE	50
SP. ATTACK	25
SP. DEFENSE	25
SPEED	50

EVOLUTIONS

LV20

+ EMPTY POKÉ BALL AND SPACE IN BELT

WHERE/HOW TO CATCH
Evolve from Nincada— must have empty Poké Ball and open slot on team

STRONG AGAINST:

| NORMAL |
| GRASS |
| FIGHTING |
| POISON |
| GROUND |
| BUG |

WEAK AGAINST:

| FIRE |
| FLYING |
| ROCK |
| GHOST |
| DARK |

MOVES LIST

LV	Move Name	Type	ST	ACC	PP
S	Scratch	Normal	40	100	35
S	Harden	Normal	—	—	30
05	Leech Life	Bug	20	100	15
09	Sand-Attack	Ground	—	100	15
14	Fury Swipes	Normal	18	80	15
19	Mind Reader	Normal	—	100	5
25	Spite	Ghost	—	100	10
31	Confuse Ray	Ghost	—	100	10
38	Shadow Ball	Ghost	80	100	15
45	Grudge	Ghost	—	100	5

TM/HM LIST

TM/HM #	Move Name	Type	ST	ACC	PP
HM01	Cut	Normal	50	95	30
HM05	Flash	Normal	—	70	20
TM06	Toxic	Poison	—	85	10
TM10	Hidden Power	Normal	—	100	15
TM11	Sunny Day	Fire	—	—	5
TM15	Hyper Beam	Normal	150	90	5
TM17	Protect	Normal	—	—	10
TM19	Giga Drain	Grass	60	100	5
TM21	Frustration	Normal	—	100	20
TM22	Solarbeam	Grass	120	100	10
TM27	Return	Normal	—	100	20
TM28	Dig	Ground	60	100	10
TM30	Shadow Ball	Ghost	60	—	20
TM32	Double Team	Normal	—	—	15
TM37	Sandstorm	Rock	—	—	10
TM40	Aerial Ace	Flying	60	—	20
TM42	Façade	Normal	70	100	20
TM43	Secret Power	Normal	70	100	20
TM44	Rest	Psychic	—	—	10
TM46	Thief	Dark	40	100	10

MOVE TUTOR LIST

Move Name	Type	ST	ACC	PP
Double-Edge	Normal	120	100	15
Dream Eater*	Psychic	100	100	15
Endure*	Normal	—	—	10
Fury Cutter	Bug	10	95	20
Mimic	Normal	—	100	10
Mud-Slap*	Ground	20	100	10
Sleep Talk	Normal	—	—	10
Snore*	Normal	40	100	15
Substitute	Normal	—	—	10
Swagger	Normal	—	90	15
Swift*	Normal	60	—	20

*Battle Frontier tutor move

045 Whismur™

NORMAL

GENERAL INFO
SPECIES: Whisper Pokémon
HEIGHT: 2'0"
WEIGHT: 36 lbs.
ABILITY: *Soundproof—Pokémon is unaffected by loud moves, such as Roar and Sing.*

STATS
HP	50
ATTACK	50
DEFENSE	25
SP. ATTACK	50
SP. DEFENSE	25
SPEED	25

EVOLUTIONS

LV20   LV40

WHERE/HOW TO CATCH
Route 116, Desert Tunnel, Rusturf Tunnel, and Victory Road

STRONG AGAINST:
GHOST

WEAK AGAINST:
FIGHTING

MOVES LIST
LV	Move Name	Type	ST	ACC	PP
S	Pound	Normal	40	100	35
05	Uproar	Normal	50	100	10
11	Astonish	Ghost	30	100	15
15	Howl	Normal	—	—	40
21	Supersonic	Normal	—	55	20
25	Stomp	Normal	65	100	20

LV	Move Name	Type	ST	ACC	PP
31	Screech	Normal	—	85	40
35	Roar	Normal	—	100	20
41	Rest	Psychic	—	—	10
41	Sleep Talk	Normal	—	—	10
45	Hyper Voice	Normal	90	100	10

TM/HM LIST
TM/HM #	Move Name	Type	ST	ACC	PP
TM03	Water Pulse	Water	60	100	20
TM05	Roar	Normal	—	100	20
TM06	Toxic	Poison	—	85	10
TM10	Hidden Power	Normal	—	100	15
TM11	Sunny Day	Fire	—	—	5
TM13	Ice Beam	Ice	95	100	10
TM14	Blizzard	Ice	120	70	5
TM17	Protect	Normal	—	—	10
TM18	Rain Dance	Water	—	—	5
TM21	Frustration	Normal	—	100	20
TM22	Solarbeam	Grass	120	100	10

TM/HM #	Move Name	Type	ST	ACC	PP
TM27	Return	Normal	—	100	20
TM30	Shadow Ball	Ghost	60	—	20
TM32	Double Team	Normal	—	—	15
TM34	Shock Wave	Electric	60	—	20
TM35	Flamethrower	Fire	95	100	15
TM38	Fire Blast	Fire	120	85	5
TM42	Façade	Normal	70	100	20
TM43	Secret Power	Normal	70	100	20
TM44	Rest	Psychic	—	—	10
TM45	Attract	Normal	—	100	15

EGG MOVES
Move Name	Type	ST	ACC	PP
Take Down	Normal	90	85	20
Snore	Normal	40	100	15
Swagger	Normal	—	90	15
Extrasensory	Psychic	80	100	30
Smellingsalt	Normal	60	100	10

MOVE TUTOR LIST
Move Name	Type	ST	ACC	PP
Body Slam*	Normal	85	100	15
Counter*	Fighting	—	100	10
Defense Curl*	Normal	—	—	40
Double-Edge	Normal	120	100	15
Dynamicpunch	Fighting	100	50	5
Endure*	Normal	—	—	10
Fire Punch*	Fire	75	100	15
Ice Punch*	Ice	75	100	15
Icy Wind*	Ice	55	95	15
Mega Kick*	Normal	120	85	5
Mega Punch*	Normal	80	75	20
Mimic	Normal	—	100	10
Mud-Slap*	Ground	20	100	10
Psych Up*	Normal	—	—	10
Rollout	Rock	30	90	20
Seismic Toss*	Fighting	—	100	20
Sleep Talk	Normal	—	—	10
Snore*	Normal	40	100	15
Substitute	Normal	—	—	10
Swagger	Normal	—	90	15
Thunderpunch*	Electric	75	100	15

*Battle Frontier tutor move

046 Loudred™

NORMAL

GENERAL INFO
SPECIES: Big Voice Pokémon
HEIGHT: 3'3"
WEIGHT: 89 lbs.
ABILITY: *Soundproof—Pokémon is unaffected by loud moves, such as Roar and Sing.*

STATS
HP	50
ATTACK	50
DEFENSE	50
SP. ATTACK	50
SP. DEFENSE	25
SPEED	50

EVOLUTIONS

LV20   LV40

WHERE/HOW TO CATCH
Evolve from Whismur; Desert Tunnel, Victory Road

STRONG AGAINST:
GHOST

WEAK AGAINST:
FIGHTING

MOVES LIST
LV	Move Name	Type	ST	ACC	PP
S	Pound	Normal	40	100	35
S	Uproar	Normal	50	100	10
S	Astonish	Ghost	30	100	15
S	Howl	Normal	—	—	40
05	Uproar	Normal	50	100	10
11	Astonish	Ghost	30	100	15
15	Howl	Normal	—	—	40

LV	Move Name	Type	ST	ACC	PP
23	Supersonic	Normal	—	55	20
29	Stomp	Normal	65	100	20
37	Screech	Normal	—	85	40
43	Roar	Normal	—	100	20
51	Rest	Psychic	—	—	10
51	Sleep Talk	Normal	—	—	10
57	Hyper Voice	Normal	90	100	10

TM/HM LIST
TM/HM #	Move Name	Type	ST	ACC	PP
HM04	Strength	Normal	80	100	15
HM06	Rock Smash	Fighting	20	100	15
TM03	Water Pulse	Water	60	100	20
TM05	Roar	Normal	—	100	20
TM06	Toxic	Poison	—	85	10
TM10	Hidden Power	Normal	—	100	15
TM11	Sunny Day	Fire	—	—	5
TM12	Taunt	Dark	—	100	20
TM13	Ice Beam	Ice	95	100	10
TM14	Blizzard	Ice	120	70	5
TM17	Protect	Normal	—	—	10
TM18	Rain Dance	Water	—	—	5
TM21	Frustration	Normal	—	100	20
TM22	Solarbeam	Grass	120	100	10

TM/HM #	Move Name	Type	ST	ACC	PP
TM26	Earthquake	Ground	100	100	10
TM27	Return	Normal	—	100	20
TM30	Shadow Ball	Ghost	60	—	20
TM31	Brick Break	Fighting	75	100	15
TM32	Double Team	Normal	—	—	15
TM34	Shock Wave	Electric	60	—	20
TM35	Flamethrower	Fire	95	100	15
TM38	Fire Blast	Fire	120	85	5
TM41	Torment	Dark	—	100	15
TM42	Façade	Normal	70	100	20
TM43	Secret Power	Normal	70	100	20
TM44	Rest	Psychic	—	—	10
TM45	Attract	Normal	—	100	15
TM50	Overheat	Fire	140	90	5

MOVE TUTOR LIST
Move Name	Type	ST	ACC	PP
Body Slam*	Normal	85	100	15
Counter*	Fighting	—	100	10
Defense Curl*	Normal	—	—	40
Double-Edge	Normal	120	100	15
Dynamicpunch	Fighting	100	50	5
Endure*	Normal	—	—	10
Fire Punch*	Fire	75	100	15
Ice Punch*	Ice	75	100	15
Icy Wind*	Ice	55	95	15
Mega Kick*	Normal	120	85	5
Mega Punch*	Normal	80	75	20
Mimic	Normal	—	100	10
Mud-Slap*	Ground	20	100	10
Psych Up*	Normal	—	—	10
Rock Slide*	Rock	75	90	10
Rollout	Rock	30	90	20
Seismic Toss*	Fighting	—	100	20
Sleep Talk	Normal	—	—	10
Snore*	Normal	40	100	15
Substitute	Normal	—	—	10
Swagger	Normal	—	90	15
Thunderpunch*	Electric	75	100	15

*Battle Frontier tutor move

047 Exploud™

NORMAL

GENERAL INFO
SPECIES: Loud Noise Pokémon
HEIGHT: 4'11"
WEIGHT: 185 lbs.
ABILITY: *Soundproof—Pokémon is unaffected by loud moves, such as Roar and Sing.*

STATS
HP	50
ATTACK	75
DEFENSE	50
SP. ATTACK	75
SP. DEFENSE	50
SPEED	50

EVOLUTIONS

LV20 → LV40

WHERE/HOW TO CATCH
Evolve from Loudred

STRONG AGAINST:
GHOST

WEAK AGAINST:
FIGHTING

MOVES LIST
LV	Move Name	Type	ST	ACC	PP
S	Pound	Normal	40	100	35
S	Uproar	Normal	50	100	10
S	Astonish	Ghost	30	100	15
S	Howl	Normal	—	—	40
05	Uproar	Normal	50	100	10
11	Astonish	Ghost	30	100	15
15	Howl	Normal	—	—	40
23	Supersonic	Normal	—	55	20
29	Stomp	Normal	65	100	20
37	Screech	Normal	—	85	40
40	Hyper Beam	Normal	150	90	5
45	Roar	Normal	—	100	20
55	Rest	Psychic	—	—	10
55	Sleep Talk	Normal	—	—	10
63	Hyper Voice	Normal	90	100	10

TM/HM LIST
TM/HM #	Move Name	Type	ST	ACC	PP
HM04	Strength	Normal	80	100	15
HM06	Rock Smash	Fighting	20	100	15
TM03	Water Pulse	Water	60	100	20
TM05	Roar	Normal	—	100	20
TM06	Toxic	Poison	—	85	10
TM10	Hidden Power	Normal	—	100	15
TM11	Sunny Day	Fire	—	—	5
TM12	Taunt	Dark	—	100	20
TM13	Ice Beam	Ice	95	100	10
TM14	Blizzard	Ice	120	70	5
TM15	Hyper Beam	Normal	150	90	5
TM17	Protect	Normal	—	—	10
TM18	Rain Dance	Water	—	—	5
TM21	Frustration	Normal	—	100	20
TM22	Solarbeam	Grass	120	100	10
TM26	Earthquake	Ground	100	100	10
TM27	Return	Normal	—	100	20
TM30	Shadow Ball	Ghost	60	—	20
TM31	Brick Break	Fighting	75	100	15
TM32	Double Team	Normal	—	—	15
TM34	Shock Wave	Electric	60	—	20
TM35	Flamethrower	Fire	95	100	15
TM38	Fire Blast	Fire	120	85	5
TM41	Torment	Dark	—	100	15
TM42	Façade	Normal	70	100	20
TM43	Secret Power	Normal	70	100	20
TM44	Rest	Psychic	—	—	10
TM45	Attract	Normal	—	100	15
TM50	Overheat	Fire	140	90	5

MOVE TUTOR LIST
Move Name	Type	ST	ACC	PP
Body Slam*	Normal	85	100	15
Counter*	Fighting	—	100	20
Defense Curl*	Normal	—	—	40
Double-Edge	Normal	120	100	15
Dynamicpunch	Fighting	100	50	5
Endure*	Normal	—	—	10
Fire Punch*	Fire	75	100	15
Ice Punch*	Ice	75	100	15
Icy Wind*	Ice	55	95	15
Mega Kick*	Normal	120	85	5
Mega Punch*	Normal	80	75	20
Mimic	Normal	—	100	10
Mud-Slap*	Ground	20	100	10
Psych Up*	Normal	—	—	10
Rock Slide*	Rock	75	90	10
Rollout	Rock	30	90	20
Seismic Toss*	Fighting	—	100	20
Sleep Talk	Normal	—	—	10
Snore*	Normal	40	100	15
Substitute	Normal	—	—	10
Swagger	Normal	—	90	15
Thunderpunch*	Electric	75	100	15

*Battle Frontier tutor move

---

048 Makuhita™

FIGHTING

GENERAL INFO
SPECIES: Guts Pokémon
HEIGHT: 3'3"
WEIGHT: 191 lbs.
ABILITIES: *Thick Fat—Fire- and Ice-type Moves inflict only 50 percent of the damage.*
Guts—The Pokémon's Attack Power rises 1.5x when inflicted with a Status condition.

STATS
HP	50
ATTACK	50
DEFENSE	25
SP. ATTACK	25
SP. DEFENSE	25
SPEED	25

EVOLUTIONS
LV24 →

WHERE/HOW TO CATCH
Granite Cave, Victory Road

STRONG AGAINST:
BUG
ROCK
DARK

WEAK AGAINST:
FLYING
PSYCHIC

MOVES LIST
LV	Move Name	Type	ST	ACC	PP
S	Tackle	Normal	35	95	35
S	Focus Energy	Normal	—	—	30
04	Sand-Attack	Ground	—	100	15
10	Arm Thrust	Fighting	15	100	20
13	Vital Throw	Fighting	70	100	10
19	Fake Out	Normal	40	100	10
22	Whirlwind	Normal	—	100	20
28	Knock Off	Dark	20	100	20
31	Smellingsalt	Normal	60	100	10
37	Belly Drum	Normal	—	—	10
40	Endure	Normal	—	—	10
46	Seismic Toss	Fighting	—	100	20
49	Reversal	Fighting	—	100	15

TM/HM LIST
TM/HM #	Move Name	Type	ST	ACC	PP
HM03	Surf	Water	95	100	15
HM04	Strength	Normal	80	100	15
HM06	Rock Smash	Fighting	20	100	15
TM01	Focus Punch	Fighting	150	100	20
TM06	Toxic	Poison	—	85	10
TM08	Bulk Up	Fighting	—	—	20
TM10	Hidden Power	Normal	—	100	15
TM11	Sunny Day	Fire	—	—	5
TM17	Protect	Normal	—	—	10
TM18	Rain Dance	Water	—	—	5
TM21	Frustration	Normal	—	100	20
TM26	Earthquake	Ground	100	100	10
TM27	Return	Normal	—	100	20
TM28	Dig	Ground	60	100	10
TM31	Brick Break	Fighting	75	100	15
TM32	Double Team	Normal	—	—	15
TM39	Rock Tomb	Rock	50	80	10
TM42	Façade	Normal	70	100	20
TM43	Secret Power	Normal	70	100	20
TM44	Rest	Psychic	—	—	10
TM45	Attract	Normal	—	100	15

EGG MOVES
Move Name	Type	ST	ACC	PP
Faint Attack	Dark	60	—	20
Detect	Fighting	—	—	5
Foresight	Normal	—	100	40
Helping Hand	Normal	—	100	20
Cross Chop	Fighting	100	80	5
Revenge	Fighting	60	100	10
Dynamicpunch	Fighting	100	50	5
Counter	Fighting	—	100	20

MOVE TUTOR LIST
Move Name	Type	ST	ACC	PP
Body Slam*	Normal	85	100	15
Counter*	Fighting	—	100	20
Double-Edge	Normal	120	100	15
Dynamicpunch	Fighting	100	50	5
Endure*	Normal	—	—	10
Fire Punch*	Fire	75	100	15
Ice Punch*	Ice	75	100	15
Mega Kick*	Normal	120	85	5
Mega Punch*	Normal	80	75	20
Metronome	Normal	—	100	10
Mimic	Normal	—	100	10
Mud-Slap*	Ground	20	100	10
Rock Slide*	Rock	75	90	10
Seismic Toss*	Fighting	—	100	20
Sleep Talk	Normal	—	—	10
Snore*	Normal	40	100	15
Substitute	Normal	—	—	10
Swagger	Normal	—	90	15
Thunderpunch*	Electric	75	100	15

*Battle Frontier tutor move

049 Hariyama™
FIGHTING

GENERAL INFO
SPECIES: Arm Thrust Pokémon
HEIGHT: 7'7"
WEIGHT: 560 lbs.
ABILITIES: *Thick Fat* — Fire- and Ice-type Moves inflict only 50 percent of the damage.
Guts — The Pokémon's Attack Power rises 1.5x when inflicted with a Status condition.

STATS
HP	75
ATTACK	100
DEFENSE	50
SP. ATTACK	50
SP. DEFENSE	50
SPEED	50

EVOLUTIONS
LV24

WHERE/HOW TO CATCH
Evolve from Makuhita; Victory Road

STRONG AGAINST:
BUG
ROCK
DARK

WEAK AGAINST:
FLYING
PSYCHIC

MOVES LIST
LV	Move Name	Type	ST	ACC	PP	LV	Move Name	Type	ST	ACC	PP
S	Tackle	Normal	35	95	35	22	Whirlwind	Normal	—	100	20
S	Focus Energy	Normal	—	—	30	29	Knock Off	Dark	20	100	20
S	Sand-Attack	Ground	—	100	15	33	Smellingsalt	Normal	60	100	10
S	Arm Thrust	Fighting	15	100	20	40	Belly Drum	Normal	—	—	10
04	Sand-Attack	Ground	—	100	15	44	Endure	Normal	—	—	10
10	Arm Thrust	Fighting	15	100	20	51	Seismic Toss	Fighting	—	100	20
13	Vital Throw	Fighting	70	100	10	55	Reversal	Fighting	—	100	15
19	Fake Out	Normal	40	100	10						

TM/HM LIST
TM/HM #	Move Name	Type	ST	ACC	PP	TM/HM #	Move Name	Type	ST	ACC	PP
HM03	Surf	Water	95	100	15	TM21	Frustration	Normal	—	100	20
HM04	Strength	Normal	80	100	15	TM26	Earthquake	Ground	100	100	10
HM06	Rock Smash	Fighting	20	100	15	TM27	Return	Normal	—	100	20
TM01	Focus Punch	Fighting	150	100	20	TM28	Dig	Ground	60	100	10
TM06	Toxic	Poison	—	85	10	TM31	Brick Break	Fighting	75	100	15
TM08	Bulk Up	Fighting	—	—	20	TM32	Double Team	Normal	—	—	15
TM10	Hidden Power	Normal	—	100	15	TM39	Rock Tomb	Rock	50	80	10
TM11	Sunny Day	Fire	—	—	5	TM42	Façade	Normal	70	100	20
TM15	Hyper Beam	Normal	150	90	5	TM43	Secret Power	Normal	70	100	20
TM17	Protect	Normal	—	—	10	TM44	Rest	Psychic	—	—	10
TM18	Rain Dance	Water	—	—	5	TM45	Attract	Normal	—	100	15

MOVE TUTOR LIST
Move Name	Type	ST	ACC	PP
Body Slam*	Normal	85	100	15
Counter*	Fighting	—	100	20
Double-Edge	Normal	120	100	15
Dynamicpunch	Fighting	100	50	5
Endure*	Normal	—	—	10
Fire Punch*	Fire	75	100	15
Ice Punch*	Ice	75	100	15
Mega Kick	Normal	120	85	5
Mega Punch*	Normal	80	75	20
Metronome	Normal	—	100	10
Mimic	Normal	—	100	10
Mud-Slap*	Ground	20	100	10
Rock Slide*	Rock	75	90	10
Seismic Toss*	Fighting	—	100	20
Sleep Talk	Normal	—	—	10
Snore*	Normal	40	100	15
Substitute	Normal	—	—	10
Swagger	Normal	—	90	15
Thunderpunch*	Electric	75	100	15

*Battle Frontier tutor move

---

050 Goldeen™
WATER

GENERAL INFO
SPECIES: Goldfish Pokémon
HEIGHT: 2'0"
WEIGHT: 33 lbs.
ABILITIES: *Swift Swim* — Doubles the Pokémon's Speed when it is raining.
Water Veil — Pokémon cannot be Burned.

STATS
HP	33
ATTACK	66
DEFENSE	33
SP. ATTACK	33
SP. DEFENSE	33
SPEED	66

EVOLUTIONS
LV33

WHERE/HOW TO CATCH
Routes 102, 111, 114, 117, and 120; Meteor Falls, Petalburg City, Safari Zone, and Victory Road

STRONG AGAINST:
FIRE
WATER
ICE
STEEL

WEAK AGAINST:
ELECTRIC
GRASS

MOVES LIST
LV	Move Name	Type	ST	ACC	PP	LV	Move Name	Type	ST	ACC	PP
S	Peck	Flying	35	100	35	24	Flail	Normal	—	100	15
S	Tail Whip	Normal	—	100	30	29	Fury Attack	Normal	15	85	20
S	Water Sport	Water	—	100	15	38	Waterfall	Water	80	100	15
10	Supersonic	Normal	—	55	20	43	Horn Drill	Normal	—	30	5
15	Horn Attack	Normal	65	100	25	52	Agility	Psychic	—	—	30

TM/HM LIST
TM/HM #	Move Name	Type	ST	ACC	PP	TM/HM #	Move Name	Type	ST	ACC	PP
HM03	Surf	Water	95	100	15	TM17	Protect	Normal	—	—	10
HM07	Waterfall	Water	80	100	15	TM18	Rain Dance	Water	—	—	5
HM08	Dive	Water	60	100	10	TM21	Frustration	Normal	—	100	20
TM03	Water Pulse	Water	60	100	20	TM27	Return	Normal	—	100	20
TM06	Toxic	Poison	—	85	10	TM32	Double Team	Normal	—	—	15
TM07	Hail	Ice	—	—	10	TM42	Façade	Normal	70	100	20
TM10	Hidden Power	Normal	—	100	15	TM43	Secret Power	Normal	70	100	20
TM13	Ice Beam	Ice	95	100	10	TM44	Rest	Psychic	—	—	10
TM14	Blizzard	Ice	120	70	5	TM45	Attract	Normal	—	100	15

EGG MOVES
Move Name	Type	ST	ACC	PP
Psybeam	Psychic	65	100	20
Hydro Pump	Water	120	80	5
Sleep Talk	Normal	—	—	10
Mud Sport	Ground	—	100	15
Haze	Ice	—	—	30

MOVE TUTOR LIST
Move Name	Type	ST	ACC	PP
Double-Edge	Normal	120	100	15
Endure*	Normal	—	—	10
Icy Wind*	Ice	55	95	15
Mimic	Normal	—	100	10
Sleep Talk	Normal	—	—	10
Snore*	Normal	40	100	15
Substitute	Normal	—	—	10
Swagger	Normal	—	90	15
Swift*	Normal	60	—	20

*Battle Frontier tutor move

051 Seaking™

WATER

GENERAL INFO
SPECIES: Goldfish Pokémon
HEIGHT: 4'3"
WEIGHT: 86 lbs.
ABILITIES: *Swift Swim*—Doubles the Pokémon's Speed when it is raining.
Water Veil—Pokémon cannot be Burned.

STATS
HP	66
ATTACK	66
DEFENSE	33
SP. ATTACK	66
SP. DEFENSE	66
SPEED	66

EVOLUTIONS
LV33

WHERE/HOW TO CATCH
Evolve from Goldeen; Safari Zone

STRONG AGAINST:
FIRE
WATER
ICE
STEEL

WEAK AGAINST:
ELECTRIC
GRASS

MOVES LIST
LV	Move Name	Type	ST	ACC	PP
S	Peck	Flying	35	100	35
S	Tail Whip	Normal	—	100	30
S	Water Sport	Water	—	100	15
S	Supersonic	Normal	—	55	20
10	Supersonic	Normal	—	55	20
15	Horn Attack	Normal	65	100	25
24	Flail	Normal	—	100	15
29	Fury Attack	Normal	15	85	20
41	Waterfall	Water	80	100	15
49	Horn Drill	Normal	—	30	5
61	Agility	Psychic	—	—	30

TM/HM LIST
TM/HM #	Move Name	Type	ST	ACC	PP
HM03	Surf	Water	95	100	15
HM07	Waterfall	Water	80	100	15
HM08	Dive	Water	60	100	10
TM03	Water Pulse	Water	60	100	20
TM06	Toxic	Poison	—	85	10
TM07	Hail	Ice	—	—	10
TM10	Hidden Power	Normal	—	100	15
TM13	Ice Beam	Ice	95	100	10
TM14	Blizzard	Ice	120	70	5
TM15	Hyper Beam	Normal	150	90	5
TM17	Protect	Normal	—	—	10
TM18	Rain Dance	Water	—	—	5
TM21	Frustration	Normal	—	100	20
TM27	Return	Normal	—	100	20
TM32	Double Team	Normal	—	—	15
TM42	Facade	Normal	70	100	20
TM43	Secret Power	Normal	70	100	20
TM44	Rest	Psychic	—	—	10
TM45	Attract	Normal	—	100	15

MOVE TUTOR LIST
Move Name	Type	ST	ACC	PP
Double-Edge	Normal	120	100	15
Endure*	Normal	—	—	10
Icy Wind*	Ice	55	95	15
Mimic	Normal	—	100	10
Sleep Talk	Normal	—	—	10
Snore*	Normal	40	100	15
Substitute	Normal	—	—	10
Swagger	Normal	—	90	15
Swift*	Normal	60	—	20

*Battle Frontier tutor move

052 Magikarp™

WATER

GENERAL INFO
SPECIES: Fish Pokémon
HEIGHT: 2'11"
WEIGHT: 22 lbs.
ABILITY: *Swift Swim*—Doubles the Pokémon's Speed when it is raining.

STATS
HP	33
ATTACK	33
DEFENSE	33
SP. ATTACK	33
SP. DEFENSE	33
SPEED	66

EVOLUTIONS
LV20

WHERE/HOW TO CATCH
All water routes with Old Rod

STRONG AGAINST:
FIRE
WATER
ICE
STEEL

WEAK AGAINST:
ELECTRIC
GRASS

MOVES LIST
LV	Move Name	Type	ST	ACC	PP
S	Splash	Normal	—	—	40
15	Tackle	Normal	35	95	35
30	Flail	Normal	—	100	15

TM/HM LIST
TM/HM #	Move Name	Type	ST	ACC	PP
None					

EGG MOVES
Move Name	Type	ST	ACC	PP
None				

MOVE TUTOR LIST
Move Name	Type	ST	ACC	PP
None				

*Battle Frontier tutor move

053 Gyarados™

WATER
FLYING

GENERAL INFO
SPECIES: Atrocious Pokémon
HEIGHT: 21'4"
WEIGHT: 518 lbs.
ABILITY: *Intimidate — Lowers the opponent's Attack by one point at the start of a battle.*

STATS

HP	66
ATTACK	100
DEFENSE	66
SP. ATTACK	60
SP. DEFENSE	60
SPEED	66

EVOLUTIONS

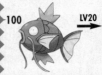 LV20

WHERE/HOW TO CATCH
Evolve from Magicarp; Sootopolis City

STRONG AGAINST:
FIRE
WATER
FIGHTING
GROUND
BUG
STEEL

WEAK AGAINST:
ELECTRIC
GRASS

MOVES LIST

LV	Move Name	Type	ST	ACC	PP
S	Thrash	Normal	90	100	20
20	Bite	Dark	60	100	25
25	Dragon Rage	Dragon	—	100	10
30	Leer	Normal	—	100	30
35	Twister	Dragon	40	100	20
40	Hydro Pump	Water	120	80	5
45	Rain Dance	Water	—	—	5
50	Dragon Dance	Dragon	—	—	20
55	Hyper Beam	Normal	150	90	5

TM/HM LIST

TM/HM #	Move Name	Type	ST	ACC	PP
HM03	Surf	Water	95	100	15
HM04	Strength	Normal	80	100	15
HM06	Rock Smash	Fighting	20	100	15
HM07	Waterfall	Water	80	100	15
HM08	Dive	Water	60	100	10
TM03	Water Pulse	Water	60	100	20
TM05	Roar	Normal	—	100	20
TM06	Toxic	Poison	—	85	10
TM07	Hail	Ice	—	—	10
TM10	Hidden Power	Normal	—	100	15
TM12	Taunt	Dark	—	100	20
TM13	Ice Beam	Ice	95	100	10
TM14	Blizzard	Ice	120	70	5
TM15	Hyper Beam	Normal	150	90	5
TM17	Protect	Normal	—	—	10
TM18	Rain Dance	Water	—	—	5
TM21	Frustration	Normal	—	100	20
TM24	Thunderbolt	Electric	95	100	15
TM25	Thunder	Electric	120	70	10
TM26	Earthquake	Ground	100	100	10
TM27	Return	Normal	—	100	20
TM32	Double Team	Normal	—	—	15
TM35	Flamethrower	Fire	95	100	15
TM37	Sandstorm	Rock	—	—	10
TM38	Fire Blast	Fire	120	85	5
TM41	Torment	Dark	—	100	15
TM42	Façade	Normal	70	100	20
TM43	Secret Power	Normal	70	100	20
TM44	Rest	Psychic	—	—	10
TM45	Attract	Normal	—	100	15

MOVE TUTOR LIST

Move Name	Type	ST	ACC	PP
Body Slam*	Normal	85	100	15
Double-Edge	Normal	120	100	15
Endure*	Normal	—	—	10
Icy Wind*	Ice	55	95	15
Mimic	Normal	—	100	10
Sleep Talk	Normal	—	—	10
Snore*	Normal	40	100	15
Swagger	Normal	—	90	15
Substitute	Normal	—	—	10
Thunder Wave*	Electric	—	100	20

*Battle Frontier tutor move

---

054 Azurill™

NORMAL

GENERAL INFO
SPECIES: Polka Dot Pokémon
HEIGHT: 0'8"
WEIGHT: 4 lbs.
ABILITIES: *Thick Fat — Fire- and Ice-type Moves inflict only 50 percent of the damage.*
Huge Power — Increases the Pokémon's Attack Power in battle. Attack Power becomes halved if Skill Swap nullifies the Ability.

STATS

HP	25
ATTACK	25
DEFENSE	25
SP. ATTACK	25
SP. DEFENSE	25
SPEED	25

EVOLUTIONS

FRIENDSHIP
LV18

WHERE/HOW TO CATCH
Breed Female Marill with Sea Incense Held Item

STRONG AGAINST:
GHOST

WEAK AGAINST:
FIGHTING

MOVES LIST

LV	Move Name	Type	ST	ACC	PP
S	Splash	Normal	—	—	40
03	Charm	Normal	—	100	20
06	Tail Whip	Normal	—	100	30
10	Bubble	Water	20	100	30
15	Slam	Normal	80	75	20
21	Water Gun	Water	40	100	25

TM/HM LIST

TM/HM #	Move Name	Type	ST	ACC	PP
HM03	Surf	Water	95	100	15
HM07	Waterfall	Water	80	100	15
TM03	Water Pulse	Water	60	100	20
TM05	Roar	Normal	—	100	20
TM06	Toxic	Poison	—	85	10
TM07	Hail	Ice	—	—	10
TM10	Hidden Power	Normal	—	100	15
TM11	Sunny Day	Fire	—	—	5
TM13	Ice Beam	Ice	95	100	10
TM14	Blizzard	Ice	120	70	5
TM17	Protect	Normal	—	—	10
TM18	Rain Dance	Water	—	—	5
TM21	Frustration	Normal	—	100	20
TM23	Iron Tail	Steel	100	75	15
TM27	Return	Normal	—	100	20
TM32	Double Team	Normal	—	—	15
TM42	Façade	Normal	70	100	20
TM43	Secret Power	Normal	70	100	20
TM44	Rest	Psychic	—	—	10
TM45	Attract	Normal	—	100	15

EGG MOVES

Move Name	Type	ST	ACC	PP
Encore	Normal	—	100	5
Sing	Normal	—	55	15
Refresh	Normal	—	100	20
Tickle	Normal	—	100	20
Slam	Normal	80	75	30

MOVE TUTOR LIST

Move Name	Type	ST	ACC	PP
Body Slam*	Normal	85	100	15
Defense Curl*	Normal	—	—	40
Double-Edge	Normal	120	100	15
Endure*	Normal	—	—	10
Icy Wind*	Ice	55	95	15
Mimic	Normal	—	100	10
Mud-Slap*	Ground	20	100	10
Rollout	Rock	30	90	20
Sleep Talk	Normal	—	—	10
Snore*	Normal	40	100	15
Substitute	Normal	—	—	10
Swagger	Normal	—	90	15
Swift*	Normal	60	—	20

*Battle Frontier tutor move

055 Marill™

WATER

GENERAL INFO
SPECIES: Aqua Mouse Pokémon
HEIGHT: 1'4"
WEIGHT: 19 lbs.

ABILITIES: *Thick Fat*—Fire- and Ice-type Moves inflict only 50 percent of the damage.
Huge Power—Increases the Pokémon's Attack Power in battle. Attack Power becomes halved if Skill Swap nullifies the Ability.

STATS
HP	66
ATTACK	33
DEFENSE	33
SP. ATTACK	33
SP. DEFENSE	33
SPEED	33

EVOLUTIONS
FRIENDSHIP

LV18

WHERE/HOW TO CATCH
Evolve from Azurill with Taming; Routes 102, 111, 112, 114, 117, and 120; Petalburg Woods and Safari Zone

STRONG AGAINST:
FIRE
WATER
ICE
STEEL

WEAK AGAINST:
ELECTRIC
GRASS

MOVES LIST
LV	Move Name	Type	ST	ACC	PP
S	Tackle	Normal	35	95	35
03	Defense Curl	Normal	—	—	40
06	Tail Whip	Normal	—	100	30
10	Water Gun	Water	40	100	25
15	Rollout	Rock	30	90	20

LV	Move Name	Type	ST	ACC	PP
21	Bubblebeam	Water	65	100	20
28	Double-Edge	Normal	120	100	15
36	Rain Dance	Water	—	—	5
45	Hydro Pump	Water	120	80	5

TM/HM LIST
TM/HM #	Move Name	Type	ST	ACC	PP
HM03	Surf	Water	95	100	15
HM04	Strength	Normal	80	100	15
HM06	Rock Smash	Fighting	20	100	15
HM07	Waterfall	Water	80	100	15
HM08	Dive	Water	60	100	10
TM01	Focus Punch	Fighting	150	100	20
TM03	Water Pulse	Water	60	100	20
TM06	Toxic	Poison	—	85	10
TM07	Hail	Ice	—	—	10
TM10	Hidden Power	Normal	—	100	15
TM13	Ice Beam	Ice	95	100	10
TM14	Blizzard	Ice	120	70	5

TM/HM #	Move Name	Type	ST	ACC	PP
TM17	Protect	Normal	—	—	10
TM18	Rain Dance	Water	—	—	5
TM21	Frustration	Normal	—	100	20
TM23	Iron Tail	Steel	100	75	15
TM27	Return	Normal	—	100	20
TM28	Dig	Ground	60	100	10
TM31	Brick Break	Fighting	75	100	15
TM32	Double Team	Normal	—	—	15
TM42	Façade	Normal	70	100	20
TM43	Secret Power	Normal	70	100	20
TM44	Rest	Psychic	—	—	10
TM45	Attract	Normal	—	100	15

EGG MOVES
Move Name	Type	ST	ACC	PP
Light Screen	Psychic	—	—	30
Amnesia	Psychic	—	—	20
Future Sight	Psychic	80	90	15
Supersonic	Normal	—	55	20
Substitute	Normal	—	—	10
Present	Normal	—	90	15
Belly Drum	Normal	—	—	10
Perish Song	Normal	—	—	5

MOVE TUTOR LIST
Move Name	Type	ST	ACC	PP
Body Slam*	Normal	85	100	15
Defense Curl*	Normal	—	—	40
Double-Edge	Normal	120	100	15
Dynamicpunch	Fighting	100	50	5
Endure*	Normal	—	—	10
Ice Punch*	Ice	75	100	15
Icy Wind*	Ice	55	95	15
Mega Kick*	Normal	120	85	5
Mega Punch*	Normal	80	75	20
Mimic	Normal	—	100	10
Mud-Slap*	Ground	20	100	10
Rollout	Rock	30	90	20
Seismic Toss*	Fighting	—	100	20
Sleep Talk	Normal	—	—	10
Snore*	Normal	40	100	15
Substitute	Normal	—	—	10
Swagger	Normal	—	90	15
Swift*	Normal	60	—	20

*Battle Frontier tutor move

056 Azumarill™

WATER

GENERAL INFO
SPECIES: Aquarabbit Pokémon
HEIGHT: 2'7"
WEIGHT: 63 lbs.

ABILITIES: *Thick Fat*—Fire- and Ice-type Moves inflict only 50 percent of the damage.
Huge Power—Increases the Pokémon's Attack Power in battle. Attack Power becomes halved if Skill Swap nullifies the Ability.

STATS
HP	66
ATTACK	33
DEFENSE	66
SP. ATTACK	33
SP. DEFENSE	66
SPEED	33

EVOLUTIONS
FRIENDSHIP

LV18

WHERE/HOW TO CATCH
Evolve from Marill

STRONG AGAINST:
FIRE
WATER
ICE
STEEL

WEAK AGAINST:
ELECTRIC
GRASS

MOVES LIST
LV	Move Name	Type	ST	ACC	PP
S	Tackle	Normal	35	95	35
S	Defense Curl	Normal	—	—	40
S	Tail Whip	Normal	—	100	30
S	Water Gun	Water	40	100	25
03	Defense Curl	Normal	—	—	40
06	Tail Whip	Normal	—	100	30

LV	Move Name	Type	ST	ACC	PP
10	Water Gun	Water	40	100	25
15	Rollout	Rock	30	90	20
24	Bubblebeam	Water	65	100	20
34	Double-Edge	Normal	120	100	15
45	Rain Dance	Water	—	—	5
57	Hydro Pump	Water	120	80	5

TM/HM LIST
TM/HM #	Move Name	Type	ST	ACC	PP
HM03	Surf	Water	95	100	15
HM04	Strength	Normal	80	100	15
HM06	Rock Smash	Fighting	20	100	15
HM07	Waterfall	Water	80	100	15
HM08	Dive	Water	60	100	10
TM01	Focus Punch	Fighting	150	100	20
TM03	Water Pulse	Water	60	100	20
TM06	Toxic	Poison	—	85	10
TM07	Hail	Ice	—	—	10
TM10	Hidden Power	Normal	—	100	15
TM13	Ice Beam	Ice	95	100	10
TM14	Blizzard	Ice	120	70	5
TM15	Hyper Beam	Normal	150	90	5

TM/HM #	Move Name	Type	ST	ACC	PP
TM17	Protect	Normal	—	—	10
TM18	Rain Dance	Water	—	—	5
TM21	Frustration	Normal	—	100	20
TM23	Iron Tail	Steel	100	75	15
TM27	Return	Normal	—	100	20
TM28	Dig	Ground	60	100	10
TM31	Brick Break	Fighting	75	100	15
TM32	Double Team	Normal	—	—	15
TM42	Façade	Normal	70	100	20
TM43	Secret Power	Normal	70	100	20
TM44	Rest	Psychic	—	—	10
TM45	Attract	Normal	—	100	15

MOVE TUTOR LIST
Move Name	Type	ST	ACC	PP
Body Slam*	Normal	85	100	15
Defense Curl*	Normal	—	—	40
Double-Edge	Normal	120	100	15
Dynamicpunch	Fighting	100	50	5
Endure*	Normal	—	—	10
Ice Punch*	Ice	75	100	15
Icy Wind*	Ice	55	95	15
Mega Kick*	Normal	120	85	5
Mega Punch*	Normal	80	75	20
Mimic	Normal	—	100	10
Mud-Slap*	Ground	20	100	10
Rollout	Rock	30	90	20
Seismic Toss*	Fighting	—	100	20
Sleep Talk	Normal	—	—	10
Snore*	Normal	40	100	15
Substitute	Normal	—	—	10
Swagger	Normal	—	90	15
Swift*	Normal	60	—	20

*Battle Frontier tutor move

057 Geodude™

ROCK
GROUND

GENERAL INFO
SPECIES: Rock Pokémon
HEIGHT: 1'4"
WEIGHT: 44 lbs.

ABILITIES: *Rock Head*—Pokémon does not receive recoil damage from moves such as Double-Edge and Body Slam.
Sturdy—One hit KO moves have no effect.

STATS
HP	33
ATTACK	66
DEFENSE	60
SP. ATTACK	33
SP. DEFENSE	30
SPEED	30

EVOLUTIONS
LV25
TRADE OVER THE GAME BOY WIRELESS ADAPTER

WHERE/HOW TO CATCH
Granite Cave, Magma Hideout, Victory Road; use Rock Smash in Routes 111 and 114, Safari Zone, and Victory Road

STRONG AGAINST:
NORMAL
FIRE
ELECTRIC
POISON
FLYING
ROCK

WEAK AGAINST:
WATER
GRASS
ICE
FIGHTING
GROUND
STEEL

MOVES LIST
LV	Move Name	Type	ST	ACC	PP
S	Tackle	Normal	35	95	35
S	Defense Curl	Normal	—	—	40
06	Mud Sport	Ground	—	100	15
11	Rock Throw	Rock	50	90	15
16	Magnitude	Ground	—	100	30
21	Selfdestruct	Normal	200	100	5

LV	Move Name	Type	ST	ACC	PP
26	Rollout	Rock	30	90	20
31	Rock Blast	Rock	25	80	10
36	Earthquake	Ground	100	100	10
41	Explosion	Normal	250	100	5
46	Double-Edge	Normal	120	100	15

TM/HM LIST
TM/HM #	Move Name	Type	ST	ACC	PP
HM04	Strength	Normal	80	100	15
HM06	Rock Smash	Fighting	20	100	15
TM01	Focus Punch	Fighting	150	100	20
TM06	Toxic	Poison	—	85	10
TM10	Hidden Power	Normal	—	100	15
TM11	Sunny Day	Fire	—	—	5
TM17	Protect	Normal	—	—	10
TM21	Frustration	Normal	—	100	20
TM26	Earthquake	Ground	100	100	10
TM27	Return	Normal	—	100	20
TM28	Dig	Ground	60	100	10

TM/HM #	Move Name	Type	ST	ACC	PP
TM31	Brick Break	Fighting	75	100	15
TM32	Double Team	Normal	—	—	15
TM35	Flamethrower	Fire	95	100	15
TM37	Sandstorm	Rock	—	—	10
TM38	Fire Blast	Fire	120	85	5
TM39	Rock Tomb	Rock	50	80	10
TM42	Façade	Normal	70	100	20
TM43	Secret Power	Normal	70	100	20
TM44	Rest	Psychic	—	—	10
TM45	Attract	Normal	—	100	15

EGG MOVES
Move Name	Type	ST	ACC	PP
Rock Slide	Rock	75	90	10
Block	Normal	—	100	5
Mega Punch	Normal	80	85	20

MOVE TUTOR LIST
Move Name	Type	ST	ACC	PP
Body Slam*	Normal	85	100	15
Counter*	Fighting	—	100	20
Defense Curl*	Normal	—	—	40
Double-Edge	Normal	120	100	15
Dynamicpunch	Fighting	100	50	5
Endure*	Normal	—	—	10
Explosion	Normal	250	100	5
Fire Punch*	Fire	75	100	15
Mega Punch*	Normal	80	75	20
Metronome	Normal	—	100	10
Mimic	Normal	—	100	10
Mud-Slap*	Ground	20	100	10
Rock Slide*	Rock	75	90	10
Rollout	Rock	30	90	20
Seismic Toss*	Fighting	—	100	20
Sleep Talk	Normal	—	—	10
Snore*	Normal	40	100	15
Substitute	Normal	—	—	10
Swagger	Normal	—	90	15

*Battle Frontier tutor move

---

058 Graveler™

ROCK
GROUND

GENERAL INFO
SPECIES: Rock Pokémon
HEIGHT: 3'3"
WEIGHT: 323 lbs.

ABILITIES: *Rock Head*—Pokémon does not receive recoil damage from moves such as Double-Edge and Body Slam.
Sturdy—One hit KO moves have no effect.

STATS
HP	33
ATTACK	100
DEFENSE	66
SP. ATTACK	33
SP. DEFENSE	33
SPEED	33

EVOLUTIONS
LV25
TRADE OVER THE GAME BOY WIRELESS ADAPTER

WHERE/HOW TO CATCH
Evolve from Golem; Magma Hideout and Victory Road

STRONG AGAINST:
NORMAL
FIRE
ELECTRIC
POISON
FLYING
ROCK

WEAK AGAINST:
WATER
GRASS
ICE
GROUND
STEEL

MOVES LIST
LV	Move Name	Type	ST	ACC	PP
S	Tackle	Normal	35	95	35
S	Defense Curl	Normal	—	—	40
S	Mud Sport	Ground	—	100	15
S	Rock Throw	Rock	50	90	15
06	Mud Sport	Ground	—	100	15
11	Rock Throw	Rock	50	90	15
16	Magnitude	Ground	—	100	30

LV	Move Name	Type	ST	ACC	PP
21	Selfdestruct	Normal	200	100	5
29	Rollout	Rock	30	90	20
37	Rock Blast	Rock	25	80	10
45	Earthquake	Ground	100	100	10
53	Explosion	Normal	250	100	5
62	Double-Edge	Normal	120	100	15

TM/HM LIST
TM/HM #	Move Name	Type	ST	ACC	PP
HM04	Strength	Normal	80	100	15
HM06	Rock Smash	Fighting	20	100	15
TM01	Focus Punch	Fighting	150	100	20
TM06	Toxic	Poison	—	85	10
TM10	Hidden Power	Normal	—	100	15
TM11	Sunny Day	Fire	—	—	5
TM17	Protect	Normal	—	—	10
TM21	Frustration	Normal	—	100	20
TM26	Earthquake	Ground	100	100	10
TM27	Return	Normal	—	100	20
TM28	Dig	Ground	60	100	10

TM/HM #	Move Name	Type	ST	ACC	PP
TM31	Brick Break	Fighting	75	100	15
TM32	Double Team	Normal	—	—	15
TM35	Flamethrower	Fire	95	100	15
TM37	Sandstorm	Rock	—	—	10
TM38	Fire Blast	Fire	120	85	5
TM39	Rock Tomb	Rock	50	80	10
TM42	Façade	Normal	70	100	20
TM43	Secret Power	Normal	70	100	20
TM44	Rest	Psychic	—	—	10
TM45	Attract	Normal	—	100	15

MOVE TUTOR LIST
Move Name	Type	ST	ACC	PP
Body Slam*	Normal	85	100	15
Counter*	Fighting	—	100	20
Defense Curl*	Normal	—	—	40
Double-Edge	Normal	120	100	15
Dynamicpunch	Fighting	100	50	5
Endure*	Normal	—	—	10
Explosion	Normal	250	100	5
Fire Punch*	Fire	75	100	15
Mega Punch*	Normal	80	75	20
Metronome	Normal	—	100	10
Mimic	Normal	—	100	10
Mud-Slap*	Ground	20	100	10
Rock Slide*	Rock	75	90	10
Rollout	Rock	30	90	20
Seismic Toss*	Fighting	—	100	20
Sleep Talk	Normal	—	—	10
Snore*	Normal	40	100	15
Substitute	Normal	—	—	10
Swagger	Normal	—	90	15

*Battle Frontier tutor move

059 Golem™

ROCK
GROUND

GENERAL INFO
SPECIES: Megaton Pokémon
HEIGHT: 4'7"
WEIGHT: 662 lbs.

ABILITIES: *Rock Head*—Pokémon does not receive recoil damage from moves such as Double-Edge and Body Slam.
Sturdy—One hit KO moves have no effect.

STATS

HP	66
ATTACK	100
DEFENSE	100
SP. ATTACK	66
SP. DEFENSE	66
SPEED	33

EVOLUTIONS

LV25

TRADE OVER THE GAME BOY WIRELESS ADAPTER

WHERE/HOW TO CATCH
Trade Graveler over Game Boy Wireless Adapter

STRONG AGAINST:
NORMAL
FIRE
ELECTRIC
POISON
FLYING
ROCK

WEAK AGAINST:
WATER
GRASS
ICE
FIGHTING
GROUND
STEEL

MOVES LIST

LV	Move Name	Type	ST	ACC	PP	LV	Move Name	Type	ST	ACC	PP
S	Tackle	Normal	35	95	35	21	Selfdestruct	Normal	200	100	5
S	Defense Curl	Normal	—	—	40	29	Rollout	Rock	30	90	20
S	Mud Sport	Ground	—	100	15	37	Rock Blast	Rock	25	80	10
S	Rock Throw	Rock	50	90	15	45	Earthquake	Ground	100	100	10
06	Mud Sport	Ground	—	100	15	53	Explosion	Normal	250	100	5
11	Rock Throw	Rock	50	90	15	62	Double-Edge	Normal	120	100	15
16	Magnitude	Ground	—	100	30						

TM/HM LIST

TM/HM #	Move Name	Type	ST	ACC	PP	TM/HM #	Move Name	Type	ST	ACC	PP
HM04	Strength	Normal	80	100	15	TM28	Dig	Ground	60	100	10
HM06	Rock Smash	Fighting	20	100	15	TM31	Brick Break	Fighting	75	100	15
TM01	Focus Punch	Fighting	150	100	20	TM32	Double Team	Normal	—	—	15
TM05	Roar	Normal	—	100	20	TM35	Flamethrower	Fire	95	100	15
TM06	Toxic	Poison	—	85	10	TM37	Sandstorm	Rock	—	—	10
TM10	Hidden Power	Normal	—	100	15	TM38	Fire Blast	Fire	120	85	5
TM11	Sunny Day	Fire	—	—	5	TM39	Rock Tomb	Rock	50	80	10
TM15	Hyper Beam	Normal	150	90	5	TM42	Façade	Normal	70	100	20
TM17	Protect	Normal	—	—	10	TM43	Secret Power	Normal	70	100	20
TM21	Frustration	Normal	—	100	20	TM44	Rest	Psychic	—	—	10
TM26	Earthquake	Ground	100	100	10	TM45	Attract	Normal	—	100	15
TM27	Return	Normal	—	100	20						

MOVE TUTOR LIST

Move Name	Type	ST	ACC	PP
Body Slam*	Normal	85	100	15
Counter*	Fighting	—	100	20
Defense Curl*	Normal	—	—	40
Double-Edge	Normal	120	100	15
Dynamicpunch	Fighting	100	50	5
Endure*	Normal	—	—	10
Explosion	Normal	250	100	5
Fire Punch*	Fire	75	100	15
Fury Cutter	Bug	10	95	20
Mega Kick*	Normal	120	85	5
Mega Punch*	Normal	80	75	20
Metronome	Normal	—	100	10
Mimic	Normal	—	100	10
Mud-Slap*	Ground	20	100	10
Rock Slide*	Rock	75	90	10
Rollout	Rock	30	90	20
Seismic Toss*	Fighting	—	100	20
Sleep Talk	Normal	—	—	10
Snore*	Normal	40	100	15
Substitute	Normal	—	—	10
Swagger	Normal	—	90	15

*Battle Frontier tutor move

060 Nosepass™

ROCK

GENERAL INFO
SPECIES: Compass Pokémon
HEIGHT: 3'3"
WEIGHT: 214 lbs.

ABILITIES: *Sturdy*—One hit KO moves have no effect.
Magnet Pull—Prevents Steel-type Pokémon from fleeing in battle.

STATS

HP	25
ATTACK	50
DEFENSE	75
SP. ATTACK	50
SP. DEFENSE	50
SPEED	25

EVOLUTIONS

NOSEPASS DOES NOT EVOLVE

WHERE/HOW TO CATCH
Granite Cave (use Rock Smash)

STRONG AGAINST:
NORMAL
FIRE
POISON
FLYING

WEAK AGAINST:
WATER
GRASS
FIGHTING
GROUND
STEEL

MOVES LIST

LV	Move Name	Type	ST	ACC	PP	LV	Move Name	Type	ST	ACC	PP
S	Tackle	Normal	35	95	35	28	Rock Slide	Rock	75	90	10
07	Harden	Normal	—	—	30	31	Sandstorm	Rock	—	—	10
13	Rock Throw	Rock	50	90	15	37	Rest	Psychic	—	—	10
16	Block	Normal	—	100	5	43	Zap Cannon	Electric	100	50	5
22	Thunder Wave	Electric	—	100	20	46	Lock-On	Normal	—	100	5

TM/HM LIST

TM/HM #	Move Name	Type	ST	ACC	PP	TM/HM #	Move Name	Type	ST	ACC	PP
HM04	Strength	Normal	80	100	15	TM27	Return	Normal	—	100	20
HM06	Rock Smash	Fighting	20	100	15	TM32	Double Team	Normal	—	—	15
TM06	Toxic	Poison	—	85	10	TM34	Shock Wave	Electric	60	—	20
TM10	Hidden Power	Normal	—	100	15	TM37	Sandstorm	Rock	—	—	10
TM11	Sunny Day	Fire	—	—	5	TM39	Rock Tomb	Rock	50	80	10
TM12	Taunt	Dark	—	100	20	TM41	Torment	Dark	—	100	15
TM17	Protect	Normal	—	—	10	TM42	Façade	Normal	70	100	20
TM21	Frustration	Normal	—	100	20	TM43	Secret Power	Normal	70	100	20
TM24	Thunderbolt	Electric	95	100	15	TM44	Rest	Psychic	—	—	10
TM25	Thunder	Electric	120	70	10	TM45	Attract	Normal	—	100	15
TM26	Earthquake	Ground	100	100	10						

EGG MOVES

Move Name	Type	ST	ACC	PP
Magnitude	Ground	—	100	30
Rollout	Rock	30	90	20
Explosion	Normal	250	100	5

MOVE TUTOR LIST

Move Name	Type	ST	ACC	PP
Body Slam*	Normal	85	100	15
Defense Curl*	Normal	—	—	40
Double-Edge	Normal	120	100	15
Dynamicpunch	Fighting	100	50	5
Explosion	Normal	250	100	5
Endure*	Normal	—	—	10
Fire Punch*	Fire	75	100	15
Ice Punch*	Ice	75	100	15
Mimic	Normal	—	100	10
Mud-Slap*	Ground	20	100	10
Rock Slide*	Rock	75	90	10
Rollout	Rock	30	90	20
Sleep Talk	Normal	—	—	10
Snore*	Normal	40	100	15
Substitute	Normal	—	—	10
Swagger	Normal	—	90	15
Thunderpunch*	Electric	75	100	15
Thunder Wave*	Electric	—	100	20

*Battle Frontier tutor move

061 Skitty™

NORMAL

GENERAL INFO
SPECIES: Kitten Pokémon
HEIGHT: 2'0"
WEIGHT: 24 lbs.
ABILITY: *Cute Charm* — *If opponent Pokémon is of the opposite gender, it may become infatuated.*

STATS
HP	25
ATTACK	50
DEFENSE	50
SP. ATTACK	50
SP. DEFENSE	25
SPEED	50

EVOLUTIONS

MOON STONE

WHERE/HOW TO CATCH
Route 116

STRONG AGAINST:
GHOST

WEAK AGAINST:
FIGHTING

MOVES LIST

LV	Move Name	Type	ST	ACC	PP	LV	Move Name	Type	ST	ACC	PP
S	Growl	Normal	—	100	40	19	Assist	Normal	—	100	20
S	Tackle	Normal	35	95	35	25	Charm	Normal	—	100	20
03	Tail Whip	Normal	—	100	30	27	Faint Attack	Dark	60	—	20
07	Attract	Normal	—	100	15	31	Covet	Normal	40	100	40
13	Sing	Normal	—	55	15	37	Heal Bell	Normal	—	—	5
15	Doubleslap	Normal	15	85	10	39	Double-Edge	Normal	120	100	15

TM/HM LIST

TM/HM #	Move Name	Type	ST	ACC	PP	TM/HM #	Move Name	Type	ST	ACC	PP
HM05	Flash	Normal	—	70	20	TM23	Iron Tail	Steel	100	75	15
TM03	Water Pulse	Water	60	100	20	TM24	Thunderbolt	Electric	95	100	15
TM04	Calm Mind	Psychic	—	—	20	TM25	Thunder	Electric	120	70	10
TM06	Toxic	Poison	—	85	10	TM27	Return	Normal	—	100	20
TM10	Hidden Power	Normal	—	100	15	TM28	Dig	Ground	60	100	10
TM11	Sunny Day	Fire	—	—	5	TM30	Shadow Ball	Ghost	60	—	20
TM13	Ice Beam	Ice	95	100	10	TM32	Double Team	Normal	—	—	15
TM14	Blizzard	Ice	120	70	5	TM34	Shock Wave	Electric	60	—	20
TM17	Protect	Normal	—	—	10	TM42	Façade	Normal	70	100	20
TM18	Rain Dance	Water	—	—	5	TM43	Secret Power	Normal	70	100	20
TM20	Safeguard	Normal	—	—	25	TM44	Rest	Psychic	—	—	10
TM21	Frustration	Normal	—	100	20	TM45	Attract	Normal	—	100	15
TM22	Solarbeam	Grass	120	100	10						

EGG MOVES

Move Name	Type	ST	ACC	PP
Helping Hand	Normal	—	100	20
Psych Up	Normal	—	—	10
Uproar	Normal	50	100	10
Fake Tears	Dark	—	100	20
Baton Pass	Normal	—	—	40
Substitute	Normal	—	—	10
Tickle	Normal	—	100	20
Wish	Normal	—	100	10

MOVE TUTOR LIST

Move Name	Type	ST	ACC	PP
Body Slam*	Normal	85	100	15
Defense Curl*	Normal	—	—	40
Double-Edge	Normal	120	100	15
Dream Eater*	Psychic	100	100	15
Endure*	Normal	—	—	10
Icy Wind*	Ice	55	95	15
Mimic	Normal	—	100	10
Mud-Slap*	Ground	20	100	10
Psych Up*	Normal	—	—	10
Rollout	Rock	30	90	20
Sleep Talk	Normal	—	—	10
Snore*	Normal	40	100	15
Substitute	Normal	—	—	10
Swagger	Normal	—	90	15
Swift*	Normal	60	—	20
Thunder Wave*	Electric	—	100	20

*Battle Frontier tutor move

062 Delcatty™

NORMAL

GENERAL INFO
SPECIES: Prim Pokémon
HEIGHT: 3'7"
WEIGHT: 72 lbs.
ABILITY: *Cute Charm* — *If opponent Pokémon is of the opposite gender, it may become infatuated.*

STATS
HP	50
ATTACK	50
DEFENSE	50
SP. ATTACK	50
SP. DEFENSE	50
SPEED	50

EVOLUTIONS
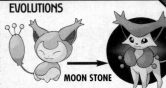
MOON STONE

WHERE/HOW TO CATCH
Evolve from Skitty with Moon Stone

STRONG AGAINST:
GHOST

WEAK AGAINST:
FIGHTING

MOVES LIST

LV	Move Name	Type	ST	ACC	PP	LV	Move Name	Type	ST	ACC	PP
S	Growl	Normal	—	100	40	S	Sing	Normal	—	55	15
S	Attract	Normal	—	100	15	S	Doubleslap	Normal	15	85	10

TM/HM LIST

TM/HM #	Move Name	Type	ST	ACC	PP	TM/HM #	Move Name	Type	ST	ACC	PP
HM04	Strength	Normal	80	100	15	TM21	Frustration	Normal	—	100	20
HM05	Flash	Normal	—	70	20	TM22	Solarbeam	Grass	120	100	10
HM06	Rock Smash	Fighting	20	100	15	TM23	Iron Tail	Steel	100	75	15
TM03	Water Pulse	Water	60	100	20	TM24	Thunderbolt	Electric	95	100	15
TM04	Calm Mind	Psychic	—	—	20	TM25	Thunder	Electric	120	70	10
TM06	Toxic	Poison	—	85	10	TM27	Return	Normal	—	100	20
TM10	Hidden Power	Normal	—	100	15	TM28	Dig	Ground	60	100	10
TM11	Sunny Day	Fire	—	—	5	TM30	Shadow Ball	Ghost	60	—	20
TM13	Ice Beam	Ice	95	100	10	TM32	Double Team	Normal	—	—	15
TM14	Blizzard	Ice	120	70	5	TM34	Shock Wave	Electric	60	—	20
TM15	Hyper Beam	Normal	150	90	5	TM42	Façade	Normal	70	100	20
TM17	Protect	Normal	—	—	10	TM43	Secret Power	Normal	70	100	20
TM18	Rain Dance	Water	—	—	5	TM44	Rest	Psychic	—	—	10
TM20	Safeguard	Normal	—	—	25	TM45	Attract	Normal	—	100	15

MOVE TUTOR LIST

Move Name	Type	ST	ACC	PP
Body Slam*	Normal	85	100	15
Defense Curl*	Normal	—	—	40
Double-Edge	Normal	120	100	15
Dream Eater*	Psychic	100	100	15
Endure*	Normal	—	—	10
Icy Wind*	Ice	55	95	15
Mimic	Normal	—	100	10
Mud-Slap*	Ground	20	100	10
Psych Up*	Normal	—	—	10
Rollout	Rock	30	90	20
Sleep Talk	Normal	—	—	10
Snore*	Normal	40	100	15
Substitute	Normal	—	—	10
Swagger	Normal	—	90	15
Swift*	Normal	60	—	20
Thunder Wave*	Electric	—	100	20

*Battle Frontier tutor move

063

Zubat™

POISON
FLYING

GENERAL INFO
SPECIES: Bat Pokémon
HEIGHT: 2'7"
WEIGHT: 17 lbs.
ABILITY: *Inner Focus* — *Prevents the Pokémon from Flinching.*

STATS
HP	→	33
ATTACK	→	33
DEFENSE	→	33
SP. ATTACK	→	33
SP. DEFENSE	→	33
SPEED	→	33

EVOLUTIONS

LV22
FRIENDSHIP

WHERE/HOW TO CATCH
Granite Cave, Meteor Falls, Seafloor Cavern, Shoal Cave, and Victory Road

STRONG AGAINST:
GRASS
FIGHTING
POISON
GROUND
BUG

WEAK AGAINST:
ELECTRIC
ICE
PSYCHIC
ROCK

MOVES LIST

LV	Move Name	Type	ST	ACC	PP
S	Leech Life	Bug	20	100	15
06	Astonish	Ghost	30	100	15
11	Supersonic	Normal	—	55	20
16	Bite	Dark	60	100	25
21	Wing Attack	Flying	60	100	35
26	Confuse Ray	Ghost	—	100	10
31	Air Cutter	Flying	55	95	25
36	Mean Look	Normal	—	100	5
41	Poison Fang	Poison	50	100	5
46	Haze	Ice	—	—	30

TM/HM LIST

TM/HM #	Move Name	Type	ST	ACC	PP
TM06	Toxic	Poison	—	85	10
TM10	Hidden Power	Normal	—	100	15
TM11	Sunny Day	Fire	—	—	5
TM12	Taunt	Dark	—	100	20
TM17	Protect	Normal	—	—	10
TM18	Rain Dance	Water	—	—	5
TM19	Giga Drain	Grass	60	100	5
TM21	Frustration	Normal	—	100	20
TM27	Return	Normal	—	100	20
TM30	Shadow Ball	Ghost	60	—	20
TM32	Double Team	Normal	—	—	15
TM36	Sludge Bomb	Poison	90	100	10
TM40	Aerial Ace	Flying	60	—	20
TM41	Torment	Dark	—	100	15
TM42	Façade	Normal	70	100	20
TM43	Secret Power	Normal	70	100	20
TM44	Rest	Psychic	—	—	10
TM45	Attract	Normal	—	100	15
TM46	Thief	Dark	40	100	10
TM47	Steel Wing	Steel	70	90	25
TM49	Snatch	Dark	—	100	10

EGG MOVES

Move Name	Type	ST	ACC	PP
Quick Attack	Normal	40	100	30
Pursuit	Dark	40	100	20
Faint Attack	Dark	60	—	20
Whirlwind	Normal	—	100	20
Curse	Normal	—	—	—

MOVE TUTOR LIST

Move Name	Type	ST	ACC	PP
Double-Edge	Normal	120	100	15
Endure*	Normal	—	—	10
Mimic	Normal	—	100	10
Sleep Talk	Normal	—	—	10
Snore*	Normal	40	100	15
Substitute	Normal	—	—	10
Swagger	Normal	—	90	15
Swift*	Normal	60	—	20

*Battle Frontier tutor move

064

Golbat™

POISON
FLYING

GENERAL INFO
SPECIES: Bat Pokémon
HEIGHT: 5'3"
WEIGHT: 121 lbs.
ABILITY: *Inner Focus* — *Prevents the Pokémon from Flinching.*

STATS
HP	→	66
ATTACK	→	66
DEFENSE	→	60
SP. ATTACK	→	60
SP. DEFENSE	→	60
SPEED	→	66

EVOLUTIONS

LV22
FRIENDSHIP

WHERE/HOW TO CATCH
Evolve from Zubat; Granite Cave, Meteor Falls, Seafloor Cavern, Shoal Cave, Sky Pillar, and Victory Road

STRONG AGAINST:
GRASS
FIGHTING
POISON
GROUND
BUG

WEAK AGAINST:
ELECTRIC
ICE
PSYCHIC
ROCK

MOVES LIST

LV	Move Name	Type	ST	ACC	PP
S	Screech	Normal	—	85	40
S	Leech Life	Bug	20	100	15
S	Supersonic	Normal	—	55	20
S	Astonish	Ghost	30	100	15
06	Astonish	Ghost	30	100	15
11	Supersonic	Normal	—	55	20
16	Bite	Dark	60	100	25
21	Wing Attack	Flying	60	100	35
28	Confuse Ray	Ghost	—	100	10
35	Air Cutter	Flying	55	95	25
42	Mean Look	Normal	—	100	5
49	Poison Fang	Poison	50	100	15
56	Haze	Ice	—	—	30

TM/HM LIST

TM/HM #	Move Name	Type	ST	ACC	PP
TM06	Toxic	Poison	—	85	10
TM10	Hidden Power	Normal	—	100	15
TM11	Sunny Day	Fire	—	—	5
TM12	Taunt	Dark	—	100	20
TM15	Hyper Beam	Normal	150	90	5
TM17	Protect	Normal	—	—	10
TM18	Rain Dance	Water	—	—	5
TM19	Giga Drain	Grass	60	100	5
TM21	Frustration	Normal	—	100	20
TM27	Return	Normal	—	100	20
TM30	Shadow Ball	Ghost	60	—	20
TM32	Double Team	Normal	—	—	15
TM36	Sludge Bomb	Poison	90	100	10
TM40	Aerial Ace	Flying	60	—	20
TM41	Torment	Dark	—	100	15
TM42	Façade	Normal	70	100	20
TM43	Secret Power	Normal	70	100	20
TM44	Rest	Psychic	—	—	10
TM45	Attract	Normal	—	100	15
TM46	Thief	Dark	40	100	10
TM47	Steel Wing	Steel	70	90	25
TM49	Snatch	Dark	—	100	10

MOVE TUTOR LIST

Move Name	Type	ST	ACC	PP
Double-Edge	Normal	120	100	15
Endure*	Normal	—	—	10
Mimic	Normal	—	100	10
Sleep Talk	Normal	—	—	10
Snore*	Normal	40	100	15
Substitute	Normal	—	—	10
Swagger	Normal	—	90	15
Swift*	Normal	60	—	20

*Battle Frontier tutor move

065 Crobat™

POISON
FLYING

GENERAL INFO
SPECIES: Bat Pokémon
HEIGHT: 5'11"
WEIGHT: 165 lbs.
ABILITY: **Inner Focus**—
Prevents the Pokémon from Flinching.

STATS

HP	66
ATTACK	66
DEFENSE	60
SP. ATTACK	60
SP. DEFENSE	66
SPEED	100

EVOLUTIONS

LV22   FRIENDSHIP

WHERE/HOW TO CATCH
Evolve from Golbat with Taming

STRONG AGAINST:
GRASS
FIGHTING
POISON
GROUND
BUG

WEAK AGAINST:
ELECTRIC
ICE
PSYCHIC
ROCK

MOVES LIST

LV	Move Name	Type	ST	ACC	PP
S	Screech	Normal	—	85	40
S	Leech Life	Bug	20	100	15
S	Supersonic	Normal	—	55	20
S	Astonish	Ghost	30	100	15
06	Astonish	Ghost	30	100	15
11	Supersonic	Normal	—	55	20
16	Bite	Dark	60	100	25

LV	Move Name	Type	ST	ACC	PP
21	Wing Attack	Flying	60	100	35
28	Confuse Ray	Ghost	—	100	10
35	Air Cutter	Flying	55	95	25
42	Mean Look	Normal	—	100	5
49	Poison Fang	Poison	50	100	15
56	Haze	Ice	—	—	30

TM/HM LIST

TM/HM #	Move Name	Type	ST	ACC	PP
HM02	Fly	Flying	70	95	15
TM06	Toxic	Poison	—	85	10
TM10	Hidden Power	Normal	—	100	15
TM11	Sunny Day	Fire	—	—	5
TM12	Taunt	Dark	—	100	20
TM15	Hyper Beam	Normal	150	90	5
TM17	Protect	Normal	—	—	10
TM18	Rain Dance	Water	—	—	5
TM19	Giga Drain	Grass	60	100	5
TM21	Frustration	Normal	—	100	20
TM27	Return	Normal	—	100	20
TM30	Shadow Ball	Ghost	60	—	20

TM/HM #	Move Name	Type	ST	ACC	PP
TM32	Double Team	Normal	—	—	15
TM36	Sludge Bomb	Poison	90	100	10
TM40	Aerial Ace	Flying	60	—	20
TM41	Torment	Dark	—	100	15
TM42	Façade	Normal	70	100	20
TM43	Secret Power	Normal	70	100	20
TM44	Rest	Psychic	—	—	10
TM45	Attract	Normal	—	100	15
TM46	Thief	Dark	40	100	10
TM47	Steel Wing	Steel	70	90	25
TM49	Snatch	Dark	—	100	10

MOVE TUTOR LIST

Move Name	Type	ST	ACC	PP
Double-Edge	Normal	120	100	15
Endure*	Normal	—	—	10
Mimic	Normal	—	100	10
Sleep Talk	Normal	—	—	10
Snore*	Normal	40	100	15
Substitute	Normal	—	—	10
Swagger	Normal	—	90	15
Swift*	Normal	60	—	20

*Battle Frontier tutor move

066 Tentacool™

WATER
POISON

GENERAL INFO
SPECIES: Jellyfish Pokémon
HEIGHT: 2'11"
WEIGHT: 100 lbs.
ABILITIES: **Clear Body**—*Moves that lower Ability values have no effect on the Pokémon.*
Liquid Ooze—*Pokémon inflicts damage on an opponent who uses HP-absorbing Moves.*

STATS

HP	33
ATTACK	33
DEFENSE	33
SP. ATTACK	33
SP. DEFENSE	66
SPEED	66

EVOLUTIONS

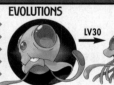
LV30

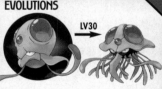

WHERE/HOW TO CATCH
All water routes and water bodies in Hoenn

STRONG AGAINST:
FIRE
WATER
ICE
FIGHTING
POISON
BUG
STEEL

WEAK AGAINST:
ELECTRIC
GROUND
PSYCHIC

MOVES LIST

LV	Move Name	Type	ST	ACC	PP
S	Poison Sting	Poison	15	100	35
06	Supersonic	Normal	—	55	20
12	Constrict	Normal	10	100	35
19	Acid	Poison	40	100	30
25	Bubblebeam	Water	65	100	20

LV	Move Name	Type	ST	ACC	PP
30	Wrap	Normal	15	85	20
36	Barrier	Psychic	—	—	30
43	Screech	Normal	—	85	40
49	Hydro Pump	Water	120	80	5

TM/HM LIST

TM/HM #	Move Name	Type	ST	ACC	PP
HM01	Cut	Normal	50	95	30
HM03	Surf	Water	95	100	15
HM07	Waterfall	Water	80	100	15
HM08	Dive	Water	60	100	10
TM03	Water Pulse	Water	60	100	20
TM06	Toxic	Poison	—	85	10
TM07	Hail	Ice	—	—	10
TM10	Hidden Power	Normal	—	100	15
TM13	Ice Beam	Ice	95	100	10
TM14	Blizzard	Ice	120	70	5
TM17	Protect	Normal	—	—	10

TM/HM #	Move Name	Type	ST	ACC	PP
TM18	Rain Dance	Water	—	—	5
TM19	Giga Drain	Grass	60	100	5
TM21	Frustration	Normal	—	100	20
TM27	Return	Normal	—	100	20
TM32	Double Team	Normal	—	—	15
TM36	Sludge Bomb	Poison	90	100	10
TM42	Façade	Normal	70	100	20
TM43	Secret Power	Normal	70	100	20
TM44	Rest	Psychic	—	—	10
TM45	Attract	Normal	—	100	15
TM46	Thief	Dark	40	100	10

EGG MOVES

Move Name	Type	ST	ACC	PP
Mirror Coat	Psychic	—	100	20
Safeguard	Normal	—	—	25
Confuse Ray	Ghost	—	100	10
Aurora Beam	Ice	65	100	20
Rapid Spin	Normal	20	100	40
Haze	Ice	—	—	30

MOVE TUTOR LIST

Move Name	Type	ST	ACC	PP
Double-Edge	Normal	120	100	15
Endure*	Normal	—	—	10
Icy Wind*	Ice	55	95	15
Mimic	Normal	—	100	10
Sleep Talk	Normal	—	—	10
Snore*	Normal	40	100	15
Substitute	Normal	—	—	10
Swagger	Normal	—	90	15
Swords Dance*	Normal	—	—	30

*Battle Frontier tutor move

067

Tentacruel™

| WATER |
| POISON |

GENERAL INFO
SPECIES: Jellyfish Pokémon
HEIGHT: 5'3"
WEIGHT: 121 lbs.
ABILITIES: *Clear Body*—Moves that lower Ability values have no effect on the Pokémon.
Liquid Ooze—Pokémon inflicts damage on an opponent who uses HP-absorbing Moves.

STATS
HP	66
ATTACK	66
DEFENSE	33
SP. ATTACK	60
SP. DEFENSE	100
SPEED	100

EVOLUTIONS
 LV30

WHERE/HOW TO CATCH
Evolve from Tentacool; Abandoned Ship (Super Rod)

STRONG AGAINST:
| FIRE |
| WATER |
| ICE |
| FIGHTING |
| POISON |
| BUG |
| STEEL |

WEAK AGAINST:
| ELECTRIC |
| GROUND |
| PSYCHIC |

MOVES LIST
LV	Move Name	Type	ST	ACC	PP
S	Poison Sting	Poison	15	100	35
S	Supersonic	Normal	—	55	20
S	Constrict	Normal	10	100	35
06	Supersonic	Normal	—	55	20
12	Constrict	Normal	10	100	35
19	Acid	Poison	40	100	30

LV	Move Name	Type	ST	ACC	PP
25	Bubblebeam	Water	65	100	20
30	Wrap	Normal	15	85	20
38	Barrier	Psychic	—	—	30
47	Screech	Normal	—	85	40
55	Hydro Pump	Water	120	80	5

TM/HM LIST
TM/HM #	Move Name	Type	ST	ACC	PP
HM01	Cut	Normal	50	95	30
HM03	Surf	Water	95	100	15
HM07	Waterfall	Water	80	100	15
HM08	Dive	Water	60	100	10
TM03	Water Pulse	Water	60	100	20
TM06	Toxic	Poison	—	85	10
TM07	Hail	Ice	—	—	10
TM10	Hidden Power	Normal	—	100	15
TM13	Ice Beam	Ice	95	100	10
TM14	Blizzard	Ice	120	70	5
TM15	Hyper Beam	Normal	150	90	5
TM17	Protect	Normal	—	—	10

TM/HM #	Move Name	Type	ST	ACC	PP
TM18	Rain Dance	Water	—	—	5
TM19	Giga Drain	Grass	60	100	5
TM21	Frustration	Normal	—	100	20
TM27	Return	Normal	—	100	20
TM32	Double Team	Normal	—	—	15
TM36	Sludge Bomb	Poison	90	100	10
TM42	Façade	Normal	70	100	20
TM43	Secret Power	Normal	70	100	20
TM44	Rest	Psychic	—	—	10
TM45	Attract	Normal	—	100	15
TM46	Thief	Dark	40	100	10

MOVE TUTOR LIST
Move Name	Type	ST	ACC	PP
Double-Edge	Normal	120	100	15
Endure*	Normal	—	—	10
Icy Wind*	Ice	55	95	15
Mimic	Normal	—	100	10
Sleep Talk	Normal	—	—	10
Snore*	Normal	40	100	15
Substitute	Normal	—	—	10
Swagger	Normal	—	90	15
Swords Dance*	Normal	—	—	30

*Battle Frontier tutor move

068

Sableye™

| DARK |
| GHOST |

GENERAL INFO
SPECIES: Darkness Pokémon
HEIGHT: 1'8"
WEIGHT: 24 lbs.
ABILITY: *Keen Eye*—Pokémon's Accuracy cannot be lowered.

STATS
HP	25
ATTACK	50
DEFENSE	50
SP. ATTACK	50
SP. DEFENSE	50
SPEED	50

EVOLUTIONS

SABLEYE DOES NOT EVOLVE

WHERE/HOW TO CATCH
Granite Cave, Sky Pillar, and Victory Road

STRONG AGAINST:
| NORMAL |
| FIGHTING |
| POISON |
| PSYCHIC |

WEAK AGAINST:
NONE

MOVES LIST
LV	Move Name	Type	ST	ACC	PP
S	Leer	Normal	—	100	30
S	Scratch	Normal	40	100	35
05	Foresight	Normal	—	100	40
09	Night Shade	Ghost	—	100	15
13	Astonish	Ghost	30	100	15
17	Fury Swipes	Normal	18	80	15
21	Fake Out	Normal	40	100	10

LV	Move Name	Type	ST	ACC	PP
25	Detect	Fighting	—	—	5
29	Faint Attack	Dark	60	—	20
33	Knock Off	Dark	20	100	20
37	Confuse Ray	Ghost	—	100	10
41	Shadow Ball	Ghost	80	100	15
45	Mean Look	Normal	—	100	5

TM/HM LIST
TM/HM #	Move Name	Type	ST	ACC	PP
HM01	Cut	Normal	50	95	30
HM05	Flash	Normal	—	70	20
HM06	Rock Smash	Fighting	20	100	15
TM01	Focus Punch	Fighting	150	100	20
TM03	Water Pulse	Water	60	100	20
TM04	Calm Mind	Psychic	—	—	20
TM06	Toxic	Poison	—	85	10
TM10	Hidden Power	Normal	—	100	15
TM11	Sunny Day	Fire	—	—	5
TM12	Taunt	Dark	—	100	20
TM17	Protect	Normal	—	—	10
TM18	Rain Dance	Water	—	—	5
TM21	Frustration	Normal	—	100	20
TM27	Return	Normal	—	100	20
TM28	Dig	Ground	60	100	10

TM/HM #	Move Name	Type	ST	ACC	PP
TM29	Psychic	Psychic	90	100	10
TM30	Shadow Ball	Ghost	60	—	20
TM31	Brick Break	Fighting	75	100	15
TM32	Double Team	Normal	—	—	15
TM34	Shock Wave	Electric	60	—	20
TM39	Rock Tomb	Rock	50	80	10
TM40	Aerial Ace	Flying	60	—	20
TM41	Torment	Dark	—	100	15
TM42	Façade	Normal	70	100	20
TM43	Secret Power	Normal	70	100	20
TM44	Rest	Psychic	—	—	10
TM45	Attract	Normal	—	100	15
TM46	Thief	Dark	40	100	10
TM49	Snatch	Dark	—	100	10

EGG MOVES
Move Name	Type	ST	ACC	PP
Psych Up	Normal	—	—	10
Recover	Normal	—	—	20
Moonlight	Normal	—	—	5

MOVE TUTOR LIST
Move Name	Type	ST	ACC	PP
Body Slam*	Normal	85	100	15
Counter*	Fighting	—	100	20
Double-Edge	Normal	120	100	15
Dream Eater*	Psychic	100	100	15
Dynamicpunch	Fighting	100	50	5
Endure*	Normal	—	—	10
Fire Punch*	Fire	75	100	15
Fury Cutter*	Bug	10	95	20
Ice Punch*	Ice	75	100	15
Mega Kick*	Normal	120	85	5
Mega Punch*	Normal	80	75	20
Metronome	Normal	—	100	10
Mimic	Normal	—	100	10
Mud-Slap*	Ground	20	100	10
Psych Up*	Normal	—	—	10
Rock Slide*	Rock	75	90	10
Seismic Toss*	Fighting	—	100	20
Sleep Talk	Normal	—	—	10
Snore*	Normal	40	100	15
Substitute	Normal	—	—	10
Swagger	Normal	—	90	15
Thunderpunch*	Electric	75	100	15

*Battle Frontier tutor move

069 Mawile™

STEEL

GENERAL INFO
SPECIES: Deceiver Pokémon
HEIGHT: 2'0"
WEIGHT: 25 lbs.
ABILITIES: *Hyper Cutter*—Pokémon's Attack Power cannot be lowered.
Intimidate—Lowers the opponent's Attack by one point at a battle's start.

STATS
HP	25
ATTACK	75
DEFENSE	50
SP. ATTACK	50
SP. DEFENSE	50
SPEED	50

EVOLUTIONS
MAWILE DOES NOT EVOLVE

WHERE/HOW TO CATCH
Victory Road

STRONG AGAINST:
NORMAL
GRASS
ICE
POISON
FLYING
PSYCHIC
BUG
ROCK
GHOST
DRAGON
DARK
STEEL

WEAK AGAINST:
FIRE
FIGHTING
GROUND

MOVES LIST
LV	Move Name	Type	ST	ACC	PP	LV	Move Name	Type	ST	ACC	PP
S	Astonish	Ghost	30	100	15	31	Baton Pass	Normal	—	—	40
06	Fake Tears	Dark	—	100	20	36	Crunch	Dark	80	100	15
11	Bite	Dark	60	100	25	41	Iron Defense	Steel	—	—	15
16	Sweet Scent	Normal	—	100	20	46	Stockpile	Normal	—	—	10
21	Vicegrip	Normal	55	100	30	46	Swallow	Normal	—	—	10
26	Faint Attack	Dark	60	—	20	46	Spit Up	Normal	100	100	10

TM/HM LIST
TM/HM #	Move Name	Type	ST	ACC	PP	TM/HM #	Move Name	Type	ST	ACC	PP
HM04	Strength	Normal	80	100	15	TM27	Return	Normal	—	100	20
HM06	Rock Smash	Fighting	20	100	15	TM31	Brick Break	Fighting	75	100	15
TM01	Focus Punch	Fighting	150	100	20	TM32	Double Team	Normal	—	—	15
TM06	Toxic	Poison	—	85	10	TM35	Flamethrower	Fire	95	100	15
TM10	Hidden Power	Normal	—	100	15	TM36	Sludge Bomb	Poison	90	100	10
TM11	Sunny Day	Fire	—	—	5	TM37	Sandstorm	Rock	—	—	10
TM12	Taunt	Dark	—	100	20	TM38	Fire Blast	Fire	120	85	5
TM13	Ice Beam	Ice	95	100	10	TM39	Rock Tomb	Rock	50	80	10
TM15	Hyper Beam	Normal	150	90	5	TM41	Torment	Dark	—	100	15
TM17	Protect	Normal	—	—	10	TM42	Facade	Normal	70	100	20
TM18	Rain Dance	Water	—	—	5	TM43	Secret Power	Normal	70	100	20
TM21	Frustration	Normal	—	100	20	TM44	Rest	Psychic	—	—	10
TM22	Solarbeam	Grass	120	100	10	TM45	Attract	Normal	—	100	15

EGG MOVES
Move Name	Type	ST	ACC	PP
Swords Dance	Normal	—	—	30
False Swipe	Normal	40	100	40
Poison Fang	Poison	50	100	15
Psych Up	Normal	—	—	10
Ancientpower	Rock	60	100	5
Tickle	Normal	—	100	20

MOVE TUTOR LIST
Move Name	Type	ST	ACC	PP
Body Slam*	Normal	85	100	15
Counter*	Fighting	—	100	20
Double-Edge	Normal	120	100	15
Dynamicpunch*	Fighting	100	50	5
Endure*	Normal	—	—	10
Ice Punch*	Ice	75	100	15
Icy Wind*	Ice	55	95	15
Mega Kick*	Normal	120	85	5
Mega Punch*	Normal	80	75	20
Mimic	Normal	—	100	10
Mud-Slap*	Ground	20	100	10
Psych Up*	Normal	—	—	10
Rock Slide*	Rock	75	90	10
Seismic Toss*	Fighting	—	100	20
Sleep Talk	Normal	—	—	10
Snore*	Normal	40	100	15
Substitute	Normal	—	—	10
Swagger	Normal	—	90	15
Swords Dance*	Normal	—	—	30
Thunderpunch*	Electric	75	100	15

*Battle Frontier tutor move

---

070 Aron™

STEEL
ROCK

GENERAL INFO
SPECIES: Iron Armor Pokémon
HEIGHT: 1'4"
WEIGHT: 132 lbs.
ABILITIES: *Sturdy*—One hit KO moves have no effect.
Rock Head—Pokémon does not receive recoil damage from moves such as Double-Edge and Body Slam.

STATS
HP	25
ATTACK	50
DEFENSE	75
SP. ATTACK	50
SP. DEFENSE	25
SPEED	25

EVOLUTIONS
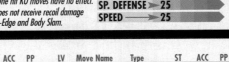LV32
LV42

WHERE/HOW TO CATCH
Granite Cave, Victory Road

STRONG AGAINST:
NORMAL
ICE
POISON
FLYING
PSYCHIC
BUG
ROCK
GHOST
DRAGON
DARK

WEAK AGAINST:
WATER
FIGHTING
GROUND

MOVES LIST
LV	Move Name	Type	ST	ACC	PP	LV	Move Name	Type	ST	ACC	PP
S	Tackle	Normal	35	95	35	21	Roar	Normal	—	100	20
04	Harden	Normal	—	—	30	25	Take Down	Normal	90	85	20
07	Mud-Slap	Ground	20	100	10	29	Iron Tail	Steel	100	75	15
10	Headbutt	Normal	70	100	15	34	Protect	Normal	—	—	10
13	Metal Claw	Steel	50	95	35	39	Metal Sound	Steel	—	85	40
17	Iron Defense	Steel	—	—	15	44	Double-Edge	Normal	120	100	15

TM/HM LIST
TM/HM #	Move Name	Type	ST	ACC	PP	TM/HM #	Move Name	Type	ST	ACC	PP
HM01	Cut	Normal	50	95	30	TM26	Earthquake	Ground	100	100	10
HM04	Strength	Normal	80	100	15	TM27	Return	Normal	—	100	20
HM06	Rock Smash	Fighting	20	100	15	TM28	Dig	Ground	60	100	10
TM03	Water Pulse	Water	60	100	20	TM32	Double Team	Normal	—	—	15
TM05	Roar	Normal	—	100	20	TM34	Shock Wave	Electric	60	—	20
TM06	Toxic	Poison	—	85	10	TM37	Sandstorm	Rock	—	—	10
TM10	Hidden Power	Normal	—	100	15	TM39	Rock Tomb	Rock	50	80	10
TM11	Sunny Day	Fire	—	—	5	TM40	Aerial Ace	Flying	60	—	20
TM17	Protect	Normal	—	—	10	TM42	Facade	Normal	70	100	20
TM18	Rain Dance	Water	—	—	5	TM43	Secret Power	Normal	70	100	20
TM21	Frustration	Normal	—	100	20	TM44	Rest	Psychic	—	—	10
TM23	Iron Tail	Steel	100	75	15	TM45	Attract	Normal	—	100	15

EGG MOVES
Move Name	Type	ST	ACC	PP
Endeavor	Normal	—	100	5
Body Slam	Normal	85	100	15
Stomp	Normal	65	100	20
Smellingsalt	Normal	60	100	10

MOVE TUTOR LIST
Move Name	Type	ST	ACC	PP
Body Slam*	Normal	85	100	15
Defense Curl*	Normal	—	—	40
Double-Edge	Normal	120	100	15
Fury Cutter*	Bug	10	95	20
Endure*	Normal	—	—	10
Mimic	Normal	—	100	10
Mud-Slap*	Ground	20	100	10
Rock Slide*	Rock	75	90	10
Rollout	Rock	30	90	20
Sleep Talk	Normal	—	—	10
Snore*	Normal	40	100	15
Substitute	Normal	—	—	10
Swagger	Normal	—	90	15

*Battle Frontier tutor move

071

Lairon™

STEEL
ROCK

GENERAL INFO
SPECIES: Iron Armor Pokémon
HEIGHT: 2'11"
WEIGHT: 265 lbs.
ABILITIES: *Sturdy* — One hit KO moves have no effect.
Rock Head — Pokémon does not receive recoil damage
from moves such as Double-Edge and Body Slam.

STATS
HP	25
ATTACK	75
DEFENSE	75
SP. ATTACK	50
SP. DEFENSE	50
SPEED	50

EVOLUTIONS

LV32
LV42

WHERE/HOW TO CATCH
Evolve from Aron;
Victory Road

STRONG AGAINST:
NORMAL
ICE
POISON
FLYING
PSYCHIC
BUG
ROCK
GHOST
DRAGON
DARK

WEAK AGAINST:
WATER
FIGHTING
GROUND

MOVES LIST

LV	Move Name	Type	ST	ACC	PP	LV	Move Name	Type	ST	ACC	PP
S	Tackle	Normal	35	95	35	17	Iron Defense	Steel	—	—	15
S	Harden	Normal	—	—	30	21	Roar	Normal	—	100	20
S	Mud-Slap	Ground	20	100	10	25	Take Down	Normal	90	85	20
S	Headbutt	Normal	70	100	15	29	Iron Tail	Steel	100	75	15
04	Harden	Normal	—	—	30	37	Protect	Normal	—	—	10
07	Mud-Slap	Ground	20	100	10	45	Metal Sound	Steel	—	85	40
10	Headbutt	Normal	70	100	15	53	Double-Edge	Normal	120	100	15
13	Metal Claw	Steel	50	95	35						

TM/HM LIST

TM/HM #	Move Name	Type	ST	ACC	PP	TM/HM #	Move Name	Type	ST	ACC	PP
HM01	Cut	Normal	50	95	30	TM26	Earthquake	Ground	100	100	10
HM04	Strength	Normal	80	100	15	TM27	Return	Normal	—	100	20
HM06	Rock Smash	Fighting	20	100	15	TM28	Dig	Ground	60	100	10
TM03	Water Pulse	Water	60	100	20	TM32	Double Team	Normal	—	—	15
TM05	Roar	Normal	—	100	20	TM34	Shock Wave	Electric	60	—	20
TM06	Toxic	Poison	—	85	10	TM37	Sandstorm	Rock	—	—	10
TM10	Hidden Power	Normal	—	100	15	TM39	Rock Tomb	Rock	50	80	10
TM11	Sunny Day	Fire	—	—	5	TM40	Aerial Ace	Flying	60	—	20
TM17	Protect	Normal	—	—	10	TM42	Façade	Normal	70	100	20
TM18	Rain Dance	Water	—	—	5	TM43	Secret Power	Normal	70	100	20
TM21	Frustration	Normal	—	100	20	TM44	Rest	Psychic	—	—	10
TM23	Iron Tail	Steel	100	75	15	TM45	Attract	Normal	—	100	15

MOVE TUTOR LIST

Move Name	Type	ST	ACC	PP
Body Slam*	Normal	85	100	15
Defense Curl*	Normal	—	—	40
Double-Edge	Normal	120	100	15
Fury Cutter	Bug	10	95	20
Endure*	Normal	—	—	10
Mimic	Normal	—	100	10
Mud-Slap*	Ground	20	100	10
Rock Slide*	Rock	75	90	10
Rollout	Rock	30	90	20
Sleep Talk	Normal	—	—	10
Snore*	Normal	40	100	15
Substitute	Normal	—	—	10
Swagger	Normal	—	90	15

*Battle Frontier tutor move

072

Aggron™

STEEL
ROCK

GENERAL INFO
SPECIES: Iron Armor Pokémon
HEIGHT: 6'11"
WEIGHT: 794 lbs.
ABILITIES: *Sturdy* — One hit KO moves have no effect.
Rock Head — Pokémon does not receive recoil damage
from moves such as Double-Edge and Body Slam.

STATS
HP	50
ATTACK	75
DEFENSE	100
SP. ATTACK	50
SP. DEFENSE	50
SPEED	50

EVOLUTIONS

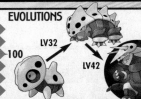

LV32
LV42

WHERE/HOW TO CATCH
Evolve from Lairon

STRONG AGAINST:
NORMAL
ICE
POISON
FLYING
PSYCHIC
BUG
ROCK
GHOST
DRAGON
DARK

WEAK AGAINST:
WATER
FIGHTING
GROUND

MOVES LIST

LV	Move Name	Type	ST	ACC	PP	LV	Move Name	Type	ST	ACC	PP
S	Tackle	Normal	35	95	35	17	Iron Defense	Steel	—	—	15
S	Harden	Normal	—	—	30	21	Roar	Normal	—	100	20
S	Mud-Slap	Ground	20	100	10	25	Take Down	Normal	90	85	20
S	Headbutt	Normal	70	100	15	29	Iron Tail	Steel	100	75	15
04	Harden	Normal	—	—	30	37	Protect	Normal	—	—	10
07	Mud-Slap	Ground	20	100	10	50	Metal Sound	Steel	—	85	40
10	Headbutt	Normal	70	100	15	63	Double-Edge	Normal	120	100	15
13	Metal Claw	Steel	50	95	35						

TM/HM LIST

TM/HM #	Move Name	Type	ST	ACC	PP	TM/HM #	Move Name	Type	ST	ACC	PP
HM01	Cut	Normal	50	95	30	TM23	Iron Tail	Steel	100	75	15
HM03	Surf	Water	95	100	15	TM24	Thunderbolt	Electric	95	100	15
HM04	Strength	Normal	80	100	15	TM25	Thunder	Electric	120	70	10
HM06	Rock Smash	Fighting	20	100	15	TM26	Earthquake	Ground	100	100	10
TM01	Focus Punch	Fighting	150	100	20	TM27	Return	Normal	—	100	20
TM02	Dragon Claw	Dragon	80	100	15	TM28	Dig	Ground	60	100	10
TM03	Water Pulse	Water	60	100	20	TM31	Brick Break	Fighting	75	100	15
TM05	Roar	Normal	—	100	20	TM32	Double Team	Normal	—	—	15
TM06	Toxic	Poison	—	85	10	TM34	Shock Wave	Electric	60	—	20
TM10	Hidden Power	Normal	—	100	15	TM35	Flamethrower	Fire	95	100	15
TM11	Sunny Day	Fire	—	—	5	TM37	Sandstorm	Rock	—	—	10
TM12	Taunt	Dark	—	100	20	TM38	Fire Blast	Fire	120	85	5
TM13	Ice Beam	Ice	95	100	10	TM39	Rock Tomb	Rock	50	80	10
TM14	Blizzard	Ice	120	70	5	TM40	Aerial Ace	Flying	60	—	20
TM15	Hyper Beam	Normal	150	90	5	TM42	Façade	Normal	70	100	20
TM17	Protect	Normal	—	—	10	TM43	Secret Power	Normal	70	100	20
TM18	Rain Dance	Water	—	—	5	TM44	Rest	Psychic	—	—	10
TM21	Frustration	Normal	—	100	20	TM45	Attract	Normal	—	100	15
TM22	Solarbeam	Grass	120	100	10						

MOVE TUTOR LIST

Move Name	Type	ST	ACC	PP
Body Slam*	Normal	85	100	15
Counter*	Fighting	—	100	20
Dynamicpunch*	Fighting	100	50	5
Defense Curl*	Normal	—	—	40
Double-Edge	Normal	120	100	15
Endure*	Normal	—	—	10
Fire Punch*	Fire	75	100	15
Fury Cutter	Bug	10	95	20
Ice Punch*	Ice	75	100	15
Icy Wind*	Ice	55	95	15
Mega Kick*	Normal	120	85	5
Mega Punch*	Normal	80	75	20
Mimic	Normal	—	100	10
Mud-Slap*	Ground	20	100	10
Rock Slide*	Rock	75	90	10
Rollout	Rock	30	90	20
Seismic Toss*	Fighting	—	100	20
Sleep Talk	Normal	—	—	10
Snore*	Normal	40	100	15
Substitute	Normal	—	—	10
Swagger	Normal	—	90	15
Thunderpunch*	Electric	75	100	15
Thunder Wave*	Electric	—	100	20

*Battle Frontier tutor move

073 Machop™

FIGHTING

GENERAL INFO
SPECIES: Superpower Pokémon
HEIGHT: 2'7"
WEIGHT: 43 lbs.
ABILITY: *Guts*—The Pokémon's Attack Power rises 1.5x when inflicted with a Status condition.

STATS
HP	66
ATTACK	66
DEFENSE	33
SP. ATTACK	33
SP. DEFENSE	33
SPEED	30

EVOLUTIONS
LV28
TRADE OVER THE GAME BOY WIRELESS ADAPTER

WHERE/HOW TO CATCH
Fiery Path

STRONG AGAINST:
BUG
ROCK
DARK

WEAK AGAINST:
FLYING
PSYCHIC

MOVES LIST
LV	Move Name	Type	ST	ACC	PP	LV	Move Name	Type	ST	ACC	PP
S	Low Kick	Fighting	—	100	20	25	Revenge	Fighting	60	100	10
S	Leer	Normal	—	100	30	31	Vital Throw	Fighting	70	100	10
07	Focus Energy	Normal	—	—	30	37	Submission	Fighting	80	80	25
13	Karate Chop	Fighting	50	100	25	40	Cross Chop	Fighting	100	80	5
19	Seismic Toss	Fighting	—	100	20	43	Scary Face	Normal	—	90	10
22	Foresight	Normal	—	100	40	49	Dynamicpunch	Fighting	100	50	5

TM/HM LIST
TM/HM #	Move Name	Type	ST	ACC	PP	TM/HM #	Move Name	Type	ST	ACC	PP
HM04	Strength	Normal	80	100	15	TM28	Dig	Ground	60	100	10
HM06	Rock Smash	Fighting	20	100	15	TM31	Brick Break	Fighting	75	100	15
TM01	Focus Punch	Fighting	150	100	20	TM32	Double Team	Normal	—	—	15
TM06	Toxic	Poison	—	85	10	TM35	Flamethrower	Fire	95	100	15
TM08	Bulk Up	Fighting	—	—	20	TM38	Fire Blast	Fire	120	85	5
TM10	Hidden Power	Normal	—	100	15	TM39	Rock Tomb	Rock	50	80	10
TM11	Sunny Day	Fire	—	—	5	TM42	Façade	Normal	70	100	20
TM17	Protect	Normal	—	—	10	TM43	Secret Power	Normal	70	100	20
TM18	Rain Dance	Water	—	—	5	TM44	Rest	Psychic	—	—	10
TM21	Frustration	Normal	—	100	20	TM45	Attract	Normal	—	100	15
TM26	Earthquake	Ground	100	100	10	TM46	Thief	Dark	40	100	10
TM27	Return	Normal	—	100	20						

EGG MOVES
Move Name	Type	ST	ACC	PP
Light Screen	Psychic	—	—	30
Meditate	Psychic	—	—	40
Encore	Normal	—	100	5
Smellingsalt	Normal	60	100	10
Counter	Fighting	—	100	20
Rock Slide	Rock	75	90	10

MOVE TUTOR LIST
Move Name	Type	ST	ACC	PP
Body Slam*	Normal	85	100	15
Counter*	Fighting	—	100	20
Defense Curl*	Normal	—	—	40
Double-Edge	Normal	120	100	15
Dynamicpunch	Fighting	100	50	5
Endure*	Normal	—	—	10
Fire Punch*	Fire	75	100	15
Ice Punch*	Ice	75	100	15
Mega Kick*	Normal	120	85	5
Mega Punch*	Normal	80	75	20
Metronome	Normal	—	100	10
Mimic	Normal	—	100	10
Mud-Slap*	Ground	20	100	10
Rock Slide*	Rock	75	90	10
Seismic Toss*	Fighting	—	100	20
Sleep Talk	Normal	—	—	10
Snore*	Normal	40	100	15
Substitute	Normal	—	—	10
Swagger	Normal	—	90	15
Thunderpunch*	Electric	75	100	15

*Battle Frontier tutor move

---

074 Machoke™

FIGHTING

GENERAL INFO
SPECIES: Superpower Pokémon
HEIGHT: 4'1"
WEIGHT: 155 lbs.
ABILITY: *Guts*—The Pokémon's Attack Power rises 1.5x when inflicted with a Status condition.

STATS
HP	66
ATTACK	100
DEFENSE	66
SP. ATTACK	30
SP. DEFENSE	33
SPEED	33

EVOLUTIONS
LV28
TRADE OVER THE GAME BOY WIRELESS ADAPTER

WHERE/HOW TO CATCH
Fiery Path

STRONG AGAINST:
BUG
ROCK
DARK

WEAK AGAINST:
FLYING
PSYCHIC

MOVES LIST
LV	Move Name	Type	ST	ACC	PP	LV	Move Name	Type	ST	ACC	PP
S	Low Kick	Fighting	—	100	20	25	Revenge	Fighting	60	100	10
S	Leer	Normal	—	100	30	33	Vital Throw	Fighting	70	100	10
S	Focus Energy	Normal	—	—	30	41	Submission	Fighting	80	80	25
07	Focus Energy	Normal	—	—	30	46	Cross Chop	Fighting	100	80	5
13	Karate Chop	Fighting	50	100	25	51	Scary Face	Normal	—	90	10
19	Seismic Toss	Fighting	—	100	20	59	Dynamicpunch	Fighting	100	50	5
22	Foresight	Normal	—	100	40						

TM/HM LIST
TM/HM #	Move Name	Type	ST	ACC	PP	TM/HM #	Move Name	Type	ST	ACC	PP
HM04	Strength	Normal	80	100	15	TM28	Dig	Ground	60	100	10
HM06	Rock Smash	Fighting	20	100	15	TM31	Brick Break	Fighting	75	100	15
TM01	Focus Punch	Fighting	150	100	20	TM32	Double Team	Normal	—	—	15
TM06	Toxic	Poison	—	85	10	TM35	Flamethrower	Fire	95	100	15
TM08	Bulk Up	Fighting	—	—	20	TM38	Fire Blast	Fire	120	85	5
TM10	Hidden Power	Normal	—	100	15	TM39	Rock Tomb	Rock	50	80	10
TM11	Sunny Day	Fire	—	—	5	TM42	Façade	Normal	70	100	20
TM17	Protect	Normal	—	—	10	TM43	Secret Power	Normal	70	100	20
TM18	Rain Dance	Water	—	—	5	TM44	Rest	Psychic	—	—	10
TM21	Frustration	Normal	—	100	20	TM45	Attract	Normal	—	100	15
TM26	Earthquake	Ground	100	100	10	TM46	Thief	Dark	40	100	10
TM27	Return	Normal	—	100	20						

MOVE TUTOR LIST
Move Name	Type	ST	ACC	PP
Body Slam*	Normal	85	100	15
Counter*	Fighting	—	100	20
Double-Edge	Normal	120	100	15
Dynamicpunch	Fighting	100	50	5
Endure*	Normal	—	—	10
Fire Punch*	Fire	75	100	15
Ice Punch*	Ice	75	100	15
Mega Kick*	Normal	120	85	5
Mega Punch*	Normal	80	75	20
Metronome	Normal	—	100	10
Mimic	Normal	—	100	10
Mud-Slap*	Ground	20	100	10
Rock Slide*	Rock	75	90	10
Seismic Toss*	Fighting	—	100	20
Sleep Talk	Normal	—	—	10
Snore*	Normal	40	100	15
Substitute	Normal	—	—	10
Swagger	Normal	—	90	15
Thunderpunch*	Electric	75	100	15

*Battle Frontier tutor move

075 Machamp™
FIGHTING

GENERAL INFO
SPECIES: Superpower Pokémon
HEIGHT: 5'3"
WEIGHT: 287 lbs.
ABILITY: *Guts*—The Pokémon's Attack Power rises 1.5x when inflicted with a Status condition.

STATS
HP	66
ATTACK	100
DEFENSE	60
SP. ATTACK	60
SP. DEFENSE	60
SPEED	33

EVOLUTIONS

LV28 → TRADE OVER THE GAME BOY WIRELESS ADAPTER

WHERE/HOW TO CATCH
Evolve from Machoke via Game Boy Wireless Adapter

STRONG AGAINST:
BUG
ROCK
DARK

WEAK AGAINST:
FLYING
PSYCHIC

MOVES LIST
LV	Move Name	Type	ST	ACC	PP
S	Low Kick	Fighting	—	100	20
S	Leer	Normal	—	100	30
S	Focus Energy	Normal	—	—	30
07	Focus Energy	Normal	—	—	30
13	Karate Chop	Fighting	50	100	25
19	Seismic Toss	Fighting	—	100	20
22	Foresight	Normal	—	100	40
25	Revenge	Fighting	60	100	10
33	Vital Throw	Fighting	70	100	10
41	Submission	Fighting	80	80	25
46	Cross Chop	Fighting	100	80	5
51	Scary Face	Normal	—	90	10
59	Dynamicpunch	Fighting	100	50	5

TM/HM LIST
TM/HM #	Move Name	Type	ST	ACC	PP
HM04	Strength	Normal	80	100	15
HM06	Rock Smash	Fighting	20	100	15
TM01	Focus Punch	Fighting	150	100	20
TM06	Toxic	Poison	—	85	10
TM08	Bulk Up	Fighting	—	—	20
TM10	Hidden Power	Normal	—	100	15
TM11	Sunny Day	Fire	—	—	5
TM15	Hyper Beam	Normal	150	90	5
TM17	Protect	Normal	—	—	10
TM18	Rain Dance	Water	—	—	5
TM21	Frustration	Normal	—	100	20
TM26	Earthquake	Ground	100	100	10
TM27	Return	Normal	—	100	20
TM28	Dig	Ground	60	100	10
TM31	Brick Break	Fighting	75	100	15
TM32	Double Team	Normal	—	—	15
TM35	Flamethrower	Fire	95	100	15
TM38	Fire Blast	Fire	120	85	5
TM39	Rock Tomb	Rock	50	80	10
TM42	Facade	Normal	70	100	20
TM43	Secret Power	Normal	70	100	20
TM44	Rest	Psychic	—	—	10
TM45	Attract	Normal	—	100	15
TM46	Thief	Dark	40	100	10

MOVE TUTOR LIST
Move Name	Type	ST	ACC	PP
Body Slam*	Normal	85	100	15
Counter*	Fighting	—	100	20
Double-Edge*	Normal	120	100	15
Dynamicpunch	Fighting	100	50	5
Endure*	Normal	—	—	10
Fire Punch*	Fire	75	100	15
Ice Punch*	Ice	75	100	15
Mega Kick*	Normal	120	85	5
Mega Punch*	Normal	80	75	20
Metronome	Normal	—	—	10
Mimic	Normal	—	100	10
Mud-Slap*	Ground	20	100	10
Rock Slide*	Rock	75	90	10
Seismic Toss*	Fighting	—	100	20
Sleep Talk	Normal	—	—	10
Snore*	Normal	40	100	15
Substitute	Normal	—	—	10
Swagger	Normal	—	90	15
Thunderpunch*	Electric	75	100	15

*Battle Frontier tutor move

---

076 Meditite™
FIGHTING
PSYCHIC

GENERAL INFO
SPECIES: Meditate Pokémon
HEIGHT: 2'0"
WEIGHT: 25 lbs.
ABILITY: *Pure Power*—Increases the Pokémon's Attack Power in battle.

STATS
HP	25
ATTACK	50
DEFENSE	50
SP. ATTACK	50
SP. DEFENSE	50
SPEED	50

EVOLUTIONS

LV37

WHERE/HOW TO CATCH
Must trade from *Pokémon Ruby* or *Pokémon Colosseum*

STRONG AGAINST:
FIGHTING
ROCK

WEAK AGAINST:
FLYING
GHOST

MOVES LIST
LV	Move Name	Type	ST	ACC	PP
S	Bide	Normal	—	100	10
04	Meditate	Psychic	—	—	40
09	Confusion	Psychic	50	100	25
12	Detect	Fighting	—	—	5
18	Hidden Power	Normal	—	100	15
25	Mind Reader	Normal	—	100	5
28	Calm Mind	Psychic	—	—	20
33	Hi Jump Kick	Fighting	85	90	20
36	Psych Up	Normal	—	—	10
41	Reversal	Fighting	—	100	15
44	Recover	Normal	—	—	20

TM/HM LIST
TM/HM #	Move Name	Type	ST	ACC	PP
HM04	Strength	Normal	80	100	15
HM05	Flash	Normal	—	70	20
HM06	Rock Smash	Fighting	20	100	15
TM01	Focus Punch	Fighting	150	100	20
TM04	Calm Mind	Psychic	—	—	20
TM06	Toxic	Poison	—	85	10
TM08	Bulk Up	Fighting	—	—	20
TM10	Hidden Power	Normal	—	100	15
TM11	Sunny Day	Fire	—	—	5
TM16	Light Screen	Psychic	—	—	30
TM17	Protect	Normal	—	—	10
TM18	Rain Dance	Water	—	—	5
TM21	Frustration	Normal	—	100	20
TM27	Return	Normal	—	100	20
TM29	Psychic	Psychic	90	100	10
TM30	Shadow Ball	Ghost	60	—	20
TM31	Brick Break	Fighting	75	100	15
TM32	Double Team	Normal	—	—	15
TM33	Reflect	Psychic	—	—	20
TM39	Rock Tomb	Rock	50	80	10
TM42	Facade	Normal	70	100	20
TM43	Secret Power	Normal	70	100	20
TM44	Rest	Psychic	—	—	10
TM45	Attract	Normal	—	100	15

EGG MOVES
Move Name	Type	ST	ACC	PP
Fire Punch	Fire	75	100	15
Thunderpunch	Electric	75	100	15
Ice Punch	Ice	75	100	15
Foresight	Normal	—	100	40
Fake Out	Normal	40	100	10
Baton Pass	Normal	—	—	40
Dynamicpunch	Fighting	100	50	5

MOVE TUTOR LIST
Move Name	Type	ST	ACC	PP
Body Slam*	Normal	85	100	15
Counter*	Fighting	—	100	20
Double-Edge*	Normal	120	100	15
Dream Eater*	Psychic	100	100	15
Dynamicpunch	Fighting	100	50	5
Endure*	Normal	—	—	10
Fire Punch*	Fire	75	100	15
Ice Punch*	Ice	75	100	15
Mega Kick*	Normal	120	85	5
Mega Punch*	Normal	80	75	20
Metronome	Normal	—	—	10
Mimic	Normal	—	100	10
Mud-Slap*	Ground	20	100	10
Psych Up*	Normal	—	—	10
Seismic Toss*	Fighting	—	100	20
Sleep Talk	Normal	—	—	10
Snore*	Normal	40	100	15
Substitute	Normal	—	—	10
Swagger	Normal	—	90	15
Swift*	Normal	60	—	20
Thunderpunch*	Electric	75	100	15

*Battle Frontier tutor move

077

Medicham™

FIGHTING
PSYCHIC

GENERAL INFO
SPECIES: **Meditate Pokémon**
HEIGHT: **4'3"**
WEIGHT: **69 lbs.**
ABILITY: **Pure Power** — *Increases the Pokémon's Attack Power in battle.*

STATS

HP	50
ATTACK	50
DEFENSE	50
SP. ATTACK	50
SP. DEFENSE	50
SPEED	75

EVOLUTIONS

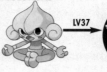 LV37

WHERE/HOW TO CATCH
Evolve from Meditite; must trade from *Pokémon Ruby* or *Pokémon Colosseum*

STRONG AGAINST:
FIGHTING
ROCK

WEAK AGAINST:
FLYING
GHOST

MOVES LIST

LV	Move Name	Type	ST	ACC	PP
S	Fire Punch	Fire	75	100	15
S	Thunderpunch	Electric	75	100	15
S	Ice Punch	Ice	75	100	15
S	Bide	Normal	—	100	10
S	Meditate	Psychic	—	—	40
S	Confusion	Psychic	50	100	25
S	Detect	Fighting	—	—	5
04	Meditate	Psychic	—	—	40
09	Confusion	Psychic	50	100	25

LV	Move Name	Type	ST	ACC	PP
12	Detect	Fighting	—	—	5
17	Hidden Power	Normal	—	100	15
25	Mind Reader	Normal	—	100	5
28	Calm Mind	Psychic	—	—	20
33	Hi Jump Kick	Fighting	85	90	20
36	Psych Up	Normal	—	—	10
44	Reversal	Fighting	—	100	15
56	Recover	Normal	—	—	20

TM/HM LIST

TM/HM #	Move Name	Type	ST	ACC	PP
HM04	Strength	Normal	80	100	15
HM05	Flash	Normal	—	70	20
HM06	Rock Smash	Fighting	20	100	15
TM01	Focus Punch	Fighting	150	100	20
TM04	Calm Mind	Psychic	—	—	20
TM06	Toxic	Poison	—	85	10
TM08	Bulk Up	Fighting	—	—	20
TM10	Hidden Power	Normal	—	100	15
TM11	Sunny Day	Fire	—	—	5
TM15	Hyper Beam	Normal	150	90	5
TM16	Light Screen	Psychic	—	—	30
TM17	Protect	Normal	—	—	10
TM18	Rain Dance	Water	—	—	5

TM/HM #	Move Name	Type	ST	ACC	PP
TM21	Frustration	Normal	—	100	20
TM27	Return	Normal	—	100	20
TM29	Psychic	Psychic	90	100	10
TM30	Shadow Ball	Ghost	60	—	20
TM31	Brick Break	Fighting	75	100	15
TM32	Double Team	Normal	—	—	15
TM33	Reflect	Psychic	—	—	20
TM39	Rock Tomb	Rock	50	80	10
TM42	Façade	Normal	70	100	20
TM43	Secret Power	Normal	70	100	20
TM44	Rest	Psychic	—	—	10
TM45	Attract	Normal	—	100	15

MOVE TUTOR LIST

Move Name	Type	ST	ACC	PP
Body Slam*	Normal	85	100	15
Counter*	Fighting	—	100	20
Double-Edge	Normal	120	100	15
Dream Eater*	Psychic	100	100	15
Dynamicpunch*	Fighting	100	50	5
Endure*	Normal	—	—	10
Fire Punch*	Fire	75	100	15
Ice Punch*	Ice	75	100	15
Mega Kick*	Normal	120	85	5
Mega Punch*	Normal	80	75	20
Metronome	Normal	—	100	10
Mimic	Normal	—	100	10
Mud-Slap*	Ground	20	100	10
Psych Up*	Normal	—	—	10
Rock Slide*	Rock	75	90	10
Seismic Toss*	Fighting	—	100	10
Sleep Talk*	Normal	—	—	10
Snore*	Normal	40	100	15
Substitute	Normal	—	—	10
Swagger	Normal	—	90	15
Swift*	Normal	60	—	20
Thunderpunch*	Electric	75	100	15
Thunder Wave*	Electric	—	100	20

*Battle Frontier tutor move

078

Electrike™

ELECTRIC

GENERAL INFO
SPECIES: **Lightning Pokémon**
HEIGHT: **2'0"**
WEIGHT: **34 lbs.**
ABILITIES: **Static** — *Gives the Pokémon's Physical Attacks a 30 percent chance of inflicting Paralysis on the opponent.*
Lightningrod — *Draws Electric-type Moves to itself.*

STATS

HP	25
ATTACK	50
DEFENSE	25
SP. ATTACK	50
SP. DEFENSE	25
SPEED	50

EVOLUTIONS

 LV26

WHERE/HOW TO CATCH
Routes 110 and 118

STRONG AGAINST:
ELECTRIC
FLYING
STEEL

WEAK AGAINST:
GROUND

MOVES LIST

LV	Move Name	Type	ST	ACC	PP
S	Tackle	Normal	35	95	35
04	Thunder Wave	Electric	—	100	20
09	Leer	Normal	—	100	30
12	Howl	Normal	—	—	40
17	Quick Attack	Normal	40	100	30
20	Spark	Electric	65	100	20

LV	Move Name	Type	ST	ACC	PP
25	Odor Sleuth	Normal	—	100	40
28	Roar	Normal	—	100	20
33	Bite	Dark	60	100	25
36	Thunder	Electric	120	70	10
41	Charge	Electric	—	100	20

TM/HM LIST

TM/HM #	Move Name	Type	ST	ACC	PP
HM04	Strength	Normal	80	100	15
HM05	Flash	Normal	—	70	20
TM05	Roar	Normal	—	100	20
TM06	Toxic	Poison	—	85	10
TM10	Hidden Power	Normal	—	100	15
TM15	Hyper Beam	Normal	150	90	5
TM17	Protect	Normal	—	—	10
TM18	Rain Dance	Water	—	—	5
TM21	Frustration	Normal	—	100	20
TM23	Iron Tail	Steel	100	75	15

TM/HM #	Move Name	Type	ST	ACC	PP
TM24	Thunderbolt	Electric	95	100	15
TM25	Thunder	Electric	120	70	10
TM27	Return	Normal	—	100	20
TM32	Double Team	Normal	—	—	15
TM34	Shock Wave	Electric	60	—	20
TM42	Façade	Normal	70	100	20
TM43	Secret Power	Normal	70	100	20
TM44	Rest	Psychic	—	—	10
TM45	Attract	Normal	—	100	15
TM46	Thief	Dark	40	100	10

EGG MOVES

Move Name	Type	ST	ACC	PP
Crunch	Dark	80	100	15
Curse	—	—	—	10
Headbutt	Normal	70	100	15
Swift	Normal	60	—	20
Uproar	Normal	50	100	10

MOVE TUTOR LIST

Move Name	Type	ST	ACC	PP
Body Slam*	Normal	85	100	15
Double-Edge	Normal	120	100	15
Endure*	Normal	—	—	10
Mimic	Normal	—	100	10
Mud-Slap*	Ground	20	100	10
Sleep Talk*	Normal	—	—	10
Snore*	Normal	40	100	15
Substitute	Normal	—	—	10
Swagger	Normal	—	90	15
Swift*	Normal	60	—	20
Thunder Wave*	Electric	—	100	20

*Battle Frontier tutor move

079 Manectric™

ELECTRIC

GENERAL INFO
SPECIES: Discharge Pokémon
HEIGHT: 4'11"
WEIGHT: 89 lbs.
ABILITIES: *Static*—*Gives the Pokémon's Physical Attacks a 30 percent chance of inflicting Paralysis on the opponent.*
Lightningrod—*Draws Electric-type Moves to itself.*

STATS

HP	50
ATTACK	75
DEFENSE	50
SP. ATTACK	75
SP. DEFENSE	50
SPEED	75

EVOLUTIONS

 LV26

WHERE/HOW TO CATCH
Evolve from Electrike; Route 118

STRONG AGAINST:
ELECTRIC
FLYING
STEEL

WEAK AGAINST:
GROUND

MOVES LIST

LV	Move Name	Type	ST	ACC	PP
S	Tackle	Normal	35	95	35
S	Thunder Wave	Electric	—	100	20
S	Leer	Normal	—	100	30
S	Howl	Normal	—	—	40
04	Thunder Wave	Electric	—	100	20
09	Leer	Normal	—	100	30
12	Howl	Normal	—	—	40

LV	Move Name	Type	ST	ACC	PP
17	Quick Attack	Normal	40	100	30
20	Spark	Electric	65	100	20
25	Odor Sleuth	Normal	—	100	40
31	Roar	Normal	—	100	20
39	Bite	Dark	60	100	25
45	Thunder	Electric	120	70	10
53	Charge	Electric	—	100	20

TM/HM LIST

TM/HM #	Move Name	Type	ST	ACC	PP
HM04	Strength	Normal	80	100	15
HM05	Flash	Normal	—	70	20
TM05	Roar	Normal	—	100	20
TM06	Toxic	Poison	—	85	10
TM10	Hidden Power	Normal	—	100	15
TM15	Hyper Beam	Normal	150	90	5
TM17	Protect	Normal	—	—	10
TM18	Rain Dance	Water	—	—	5
TM21	Frustration	Normal	—	100	20
TM23	Iron Tail	Steel	100	75	15

TM/HM #	Move Name	Type	ST	ACC	PP
TM24	Thunderbolt	Electric	95	100	15
TM25	Thunder	Electric	120	70	10
TM27	Return	Normal	—	100	20
TM32	Double Team	Normal	—	—	15
TM34	Shock Wave	Electric	60	—	20
TM42	Façade	Normal	70	100	20
TM43	Secret Power	Normal	70	100	20
TM44	Rest	Psychic	—	—	10
TM45	Attract	Normal	—	100	15
TM46	Thief	Dark	40	100	10

MOVE TUTOR LIST

Move Name	Type	ST	ACC	PP
Body Slam*	Normal	85	100	15
Double-Edge	Normal	120	100	15
Endure*	Normal	—	—	10
Mimic	Normal	—	100	10
Mud-Slap*	Ground	20	100	10
Sleep Talk	Normal	—	—	10
Snore*	Normal	40	100	15
Substitute	Normal	—	—	10
Swagger	Normal	—	90	15
Swift*	Normal	60	—	20
Thunder Wave*	Electric	—	100	20

*Battle Frontier tutor move

---

080 Plusle™

ELECTRIC

GENERAL INFO
SPECIES: Cheering Pokémon
HEIGHT: 1'4"
WEIGHT: 9 lbs.
ABILITY: *Plus*—*Increases Special Attack 1.5x when faced with a Pokémon with the Minus Ability in battle.*

STATS

HP	50
ATTACK	50
DEFENSE	25
SP. ATTACK	75
SP. DEFENSE	50
SPEED	75

EVOLUTIONS

PLUSLE DOES NOT EVOLVE

WHERE/HOW TO CATCH
Route 110

STRONG AGAINST:
ELECTRIC
FLYING
STEEL

WEAK AGAINST:
GROUND

MOVES LIST

LV	Move Name	Type	ST	ACC	PP
S	Growl	Normal	—	100	40
04	Thunder Wave	Electric	—	100	20
10	Quick Attack	Normal	40	100	30
13	Helping Hand	Normal	—	100	20
19	Spark	Electric	65	100	20
22	Encore	Normal	—	100	5

LV	Move Name	Type	ST	ACC	PP
28	Fake Tears	Dark	—	100	20
31	Charge	Electric	—	100	20
37	Thunder	Electric	120	70	10
40	Baton Pass	Normal	—	—	40
47	Agility	Psychic	—	—	30

TM/HM LIST

TM/HM #	Move Name	Type	ST	ACC	PP
HM05	Flash	Normal	—	70	20
TM06	Toxic	Poison	—	85	10
TM10	Hidden Power	Normal	—	100	15
TM16	Light Screen	Psychic	—	—	30
TM17	Protect	Normal	—	—	10
TM18	Rain Dance	Water	—	—	5
TM21	Frustration	Normal	—	100	20
TM23	Iron Tail	Steel	100	75	15
TM24	Thunderbolt	Electric	95	100	15

TM/HM #	Move Name	Type	ST	ACC	PP
TM25	Thunder	Electric	120	70	10
TM27	Return	Normal	—	100	20
TM32	Double Team	Normal	—	—	15
TM34	Shock Wave	Electric	60	—	20
TM42	Façade	Normal	70	100	20
TM43	Secret Power	Normal	70	100	20
TM44	Rest	Psychic	—	—	10
TM45	Attract	Normal	—	100	15

EGG MOVES

Move Name	Type	ST	ACC	PP
Substitute	Normal	—	—	10
Wish	Normal	—	100	10

MOVE TUTOR LIST

Move Name	Type	ST	ACC	PP
Body Slam*	Normal	85	100	15
Counter*	Fighting	—	100	20
Defense Curl*	Normal	—	—	40
Double-Edge	Normal	120	100	15
Dynamicpunch	Fighting	100	50	5
Endure*	Normal	—	—	10
Mega Kick*	Normal	120	85	5
Mega Punch*	Normal	80	75	20
Metronome	Normal	—	100	10
Mimic	Normal	—	100	10
Mud-Slap*	Ground	20	100	10
Rollout	Rock	30	90	20
Seismic Toss*	Fighting	—	100	20
Sleep Talk	Normal	—	—	10
Snore*	Normal	40	100	15
Substitute	Normal	—	—	10
Swagger	Normal	—	90	15
Swift*	Normal	60	—	20
Thunderpunch*	Electric	75	100	15
Thunder Wave*	Electric	—	100	20

*Battle Frontier tutor move

081 Minun™

ELECTRIC

GENERAL INFO
SPECIES: Cheering Pokémon
HEIGHT: 1'4"
WEIGHT: 9 lbs.
ABILITY: *Minus*—Increases
Special Attack 1.5x when faced with a
Pokémon with the Plus Ability in battle.

STATS
HP	50
ATTACK	50
DEFENSE	50
SP. ATTACK	75
SP. DEFENSE	50
SPEED	75

EVOLUTIONS

MINUN DOES NOT EVOLVE

WHERE/HOW TO CATCH
Route 110

STRONG AGAINST:
ELECTRIC
FLYING
STEEL

WEAK AGAINST:
GROUND

MOVES LIST
LV	Move Name	Type	ST	ACC	PP	LV	Move Name	Type	ST	ACC	PP
S	Growl	Normal	—	100	40	28	Charm	Normal	—	100	20
04	Thunder Wave	Electric	—	100	20	31	Charge	Electric	—	100	20
10	Quick Attack	Normal	40	100	30	37	Thunder	Electric	120	70	10
13	Helping Hand	Normal	—	100	20	40	Baton Pass	Normal	—	—	40
19	Spark	Electric	65	100	20	47	Agility	Psychic	—	—	30
22	Encore	Normal	—	100	5						

TM/HM LIST
TM/HM #	Move Name	Type	ST	ACC	PP	TM/HM #	Move Name	Type	ST	ACC	PP
HM05	Flash	Normal	—	70	20	TM25	Thunder	Electric	120	70	10
TM06	Toxic	Poison	—	85	10	TM27	Return	Normal	—	100	20
TM10	Hidden Power	Normal	—	100	15	TM32	Double Team	Normal	—	—	15
TM16	Light Screen	Psychic	—	—	30	TM34	Shock Wave	Electric	60	—	20
TM17	Protect	Normal	—	—	10	TM42	Façade	Normal	70	100	20
TM18	Rain Dance	Water	—	—	5	TM43	Secret Power	Normal	70	100	20
TM21	Frustration	Normal	—	100	20	TM44	Rest	Psychic	—	—	10
TM23	Iron Tail	Steel	100	75	15	TM45	Attract	Normal	—	100	15
TM24	Thunderbolt	Electric	95	100	15						

EGG MOVES
Move Name	Type	ST	ACC	PP
Substitute	Normal	—	—	10
Wish	Normal	—	100	10

MOVE TUTOR LIST
Move Name	Type	ST	ACC	PP
Body Slam*	Normal	85	100	15
Counter*	Fighting	—	100	20
Defense Curl*	Normal	—	—	40
Double-Edge	Normal	120	100	15
Dynamicpunch*	Fighting	100	50	5
Endure*	Normal	—	—	10
Mega Kick*	Normal	120	85	5
Mega Punch*	Normal	80	75	20
Metronome	Normal	—	100	10
Mimic	Normal	—	100	10
Mud-Slap*	Ground	20	100	10
Rollout	Rock	30	90	20
Seismic Toss*	Fighting	—	100	20
Sleep Talk	Normal	—	—	10
Snore*	Normal	40	100	15
Substitute	Normal	—	—	10
Swagger	Normal	—	90	15
Swift*	Normal	60	—	20
Thunderpunch*	Electric	75	100	15
Thunder Wave*	Electric	—	100	20

*Battle Frontier tutor move

082 Magnemite™

ELECTRIC
STEEL

GENERAL INFO
SPECIES: Magnet Pokémon
HEIGHT: 1'0"
WEIGHT: 13 lbs.
ABILITIES: *Magnet Pull*—Prevents
Steel-type Pokémon from fleeing in battle.
Sturdy—One hit KO moves have no effect.

STATS
HP	33
ATTACK	33
DEFENSE	66
SP. ATTACK	100
SP. DEFENSE	30
SPEED	33

EVOLUTIONS

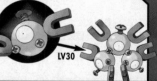

LV30

WHERE/HOW TO CATCH
New Mauville

STRONG AGAINST:
NORMAL
ELECTRIC
GRASS
ICE
POISON
FLYING
PSYCHIC
BUG
ROCK
GHOST
DRAGON
DARK
STEEL

WEAK AGAINST:
FIRE
FIGHTING
GROUND

MOVES LIST
LV	Move Name	Type	ST	ACC	PP	LV	Move Name	Type	ST	ACC	PP
S	Metal Sound	Steel	—	85	40	26	Spark	Electric	65	100	20
S	Tackle	Normal	35	95	35	32	Lock-On	Normal	—	100	5
06	Thundershock	Electric	40	100	30	38	Swift	Normal	60	—	20
11	Supersonic	Normal	—	55	20	44	Screech	Normal	—	85	40
16	Sonicboom	Normal	—	90	20	50	Zap Cannon	Electric	100	50	5
21	Thunder Wave	Electric	—	100	20						

TM/HM LIST
TM/HM #	Move Name	Type	ST	ACC	PP	TM/HM #	Move Name	Type	ST	ACC	PP
HM05	Flash	Normal	—	70	20	TM25	Thunder	Electric	120	70	10
TM06	Toxic	Poison	—	85	10	TM27	Return	Normal	—	100	20
TM10	Hidden Power	Normal	—	100	15	TM32	Double Team	Normal	—	—	15
TM11	Sunny Day	Fire	—	—	5	TM33	Reflect	Psychic	—	—	20
TM17	Protect	Normal	—	—	10	TM34	Shock Wave	Electric	60	—	20
TM18	Rain Dance	Water	—	—	5	TM42	Façade	Normal	70	100	20
TM21	Frustration	Normal	—	100	20	TM43	Secret Power	Normal	70	100	20
TM24	Thunderbolt	Electric	95	100	15	TM44	Rest	Psychic	—	—	10

EGG MOVES
Move Name	Type	ST	ACC	PP
None				

MOVE TUTOR LIST
Move Name	Type	ST	ACC	PP
Double-Edge	Normal	120	100	15
Endure*	Normal	—	—	10
Mimic	Normal	—	100	10
Rollout	Rock	30	90	20
Sleep Talk	Normal	—	—	10
Snore*	Normal	40	100	15
Substitute	Normal	—	—	10
Swagger	Normal	—	90	15
Swift*	Normal	60	—	20
Thunder Wave*	Electric	—	100	20

*Battle Frontier tutor move

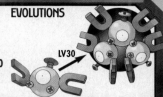

083 Magneton™

ELECTRIC
STEEL

GENERAL INFO
SPECIES: Magnet Pokémon
HEIGHT: 3'3"
WEIGHT: 132 lbs.
ABILITIES: *Magnet Pull*—Prevents Steel-type Pokémon from fleeing in battle.
Sturdy—One hit KO moves have no effect.

STATS
HP	33
ATTACK	66
DEFENSE	66
SP. ATTACK	100
SP. DEFENSE	66
SPEED	66

EVOLUTIONS
LV30

WHERE/HOW TO CATCH
Evolve from Magnemite; New Mauville

STRONG AGAINST:
NORMAL
ELECTRIC
GRASS
ICE
POISON
FLYING
PSYCHIC
BUG
ROCK
GHOST
DRAGON
DARK
STEEL

WEAK AGAINST:
FIRE
FIGHTING
GROUND

MOVES LIST
LV	Move Name	Type	ST	ACC	PP
S	Metal Sound	Steel	—	85	40
S	Tackle	Normal	35	95	35
S	Thundershock	Electric	40	100	30
S	Supersonic	Normal	—	55	20
06	Thundershock	Electric	40	100	30
11	Supersonic	Normal	—	55	20
16	Sonicboom	Normal	—	90	20

LV	Move Name	Type	ST	ACC	PP
21	Thunder Wave	Electric	—	100	20
26	Spark	Electric	65	100	20
35	Lock-On	Normal	—	100	5
44	Tri Attack	Normal	80	100	10
53	Screech	Normal	—	85	40
62	Zap Cannon	Electric	100	50	5

TM/HM LIST
TM/HM #	Move Name	Type	ST	ACC	PP
HM05	Flash	Normal	—	70	20
TM06	Toxic	Poison	—	85	10
TM10	Hidden Power	Normal	—	100	15
TM11	Sunny Day	Fire	—	—	5
TM15	Hyper Beam	Normal	150	90	5
TM17	Protect	Normal	—	—	10
TM18	Rain Dance	Water	—	—	5
TM21	Frustration	Normal	—	100	20
TM24	Thunderbolt	Electric	95	100	15

TM/HM #	Move Name	Type	ST	ACC	PP
TM25	Thunder	Electric	120	70	10
TM27	Return	Normal	—	100	20
TM32	Double Team	Normal	—	—	15
TM33	Reflect	Psychic	—	—	20
TM34	Shock Wave	Electric	60	—	20
TM42	Façade	Normal	70	100	20
TM43	Secret Power	Normal	70	100	20
TM44	Rest	Psychic	—	—	10

MOVE TUTOR LIST
Move Name	Type	ST	ACC	PP
Double-Edge	Normal	120	100	15
Endure*	Normal	—	—	10
Mimic	Normal	—	100	10
Rollout	Rock	30	90	20
Sleep Talk	Normal	—	—	10
Snore*	Normal	40	100	15
Substitute	Normal	—	—	10
Swagger	Normal	—	90	15
Swift*	Normal	60	—	20
Thunder Wave*	Electric	—	100	20

*Battle Frontier tutor move

---

084 Voltorb™

ELECTRIC

GENERAL INFO
SPECIES: Ball Pokémon
HEIGHT: 1'8"
WEIGHT: 23 lbs.
ABILITIES: *Soundproof*—Pokémon is unaffected by loud moves such as Roar and Sing.
Static—Gives the Pokémon's Physical Attacks a 30 percent chance of inflicting Paralysis on the opponent.

STATS
HP	33
ATTACK	33
DEFENSE	33
SP. ATTACK	66
SP. DEFENSE	33
SPEED	100

EVOLUTIONS
LV30

WHERE/HOW TO CATCH
New Mauville

STRONG AGAINST:
ELECTRIC
FLYING
STEEL

WEAK AGAINST:
GROUND

MOVES LIST
LV	Move Name	Type	ST	ACC	PP
S	Charge	Electric	—	100	20
S	Tackle	Normal	35	95	35
08	Screech	Normal	—	85	40
15	Sonicboom	Normal	—	90	20
21	Spark	Electric	65	100	20
27	Selfdestruct	Normal	200	100	5

LV	Move Name	Type	ST	ACC	PP
32	Rollout	Rock	30	90	20
37	Light Screen	Psychic	—	—	30
42	Swift	Normal	60	—	20
46	Explosion	Normal	250	100	5
49	Mirror Coat	Psychic	—	100	20

TM/HM LIST
TM/HM #	Move Name	Type	ST	ACC	PP
HM05	Flash	Normal	—	70	20
TM06	Toxic	Poison	—	85	10
TM10	Hidden Power	Normal	—	100	15
TM12	Taunt	Dark	—	100	20
TM16	Light Screen	Psychic	—	—	30
TM17	Protect	Normal	—	—	10
TM18	Rain Dance	Water	—	—	5
TM21	Frustration	Normal	—	100	20
TM24	Thunderbolt	Electric	95	100	15

TM/HM #	Move Name	Type	ST	ACC	PP
TM25	Thunder	Electric	120	70	10
TM27	Return	Normal	—	100	20
TM32	Double Team	Normal	—	—	15
TM34	Shock Wave	Electric	60	—	20
TM41	Torment	Dark	—	100	15
TM42	Façade	Normal	70	100	20
TM43	Secret Power	Normal	70	100	20
TM44	Rest	Psychic	—	—	10
TM46	Thief	Dark	40	100	10

EGG MOVES
Move Name	Type	ST	ACC	PP
None				

MOVE TUTOR LIST
Move Name	Type	ST	ACC	PP
Endure*	Normal	—	—	10
Explosion	Normal	250	100	5
Mimic	Normal	—	100	10
Rollout	Rock	30	90	20
Sleep Talk	Normal	—	—	10
Snore*	Normal	40	100	15
Substitute	Normal	—	—	10
Swagger	Normal	—	90	15
Swift*	Normal	60	—	20
Thunder Wave*	Electric	—	100	20

*Battle Frontier tutor move

085 Electrode™

ELECTRIC

GENERAL INFO
SPECIES: **Ball Pokémon**
HEIGHT: **3'11"**
WEIGHT: **147 lbs.**
ABILITIES: *Soundproof*—*Pokémon is unaffected by loud moves such as Roar and Sing.*
Static—*Gives the Pokémon's Physical Attacks a 30 percent chance of inflicting Paralysis on the opponent.*

STATS

HP	33
ATTACK	33
DEFENSE	66
SP. ATTACK	66
SP. DEFENSE	66
SPEED	100

EVOLUTIONS

LV30

WHERE/HOW TO CATCH
Evolve from Voltorb; New Mauville

STRONG AGAINST:
ELECTRIC
FLYING
STEEL

WEAK AGAINST:
GROUND

MOVES LIST

LV	Move Name	Type	ST	ACC	PP		LV	Move Name	Type	ST	ACC	PP
S	Charge	Electric	—	100	20		27	Selfdestruct	Normal	200	100	5
S	Tackle	Normal	35	95	35		34	Rollout	Rock	30	90	20
S	Screech	Normal	—	85	40		41	Light Screen	Psychic	—	—	30
S	Sonicboom	Normal	—	90	20		48	Swift	Normal	60	—	20
08	Screech	Normal	—	85	40		54	Explosion	Normal	250	100	5
15	Sonicboom	Normal	—	90	20		59	Mirror Coat	Psychic	—	100	20
21	Spark	Electric	65	100	20							

TM/HM LIST

TM/HM #	Move Name	Type	ST	ACC	PP		TM/HM #	Move Name	Type	ST	ACC	PP
HM05	Flash	Normal	—	70	20		TM25	Thunder	Electric	120	70	10
TM06	Toxic	Poison	—	85	10		TM27	Return	Normal	—	100	20
TM10	Hidden Power	Normal	—	100	15		TM32	Double Team	Normal	—	—	15
TM12	Taunt	Dark	—	100	20		TM34	Shock Wave	Electric	60	—	20
TM15	Hyper Beam	Normal	150	90	5		TM41	Torment	Dark	—	100	15
TM16	Light Screen	Psychic	—	—	30		TM42	Façade	Normal	70	100	20
TM17	Protect	Normal	—	—	10		TM43	Secret Power	Normal	70	100	20
TM18	Rain Dance	Water	—	—	5		TM44	Rest	Psychic	—	—	10
TM21	Frustration	Normal	—	100	20		TM46	Thief	Dark	40	100	10
TM24	Thunderbolt	Electric	95	100	15							

MOVE TUTOR LIST

Move Name	Type	ST	ACC	PP
Endure*	Normal	—	—	10
Explosion	Normal	250	100	5
Mimic	Normal	—	100	10
Rollout	Rock	30	90	20
Sleep Talk	Normal	—	—	10
Snore*	Normal	40	100	15
Substitute	Normal	—	—	10
Swagger	Normal	—	90	15
Swift*	Normal	60	—	20
Thunder Wave*	Electric	—	100	20

*Battle Frontier tutor move

086 Volbeat™

BUG

GENERAL INFO
SPECIES: **Firefly Pokémon**
HEIGHT: **2'4"**
WEIGHT: **39 lbs.**
ABILITIES: *Illuminate*—*Increases the chance of encountering wild Pokémon.*
Swarm—*When the Pokémon's HP falls below 1/3, the power of Bug-type Moves increases 1.5x.*

STATS

HP	50
ATTACK	50
DEFENSE	50
SP. ATTACK	50
SP. DEFENSE	50
SPEED	75

EVOLUTIONS

VOLBEAT DOES NOT EVOLVE

WHERE/HOW TO CATCH
Route 117

STRONG AGAINST:
GRASS
FIGHTING
GROUND

WEAK AGAINST:
FIRE
FLYING
ROCK

MOVES LIST

LV	Move Name	Type	ST	ACC	PP		LV	Move Name	Type	ST	ACC	PP
S	Tackle	Normal	35	95	35		21	Tail Glow	Bug	—	100	20
05	Confuse Ray	Ghost	—	100	10		25	Signal Beam	Bug	75	100	15
09	Double Team	Normal	—	—	15		29	Protect	Normal	—	—	10
13	Moonlight	Normal	—	—	5		33	Helping Hand	Normal	—	100	20
17	Quick Attack	Normal	40	100	30		37	Double-Edge	Normal	120	100	15

TM/HM LIST

TM/HM #	Move Name	Type	ST	ACC	PP		TM/HM #	Move Name	Type	ST	ACC	PP
HM05	Flash	Normal	—	70	20		TM25	Thunder	Electric	120	70	10
TM01	Focus Punch	Fighting	150	100	20		TM27	Return	Normal	—	100	20
TM03	Water Pulse	Water	60	100	20		TM30	Shadow Ball	Ghost	60	—	20
TM06	Toxic	Poison	—	85	10		TM31	Brick Break	Fighting	75	100	15
TM10	Hidden Power	Normal	—	100	15		TM32	Double Team	Normal	—	—	15
TM11	Sunny Day	Fire	—	—	5		TM34	Shock Wave	Electric	60	—	20
TM16	Light Screen	Psychic	—	—	30		TM40	Aerial Ace	Flying	60	—	20
TM17	Protect	Normal	—	—	10		TM42	Façade	Normal	70	100	20
TM18	Rain Dance	Water	—	—	5		TM43	Secret Power	Normal	70	100	20
TM19	Giga Drain	Grass	60	100	5		TM44	Rest	Psychic	—	—	10
TM21	Frustration	Normal	—	100	20		TM45	Attract	Normal	—	100	15
TM22	Solarbeam	Grass	120	100	10		TM46	Thief	Dark	40	100	10
TM24	Thunderbolt	Electric	95	100	15							

EGG MOVES

Move Name	Type	ST	ACC	PP
Baton Pass	Normal	—	—	40
Silver Wind	Bug	60	100	5
Trick	Psychic	—	100	10

MOVE TUTOR LIST

Move Name	Type	ST	ACC	PP
Body Slam*	Normal	85	100	15
Counter*	Fighting	—	100	20
Double-Edge	Normal	120	100	15
Dynamicpunch	Fighting	100	50	5
Endure*	Normal	—	—	10
Ice Punch*	Ice	75	100	15
Mega Kick*	Normal	120	85	5
Mega Punch*	Normal	80	75	20
Metronome	Normal	—	100	10
Mimic	Normal	—	100	10
Mud-Slap*	Ground	20	100	10
Psych Up*	Normal	—	—	10
Seismic Toss*	Fighting	—	100	20
Sleep Talk	Normal	—	—	10
Snore*	Normal	40	100	15
Substitute	Normal	—	—	10
Swagger	Normal	—	90	15
Swift*	Normal	60	—	20
Thunderpunch*	Electric	75	100	15
Thunder Wave*	Electric	—	100	20

*Battle Frontier tutor move

087 Illumise

BUG

GENERAL INFO
SPECIES: Firefly Pokémon
HEIGHT: 2'0"
WEIGHT: 39 lbs.
ABILITY: *Oblivious — Pokémon is not affected by the Attract condition.*

STATS
HP	50
ATTACK	50
DEFENSE	50
SP. ATTACK	50
SP. DEFENSE	50
SPEED	75

EVOLUTIONS

ILLUMISE DOES NOT EVOLVE

WHERE/HOW TO CATCH
Route 117

STRONG AGAINST:
GRASS
FIGHTING
GROUND

WEAK AGAINST:
FIRE
FLYING
ROCK

MOVES LIST
LV	Move Name	Type	ST	ACC	PP	LV	Move Name	Type	ST	ACC	PP
S	Tackle	Normal	35	95	35	21	Wish	Normal	—	100	10
05	Sweet Scent	Normal	—	100	20	25	Encore	Normal	—	100	5
09	Charm	Normal	—	100	20	29	Flatter	Dark	—	100	15
13	Moonlight	Normal	—	—	5	33	Helping Hand	Normal	—	100	20
17	Quick Attack	Normal	40	100	30	37	Covet	Normal	40	100	40

TM/HM LIST
TM/HM #	Move Name	Type	ST	ACC	PP	TM/HM #	Move Name	Type	ST	ACC	PP
HM05	Flash	Normal	—	70	20	TM25	Thunder	Electric	120	70	10
TM01	Focus Punch	Fighting	150	100	20	TM27	Return	Normal	—	100	20
TM03	Water Pulse	Water	60	100	20	TM30	Shadow Ball	Ghost	60	—	20
TM06	Toxic	Poison	—	85	10	TM31	Brick Break	Fighting	75	100	15
TM10	Hidden Power	Normal	—	100	15	TM32	Double Team	Normal	—	—	15
TM11	Sunny Day	Fire	—	—	5	TM34	Shock Wave	Electric	60	—	20
TM16	Light Screen	Psychic	—	—	30	TM40	Aerial Ace	Flying	60	—	20
TM17	Protect	Normal	—	—	10	TM42	Façade	Normal	70	100	20
TM18	Rain Dance	Water	—	—	5	TM43	Secret Power	Normal	70	100	20
TM19	Giga Drain	Grass	60	100	5	TM44	Rest	Psychic	—	—	10
TM21	Frustration	Normal	—	100	20	TM45	Attract	Normal	—	100	15
TM22	Solarbeam	Grass	120	100	10	TM46	Thief	Dark	40	100	10
TM24	Thunderbolt	Electric	95	100	15						

EGG MOVES
Move Name	Type	ST	ACC	PP
Baton Pass	Normal	—	—	40
Silver Wind	Bug	60	100	5
Growth	Normal	—	—	40

MOVE TUTOR LIST
Move Name	Type	ST	ACC	PP
Body Slam*	Normal	85	100	15
Counter*	Fighting	—	100	20
Double-Edge	Normal	120	100	15
Dynamicpunch*	Fighting	100	50	5
Endure*	Normal	—	—	10
Ice Punch*	Ice	75	100	15
Mega Kick*	Normal	120	85	5
Mega Punch*	Normal	80	75	20
Metronome	Normal	—	—	10
Mimic	Normal	—	100	10
Mud-Slap*	Ground	20	100	10
Psych Up*	Normal	—	—	10
Seismic Toss*	Fighting	—	100	20
Sleep Talk	Normal	—	—	10
Snore*	Normal	40	100	15
Substitute	Normal	—	—	10
Swagger	Normal	—	90	15
Swift*	Normal	60	—	20
Thunderpunch*	Electric	75	100	15
Thunder Wave*	Electric	—	100	20

*Battle Frontier tutor move

088 Oddish

GRASS
POISON

GENERAL INFO
SPECIES: Weed Pokémon
HEIGHT: 1'8"
WEIGHT: 12 lbs.
ABILITY: *Chlorophyll — Doubles the Pokémon's Speed when it is sunny.*

STATS
HP	33
ATTACK	33
DEFENSE	33
SP. ATTACK	60
SP. DEFENSE	60
SPEED	33

EVOLUTIONS
 LV21

LEAF STONE
SUN STONE

WHERE/HOW TO CATCH
Routes 110, 117, 119, 120, 121, and 123; Safari Zone

STRONG AGAINST:
WATER
ELECTRIC
GRASS
FIGHTING

WEAK AGAINST:
FIRE
ICE
FLYING
PSYCHIC

MOVES LIST
LV	Move Name	Type	ST	ACC	PP	LV	Move Name	Type	ST	ACC	PP
S	Absorb	Grass	20	100	20	18	Sleep Powder	Grass	—	75	15
07	Sweet Scent	Normal	—	100	20	23	Acid	Poison	40	100	30
14	Poisonpowder	Poison	—	75	35	32	Moonlight	Normal	—	—	5
16	Stun Spore	Grass	—	75	30	39	Petal Dance	Grass	70	100	20

TM/HM LIST
TM/HM #	Move Name	Type	ST	ACC	PP	TM/HM #	Move Name	Type	ST	ACC	PP
HM01	Cut	Normal	50	95	30	TM22	Solarbeam	Grass	120	100	10
HM05	Flash	Normal	—	70	20	TM27	Return	Normal	—	100	20
TM06	Toxic	Poison	—	85	10	TM32	Double Team	Normal	—	—	15
TM09	Bullet Seed	Grass	10	100	30	TM36	Sludge Bomb	Poison	90	100	10
TM10	Hidden Power	Normal	—	100	15	TM42	Façade	Normal	70	100	20
TM11	Sunny Day	Fire	—	—	5	TM43	Secret Power	Normal	70	100	20
TM17	Protect	Normal	—	—	10	TM44	Rest	Psychic	—	—	10
TM19	Giga Drain	Grass	60	100	5	TM45	Attract	Normal	—	100	15
TM21	Frustration	Normal	—	100	20						

EGG MOVES
Move Name	Type	ST	ACC	PP
Razor Leaf	Grass	55	95	25
Flail	Normal	—	100	15
Synthesis	Grass	—	—	5
Charm	Normal	—	100	20
Ingrain	Normal	—	100	20
Swords Dance	Normal	—	—	30

MOVE TUTOR LIST
Move Name	Type	ST	ACC	PP
Double-Edge	Normal	120	100	15
Endure*	Normal	—	—	10
Mimic	Normal	—	100	10
Sleep Talk	Normal	—	—	10
Snore*	Normal	40	100	15
Substitute	Normal	—	—	10
Swagger	Normal	—	90	15
Swords Dance*	Normal	—	—	30

*Battle Frontier tutor move

089 Gloom™

GRASS
POISON

GENERAL INFO
SPECIES: Weed Pokémon
HEIGHT: 2'7"
WEIGHT: 19 lbs.
ABILITY: *Chlorophyll—Doubles the Pokémon's Speed when it is sunny.*

STATS
HP	30
ATTACK	66
DEFENSE	66
SP. ATTACK	66
SP. DEFENSE	66
SPEED	33

EVOLUTIONS

LV21

LEAF STONE

SUN STONE

WHERE/HOW TO CATCH
Evolve from Oddish; Routes 121 and 123, Safari Zone

STRONG AGAINST:
WATER
ELECTRIC
GRASS
FIGHTING

WEAK AGAINST:
FIRE
ICE
FLYING
PSYCHIC

MOVES LIST
LV	Move Name	Type	ST	ACC	PP
S	Absorb	Grass	20	100	20
S	Sweet Scent	Normal	—	100	20
S	Poisonpowder	Poison	—	75	35
07	Sweet Scent	Normal	—	100	20
14	Poisonpowder	Poison	—	75	35

LV	Move Name	Type	ST	ACC	PP
16	Stun Spore	Grass	—	75	30
18	Sleep Powder	Grass	—	75	15
24	Acid	Poison	40	100	30
35	Moonlight	Normal	—	—	5
44	Petal Dance	Grass	70	100	20

TM/HM LIST
TM/HM #	Move Name	Type	ST	ACC	PP
HM01	Cut	Normal	50	95	30
HM05	Flash	Normal	—	70	20
TM06	Toxic	Poison	—	85	10
TM09	Bullet Seed	Grass	10	100	30
TM10	Hidden Power	Normal	—	100	15
TM11	Sunny Day	Fire	—	—	5
TM17	Protect	Normal	—	—	10
TM19	Giga Drain	Grass	60	100	5
TM21	Frustration	Normal	—	100	20

TM/HM #	Move Name	Type	ST	ACC	PP
TM22	Solarbeam	Grass	120	100	10
TM27	Return	Normal	—	100	20
TM32	Double Team	Normal	—	—	15
TM36	Sludge Bomb	Poison	90	100	10
TM42	Façade	Normal	70	100	20
TM43	Secret Power	Normal	70	100	20
TM44	Rest	Psychic	—	—	10
TM45	Attract	Normal	—	100	15

MOVE TUTOR LIST
Move Name	Type	ST	ACC	PP
Double-Edge	Normal	120	100	15
Endure*	Normal	—	—	10
Mimic	Normal	—	100	10
Sleep Talk	Normal	—	—	10
Snore*	Normal	40	100	15
Substitute	Normal	—	—	10
Swagger	Normal	—	90	15
Swords Dance*	Normal	—	—	30

*Battle Frontier tutor move

090 Vileplume™

GRASS
POISON

GENERAL INFO
SPECIES: Flower Pokémon
HEIGHT: 3'11"
WEIGHT: 41 lbs.
ABILITY: *Chlorophyll—Doubles the Pokémon's Speed when it is sunny.*

STATS
HP	66
ATTACK	66
DEFENSE	66
SP. ATTACK	100
SP. DEFENSE	66
SPEED	33

EVOLUTIONS

LV21

LEAF STONE

SUN STONE

WHERE/HOW TO CATCH
Evolve from Gloom with Leaf Stone

STRONG AGAINST:
WATER
ELECTRIC
GRASS
FIGHTING

WEAK AGAINST:
FIRE
ICE
FLYING
PSYCHIC

MOVES LIST
LV	Move Name	Type	ST	ACC	PP
S	Absorb	Grass	20	100	20
S	Aromatherapy	Grass	—	—	5
S	Stun Spore	Grass	—	75	30

LV	Move Name	Type	ST	ACC	PP
S	Mega Drain	Grass	40	100	10
44	Petal Dance	Grass	70	100	20

TM/HM LIST
TM/HM #	Move Name	Type	ST	ACC	PP
HM01	Cut	Normal	50	95	30
HM05	Flash	Normal	—	70	20
TM06	Toxic	Poison	—	85	10
TM09	Bullet Seed	Grass	10	100	30
TM10	Hidden Power	Normal	—	100	15
TM11	Sunny Day	Fire	—	—	5
TM15	Hyper Beam	Normal	150	90	5
TM17	Protect	Normal	—	—	10
TM19	Giga Drain	Grass	60	100	5

TM/HM #	Move Name	Type	ST	ACC	PP
TM21	Frustration	Normal	—	100	20
TM22	Solarbeam	Grass	120	100	10
TM27	Return	Normal	—	100	20
TM32	Double Team	Normal	—	—	15
TM36	Sludge Bomb	Poison	90	100	10
TM42	Façade	Normal	70	100	20
TM43	Secret Power	Normal	70	100	20
TM44	Rest	Psychic	—	—	10
TM45	Attract	Normal	—	100	15

MOVE TUTOR LIST
Move Name	Type	ST	ACC	PP
Body Slam*	Normal	85	100	15
Double-Edge	Normal	120	100	15
Endure*	Normal	—	—	10
Mimic	Normal	—	100	10
Sleep Talk	Normal	—	—	10
Snore*	Normal	40	100	15
Substitute	Normal	—	—	10
Swagger	Normal	—	90	15
Swords Dance*	Normal	—	—	30

*Battle Frontier tutor move

091

Bellossom™

GRASS

GENERAL INFO
SPECIES: Flower Pokémon
HEIGHT: 1'4"
WEIGHT: 13 lbs.
ABILITY: *Chlorophyll—Doubles the Pokémon's Speed when it is sunny.*

STATS

HP	66
ATTACK	66
DEFENSE	45
SP. ATTACK	60
SP. DEFENSE	60
SPEED	33

EVOLUTIONS

LEAF STONE

LV21

SUN STONE

WHERE/HOW TO CATCH
Evolve from Gloom with Sun Stone

STRONG AGAINST:
WATER
ELECTRIC
GRASS
GROUND

WEAK AGAINST:
FIRE
ICE
POISON
FLYING
BUG

MOVES LIST

LV	Move Name	Type	ST	ACC	PP
S	Absorb	Grass	20	100	20
S	Sweet Scent	Normal	—	100	20
S	Stun Spore	Grass	—	75	30

LV	Move Name	Type	ST	ACC	PP
S	Magical Leaf	Grass	60	—	20
44	Petal Dance	Grass	70	100	20
55	Solarbeam	Grass	120	100	10

TM/HM LIST

TM/HM #	Move Name	Type	ST	ACC	PP
HM01	Cut	Normal	50	95	30
HM05	Flash	Normal	—	70	20
TM06	Toxic	Poison	—	85	10
TM09	Bullet Seed	Grass	10	100	30
TM10	Hidden Power	Normal	—	100	15
TM11	Sunny Day	Fire	—	—	5
TM15	Hyper Beam	Normal	150	90	5
TM17	Protect	Normal	—	—	10
TM19	Giga Drain	Grass	60	100	5
TM20	Safeguard	Normal	—	—	25

TM/HM #	Move Name	Type	ST	ACC	PP
TM21	Frustration	Normal	—	100	20
TM22	Solarbeam	Grass	120	100	10
TM27	Return	Normal	—	100	20
TM32	Double Team	Normal	—	—	15
TM36	Sludge Bomb	Poison	90	100	10
TM42	Façade	Normal	70	100	20
TM43	Secret Power	Normal	70	100	20
TM44	Rest	Psychic	—	—	10
TM45	Attract	Normal	—	100	15

MOVE TUTOR LIST

Move Name	Type	ST	ACC	PP
Double-Edge	Normal	120	100	15
Endure*	Normal	—	—	10
Mimic	Normal	—	100	10
Sleep Talk	Normal	—	—	10
Snore*	Normal	40	100	15
Substitute	Normal	—	—	10
Swagger	Normal	—	90	15
Swords Dance*	Normal	—	—	30

*Battle Frontier tutor move

092

Doduo™

NORMAL
FLYING

GENERAL INFO
SPECIES: Twin Bird Pokémon
HEIGHT: 4'7"
WEIGHT: 86 lbs.
ABILITIES: *Run Away—Pokémon can flee from battle (except Trainer battles).*
Early Bird—The Pokémon recovers from Sleep earlier.

STATS

HP	33
ATTACK	66
DEFENSE	33
SP. ATTACK	33
SP. DEFENSE	30
SPEED	66

EVOLUTIONS

LV31

WHERE/HOW TO CATCH
Safari Zone

STRONG AGAINST:
GRASS
GROUND
BUG
GHOST

WEAK AGAINST:
ELECTRIC
ICE
ROCK

MOVES LIST

LV	Move Name	Type	ST	ACC	PP
S	Peck	Flying	35	100	35
S	Growl	Normal	—	100	40
09	Pursuit	Dark	40	100	20
13	Fury Attack	Normal	15	85	20
21	Tri Attack	Normal	80	100	10

LV	Move Name	Type	ST	ACC	PP
25	Rage	Normal	20	100	20
33	Uproar	Normal	50	100	10
37	Drill Peck	Flying	80	100	20
45	Agility	Psychic	—	—	30

TM/HM LIST

TM/HM #	Move Name	Type	ST	ACC	PP
HM02	Fly	Flying	70	95	15
TM06	Toxic	Poison	—	85	10
TM10	Hidden Power	Normal	—	100	15
TM11	Sunny Day	Fire	—	—	5
TM17	Protect	Normal	—	—	10
TM21	Frustration	Normal	—	100	20
TM27	Return	Normal	—	100	20
TM32	Double Team	Normal	—	—	15

TM/HM #	Move Name	Type	ST	ACC	PP
TM40	Aerial Ace	Flying	60	—	20
TM42	Façade	Normal	70	100	20
TM43	Secret Power	Normal	70	100	20
TM44	Rest	Psychic	—	—	10
TM45	Attract	Normal	—	100	15
TM46	Thief	Dark	40	100	10
TM47	Steel Wing	Steel	70	90	25

EGG MOVES

Move Name	Type	ST	ACC	PP
Quick Attack	Normal	40	100	30
Supersonic	Normal	—	55	20
Haze	Ice	—	—	30
Endeavor	Normal	—	100	5
Faint Attack	Dark	60	—	20
Flail	Normal	—	100	15

MOVE TUTOR LIST

Move Name	Type	ST	ACC	PP
Body Slam*	Normal	85	100	15
Double-Edge	Normal	120	100	15
Endure*	Normal	—	—	10
Mimic	Normal	—	100	10
Mud-Slap*	Ground	20	100	10
Sleep Talk	Normal	—	—	10
Snore*	Normal	40	100	15
Substitute	Normal	—	—	10
Swagger	Normal	—	90	15
Swift*	Normal	60	—	20

*Battle Frontier tutor move

093

Dodrio™

NORMAL
FLYING

GENERAL INFO
SPECIES: Triple Bird Pokémon
HEIGHT: 5'11"
WEIGHT: 188 lbs.
ABILITIES: **Run Away** — *Pokémon can flee from battle (except Trainer battles).*
Early Bird — *The Pokémon recovers from Sleep earlier.*

STATS

HP	30
ATTACK	100
DEFENSE	66
SP. ATTACK	66
SP. DEFENSE	30
SPEED	100

EVOLUTIONS

 LV31

WHERE/HOW TO CATCH
Evolve from Doduo;
Safari Zone

STRONG AGAINST:
GRASS
GROUND
BUG
GHOST

WEAK AGAINST:
ELECTRIC
ICE
ROCK

MOVES LIST

LV	Move Name	Type	ST	ACC	PP	LV	Move Name	Type	ST	ACC	PP
S	Peck	Flying	35	100	35	21	Tri Attack	Normal	80	100	10
S	Growl	Normal	—	100	40	25	Rage	Normal	20	100	20
S	Pursuit	Dark	40	100	20	38	Uproar	Normal	50	100	10
S	Fury Attack	Normal	15	85	20	47	Drill Peck	Flying	80	100	20
09	Pursuit	Dark	40	100	20	60	Agility	Psychic	—	—	30
13	Fury Attack	Normal	15	85	20						

TM/HM LIST

TM/HM #	Move Name	Type	ST	ACC	PP	TM/HM #	Move Name	Type	ST	ACC	PP
HM02	Fly	Flying	70	95	15	TM32	Double Team	Normal	—	—	15
TM06	Toxic	Poison	—	85	10	TM40	Aerial Ace	Flying	60	—	20
TM10	Hidden Power	Normal	—	100	15	TM41	Torment	Dark	—	100	15
TM11	Sunny Day	Fire	—	—	5	TM42	Façade	Normal	70	100	20
TM12	Taunt	Dark	—	100	20	TM43	Secret Power	Normal	70	100	20
TM15	Hyper Beam	Normal	150	90	5	TM44	Rest	Psychic	—	—	10
TM17	Protect	Normal	—	—	10	TM45	Attract	Normal	—	100	15
TM21	Frustration	Normal	—	100	20	TM46	Thief	Dark	40	100	10
TM27	Return	Normal	—	100	20	TM47	Steel Wing	Steel	70	90	25

MOVE TUTOR LIST

Move Name	Type	ST	ACC	PP
Body Slam*	Normal	85	100	15
Double-Edge	Normal	120	100	15
Endure*	Normal	—	—	10
Mimic	Normal	—	100	10
Mud-Slap*	Ground	20	100	10
Sleep Talk	Normal	—	—	10
Snore*	Normal	40	100	15
Substitute	Normal	—	—	10
Swagger	Normal	—	90	15
Swift*	Normal	60	—	20

*Battle Frontier tutor move

094

Roselia™

GRASS
POISON

GENERAL INFO
SPECIES: Thorn Pokémon
HEIGHT: 1'0"
WEIGHT: 4 lbs.
ABILITIES: **Natural Cure** — *Any negative Status conditions are automatically healed when you remove the Pokémon from battle.*
Poison Point — *Gives the Pokémon's Physical Attacks a 30 percent chance of Poisoning the opponent.*

STATS

HP	25
ATTACK	50
DEFENSE	50
SP. ATTACK	75
SP. DEFENSE	50
SPEED	50

EVOLUTIONS

ROSELIA DOES
NOT EVOLVE

WHERE/HOW TO CATCH
Must trade from
Pokémon Ruby

STRONG AGAINST:
WATER
ELECTRIC
GRASS
FIGHTING

WEAK AGAINST:
FIRE
ICE
FLYING
PSYCHIC

MOVES LIST

LV	Move Name	Type	ST	ACC	PP	LV	Move Name	Type	ST	ACC	PP
S	Absorb	Grass	20	100	20	33	Giga Drain	Grass	60	100	5
05	Growth	Normal	—	—	40	37	Sweet Scent	Normal	—	100	20
09	Poison Sting	Poison	15	100	35	41	Ingrain	Grass	—	100	20
13	Stun Spore	Grass	—	75	30	45	Toxic	Poison	—	85	10
17	Mega Drain	Grass	40	100	10	49	Petal Dance	Grass	70	100	20
21	Leech Seed	Grass	—	90	10	53	Aromatherapy	Grass	—	—	5
25	Magical Leaf	Grass	60	—	20	57	Synthesis	Grass	—	—	5
29	Grasswhistle	Grass	—	55	15						

TM/HM LIST

TM/HM #	Move Name	Type	ST	ACC	PP	TM/HM #	Move Name	Type	ST	ACC	PP
HM01	Cut	Normal	50	95	30	TM22	Solarbeam	Grass	120	100	10
HM05	Flash	Normal	—	70	20	TM27	Return	Normal	—	100	20
TM06	Toxic	Poison	—	85	10	TM30	Shadow Ball	Ghost	60	—	20
TM09	Bullet Seed	Grass	10	100	30	TM32	Double Team	Normal	—	—	15
TM10	Hidden Power	Normal	—	100	15	TM36	Sludge Bomb	Poison	90	100	10
TM11	Sunny Day	Fire	—	—	5	TM42	Façade	Normal	70	100	20
TM17	Protect	Normal	—	—	10	TM43	Secret Power	Normal	70	100	20
TM19	Giga Drain	Grass	60	100	5	TM44	Rest	Psychic	—	—	10
TM21	Frustration	Normal	—	100	20	TM45	Attract	Normal	—	100	15

EGG MOVES

Move Name	Type	ST	ACC	PP
Spikes	Ground	—	—	20
Pin Missile	Bug	14	85	20
Cotton Spore	Grass	—	85	40
Synthesis	Grass	—	—	5

MOVE TUTOR LIST

Move Name	Type	ST	ACC	PP
Body Slam*	Normal	85	100	15
Double-Edge	Normal	120	100	15
Endure*	Normal	—	—	10
Mimic	Normal	—	100	10
Mud-Slap*	Ground	20	100	10
Psych Up*	Normal	—	—	10
Sleep Talk	Normal	—	—	10
Snore*	Normal	40	100	15
Substitute	Normal	—	—	10
Swagger	Normal	—	90	15
Swift*	Normal	60	—	20
Swords Dance*	Normal	—	—	30

*Battle Frontier tutor move

095

Gulpin™

POISON

GENERAL INFO
SPECIES: Stomach Pokémon
HEIGHT: 1'4"
WEIGHT: 23 lbs.
ABILITIES: *Liquid Ooze* — Pokémon inflicts damage on an opponent who uses HP-absorbing Moves.
Sticky Hold — Protects the Pokémon's Held Item from Theft.

STATS

HP		50
ATTACK		50
DEFENSE		50
SP. ATTACK		50
SP. DEFENSE		50
SPEED		50

EVOLUTIONS

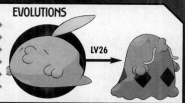

LV26

WHERE/HOW TO CATCH
Route 110

MOVES LIST

LV	Move Name	Type	ST	ACC	PP		LV	Move Name	Type	ST	ACC	PP
S	Pound	Normal	40	100	35		28	Toxic	Poison	—	85	10
06	Yawn	Normal	—	100	10		34	Stockpile	Normal	—	—	10
09	Poison Gas	Poison	—	55	40		34	Spit Up	Normal	100	100	10
14	Sludge	Poison	65	100	20		34	Swallow	Normal	—	—	10
17	Amnesia	Psychic	—	—	20		39	Sludge Bomb	Poison	90	100	10
23	Encore	Normal	—	100	5							

STRONG AGAINST:
GRASS
FIGHTING
POISON
BUG

WEAK AGAINST:
GROUND
PSYCHIC

TM/HM LIST

TM/HM #	Move Name	Type	ST	ACC	PP		TM/HM #	Move Name	Type	ST	ACC	PP
HM04	Strength	Normal	80	100	15		TM22	Solarbeam	Grass	120	100	10
HM06	Rock Smash	Fighting	20	100	15		TM27	Return	Normal	—	100	20
TM03	Water Pulse	Water	60	100	20		TM30	Shadow Ball	Ghost	60	—	20
TM06	Toxic	Poison	—	85	10		TM32	Double Team	Normal	—	—	15
TM09	Bullet Seed	Grass	10	100	30		TM34	Shock Wave	Electric	60	—	20
TM10	Hidden Power	Normal	—	100	15		TM36	Sludge Bomb	Poison	90	100	10
TM11	Sunny Day	Fire	—	—	5		TM42	Façade	Normal	70	100	20
TM13	Ice Beam	Ice	95	100	10		TM43	Secret Power	Normal	70	100	20
TM17	Protect	Normal	—	—	10		TM44	Rest	Psychic	—	—	10
TM18	Rain Dance	Water	—	—	5		TM45	Attract	Normal	—	100	15
TM19	Giga Drain	Grass	60	100	5		TM49	Snatch	Dark	—	100	10
TM21	Frustration	Normal	—	100	20							

EGG MOVES

Move Name	Type	ST	ACC	PP
Dream Eater	Psychic	100	100	15
Acid Armor	Poison	—	—	40
Smog	Poison	20	70	20
Pain Split	Normal	—	100	20

MOVE TUTOR LIST

Move Name	Type	ST	ACC	PP
Body Slam*	Normal	85	100	15
Counter*	Fighting	—	100	20
Defense Curl*	Normal	—	—	40
Double-Edge	Normal	120	100	15
Dream Eater*	Psychic	100	100	15
Dynamicpunch	Fighting	100	50	5
Endure*	Normal	—	—	10
Explosion	Normal	250	100	5
Fire Punch*	Fire	75	100	15
Mimic	Normal	—	100	10
Mud-Slap*	Ground	20	100	10
Rollout	Rock	30	90	20
Sleep Talk	Normal	—	—	10
Snore*	Normal	40	100	15
Substitute	Normal	—	—	10
Swagger	Normal	—	90	15
Thunderpunch*	Electric	75	100	15

*Battle Frontier tutor move

096

Swalot™

POISON

GENERAL INFO
SPECIES: Poison Bag Pokémon
HEIGHT: 5'7"
WEIGHT: 176 lbs.
ABILITIES: *Liquid Ooze* — Pokémon inflicts damage on an opponent who uses HP-absorbing Moves.
Sticky Hold — Protects the Pokémon's Held Item from Theft.

STATS

HP		50
ATTACK		50
DEFENSE		50
SP. ATTACK		50
SP. DEFENSE		50
SPEED		50

EVOLUTIONS

LV26

WHERE/HOW TO CATCH
Evolve from Gulpin

MOVES LIST

LV	Move Name	Type	ST	ACC	PP		LV	Move Name	Type	ST	ACC	PP
S	Pound	Normal	40	100	35		23	Encore	Normal	—	100	5
S	Yawn	Normal	—	100	10		26	Body Slam	Normal	85	100	15
S	Poison Gas	Poison	—	55	40		31	Toxic	Poison	—	85	10
S	Sludge	Poison	65	100	20		40	Stockpile	Normal	—	—	10
06	Yawn	Normal	—	100	10		40	Spit Up	Normal	100	100	10
09	Poison Gas	Poison	—	55	40		40	Swallow	Normal	—	—	10
14	Sludge	Poison	65	100	20		48	Sludge Bomb	Poison	90	100	10
17	Amnesia	Psychic	—	—	20							

STRONG AGAINST:
GRASS
FIGHTING
POISON
BUG

WEAK AGAINST:
GROUND
PSYCHIC

TM/HM LIST

TM/HM #	Move Name	Type	ST	ACC	PP		TM/HM #	Move Name	Type	ST	ACC	PP
HM04	Strength	Normal	80	100	15		TM21	Frustration	Normal	—	100	20
HM06	Rock Smash	Fighting	20	100	15		TM22	Solarbeam	Grass	120	100	10
TM03	Water Pulse	Water	60	100	20		TM27	Return	Normal	—	100	20
TM06	Toxic	Poison	—	85	10		TM30	Shadow Ball	Ghost	60	—	20
TM09	Bullet Seed	Grass	10	100	30		TM32	Double Team	Normal	—	—	15
TM10	Hidden Power	Normal	—	100	15		TM34	Shock Wave	Electric	60	—	20
TM11	Sunny Day	Fire	—	—	5		TM36	Sludge Bomb	Poison	90	100	10
TM13	Ice Beam	Ice	95	100	10		TM42	Façade	Normal	70	100	20
TM15	Hyper Beam	Normal	150	90	5		TM43	Secret Power	Normal	70	100	20
TM17	Protect	Normal	—	—	10		TM44	Rest	Psychic	—	—	10
TM18	Rain Dance	Water	—	—	5		TM45	Attract	Normal	—	100	15
TM19	Giga Drain	Grass	60	100	5		TM49	Snatch	Dark	—	100	10

MOVE TUTOR LIST

Move Name	Type	ST	ACC	PP
Body Slam*	Normal	85	100	15
Counter*	Fighting	—	100	20
Defense Curl*	Normal	—	—	40
Double-Edge	Normal	120	100	15
Dream Eater*	Psychic	100	100	15
Dynamicpunch	Fighting	100	50	5
Endure*	Normal	—	—	10
Explosion	Normal	250	100	5
Fire Punch*	Fire	75	100	15
Mimic	Normal	—	100	10
Mud-Slap*	Ground	20	100	10
Rollout	Rock	30	90	20
Sleep Talk	Normal	—	—	10
Snore*	Normal	40	100	15
Substitute	Normal	—	—	10
Swagger	Normal	—	90	15
Thunderpunch*	Electric	75	100	15

*Battle Frontier tutor move

097 Carvanha™

WATER
DARK

GENERAL INFO
SPECIES: Savage Pokémon
HEIGHT: 2'7"
WEIGHT: 46 lbs.
ABILITY: *Rough Skin*—Recoil hurts the opponent Pokémon when it uses a Physical Attack.

STATS
HP	25
ATTACK	75
DEFENSE	25
SP. ATTACK	50
SP. DEFENSE	25
SPEED	50

EVOLUTIONS
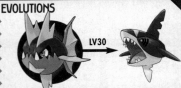
LV30

WHERE/HOW TO CATCH
Routes 118 and 119

STRONG AGAINST:
FIRE
WATER
ICE
PSYCHIC
GHOST
DARK
STEEL

WEAK AGAINST:
ELECTRIC
GRASS
FIGHTING
BUG

MOVES LIST
LV	Move Name	Type	ST	ACC	PP
S	Leer	Normal	—	100	30
S	Bite	Dark	60	100	25
07	Rage	Normal	20	100	20
13	Focus Energy	Normal	—	—	30
16	Scary Face	Normal	—	90	10
22	Crunch	Dark	80	100	15
28	Screech	Normal	—	85	40
31	Take Down	Normal	90	85	20
37	Swagger	Normal	—	90	15
43	Agility	Psychic	—	—	30

TM/HM LIST
TM/HM #	Move Name	Type	ST	ACC	PP
HM03	Surf	Water	95	100	15
HM07	Waterfall	Water	80	100	15
HM08	Dive	Water	60	100	10
TM03	Water Pulse	Water	60	100	20
TM06	Toxic	Poison	—	85	10
TM07	Hail	Ice	—	—	10
TM10	Hidden Power	Normal	—	100	15
TM12	Taunt	Dark	—	100	20
TM13	Ice Beam	Ice	95	100	10
TM14	Blizzard	Ice	120	70	5
TM17	Protect	Normal	—	—	10
TM18	Rain Dance	Water	—	—	5
TM21	Frustration	Normal	—	100	20
TM27	Return	Normal	—	100	20
TM32	Double Team	Normal	—	—	15
TM41	Torment	Dark	—	100	15
TM42	Façade	Normal	70	100	20
TM43	Secret Power	Normal	70	100	20
TM44	Rest	Psychic	—	—	10
TM45	Attract	Normal	—	100	15
TM46	Thief	Dark	40	100	10

EGG MOVES
Move Name	Type	ST	ACC	PP
Hydro Pump	Water	120	80	5
Double-Edge	Normal	120	100	15
Thrash	Normal	90	100	20

MOVE TUTOR LIST
Move Name	Type	ST	ACC	PP
Double-Edge	Normal	120	100	15
Endure*	Normal	—	—	10
Fury Cutter	Bug	10	95	20
Icy Wind*	Ice	55	95	15
Mimic	Normal	—	100	10
Mud-Slap*	Ground	20	100	10
Sleep Talk	Normal	—	—	10
Snore*	Normal	40	100	15
Substitute	Normal	—	—	10
Swagger	Normal	—	90	15
Swift*	Normal	60	—	20

*Battle Frontier tutor move

098 Sharpedo™

WATER
DARK

GENERAL INFO
SPECIES: Brutal Pokémon
HEIGHT: 5'11"
WEIGHT: 196 lbs.
ABILITY: *Rough Skin*—Recoil hurts the opponent Pokémon when it uses a Physical Attack.

STATS
HP	50
ATTACK	100
DEFENSE	25
SP. ATTACK	75
SP. DEFENSE	25
SPEED	75

EVOLUTIONS

LV30
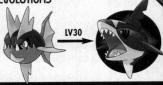

WHERE/HOW TO CATCH
Evolve from Carvanha; Routes 103, 118, 122, 124, 125, 126, 127, 128, 129, 130, 131, 132, 133, and 134

STRONG AGAINST:
FIRE
WATER
ICE
PSYCHIC
GHOST
DARK
STEEL

WEAK AGAINST:
ELECTRIC
GRASS
FIGHTING
BUG

MOVES LIST
LV	Move Name	Type	ST	ACC	PP
S	Leer	Normal	—	100	30
S	Bite	Dark	60	100	25
S	Rage	Normal	20	100	20
S	Focus Energy	Normal	—	—	30
07	Rage	Normal	20	100	20
13	Focus Energy	Normal	—	—	30
16	Scary Face	Normal	—	90	10
22	Crunch	Dark	80	100	15
28	Screech	Normal	—	85	40
33	Slash	Normal	70	100	20
38	Taunt	Dark	—	100	20
43	Swagger	Normal	—	90	15
48	Skull Bash	Normal	100	100	15
53	Agility	Psychic	—	—	30

TM/HM LIST
TM/HM #	Move Name	Type	ST	ACC	PP
HM03	Surf	Water	95	100	15
HM04	Strength	Normal	80	100	15
HM06	Rock Smash	Fighting	20	100	15
HM07	Waterfall	Water	80	100	15
HM08	Dive	Water	60	100	10
TM03	Water Pulse	Water	60	100	20
TM05	Roar	Normal	—	100	20
TM06	Toxic	Poison	—	85	10
TM07	Hail	Ice	—	—	10
TM10	Hidden Power	Normal	—	100	15
TM12	Taunt	Dark	—	100	20
TM13	Ice Beam	Ice	95	100	10
TM14	Blizzard	Ice	120	70	5
TM15	Hyper Beam	Normal	150	90	5
TM17	Protect	Normal	—	—	10
TM18	Rain Dance	Water	—	—	5
TM21	Frustration	Normal	—	100	20
TM26	Earthquake	Ground	100	100	10
TM27	Return	Normal	—	100	20
TM32	Double Team	Normal	—	—	15
TM39	Rock Tomb	Rock	50	80	10
TM41	Torment	Dark	—	100	15
TM42	Façade	Normal	70	100	20
TM43	Secret Power	Normal	70	100	20
TM44	Rest	Psychic	—	—	10
TM45	Attract	Normal	—	100	15
TM46	Thief	Dark	40	100	10

MOVE TUTOR LIST
Move Name	Type	ST	ACC	PP
Double-Edge	Normal	120	100	15
Endure*	Normal	—	—	10
Fury Cutter	Bug	10	95	20
Icy Wind*	Ice	55	95	15
Mimic	Normal	—	100	10
Mud-Slap*	Ground	20	100	10
Sleep Talk	Normal	—	—	10
Snore*	Normal	40	100	15
Substitute	Normal	—	—	10
Swagger	Normal	—	90	15
Swift*	Normal	60	—	20

*Battle Frontier tutor move

099

Wailmer™

WATER

GENERAL INFO
SPECIES: Ball Whale Pokémon
HEIGHT: 6'7"
WEIGHT: 287 lbs.
ABILITIES: *Water Veil*—Pokémon cannot be Burned.
Oblivious—The Attract condition does not affect Pokémon.

STATS
HP	75
ATTACK	50
DEFENSE	25
SP. ATTACK	50
SP. DEFENSE	25
SPEED	50

EVOLUTIONS

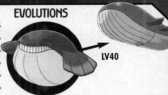

LV40

WHERE/HOW TO CATCH
Routes 103, 105, 106, 107, 108, 109, 110, 115, 121, 122, 123, 124, 125, 126, 127, 128, 129, 130, 131, 132, 133, 134, and 135; Ever Grande City, Mossdeep City, Lilycove City, Seafloor Cavern, Shoal Cave, Slateport City, and Sootopolis City

STRONG AGAINST:
FIRE
WATER
ICE
STEEL

WEAK AGAINST:
ELECTRIC
GRASS

MOVES LIST

LV	Move Name	Type	ST	ACC	PP
S	Splash	Normal	—	—	40
05	Growl	Normal	—	100	40
10	Water Gun	Water	40	100	25
14	Rollout	Rock	30	90	20
19	Whirlpool	Water	15	70	15
23	Astonish	Ghost	30	100	15
28	Water Pulse	Water	60	100	20
32	Mist	Ice	—	—	30
37	Rest	Psychic	—	—	10
41	Water Spout	Water	150	100	5
46	Amnesia	Psychic	—	—	20
50	Hydro Pump	Water	120	80	5

TM/HM LIST

TM/HM #	Move Name	Type	ST	ACC	PP
HM03	Surf	Water	95	100	15
HM04	Strength	Normal	80	100	15
HM06	Rock Smash	Fighting	20	100	15
HM07	Waterfall	Water	80	100	15
HM08	Dive	Water	60	100	10
TM03	Water Pulse	Water	60	100	20
TM05	Roar	Normal	—	100	20
TM06	Toxic	Poison	—	85	10
TM07	Hail	Ice	—	—	10
TM10	Hidden Power	Normal	—	100	15
TM13	Ice Beam	Ice	95	100	10
TM14	Blizzard	Ice	120	70	5
TM17	Protect	Normal	—	—	10
TM18	Rain Dance	Water	—	—	5
TM21	Frustration	Normal	—	100	20
TM26	Earthquake	Ground	100	100	10
TM27	Return	Normal	—	100	20
TM32	Double Team	Normal	—	—	15
TM39	Rock Tomb	Rock	50	80	10
TM42	Façade	Normal	70	100	20
TM43	Secret Power	Normal	70	100	20
TM44	Rest	Psychic	—	—	10
TM45	Attract	Normal	—	100	15

EGG MOVES

Move Name	Type	ST	ACC	PP
Double-Edge	Normal	120	100	15
Thrash	Normal	90	100	20
Swagger	Normal	—	90	15
Snore	Normal	40	100	15
Sleep Talk	Normal	—	—	10
Curse	—	—	—	10
Fissure	Ground	—	30	5
Tickle	Normal	—	100	20

MOVE TUTOR LIST

Move Name	Type	ST	ACC	PP
Body Slam*	Normal	85	100	15
Defense Curl*	Normal	—	—	40
Double-Edge	Normal	120	100	15
Dynamicpunch	Fighting	100	50	5
Endure*	Normal	—	—	10
Icy Wind*	Ice	55	95	15
Mimic	Normal	—	100	10
Rollout	Rock	30	90	20
Sleep Talk	Normal	—	—	10
Snore*	Normal	40	100	15
Substitute	Normal	—	—	10
Swagger	Normal	—	90	15

*Battle Frontier tutor move

100

Wailord™

WATER

GENERAL INFO
SPECIES: Float Whale Pokémon
HEIGHT: 47'7"
WEIGHT: 878 lbs.
ABILITIES: *Water Veil*—Pokémon cannot be Burned.
Oblivious—The Attract condition does not affect Pokémon.

STATS
HP	75
ATTACK	75
DEFENSE	50
SP. ATTACK	75
SP. DEFENSE	25
SPEED	50

EVOLUTIONS

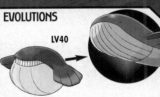

LV40

WHERE/HOW TO CATCH
Evolve from Wailmer; Route 129

STRONG AGAINST:
FIRE
WATER
ICE
STEEL

WEAK AGAINST:
ELECTRIC
GRASS

MOVES LIST

LV	Move Name	Type	ST	ACC	PP
S	Splash	Normal	—	—	40
S	Growl	Normal	—	100	40
S	Water Gun	Water	40	100	25
S	Rollout	Rock	30	90	20
05	Growl	Normal	—	100	40
10	Water Gun	Water	40	100	25
14	Rollout	Rock	30	90	20
19	Whirlpool	Water	15	70	15
23	Astonish	Ghost	30	100	15
28	Water Pulse	Water	60	100	20
32	Mist	Ice	—	—	30
37	Rest	Psychic	—	—	10
44	Water Spout	Water	150	100	5
52	Amnesia	Psychic	—	—	20
59	Hydro Pump	Water	120	80	5

TM/HM LIST

TM/HM #	Move Name	Type	ST	ACC	PP
HM03	Surf	Water	95	100	15
HM04	Strength	Normal	80	100	15
HM06	Rock Smash	Fighting	20	100	15
HM07	Waterfall	Water	80	100	15
HM08	Dive	Water	60	100	10
TM03	Water Pulse	Water	60	100	20
TM05	Roar	Normal	—	100	20
TM06	Toxic	Poison	—	85	10
TM07	Hail	Ice	—	—	10
TM10	Hidden Power	Normal	—	100	15
TM13	Ice Beam	Ice	95	100	10
TM14	Blizzard	Ice	120	70	5
TM15	Hyper Beam	Normal	150	90	5
TM17	Protect	Normal	—	—	10
TM18	Rain Dance	Water	—	—	5
TM21	Frustration	Normal	—	100	20
TM26	Earthquake	Ground	100	100	10
TM27	Return	Normal	—	100	20
TM32	Double Team	Normal	—	—	15
TM39	Rock Tomb	Rock	50	80	10
TM42	Façade	Normal	70	100	20
TM43	Secret Power	Normal	70	100	20
TM44	Rest	Psychic	—	—	10
TM45	Attract	Normal	—	100	15

MOVE TUTOR LIST

Move Name	Type	ST	ACC	PP
Body Slam*	Normal	85	100	15
Defense Curl*	Normal	—	—	40
Double-Edge	Normal	120	100	15
Dynamicpunch	Fighting	100	50	5
Endure*	Normal	—	—	10
Icy Wind*	Ice	55	95	15
Mimic	Normal	—	100	10
Rollout	Rock	30	90	20
Sleep Talk	Normal	—	—	10
Snore*	Normal	40	100	15
Substitute	Normal	—	—	10
Swagger	Normal	—	90	15

*Battle Frontier tutor move

101 Numel™

FIRE
GROUND

GENERAL INFO
SPECIES: Numb Pokémon
HEIGHT: 2'4"
WEIGHT: 53 lbs.
ABILITY: *Oblivious* — Pokémon is not affected by the Attract condition.

STATS
HP	50
ATTACK	50
DEFENSE	25
SP. ATTACK	50
SP. DEFENSE	25
SPEED	25

EVOLUTIONS

LV33

WHERE/HOW TO CATCH
Route 122 and Fiery Path

STRONG AGAINST:
FIRE
ELECTRIC
POISON
BUG
STEEL

WEAK AGAINST:
WATER
GROUND

MOVES LIST
LV	Move Name	Type	ST	ACC	PP
S	Growl	Normal	—	100	40
S	Tackle	Normal	35	95	35
11	Ember	Fire	40	100	25
19	Magnitude	Ground	—	100	30
25	Focus Energy	Normal	—	—	30

LV	Move Name	Type	ST	ACC	PP
29	Take Down	Normal	90	85	20
31	Amnesia	Psychic	—	—	20
35	Earthquake	Ground	100	100	10
41	Flamethrower	Fire	95	100	15
49	Double-Edge	Normal	120	100	15

TM/HM LIST
TM/HM #	Move Name	Type	ST	ACC	PP
HM04	Strength	Normal	80	100	15
HM06	Rock Smash	Fighting	20	100	15
TM06	Toxic	Poison	—	85	10
TM10	Hidden Power	Normal	—	100	15
TM11	Sunny Day	Fire	—	—	5
TM17	Protect	Normal	—	—	10
TM21	Frustration	Normal	—	100	20
TM26	Earthquake	Ground	100	100	10
TM27	Return	Normal	—	100	20
TM28	Dig	Ground	60	100	10

TM/HM #	Move Name	Type	ST	ACC	PP
TM32	Double Team	Normal	—	—	15
TM35	Flamethrower	Fire	95	100	15
TM37	Sandstorm	Rock	—	—	10
TM38	Fire Blast	Fire	120	85	5
TM39	Rock Tomb	Rock	50	80	10
TM42	Façade	Normal	70	100	20
TM43	Secret Power	Normal	70	100	20
TM44	Rest	Psychic	—	—	10
TM45	Attract	Normal	—	100	15
TM50	Overheat	Fire	140	90	5

EGG MOVES
Move Name	Type	ST	ACC	PP
Howl	Normal	—	—	40
Scary Face	Normal	—	90	10
Body Slam	Normal	85	100	15
Rollout	Rock	30	90	20
Defense Curl	Normal	—	—	40
Stomp	Normal	65	100	20

MOVE TUTOR LIST
Move Name	Type	ST	ACC	PP
Body Slam*	Normal	85	100	15
Defense Curl*	Normal	—	—	40
Double-Edge	Normal	120	100	15
Endure*	Normal	—	—	10
Mimic	Normal	—	100	10
Mud-Slap*	Ground	20	100	10
Rock Slide*	Rock	75	90	10
Rollout	Rock	30	90	20
Sleep Talk	Normal	—	—	10
Snore*	Normal	40	100	15
Substitute	Normal	—	—	10
Swagger	Normal	—	90	15

*Battle Frontier tutor move

102 Camerupt™

FIRE
GROUND

GENERAL INFO
SPECIES: Eruption Pokémon
HEIGHT: 6'3"
WEIGHT: 485 lbs.
ABILITY: *Magma Armor* — Pokémon cannot be Frozen.

STATS
HP	50
ATTACK	75
DEFENSE	50
SP. ATTACK	75
SP. DEFENSE	50
SPEED	50

EVOLUTIONS
 LV33

WHERE/HOW TO CATCH
Evolve from Numel

STRONG AGAINST:
FIRE
ELECTRIC
POISON
BUG
STEEL

WEAK AGAINST:
WATER
GROUND

MOVES LIST
LV	Move Name	Type	ST	ACC	PP
S	Growl	Normal	—	100	40
S	Tackle	Normal	35	95	35
S	Ember	Fire	40	100	25
S	Magnitude	Ground	—	100	30
11	Ember	Fire	40	100	25
19	Magnitude	Ground	—	100	30
25	Focus Energy	Normal	—	—	30

LV	Move Name	Type	ST	ACC	PP
29	Take Down	Normal	90	85	20
31	Amnesia	Psychic	—	—	20
33	Rock Slide	Rock	75	90	10
37	Earthquake	Ground	100	100	10
45	Eruption	Fire	150	100	5
55	Fissure	Ground	—	30	5

TM/HM LIST
TM/HM #	Move Name	Type	ST	ACC	PP
HM04	Strength	Normal	80	100	15
HM06	Rock Smash	Fighting	20	100	15
TM05	Roar	Normal	—	100	20
TM06	Toxic	Poison	—	85	10
TM10	Hidden Power	Normal	—	100	15
TM11	Sunny Day	Fire	—	—	5
TM15	Hyper Beam	Normal	150	90	5
TM17	Protect	Normal	—	—	10
TM21	Frustration	Normal	—	100	20
TM26	Earthquake	Ground	100	100	10
TM27	Return	Normal	—	100	20

TM/HM #	Move Name	Type	ST	ACC	PP
TM28	Dig	Ground	60	100	10
TM32	Double Team	Normal	—	—	15
TM35	Flamethrower	Fire	95	100	15
TM37	Sandstorm	Rock	—	—	10
TM38	Fire Blast	Fire	120	85	5
TM39	Rock Tomb	Rock	50	80	10
TM42	Façade	Normal	70	100	20
TM43	Secret Power	Normal	70	100	20
TM44	Rest	Psychic	—	—	10
TM45	Attract	Normal	—	100	15
TM50	Overheat	Fire	140	90	5

MOVE TUTOR LIST
Move Name	Type	ST	ACC	PP
Body Slam*	Normal	85	100	15
Defense Curl*	Normal	—	—	40
Double-Edge	Normal	120	100	15
Endure*	Normal	—	—	10
Explosion	Normal	250	100	5
Mimic	Normal	—	100	10
Mud-Slap*	Ground	20	100	10
Rock Slide*	Rock	75	90	10
Rollout	Rock	30	90	20
Sleep Talk	Normal	—	—	10
Snore*	Normal	40	100	15
Substitute	Normal	—	—	10
Swagger	Normal	—	90	15

*Battle Frontier tutor move

103 Slugma™

FIRE

GENERAL INFO
SPECIES: Lava Pokémon
HEIGHT: 2'4"
WEIGHT: 77 lbs.

ABILITIES: *Magma Armor* — *Pokémon cannot be Frozen.*
Flame Body — *Gives the Pokémon's Physical Attacks a 30 percent chance of Burning the opponent.*

STATS

HP	33
ATTACK	33
DEFENSE	33
SP. ATTACK	66
SP. DEFENSE	33
SPEED	33

EVOLUTIONS

 LV38

WHERE/HOW TO CATCH
Route 113 and Fiery Path

STRONG AGAINST:
FIRE
GRASS
ICE
BUG
STEEL

WEAK AGAINST:
BUG
GROUND
ROCK

MOVES LIST

LV	Move Name	Type	ST	ACC	PP
S	Yawn	Normal	—	100	10
S	Smog	Poison	20	70	20
08	Ember	Fire	40	100	25
15	Rock Throw	Rock	50	90	15
22	Harden	Normal	—	—	30

LV	Move Name	Type	ST	ACC	PP
29	Amnesia	Psychic	—	—	20
36	Flamethrower	Fire	95	100	15
43	Rock Slide	Rock	75	90	10
50	Body Slam	Normal	85	100	15

TM/HM LIST

TM/HM #	Move Name	Type	ST	ACC	PP
HM06	Rock Smash	Fighting	20	100	15
TM06	Toxic	Poison	—	85	10
TM10	Hidden Power	Normal	—	100	15
TM11	Sunny Day	Fire	—	—	5
TM16	Light Screen	Psychic	—	—	30
TM17	Protect	Normal	—	—	10
TM21	Frustration	Normal	—	100	20
TM27	Return	Normal	—	100	20
TM32	Double Team	Normal	—	—	15

TM/HM #	Move Name	Type	ST	ACC	PP
TM33	Reflect	Psychic	—	—	20
TM35	Flamethrower	Fire	95	100	15
TM38	Fire Blast	Fire	120	85	5
TM42	Façade	Normal	70	100	20
TM43	Secret Power	Normal	70	100	20
TM44	Rest	Psychic	—	—	10
TM45	Attract	Normal	—	100	15
TM50	Overheat	Fire	140	90	5

EGG MOVES

Move Name	Type	ST	ACC	PP
Acid Armor	Poison	—	—	40

MOVE TUTOR LIST

Move Name	Type	ST	ACC	PP
Body Slam*	Normal	85	100	15
Defense Curl*	Normal	—	—	40
Double-Edge	Normal	120	100	15
Endure*	Normal	—	—	10
Mimic	Normal	—	100	10
Mud-Slap*	Ground	20	100	10
Rock Slide*	Rock	75	90	10
Rollout	Rock	30	90	20
Sleep Talk	Normal	—	—	10
Snore*	Normal	40	100	15
Substitute	Normal	—	—	10
Swagger	Normal	—	90	15

*Battle Frontier tutor move

104 Magcargo™

FIRE
ROCK

GENERAL INFO
SPECIES: Lava Pokémon
HEIGHT: 2'7"
WEIGHT: 121 lbs.

ABILITIES: *Magma Armor* — *Pokémon cannot be Frozen.*
Flame Body — *Gives the Pokémon's Physical Attacks a 30 percent chance of Burning the opponent.*

STATS

HP	33
ATTACK	33
DEFENSE	66
SP. ATTACK	66
SP. DEFENSE	66
SPEED	33

EVOLUTIONS

 LV38

WHERE/HOW TO CATCH
Evolve from Slugma

STRONG AGAINST:
NORMAL
FIRE
ICE
POISON
FLYING
BUG

WEAK AGAINST:
ROCK
GROUND
FIGHTING
WATER

MOVES LIST

LV	Move Name	Type	ST	ACC	PP
S	Yawn	Normal	—	100	10
S	Smog	Poison	20	70	20
S	Ember	Fire	40	100	25
S	Rock Throw	Rock	50	90	15
08	Ember	Fire	40	100	25
15	Rock Throw	Rock	50	90	15

LV	Move Name	Type	ST	ACC	PP
22	Harden	Normal	—	—	30
29	Amnesia	Psychic	—	—	20
36	Flamethrower	Fire	95	100	15
48	Rock Slide	Rock	75	90	10
60	Body Slam	Normal	85	100	15

TM/HM LIST

TM/HM #	Move Name	Type	ST	ACC	PP
HM04	Strength	Normal	80	100	15
HM06	Rock Smash	Fighting	20	100	15
TM06	Toxic	Poison	—	85	10
TM10	Hidden Power	Normal	—	100	15
TM11	Sunny Day	Fire	—	—	5
TM15	Hyper Beam	Normal	150	90	5
TM16	Light Screen	Psychic	—	—	30
TM17	Protect	Normal	—	—	10
TM21	Frustration	Normal	—	100	20
TM26	Earthquake	Ground	100	100	10
TM27	Return	Normal	—	100	20

TM/HM #	Move Name	Type	ST	ACC	PP
TM32	Double Team	Normal	—	—	15
TM33	Reflect	Psychic	—	—	20
TM35	Flamethrower	Fire	95	100	15
TM37	Sandstorm	Rock	—	—	10
TM38	Fire Blast	Fire	120	85	5
TM39	Rock Tomb	Rock	50	80	10
TM42	Façade	Normal	70	100	20
TM43	Secret Power	Normal	70	100	20
TM44	Rest	Psychic	—	—	10
TM45	Attract	Normal	—	100	15
TM50	Overheat	Fire	140	90	5

MOVE TUTOR LIST

Move Name	Type	ST	ACC	PP
Body Slam*	Normal	85	100	15
Defense Curl*	Normal	—	—	40
Double-Edge	Normal	120	100	15
Endure*	Normal	—	—	10
Mimic	Normal	—	100	10
Mud-Slap*	Ground	20	100	10
Rock Slide*	Rock	75	90	10
Rollout	Rock	30	90	20
Sleep Talk	Normal	—	—	10
Snore*	Normal	40	100	15
Substitute	Normal	—	—	10
Swagger	Normal	—	90	15

*Battle Frontier tutor move

105 Torkoal™

FIRE

GENERAL INFO
SPECIES: Coal Pokémon
HEIGHT: 1'8"
WEIGHT: 177 lbs.
ABILITY: *White Smoke*— Pokémon is not affected by moves that lower stats.

STATS
HP	50
ATTACK	75
DEFENSE	75
SP. ATTACK	75
SP. DEFENSE	50
SPEED	25

EVOLUTIONS

TORKOAL DOES NOT EVOLVE

WHERE/HOW TO CATCH
Fiery Path and Magma Hideout

STRONG AGAINST:
FIRE
GRASS
ICE
BUG
STEEL

WEAK AGAINST:
WATER
GROUND
ROCK

MOVES LIST
LV	Move Name	Type	ST	ACC	PP
S	Ember	Fire	40	100	25
04	Smog	Poison	20	70	20
07	Curse	—	—	—	10
14	Smokescreen	Normal	—	100	20
17	Fire Spin	Fire	15	70	15
20	Body Slam	Normal	85	100	15
27	Protect	Normal	—	—	10
30	Flamethrower	Fire	95	100	15
33	Iron Defense	Steel	—	—	15
40	Amnesia	Psychic	—	—	20
43	Flail	Normal	—	100	15
46	Heat Wave	Fire	100	90	10

TM/HM LIST
TM/HM #	Move Name	Type	ST	ACC	PP
HM04	Strength	Normal	80	100	15
HM06	Rock Smash	Fighting	20	100	15
TM06	Toxic	Poison	—	85	10
TM10	Hidden Power	Normal	—	100	15
TM11	Sunny Day	Fire	—	—	5
TM17	Protect	Normal	—	—	10
TM21	Frustration	Normal	—	100	20
TM23	Iron Tail	Steel	100	75	15
TM27	Return	Normal	—	100	20
TM32	Double Team	Normal	—	—	15
TM35	Flamethrower	Fire	95	100	15
TM36	Sludge Bomb	Poison	90	100	10
TM38	Fire Blast	Fire	120	85	5
TM42	Façade	Normal	70	100	20
TM43	Secret Power	Normal	70	100	20
TM44	Rest	Psychic	—	—	10
TM45	Attract	Normal	—	100	15
TM50	Overheat	Fire	140	90	5

EGG MOVES
Move Name	Type	ST	ACC	PP
Eruption	Fire	150	100	5
Endure	Normal	—	—	10
Sleep Talk	Normal	—	—	10
Yawn	Normal	—	100	10

MOVE TUTOR LIST
Move Name	Type	ST	ACC	PP
Body Slam*	Normal	85	100	15
Double-Edge	Normal	120	100	15
Endure*	Normal	—	—	10
Explosion	Normal	250	100	5
Mimic	Normal	—	100	10
Mud-Slap*	Ground	20	100	10
Rock Slide*	Rock	75	90	10
Sleep Talk	Normal	—	—	10
Snore*	Normal	40	100	15
Substitute	Normal	—	—	10
Swagger	Normal	—	90	15

*Battle Frontier tutor move

106 Grimer™

POISON

GENERAL INFO
SPECIES: Sludge Pokémon
HEIGHT: 2'11"
WEIGHT: 66 lbs.
ABILITIES: *Stench*— Lowers the chance of encountering wild Pokémon.
Sticky Hold— Protects the Pokémon's Held Item from Theft.

STATS
HP	66
ATTACK	100
DEFENSE	66
SP. ATTACK	66
SP. DEFENSE	60
SPEED	30

EVOLUTIONS
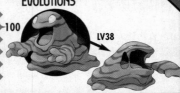

LV38

WHERE/HOW TO CATCH
Fiery Path

STRONG AGAINST:
GRASS
FIGHTING
POISON
BUG

WEAK AGAINST:
GROUND
PSYCHIC

MOVES LIST
LV	Move Name	Type	ST	ACC	PP
S	Poison Gas	Poison	—	55	40
S	Pound	Normal	40	100	35
04	Harden	Normal	—	—	30
08	Disable	Normal	—	55	20
13	Sludge	Poison	65	100	20
19	Minimize	Normal	—	—	20
26	Screech	Normal	—	85	40
34	Acid Armor	Poison	—	—	40
43	Sludge Bomb	Poison	90	100	10
53	Memento	Dark	—	100	10

TM/HM LIST
TM/HM #	Move Name	Type	ST	ACC	PP
TM06	Toxic	Poison	—	85	10
TM10	Hidden Power	Normal	—	100	15
TM11	Sunny Day	Fire	—	—	5
TM12	Taunt	Dark	—	100	20
TM17	Protect	Normal	—	—	10
TM18	Rain Dance	Water	—	—	5
TM19	Giga Drain	Grass	60	100	5
TM21	Frustration	Normal	—	100	20
TM24	Thunderbolt	Electric	95	100	15
TM25	Thunder	Electric	120	70	10
TM27	Return	Normal	—	100	20
TM28	Dig	Ground	60	100	10
TM32	Double Team	Normal	—	—	15
TM34	Shock Wave	Electric	60	—	20
TM35	Flamethrower	Fire	95	100	15
TM36	Sludge Bomb	Poison	90	100	10
TM38	Fire Blast	Fire	120	85	5
TM39	Rock Tomb	Rock	50	80	10
TM41	Torment	Dark	—	100	15
TM42	Façade	Normal	70	100	20
TM43	Secret Power	Normal	70	100	20
TM44	Rest	Psychic	—	—	10
TM45	Attract	Normal	—	100	15
TM46	Thief	Dark	40	100	10

EGG MOVES
Move Name	Type	ST	ACC	PP
Haze	Ice	—	—	30
Mean Look	Normal	—	100	5
Imprison	Psychic	—	100	15
Curse	—	—	—	10
Shadow Ball	Ghost	60	—	20
Explosion	Normal	250	100	5
Lick	Ghost	20	100	30

MOVE TUTOR LIST
Move Name	Type	ST	ACC	PP
Body Slam*	Normal	85	100	15
Dynamicpunch	Fighting	100	50	5
Endure*	Normal	—	—	10
Explosion	Normal	250	100	5
Fire Punch*	Fire	75	100	15
Ice Punch*	Ice	75	100	15
Mimic	Normal	—	100	10
Mud-Slap*	Ground	20	100	10
Sleep Talk	Normal	—	—	10
Snore*	Normal	40	100	15
Substitute	Normal	—	—	10
Swagger	Normal	—	90	15
Thunderpunch*	Electric	75	100	15

*Battle Frontier tutor move

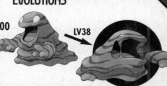

107 Muk™
POISON

GENERAL INFO
SPECIES: Sludge Pokémon
HEIGHT: 3'11"
WEIGHT: 66 lbs.

ABILITIES: *Stench* — Lowers the chance of encountering wild Pokémon.
Sticky Hold — Protects the Pokémon's Held Item from Theft.

STATS

HP	66
ATTACK	100
DEFENSE	66
SP. ATTACK	66
SP. DEFENSE	60
SPEED	33

EVOLUTIONS LV38

WHERE/HOW TO CATCH
Evolve from Grimer

STRONG AGAINST:
GRASS
FIGHTING
POISON
BUG

WEAK AGAINST:
GROUND
PSYCHIC

MOVES LIST

LV	Move Name	Type	ST	ACC	PP
S	Poison Gas	Poison	—	55	40
S	Pound	Normal	40	100	35
S	Harden	Normal	—	—	30
04	Harden	Normal	—	—	30
08	Disable	Normal	—	55	20
13	Sludge	Poison	65	100	20
19	Minimize	Normal	—	—	20
26	Screech	Normal	—	85	40
34	Acid Armor	Poison	—	—	40
47	Sludge Bomb	Poison	90	100	10
61	Memento	Dark	—	100	10

TM/HM LIST

TM/HM #	Move Name	Type	ST	ACC	PP
HM04	Strength	Normal	80	100	15
HM06	Rock Smash	Fighting	20	100	15
TM01	Focus Punch	Fighting	150	100	20
TM06	Toxic	Poison	—	85	10
TM10	Hidden Power	Normal	—	100	15
TM11	Sunny Day	Fire	—	—	5
TM12	Taunt	Dark	—	100	20
TM15	Hyper Beam	Normal	150	90	5
TM17	Protect	Normal	—	—	10
TM18	Rain Dance	Water	—	—	5
TM19	Giga Drain	Grass	60	100	5
TM21	Frustration	Normal	—	100	20
TM24	Thunderbolt	Electric	95	100	15
TM25	Thunder	Electric	120	70	10
TM27	Return	Normal	—	100	20
TM28	Dig	Ground	60	100	10
TM31	Brick Break	Fighting	75	100	15
TM32	Double Team	Normal	—	—	15
TM34	Shock Wave	Electric	60	—	20
TM35	Flamethrower	Fire	95	100	15
TM36	Sludge Bomb	Poison	90	100	10
TM38	Fire Blast	Fire	120	85	5
TM39	Rock Tomb	Rock	50	80	10
TM41	Torment	Dark	—	100	15
TM42	Façade	Normal	70	100	20
TM43	Secret Power	Normal	70	100	20
TM44	Rest	Psychic	—	—	10
TM45	Attract	Normal	—	100	15
TM46	Thief	Dark	40	100	10

MOVE TUTOR LIST

Move Name	Type	ST	ACC	PP
Body Slam*	Normal	85	100	15
Dynamicpunch	Fighting	100	50	5
Endure*	Normal	—	—	10
Explosion	Normal	250	100	5
Fire Punch*	Fire	75	100	15
Ice Punch*	Ice	75	100	15
Mimic	Normal	—	100	10
Mud-Slap*	Ground	20	100	10
Sleep Talk	Normal	—	—	10
Snore*	Normal	40	100	15
Substitute	Normal	—	—	10
Swagger	Normal	—	90	15
Thunderpunch*	Electric	75	100	15

*Battle Frontier tutor move

108 Koffing™
POISON

GENERAL INFO
SPECIES: Poison Gas Pokémon
HEIGHT: 2'0"
WEIGHT: 2 lbs.

ABILITY: *Levitate* — Pokémon is not affected by Ground-type Moves.

STATS

HP	33
ATTACK	66
DEFENSE	60
SP. ATTACK	60
SP. DEFENSE	33
SPEED	33

EVOLUTIONS LV35

WHERE/HOW TO CATCH
Fiery Path

STRONG AGAINST:
GRASS
FIGHTING
POISON
BUG
GROUND

WEAK AGAINST:
PSYCHIC

MOVES LIST

LV	Move Name	Type	ST	ACC	PP
S	Poison Gas	Poison	—	55	40
S	Tackle	Normal	35	95	35
09	Smog	Poison	20	70	20
17	Selfdestruct	Normal	200	100	5
21	Sludge	Poison	65	100	20
25	Smokescreen	Normal	—	100	20
33	Haze	Ice	—	—	30
41	Explosion	Normal	250	100	5
45	Destiny Bond	Ghost	—	—	5
49	Memento	Dark	—	100	10

TM/HM LIST

TM/HM #	Move Name	Type	ST	ACC	PP
HM05	Flash	Normal	—	70	20
TM06	Toxic	Poison	—	85	10
TM10	Hidden Power	Normal	—	100	15
TM11	Sunny Day	Fire	—	—	5
TM12	Taunt	Dark	—	100	20
TM17	Protect	Normal	—	—	10
TM18	Rain Dance	Water	—	—	5
TM21	Frustration	Normal	—	100	20
TM24	Thunderbolt	Electric	95	100	15
TM25	Thunder	Electric	120	70	10
TM27	Return	Normal	—	100	20
TM30	Shadow Ball	Ghost	60	—	20
TM32	Double Team	Normal	—	—	15
TM34	Shock Wave	Electric	60	—	20
TM35	Flamethrower	Fire	95	100	15
TM36	Sludge Bomb	Poison	90	100	10
TM38	Fire Blast	Fire	120	85	5
TM41	Torment	Dark	—	100	15
TM42	Façade	Normal	70	100	20
TM43	Secret Power	Normal	70	100	20
TM44	Rest	Psychic	—	—	10
TM45	Attract	Normal	—	100	15
TM46	Thief	Dark	40	100	10

EGG MOVES

Move Name	Type	ST	ACC	PP
Screech	Normal	—	85	40
Psywave	Psychic	—	80	15
Destiny Bond	Ghost	—	—	5
Will-O-Wisp	Fire	—	75	15
Psybeam	Psychic	65	100	20
Pain Split	Normal	—	100	10

MOVE TUTOR LIST

Move Name	Type	ST	ACC	PP
Endure*	Normal	—	—	10
Explosion	Normal	250	100	5
Mimic	Normal	—	100	10
Rollout	Rock	30	90	20
Sleep Talk*	Normal	—	—	10
Snore*	Normal	40	100	15
Substitute	Normal	—	—	10
Swagger	Normal	—	90	15

*Battle Frontier tutor move

109 Weezing™

POISON

GENERAL INFO
SPECIES: Poison Gas Pokémon
HEIGHT: 3'11"
WEIGHT: 21 lbs.
ABILITY: *Levitate — Pokémon is not affected by Ground-type Moves.*

STATS
HP	33
ATTACK	60
DEFENSE	60
SP. ATTACK	60
SP. DEFENSE	60
SPEED	66

EVOLUTIONS

LV35

WHERE/HOW TO CATCH
Evolve from Koffing

STRONG AGAINST:
- GRASS
- FIGHTING
- POISON
- BUG
- GROUND

WEAK AGAINST:
- PSYCHIC

MOVES LIST

LV	Move Name	Type	ST	ACC	PP	LV	Move Name	Type	ST	ACC	PP
S	Poison Gas	Poison	—	55	40	21	Sludge	Poison	65	100	20
S	Tackle	Normal	35	95	35	25	Smokescreen	Normal	—	100	20
S	Smog	Poison	20	70	20	33	Haze	Ice	—	—	30
S	Selfdestruct	Normal	200	100	5	44	Explosion	Normal	250	100	5
09	Smog	Poison	20	70	20	51	Destiny Bond	Ghost	—	—	5
17	Selfdestruct	Normal	200	100	5	58	Memento	Dark	—	100	10

TM/HM LIST

TM/HM #	Move Name	Type	ST	ACC	PP	TM/HM #	Move Name	Type	ST	ACC	PP
HM05	Flash	Normal	—	70	20	TM30	Shadow Ball	Ghost	60	—	20
TM06	Toxic	Poison	—	85	10	TM32	Double Team	Normal	—	—	15
TM10	Hidden Power	Normal	—	100	15	TM34	Shock Wave	Electric	60	—	20
TM11	Sunny Day	Fire	—	—	5	TM35	Flamethrower	Fire	95	100	15
TM12	Taunt	Dark	—	100	20	TM36	Sludge Bomb	Poison	90	100	10
TM15	Hyper Beam	Normal	150	90	5	TM38	Fire Blast	Fire	120	85	5
TM17	Protect	Normal	—	—	10	TM41	Torment	Dark	—	100	15
TM18	Rain Dance	Water	—	—	5	TM42	Façade	Normal	70	100	20
TM21	Frustration	Normal	—	100	20	TM43	Secret Power	Normal	70	100	20
TM24	Thunderbolt	Electric	95	100	15	TM44	Rest	Psychic	—	—	10
TM25	Thunder	Electric	120	70	10	TM45	Attract	Normal	—	100	15
TM27	Return	Normal	—	100	20	TM46	Thief	Dark	40	100	10

MOVE TUTOR LIST

Move Name	Type	ST	ACC	PP
Endure*	Normal	—	—	10
Explosion	Normal	250	100	5
Mimic	Normal	—	100	10
Rollout	Rock	30	90	20
Sleep Talk*	Normal	—	—	10
Snore*	Normal	40	100	15
Substitute	Normal	—	—	10
Swagger	Normal	—	90	15

*Battle Frontier tutor move

110 Spoink™

PSYCHIC

GENERAL INFO
SPECIES: Bounce Pokémon
HEIGHT: 2'4"
WEIGHT: 67 lbs.
ABILITIES: *Thick Fat — Fire- and Ice-type Moves inflict only 50 percent of the damage.*
Own Tempo — Pokémon cannot become Confused.

STATS
HP	50
ATTACK	25
DEFENSE	25
SP. ATTACK	50
SP. DEFENSE	50
SPEED	50

EVOLUTIONS

LV32

WHERE/HOW TO CATCH
Jagged Pass

STRONG AGAINST:
- FIGHTING
- PSYCHIC

WEAK AGAINST:
- BUG
- GHOST
- DARK

MOVES LIST

LV	Move Name	Type	ST	ACC	PP	LV	Move Name	Type	ST	ACC	PP
S	Splash	Normal	—	—	40	28	Magic Coat	Psychic	—	100	15
07	Psywave	Psychic	—	80	15	34	Psychic	Psychic	90	100	10
10	Odor Sleuth	Normal	—	100	40	37	Rest	Psychic	—	—	10
16	Psybeam	Psychic	65	100	20	37	Snore	Normal	40	100	15
19	Psych Up	Normal	—	—	10	43	Bounce	Flying	85	85	5
25	Confuse Ray	Ghost	—	100	10						

TM/HM LIST

TM/HM #	Move Name	Type	ST	ACC	PP	TM/HM #	Move Name	Type	ST	ACC	PP
HM05	Flash	Normal	—	70	20	TM30	Shadow Ball	Ghost	60	—	20
TM04	Calm Mind	Psychic	—	—	20	TM32	Double Team	Normal	—	—	15
TM06	Toxic	Poison	—	85	10	TM33	Reflect	Psychic	—	—	20
TM10	Hidden Power	Normal	—	100	15	TM34	Shock Wave	Electric	60	—	20
TM11	Sunny Day	Fire	—	—	5	TM41	Torment	Dark	—	100	15
TM12	Taunt	Dark	—	100	20	TM42	Façade	Normal	70	100	20
TM16	Light Screen	Psychic	—	—	30	TM43	Secret Power	Normal	70	100	20
TM17	Protect	Normal	—	—	10	TM44	Rest	Psychic	—	—	10
TM18	Rain Dance	Water	—	—	5	TM45	Attract	Normal	—	100	15
TM21	Frustration	Normal	—	100	20	TM46	Thief	Dark	40	100	10
TM23	Iron Tail	Steel	100	75	15	TM48	Skill Swap	Psychic	—	100	10
TM27	Return	Normal	—	100	20	TM49	Snatch	Dark	—	100	10
TM29	Psychic	Psychic	90	100	10						

EGG MOVES

Move Name	Type	ST	ACC	PP
Future Sight	Psychic	80	90	15
Extrasensory	Psychic	80	100	30
Substitute	Normal	—	—	10
Trick	Psychic	—	100	10

MOVE TUTOR LIST

Move Name	Type	ST	ACC	PP
Body Slam*	Normal	85	100	15
Double-Edge	Normal	120	100	15
Endure*	Normal	—	—	10
Icy Wind*	Ice	55	95	15
Mimic	Normal	—	100	10
Psych Up*	Normal	—	—	10
Sleep Talk	Normal	—	—	10
Snore*	Normal	40	100	15
Substitute	Normal	—	—	10
Swagger	Normal	—	90	15
Swift*	Normal	60	—	20

*Battle Frontier tutor move

111 Grumpig™

PSYCHIC

GENERAL INFO
SPECIES: Manipulate Pokémon
HEIGHT: 2'11"
WEIGHT: 158 lbs.
ABILITIES: *Thick Fat*—Fire- and Ice-type Moves inflict only 50 percent of the damage.
Own Tempo—Pokémon cannot become Confused.

STATS
HP	50
ATTACK	50
DEFENSE	50
SP. ATTACK	75
SP. DEFENSE	75
SPEED	75

EVOLUTIONS
 LV32

WHERE/HOW TO CATCH
Evolve from Spoink

STRONG AGAINST:
FIGHTING
PSYCHIC

WEAK AGAINST:
BUG
GHOST
DARK

MOVES LIST
LV	Move Name	Type	ST	ACC	PP		LV	Move Name	Type	ST	ACC	PP
S	Splash	Normal	—	—	40		19	Psych Up	Normal	—	—	10
S	Psywave	Psychic	—	80	15		25	Confuse Ray	Ghost	—	100	10
S	Odor Sleuth	Normal	—	100	40		28	Magic Coat	Psychic	—	100	15
S	Psybeam	Psychic	65	100	20		37	Psychic	Psychic	90	100	10
07	Psywave	Psychic	—	80	15		43	Rest	Psychic	—	—	10
10	Odor Sleuth	Normal	—	100	40		43	Snore	Normal	40	100	15
16	Psybeam	Psychic	65	100	20		55	Bounce	Flying	85	85	5

TM/HM LIST
TM/HM #	Move Name	Type	ST	ACC	PP		TM/HM #	Move Name	Type	ST	ACC	PP
HM05	Flash	Normal	—	70	20		TM29	Psychic	Psychic	90	100	10
TM01	Focus Punch	Fighting	150	100	20		TM30	Shadow Ball	Ghost	60	—	20
TM04	Calm Mind	Psychic	—	—	20		TM32	Double Team	Normal	—	—	15
TM06	Toxic	Poison	—	85	10		TM33	Reflect	Psychic	—	—	20
TM10	Hidden Power	Normal	—	100	15		TM34	Shock Wave	Electric	60	—	20
TM11	Sunny Day	Fire	—	—	5		TM41	Torment	Dark	—	100	15
TM12	Taunt	Dark	—	100	20		TM42	Façade	Normal	70	100	20
TM15	Hyper Beam	Normal	150	90	5		TM43	Secret Power	Normal	70	100	20
TM16	Light Screen	Psychic	—	—	30		TM44	Rest	Psychic	—	—	10
TM17	Protect	Normal	—	—	10		TM45	Attract	Normal	—	100	15
TM18	Rain Dance	Water	—	—	5		TM46	Thief	Dark	40	100	10
TM21	Frustration	Normal	—	100	20		TM48	Skill Swap	Psychic	—	100	10
TM23	Iron Tail	Steel	100	75	15		TM49	Snatch	Dark	—	100	10
TM27	Return	Normal	—	100	20							

MOVE TUTOR LIST
Move Name	Type	ST	ACC	PP
Body Slam*	Normal	85	100	15
Counter*	Fighting	—	100	20
Double-Edge	Normal	120	100	15
Dream Eater*	Psychic	100	100	15
Dynamicpunch	Fighting	100	50	5
Endure*	Normal	—	—	10
Fire Punch*	Fire	75	100	15
Ice Punch*	Ice	75	100	15
Icy Wind*	Ice	55	95	15
Mega Kick*	Normal	120	85	5
Mega Punch*	Normal	80	75	20
Metronome	Normal	—	100	10
Mimic	Normal	—	100	10
Mud-Slap*	Ground	20	100	10
Psych Up*	Normal	—	—	10
Seismic Toss*	Fighting	—	100	20
Sleep Talk	Normal	—	—	10
Snore*	Normal	40	100	15
Substitute	Normal	—	—	10
Swagger	Normal	—	90	15
Swift*	Normal	60	—	20
Thunderpunch*	Electric	75	100	15

*Battle Frontier tutor move

---

112 Sandshrew™

GROUND

GENERAL INFO
SPECIES: Mouse Pokémon
HEIGHT: 2'0"
WEIGHT: 26 lbs.
ABILITY: *Sand Veil*—The Pokémon's Evasion stat rises when a Sandstorm blows.

STATS
HP	30
ATTACK	66
DEFENSE	66
SP. ATTACK	33
SP. DEFENSE	33
SPEED	33

EVOLUTIONS
 LV22

WHERE/HOW TO CATCH
Routes 111 and 113, Mirage Tower

STRONG AGAINST:
ELECTRIC
POISON
ROCK

WEAK AGAINST:
WATER
GRASS
ICE

MOVES LIST
LV	Move Name	Type	ST	ACC	PP		LV	Move Name	Type	ST	ACC	PP
S	Scratch	Normal	40	100	35		30	Swift	Normal	60	—	20
06	Defense Curl	Normal	—	—	40		37	Fury Swipes	Normal	18	80	15
11	Sand-Attack	Ground	—	100	15		45	Sand Tomb	Ground	15	70	15
17	Poison Sting	Poison	15	100	35		53	Sandstorm	Rock	—	—	10
23	Slash	Normal	70	100	20							

TM/HM LIST
TM/HM #	Move Name	Type	ST	ACC	PP		TM/HM #	Move Name	Type	ST	ACC	PP
HM01	Cut	Normal	50	95	30		TM28	Dig	Ground	60	100	10
HM04	Strength	Normal	80	100	15		TM31	Brick Break	Fighting	75	100	15
HM06	Rock Smash	Fighting	20	100	15		TM32	Double Team	Normal	—	—	15
TM01	Focus Punch	Fighting	150	100	20		TM37	Sandstorm	Rock	—	—	10
TM06	Toxic	Poison	—	85	10		TM39	Rock Tomb	Rock	50	80	10
TM10	Hidden Power	Normal	—	100	15		TM40	Aerial Ace	Flying	60	—	20
TM11	Sunny Day	Fire	—	—	5		TM42	Facade	Normal	70	100	20
TM17	Protect	Normal	—	—	10		TM43	Secret Power	Normal	70	100	20
TM21	Frustration	Normal	—	100	20		TM44	Rest	Psychic	—	—	10
TM23	Iron Tail	Steel	100	75	15		TM45	Attract	Normal	—	100	15
TM26	Earthquake	Ground	100	100	10		TM46	Thief	Dark	40	100	10
TM27	Return	Normal	—	100	20							

EGG MOVES
Move Name	Type	ST	ACC	PP
Flail	Normal	—	100	15
Safeguard	Normal	—	—	25
Counter	Fighting	—	100	20
Rapid Spin	Normal	20	100	40
Rock Slide	Rock	75	90	10
Swords Dance	Normal	—	—	30
Crush Claw	Normal	75	95	10
Metal Claw	Spell	50	95	35

MOVE TUTOR LIST
Move Name	Type	ST	ACC	PP
Body Slam*	Normal	85	100	15
Counter*	Fighting	—	100	20
Defense Curl*	Normal	—	—	40
Double-Edge	Normal	120	100	15
Dynamicpunch	Fighting	100	50	5
Endure*	Normal	—	—	10
Fury Cutter	Bug	10	95	20
Mimic	Normal	—	100	10
Mud-Slap*	Ground	20	100	10
Rock Slide*	Rock	75	90	10
Rollout	Rock	30	90	20
Seismic Toss*	Fighting	—	100	20
Sleep Talk	Normal	—	—	10
Snore*	Normal	40	100	15
Substitute	Normal	—	—	10
Swagger	Normal	—	90	15
Swift*	Normal	60	—	20
Swords Dance*	Normal	—	—	30

*Battle Frontier tutor move

113 Sandslash™

GROUND

GENERAL INFO
SPECIES: Mouse Pokémon
HEIGHT: 3'3"
WEIGHT: 65 lbs.
ABILITY: *Sand Veil*—The Pokémon's Evasion stat rises when a Sandstorm blows.

STATS
HP	66
ATTACK	100
DEFENSE	66
SP. ATTACK	33
SP. DEFENSE	33
SPEED	66

EVOLUTIONS
LV22

WHERE/HOW TO CATCH
Evolve from Sandshrew

STRONG AGAINST:
ELECTRIC
POISON
ROCK

WEAK AGAINST:
WATER
GRASS
ICE

MOVES LIST
LV	Move Name	Type	ST	ACC	PP
S	Scratch	Normal	40	100	35
S	Defense Curl	Normal	—	—	40
S	Sand-Attack	Ground	—	100	15
06	Defense Curl	Normal	—	—	40
11	Sand-Attack	Ground	—	100	15
17	Poison Sting	Poison	15	100	35
24	Slash	Normal	70	100	20
33	Swift	Normal	60	—	20
42	Fury Swipes	Normal	18	80	15
52	Sand Tomb	Ground	15	70	15
62	Sandstorm	Rock	—	—	10

TM/HM LIST
TM/HM #	Move Name	Type	ST	ACC	PP
HM01	Cut	Normal	50	95	30
HM04	Strength	Normal	80	100	15
HM06	Rock Smash	Fighting	20	100	15
TM01	Focus Punch	Fighting	150	100	20
TM06	Toxic	Poison	—	85	10
TM10	Hidden Power	Normal	—	100	15
TM11	Sunny Day	Fire	—	—	5
TM15	Hyper Beam	Normal	150	90	5
TM17	Protect	Normal	—	—	10
TM21	Frustration	Normal	—	100	20
TM23	Iron Tail	Steel	100	75	15
TM26	Earthquake	Ground	100	100	10
TM27	Return	Normal	—	100	20
TM28	Dig	Ground	60	100	10
TM31	Brick Break	Fighting	75	100	15
TM32	Double Team	Normal	—	—	15
TM37	Sandstorm	Rock	—	—	10
TM39	Rock Tomb	Rock	50	80	10
TM40	Aerial Ace	Flying	60	—	20
TM42	Façade	Normal	70	100	20
TM43	Secret Power	Normal	70	100	20
TM44	Rest	Psychic	—	—	10
TM45	Attract	Normal	—	100	15
TM46	Thief	Dark	40	100	10

MOVE TUTOR LIST
Move Name	Type	ST	ACC	PP
Body Slam*	Normal	85	100	15
Counter*	Fighting	—	100	20
Defense Curl*	Normal	—	—	40
Double-Edge	Normal	120	100	15
Dynamicpunch	Fighting	100	50	5
Endure*	Normal	—	—	10
Fury Cutter	Bug	10	95	20
Mimic	Normal	—	100	10
Mud-Slap*	Ground	20	100	10
Rock Slide*	Rock	75	90	10
Rollout	Rock	30	90	20
Seismic Toss*	Fighting	—	100	20
Sleep Talk	Normal	—	—	10
Snore*	Normal	40	100	15
Substitute	Normal	—	—	10
Swagger	Normal	—	90	15
Swift*	Normal	60	—	20
Swords Dance*	Normal	—	—	30

*Battle Frontier tutor move

114 Spinda™

NORMAL

GENERAL INFO
SPECIES: Spot Panda Pokémon
HEIGHT: 3'7"
WEIGHT: 11 lbs.
ABILITY: *Own Tempo*—Pokémon cannot become Confused.

STATS
HP	50
ATTACK	50
DEFENSE	50
SP. ATTACK	50
SP. DEFENSE	50
SPEED	50

EVOLUTIONS
SPINDA DOES NOT EVOLVE

WHERE/HOW TO CATCH
Route 113

STRONG AGAINST:
GHOST

WEAK AGAINST:
FIGHTING

MOVES LIST
LV	Move Name	Type	ST	ACC	PP
S	Tackle	Normal	35	95	35
05	Uproar	Normal	50	100	10
12	Faint Attack	Dark	60	—	20
16	Psybeam	Psychic	65	100	20
23	Hypnosis	Psychic	—	60	20
27	Dizzy Punch	Normal	70	100	10
34	Teeter Dance	Normal	—	100	20
38	Psych Up	Normal	—	—	10
45	Double-Edge	Normal	120	100	15
49	Flail	Normal	—	100	15
56	Thrash	Normal	90	100	20

TM/HM LIST
TM/HM #	Move Name	Type	ST	ACC	PP
HM04	Strength	Normal	80	100	15
HM05	Flash	Normal	—	70	20
HM06	Rock Smash	Fighting	20	100	15
TM01	Focus Punch	Fighting	150	100	20
TM03	Water Pulse	Water	60	100	20
TM04	Calm Mind	Psychic	—	—	20
TM06	Toxic	Poison	—	85	10
TM10	Hidden Power	Normal	—	100	15
TM11	Sunny Day	Fire	—	—	5
TM17	Protect	Normal	—	—	10
TM18	Rain Dance	Water	—	—	5
TM20	Safeguard	Normal	—	—	25
TM21	Frustration	Normal	—	100	20
TM27	Return	Normal	—	100	20
TM28	Dig	Ground	60	100	10
TM29	Psychic	Psychic	90	100	10
TM30	Shadow Ball	Ghost	60	—	20
TM31	Brick Break	Fighting	75	100	15
TM32	Double Team	Normal	—	—	15
TM34	Shock Wave	Electric	60	—	20
TM39	Rock Tomb	Rock	50	80	10
TM42	Façade	Normal	70	100	20
TM43	Secret Power	Normal	70	100	20
TM44	Rest	Psychic	—	—	10
TM45	Attract	Normal	—	100	15
TM46	Thief	Dark	40	100	10
TM48	Skill Swap	Psychic	—	100	10
TM49	Snatch	Dark	—	100	10

EGG MOVES
Move Name	Type	ST	ACC	PP
Encore	Normal	—	100	5
Rock Slide	Rock	75	90	10
Assist	Normal	—	100	20
Disable	Normal	—	55	20
Baton Pass	Normal	—	—	40
Trick	Psychic	—	100	10
Smellingsalt	Normal	60	100	10
Wish	Normal	—	100	10

MOVE TUTOR LIST
Move Name	Type	ST	ACC	PP
Body Slam*	Normal	85	100	15
Counter*	Fighting	—	100	20
Defense Curl*	Normal	—	—	40
Double-Edge	Normal	120	100	15
Dream Eater*	Psychic	100	100	15
Dynamicpunch	Fighting	100	50	5
Endure*	Normal	—	—	10
Fire Punch*	Fire	75	100	15
Ice Punch*	Ice	75	100	15
Icy Wind*	Ice	55	95	15
Mega Kick*	Normal	120	85	5
Mega Punch*	Normal	80	75	20
Metronome	Normal	—	100	10
Mimic	Normal	—	100	10
Mud-Slap*	Ground	20	100	10
Psych Up*	Normal	—	—	10
Rock Slide*	Rock	75	90	10
Rollout	Rock	30	90	20
Seismic Toss*	Fighting	—	100	20
Sleep Talk	Normal	—	—	10
Snore*	Normal	40	100	15
Substitute	Normal	—	—	10
Swagger	Normal	—	90	15
Swift*	Normal	60	—	20
Thunderpunch*	Electric	75	100	15

*Battle Frontier tutor move

115

Skarmory™

STEEL
FLYING

GENERAL INFO
SPECIES: Armor Bird Pokémon
HEIGHT: 5'7"
WEIGHT: 111 lbs.
ABILITIES: *Keen Eye*—Pokémon's Accuracy cannot be lowered.
Sturdy—One hit KO moves have no effect.

STATS
HP	33
ATTACK	66
DEFENSE	100
SP. ATTACK	33
SP. DEFENSE	66
SPEED	66

EVOLUTIONS

SKARMORY DOES NOT EVOLVE

WHERE/HOW TO CATCH
Route 113

STRONG AGAINST:
NORMAL
GRASS
POISON
GROUND
FLYING
PSYCHIC
BUG
GHOST
DRAGON
DARK
STEEL

WEAK AGAINST:
FIRE
ELECTRIC

MOVES LIST
LV	Move Name	Type	ST	ACC	PP
S	Leer	Normal	—	100	30
S	Peck	Flying	35	100	35
10	Sand-Attack	Ground	—	100	15
13	Swift	Normal	60	—	20
16	Agility	Psychic	—	—	30
26	Fury Attack	Normal	15	85	20
29	Air Cutter	Flying	55	95	25
32	Steel Wing	Steel	70	90	25
42	Spikes	Ground	—	—	20
45	Metal Sound	Steel	—	85	40

TM/HM LIST
TM/HM #	Move Name	Type	ST	ACC	PP
HM01	Cut	Normal	50	95	30
HM02	Fly	Flying	70	95	15
HM06	Rock Smash	Fighting	20	100	15
TM05	Roar	Normal	—	—	20
TM06	Toxic	Poison	—	85	10
TM10	Hidden Power	Normal	—	100	15
TM11	Sunny Day	Fire	—	—	5
TM12	Taunt	Dark	—	100	20
TM17	Protect	Normal	—	—	10
TM21	Frustration	Normal	—	100	20
TM27	Return	Normal	—	100	20
TM32	Double Team	Normal	—	—	15
TM37	Sandstorm	Rock	—	—	10
TM40	Aerial Ace	Flying	60	—	20
TM41	Torment	Dark	—	100	15
TM42	Facade	Normal	70	100	20
TM43	Secret Power	Normal	70	100	20
TM44	Rest	Psychic	—	—	10
TM45	Attract	Normal	—	100	15
TM46	Thief	Dark	40	100	10
TM47	Steel Wing	Steel	70	90	25

EGG MOVES
Move Name	Type	ST	ACC	PP
Drill Peck	Flying	80	100	20
Pursuit	Dark	40	100	20
Sky Attack	Flying	140	90	5
Whirlwind	Normal	—	100	20
Curse	—	—	—	10

MOVE TUTOR LIST
Move Name	Type	ST	ACC	PP
Counter*	Fighting	—	100	20
Double-Edge	Normal	120	100	15
Endure*	Normal	—	—	10
Mimic	Normal	—	100	10
Mud-Slap*	Ground	20	100	10
Rock Slide*	Rock	75	90	10
Sleep Talk	Normal	—	—	10
Snore*	Normal	40	100	15
Substitute	Normal	—	—	10
Swagger	Normal	—	90	15
Swift*	Normal	60	—	20

*Battle Frontier tutor move

116

Trapinch™

GROUND

GENERAL INFO
SPECIES: Ant Pit Pokémon
HEIGHT: 2'4"
WEIGHT: 33 lbs.
ABILITIES: *Hyper Cutter*—Pokémon's Attack Power cannot be lowered.
Arena Trap—Prevents the opponent Pokémon from fleeing or switching out of battle. Does not affect Flying-type Pokémon or Pokémon with the Levitate Ability.

STATS
HP	25
ATTACK	75
DEFENSE	50
SP. ATTACK	50
SP. DEFENSE	25
SPEED	25

EVOLUTIONS
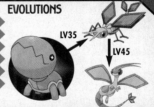
LV35
LV45

WHERE/HOW TO CATCH
Route 111 and Mirage Tower

STRONG AGAINST:
ELECTRIC
POISON
ROCK

WEAK AGAINST:
WATER
GRASS
ICE

MOVES LIST
LV	Move Name	Type	ST	ACC	PP
S	Bite	Dark	60	100	25
09	Sand-Attack	Ground	—	100	15
17	Faint Attack	Dark	60	—	20
25	Sand Tomb	Ground	15	70	15
33	Crunch	Dark	80	100	15
41	Dig	Ground	60	100	10
49	Sandstorm	Rock	—	—	10
57	Hyper Beam	Normal	150	90	5

TM/HM LIST
TM/HM #	Move Name	Type	ST	ACC	PP
HM04	Strength	Normal	80	100	15
HM06	Rock Smash	Fighting	20	100	15
TM06	Toxic	Poison	—	85	10
TM10	Hidden Power	Normal	—	100	15
TM11	Sunny Day	Fire	—	—	5
TM15	Hyper Beam	Normal	150	90	5
TM17	Protect	Normal	—	—	10
TM19	Giga Drain	Grass	60	100	5
TM21	Frustration	Normal	—	100	20
TM22	Solarbeam	Grass	120	100	10
TM26	Earthquake	Ground	100	100	10
TM27	Return	Normal	—	100	20
TM28	Dig	Ground	60	100	10
TM32	Double Team	Normal	—	—	15
TM37	Sandstorm	Rock	—	—	10
TM39	Rock Tomb	Rock	50	80	10
TM42	Facade	Normal	70	100	20
TM43	Secret Power	Normal	70	100	20
TM44	Rest	Psychic	—	—	10
TM45	Attract	Normal	—	100	15

EGG MOVES
Move Name	Type	ST	ACC	PP
Focus Energy	Normal	—	—	30
Quick Attack	Normal	40	100	30
Whirlwind	Normal	—	100	20

MOVE TUTOR LIST
Move Name	Type	ST	ACC	PP
Body Slam*	Normal	85	100	15
Double-Edge	Normal	120	100	15
Endure*	Normal	—	—	10
Mimic	Normal	—	100	10
Mud-Slap*	Ground	20	100	10
Rock Slide*	Rock	75	90	10
Sleep Talk	Normal	—	—	10
Snore*	Normal	40	100	15
Substitute	Normal	—	—	10
Swagger	Normal	—	90	15

*Battle Frontier tutor move

117

Vibrava™

GROUND
DRAGON

GENERAL INFO
SPECIES: Vibration Pokémon
HEIGHT: 3'7"
WEIGHT: 34 lbs.
ABILITY: *Levitate—Pokémon is not affected by Ground-type Moves.*

STATS

HP	25
ATTACK	75
DEFENSE	50
SP. ATTACK	50
SP. DEFENSE	50
SPEED	50

EVOLUTIONS

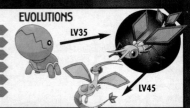

LV35

LV45

WHERE/HOW TO CATCH
Evolve from Trapinch

STRONG AGAINST:
FIRE
ELECTRIC
POISON
ROCK
GROUND

WEAK AGAINST:
ICE
DRAGON

MOVES LIST

LV	Move Name	Type	ST	ACC	PP	LV	Move Name	Type	ST	ACC	PP
S	Bite	Dark	60	100	25	25	Sand Tomb	Ground	15	70	15
S	Sand-Attack	Ground	—	100	15	33	Crunch	Dark	80	100	15
S	Faint Attack	Dark	60	—	20	35	Dragonbreath	Dragon	60	100	20
S	Sand Tomb	Ground	15	70	15	41	Screech	Normal	—	85	40
09	Sand-Attack	Ground	—	100	15	49	Sandstorm	Rock	—	—	10
17	Faint Attack	Dark	60	—	20	57	Hyper Beam	Normal	150	90	5

TM/HM LIST

TM/HM #	Move Name	Type	ST	ACC	PP	TM/HM #	Move Name	Type	ST	ACC	PP
HM02	Fly	Flying	70	95	15	TM26	Earthquake	Ground	100	100	10
HM04	Strength	Normal	80	100	15	TM27	Return	Normal	—	100	20
HM06	Rock Smash	Fighting	20	100	15	TM28	Dig	Ground	60	100	10
TM06	Toxic	Poison	—	85	10	TM32	Double Team	Normal	—	—	15
TM10	Hidden Power	Normal	—	100	15	TM37	Sandstorm	Rock	—	—	10
TM11	Sunny Day	Fire	—	—	5	TM39	Rock Tomb	Rock	50	80	10
TM15	Hyper Beam	Normal	150	90	5	TM42	Façade	Normal	70	100	20
TM17	Protect	Normal	—	—	10	TM43	Secret Power	Normal	70	100	20
TM19	Giga Drain	Grass	60	100	5	TM44	Rest	Psychic	—	—	10
TM21	Frustration	Normal	—	100	20	TM45	Attract	Normal	—	100	15
TM22	Solarbeam	Grass	120	100	10	TM47	Steel Wing	Steel	70	90	25

MOVE TUTOR LIST

Move Name	Type	ST	ACC	PP
Body Slam*	Normal	85	100	15
Double-Edge	Normal	120	100	15
Endure*	Normal	—	—	10
Mimic	Normal	—	100	10
Mud-Slap*	Ground	20	100	10
Rock Slide*	Rock	75	90	10
Sleep Talk	Normal	—	—	10
Snore*	Normal	40	100	15
Substitute	Normal	—	—	10
Swagger	Normal	—	90	15
Swift*	Normal	60	—	20

*Battle Frontier tutor move

118

Flygon™

GROUND
DRAGON

GENERAL INFO
SPECIES: Mystic Pokémon
HEIGHT: 6'7"
WEIGHT: 181 lbs.
ABILITY: *Levitate—Pokémon is not affected by Ground-type Moves.*

STATS

HP	25
ATTACK	75
DEFENSE	50
SP. ATTACK	75
SP. DEFENSE	50
SPEED	75

EVOLUTIONS

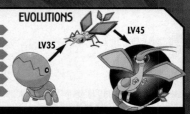

LV35

LV45

WHERE/HOW TO CATCH
Evolve from Vibrava

STRONG AGAINST:
FIRE
ELECTRIC
POISON
ROCK
GROUND

WEAK AGAINST:
ICE
DRAGON

MOVES LIST

LV	Move Name	Type	ST	ACC	PP	LV	Move Name	Type	ST	ACC	PP
S	Bite	Dark	60	100	25	25	Sand Tomb	Ground	15	70	15
S	Sand-Attack	Ground	—	100	15	33	Crunch	Dark	80	100	15
S	Faint Attack	Dark	60	—	20	35	Dragonbreath	Dragon	60	100	20
S	Sand Tomb	Ground	15	70	15	41	Screech	Normal	—	85	40
09	Sand-Attack	Ground	—	100	15	53	Sandstorm	Rock	—	—	10
17	Faint Attack	Dark	60	—	20	65	Hyper Beam	Normal	150	90	5

TM/HM LIST

TM/HM #	Move Name	Type	ST	ACC	PP	TM/HM #	Move Name	Type	ST	ACC	PP
HM02	Fly	Flying	70	95	15	TM26	Earthquake	Ground	100	100	10
HM04	Strength	Normal	80	100	15	TM27	Return	Normal	—	100	20
HM06	Rock Smash	Fighting	20	100	15	TM28	Dig	Ground	60	100	10
TM02	Dragon Claw	Dragon	80	100	15	TM32	Double Team	Normal	—	—	15
TM06	Toxic	Poison	—	85	10	TM35	Flamethrower	Fire	95	100	15
TM10	Hidden Power	Normal	—	100	15	TM37	Sandstorm	Rock	—	—	10
TM11	Sunny Day	Fire	—	—	5	TM38	Fire Blast	Fire	120	85	5
TM15	Hyper Beam	Normal	150	90	5	TM39	Rock Tomb	Rock	50	80	10
TM17	Protect	Normal	—	—	10	TM42	Façade	Normal	70	100	20
TM19	Giga Drain	Grass	60	100	5	TM43	Secret Power	Normal	70	100	20
TM21	Frustration	Normal	—	100	20	TM44	Rest	Psychic	—	—	10
TM22	Solarbeam	Grass	120	100	10	TM45	Attract	Normal	—	100	15
TM23	Iron Tail	Steel	100	75	15	TM47	Steel Wing	Steel	70	90	25

MOVE TUTOR LIST

Move Name	Type	ST	ACC	PP
Body Slam*	Normal	85	100	15
Double-Edge	Normal	120	100	15
Endure*	Normal	—	—	10
Fire Punch*	Fire	75	100	15
Fury Cutter	Bug	10	95	20
Mimic	Normal	—	100	10
Mud-Slap*	Ground	20	100	10
Rock Slide*	Rock	75	90	10
Sleep Talk	Normal	—	—	10
Snore*	Normal	40	100	15
Substitute	Normal	—	—	10
Swagger	Normal	—	90	15
Swift*	Normal	60	—	20

*Battle Frontier tutor move

119

Cacnea™
GRASS

GENERAL INFO
SPECIES: Cactus Pokémon
HEIGHT: 1'4"
WEIGHT: 133 lbs.
ABILITY: Sand Veil—
The Pokémon's Evasion stat rises when a Sandstorm blows.

STATS

HP	25
ATTACK	75
DEFENSE	25
SP. ATTACK	75
SP. DEFENSE	25
SPEED	25

EVOLUTIONS

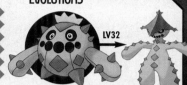

LV32

WHERE/HOW TO CATCH
Route 111

STRONG AGAINST:
GRASS
ELECTRIC
WATER
GROUND

WEAK AGAINST:
FIRE
ICE
POISON
FLYING
BUG

MOVES LIST

LV	Move Name	Type	ST	ACC	PP
S	Poison Sting	Poison	15	100	35
S	Leer	Normal	—	100	30
05	Absorb	Grass	20	100	20
09	Growth	Normal	—	—	40
13	Leech Seed	Grass	—	90	10
17	Sand-Attack	Ground	—	100	15
21	Pin Missile	Bug	14	85	20
25	Ingrain	Grass	—	100	20
29	Faint Attack	Dark	60	—	20
33	Spikes	Ground	—	—	20
37	Needle Arm	Grass	60	100	15
41	Cotton Spore	Grass	—	85	40
45	Sandstorm	Rock	—	—	10

TM/HM LIST

TM/HM #	Move Name	Type	ST	ACC	PP
HM01	Cut	Normal	50	95	30
HM05	Flash	Normal	—	70	20
TM01	Focus Punch	Fighting	150	100	20
TM06	Toxic	Poison	—	85	10
TM09	Bullet Seed	Grass	10	100	30
TM10	Hidden Power	Normal	—	100	15
TM11	Sunny Day	Fire	—	—	5
TM17	Protect	Normal	—	—	10
TM19	Giga Drain	Grass	60	100	5
TM21	Frustration	Normal	—	100	20
TM22	Solarbeam	Grass	120	100	10
TM27	Return	Normal	—	100	20
TM32	Double Team	Normal	—	—	15
TM37	Sandstorm	Rock	—	—	10
TM42	Façade	Normal	70	100	20
TM43	Secret Power	Normal	70	100	20
TM44	Rest	Psychic	—	—	10
TM45	Attract	Normal	—	100	15

EGG MOVES

Move Name	Type	ST	ACC	PP
Grasswhistle	Grass	—	55	15
Acid	Poison	40	100	30
Teeter Dance	Normal	—	100	20
Dynamicpunch	Fighting	100	50	5
Counter	Fighting	—	100	20

MOVE TUTOR LIST

Move Name	Type	ST	ACC	PP
Body Slam*	Normal	85	100	15
Counter*	Fighting	—	100	20
Double-Edge	Normal	120	100	15
Dynamicpunch	Fighting	100	50	5
Endure*	Normal	—	—	10
Fury Cutter	Bug	10	95	20
Mega Punch*	Normal	80	75	20
Mimic	Normal	—	100	10
Mud-Slap*	Ground	20	100	10
Seismic Toss*	Fighting	—	100	20
Sleep Talk	Normal	—	—	10
Snore*	Normal	40	100	15
Substitute	Normal	—	—	10
Swagger	Normal	—	90	15
Swords Dance*	Normal	—	—	30
Thunderpunch*	Electric	75	100	15

*Battle Frontier tutor move

120

Cacturne™
GRASS
DARK

GENERAL INFO
SPECIES: Scarecrow Pokémon
HEIGHT: 4'3"
WEIGHT: 171 lbs.
ABILITY: Sand Veil—
The Pokémon's Evasion stat rises when a Sandstorm blows.

STATS

HP	50
ATTACK	75
DEFENSE	50
SP. ATTACK	100
SP. DEFENSE	50
SPEED	50

EVOLUTIONS

 LV32

WHERE/HOW TO CATCH
Evolve from Cacnea

STRONG AGAINST:
WATER
ELECTRIC
GRASS
GROUND
PSYCHIC
GHOST
DARK

WEAK AGAINST:
FIRE
ICE
FIGHTING
POISON
FLYING
BUG

MOVES LIST

LV	Move Name	Type	ST	ACC	PP
S	Poison Sting	Poison	15	100	35
S	Leer	Normal	—	100	30
S	Absorb	Grass	20	100	20
S	Growth	Normal	—	—	40
05	Absorb	Grass	20	100	20
09	Growth	Normal	—	—	40
13	Leech Seed	Grass	—	90	10
17	Sand-Attack	Ground	—	100	15
21	Pin Missile	Bug	14	85	20
25	Ingrain	Grass	—	100	20
29	Faint Attack	Dark	60	—	20
35	Spikes	Ground	—	—	20
41	Needle Arm	Grass	60	100	15
47	Cotton Spore	Grass	—	85	40
53	Sandstorm	Rock	—	—	10

TM/HM LIST

TM/HM #	Move Name	Type	ST	ACC	PP
HM01	Cut	Normal	50	95	30
HM04	Strength	Normal	80	100	15
HM05	Flash	Normal	—	70	20
TM01	Focus Punch	Fighting	150	100	20
TM06	Toxic	Poison	—	85	10
TM09	Bullet Seed	Grass	10	100	30
TM10	Hidden Power	Normal	—	100	15
TM11	Sunny Day	Fire	—	—	5
TM15	Hyper Beam	Normal	150	90	5
TM17	Protect	Normal	—	—	10
TM19	Giga Drain	Grass	60	100	5
TM21	Frustration	Normal	—	100	20
TM22	Solarbeam	Grass	120	100	10
TM27	Return	Normal	—	100	20
TM32	Double Team	Normal	—	—	15
TM37	Sandstorm	Rock	—	—	10
TM42	Façade	Normal	70	100	20
TM43	Secret Power	Normal	70	100	20
TM44	Rest	Psychic	—	—	10
TM45	Attract	Normal	—	100	15

MOVE TUTOR LIST

Move Name	Type	ST	ACC	PP
Body Slam*	Normal	85	100	15
Counter*	Fighting	—	100	20
Double-Edge	Normal	120	100	15
Dynamicpunch	Fighting	100	50	5
Endure*	Normal	—	—	10
Fury Cutter	Bug	10	95	20
Mega Kick*	Normal	120	75	15
Mega Punch*	Normal	80	75	20
Mimic	Normal	—	100	10
Mud-Slap*	Ground	20	100	10
Seismic Toss*	Fighting	—	100	20
Sleep Talk	Normal	—	—	10
Snore*	Normal	40	100	15
Substitute	Normal	—	—	10
Swagger	Normal	—	90	15
Swords Dance*	Normal	—	—	30
Thunderpunch*	Electric	75	100	15

*Battle Frontier tutor move

121 Swablu

NORMAL
FLYING

GENERAL INFO
SPECIES: Cotton Bird Pokémon
HEIGHT: 1'4"
WEIGHT: 3 lbs.
ABILITY: *Natural Cure*—*Any negative Status conditions are healed when the Pokémon is removed from battle.*

STATS
HP	25
ATTACK	50
DEFENSE	50
SP. ATTACK	50
SP. DEFENSE	50
SPEED	50

EVOLUTIONS
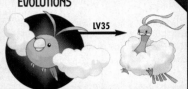

LV35

WHERE/HOW TO CATCH
Routes 114 and 115

STRONG AGAINST:
GRASS
GROUND
BUG
GHOST

WEAK AGAINST:
ELECTRIC
ICE
ROCK

MOVES LIST
LV	Move Name	Type	ST	ACC	PP
S	Peck	Flying	35	100	35
S	Growl	Normal	—	100	40
08	Astonish	Ghost	30	100	15
11	Sing	Normal	—	55	15
18	Fury Attack	Normal	15	85	20
21	Safeguard	Normal	—	—	25

LV	Move Name	Type	ST	ACC	PP
28	Mist	Ice	—	—	30
31	Take Down	Normal	90	85	20
38	Mirror Move	Flying	—	—	20
41	Refresh	Normal	—	100	20
48	Perish Song	Normal	—	—	5

TM/HM LIST
TM/HM #	Move Name	Type	ST	ACC	PP
HM02	Fly	Flying	70	95	15
TM06	Toxic	Poison	—	85	10
TM10	Hidden Power	Normal	—	100	15
TM11	Sunny Day	Fire	—	—	5
TM13	Ice Beam	Ice	95	100	10
TM17	Protect	Normal	—	—	10
TM18	Rain Dance	Water	—	—	5
TM20	Safeguard	Normal	—	—	25
TM21	Frustration	Normal	—	100	20
TM22	Solarbeam	Grass	120	100	10

TM/HM #	Move Name	Type	ST	ACC	PP
TM27	Return	Normal	—	100	20
TM32	Double Team	Normal	—	—	15
TM40	Aerial Ace	Flying	60	—	20
TM42	Façade	Normal	70	100	20
TM43	Secret Power	Normal	70	100	20
TM44	Rest	Psychic	—	—	10
TM45	Attract	Normal	—	100	15
TM46	Thief	Dark	40	100	10
TM47	Steel Wing	Steel	70	90	25

EGG MOVES
Move Name	Type	ST	ACC	PP
Agility	Psychic	—	—	30
Haze	Ice	—	—	30
Pursuit	Dark	40	100	20
Rage	Normal	20	100	20

MOVE TUTOR LIST
Move Name	Type	ST	ACC	PP
Body Slam*	Normal	85	100	15
Double-Edge	Normal	120	100	15
Dream Eater*	Psychic	100	100	15
Endure*	Normal	—	—	10
Mimic	Normal	—	100	10
Mud-Slap*	Ground	20	100	10
Psych Up*	Normal	—	—	10
Sleep Talk	Normal	—	—	10
Snore*	Normal	40	100	15
Substitute	Normal	—	—	10
Swagger	Normal	—	90	15
Swift*	Normal	60	—	20

*Battle Frontier tutor move

122 Altaria

DRAGON
FLYING

GENERAL INFO
SPECIES: Humming Pokémon
HEIGHT: 3'7"
WEIGHT: 45 lbs.
ABILITY: *Natural Cure*—*Any negative Status conditions are healed when the Pokémon is removed from battle.*

STATS
HP	50
ATTACK	50
DEFENSE	50
SP. ATTACK	50
SP. DEFENSE	75
SPEED	75

EVOLUTIONS
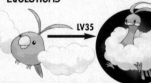

LV35

WHERE/HOW TO CATCH
Evolve from Swablu; Sky Pillar

STRONG AGAINST:
FIRE
WATER
GRASS
FIGHTING
GROUND
BUG

WEAK AGAINST:
ICE
ROCK
DRAGON

MOVES LIST
LV	Move Name	Type	ST	ACC	PP
S	Peck	Flying	35	100	35
S	Growl	Normal	—	100	40
S	Astonish	Ghost	30	100	15
S	Sing	Normal	—	55	15
08	Astonish	Ghost	30	100	15
11	Sing	Normal	—	55	15
18	Fury Attack	Normal	15	85	20
21	Safeguard	Normal	—	—	25

LV	Move Name	Type	ST	ACC	PP
28	Mist	Ice	—	—	30
31	Take Down	Normal	90	85	20
35	Dragonbreath	Dragon	60	100	20
40	Dragon Dance	Dragon	—	—	20
45	Refresh	Normal	—	100	20
54	Perish Song	Normal	—	—	5
59	Sky Attack	Flying	140	90	5

TM/HM LIST
TM/HM #	Move Name	Type	ST	ACC	PP
HM02	Fly	Flying	70	95	15
HM06	Rock Smash	Fighting	20	100	15
TM02	Dragon Claw	Dragon	80	100	15
TM05	Roar	Normal	—	100	20
TM06	Toxic	Poison	—	85	10
TM10	Hidden Power	Normal	—	100	15
TM11	Sunny Day	Fire	—	—	5
TM13	Ice Beam	Ice	95	100	10
TM15	Hyper Beam	Normal	150	90	5
TM17	Protect	Normal	—	—	10
TM18	Rain Dance	Water	—	—	5
TM20	Safeguard	Normal	—	—	25
TM21	Frustration	Normal	—	100	20
TM22	Solarbeam	Grass	120	100	10

TM/HM #	Move Name	Type	ST	ACC	PP
TM23	Iron Tail	Steel	100	75	15
TM26	Earthquake	Ground	100	100	10
TM27	Return	Normal	—	100	20
TM32	Double Team	Normal	—	—	15
TM35	Flamethrower	Fire	95	100	15
TM38	Fire Blast	Fire	120	85	5
TM40	Aerial Ace	Flying	60	—	20
TM42	Façade	Normal	70	100	20
TM43	Secret Power	Normal	70	100	20
TM44	Rest	Psychic	—	—	10
TM45	Attract	Normal	—	100	15
TM46	Thief	Dark	40	100	10
TM47	Steel Wing	Steel	70	90	25

MOVE TUTOR LIST
Move Name	Type	ST	ACC	PP
Body Slam*	Normal	85	100	15
Double-Edge	Normal	120	100	15
Dream Eater*	Psychic	100	100	15
Endure*	Normal	—	—	10
Mimic	Normal	—	100	10
Mud-Slap*	Ground	20	100	10
Psych Up*	Normal	—	—	10
Sleep Talk	Normal	—	—	10
Snore*	Normal	40	100	15
Substitute	Normal	—	—	10
Swagger	Normal	—	90	15
Swift*	Normal	60	—	20

*Battle Frontier tutor move

123

Zangoose™

NORMAL

GENERAL INFO
SPECIES: Cat Ferret Pokémon
HEIGHT: 4'3"
WEIGHT: 89 lbs.
ABILITY: *Immunity* — Pokémon cannot be Poisoned.

STATS

HP	50
ATTACK	75
DEFENSE	50
SP. ATTACK	50
SP. DEFENSE	50
SPEED	75

EVOLUTIONS

ZANGOOSE DOES NOT EVOLVE

WHERE/HOW TO CATCH
Must trade from *Pokémon Ruby*

MOVES LIST

LV	Move Name	Type	ST	ACC	PP
S	Scratch	Normal	40	100	35
04	Leer	Normal	—	100	30
07	Quick Attack	Normal	40	100	30
10	Swords Dance	Normal	—	—	30
13	Fury Cutter	Bug	10	95	20
19	Slash	Normal	70	100	20
25	Pursuit	Dark	40	100	20
31	Crush Claw	Normal	75	95	10
37	Taunt	Dark	—	100	20
46	Detect	Fighting	—	—	5
55	False Swipe	Normal	40	100	40

STRONG AGAINST:
GHOST

WEAK AGAINST:
FIGHTING

TM/HM LIST

TM/HM #	Move Name	Type	ST	ACC	PP
HM04	Strength	Normal	80	100	15
HM06	Rock Smash	Fighting	20	100	15
TM01	Focus Punch	Fighting	150	100	20
TM03	Water Pulse	Water	60	100	20
TM05	Roar	Normal	—	100	20
TM06	Toxic	Poison	—	85	10
TM10	Hidden Power	Normal	—	100	15
TM11	Sunny Day	Fire	—	—	5
TM12	Taunt	Dark	—	100	20
TM13	Ice Beam	Ice	95	100	10
TM14	Blizzard	Ice	120	70	5
TM17	Protect	Normal	—	—	10
TM18	Rain Dance	Water	—	—	5
TM19	Giga Drain	Grass	60	100	5
TM21	Frustration	Normal	—	100	20
TM22	Solarbeam	Grass	120	100	10
TM23	Iron Tail	Steel	100	75	15
TM24	Thunderbolt	Electric	95	100	15
TM25	Thunder	Electric	120	70	10
TM27	Return	Normal	—	100	20
TM28	Dig	Ground	60	100	10
TM30	Shadow Ball	Ghost	60	—	20
TM31	Brick Break	Fighting	75	100	15
TM32	Double Team	Normal	—	—	15
TM34	Shock Wave	Electric	60	—	20
TM35	Flamethrower	Fire	95	100	15
TM38	Fire Blast	Fire	120	85	5
TM40	Aerial Ace	Flying	60	—	20
TM42	Façade	Normal	70	100	20
TM43	Secret Power	Normal	70	100	20
TM44	Rest	Psychic	—	—	10
TM45	Attract	Normal	—	100	15
TM46	Thief	Dark	40	100	10

EGG MOVES

Move Name	Type	ST	ACC	PP
Flail	Normal	—	100	15
Double Kick	Fighting	30	100	30
Razor Wind	Normal	80	100	10
Counter	Fighting	—	100	20
Roar	Normal	—	100	20
Curse	—	—	—	10

MOVE TUTOR LIST

Move Name	Type	ST	ACC	PP
Body Slam*	Normal	85	100	15
Counter*	Fighting	—	100	20
Defense Curl*	Normal	—	—	40
Double-Edge	Normal	120	100	15
Dynamicpunch	Fighting	100	50	5
Endure*	Normal	—	—	10
Fire Punch*	Fire	75	100	15
Fury Cutter	Bug	10	95	20
Ice Punch*	Ice	75	100	15
Icy Wind*	Ice	55	95	15
Mega Kick*	Normal	120	85	5
Mega Punch*	Normal	80	75	20
Mimic	Normal	—	100	10
Mud-Slap*	Ground	20	100	10
Rock Slide*	Rock	75	90	10
Rollout	Rock	30	90	20
Seismic Toss*	Fighting	—	100	20
Sleep Talk	Normal	—	—	10
Snore*	Normal	40	100	15
Substitute	Normal	—	—	10
Swagger	Normal	—	90	15
Swift*	Normal	60	—	20
Swords Dance*	Normal	—	—	30
Thunderpunch*	Electric	75	100	15
Thunder Wave*	Electric	—	100	20

*Battle Frontier tutor move

124

Seviper™

POISON

GENERAL INFO
SPECIES: Fang Snake Pokémon
HEIGHT: 8'10"
WEIGHT: 116 lbs.
ABILITY: *Shed Skin* — Every turn, the Pokémon has a 1/3 chance of recovering from a Status condition.

STATS

HP	50
ATTACK	75
DEFENSE	50
SP. ATTACK	75
SP. DEFENSE	50
SPEED	50

EVOLUTIONS

SEVIPER DOES NOT EVOLVE

WHERE/HOW TO CATCH
Route 114

MOVES LIST

LV	Move Name	Type	ST	ACC	PP
S	Wrap	Normal	15	85	20
07	Lick	Ghost	20	100	30
10	Bite	Dark	60	100	25
16	Poison Tail	Poison	50	100	25
19	Screech	Normal	—	85	40
25	Glare	Normal	—	75	30
28	Crunch	Dark	80	100	15
34	Poison Fang	Poison	50	100	15
37	Swagger	Normal	—	90	15
43	Haze	Ice	—	—	30

STRONG AGAINST:
GRASS
FIGHTING
POISON
BUG

WEAK AGAINST:
GROUND
PSYCHIC

TM/HM LIST

TM/HM #	Move Name	Type	ST	ACC	PP
HM04	Strength	Normal	80	100	15
HM06	Rock Smash	Fighting	20	100	15
TM06	Toxic	Poison	—	85	10
TM10	Hidden Power	Normal	—	100	15
TM11	Sunny Day	Fire	—	—	5
TM12	Taunt	Dark	—	100	20
TM17	Protect	Normal	—	—	10
TM18	Rain Dance	Water	—	—	5
TM19	Giga Drain	Grass	60	100	5
TM21	Frustration	Normal	—	100	20
TM23	Iron Tail	Steel	100	75	15
TM26	Earthquake	Ground	100	100	10
TM27	Return	Normal	—	100	20
TM28	Dig	Ground	60	100	10
TM32	Double Team	Normal	—	—	15
TM35	Flamethrower	Fire	95	100	15
TM36	Sludge Bomb	Poison	90	100	10
TM42	Façade	Normal	70	100	20
TM43	Secret Power	Normal	70	100	20
TM44	Rest	Psychic	—	—	10
TM45	Attract	Normal	—	100	15
TM46	Thief	Dark	40	100	10
TM49	Snatch	Dark	—	100	10

EGG MOVES

Move Name	Type	ST	ACC	PP
Stockpile	Normal	—	—	10
Swallow	Normal	—	—	10
Spit Up	Normal	100	100	10
Body Slam	Normal	85	100	15

MOVE TUTOR LIST

Move Name	Type	ST	ACC	PP
Body Slam*	Normal	85	100	15
Double-Edge	Normal	120	100	15
Endure*	Normal	—	—	10
Fury Cutter	Bug	10	95	20
Mimic	Normal	—	100	10
Mud-Slap*	Ground	20	100	10
Sleep Talk	Normal	—	—	10
Snore*	Normal	40	100	15
Substitute	Normal	—	—	10
Swagger	Normal	—	90	15
Swift*	Normal	60	—	20

*Battle Frontier tutor move

125

Lunatone™

ROCK
PSYCHIC

GENERAL INFO
SPECIES: Meteorite Pokémon
HEIGHT: 3'3"
WEIGHT: 370 lbs.
ABILITY: Levitate—Pokémon
is not affected by Ground-type Moves.

STATS
HP	50
ATTACK	50
DEFENSE	50
SP. ATTACK	75
SP. DEFENSE	50
SPEED	50

EVOLUTIONS

LUNATONE DOES
NOT EVOLVE

WHERE/HOW TO CATCH
Must trade from
Pokémon Ruby

STRONG AGAINST:
NORMAL
FIRE
POISON
FLYING
PSYCHIC
GROUND

WEAK AGAINST:
WATER
GRASS
BUG
GHOST
DARK
STEEL

MOVES LIST
LV	Move Name	Type	ST	ACC	PP
S	Tackle	Normal	35	95	35
S	Harden	Normal	—	—	30
07	Confusion	Psychic	50	100	25
13	Rock Throw	Rock	50	90	15
19	Hypnosis	Psychic	—	60	20
25	Psywave	Psychic	—	80	15
31	Cosmic Power	Normal	—	—	20
37	Psychic	Psychic	90	100	10
43	Future Sight	Psychic	80	90	15
49	Explosion	Normal	250	100	5

TM/HM LIST
TM/HM #	Move Name	Type	ST	ACC	PP
HM05	Flash	Normal	—	70	20
TM04	Calm Mind	Psychic	—	—	20
TM06	Toxic	Poison	—	85	10
TM10	Hidden Power	Normal	—	100	15
TM13	Ice Beam	Ice	95	100	10
TM15	Hyper Beam	Normal	150	90	5
TM16	Light Screen	Psychic	—	—	30
TM17	Protect	Normal	—	—	10
TM18	Rain Dance	Water	—	—	5
TM20	Safeguard	Normal	—	—	25
TM21	Frustration	Normal	—	100	20
TM26	Earthquake	Ground	100	100	10
TM27	Return	Normal	—	100	20
TM29	Psychic	Psychic	90	100	10
TM30	Shadow Ball	Ghost	60	—	20
TM32	Double Team	Normal	—	—	15
TM33	Reflect	Psychic	—	—	20
TM37	Sandstorm	Rock	—	—	10
TM39	Rock Tomb	Rock	50	80	10
TM42	Façade	Normal	70	100	20
TM43	Secret Power	Normal	70	100	20
TM44	Rest	Psychic	—	—	10
TM48	Skill Swap	Psychic	—	100	10

EGG MOVES
Move Name	Type	ST	ACC	PP
None				

MOVE TUTOR LIST
Move Name	Type	ST	ACC	PP
Body Slam*	Normal	85	100	15
Defense Curl*	Normal	—	—	40
Double-Edge	Normal	120	100	15
Dream Eater*	Psychic	100	100	15
Endure*	Normal	—	—	10
Explosion	Normal	250	100	5
Mimic	Normal	—	100	10
Psych Up*	Normal	—	—	10
Rock Slide*	Rock	75	90	10
Rollout	Rock	30	90	20
Sleep Talk	Normal	—	—	10
Snore*	Normal	40	100	15
Substitute	Normal	—	—	10
Swagger	Normal	—	90	15
Swift*	Normal	60	—	20

*Battle Frontier tutor move

126

Solrock™

ROCK
PSYCHIC

GENERAL INFO
SPECIES: Meteorite Pokémon
HEIGHT: 3'11"
WEIGHT: 340 lbs.
ABILITY: Levitate—Pokémon
is not affected by Ground-type Moves.

STATS
HP	50
ATTACK	75
DEFENSE	50
SP. ATTACK	50
SP. DEFENSE	50
SPEED	50

EVOLUTIONS

SOLROCK DOES
NOT EVOLVE

WHERE/HOW TO CATCH
Meteor Falls

STRONG AGAINST:
NORMAL
FIRE
POISON
FLYING
PSYCHIC
GROUND

WEAK AGAINST:
WATER
GRASS
BUG
GHOST
DARK
STEEL

MOVES LIST
LV	Move Name	Type	ST	ACC	PP
S	Tackle	Normal	35	95	35
S	Harden	Normal	—	—	30
07	Confusion	Psychic	50	100	25
13	Rock Throw	Rock	50	90	15
19	Fire Spin	Fire	15	70	15
25	Psywave	Psychic	—	80	15
31	Cosmic Power	Normal	—	—	20
37	Rock Slide	Rock	75	90	10
43	Solarbeam	Grass	120	100	10
49	Explosion	Normal	250	100	5

TM/HM LIST
TM/HM #	Move Name	Type	ST	ACC	PP
HM05	Flash	Normal	—	70	20
TM04	Calm Mind	Psychic	—	—	20
TM06	Toxic	Poison	—	85	10
TM10	Hidden Power	Normal	—	100	15
TM11	Sunny Day	Fire	—	—	5
TM15	Hyper Beam	Normal	150	90	5
TM16	Light Screen	Psychic	—	—	30
TM17	Protect	Normal	—	—	10
TM20	Safeguard	Normal	—	—	25
TM21	Frustration	Normal	—	100	20
TM22	Solarbeam	Grass	120	100	10
TM26	Earthquake	Ground	100	100	10
TM27	Return	Normal	—	100	20
TM29	Psychic	Psychic	90	100	10
TM30	Shadow Ball	Ghost	60	—	20
TM32	Double Team	Normal	—	—	15
TM33	Reflect	Psychic	—	—	20
TM35	Flamethrower	Fire	95	100	15
TM37	Sandstorm	Rock	—	—	10
TM38	Fire Blast	Fire	120	85	5
TM39	Rock Tomb	Rock	50	80	10
TM42	Façade	Normal	70	100	20
TM43	Secret Power	Normal	70	100	20
TM44	Rest	Psychic	—	—	10
TM48	Skill Swap	Psychic	—	100	10
TM50	Overheat	Fire	140	90	5

EGG MOVES
Move Name	Type	ST	ACC	PP
None				

MOVE TUTOR LIST
Move Name	Type	ST	ACC	PP
Body Slam*	Normal	85	100	15
Defense Curl*	Normal	—	—	40
Double-Edge	Normal	120	100	15
Dream Eater*	Psychic	100	100	15
Endure*	Normal	—	—	10
Explosion	Normal	250	100	5
Mimic	Normal	—	100	10
Psych Up*	Normal	—	—	10
Rock Slide*	Rock	75	90	10
Rollout	Rock	30	90	20
Sleep Talk	Normal	—	—	10
Snore*	Normal	40	100	15
Substitute	Normal	—	—	10
Swagger	Normal	—	90	15
Swift*	Normal	60	—	20

*Battle Frontier tutor move

127

Barboach™

WATER
GROUND

GENERAL INFO
SPECIES: Whiskers Pokémon
HEIGHT: 1'4"
WEIGHT: 4 lbs.
ABILITY: *Oblivious*—Pokémon is not affected by the Attract condition.

STATS

HP	25
ATTACK	50
DEFENSE	50
SP. ATTACK	50
SP. DEFENSE	25
SPEED	50

EVOLUTIONS

LV30

WHERE/HOW TO CATCH
Routes 111, 114, and 120; Meteor Falls and Victory Road

STRONG AGAINST:
FIRE
ELECTRIC
POISON
ROCK
STEEL

WEAK AGAINST:
GRASS

MOVES LIST

LV	Move Name	Type	ST	ACC	PP
S	Mud-Slap	Ground	20	100	10
06	Mud Sport	Ground	—	100	15
06	Water Sport	Water	—	100	15
11	Water Gun	Water	40	100	25
16	Magnitude	Ground	—	100	30
21	Amnesia	Psychic	—	—	20
26	Rest	Psychic	—	—	10
26	Snore	Normal	40	100	15
31	Earthquake	Ground	100	100	10
36	Future Sight	Psychic	80	90	15
41	Fissure	Ground	—	30	5

TM/HM LIST

TM/HM #	Move Name	Type	ST	ACC	PP
HM03	Surf	Water	95	100	15
HM07	Waterfall	Water	80	100	15
HM08	Dive	Water	60	100	10
TM03	Water Pulse	Water	60	100	20
TM06	Toxic	Poison	—	85	10
TM07	Hail	Ice	—	—	10
TM10	Hidden Power	Normal	—	100	15
TM13	Ice Beam	Ice	95	100	10
TM14	Blizzard	Ice	120	70	5
TM17	Protect	Normal	—	—	10
TM18	Rain Dance	Water	—	—	5

TM/HM #	Move Name	Type	ST	ACC	PP
TM21	Frustration	Normal	—	100	20
TM26	Earthquake	Ground	100	100	10
TM27	Return	Normal	—	100	20
TM32	Double Team	Normal	—	—	15
TM37	Sandstorm	Rock	—	—	10
TM39	Rock Tomb	Rock	50	80	10
TM42	Façade	Normal	70	100	20
TM43	Secret Power	Normal	70	100	20
TM44	Rest	Psychic	—	—	10
TM45	Attract	Normal	—	100	15

EGG MOVES

Move Name	Type	ST	ACC	PP
Thrash	Normal	90	100	20
Whirlpool	Water	15	70	15
Spark	Electric	65	100	20

MOVE TUTOR LIST

Move Name	Type	ST	ACC	PP
Double-Edge	Normal	120	100	15
Endure*	Normal	—	—	10
Icy Wind*	Ice	55	95	15
Mimic	Normal	—	100	10
Mud-Slap*	Ground	20	100	10
Sleep Talk	Normal	—	—	10
Snore*	Normal	40	100	15
Substitute	Normal	—	—	10
Swagger	Normal	—	90	15

*Battle Frontier tutor move

128

Whiscash™

WATER
GROUND

GENERAL INFO
SPECIES: Whiskers Pokémon
HEIGHT: 2'11"
WEIGHT: 52 lbs.
ABILITY: *Oblivious*—Pokémon is not affected by the Attract condition.

STATS

HP	50
ATTACK	75
DEFENSE	50
SP. ATTACK	75
SP. DEFENSE	50
SPEED	50

EVOLUTIONS

LV30

WHERE/HOW TO CATCH
Evolve from Barboach

STRONG AGAINST:
FIRE
ELECTRIC
POISON
ROCK
STEEL

WEAK AGAINST:
GRASS

MOVES LIST

LV	Move Name	Type	ST	ACC	PP
S	Tickle	Normal	—	100	20
S	Mud-Slap	Ground	20	100	10
S	Mud Sport	Ground	—	100	15
S	Water Sport	Water	—	100	15
06	Mud Sport	Ground	—	100	15
06	Water Sport	Water	—	100	15
11	Water Gun	Water	40	100	25

LV	Move Name	Type	ST	ACC	PP
16	Magnitude	Ground	—	100	30
21	Amnesia	Psychic	—	—	20
26	Rest	Psychic	—	—	10
26	Snore	Normal	40	100	15
36	Earthquake	Ground	100	100	10
46	Future Sight	Psychic	80	90	15
56	Fissure	Ground	—	30	5

TM/HM LIST

TM/HM #	Move Name	Type	ST	ACC	PP
HM03	Surf	Water	95	100	15
HM04	Strength	Normal	80	100	15
HM06	Rock Smash	Fighting	20	100	15
HM07	Waterfall	Water	80	100	15
HM08	Dive	Water	60	100	10
TM03	Water Pulse	Water	60	100	20
TM06	Toxic	Poison	—	85	10
TM07	Hail	Ice	—	—	10
TM10	Hidden Power	Normal	—	100	15
TM13	Ice Beam	Ice	95	100	10
TM14	Blizzard	Ice	120	70	5
TM15	Hyper Beam	Normal	150	90	5

TM/HM #	Move Name	Type	ST	ACC	PP
TM17	Protect	Normal	—	—	10
TM18	Rain Dance	Water	—	—	5
TM21	Frustration	Normal	—	100	20
TM26	Earthquake	Ground	100	100	10
TM27	Return	Normal	—	100	20
TM32	Double Team	Normal	—	—	15
TM37	Sandstorm	Rock	—	—	10
TM39	Rock Tomb	Rock	50	80	10
TM42	Façade	Normal	70	100	20
TM43	Secret Power	Normal	70	100	20
TM44	Rest	Psychic	—	—	10
TM45	Attract	Normal	—	100	15

MOVE TUTOR LIST

Move Name	Type	ST	ACC	PP
Double-Edge	Normal	120	100	15
Endure*	Normal	—	—	10
Icy Wind*	Ice	55	95	15
Mimic	Normal	—	100	10
Mud-Slap*	Ground	20	100	10
Rock Slide*	Rock	75	90	10
Sleep Talk	Normal	—	—	10
Snore*	Normal	40	100	15
Substitute	Normal	—	—	10
Swagger	Normal	—	90	15

*Battle Frontier tutor move

129

Corphish™

WATER

GENERAL INFO
SPECIES: **Ruffian Pokémon**
HEIGHT: **2'0"**
WEIGHT: **25 lbs.**
ABILITIES: *Hyper Cutter*—*Pokémon's Attack Power cannot be lowered.*
Shell Armor—*Prevents the opponent Pokémon from scoring a Critical Hit.*

STATS

HP	25
ATTACK	75
DEFENSE	50
SP. ATTACK	50
SP. DEFENSE	25
SPEED	25

EVOLUTIONS

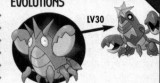

LV30

WHERE/HOW TO CATCH
Routes 102 and 117, Petalburg City

STRONG AGAINST:
FIRE
WATER
ICE
STEEL

WEAK AGAINST:
ELECTRIC
GRASS

MOVES LIST

LV	Move Name	Type	ST	ACC	PP	LV	Move Name	Type	ST	ACC	PP
S	Bubble	Water	20	100	30	25	Knock Off	Dark	20	100	20
07	Harden	Normal	—	—	30	31	Taunt	Dark	—	100	20
10	Vicegrip	Normal	55	100	30	34	Crabhammer	Water	90	85	10
13	Leer	Normal	—	100	30	37	Swords Dance	Normal	—	—	30
19	Bubblebeam	Water	65	100	20	46	Guillotine	Normal	—	30	5
22	Protect	Normal	—	—	10						

TM/HM LIST

TM/HM #	Move Name	Type	ST	ACC	PP	TM/HM #	Move Name	Type	ST	ACC	PP
HM01	Cut	Normal	50	95	30	TM18	Rain Dance	Water	—	—	5
HM03	Surf	Water	95	100	15	TM21	Frustration	Normal	—	100	20
HM04	Strength	Normal	80	100	15	TM27	Return	Normal	—	100	20
HM06	Rock Smash	Fighting	20	100	15	TM28	Dig	Ground	60	100	10
HM07	Waterfall	Water	80	100	15	TM31	Brick Break	Fighting	75	100	15
TM03	Water Pulse	Water	60	100	20	TM32	Double Team	Normal	—	—	15
TM06	Toxic	Poison	—	85	10	TM36	Sludge Bomb	Poison	90	100	10
TM07	Hail	Ice	—	—	10	TM39	Rock Tomb	Rock	50	80	10
TM10	Hidden Power	Normal	—	100	15	TM40	Aerial Ace	Flying	60	—	20
TM12	Taunt	Dark	—	100	20	TM42	Façade	Normal	70	100	20
TM13	Ice Beam	Ice	95	100	10	TM43	Secret Power	Normal	70	100	20
TM14	Blizzard	Ice	120	70	5	TM44	Rest	Psychic	—	—	10
TM17	Protect	Normal	—	—	10	TM45	Attract	Normal	—	100	15

EGG MOVES

Move Name	Type	ST	ACC	PP
Mud Sport	Ground	—	100	15
Endeavor	Normal	—	100	5
Body Slam	Normal	85	100	15
Ancientpower	Rock	60	100	5

MOVE TUTOR LIST

Move Name	Type	ST	ACC	PP
Body Slam*	Normal	85	100	15
Counter*	Fighting	—	100	20
Double-Edge	Normal	120	100	15
Endure*	Normal	—	—	10
Fury Cutter	Bug	10	95	20
Icy Wind*	Ice	55	95	15
Mimic	Normal	—	100	10
Mud-Slap*	Ground	20	100	10
Sleep Talk	Normal	—	—	10
Snore*	Normal	40	100	15
Substitute	Normal	—	—	10
Swagger	Normal	—	90	15
Swords Dance*	Normal	—	—	30

*Battle Frontier tutor move

130

Crawdaunt™

WATER
DARK

GENERAL INFO
SPECIES: **Rogue Pokémon**
HEIGHT: **3'7"**
WEIGHT: **72 lbs.**
ABILITIES: *Hyper Cutter*—*Pokémon's Attack Power cannot be lowered.*
Shell Armor—*Prevents the opponent Pokémon from scoring a Critical Hit.*

STATS

HP	50
ATTACK	100
DEFENSE	50
SP. ATTACK	75
SP. DEFENSE	50
SPEED	50

EVOLUTIONS

LV30

WHERE/HOW TO CATCH
Evolve from Corphish

STRONG AGAINST:
FIRE
WATER
ICE
PSYCHIC
GHOST
DARK
STEEL

WEAK AGAINST:
ELECTRIC
GRASS
FIGHTING
BUG

MOVES LIST

LV	Move Name	Type	ST	ACC	PP	LV	Move Name	Type	ST	ACC	PP
S	Bubble	Water	20	100	30	19	Bubblebeam	Water	65	100	20
S	Harden	Normal	—	—	30	22	Protect	Normal	—	—	10
S	Vicegrip	Normal	55	100	30	25	Knock Off	Dark	20	100	20
S	Leer	Normal	—	100	30	33	Taunt	Dark	—	100	20
07	Harden	Normal	—	—	30	38	Crabhammer	Water	90	85	10
10	Vicegrip	Normal	55	100	30	43	Swords Dance	Normal	—	—	30
13	Leer	Normal	—	100	30	56	Guillotine	Normal	—	30	5

TM/HM LIST

TM/HM #	Move Name	Type	ST	ACC	PP	TM/HM #	Move Name	Type	ST	ACC	PP
HM01	Cut	Normal	50	95	30	TM17	Protect	Normal	—	—	10
HM03	Surf	Water	95	100	15	TM18	Rain Dance	Water	—	—	5
HM04	Strength	Normal	80	100	15	TM21	Frustration	Normal	—	100	20
HM06	Rock Smash	Fighting	20	100	15	TM27	Return	Normal	—	100	20
HM07	Waterfall	Water	80	100	15	TM28	Dig	Ground	60	100	10
HM08	Dive	Water	60	100	10	TM31	Brick Break	Fighting	75	100	15
TM03	Water Pulse	Water	60	100	20	TM32	Double Team	Normal	—	—	15
TM06	Toxic	Poison	—	85	10	TM36	Sludge Bomb	Poison	90	100	10
TM07	Hail	Ice	—	—	10	TM39	Rock Tomb	Rock	50	80	10
TM10	Hidden Power	Normal	—	100	15	TM40	Aerial Ace	Flying	60	—	20
TM12	Taunt	Dark	—	100	20	TM42	Façade	Normal	70	100	20
TM13	Ice Beam	Ice	95	100	10	TM43	Secret Power	Normal	70	100	20
TM14	Blizzard	Ice	120	70	5	TM44	Rest	Psychic	—	—	10
TM15	Hyper Beam	Normal	150	90	5	TM45	Attract	Normal	—	100	15

MOVE TUTOR LIST

Move Name	Type	ST	ACC	PP
Body Slam*	Normal	85	100	15
Counter*	Fighting	—	100	20
Double-Edge	Normal	120	100	15
Endure*	Normal	—	—	10
Fury Cutter	Bug	10	95	20
Icy Wind*	Ice	55	95	15
Mimic	Normal	—	100	10
Mud-Slap*	Ground	20	100	10
Sleep Talk	Normal	—	—	10
Snore*	Normal	40	100	15
Substitute	Normal	—	—	10
Swagger	Normal	—	90	15
Swift*	Normal	60	—	20
Swords Dance*	Normal	—	—	30

*Battle Frontier tutor move

131

Baltoy™

GROUND
PSYCHIC

GENERAL INFO
SPECIES: **Clay Doll Pokémon**
HEIGHT: **1'8"**
WEIGHT: **47 lbs.**
ABILITY: *Levitate—Pokémon is not affected by Ground-type Moves.*

STATS

HP	25
ATTACK	50
DEFENSE	50
SP. ATTACK	50
SP. DEFENSE	50
SPEED	50

EVOLUTIONS

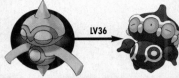

LV36

WHERE/HOW TO CATCH
Route 111

STRONG AGAINST:
ELECTRIC
FIGHTING
POISON
PSYCHIC
ROCK
GROUND

WEAK AGAINST:
WATER
GRASS
ICE
BUG
GHOST
DARK

MOVES LIST

LV	Move Name	Type	ST	ACC	PP
S	Confusion	Psychic	50	100	25
03	Harden	Normal	—	—	30
05	Rapid Spin	Normal	20	100	40
07	Mud-Slap	Ground	20	100	10
11	Psybeam	Psychic	65	100	20
15	Rock Tomb	Rock	50	80	10

LV	Move Name	Type	ST	ACC	PP
19	Selfdestruct	Normal	200	100	5
25	Ancientpower	Rock	60	100	5
31	Sandstorm	Rock	—	—	10
37	Cosmic Power	Normal	—	—	20
45	Explosion	Normal	250	100	5

TM/HM LIST

TM/HM #	Move Name	Type	ST	ACC	PP
HM05	Flash	Normal	—	70	20
TM06	Toxic	Poison	—	85	10
TM10	Hidden Power	Normal	—	100	15
TM11	Sunny Day	Fire	—	—	5
TM13	Ice Beam	Ice	95	100	10
TM16	Light Screen	Psychic	—	—	30
TM17	Protect	Normal	—	—	10
TM18	Rain Dance	Water	—	—	5
TM21	Frustration	Normal	—	100	20
TM22	Solarbeam	Grass	120	100	10
TM26	Earthquake	Ground	100	100	10
TM27	Return	Normal	—	100	20

TM/HM #	Move Name	Type	ST	ACC	PP
TM28	Dig	Ground	60	100	10
TM29	Psychic	Psychic	90	100	10
TM30	Shadow Ball	Ghost	60	—	20
TM32	Double Team	Normal	—	—	15
TM33	Reflect	Psychic	—	—	20
TM37	Sandstorm	Rock	—	—	10
TM39	Rock Tomb	Rock	50	80	10
TM42	Façade	Normal	70	100	20
TM43	Secret Power	Normal	70	100	20
TM44	Rest	Psychic	—	—	10
TM48	Skill Swap	Psychic	—	100	10

EGG MOVES

Move Name	Type	ST	ACC	PP
None				

MOVE TUTOR LIST

Move Name	Type	ST	ACC	PP
Double-Edge	Normal	120	100	15
Dream Eater*	Psychic	100	100	15
Endure*	Normal	—	—	10
Explosion	Normal	250	100	5
Mimic	Normal	—	100	10
Mud-Slap*	Ground	20	100	10
Psych Up*	Normal	—	—	10
Rock Slide*	Rock	75	90	10
Sleep Talk	Normal	—	—	10
Snore*	Normal	40	100	15
Substitute	Normal	—	—	10
Swagger	Normal	—	90	15

*Battle Frontier tutor move

132

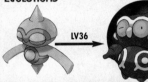

Claydol™

GROUND
PSYCHIC

GENERAL INFO
SPECIES: **Clay Doll Pokémon**
HEIGHT: **4'11"**
WEIGHT: **238 lbs.**
ABILITY: *Levitate—Pokémon is not affected by Ground-type Moves.*

STATS

HP	50
ATTACK	50
DEFENSE	75
SP. ATTACK	50
SP. DEFENSE	75
SPEED	50

EVOLUTIONS

LV36

WHERE/HOW TO CATCH
Evolve from Baltoy;
Sky Pillar

STRONG AGAINST:
ELECTRIC
FIGHTING
POISON
PSYCHIC
ROCK
GROUND

WEAK AGAINST:
WATER
GRASS
ICE
BUG
GHOST
DARK

MOVES LIST

LV	Move Name	Type	ST	ACC	PP
S	Teleport	Psychic	—	—	20
S	Confusion	Psychic	50	100	25
S	Harden	Normal	—	—	30
S	Rapid Spin	Normal	20	100	40
03	Harden	Normal	—	—	30
05	Rapid Spin	Normal	20	100	40
07	Mud-Slap	Ground	20	100	10
11	Psybeam	Psychic	65	100	20

LV	Move Name	Type	ST	ACC	PP
15	Rock Tomb	Rock	50	80	10
19	Selfdestruct	Normal	200	100	5
25	Ancientpower	Rock	60	100	5
31	Sandstorm	Rock	—	—	10
36	Hyper Beam	Normal	150	90	5
42	Cosmic Power	Normal	—	—	20
55	Explosion	Normal	250	100	5

TM/HM LIST

TM/HM #	Move Name	Type	ST	ACC	PP
HM04	Strength	Normal	80	100	15
HM05	Flash	Normal	—	70	20
HM06	Rock Smash	Fighting	20	100	15
TM06	Toxic	Poison	—	85	10
TM10	Hidden Power	Normal	—	100	15
TM11	Sunny Day	Fire	—	—	5
TM13	Ice Beam	Ice	95	100	10
TM15	Hyper Beam	Normal	150	90	5
TM16	Light Screen	Psychic	—	—	30
TM17	Protect	Normal	—	—	10
TM18	Rain Dance	Water	—	—	5
TM21	Frustration	Normal	—	100	20
TM22	Solarbeam	Grass	120	100	10

TM/HM #	Move Name	Type	ST	ACC	PP
TM26	Earthquake	Ground	100	100	10
TM27	Return	Normal	—	100	20
TM28	Dig	Ground	60	100	10
TM29	Psychic	Psychic	90	100	10
TM30	Shadow Ball	Ghost	60	—	20
TM32	Double Team	Normal	—	—	15
TM33	Reflect	Psychic	—	—	20
TM37	Sandstorm	Rock	—	—	10
TM39	Rock Tomb	Rock	50	80	10
TM42	Façade	Normal	70	100	20
TM43	Secret Power	Normal	70	100	20
TM44	Rest	Psychic	—	—	10
TM48	Skill Swap	Psychic	—	100	10

MOVE TUTOR LIST

Move Name	Type	ST	ACC	PP
Double-Edge	Normal	120	100	15
Dream Eater*	Psychic	100	100	15
Endure*	Normal	—	—	10
Explosion	Normal	250	100	5
Mimic	Normal	—	100	10
Mud-Slap*	Ground	20	100	10
Psych Up*	Normal	—	—	10
Rock Slide*	Rock	75	90	10
Sleep Talk	Normal	—	—	10
Snore*	Normal	40	100	15
Substitute	Normal	—	—	10
Swagger	Normal	—	90	15

*Battle Frontier tutor move

133 Lileep™

ROCK
GRASS

GENERAL INFO
SPECIES: Sea Lily Pokémon
HEIGHT: 3'3"
WEIGHT: 52 lbs.
ABILITY: *Suction Cups* — *Pokémon cannot be switched out of the battle by Roar or Whirlwind.*

STATS

HP	50
ATTACK	50
DEFENSE	50
SP. ATTACK	50
SP. DEFENSE	50
SPEED	25

EVOLUTIONS

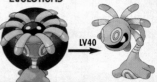

LV40

WHERE/HOW TO CATCH
Resurrect Root Fossil

STRONG AGAINST:
NORMAL
ELECTRIC

WEAK AGAINST:
ICE
FIGHTING
BUG
STEEL

MOVES LIST

LV	Move Name	Type	ST	ACC	PP		LV	Move Name	Type	ST	ACC	PP
S	Astonish	Ghost	30	100	15		36	Amnesia	Psychic	—	—	20
08	Constrict	Normal	10	100	35		43	Ancientpower	Rock	60	100	5
15	Acid	Poison	40	100	30		50	Stockpile	Normal	—	—	10
22	Ingrain	Grass	—	100	20		50	Spit Up	Normal	100	100	10
29	Confuse Ray	Ghost	—	100	10		50	Swallow	Normal	—	—	10

TM/HM LIST

TM/HM #	Move Name	Type	ST	ACC	PP		TM/HM #	Move Name	Type	ST	ACC	PP
TM06	Toxic	Poison	—	85	10		TM27	Return	Normal	—	100	20
TM09	Bullet Seed	Grass	10	100	30		TM32	Double Team	Normal	—	—	15
TM10	Hidden Power	Normal	—	100	15		TM36	Sludge Bomb	Poison	90	100	10
TM11	Sunny Day	Fire	—	—	5		TM37	Sandstorm	Rock	—	—	10
TM17	Protect	Normal	—	—	10		TM42	Façade	Normal	70	100	20
TM19	Giga Drain	Grass	60	100	5		TM43	Secret Power	Normal	70	100	20
TM21	Frustration	Normal	—	100	20		TM44	Rest	Psychic	—	—	10
TM22	Solarbeam	Grass	120	100	10		TM45	Attract	Normal	—	100	15

EGG MOVES

Move Name	Type	ST	ACC	PP
Barrier	Psychic	—	—	30
Recover	Normal	—	—	20
Mirror Coat	Psychic	—	100	20
Rock Slide	Rock	75	90	10

MOVE TUTOR LIST

Move Name	Type	ST	ACC	PP
Body Slam*	Normal	85	100	15
Double-Edge	Normal	120	100	15
Endure*	Normal	—	—	10
Mimic	Normal	—	100	10
Mud-Slap*	Ground	20	100	10
Psych Up*	Normal	—	—	10
Rock Slide*	Rock	75	90	10
Sleep Talk	Normal	—	—	10
Snore*	Normal	40	100	15
Substitute	Normal	—	—	10
Swagger	Normal	—	90	15

*Battle Frontier tutor move

134 Cradily™

ROCK
GRASS

GENERAL INFO
SPECIES: Barnacle Pokémon
HEIGHT: 4'11"
WEIGHT: 133 lbs.
ABILITY: *Suction Cups* — *Pokémon cannot be switched out of the battle by Roar or Whirlwind.*

STATS

HP	50
ATTACK	75
DEFENSE	75
SP. ATTACK	75
SP. DEFENSE	75
SPEED	50

EVOLUTIONS

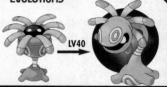

LV40

WHERE/HOW TO CATCH
Evolve from Lileep

STRONG AGAINST:
NORMAL
ELECTRIC

WEAK AGAINST:
ICE
FIGHTING
BUG
STEEL

MOVES LIST

LV	Move Name	Type	ST	ACC	PP		LV	Move Name	Type	ST	ACC	PP
S	Astonish	Ghost	30	100	15		29	Confuse Ray	Ghost	—	100	10
S	Constrict	Normal	10	100	35		36	Amnesia	Psychic	—	—	20
S	Acid	Poison	40	100	30		48	Ancientpower	Rock	60	100	5
S	Ingrain	Grass	—	100	20		60	Stockpile	Normal	—	—	10
08	Constrict	Normal	10	100	35		60	Spit Up	Normal	100	100	10
15	Acid	Poison	40	100	30		60	Swallow	Normal	—	—	10
22	Ingrain	Grass	—	100	20							

TM/HM LIST

TM/HM #	Move Name	Type	ST	ACC	PP		TM/HM #	Move Name	Type	ST	ACC	PP
HM04	Strength	Normal	80	100	15		TM26	Earthquake	Ground	100	100	10
HM06	Rock Smash	Fighting	20	100	15		TM27	Return	Normal	—	100	20
TM06	Toxic	Poison	—	85	10		TM32	Double Team	Normal	—	—	15
TM09	Bullet Seed	Grass	10	100	30		TM36	Sludge Bomb	Poison	90	100	10
TM10	Hidden Power	Normal	—	100	15		TM37	Sandstorm	Rock	—	—	10
TM11	Sunny Day	Fire	—	—	5		TM39	Rock Tomb	Rock	50	80	10
TM15	Hyper Beam	Normal	150	90	5		TM42	Façade	Normal	70	100	20
TM17	Protect	Normal	—	—	10		TM43	Secret Power	Normal	70	100	20
TM19	Giga Drain	Grass	60	100	5		TM44	Rest	Psychic	—	—	10
TM21	Frustration	Normal	—	100	20		TM45	Attract	Normal	—	100	15
TM22	Solarbeam	Grass	120	100	10							

MOVE TUTOR LIST

Move Name	Type	ST	ACC	PP
Body Slam*	Normal	85	100	15
Double-Edge	Normal	120	100	15
Endure*	Normal	—	—	10
Mimic	Normal	—	100	10
Mud-Slap*	Ground	20	100	10
Psych Up*	Normal	—	—	10
Rock Slide*	Rock	75	90	10
Sleep Talk	Normal	—	—	10
Snore*	Normal	40	100	15
Substitute	Normal	—	—	10
Swagger	Normal	—	90	15

*Battle Frontier tutor move

135

Anorith™

ROCK
BUG

WHERE/HOW TO CATCH
Resurrect Claw Fossil

STRONG AGAINST:
NORMAL
POISON

WEAK AGAINST:
WATER
ROCK
STEEL

GENERAL INFO
SPECIES: Old Shrimp Pokémon
HEIGHT: 2'4"
WEIGHT: 28 lbs.
ABILITY: *Battle Armor—*
Prevents the opponent Pokémon
from scoring a Critical Hit.

STATS

HP	25
ATTACK	75
DEFENSE	50
SP. ATTACK	50
SP. DEFENSE	50
SPEED	50

EVOLUTIONS

 LV40

MOVES LIST

LV	Move Name	Type	ST	ACC	PP	LV	Move Name	Type	ST	ACC	PP
S	Scratch	Normal	40	100	35	31	Protect	Normal	—	—	10
07	Harden	Normal	—	—	30	37	Ancientpower	Rock	60	100	5
13	Mud Sport	Ground	—	100	15	43	Fury Cutter	Bug	10	95	20
19	Water Gun	Water	40	100	25	49	Slash	Normal	70	100	20
25	Metal Claw	Steel	50	95	35	55	Rock Blast	Rock	25	80	10

TM/HM LIST

TM/HM #	Move Name	Type	ST	ACC	PP	TM/HM #	Move Name	Type	ST	ACC	PP
HM01	Cut	Normal	50	95	30	TM31	Brick Break	Fighting	75	100	15
HM06	Rock Smash	Fighting	20	100	15	TM32	Double Team	Normal	—	—	15
TM03	Water Pulse	Water	60	100	20	TM37	Sandstorm	Rock	—	—	10
TM06	Toxic	Poison	—	85	10	TM39	Rock Tomb	Rock	50	80	10
TM10	Hidden Power	Normal	—	100	15	TM40	Aerial Ace	Flying	60	—	20
TM11	Sunny Day	Fire	—	—	5	TM42	Façade	Normal	70	100	20
TM17	Protect	Normal	—	—	10	TM43	Secret Power	Normal	70	100	20
TM21	Frustration	Normal	—	100	20	TM44	Rest	Psychic	—	—	10
TM27	Return	Normal	—	100	20	TM45	Attract	Normal	—	100	15
TM28	Dig	Ground	60	100	10						

EGG MOVES

Move Name	Type	ST	ACC	PP
Knock Off	Dark	20	100	20
Rock Slide	Rock	75	90	10
Rapid Spin	Normal	20	100	40
Swords Dance	Normal	—	—	30

MOVE TUTOR LIST

Move Name	Type	ST	ACC	PP
Body Slam*	Normal	85	100	15
Double-Edge	Normal	120	100	15
Endure*	Normal	—	—	10
Fury Cutter	Bug	10	95	20
Mimic	Normal	—	100	10
Mud-Slap*	Ground	20	100	10
Rock Slide*	Rock	75	90	10
Sleep Talk	Normal	—	—	10
Snore*	Normal	40	100	15
Substitute	Normal	—	—	10
Swagger	Normal	—	90	15
Swords Dance*	Normal	—	—	30

*Battle Frontier tutor move

136

Armaldo™

ROCK
BUG

WHERE/HOW TO CATCH
Evolve from Anorith

STRONG AGAINST:
NORMAL
POISON

WEAK AGAINST:
WATER
ROCK
STEEL

GENERAL INFO
SPECIES: Plate Pokémon
HEIGHT: 4'11"
WEIGHT: 150 lbs.
ABILITY: *Battle Armor—*
Prevents the opponent Pokémon
from scoring a Critical Hit.

STATS

HP	50
ATTACK	100
DEFENSE	75
SP. ATTACK	50
SP. DEFENSE	50
SPEED	50

EVOLUTIONS

 LV40

MOVES LIST

LV	Move Name	Type	ST	ACC	PP	LV	Move Name	Type	ST	ACC	PP
S	Scratch	Normal	40	100	35	25	Metal Claw	Steel	50	95	35
S	Harden	Normal	—	—	30	31	Protect	Normal	—	—	10
S	Mud Sport	Ground	—	100	15	37	Ancientpower	Rock	60	100	5
S	Water Gun	Water	40	100	25	46	Fury Cutter	Bug	10	95	20
07	Harden	Normal	—	—	30	55	Slash	Normal	70	100	20
13	Mud Sport	Ground	—	100	15	64	Rock Blast	Rock	25	80	10
19	Water Gun	Water	40	100	25						

TM/HM LIST

TM/HM #	Move Name	Type	ST	ACC	PP	TM/HM #	Move Name	Type	ST	ACC	PP
HM01	Cut	Normal	50	95	30	TM27	Return	Normal	—	100	20
HM04	Strength	Normal	80	100	15	TM28	Dig	Ground	60	100	10
HM06	Rock Smash	Fighting	20	100	15	TM31	Brick Break	Fighting	75	100	15
TM03	Water Pulse	Water	60	100	20	TM32	Double Team	Normal	—	—	15
TM06	Toxic	Poison	—	85	10	TM37	Sandstorm	Rock	—	—	10
TM10	Hidden Power	Normal	—	100	15	TM39	Rock Tomb	Rock	50	80	10
TM11	Sunny Day	Fire	—	—	5	TM40	Aerial Ace	Flying	60	—	20
TM15	Hyper Beam	Normal	150	90	5	TM42	Façade	Normal	70	100	20
TM17	Protect	Normal	—	—	10	TM43	Secret Power	Normal	70	100	20
TM21	Frustration	Normal	—	100	20	TM44	Rest	Psychic	—	—	10
TM23	Iron Tail	Steel	100	75	15	TM45	Attract	Normal	—	100	15
TM26	Earthquake	Ground	100	100	10						

MOVE TUTOR LIST

Move Name	Type	ST	ACC	PP
Body Slam*	Normal	85	100	15
Double-Edge	Normal	120	100	15
Endure*	Normal	—	—	10
Fury Cutter	Bug	10	95	20
Mimic	Normal	—	100	10
Mud-Slap*	Ground	20	100	10
Rock Slide*	Rock	75	90	10
Seismic Toss*	Fighting	—	100	20
Sleep Talk	Normal	—	—	10
Snore*	Normal	40	100	15
Substitute	Normal	—	—	10
Swagger	Normal	—	90	15
Swords Dance*	Normal	—	—	30

*Battle Frontier tutor move

137 Igglybuff™

NORMAL

GENERAL INFO
SPECIES: Balloon Pokémon
HEIGHT: 1'0"
WEIGHT: 2 lbs.
ABILITY: *Cute Charm*—Gives the Pokémon's Physical Attacks a 30 percent chance of Attracting the opponent.

STATS
HP	66
ATTACK	33
DEFENSE	33
SP. ATTACK	33
SP. DEFENSE	33
SPEED	33

EVOLUTIONS

FRIENDSHIP

MOON STONE

WHERE/HOW TO CATCH
Breed from Jigglypuff

STRONG AGAINST:
GHOST

WEAK AGAINST:
FIGHTING

MOVES LIST
LV	Move Name	Type	ST	ACC	PP
S	Sing	Normal	—	55	15
S	Charm	Normal	—	100	20
04	Defense Curl	Normal	—	—	40

LV	Move Name	Type	ST	ACC	PP
09	Pound	Normal	40	100	35
14	Sweet Kiss	Normal	—	75	10

TM/HM LIST
TM/HM #	Move Name	Type	ST	ACC	PP
HM05	Flash	Normal	—	70	20
TM03	Water Pulse	Water	60	100	20
TM06	Toxic	Poison	—	85	10
TM10	Hidden Power	Normal	—	100	15
TM11	Sunny Day	Fire	—	—	5
TM16	Light Screen	Psychic	—	—	30
TM17	Protect	Normal	—	—	10
TM18	Rain Dance	Water	—	—	5
TM20	Safeguard	Normal	—	—	25
TM21	Frustration	Normal	—	100	20
TM22	Solarbeam	Grass	120	100	10
TM27	Return	Normal	—	100	20

TM/HM #	Move Name	Type	ST	ACC	PP
TM28	Dig	Ground	60	100	10
TM29	Psychic	Psychic	90	100	10
TM30	Shadow Ball	Ghost	60	—	20
TM32	Double Team	Normal	—	—	15
TM33	Reflect	Psychic	—	—	20
TM34	Shock Wave	Electric	60	—	20
TM35	Flamethrower	Fire	95	100	15
TM38	Fire Blast	Fire	120	85	5
TM42	Façade	Normal	70	100	20
TM43	Secret Power	Normal	70	100	20
TM44	Rest	Psychic	—	—	10
TM45	Attract	Normal	—	100	15

EGG MOVES
Move Name	Type	ST	ACC	PP
Faint Attack	Dark	60	—	20
Fake Tears	Dark	—	100	20
Perish Song	Normal	—	90	5
Present	Normal	—	90	15
Wish	Normal	—	100	10

MOVE TUTOR LIST
Move Name	Type	ST	ACC	PP
Body Slam*	Normal	85	100	15
Counter*	Fighting	—	100	20
Defense Curl*	Normal	—	—	40
Double-Edge	Normal	120	100	15
Dream Eater*	Psychic	100	100	15
Endure*	Normal	—	—	10
Icy Wind*	Ice	55	95	15
Mega Kick*	Normal	120	85	5
Mega Punch*	Normal	80	75	20
Mimic	Normal	—	100	10
Mud-Slap*	Ground	20	100	10
Psych Up*	Normal	—	—	10
Rollout	Rock	30	90	20
Seismic Toss*	Fighting	—	100	20
Sleep Talk	Normal	—	—	10
Snore*	Normal	40	100	15
Substitute	Normal	—	—	10
Swagger	Normal	—	90	15
Thunder Wave*	Electric	—	100	20

*Battle Frontier tutor move

138 Jigglypuff™

NORMAL

GENERAL INFO
SPECIES: Balloon Pokémon
HEIGHT: 1'8"
WEIGHT: 12 lbs.
ABILITY: *Cute Charm*—Gives the Pokémon's Physical Attacks a 30 percent chance of Attracting the opponent.

STATS
HP	66
ATTACK	33
DEFENSE	33
SP. ATTACK	33
SP. DEFENSE	33
SPEED	33

EVOLUTIONS

FRIENDSHIP

MOON STONE

WHERE/HOW TO CATCH
Evolve from Igglybuff with Friendship; Route 115

STRONG AGAINST:
GHOST

WEAK AGAINST:
FIGHTING

MOVES LIST
LV	Move Name	Type	ST	ACC	PP
S	Sing	Normal	—	55	15
04	Defense Curl	Normal	—	—	40
09	Pound	Normal	40	100	35
14	Disable	Normal	—	55	20
19	Rollout	Rock	30	90	20
24	Doubleslap	Normal	15	85	10

LV	Move Name	Type	ST	ACC	PP
29	Rest	Psychic	—	—	10
34	Body Slam	Normal	85	100	15
39	Mimic	Normal	—	100	10
44	Hyper Voice	Normal	90	100	10
49	Double-Edge	Normal	120	100	15

TM/HM LIST
TM/HM #	Move Name	Type	ST	ACC	PP
HM04	Strength	Normal	80	100	15
HM05	Flash	Normal	—	70	20
TM01	Focus Punch	Fighting	150	100	20
TM03	Water Pulse	Water	60	100	20
TM06	Toxic	Poison	—	85	10
TM10	Hidden Power	Normal	—	100	15
TM11	Sunny Day	Fire	—	—	5
TM13	Ice Beam	Ice	95	100	10
TM14	Blizzard	Ice	120	70	5
TM16	Light Screen	Psychic	—	—	30
TM17	Protect	Normal	—	—	10
TM18	Rain Dance	Water	—	—	5
TM20	Safeguard	Normal	—	—	25
TM21	Frustration	Normal	—	100	20
TM22	Solarbeam	Grass	120	100	10
TM24	Thunderbolt	Electric	95	100	15

TM/HM #	Move Name	Type	ST	ACC	PP
TM25	Thunder	Electric	120	70	10
TM27	Return	Normal	—	100	20
TM28	Dig	Ground	60	100	10
TM29	Psychic	Psychic	90	100	10
TM30	Shadow Ball	Ghost	60	—	20
TM31	Brick Break	Fighting	75	100	15
TM32	Double Team	Normal	—	—	15
TM33	Reflect	Psychic	—	—	20
TM34	Shock Wave	Electric	60	—	20
TM35	Flamethrower	Fire	95	100	15
TM38	Fire Blast	Fire	120	85	5
TM42	Façade	Normal	70	100	20
TM43	Secret Power	Normal	70	100	20
TM44	Rest	Psychic	—	—	10
TM45	Attract	Normal	—	100	15
TM49	Snatch	Dark	—	100	10

MOVE TUTOR LIST
Move Name	Type	ST	ACC	PP
Body Slam*	Normal	85	100	15
Counter*	Fighting	—	100	20
Defense Curl*	Normal	—	—	40
Double-Edge	Normal	120	100	15
Dream Eater*	Psychic	100	100	15
Dynamicpunch	Fighting	100	50	5
Endure*	Normal	—	—	10
Fire Punch*	Fire	75	100	15
Ice Punch*	Ice	75	100	15
Mega Kick*	Normal	120	85	5
Mega Punch*	Normal	80	75	20
Metronome	Normal	—	100	10
Mimic	Normal	—	100	10
Mud-Slap*	Ground	20	100	10
Psych Up*	Normal	—	—	10
Rollout	Rock	30	90	20
Seismic Toss*	Fighting	—	100	20
Sleep Talk	Normal	—	—	10
Snore*	Normal	40	100	15
Substitute	Normal	—	—	10
Swagger	Normal	—	90	15
Thunderpunch*	Electric	75	100	15
Thunder Wave*	Electric	—	100	20

*Battle Frontier tutor move

139

Wigglytuff™

NORMAL

GENERAL INFO
SPECIES: Balloon Pokémon
HEIGHT: 3'3"
WEIGHT: 26 lbs.
ABILITY: *Cute Charm*—Gives the Pokémon's Physical Attacks a 30 percent chance of Attracting the opponent.

STATS

HP	100
ATTACK	66
DEFENSE	33
SP. ATTACK	66
SP. DEFENSE	33
SPEED	33

EVOLUTIONS

FRIENDSHIP

MOON STONE

WHERE/HOW TO CATCH
Evolve from Jigglypuff with Moon Stone

STRONG AGAINST:
GHOST

WEAK AGAINST:
FIGHTING

MOVES LIST

LV	Move Name	Type	ST	ACC	PP
S	Sing	Normal	—	55	15
S	Disable	Normal	—	55	20

LV	Move Name	Type	ST	ACC	PP
S	Defense Curl	Normal	—	—	40
S	Doubleslap	Normal	15	85	10

TM/HM LIST

TM/HM #	Move Name	Type	ST	ACC	PP
HM04	Strength	Normal	80	100	15
HM05	Flash	Normal	—	70	20
TM01	Focus Punch	Fighting	150	100	20
TM03	Water Pulse	Water	60	100	20
TM06	Toxic	Poison	—	85	10
TM10	Hidden Power	Normal	—	100	15
TM11	Sunny Day	Fire	—	—	5
TM13	Ice Beam	Ice	95	100	10
TM14	Blizzard	Ice	120	70	5
TM15	Hyper Beam	Normal	150	90	5
TM16	Light Screen	Psychic	—	—	30
TM17	Protect	Normal	—	—	10
TM18	Rain Dance	Water	—	—	5
TM20	Safeguard	Normal	—	—	25
TM21	Frustration	Normal	—	100	20
TM22	Solarbeam	Grass	120	100	10
TM24	Thunderbolt	Electric	95	100	15

TM/HM #	Move Name	Type	ST	ACC	PP
TM25	Thunder	Electric	120	70	10
TM27	Return	Normal	—	100	20
TM28	Dig	Ground	60	100	10
TM29	Psychic	Psychic	90	100	10
TM30	Shadow Ball	Ghost	60	—	20
TM31	Brick Break	Fighting	75	100	15
TM32	Double Team	Normal	—	—	15
TM33	Reflect	Psychic	—	—	20
TM34	Shock Wave	Electric	60	—	20
TM35	Flamethrower	Fire	95	100	15
TM38	Fire Blast	Fire	120	85	5
TM42	Façade	Normal	70	100	20
TM43	Secret Power	Normal	70	100	20
TM44	Rest	Psychic	—	—	10
TM45	Attract	Normal	—	100	15
TM49	Snatch	Dark	—	100	10

MOVE TUTOR LIST

Move Name	Type	ST	ACC	PP
Body Slam*	Normal	85	100	15
Counter*	Fighting	—	100	20
Defense Curl*	Normal	—	—	40
Double-Edge	Normal	120	100	15
Dream Eater*	Psychic	100	100	15
Dream Eater*	Psychic	100	100	15
Dynamicpunch	Fighting	100	50	5
Endure*	Normal	—	—	10
Fire Punch*	Fire	75	100	15
Ice Punch*	Ice	75	100	15
Mega Kick*	Normal	120	85	5
Mega Punch*	Normal	80	75	20
Mimic	Normal	—	100	10
Mud-Slap*	Ground	20	100	10
Psych Up*	Normal	—	—	10
Rollout	Rock	30	90	20
Seismic Toss*	Fighting	—	100	20
Sleep Talk	Normal	—	—	10
Snore*	Normal	40	100	15
Substitute	Normal	—	—	10
Swagger	Normal	—	90	15
Thunderpunch*	Electric	75	100	15
Thunder Wave*	Electric	—	100	20

*Battle Frontier tutor move

140

Feebas™

WATER

GENERAL INFO
SPECIES: Fish Pokémon
HEIGHT: 2'0"
WEIGHT: 16 lbs.
ABILITY: *Swift Swim*—Doubles the Pokémon's Speed when it rains.

STATS

HP	25
ATTACK	25
DEFENSE	25
SP. ATTACK	25
SP. DEFENSE	50
SPEED	75

EVOLUTIONS

MAX OUT BEAUTY CONDITION

WHERE/HOW TO CATCH
Route 119

STRONG AGAINST:
FIRE
WATER
ICE
STEEL

WEAK AGAINST:
ELECTRIC
GRASS

MOVES LIST

LV	Move Name	Type	ST	ACC	PP
S	Splash	Normal	—	—	40
15	Tackle	Normal	35	95	35

LV	Move Name	Type	ST	ACC	PP
30	Flail	Normal	—	100	15

TM/HM LIST

TM/HM #	Move Name	Type	ST	ACC	PP
HM03	Surf	Water	95	100	15
HM07	Waterfall	Water	80	100	15
HM08	Dive	Water	60	100	10
TM03	Water Pulse	Water	60	100	20
TM06	Toxic	Poison	—	85	10
TM07	Hail	Ice	—	—	10
TM10	Hidden Power	Normal	—	100	15
TM13	Ice Beam	Ice	95	100	10
TM14	Blizzard	Ice	120	70	5

TM/HM #	Move Name	Type	ST	ACC	PP
TM17	Protect	Normal	—	—	10
TM18	Rain Dance	Water	—	—	5
TM21	Frustration	Normal	—	100	20
TM27	Return	Normal	—	100	20
TM32	Double Team	Normal	—	—	15
TM42	Façade	Normal	70	100	20
TM43	Secret Power	Normal	70	100	20
TM44	Rest	Psychic	—	—	10
TM45	Attract	Normal	—	100	15

EGG MOVES

Move Name	Type	ST	ACC	PP
Mirror Coat	Psychic	—	100	20
Dragonbreath	Dragon	60	100	20
Mud Sport	Ground	—	100	15
Hypnosis	Psychic	—	60	20
Light Screen	Psychic	—	—	30
Confuse Ray	Ghost	—	100	10

MOVE TUTOR LIST

Move Name	Type	ST	ACC	PP
Body Slam*	Normal	85	100	15
Double-Edge	Normal	120	100	15
Endure*	Normal	—	—	10
Icy Wind*	Ice	55	95	15
Mimic	Normal	—	100	10
Mud-Slap*	Ground	20	100	10
Sleep Talk	Normal	—	—	10
Snore*	Normal	40	100	15
Substitute	Normal	—	—	10
Swagger	Normal	—	90	15
Swift*	Normal	60	—	20

*Battle Frontier tutor move

141 Milotic™

WATER

GENERAL INFO
SPECIES: Tender Pokémon
HEIGHT: 20'4"
WEIGHT: 357 lbs.
ABILITY: *Marvel Scale* — *Multiplies defense by 1.5 when Pokémon has a Status condition.*

STATS
HP	50
ATTACK	50
DEFENSE	50
SP. ATTACK	75
SP. DEFENSE	75
SPEED	75

EVOLUTIONS

 MAX OUT BEAUTY CONDITION →

WHERE/HOW TO CATCH
Evolve from Feebas by maxing out Beauty condition

STRONG AGAINST:
FIRE
WATER
ICE
STEEL

WEAK AGAINST:
ELECTRIC
GRASS

MOVES LIST
LV	Move Name	Type	ST	ACC	PP
S	Water Gun	Water	40	100	25
05	Wrap	Normal	15	85	20
10	Water Sport	Water	—	100	15
15	Refresh	Normal	—	100	20
20	Water Pulse	Water	60	100	20
25	Twister	Dragon	40	100	20

LV	Move Name	Type	ST	ACC	PP
30	Recover	Normal	—	—	20
35	Rain Dance	Water	—	—	5
40	Hydro Pump	Water	120	80	5
45	Attract	Normal	—	100	15
50	Safeguard	Normal	—	—	25

TM/HM LIST
TM/HM #	Move Name	Type	ST	ACC	PP
HM03	Surf	Water	95	100	15
HM07	Waterfall	Water	80	100	15
HM08	Dive	Water	60	100	20
TM03	Water Pulse	Water	60	100	20
TM06	Toxic	Poison	—	85	10
TM07	Hail	Ice	—	—	10
TM10	Hidden Power	Normal	—	100	15
TM13	Ice Beam	Ice	95	100	10
TM14	Blizzard	Ice	120	70	5
TM15	Hyper Beam	Normal	150	90	5
TM17	Protect	Normal	—	—	10

TM/HM #	Move Name	Type	ST	ACC	PP
TM18	Rain Dance	Water	—	—	5
TM20	Safeguard	Normal	—	—	25
TM21	Frustration	Normal	—	100	20
TM23	Iron Tail	Steel	100	75	15
TM27	Return	Normal	—	100	20
TM32	Double Team	Normal	—	—	15
TM42	Façade	Normal	70	100	20
TM43	Secret Power	Normal	70	100	20
TM44	Rest	Psychic	—	—	10
TM45	Attract	Normal	—	100	15

MOVE TUTOR LIST
Move Name	Type	ST	ACC	PP
Body Slam*	Normal	85	100	15
Double-Edge	Normal	120	100	15
Endure*	Normal	—	—	10
Icy Wind*	Ice	55	95	15
Mimic	Normal	—	100	10
Mud-Slap*	Ground	20	100	10
Psych Up*	Normal	—	—	10
Sleep Talk	Normal	—	—	10
Snore*	Normal	40	100	15
Substitute	Normal	—	—	10
Swagger	Normal	—	90	15
Swift*	Normal	60	—	20

*Battle Frontier tutor move

---

142 Castform™

NORMAL

GENERAL INFO
SPECIES: Weather Pokémon
HEIGHT: 1'0"
WEIGHT: 2 lbs.
ABILITY: *Forecast* — *Changes the Pokémon's type and shape depending upon the weather.*

STATS
HP	50
ATTACK	50
DEFENSE	50
SP. ATTACK	50
SP. DEFENSE	50
SPEED	50

EVOLUTIONS

 CASTFORM DOES NOT EVOLVE

WHERE/HOW TO CATCH
Receive at Weather Institute

STRONG AGAINST:
GHOST

WEAK AGAINST:
FIGHTING

MOVES LIST
LV	Move Name	Type	ST	ACC	PP
S	Tackle	Normal	35	95	35
10	Water Gun	Water	40	100	25
10	Ember	Fire	40	100	25
10	Powder Snow	Ice	40	100	25

LV	Move Name	Type	ST	ACC	PP
20	Rain Dance	Water	—	—	5
20	Sunny Day	Fire	—	—	5
20	Hail	Ice	—	—	10
30	Weather Ball	Normal	50	100	10

TM/HM LIST
TM/HM #	Move Name	Type	ST	ACC	PP
HM05	Flash	Normal	—	70	20
TM03	Water Pulse	Water	60	100	20
TM06	Toxic	Poison	—	85	10
TM07	Hail	Ice	—	—	10
TM10	Hidden Power	Normal	—	100	15
TM11	Sunny Day	Fire	—	—	5
TM13	Ice Beam	Ice	95	100	10
TM14	Blizzard	Ice	120	70	5
TM17	Protect	Normal	—	—	10
TM18	Rain Dance	Water	—	—	5
TM21	Frustration	Normal	—	100	20
TM22	Solarbeam	Grass	120	100	10
TM24	Thunderbolt	Electric	95	100	15

TM/HM #	Move Name	Type	ST	ACC	PP
TM25	Thunder	Electric	120	70	10
TM27	Return	Normal	—	100	20
TM30	Shadow Ball	Ghost	60	—	20
TM32	Double Team	Normal	—	—	15
TM34	Shock Wave	Electric	60	—	20
TM35	Flamethrower	Fire	95	100	15
TM37	Sandstorm	Rock	—	—	10
TM38	Fire Blast	Fire	120	85	5
TM42	Façade	Normal	70	100	20
TM43	Secret Power	Normal	70	100	20
TM44	Rest	Psychic	—	—	10
TM45	Attract	Normal	—	100	15
TM46	Thief	Dark	40	100	10

EGG MOVES
Move Name	Type	ST	ACC	PP
Future Sight	Psychic	80	90	15
Psych Up	Normal	—	—	10

MOVE TUTOR LIST
Move Name	Type	ST	ACC	PP
Body Slam*	Normal	85	100	15
Defense Curl*	Normal	—	—	40
Double-Edge	Normal	120	100	15
Endure*	Normal	—	—	10
Icy Wind*	Ice	55	95	15
Mimic	Normal	—	100	10
Psych Up*	Normal	—	—	10
Sleep Talk	Normal	—	—	10
Snore*	Normal	40	100	15
Substitute	Normal	—	—	10
Swagger	Normal	—	90	15
Swift*	Normal	60	—	20
Thunder Wave*	Electric	—	100	20

*Battle Frontier tutor move

143

Staryu™

WATER

GENERAL INFO
SPECIES: Star Shape Pokémon
HEIGHT: 2'7"
WEIGHT: 76 lbs.
ABILITIES: *Illuminate* — Increases the chance of encountering wild Pokémon.
Natural Cure — Any negative Status conditions are healed when the Pokémon is removed from battle.

STATS
HP	33
ATTACK	33
DEFENSE	33
SP. ATTACK	66
SP. DEFENSE	33
SPEED	66

EVOLUTIONS

WATER STONE

WHERE/HOW TO CATCH
Lilycove City

STRONG AGAINST:
FIRE
WATER
ICE
STEEL

WEAK AGAINST:
ELECTRIC
GRASS

MOVES LIST
LV	Move Name	Type	ST	ACC	PP
S	Tackle	Normal	35	95	35
S	Harden	Normal	—	—	30
06	Water Gun	Water	40	100	25
10	Rapid Spin	Normal	20	100	40
15	Recover	Normal	—	—	20
19	Camouflage	Normal	—	100	20

LV	Move Name	Type	ST	ACC	PP
24	Swift	Normal	60	—	20
28	Bubblebeam	Water	65	100	20
33	Minimize	Normal	—	—	20
37	Light Screen	Psychic	—	—	30
42	Cosmic Power	Normal	—	—	20
46	Hydro Pump	Water	120	80	5

TM/HM LIST
TM/HM #	Move Name	Type	ST	ACC	PP
HM03	Surf	Water	95	100	15
HM05	Flash	Normal	—	70	20
HM07	Waterfall	Water	80	100	15
HM08	Dive	Water	60	100	10
TM03	Water Pulse	Water	60	100	20
TM06	Toxic	Poison	—	85	10
TM07	Hail	Ice	—	—	10
TM10	Hidden Power	Normal	—	100	15
TM13	Ice Beam	Ice	95	100	10
TM14	Blizzard	Ice	120	70	5
TM16	Light Screen	Psychic	—	—	30
TM17	Protect	Normal	—	—	10

TM/HM #	Move Name	Type	ST	ACC	PP
TM18	Rain Dance	Water	—	—	5
TM21	Frustration	Normal	—	100	20
TM24	Thunderbolt	Electric	95	100	15
TM25	Thunder	Electric	120	70	10
TM27	Return	Normal	—	100	20
TM29	Psychic	Psychic	90	100	10
TM32	Double Team	Normal	—	—	15
TM33	Reflect	Psychic	—	—	20
TM42	Façade	Normal	70	100	20
TM43	Secret Power	Normal	70	100	20
TM44	Rest	Psychic	—	—	10

EGG MOVES
Move Name	Type	ST	ACC	PP
None				

MOVE TUTOR LIST
Move Name	Type	ST	ACC	PP
Double-Edge	Normal	120	100	15
Endure*	Normal	—	—	10
Icy Wind*	Ice	55	95	15
Mimic	Normal	—	100	10
Psych Up*	Normal	—	—	10
Sleep Talk	Normal	—	—	10
Snore*	Normal	40	100	15
Substitute	Normal	—	—	10
Swagger	Normal	—	90	15
Swift*	Normal	60	—	20
Thunder Wave*	Electric	—	100	20

*Battle Frontier tutor move

144

Starmie™

WATER
PSYCHIC

GENERAL INFO
SPECIES: Mysterious Pokémon
HEIGHT: 3'7"
WEIGHT: 176 lbs.
ABILITIES: *Illuminate* — Increases the chance of encountering wild Pokémon.
Natural Cure — Any negative Status conditions are healed when the Pokémon is removed from battle.

STATS
HP	33
ATTACK	66
DEFENSE	60
SP. ATTACK	100
SP. DEFENSE	66
SPEED	100

EVOLUTIONS

WATER STONE

WHERE/HOW TO CATCH
Evolve from Staryu with Water Stone

STRONG AGAINST:
FIRE
WATER
ICE
FIGHTING
PSYCHIC
STEEL

WEAK AGAINST:
ELECTRIC
GRASS
BUG
GHOST
DARK

MOVES LIST
LV	Move Name	Type	ST	ACC	PP
S	Water Gun	Water	40	100	25
S	Rapid Spin	Normal	20	100	40
S	Recover	Normal	—	—	20

LV	Move Name	Type	ST	ACC	PP
S	Swift	Normal	60	—	20
33	Confuse Ray	Ghost	—	100	10

TM/HM LIST
TM/HM #	Move Name	Type	ST	ACC	PP
HM03	Surf	Water	95	100	15
HM05	Flash	Normal	—	70	20
HM07	Waterfall	Water	80	100	15
HM08	Dive	Water	60	100	10
TM03	Water Pulse	Water	60	100	20
TM06	Toxic	Poison	—	85	10
TM07	Hail	Ice	—	—	10
TM10	Hidden Power	Normal	—	100	15
TM13	Ice Beam	Ice	95	100	10
TM14	Blizzard	Ice	120	70	5
TM15	Hyper Beam	Normal	150	90	5
TM16	Light Screen	Psychic	—	—	30
TM17	Protect	Normal	—	—	10

TM/HM #	Move Name	Type	ST	ACC	PP
TM18	Rain Dance	Water	—	—	5
TM21	Frustration	Normal	—	100	20
TM24	Thunderbolt	Electric	95	100	15
TM25	Thunder	Electric	120	70	10
TM27	Return	Normal	—	100	20
TM29	Psychic	Psychic	90	100	10
TM32	Double Team	Normal	—	—	15
TM33	Reflect	Psychic	—	—	20
TM42	Façade	Normal	70	100	20
TM43	Secret Power	Normal	70	100	20
TM44	Rest	Psychic	—	—	10
TM48	Skill Swap	Psychic	—	100	10

MOVE TUTOR LIST
Move Name	Type	ST	ACC	PP
Double-Edge	Normal	120	100	15
Dream Eater*	Psychic	100	100	15
Endure*	Normal	—	—	10
Icy Wind*	Ice	55	95	15
Mimic	Normal	—	100	10
Psych Up*	Normal	—	—	10
Sleep Talk	Normal	—	—	10
Snore*	Normal	40	100	15
Substitute	Normal	—	—	10
Swagger	Normal	—	90	15
Swift*	Normal	60	—	20
Thunder Wave*	Electric	—	100	20

*Battle Frontier tutor move

145 Kecleon

NORMAL

GENERAL INFO
SPECIES: Color Swap Pokémon
HEIGHT: 3'3"
WEIGHT: 49 lbs.
ABILITY: *Color Change—*
Changes the Pokémon's type to the
type of the move that hits it.

STATS

HP	50
ATTACK	75
DEFENSE	50
SP. ATTACK	50
SP. DEFENSE	75
SPEED	50

EVOLUTIONS

KECLEON DOES
NOT EVOLVE

WHERE/HOW TO CATCH
Routes 118, 119, 120, 121, and 123

STRONG AGAINST:
GHOST

WEAK AGAINST:
FIGHTING

MOVES LIST

LV	Move Name	Type	ST	ACC	PP		LV	Move Name	Type	ST	ACC	PP
S	Thief	Dark	40	100	10		12	Fury Swipes	Normal	18	80	15
S	Tail Whip	Normal	—	100	30		17	Psybeam	Psychic	65	100	20
S	Astonish	Ghost	30	100	15		24	Screech	Normal	—	85	40
S	Lick	Ghost	20	100	30		31	Slash	Normal	70	100	20
S	Scratch	Normal	40	100	35		40	Substitute	Normal	—	—	10
04	Bind	Normal	15	75	20		49	Ancientpower	Rock	60	100	5
07	Faint Attack	Dark	60	—	20							

TM/HM LIST

TM/HM #	Move Name	Type	ST	ACC	PP		TM/HM #	Move Name	Type	ST	ACC	PP
HM01	Cut	Normal	50	95	30		TM27	Return	Normal	—	100	20
HM04	Strength	Normal	80	100	15		TM28	Dig	Ground	60	100	10
HM05	Flash	Normal	—	70	20		TM30	Shadow Ball	Ghost	60	—	20
HM06	Rock Smash	Fighting	20	100	15		TM31	Brick Break	Fighting	75	100	15
TM01	Focus Punch	Fighting	150	100	20		TM32	Double Team	Normal	—	—	15
TM03	Water Pulse	Water	60	100	20		TM34	Shock Wave	Electric	60	—	20
TM06	Toxic	Poison	—	85	10		TM35	Flamethrower	Fire	95	100	15
TM10	Hidden Power	Normal	—	100	15		TM38	Fire Blast	Fire	120	85	5
TM11	Sunny Day	Fire	—	—	5		TM39	Rock Tomb	Rock	50	80	10
TM13	Ice Beam	Ice	95	100	10		TM40	Aerial Ace	Flying	60	—	20
TM14	Blizzard	Ice	120	70	5		TM42	Façade	Normal	70	100	20
TM17	Protect	Normal	—	—	10		TM43	Secret Power	Normal	70	100	20
TM18	Rain Dance	Water	—	—	5		TM44	Rest	Psychic	—	—	10
TM21	Frustration	Normal	—	100	20		TM45	Attract	Normal	—	100	15
TM22	Solarbeam	Grass	120	100	10		TM46	Thief	Dark	40	100	10
TM23	Iron Tail	Steel	100	75	15		TM48	Skill Swap	Psychic	—	100	10
TM24	Thunderbolt	Electric	95	100	15		TM49	Snatch	Dark	—	100	10
TM25	Thunder	Electric	120	70	10							

EGG MOVES

Move Name	Type	ST	ACC	PP
Disable	Normal	—	55	20
Magic Coat	Psychic	—	100	15
Trick	Psychic	—	100	10

MOVE TUTOR LIST

Move Name	Type	ST	ACC	PP
Body Slam*	Normal	85	100	15
Counter*	Fighting	—	100	20
Defense Curl*	Normal	—	—	40
Double-Edge	Normal	120	100	15
Dynamicpunch	Fighting	100	50	5
Endure*	Normal	—	—	10
Fire Punch*	Fire	75	100	15
Fury Cutter	Bug	10	95	20
Ice Punch*	Ice	75	100	15
Icy Wind*	Ice	55	95	15
Mega Kick*	Normal	120	85	5
Mega Punch*	Normal	80	75	20
Metronome	Normal	—	100	10
Mimic	Normal	—	100	10
Mud-Slap*	Ground	20	100	10
Psych Up*	Normal	—	—	10
Rock Slide*	Rock	75	90	10
Rollout	Rock	30	90	20
Seismic Toss*	Fighting	—	100	20
Sleep Talk	Normal	—	—	10
Snore*	Normal	40	100	15
Substitute	Normal	—	—	10
Swagger	Normal	—	90	15
Swift*	Normal	60	—	20
Thunderpunch*	Electric	75	100	15
Thunder Wave*	Electric	—	100	20

*Battle Frontier tutor move

146 Shuppet

GHOST

GENERAL INFO
SPECIES: Puppet Pokémon
HEIGHT: 2'0"
WEIGHT: 5 lbs.
ABILITY: *Insomnia—*
Pokémon cannot be put to Sleep.

STATS

HP	25
ATTACK	50
DEFENSE	25
SP. ATTACK	75
SP. DEFENSE	25
SPEED	50

EVOLUTIONS

LV37

WHERE/HOW TO CATCH
Routes 121 and 123,
Mt. Pyre

STRONG AGAINST:
NORMAL
FLYING
POISON
BUG

WEAK AGAINST:
GHOST
DARK

MOVES LIST

LV	Move Name	Type	ST	ACC	PP		LV	Move Name	Type	ST	ACC	PP
S	Knock Off	Dark	20	100	20		32	Will-O-Wisp	Fire	—	75	15
08	Screech	Normal	—	85	40		37	Faint Attack	Dark	60	—	20
13	Night Shade	Ghost	—	100	15		44	Shadow Ball	Ghost	80	100	15
20	Curse	—	—	—	10		49	Snatch	Dark	—	100	10
25	Spite	Ghost	—	100	10		56	Grudge	Ghost	—	100	5

TM/HM LIST

TM/HM #	Move Name	Type	ST	ACC	PP		TM/HM #	Move Name	Type	ST	ACC	PP
HM05	Flash	Normal	—	70	20		TM29	Psychic	Psychic	90	100	10
TM04	Calm Mind	Psychic	—	—	20		TM30	Shadow Ball	Ghost	60	—	20
TM06	Toxic	Poison	—	85	10		TM32	Double Team	Normal	—	—	15
TM10	Hidden Power	Normal	—	100	15		TM34	Shock Wave	Electric	60	—	20
TM11	Sunny Day	Fire	—	—	5		TM41	Torment	Dark	—	100	15
TM12	Taunt	Dark	—	100	20		TM42	Façade	Normal	70	100	20
TM17	Protect	Normal	—	—	10		TM43	Secret Power	Normal	70	100	20
TM18	Rain Dance	Water	—	—	5		TM44	Rest	Psychic	—	—	10
TM21	Frustration	Normal	—	100	20		TM45	Attract	Normal	—	100	15
TM24	Thunderbolt	Electric	95	100	15		TM46	Thief	Dark	40	100	10
TM25	Thunder	Electric	120	70	10		TM48	Skill Swap	Psychic	—	100	10
TM27	Return	Normal	—	100	20		TM49	Snatch	Dark	—	100	10

EGG MOVES

Move Name	Type	ST	ACC	PP
Disable	Normal	—	55	20
Destiny Bond	Ghost	—	—	5
Foresight	Normal	—	100	40
Astonish	Ghost	30	100	15
Imprison	Psychic	—	100	15

MOVE TUTOR LIST

Move Name	Type	ST	ACC	PP
Body Slam*	Normal	85	100	15
Double-Edge	Normal	120	100	15
Dream Eater*	Psychic	100	100	15
Endure*	Normal	—	—	10
Icy Wind*	Ice	55	95	15
Mimic	Normal	—	100	10
Psych Up*	Normal	—	—	10
Rock Slide*	Rock	75	90	10
Sleep Talk	Normal	—	—	10
Snore*	Normal	40	100	15
Substitute	Normal	—	—	10
Swagger	Normal	—	90	15
Thunder Wave*	Electric	—	100	20

*Battle Frontier tutor move

147

Banette™

GHOST

GENERAL INFO
SPECIES: Marionette Pokémon
HEIGHT: 3'7"
WEIGHT: 28 lbs.
ABILITY: *Insomnia*— *Pokémon cannot be put to Sleep.*

STATS
HP	50
ATTACK	75
DEFENSE	50
SP. ATTACK	75
SP. DEFENSE	50
SPEED	50

EVOLUTIONS
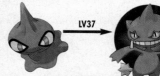
LV37

WHERE/HOW TO CATCH
Evolve from Shuppet; Sky Pillar

STRONG AGAINST:
NORMAL
FLYING
POISON
BUG

WEAK AGAINST:
GHOST
DARK

MOVES LIST
LV	Move Name	Type	ST	ACC	PP
S	Knock Off	Dark	20	100	20
S	Screech	Normal	—	85	40
S	Night Shade	Ghost	—	100	15
S	Curse	—	—	—	10
08	Screech	Normal	—	85	40
13	Night Shade	Ghost	—	100	15
20	Curse	—	—	—	10
25	Spite	Ghost	—	100	10
32	Will-O-Wisp	Fire	—	75	15
39	Faint Attack	Dark	60	—	20
48	Shadow Ball	Ghost	80	100	15
55	Snatch	Dark	—	100	10
64	Grudge	Ghost	—	100	5

TM/HM LIST
TM/HM #	Move Name	Type	ST	ACC	PP
HM05	Flash	Normal	—	70	20
TM04	Calm Mind	Psychic	—	—	20
TM06	Toxic	Poison	—	85	10
TM10	Hidden Power	Normal	—	100	15
TM11	Sunny Day	Fire	—	—	5
TM12	Taunt	Dark	—	100	20
TM15	Hyper Beam	Normal	150	90	5
TM17	Protect	Normal	—	—	10
TM18	Rain Dance	Water	—	—	5
TM21	Frustration	Normal	—	100	20
TM24	Thunderbolt	Electric	95	100	15
TM25	Thunder	Electric	120	70	10
TM27	Return	Normal	—	100	20
TM29	Psychic	Psychic	90	100	10
TM30	Shadow Ball	Ghost	60	—	20
TM32	Double Team	Normal	—	—	15
TM34	Shock Wave	Electric	60	—	20
TM41	Torment	Dark	—	100	15
TM42	Façade	Normal	70	100	20
TM43	Secret Power	Normal	70	100	20
TM44	Rest	Psychic	—	—	10
TM45	Attract	Normal	—	100	15
TM46	Thief	Dark	40	100	10
TM48	Skill Swap	Psychic	—	100	10
TM49	Snatch	Dark	—	100	10

MOVE TUTOR LIST
Move Name	Type	ST	ACC	PP
Body Slam*	Normal	85	100	15
Double-Edge	Normal	120	100	15
Dream Eater*	Psychic	100	100	15
Endure*	Normal	—	—	10
Icy Wind*	Ice	55	95	15
Metronome	Normal	—	100	10
Mimic	Normal	—	100	10
Mud-Slap*	Ground	20	100	10
Psych Up*	Normal	—	—	10
Rock Slide*	Rock	75	90	10
Sleep Talk	Normal	—	—	10
Snore*	Normal	40	100	15
Substitute	Normal	—	—	10
Swagger	Normal	—	90	15
Thunder Wave*	Electric	—	100	20

*Battle Frontier tutor move

148

Duskull™

GHOST

GENERAL INFO
SPECIES: Requiem Pokémon
HEIGHT: 2'7"
WEIGHT: 33 lbs.
ABILITY: *Levitate*— *Pokémon is not affected by Ground-type Moves.*

STATS
HP	25
ATTACK	50
DEFENSE	50
SP. ATTACK	25
SP. DEFENSE	50
SPEED	25

EVOLUTIONS

LV37

WHERE/HOW TO CATCH
Mt. Pyre

STRONG AGAINST:
NORMAL
FLYING
POISON
BUG

WEAK AGAINST:
GHOST
DARK

MOVES LIST
LV	Move Name	Type	ST	ACC	PP
S	Leer	Normal	—	100	30
S	Night Shade	Ghost	—	100	15
05	Disable	Normal	—	55	20
12	Foresight	Normal	—	100	40
16	Astonish	Ghost	30	100	15
23	Confuse Ray	Ghost	—	100	10
27	Pursuit	Dark	40	100	20
34	Curse	—	—	—	10
38	Will-O-Wisp	Fire	—	75	15
45	Mean Look	Normal	—	100	5
49	Future Sight	Psychic	80	90	15

TM/HM LIST
TM/HM #	Move Name	Type	ST	ACC	PP
HM05	Flash	Normal	—	70	20
TM04	Calm Mind	Psychic	—	—	20
TM06	Toxic	Poison	—	85	10
TM10	Hidden Power	Normal	—	100	15
TM11	Sunny Day	Fire	—	—	5
TM12	Taunt	Dark	—	100	20
TM13	Ice Beam	Ice	95	100	10
TM14	Blizzard	Ice	120	70	5
TM17	Protect	Normal	—	—	10
TM18	Rain Dance	Water	—	—	5
TM21	Frustration	Normal	—	100	20
TM27	Return	Normal	—	100	20
TM29	Psychic	Psychic	90	100	10
TM30	Shadow Ball	Ghost	60	—	20
TM32	Double Team	Normal	—	—	15
TM41	Torment	Dark	—	100	15
TM42	Façade	Normal	70	100	20
TM43	Secret Power	Normal	70	100	20
TM44	Rest	Psychic	—	—	10
TM45	Attract	Normal	—	100	15
TM46	Thief	Dark	40	100	10
TM48	Skill Swap	Psychic	—	100	10
TM49	Snatch	Dark	—	100	10

EGG MOVES
Move Name	Type	ST	ACC	PP
Imprison	Psychic	—	100	15
Destiny Bond	Ghost	—	—	5
Grudge	Ghost	—	100	5
Memento	Dark	—	100	10
Faint Attack	Dark	60	—	20
Pain Split	Normal	—	100	60

MOVE TUTOR LIST
Move Name	Type	ST	ACC	PP
Body Slam*	Normal	85	100	15
Double-Edge	Normal	120	100	15
Dream Eater*	Psychic	100	100	15
Endure*	Normal	—	—	10
Icy Wind*	Ice	55	95	15
Mimic	Normal	—	100	10
Psych Up*	Normal	—	—	10
Sleep Talk	Normal	—	—	10
Snore*	Normal	40	100	15
Substitute	Normal	—	—	10
Swagger	Normal	—	90	15

*Battle Frontier tutor move

PRIMA OFFICIAL GAME GUIDE

149 Dusclops

GHOST

GENERAL INFO
SPECIES: Beckon Pokémon
HEIGHT: 5'3"
WEIGHT: 67 lbs.
ABILITY: *Pressure*—When hit by a move, the opponent's Pokémon loses 2 PP.

STATS
HP	25
ATTACK	50
DEFENSE	75
SP. ATTACK	50
SP. DEFENSE	75
SPEED	25

EVOLUTIONS
 LV37 →

WHERE/HOW TO CATCH
Evolve from Duskull

STRONG AGAINST:
NORMAL
FLYING
POISON
BUG

WEAK AGAINST:
GHOST
DARK

MOVES LIST
LV	Move Name	Type	ST	ACC	PP
S	Leer	Normal	—	100	30
S	Night Shade	Ghost	—	100	15
S	Disable	Normal	—	55	20
05	Disable	Normal	—	55	20
12	Foresight	Normal	—	100	40
16	Astonish	Ghost	30	100	15
23	Confuse Ray	Ghost	—	100	10

LV	Move Name	Type	ST	ACC	PP
27	Pursuit	Dark	40	100	20
34	Curse	—	—	—	10
37	Shadow Ball	Ghost	60	—	20
41	Will-O-Wisp	Fire	—	75	15
51	Mean Look	Normal	—	100	5
58	Future Sight	Psychic	80	90	15

TM/HM LIST
TM/HM #	Move Name	Type	ST	ACC	PP
HM04	Strength	Normal	80	100	15
HM05	Flash	Normal	—	70	20
HM06	Rock Smash	Fighting	20	100	15
TM01	Focus Punch	Fighting	150	100	20
TM04	Calm Mind	Psychic	—	—	20
TM06	Toxic	Poison	—	85	10
TM10	Hidden Power	Normal	—	100	15
TM11	Sunny Day	Fire	—	—	5
TM12	Taunt	Dark	—	100	20
TM13	Ice Beam	Ice	95	100	10
TM14	Blizzard	Ice	120	70	5
TM15	Hyper Beam	Normal	150	90	5
TM17	Protect	Normal	—	—	10
TM18	Rain Dance	Water	—	—	5
TM21	Frustration	Normal	—	100	20

TM/HM #	Move Name	Type	ST	ACC	PP
TM26	Earthquake	Ground	100	100	10
TM27	Return	Normal	—	100	20
TM29	Psychic	Psychic	90	100	10
TM30	Shadow Ball	Ghost	60	—	20
TM32	Double Team	Normal	—	—	15
TM39	Rock Tomb	Rock	50	80	10
TM41	Torment	Dark	—	100	15
TM42	Façade	Normal	70	100	20
TM43	Secret Power	Normal	70	100	20
TM44	Rest	Psychic	—	—	10
TM45	Attract	Normal	—	100	15
TM46	Thief	Dark	40	100	10
TM48	Skill Swap	Psychic	—	100	10
TM49	Snatch	Dark	—	100	10

MOVE TUTOR LIST
Move Name	Type	ST	ACC	PP
Body Slam*	Normal	85	100	15
Counter*	Fighting	—	100	20
Double-Edge	Normal	120	100	15
Dream Eater*	Psychic	100	100	15
Dynamicpunch	Fighting	100	50	5
Endure*	Normal	—	—	10
Fire Punch*	Fire	75	100	15
Ice Punch*	Ice	75	100	15
Icy Wind*	Ice	55	95	15
Mega Kick*	Normal	120	85	5
Mega Punch*	Normal	80	75	20
Metronome	Normal	—	100	10
Mimic	Normal	—	100	10
Mud-Slap*	Ground	20	100	10
Psych Up*	Normal	—	—	10
Rock Slide*	Rock	75	90	10
Seismic Toss*	Fighting	—	100	20
Sleep Talk	Normal	—	—	10
Snore*	Normal	40	100	15
Substitute	Normal	—	—	10
Swagger	Normal	—	90	15
Thunderpunch*	Electric	75	100	15

*Battle Frontier tutor move

150 Tropius

GRASS
FLYING

GENERAL INFO
SPECIES: Fruit Pokémon
HEIGHT: 6'7"
WEIGHT: 221 lbs.
ABILITY: *Chlorophyll*—Doubles the Pokémon's Speed when it is sunny.

STATS
HP	50
ATTACK	50
DEFENSE	50
SP. ATTACK	75
SP. DEFENSE	50
SPEED	50

EVOLUTIONS

TROPIUS DOES NOT EVOLVE

WHERE/HOW TO CATCH
Route 119

STRONG AGAINST:
WATER
GRASS
FIGHTING
GROUND

WEAK AGAINST:
FIRE
ICE
POISON
FLYING
ROCK

MOVES LIST
LV	Move Name	Type	ST	ACC	PP
S	Leer	Normal	—	100	30
S	Gust	Flying	40	100	35
07	Growth	Normal	—	—	40
11	Razor Leaf	Grass	55	95	25
17	Stomp	Normal	65	100	20
21	Sweet Scent	Normal	—	100	20

LV	Move Name	Type	ST	ACC	PP
27	Whirlwind	Normal	—	100s	20
31	Magical Leaf	Grass	60	—	20
37	Body Slam	Normal	85	100	15
41	Solarbeam	Grass	120	100	10
47	Synthesis	Grass	—	—	5

TM/HM LIST
TM/HM #	Move Name	Type	ST	ACC	PP
HM01	Cut	Normal	50	95	30
HM02	Fly	Flying	70	95	15
HM04	Strength	Normal	80	100	15
HM05	Flash	Normal	—	70	20
HM06	Rock Smash	Fighting	20	100	15
TM05	Roar	Normal	—	100	20
TM06	Toxic	Poison	—	85	10
TM09	Bullet Seed	Grass	10	100	30
TM10	Hidden Power	Normal	—	100	15
TM11	Sunny Day	Fire	—	—	5
TM15	Hyper Beam	Normal	150	90	5
TM17	Protect	Normal	—	—	10
TM19	Giga Drain	Grass	60	100	5

TM/HM #	Move Name	Type	ST	ACC	PP
TM20	Safeguard	Normal	—	—	25
TM21	Frustration	Normal	—	100	20
TM22	Solarbeam	Grass	120	100	10
TM26	Earthquake	Ground	100	100	10
TM27	Return	Normal	—	100	20
TM32	Double Team	Normal	—	—	15
TM40	Aerial Ace	Flying	60	—	20
TM42	Façade	Normal	70	100	20
TM43	Secret Power	Normal	70	100	20
TM44	Rest	Psychic	—	—	10
TM45	Attract	Normal	—	100	15
TM47	Steel Wing	Steel	70	90	25

EGG MOVES
Move Name	Type	ST	ACC	PP
Headbutt	Normal	70	100	15
Slam	Normal	80	75	20
Razor Wind	Normal	80	100	10
Leech Seed	Grass	—	90	10
Nature Power	Normal	—	95	20

MOVE TUTOR LIST
Move Name	Type	ST	ACC	PP
Body Slam*	Normal	85	100	15
Double-Edge	Normal	120	100	15
Endure*	Normal	—	—	10
Fury Cutter	Bug	10	95	20
Mimic	Normal	—	100	10
Mud-Slap*	Ground	20	100	10
Sleep Talk	Normal	—	—	10
Snore*	Normal	40	100	15
Substitute	Normal	—	—	10
Swagger	Normal	—	90	15
Swords Dance*	Normal	—	—	30

*Battle Frontier tutor move

151 Chimecho™

PSYCHIC

GENERAL INFO
SPECIES: Wind Chime Pokémon
HEIGHT: 2'0"
WEIGHT: 2 lbs.
ABILITY: *Levitate* — Pokémon is not affected by Ground-type Moves.

STATS
HP	50
ATTACK	50
DEFENSE	50
SP. ATTACK	25
SP. DEFENSE	25
SPEED	25

EVOLUTIONS
CHIMECHO DOES NOT EVOLVE

WHERE/HOW TO CATCH
Mt. Pyre

STRONG AGAINST:
FIRE
PSYCHIC
GROUND

WEAK AGAINST:
BUG
GHOST
DARK

MOVES LIST
LV	Move Name	Type	ST	ACC	PP
S	Wrap	Normal	15	85	20
06	Growl	Normal	—	100	40
09	Astonish	Ghost	30	100	15
14	Confusion	Psychic	50	100	25
17	Take Down	Normal	90	85	20
22	Uproar	Normal	50	100	10
25	Yawn	Normal	—	100	10
30	Psywave	Psychic	—	80	15
33	Double-Edge	Normal	120	100	15
38	Heal Bell	Normal	—	—	5
41	Safeguard	Normal	—	—	25
46	Psychic	Psychic	90	100	10

TM/HM LIST
TM/HM #	Move Name	Type	ST	ACC	PP
HM05	Flash	Normal	—	70	20
TM04	Calm Mind	Psychic	—	—	20
TM06	Toxic	Poison	—	85	10
TM10	Hidden Power	Normal	—	100	15
TM11	Sunny Day	Fire	—	—	5
TM12	Taunt	Dark	—	100	20
TM16	Light Screen	Psychic	—	—	30
TM17	Protect	Normal	—	—	10
TM18	Rain Dance	Water	—	—	5
TM20	Safeguard	Normal	—	—	25
TM21	Frustration	Normal	—	100	20
TM27	Return	Normal	—	100	20
TM29	Psychic	Psychic	90	100	10
TM30	Shadow Ball	Ghost	60	—	15
TM32	Double Team	Normal	—	—	15
TM33	Reflect	Psychic	—	—	20
TM34	Shock Wave	Electric	60	—	20
TM41	Torment	Dark	—	100	15
TM42	Façade	Normal	70	100	20
TM43	Secret Power	Normal	70	100	20
TM44	Rest	Psychic	—	—	10
TM45	Attract	Normal	—	100	15
TM48	Skill Swap	Psychic	—	100	10
TM49	Snatch	Dark	—	100	10

EGG MOVES
Move Name	Type	ST	ACC	PP
Disable	Normal	—	55	20
Curse	—	—	—	10
Hypnosis	Psychic	—	60	20
Dream Eater	Psychic	100	100	15

MOVE TUTOR LIST
Move Name	Type	ST	ACC	PP
Defense Curl*	Normal	—	—	40
Double-Edge	Normal	120	100	15
Dream Eater*	Psychic	100	100	15
Endure*	Normal	—	—	10
Icy Wind*	Ice	55	95	15
Mimic	Normal	—	100	10
Psych Up*	Normal	—	—	10
Rock Slide*	Rock	75	90	10
Rollout	Rock	30	90	20
Sleep Talk	Normal	—	—	10
Snore*	Normal	40	100	15
Substitute	Normal	—	—	10
Swagger	Normal	—	90	15

*Battle Frontier tutor move

---

152 Absol™

DARK

GENERAL INFO
SPECIES: Disaster Pokémon
HEIGHT: 3'11"
WEIGHT: 104 lbs.
ABILITY: *Pressure* — When hit by a move, the opponent's Pokémon loses 2 PP.

STATS
HP	50
ATTACK	100
DEFENSE	50
SP. ATTACK	75
SP. DEFENSE	50
SPEED	50

EVOLUTIONS
ABSOL DOES NOT EVOLVE

WHERE/HOW TO CATCH
Route 120

STRONG AGAINST:
PSYCHIC
GHOST
DARK

WEAK AGAINST:
FIGHTING
BUG

MOVES LIST
LV	Move Name	Type	ST	ACC	PP
S	Scratch	Normal	40	100	35
05	Leer	Normal	—	100	30
09	Taunt	Dark	—	100	20
13	Quick Attack	Normal	40	100	30
17	Razor Wind	Normal	80	100	10
21	Bite	Dark	60	100	25
26	Swords Dance	Normal	—	—	30
31	Double Team	Normal	—	—	15
36	Slash	Normal	70	100	20
41	Future Sight	Psychic	80	90	15
46	Perish Song	Normal	—	—	5

TM/HM LIST
TM/HM #	Move Name	Type	ST	ACC	PP
HM01	Cut	Normal	50	95	30
HM04	Strength	Normal	80	100	15
HM05	Flash	Normal	—	70	20
HM06	Rock Smash	Fighting	20	100	15
TM03	Water Pulse	Water	60	100	20
TM04	Calm Mind	Psychic	—	—	20
TM06	Toxic	Poison	—	85	10
TM07	Hail	Ice	—	—	10
TM10	Hidden Power	Normal	—	100	15
TM11	Sunny Day	Fire	—	—	5
TM12	Taunt	Dark	—	100	20
TM13	Ice Beam	Ice	95	100	10
TM14	Blizzard	Ice	120	70	5
TM15	Hyper Beam	Normal	150	90	5
TM17	Protect	Normal	—	—	10
TM18	Rain Dance	Water	—	—	5
TM21	Frustration	Normal	—	100	20
TM23	Iron Tail	Steel	100	75	15
TM24	Thunderbolt	Electric	95	100	15
TM25	Thunder	Electric	120	70	10
TM27	Return	Normal	—	100	20
TM30	Shadow Ball	Ghost	60	—	20
TM32	Double Team	Normal	—	—	15
TM34	Shock Wave	Electric	60	—	20
TM35	Flamethrower	Fire	95	100	15
TM37	Sandstorm	Rock	—	—	10
TM38	Fire Blast	Fire	120	85	5
TM40	Aerial Ace	Flying	60	—	20
TM41	Torment	Dark	—	100	15
TM42	Façade	Normal	70	100	20
TM43	Secret Power	Normal	70	100	20
TM44	Rest	Psychic	—	—	10
TM45	Attract	Normal	—	100	15
TM46	Thief	Dark	40	100	10
TM49	Snatch	Dark	—	100	10

EGG MOVES
Move Name	Type	ST	ACC	PP
Baton Pass	Normal	—	—	40
Faint Attack	Dark	60	—	20
Double-Edge	Normal	120	100	15
Magic Coat	Psychic	—	100	15
Curse	—	—	—	10
Substitute	Normal	—	—	10

MOVE TUTOR LIST
Move Name	Type	ST	ACC	PP
Body Slam*	Normal	85	100	15
Counter*	Fighting	—	100	20
Double-Edge*	Normal	120	100	15
Dream Eater*	Psychic	100	100	15
Endure*	Normal	—	—	10
Fury Cutter	Bug	10	95	20
Icy Wind*	Ice	55	95	15
Mimic	Normal	—	100	10
Mud-Slap*	Ground	20	100	10
Psych Up*	Normal	—	—	10
Rock Slide*	Rock	75	90	10
Sleep Talk	Normal	—	—	10
Snore*	Normal	40	100	15
Substitute	Normal	—	—	10
Swagger	Normal	—	90	15
Swift*	Normal	60	—	20
Swords Dance*	Normal	—	—	30
Thunder Wave*	Electric	—	100	20

*Battle Frontier tutor move

153 Vulpix™

FIRE

GENERAL INFO
SPECIES: Fox Pokémon
HEIGHT: 2'0"
WEIGHT: 22 lbs.
ABILITY: *Flash Fire*—The Pokémon's Attack is increased a point when a Fire-type Move hits the Pokémon.

STATS

HP	33
ATTACK	33
DEFENSE	33
SP. ATTACK	33
SP. DEFENSE	66
SPEED	66

EVOLUTIONS

 FIRE STONE

WHERE/HOW TO CATCH
Mt. Pyre

STRONG AGAINST:
FIRE
GRASS
ICE
BUG
STEEL

WEAK AGAINST:
WATER
GROUND
ROCK

MOVES LIST

LV	Move Name	Type	ST	ACC	PP		LV	Move Name	Type	ST	ACC	PP
S	Ember	Fire	40	100	25		25	Imprison	Psychic	—	100	15
05	Tail Whip	Normal	—	100	30		29	Flamethrower	Fire	95	100	15
09	Roar	Normal	—	100	20		33	Safeguard	Normal	—	—	25
13	Quick Attack	Normal	40	100	30		37	Grudge	Ghost	—	100	5
17	Will-O-Wisp	Fire	—	75	15		41	Fire Spin	Fire	15	70	15
21	Confuse Ray	Ghost	—	100	10							

TM/HM LIST

TM/HM #	Move Name	Type	ST	ACC	PP		TM/HM #	Move Name	Type	ST	ACC	PP
TM05	Roar	Normal	—	100	20		TM28	Dig	Ground	60	100	10
TM06	Toxic	Poison	—	85	10		TM32	Double Team	Normal	—	—	15
TM10	Hidden Power	Normal	—	100	15		TM35	Flamethrower	Fire	95	100	15
TM11	Sunny Day	Fire	—	—	5		TM38	Fire Blast	Fire	120	85	5
TM17	Protect	Normal	—	—	10		TM42	Façade	Normal	70	100	20
TM20	Safeguard	Normal	—	—	25		TM43	Secret Power	Normal	70	100	20
TM21	Frustration	Normal	—	100	20		TM44	Rest	Psychic	—	—	10
TM23	Iron Tail	Steel	100	75	15		TM45	Attract	Normal	—	100	15
TM27	Return	Normal	—	100	20		TM50	Overheat	Fire	140	90	5

EGG MOVES

Move Name	Type	ST	ACC	PP
Faint Attack	Dark	60	—	20
Hypnosis	Psychic	—	60	20
Flail	Normal	—	100	15
Disable	Normal	—	55	20
Howl	Normal	—	—	40
Psych Up	Normal	—	—	10
Heat Wave	Fire	100	90	10

MOVE TUTOR LIST

Move Name	Type	ST	ACC	PP
Body Slam*	Normal	85	100	15
Double-Edge	Normal	120	100	15
Endure*	Normal	—	—	10
Mimic	Normal	—	100	10
Sleep Talk	Normal	—	—	10
Snore*	Normal	40	100	15
Substitute	Normal	—	—	10
Swagger	Normal	—	90	15
Swift*	Normal	60	—	20

*Battle Frontier tutor move

---

154 Ninetales

FIRE

GENERAL INFO
SPECIES: Fox Pokémon
HEIGHT: 3'7"
WEIGHT: 44 lbs.
ABILITY: *Flash Fire*—The Pokémon's Attack is increased a point when a Fire-type Move hits the Pokémon.

STATS

HP	66
ATTACK	66
DEFENSE	66
SP. ATTACK	66
SP. DEFENSE	66
SPEED	100

EVOLUTIONS

 FIRE STONE

WHERE/HOW TO CATCH
Evolve from Vulpix with Fire Stone

STRONG AGAINST:
FIRE
GRASS
ICE
BUG
STEEL

WEAK AGAINST:
WATER
GROUND
ROCK

MOVES LIST

LV	Move Name	Type	ST	ACC	PP		LV	Move Name	Type	ST	ACC	PP
S	Ember	Fire	40	100	25		S	Safeguard	Normal	—	—	25
S	Quick Attack	Normal	40	100	30		45	Fire Spin	Fire	15	70	15
S	Confuse Ray	Ghost	—	100	10							

TM/HM LIST

TM/HM #	Move Name	Type	ST	ACC	PP		TM/HM #	Move Name	Type	ST	ACC	PP
TM05	Roar	Normal	—	100	20		TM28	Dig	Ground	60	100	10
TM06	Toxic	Poison	—	85	10		TM32	Double Team	Normal	—	—	15
TM10	Hidden Power	Normal	—	100	15		TM35	Flamethrower	Fire	95	100	15
TM11	Sunny Day	Fire	—	—	5		TM38	Fire Blast	Fire	120	85	5
TM15	Hyper Beam	Normal	150	90	5		TM42	Façade	Normal	70	100	20
TM17	Protect	Normal	—	—	10		TM43	Secret Power	Normal	70	100	20
TM20	Safeguard	Normal	—	—	25		TM44	Rest	Psychic	—	—	10
TM21	Frustration	Normal	—	100	20		TM45	Attract	Normal	—	100	15
TM23	Iron Tail	Steel	100	75	15		TM50	Overheat	Fire	140	90	5
TM27	Return	Normal	—	100	20							

MOVE TUTOR LIST

Move Name	Type	ST	ACC	PP
Body Slam*	Normal	85	100	15
Double-Edge	Normal	120	100	15
Endure*	Normal	—	—	10
Mimic	Normal	—	100	10
Sleep Talk	Normal	—	—	10
Snore*	Normal	40	100	15
Substitute	Normal	—	—	10
Swagger	Normal	—	90	15
Swift*	Normal	60	—	20

*Battle Frontier tutor move

155 Pichu™
ELECTRIC

GENERAL INFO
SPECIES: Tiny Mouse Pokémon
HEIGHT: 1'0"
WEIGHT: 4 lbs.
ABILITY: *Static*—Gives the Pokémon's Physical Attacks a 30 percent chance of inflicting Paralysis on the opponent.

STATS

HP	33
ATTACK	33
DEFENSE	33
SP. ATTACK	33
SP. DEFENSE	33
SPEED	66

EVOLUTIONS

FRIENDSHIP

THUNDERSTONE

WHERE/HOW TO CATCH
Breed from Pikachu

STRONG AGAINST:
ELECTRIC
FLYING
STEEL

WEAK AGAINST:
GROUND

MOVES LIST

LV	Move Name	Type	ST	ACC	PP
S	Thundershock	Electric	40	100	30
S	Charm	Normal	—	100	20
06	Tail Whip	Normal	—	100	30
08	Thunder Wave	Electric	—	100	20
11	Sweet Kiss	Normal	—	75	10

TM/HM LIST

TM/HM #	Move Name	Type	ST	ACC	PP
HM05	Flash	Normal	—	70	20
TM06	Toxic	Poison	—	85	10
TM10	Hidden Power	Normal	—	100	15
TM16	Light Screen	Psychic	—	—	30
TM17	Protect	Normal	—	—	10
TM18	Rain Dance	Water	—	—	5
TM21	Frustration	Normal	—	100	20
TM23	Iron Tail	Steel	100	75	15
TM24	Thunderbolt	Electric	95	100	15
TM25	Thunder	Electric	120	70	10
TM27	Return	Normal	—	100	20
TM32	Double Team	Normal	—	—	15
TM34	Shock Wave	Electric	60	—	20
TM42	Façade	Normal	70	100	20
TM43	Secret Power	Normal	70	100	20
TM44	Rest	Psychic	—	—	10
TM45	Attract	Normal	—	100	15

EGG MOVES

Move Name	Type	ST	ACC	PP
Reversal	Fighting	—	100	15
Bide	Normal	—	100	10
Encore	Normal	—	100	5
Doubleslap	Normal	15	85	10
Charge	Electric	—	100	20
Present	Normal	—	90	15
Wish	Normal	—	100	10

MOVE TUTOR LIST

Move Name	Type	ST	ACC	PP
Body Slam*	Normal	85	100	15
Defense Curl*	Normal	—	—	40
Double-Edge	Normal	120	100	15
Endure*	Normal	—	—	10
Mega Kick*	Normal	120	85	5
Mega Punch*	Normal	80	75	20
Metronome	Normal	—	100	10
Mimic	Normal	—	100	10
Mud-Slap*	Ground	20	100	10
Rollout	Rock	30	90	20
Seismic Toss*	Fighting	—	100	20
Sleep Talk	Normal	—	—	10
Snore*	Normal	40	100	15
Substitute	Normal	—	—	10
Swagger	Normal	—	90	15
Swift*	Normal	60	—	20
Thunder Wave*	Electric	—	100	20

*Battle Frontier tutor move

156 Pikachu™
ELECTRIC

GENERAL INFO
SPECIES: Mouse Pokémon
HEIGHT: 1'4"
WEIGHT: 13 lbs.
ABILITY: *Static*—Gives the Pokémon's Physical Attacks a 30 percent chance of inflicting Paralysis on the opponent.

STATS

HP	33
ATTACK	66
DEFENSE	33
SP. ATTACK	33
SP. DEFENSE	33
SPEED	66

EVOLUTIONS

FRIENDSHIP

THUNDERSTONE

WHERE/HOW TO CATCH
Evolve from Pichu with Friendship; Safari Zone

STRONG AGAINST:
ELECTRIC
FLYING
STEEL

WEAK AGAINST:
GROUND

MOVES LIST

LV	Move Name	Type	ST	ACC	PP
S	Thundershock	Electric	40	100	30
S	Growl	Normal	—	100	40
06	Tail Whip	Normal	—	100	30
08	Thunder Wave	Electric	—	100	20
11	Quick Attack	Normal	40	100	30
15	Double Team	Normal	—	—	15
20	Slam	Normal	80	75	20
26	Thunderbolt	Electric	95	100	15
33	Agility	Psychic	—	—	30
41	Thunder	Electric	120	70	10
50	Light Screen	Psychic	—	—	30

TM/HM LIST

TM/HM #	Move Name	Type	ST	ACC	PP
HM04	Strength	Normal	80	100	15
HM05	Flash	Normal	—	70	20
HM06	Rock Smash	Fighting	20	100	15
TM01	Focus Punch	Fighting	150	100	20
TM06	Toxic	Poison	—	85	10
TM10	Hidden Power	Normal	—	100	15
TM16	Light Screen	Psychic	—	—	30
TM17	Protect	Normal	—	—	10
TM18	Rain Dance	Water	—	—	5
TM21	Frustration	Normal	—	100	20
TM23	Iron Tail	Steel	100	75	15
TM24	Thunderbolt	Electric	95	100	15
TM25	Thunder	Electric	120	70	10
TM27	Return	Normal	—	100	20
TM28	Dig	Ground	60	100	10
TM31	Brick Break	Fighting	75	100	15
TM32	Double Team	Normal	—	—	15
TM34	Shock Wave	Electric	60	—	20
TM42	Façade	Normal	70	100	20
TM43	Secret Power	Normal	70	100	20
TM44	Rest	Psychic	—	—	10
TM45	Attract	Normal	—	100	15

MOVE TUTOR LIST

Move Name	Type	ST	ACC	PP
Body Slam*	Normal	85	100	15
Counter*	Fighting	—	100	20
Defense Curl*	Normal	—	—	40
Double-Edge	Normal	120	100	15
Dynamicpunch	Fighting	100	50	5
Endure*	Normal	—	—	10
Mega Kick*	Normal	120	85	5
Mega Punch*	Normal	80	75	20
Mimic	Normal	—	100	10
Mud-Slap*	Ground	20	100	10
Rollout	Rock	30	90	20
Seismic Toss*	Fighting	—	100	20
Sleep Talk	Normal	—	—	10
Snore*	Normal	40	100	15
Substitute	Normal	—	—	10
Swagger	Normal	—	90	15
Swift*	Normal	60	—	20
Thunderpunch*	Electric	75	100	15
Thunder Wave*	Electric	—	100	20

*Battle Frontier tutor move

157

Raichu™

ELECTRIC

GENERAL INFO
SPECIES: Mouse Pokémon
HEIGHT: 2'7"
WEIGHT: 66 lbs.
ABILITY: *Static* — Gives the Pokémon's Physical Attacks a 30 percent chance of inflicting Paralysis on the opponent.

STATS
HP	33
ATTACK	66
DEFENSE	33
SP. ATTACK	66
SP. DEFENSE	66
SPEED	100

EVOLUTIONS

FRIENDSHIP   THUNDERSTONE

WHERE/HOW TO CATCH
Evolve from Pikachu with Thunder Stone

STRONG AGAINST:
ELECTRIC
FLYING
STEEL

WEAK AGAINST:
GROUND

MOVES LIST
LV	Move Name	Type	ST	ACC	PP	LV	Move Name	Type	ST	ACC	PP
S	Thundershock	Electric	40	100	30	S	Quick Attack	Normal	40	100	30
S	Tail Whip	Normal	—	100	30	S	Thunderbolt	Electric	95	100	15

TM/HM LIST
TM/HM #	Move Name	Type	ST	ACC	PP	TM/HM #	Move Name	Type	ST	ACC	PP
HM04	Strength	Normal	80	100	15	TM24	Thunderbolt	Electric	95	100	15
HM05	Flash	Normal	—	70	20	TM25	Thunder	Electric	120	70	10
HM06	Rock Smash	Fighting	20	100	15	TM27	Return	Normal	—	100	20
TM01	Focus Punch	Fighting	150	100	20	TM28	Dig	Ground	60	100	10
TM06	Toxic	Poison	—	85	10	TM31	Brick Break	Fighting	75	100	15
TM10	Hidden Power	Normal	—	100	15	TM32	Double Team	Normal	—	—	15
TM15	Hyper Beam	Normal	150	90	5	TM34	Shock Wave	Electric	60	—	20
TM16	Light Screen	Psychic	—	—	30	TM42	Façade	Normal	70	100	20
TM17	Protect	Normal	—	—	10	TM43	Secret Power	Normal	70	100	20
TM18	Rain Dance	Water	—	—	5	TM44	Rest	Psychic	—	—	10
TM21	Frustration	Normal	—	100	20	TM45	Attract	Normal	—	100	15
TM23	Iron Tail	Steel	100	75	15	TM46	Thief	Dark	40	100	10

MOVE TUTOR LIST
Move Name	Type	ST	ACC	PP
Body Slam*	Normal	85	100	15
Counter*	Fighting	—	100	20
Defense Curl*	Normal	—	—	40
Double-Edge	Normal	120	100	15
Dynamicpunch*	Fighting	100	50	5
Endure*	Normal	—	—	10
Mega Kick*	Normal	120	85	5
Mega Punch*	Normal	80	75	20
Mimic	Normal	—	100	10
Mud-Slap*	Ground	20	100	10
Rollout	Rock	30	90	20
Seismic Toss*	Fighting	—	100	20
Sleep Talk	Normal	—	—	10
Snore*	Normal	40	100	15
Substitute	Normal	—	—	10
Swagger	Normal	—	90	15
Swift*	Normal	60	—	20
Thunderpunch*	Electric	75	100	15
Thunder Wave*	Electric	—	100	20

*Battle Frontier tutor move

158

Psyduck™

WATER

GENERAL INFO
SPECIES: Duck Pokémon
HEIGHT: 2'7"
WEIGHT: 43 lbs.
ABILITIES: *Damp* — Prevents opponent Pokémon from using either Explosion or Selfdestruct.
Cloud Nine — Causes weather effects to disappear.

STATS
HP	30
ATTACK	66
DEFENSE	33
SP. ATTACK	60
SP. DEFENSE	30
SPEED	30

EVOLUTIONS
 LV33

WHERE/HOW TO CATCH
Safari Zone

STRONG AGAINST:
FIRE
WATER
ICE
STEEL

WEAK AGAINST:
ELECTRIC
GRASS

MOVES LIST
LV	Move Name	Type	ST	ACC	PP	LV	Move Name	Type	ST	ACC	PP
S	Water Sport	Water	—	100	15	23	Screech	Normal	—	85	40
S	Scratch	Normal	40	100	35	31	Psych Up	Normal	—	—	10
05	Tail Whip	Normal	—	100	30	40	Fury Swipes	Normal	18	80	15
10	Disable	Normal	—	55	20	50	Hydro Pump	Water	120	80	5
16	Confusion	Psychic	50	100	25						

TM/HM LIST
TM/HM #	Move Name	Type	ST	ACC	PP	TM/HM #	Move Name	Type	ST	ACC	PP
HM03	Surf	Water	95	100	15	TM17	Protect	Normal	—	—	10
HM04	Strength	Normal	80	100	15	TM18	Rain Dance	Water	—	—	5
HM05	Flash	Normal	—	70	20	TM21	Frustration	Normal	—	100	20
HM06	Rock Smash	Fighting	20	100	15	TM23	Iron Tail	Steel	100	75	15
HM07	Waterfall	Water	80	100	15	TM27	Return	Normal	—	100	20
HM08	Dive	Water	60	100	10	TM28	Dig	Ground	60	100	10
TM01	Focus Punch	Fighting	150	100	20	TM31	Brick Break	Fighting	75	100	15
TM03	Water Pulse	Water	60	100	20	TM32	Double Team	Normal	—	—	15
TM04	Calm Mind	Psychic	—	—	20	TM40	Aerial Ace	Flying	60	—	20
TM06	Toxic	Poison	—	85	10	TM42	Façade	Normal	70	100	20
TM07	Hail	Ice	—	—	10	TM43	Secret Power	Normal	70	100	20
TM10	Hidden Power	Normal	—	100	15	TM44	Rest	Psychic	—	—	10
TM13	Ice Beam	Ice	95	100	10	TM45	Attract	Normal	—	100	15
TM14	Blizzard	Ice	120	70	5						

EGG MOVES
Move Name	Type	ST	ACC	PP
Hypnosis	Psychic	—	60	20
Psybeam	Psychic	65	100	20
Foresight	Normal	—	100	40
Light Screen	Psychic	—	—	30
Future Sight	Psychic	80	90	15
Psychic	Psychic	90	100	10
Refresh	Normal	—	100	20
Cross Chop	Fighting	100	80	5

MOVE TUTOR LIST
Move Name	Type	ST	ACC	PP
Body Slam*	Normal	85	100	15
Counter*	Fighting	—	100	20
Double-Edge	Normal	120	100	15
Dynamicpunch*	Fighting	100	50	5
Endure*	Normal	—	—	10
Ice Punch*	Ice	75	100	15
Icy Wind*	Ice	55	95	15
Mega Kick*	Normal	120	85	5
Mega Punch*	Normal	80	75	20
Mimic	Normal	—	100	10
Mud-Slap*	Ground	20	100	10
Psych Up*	Normal	—	—	10
Seismic Toss*	Fighting	—	100	20
Sleep Talk	Normal	—	—	10
Snore*	Normal	40	100	15
Substitute	Normal	—	—	10
Swagger	Normal	—	90	15
Swift*	Normal	60	—	20

*Battle Frontier tutor move

159

Golduck™

WATER

GENERAL INFO
SPECIES: Duck Pokémon
HEIGHT: 5'7"
WEIGHT: 169 lbs.

ABILITIES: *Damp* — *Prevents opponent Pokémon from using either Explosion or Selfdestruct.*
Cloud Nine — *Causes weather effects to disappear.*

STATS

HP	66
ATTACK	66
DEFENSE	66
SP. ATTACK	100
SP. DEFENSE	66
SPEED	66

EVOLUTIONS

LV33

WHERE/HOW TO CATCH
Evolve from Psyduck; Safari Zone

STRONG AGAINST:
FIRE
WATER
ICE
STEEL

WEAK AGAINST:
ELECTRIC
GRASS

MOVES LIST

LV	Move Name	Type	ST	ACC	PP
S	Water Sport	Water	—	100	15
S	Scratch	Normal	40	100	35
S	Tail Whip	Normal	—	100	30
S	Disable	Normal	—	55	20
05	Tail Whip	Normal	—	100	30
10	Disable	Normal	—	55	20

LV	Move Name	Type	ST	ACC	PP
16	Confusion	Psychic	50	100	25
23	Screech	Normal	—	85	40
31	Psych Up	Normal	—	—	10
44	Fury Swipes	Normal	18	80	15
58	Hydro Pump	Water	120	80	5

TM/HM LIST

TM/HM #	Move Name	Type	ST	ACC	PP
HM03	Surf	Water	95	100	15
HM04	Strength	Normal	80	100	15
HM05	Flash	Normal	—	70	20
HM06	Rock Smash	Fighting	20	100	15
HM07	Waterfall	Water	80	100	15
HM08	Dive	Water	60	100	10
TM01	Focus Punch	Fighting	150	100	20
TM03	Water Pulse	Water	60	100	20
TM04	Calm Mind	Psychic	—	—	20
TM06	Toxic	Poison	—	85	10
TM07	Hail	Ice	—	—	10
TM10	Hidden Power	Normal	—	100	15
TM13	Ice Beam	Ice	95	100	10
TM14	Blizzard	Ice	120	70	5

TM/HM #	Move Name	Type	ST	ACC	PP
TM15	Hyper Beam	Normal	150	90	5
TM17	Protect	Normal	—	—	10
TM18	Rain Dance	Water	—	—	5
TM21	Frustration	Normal	—	100	20
TM23	Iron Tail	Steel	100	75	15
TM27	Return	Normal	—	100	20
TM28	Dig	Ground	60	100	10
TM31	Brick Break	Fighting	75	100	15
TM32	Double Team	Normal	—	—	15
TM40	Aerial Ace	Flying	60	—	20
TM42	Façade	Normal	70	100	20
TM43	Secret Power	Normal	70	100	20
TM44	Rest	Psychic	—	—	10
TM45	Attract	Normal	—	100	15

MOVE TUTOR LIST

Move Name	Type	ST	ACC	PP
Body Slam*	Normal	85	100	15
Counter*	Fighting	—	100	20
Double-Edge	Normal	120	100	15
Dynamicpunch	Fighting	100	50	5
Endure*	Normal	—	—	10
Fury Cutter	Bug	10	95	20
Ice Punch*	Ice	75	100	15
Icy Wind*	Ice	55	95	15
Mega Kick*	Normal	120	85	5
Mega Punch*	Normal	80	75	20
Mimic	Normal	—	100	10
Mud-Slap*	Ground	20	100	10
Psych Up*	Normal	—	—	10
Seismic Toss*	Fighting	—	100	20
Sleep Talk*	Normal	—	—	10
Snore*	Normal	40	100	15
Substitute	Normal	—	—	10
Swagger	Normal	—	90	15
Swift*	Normal	60	—	20

*Battle Frontier tutor move

160

Wynaut™

PSYCHIC

GENERAL INFO
SPECIES: Bright Pokémon
HEIGHT: 2'0"
WEIGHT: 31 lbs.

ABILITY: *Shadow Tag* —
The opponent Pokémon cannot run or switch out from the battle.

STATS

HP	50
ATTACK	25
DEFENSE	50
SP. ATTACK	25
SP. DEFENSE	50
SPEED	25

EVOLUTIONS

 LV15

WHERE/HOW TO CATCH
Mirage Island and Lavaridge Town

STRONG AGAINST:
FIGHTING
PSYCHIC

WEAK AGAINST:
BUG
GHOST
DARK

MOVES LIST

LV	Move Name	Type	ST	ACC	PP
S	Splash	Normal	—	—	40
S	Charm	Normal	—	100	20
S	Encore	Normal	—	100	5
15	Counter	Fighting	—	100	20

LV	Move Name	Type	ST	ACC	PP
15	Mirror Coat	Psychic	—	100	20
15	Safeguard	Normal	—	—	25
15	Destiny Bond	Ghost	—	—	5

TM/HM LIST

TM/HM #	Move Name	Type	ST	ACC	PP
None					

EGG MOVES

Move Name	Type	ST	ACC	PP
None				

MOVE TUTOR LIST

Move Name	Type	ST	ACC	PP
None				

161

Wobbuffet™

PSYCHIC

GENERAL INFO
SPECIES: Patient Pokémon
HEIGHT: 4'3"
WEIGHT: 63 lbs.
ABILITY: *Shadow Tag—*
The opponent Pokémon cannot run
or switch out from the battle.

STATS

HP		100
ATTACK		33
DEFENSE		33
SP. ATTACK		33
SP. DEFENSE		33
SPEED		33

EVOLUTIONS

 LV15

WHERE/HOW TO CATCH
Evolve from Wynaut;
Safari Zone

STRONG AGAINST:

FIGHTING
PSYCHIC

WEAK AGAINST:

BUG
GHOST
DARK

MOVES LIST

LV	Move Name	Type	ST	ACC	PP	LV	Move Name	Type	ST	ACC	PP
S	Counter	Fighting	—	100	20	S	Safeguard	Normal	—	—	25
S	Mirror Coat	Psychic	—	100	20	S	Destiny Bond	Ghost	—	—	5

TM/HM LIST

TM/HM #	Move Name	Type	ST	ACC	PP
None					

MOVE TUTOR LIST

Move Name	Type	ST	ACC	PP
None				

162

Natu™

PSYCHIC
FLYING

GENERAL INFO
SPECIES: Tiny Bird Pokémon
HEIGHT: 0'8"
WEIGHT: 4 lbs.
ABILITIES: *Synchronize—Shares the*
Pokémon's Poison, Paralysis, or Burn condition
with the opponent Pokémon.
Early Bird—The Pokémon recovers from Sleep earlier.

STATS

HP		33
ATTACK		33
DEFENSE		33
SP. ATTACK		66
SP. DEFENSE		33
SPEED		66

EVOLUTIONS

 LV25

WHERE/HOW TO CATCH
Safari Zone

STRONG AGAINST:

GRASS
PSYCHIC
GROUND
FIGHTING

WEAK AGAINST:

ELECTRIC
ICE
ROCK
GHOST
DARK

MOVES LIST

LV	Move Name	Type	ST	ACC	PP	LV	Move Name	Type	ST	ACC	PP
S	Peck	Flying	35	100	35	30	Wish	Normal	—	100	10
S	Leer	Normal	—	100	30	30	Future Sight	Psychic	80	90	15
10	Night Shade	Ghost	—	100	15	40	Confuse Ray	Ghost	—	100	10
20	Teleport	Psychic	—	—	20	50	Psychic	Psychic	90	100	10

TM/HM LIST

TM/HM #	Move Name	Type	ST	ACC	PP	TM/HM #	Move Name	Type	ST	ACC	PP
HM05	Flash	Normal	—	70	20	TM29	Psychic	Psychic	90	100	10
TM04	Calm Mind	Psychic	—	—	20	TM30	Shadow Ball	Ghost	60	—	20
TM06	Toxic	Poison	—	85	10	TM32	Double Team	Normal	—	—	15
TM10	Hidden Power	Normal	—	100	15	TM33	Reflect	Psychic	—	—	20
TM11	Sunny Day	Fire	—	—	5	TM40	Aerial Ace	Flying	60	—	20
TM16	Light Screen	Psychic	—	—	30	TM42	Façade	Normal	70	100	20
TM17	Protect	Normal	—	—	10	TM43	Secret Power	Normal	70	100	20
TM18	Rain Dance	Water	—	—	5	TM44	Rest	Psychic	—	—	10
TM19	Giga Drain	Grass	60	100	5	TM45	Attract	Normal	—	100	15
TM21	Frustration	Normal	—	100	20	TM46	Thief	Dark	40	100	10
TM22	Solarbeam	Grass	120	100	10	TM47	Steel Wing	Steel	70	90	25
TM27	Return	Normal	—	100	20	TM48	Skill Swap	Psychic	—	100	10

EGG MOVES

Move Name	Type	ST	ACC	PP
Haze	Ice	—	—	30
Drill Peck	Flying	80	100	20
Quick Attack	Normal	40	100	30
Steel Wing	Steel	70	90	25
Refresh	Normal	—	100	20
Faint Attack	Dark	60	—	20
Psych Up	Normal	—	—	10
Featherdance	Flying	—	100	15

MOVE TUTOR LIST

Move Name	Type	ST	ACC	PP
Double-Edge	Normal	120	100	15
Dream Eater*	Psychic	100	100	15
Endure*	Normal	—	—	10
Mimic	Normal	—	100	10
Psych Up*	Normal	—	—	10
Sleep Talk	Normal	—	—	10
Snore*	Normal	40	100	15
Substitute	Normal	—	—	10
Swagger	Normal	—	90	15
Swift*	Normal	60	—	20
Thunder Wave*	Electric	—	100	20

*Battle Frontier tutor move

163 Xatu™

PSYCHIC
FLYING

GENERAL INFO
SPECIES: Mystic Pokémon
HEIGHT: 4'11"
WEIGHT: 33 lbs.
ABILITIES: *Synchronize*—Shares the Pokémon's Poison, Paralysis, or Burn condition with the opponent Pokémon.
Early Bird—The Pokémon recovers from Sleep earlier.

STATS
HP	33
ATTACK	66
DEFENSE	66
SP. ATTACK	100
SP. DEFENSE	66
SPEED	100

EVOLUTIONS

 LV25

WHERE/HOW TO CATCH
Evolve from Natu; Safari Zone

STRONG AGAINST:
GRASS
PSYCHIC
GROUND
FIGHTING

WEAK AGAINST:
ELECTRIC
ICE
ROCK
GHOST
DARK

MOVES LIST
LV	Move Name	Type	ST	ACC	PP
S	Peck	Flying	35	100	35
S	Leer	Normal	—	100	30
10	Night Shade	Ghost	—	100	15
20	Teleport	Psychic	—	—	20
35	Wish	Normal	—	100	10
35	Future Sight	Psychic	80	90	15
50	Confuse Ray	Ghost	—	100	10
65	Psychic	Psychic	90	100	10

TM/HM LIST
TM/HM #	Move Name	Type	ST	ACC	PP
HM02	Fly	Flying	70	95	15
HM05	Flash	Normal	—	70	20
TM04	Calm Mind	Psychic	—	—	20
TM06	Toxic	Poison	—	85	10
TM10	Hidden Power	Normal	—	100	15
TM11	Sunny Day	Fire	—	—	5
TM15	Hyper Beam	Normal	150	90	5
TM16	Light Screen	Psychic	—	—	30
TM17	Protect	Normal	—	—	10
TM18	Rain Dance	Water	—	—	5
TM19	Giga Drain	Grass	60	100	5
TM21	Frustration	Normal	—	100	20
TM22	Solarbeam	Grass	120	100	10
TM27	Return	Normal	—	100	20
TM29	Psychic	Psychic	90	100	10
TM30	Shadow Ball	Ghost	60	—	20
TM32	Double Team	Normal	—	—	15
TM33	Reflect	Psychic	—	—	20
TM40	Aerial Ace	Flying	60	—	20
TM42	Façade	Normal	70	100	20
TM43	Secret Power	Normal	70	100	20
TM44	Rest	Psychic	—	—	10
TM45	Attract	Normal	—	100	15
TM46	Thief	Dark	40	100	10
TM47	Steel Wing	Steel	70	90	25
TM48	Skill Swap	Psychic	—	100	10

MOVE TUTOR LIST
Move Name	Type	ST	ACC	PP
Double-Edge	Normal	120	100	15
Dream Eater*	Psychic	100	100	15
Endure*	Normal	—	—	10
Mimic	Normal	—	100	10
Psych Up*	Normal	—	—	10
Sleep Talk	Normal	—	—	10
Snore*	Normal	40	100	15
Substitute	Normal	—	—	10
Swagger	Normal	—	90	15
Swift*	Normal	60	—	20
Thunder Wave*	Electric	—	100	20

*Battle Frontier tutor move

164 Girafarig™

NORMAL
PSYCHIC

GENERAL INFO
SPECIES: Long Neck Pokémon
HEIGHT: 4'11"
WEIGHT: 91 lbs.
ABILITIES: *Inner Focus*—Prevents the Pokémon from Flinching.
Early Bird—The Pokémon recovers from Sleep earlier.

STATS
HP	66
ATTACK	66
DEFENSE	33
SP. ATTACK	66
SP. DEFENSE	66
SPEED	66

EVOLUTIONS

GIRAFARIG DOES NOT EVOLVE

WHERE/HOW TO CATCH
Safari Zone

STRONG AGAINST:
PSYCHIC
GHOST

WEAK AGAINST:
BUG
DARK

MOVES LIST
LV	Move Name	Type	ST	ACC	PP
S	Tackle	Normal	35	95	35
S	Growl	Normal	—	100	40
07	Astonish	Ghost	30	100	15
13	Confusion	Psychic	50	100	25
19	Stomp	Normal	65	100	20
25	Odor Sleuth	Normal	—	100	40
31	Agility	Psychic	—	—	30
37	Baton Pass	Normal	—	—	40
43	Psybeam	Psychic	65	100	20
49	Crunch	Dark	80	100	15

TM/HM LIST
TM/HM #	Move Name	Type	ST	ACC	PP
HM04	Strength	Normal	80	100	15
HM05	Flash	Normal	—	70	20
HM06	Rock Smash	Fighting	20	100	15
TM04	Calm Mind	Psychic	—	—	20
TM06	Toxic	Poison	—	85	10
TM10	Hidden Power	Normal	—	100	15
TM11	Sunny Day	Fire	—	—	5
TM16	Light Screen	Psychic	—	—	30
TM17	Protect	Normal	—	—	10
TM18	Rain Dance	Water	—	—	5
TM21	Frustration	Normal	—	100	20
TM23	Iron Tail	Steel	100	75	15
TM24	Thunderbolt	Electric	95	100	15
TM25	Thunder	Electric	120	70	10
TM26	Earthquake	Ground	100	100	10
TM27	Return	Normal	—	100	20
TM29	Psychic	Psychic	90	100	10
TM30	Shadow Ball	Ghost	60	—	20
TM32	Double Team	Normal	—	—	15
TM33	Reflect	Psychic	—	—	20
TM34	Shock Wave	Electric	60	—	20
TM42	Façade	Normal	70	100	20
TM43	Secret Power	Normal	70	100	20
TM44	Rest	Psychic	—	—	10
TM45	Attract	Normal	—	100	15
TM46	Thief	Dark	40	100	10
TM48	Skill Swap	Psychic	—	100	10

EGG MOVES
Move Name	Type	ST	ACC	PP
Take Down	Normal	90	85	20
Amnesia	Psychic	—	—	20
Foresight	Normal	—	100	40
Future Sight	Psychic	80	90	15
Psych Up	Normal	—	—	10
Beat Up	Dark	10	100	10
Wish	Normal	—	100	10
Magic Coat	Psychic	—	—	15

MOVE TUTOR LIST
Move Name	Type	ST	ACC	PP
Body Slam*	Normal	85	100	15
Double-Edge*	Normal	120	100	15
Dream Eater*	Psychic	100	100	15
Endure*	Normal	—	—	10
Mimic	Normal	—	100	10
Mud-Slap*	Ground	20	100	10
Psych Up*	Normal	—	—	10
Sleep Talk	Normal	—	—	10
Snore*	Normal	40	100	15
Substitute	Normal	—	—	10
Swagger	Normal	—	90	15
Swift*	Normal	60	—	20
Thunder Wave*	Electric	—	100	20

*Battle Frontier tutor move

165 Phanpy

GROUND

GENERAL INFO
SPECIES: Long Nose Pokémon
HEIGHT: 1'8"
WEIGHT: 74 lbs.
ABILITY: *Pickup*—*Pokémon may find an Item at the end of the battle.*

STATS
HP	66
ATTACK	66
DEFENSE	33
SP. ATTACK	33
SP. DEFENSE	33
SPEED	33

EVOLUTIONS

LV25

WHERE/HOW TO CATCH
Safari Zone

STRONG AGAINST:
ELECTRIC
POISON
ROCK

WEAK AGAINST:
WATER
GRASS
ICE

MOVES LIST
LV	Move Name	Type	ST	ACC	PP
S	Odor Sleuth	Normal	—	100	40
S	Tackle	Normal	35	95	35
S	Growl	Normal	—	100	40
09	Defense Curl	Normal	—	—	40
17	Flail	Normal	—	100	15
25	Take Down	Normal	90	85	20
33	Rollout	Rock	30	90	20
41	Endure	Normal	—	—	10
49	Double-Edge	Normal	120	100	15

TM/HM LIST
TM/HM #	Move Name	Type	ST	ACC	PP
HM04	Strength	Normal	80	100	15
HM06	Rock Smash	Fighting	20	100	15
TM05	Roar	Normal	—	100	20
TM06	Toxic	Poison	—	85	10
TM10	Hidden Power	Normal	—	100	15
TM11	Sunny Day	Fire	—	—	5
TM17	Protect	Normal	—	—	10
TM21	Frustration	Normal	—	100	20
TM23	Iron Tail	Steel	100	75	15
TM26	Earthquake	Ground	100	100	10
TM27	Return	Normal	—	100	20
TM32	Double Team	Normal	—	—	15
TM37	Sandstorm	Rock	—	—	10
TM39	Rock Tomb	Rock	50	80	10
TM42	Façade	Normal	70	100	20
TM43	Secret Power	Normal	70	100	20
TM44	Rest	Psychic	—	—	10
TM45	Attract	Normal	—	100	15

EGG MOVES
Move Name	Type	ST	ACC	PP
Focus Energy	Normal	—	—	30
Body Slam	Normal	85	100	15
Ancientpower	Rock	60	100	5
Snore	Normal	40	100	15
Counter	Fighting	—	100	20
Fissure	Ground	—	30	5

MOVE TUTOR LIST
Move Name	Type	ST	ACC	PP
Body Slam*	Normal	85	100	15
Counter*	Fighting	—	100	20
Double-Edge	Normal	120	100	15
Endure*	Normal	—	—	10
Mimic	Normal	—	100	10
Mud-Slap*	Ground	20	100	10
Rollout	Rock	30	90	20
Sleep Talk	Normal	—	—	10
Snore*	Normal	40	100	15
Substitute	Normal	—	—	10
Swagger	Normal	—	90	15

*Battle Frontier tutor move

166 Donphan

GROUND

GENERAL INFO
SPECIES: Armor Pokémon
HEIGHT: 3'7"
WEIGHT: 265 lbs.
ABILITY: *Sturdy*—*One hit KO moves have no effect.*

STATS
HP	66
ATTACK	100
DEFENSE	66
SP. ATTACK	66
SP. DEFENSE	33
SPEED	33

EVOLUTIONS

LV25

WHERE/HOW TO CATCH
Evolve from Phanpy

STRONG AGAINST:
ELECTRIC
POISON
ROCK

WEAK AGAINST:
WATER
GRASS
ICE

MOVES LIST
LV	Move Name	Type	ST	ACC	PP
S	Odor Sleuth	Normal	—	100	40
S	Horn Attack	Normal	65	100	25
S	Growl	Normal	—	100	40
09	Defense Curl	Normal	—	—	40
17	Flail	Normal	—	100	15
25	Fury Attack	Normal	15	85	20
33	Rollout	Rock	30	90	20
41	Rapid Spin	Normal	20	100	40
49	Earthquake	Ground	100	100	10

TM/HM LIST
TM/HM #	Move Name	Type	ST	ACC	PP
HM04	Strength	Normal	80	100	15
HM06	Rock Smash	Fighting	20	100	15
TM05	Roar	Normal	—	100	20
TM06	Toxic	Poison	—	85	10
TM10	Hidden Power	Normal	—	100	15
TM11	Sunny Day	Fire	—	—	5
TM15	Hyper Beam	Normal	150	90	5
TM17	Protect	Normal	—	—	10
TM21	Frustration	Normal	—	100	20
TM23	Iron Tail	Steel	100	75	15
TM26	Earthquake	Ground	100	100	10
TM27	Return	Normal	—	100	20
TM32	Double Team	Normal	—	—	15
TM37	Sandstorm	Rock	—	—	10
TM39	Rock Tomb	Rock	50	80	10
TM42	Façade	Normal	70	100	20
TM43	Secret Power	Normal	70	100	20
TM44	Rest	Psychic	—	—	10
TM45	Attract	Normal	—	100	15

MOVE TUTOR LIST
Move Name	Type	ST	ACC	PP
Body Slam*	Normal	85	100	15
Counter*	Fighting	—	100	20
Defense Curl*	Normal	—	—	40
Double-Edge	Normal	120	100	15
Endure*	Normal	—	—	10
Mimic	Normal	—	100	10
Mud-Slap*	Ground	20	100	10
Rock Slide*	Rock	75	90	10
Rollout	Rock	30	90	20
Sleep Talk	Normal	—	—	10
Snore*	Normal	40	100	15
Substitute	Normal	—	—	10
Swagger	Normal	—	90	15

*Battle Frontier tutor move

167 Pinsir™

BUG

GENERAL INFO
SPECIES: **Stag Beetle Pokémon**
HEIGHT: **4'11"**
WEIGHT: **121 lbs.**
ABILITY: *Hyper Cutter* — *Pokémon's Attack Power cannot be lowered.*

STATS
HP	33
ATTACK	100
DEFENSE	66
SP. ATTACK	66
SP. DEFENSE	66
SPEED	66

EVOLUTIONS

PINSIR DOES NOT EVOLVE

WHERE/HOW TO CATCH
Safari Zone

STRONG AGAINST:
GRASS
FIGHTING
GROUND

WEAK AGAINST:
FIRE
FLYING
ROCK

MOVES LIST
LV	Move Name	Type	ST	ACC	PP
S	Vicegrip	Normal	55	100	30
S	Focus Energy	Normal	—	—	30
07	Bind	Normal	15	75	20
13	Seismic Toss	Fighting	—	100	20
19	Harden	Normal	—	—	30
25	Revenge	Fighting	60	100	10
31	Brick Break	Fighting	75	100	15
37	Guillotine	Normal	—	30	5
43	Submission	Fighting	80	80	25
49	Swords Dance	Normal	—	—	30

TM/HM LIST
TM/HM #	Move Name	Type	ST	ACC	PP
HM01	Cut	Normal	50	95	30
HM04	Strength	Normal	80	100	15
HM06	Rock Smash	Fighting	20	100	15
TM01	Focus Punch	Fighting	150	100	20
TM06	Toxic	Poison	—	85	10
TM08	Bulk Up	Fighting	—	—	20
TM10	Hidden Power	Normal	—	100	15
TM11	Sunny Day	Fire	—	—	5
TM15	Hyper Beam	Normal	150	90	5
TM17	Protect	Normal	—	—	10
TM18	Rain Dance	Water	—	—	5
TM21	Frustration	Normal	—	100	20
TM26	Earthquake	Ground	100	100	10
TM27	Return	Normal	—	100	20
TM28	Dig	Ground	60	100	10
TM31	Brick Break	Fighting	75	100	15
TM32	Double Team	Normal	—	—	15
TM39	Rock Tomb	Rock	50	80	10
TM42	Facade	Normal	70	100	20
TM43	Secret Power	Normal	70	100	20
TM44	Rest	Psychic	—	—	10
TM45	Attract	Normal	—	100	15
TM46	Thief	Dark	40	100	10

EGG MOVES
Move Name	Type	ST	ACC	PP
Fury Attack	Normal	15	85	20
False Swipe	Normal	40	100	40
Flail	Normal	—	100	15
Faint Attack	Dark	60	—	20

MOVE TUTOR LIST
Move Name	Type	ST	ACC	PP
Body Slam*	Normal	85	100	15
Double-Edge	Normal	120	100	15
Endure*	Normal	—	—	10
Fury Cutter	Bug	10	95	20
Mimic	Normal	—	100	10
Rock Slide*	Rock	75	90	10
Seismic Toss*	Fighting	—	100	20
Sleep Talk	Normal	—	—	10
Snore*	Normal	40	100	15
Substitute	Normal	—	—	10
Swagger	Normal	—	90	15
Swords Dance*	Normal	—	—	30

*Battle Frontier tutor move

168 Heracross™

BUG
FIGHTING

GENERAL INFO
SPECIES: **Single Horn Pokémon**
HEIGHT: **4'11"**
WEIGHT: **120 lbs.**
ABILITIES: *Swarm* — *When the Pokémon's HP falls below 1/3, the power of Bug-type Moves increases 1.5x.*
Guts — *The Pokémon's Attack Power rises 1.5x when inflicted with a Status condition.*

STATS
HP	66
ATTACK	100
DEFENSE	66
SP. ATTACK	33
SP. DEFENSE	66
SPEED	66

EVOLUTIONS

HERACROSS DOES NOT EVOLVE

WHERE/HOW TO CATCH
Safari Zone

STRONG AGAINST:
GRASS
FIGHTING
GROUND

WEAK AGAINST:
FIRE
FLYING
ROCK

MOVES LIST
LV	Move Name	Type	ST	ACC	PP
S	Tackle	Normal	35	95	35
S	Leer	Normal	—	100	30
06	Horn Attack	Normal	65	100	25
11	Endure	Normal	—	—	10
17	Fury Attack	Normal	15	85	20
23	Brick Break	Fighting	75	100	15
30	Counter	Normal	—	100	20
37	Take Down	Normal	90	85	20
45	Reversal	Fighting	—	100	15
53	Megahorn	Bug	120	85	10

TM/HM LIST
TM/HM #	Move Name	Type	ST	ACC	PP
HM01	Cut	Normal	50	95	30
HM04	Strength	Normal	80	100	15
HM06	Rock Smash	Fighting	20	100	15
TM01	Focus Punch	Fighting	150	100	20
TM06	Toxic	Poison	—	85	10
TM08	Bulk Up	Fighting	—	—	20
TM10	Hidden Power	Normal	—	100	15
TM11	Sunny Day	Fire	—	—	5
TM15	Hyper Beam	Normal	150	90	5
TM17	Protect	Normal	—	—	10
TM18	Rain Dance	Water	—	—	5
TM21	Frustration	Normal	—	100	20
TM26	Earthquake	Ground	100	100	10
TM27	Return	Normal	—	100	20
TM28	Dig	Ground	60	100	10
TM31	Brick Break	Fighting	75	100	15
TM32	Double Team	Normal	—	—	15
TM39	Rock Tomb	Rock	50	80	10
TM42	Facade	Normal	70	100	20
TM43	Secret Power	Normal	70	100	20
TM44	Rest	Psychic	—	—	10
TM45	Attract	Normal	—	100	15
TM46	Thief	Dark	40	100	10

EGG MOVES
Move Name	Type	ST	ACC	PP
Harden	Normal	—	—	30
False Swipe	Normal	40	100	40
Bide	Normal	15	75	20
Flail	Normal	—	100	15

MOVE TUTOR LIST
Move Name	Type	ST	ACC	PP
Body Slam*	Normal	85	100	15
Counter*	Fighting	—	100	20
Double-Edge	Normal	120	100	15
Endure*	Normal	—	—	10
Fury Cutter	Bug	10	95	20
Mimic	Normal	—	100	10
Rock Slide*	Rock	75	90	10
Seismic Toss*	Fighting	—	100	20
Sleep Talk	Normal	—	—	10
Snore*	Normal	40	100	15
Substitute	Normal	—	—	10
Swagger	Normal	—	90	15
Swords Dance*	Normal	—	—	30

*Battle Frontier tutor move

169 Rhyhorn™

GROUND
ROCK

GENERAL INFO
SPECIES: Spikes Pokémon
HEIGHT: 3'3"
WEIGHT: 256 lbs.
ABILITIES: *Lightningrod*—Draws all Electric-type Moves to itself.
Rock Head—Pokémon does not receive recoil damage from moves such as Double-Edge and Body Slam.

STATS
HP	66
ATTACK	66
DEFENSE	66
SP. ATTACK	33
SP. DEFENSE	33
SPEED	33

EVOLUTIONS

LV42

WHERE/HOW TO CATCH
Safari Zone

STRONG AGAINST:
NORMAL
FIRE
ELECTRIC
POISON
FLYING
ROCK

WEAK AGAINST:
WATER
GRASS
ICE
FIGHTING
GROUND
STEEL

MOVES LIST

LV	Move Name	Type	ST	ACC	PP
S	Horn Attack	Normal	65	100	25
S	Tail Whip	Normal	—	100	30
10	Stomp	Normal	65	100	20
15	Fury Attack	Normal	15	85	20
24	Scary Face	Normal	—	90	10
29	Rock Blast	Rock	25	80	10
38	Horn Drill	Normal	—	30	5
43	Take Down	Normal	90	85	20
52	Earthquake	Ground	100	100	10
57	Megahorn	Bug	120	85	10

TM/HM LIST

TM/HM #	Move Name	Type	ST	ACC	PP
HM04	Strength	Normal	80	100	15
HM06	Rock Smash	Fighting	20	100	15
TM05	Roar	Normal	—	100	20
TM06	Toxic	Poison	—	85	10
TM10	Hidden Power	Normal	—	100	15
TM11	Sunny Day	Fire	—	—	5
TM13	Ice Beam	Ice	95	100	10
TM14	Blizzard	Ice	120	70	5
TM17	Protect	Normal	—	—	10
TM18	Rain Dance	Water	—	—	5
TM21	Frustration	Normal	—	100	20
TM23	Iron Tail	Steel	100	75	15
TM24	Thunderbolt	Electric	95	100	15
TM25	Thunder	Electric	120	70	10
TM26	Earthquake	Ground	100	100	10
TM27	Return	Normal	—	100	20
TM28	Dig	Ground	60	100	10
TM32	Double Team	Normal	—	—	15
TM34	Shock Wave	Electric	60	—	20
TM35	Flamethrower	Fire	95	100	15
TM37	Sandstorm	Rock	—	—	10
TM38	Fire Blast	Fire	120	85	5
TM39	Rock Tomb	Rock	50	80	10
TM42	Façade	Normal	70	100	20
TM43	Secret Power	Normal	70	100	20
TM44	Rest	Psychic	—	—	10
TM45	Attract	Normal	—	100	15
TM46	Thief	Dark	40	100	10

EGG MOVES

Move Name	Type	ST	ACC	PP
Crunch	Dark	80	100	15
Reversal	Fighting	—	100	15
Rock Slide	Rock	75	90	10
Counter	Fighting	—	100	20
Magnitude	Ground	—	100	30
Swords Dance	Normal	—	—	30
Curse	—	—	—	10
Crush Claw	Normal	75	95	10

MOVE TUTOR LIST

Move Name	Type	ST	ACC	PP
Body Slam*	Normal	85	100	15
Counter*	Fighting	—	100	20
Double-Edge	Normal	120	100	15
Endure*	Normal	—	—	10
Icy Wind*	Ice	55	95	15
Mimic	Normal	—	100	10
Mud-Slap*	Ground	20	100	10
Rock Slide*	Rock	75	90	10
Rollout	Rock	30	90	20
Sleep Talk	Normal	—	—	10
Substitute	Normal	—	—	10
Swagger	Normal	—	90	15
Swords Dance*	Normal	—	—	30

*Battle Frontier tutor move

170 Rhydon™

GROUND
ROCK

GENERAL INFO
SPECIES: Drill Pokémon
HEIGHT: 6'3"
WEIGHT: 256 lbs.
ABILITIES: *Lightningrod*—Draws all Electric-type Moves to itself.
Rock Head—Pokémon does not receive recoil damage from moves such as Double-Edge and Body Slam.

STATS
HP	66
ATTACK	66
DEFENSE	66
SP. ATTACK	33
SP. DEFENSE	33
SPEED	33

EVOLUTIONS

LV42

WHERE/HOW TO CATCH
Evolve from Rhyhorn

STRONG AGAINST:
NORMAL
FIRE
ELECTRIC
POISON
FLYING
ROCK

WEAK AGAINST:
WATER
GRASS
ICE
FIGHTING
GROUND
STEEL

MOVES LIST

LV	Move Name	Type	ST	ACC	PP
S	Horn Attack	Normal	65	100	25
S	Tail Whip	Normal	—	100	30
S	Stomp	Normal	65	100	20
S	Fury Attack	Normal	15	85	20
10	Stomp	Normal	65	100	20
15	Fury Attack	Normal	15	85	20
24	Scary Face	Normal	—	90	10
29	Rock Blast	Rock	25	80	10
38	Horn Drill	Normal	—	30	5
46	Take Down	Normal	90	85	20
58	Earthquake	Ground	100	100	10
66	Megahorn	Bug	120	85	10

TM/HM LIST

TM/HM #	Move Name	Type	ST	ACC	PP
HM01	Cut	Normal	50	95	30
HM03	Surf	Water	95	100	15
HM04	Strength	Normal	80	100	15
HM06	Rock Smash	Fighting	20	100	15
TM01	Focus Punch	Fighting	150	100	20
TM05	Roar	Normal	—	100	20
TM06	Toxic	Poison	—	85	10
TM10	Hidden Power	Normal	—	100	15
TM11	Sunny Day	Fire	—	—	5
TM13	Ice Beam	Ice	95	100	10
TM14	Blizzard	Ice	120	70	5
TM15	Hyper Beam	Normal	150	90	5
TM17	Protect	Normal	—	—	10
TM18	Rain Dance	Water	—	—	5
TM21	Frustration	Normal	—	100	20
TM23	Iron Tail	Steel	100	75	15
TM24	Thunderbolt	Electric	95	100	15
TM25	Thunder	Electric	120	70	10
TM26	Earthquake	Ground	100	100	10
TM27	Return	Normal	—	100	20
TM28	Dig	Ground	60	100	10
TM31	Brick Break	Fighting	75	100	15
TM32	Double Team	Normal	—	—	15
TM34	Shock Wave	Electric	60	—	20
TM35	Flamethrower	Fire	95	100	15
TM37	Sandstorm	Rock	—	—	10
TM38	Fire Blast	Fire	120	85	5
TM39	Rock Tomb	Rock	50	80	10
TM42	Façade	Normal	70	100	20
TM43	Secret Power	Normal	70	100	20
TM44	Rest	Psychic	—	—	10
TM45	Attract	Normal	—	100	15
TM46	Thief	Dark	40	100	10

MOVE TUTOR LIST

Move Name	Type	ST	ACC	PP
Body Slam*	Normal	85	100	15
Counter*	Fighting	—	100	20
Double-Edge	Normal	120	100	15
Dynamicpunch	Fighting	100	50	5
Endure*	Normal	—	—	10
Fire Punch*	Fire	75	100	15
Fury Cutter	Bug	10	95	20
Icy Wind*	Ice	55	95	15
Mega Kick*	Normal	120	85	5
Mega Punch*	Normal	80	75	20
Mimic	Normal	—	100	10
Mud-Slap*	Ground	20	100	10
Rock Slide*	Rock	75	90	10
Rollout	Rock	30	90	20
Seismic Toss*	Fighting	—	100	20
Sleep Talk	Normal	—	—	10
Snore*	Normal	40	100	15
Substitute	Normal	—	—	10
Swagger	Normal	—	90	15
Swords Dance*	Normal	—	—	30
Thunderpunch*	Electric	75	100	15

*Battle Frontier tutor move

171 Snorunt™

ICE

GENERAL INFO
SPECIES: Snow Hat Pokémon
HEIGHT: 2'4"
WEIGHT: 37 lbs.
ABILITY: *Inner Focus —Prevents the Pokémon from Flinching.*

STATS
HP	50
ATTACK	25
DEFENSE	50
SP. ATTACK	25
SP. DEFENSE	50
SPEED	25

EVOLUTIONS
LV42

WHERE/HOW TO CATCH
Shoal Cave

STRONG AGAINST:
ICE

WEAK AGAINST:
FIRE
FIGHTING
ROCK
STEEL

MOVES LIST
LV	Move Name	Type	ST	ACC	PP
S	Powder Snow	Ice	40	100	25
S	Leer	Normal	—	100	30
07	Double Team	Normal	—	—	15
10	Bite	Dark	60	100	25
16	Icy Wind	Ice	55	95	15
19	Headbutt	Normal	70	100	15
25	Protect	Normal	—	—	10
28	Crunch	Dark	80	100	15
34	Ice Beam	Ice	95	100	10
37	Hail	Ice	—	—	10
43	Blizzard	Ice	120	70	5

TM/HM LIST
TM/HM #	Move Name	Type	ST	ACC	PP
HM05	Flash	Normal	—	70	20
TM03	Water Pulse	Water	60	100	20
TM06	Toxic	Poison	—	85	10
TM07	Hail	Ice	—	—	10
TM10	Hidden Power	Normal	—	100	15
TM13	Ice Beam	Ice	95	100	10
TM14	Blizzard	Ice	120	70	5
TM16	Light Screen	Psychic	—	—	30
TM17	Protect	Normal	—	—	10
TM18	Rain Dance	Water	—	—	5
TM20	Safeguard	Normal	—	—	25
TM21	Frustration	Normal	—	100	20
TM27	Return	Normal	—	100	20
TM30	Shadow Ball	Ghost	60	—	20
TM32	Double Team	Normal	—	—	15
TM42	Façade	Normal	70	100	20
TM43	Secret Power	Normal	70	100	20
TM44	Rest	Psychic	—	—	10
TM45	Attract	Normal	—	100	15

EGG MOVES
Move Name	Type	ST	ACC	PP
Block	Normal	—	100	5
Spikes	Ground	—	—	20

MOVE TUTOR LIST
Move Name	Type	ST	ACC	PP
Body Slam*	Normal	85	100	15
Double-Edge	Normal	120	100	15
Endure*	Normal	—	—	10
Icy Wind*	Ice	55	95	15
Mimic	Normal	—	100	10
Sleep Talk	Normal	—	—	10
Snore*	Normal	40	100	15
Substitute	Normal	—	—	10
Swagger	Normal	—	90	15

*Battle Frontier tutor move

172 Glalie™

ICE

GENERAL INFO
SPECIES: Face Pokémon
HEIGHT: 4'11"
WEIGHT: 566 lbs.
ABILITY: *Inner Focus —Prevents the Pokémon from Flinching.*

STATS
HP	50
ATTACK	75
DEFENSE	50
SP. ATTACK	75
SP. DEFENSE	50
SPEED	75

EVOLUTIONS
LV42

WHERE/HOW TO CATCH
Evolve from Snorunt

STRONG AGAINST:
ICE

WEAK AGAINST:
FIRE
FIGHTING
ROCK
STEEL

MOVES LIST
LV	Move Name	Type	ST	ACC	PP
S	Powder Snow	Ice	40	100	25
S	Leer	Normal	—	100	30
S	Double Team	Normal	—	—	15
S	Bite	Dark	60	100	25
07	Double Team	Normal	—	—	15
10	Bite	Dark	60	100	25
16	Icy Wind	Ice	55	95	15
19	Headbutt	Normal	70	100	15
25	Protect	Normal	—	—	10
28	Crunch	Dark	80	100	15
34	Ice Beam	Ice	95	100	10
42	Hail	Ice	—	—	10
53	Blizzard	Ice	120	70	5
61	Sheer Cold	Ice	—	30	5

TM/HM LIST
TM/HM #	Move Name	Type	ST	ACC	PP
HM05	Flash	Normal	—	70	20
TM03	Water Pulse	Water	60	100	20
TM06	Toxic	Poison	—	85	10
TM07	Hail	Ice	—	—	10
TM10	Hidden Power	Normal	—	100	15
TM12	Taunt	Dark	—	100	20
TM13	Ice Beam	Ice	95	100	10
TM14	Blizzard	Ice	120	70	5
TM15	Hyper Beam	Normal	150	90	5
TM16	Light Screen	Psychic	—	—	30
TM17	Protect	Normal	—	—	10
TM18	Rain Dance	Water	—	—	5
TM20	Safeguard	Normal	—	—	25
TM21	Frustration	Normal	—	100	20
TM26	Earthquake	Ground	100	100	10
TM27	Return	Normal	—	100	20
TM30	Shadow Ball	Ghost	60	—	20
TM32	Double Team	Normal	—	—	15
TM41	Torment	Dark	—	100	15
TM42	Façade	Normal	70	100	20
TM43	Secret Power	Normal	70	100	20
TM44	Rest	Psychic	—	—	10
TM45	Attract	Normal	—	100	15

MOVE TUTOR LIST
Move Name	Type	ST	ACC	PP
Body Slam*	Normal	85	100	15
Defense Curl*	Normal	—	—	40
Double-Edge	Normal	120	100	15
Endure*	Normal	—	—	10
Explosion	Normal	250	100	5
Icy Wind*	Ice	55	95	15
Mimic	Normal	—	100	10
Rollout	Rock	30	90	20
Sleep Talk	Normal	—	—	10
Snore*	Normal	40	100	15
Substitute	Normal	—	—	10
Swagger	Normal	—	90	15

*Battle Frontier tutor move

173 Spheal™

ICE
WATER

GENERAL INFO
SPECIES: Clap Pokémon
HEIGHT: 2'7"
WEIGHT: 87 lbs.
ABILITY: *Thick Fat* — Fire- and Ice-type Moves inflict only 50 percent of the damage.

STATS
Stat	Value
HP	50
ATTACK	50
DEFENSE	50
SP. ATTACK	50
SP. DEFENSE	50
SPEED	25

EVOLUTIONS

LV32, LV44

WHERE/HOW TO CATCH
Shoal Cave

STRONG AGAINST:
WATER
ICE
FIRE

WEAK AGAINST:
ELECTRIC
GRASS
FIGHTING
ROCK

MOVES LIST
LV	Move Name	Type	ST	ACC	PP
S	Powder Snow	Ice	40	100	25
S	Growl	Normal	—	100	40
S	Water Gun	Water	40	100	25
07	Encore	Normal	—	100	5
13	Ice Ball	Ice	30	90	20
19	Body Slam	Normal	85	100	15
25	Aurora Beam	Ice	65	100	20
31	Hail	Ice	—	—	10
37	Rest	Psychic	—	—	10
37	Snore	Normal	40	100	15
43	Blizzard	Ice	120	70	5
49	Sheer Cold	Ice	—	30	5

TM/HM LIST
TM/HM #	Move Name	Type	ST	ACC	PP
HM03	Surf	Water	95	100	15
HM04	Strength	Normal	80	100	15
HM06	Rock Smash	Fighting	20	100	15
HM07	Waterfall	Water	80	100	15
HM08	Dive	Water	60	100	10
TM03	Water Pulse	Water	60	100	20
TM06	Toxic	Poison	—	85	10
TM07	Hail	Ice	—	—	10
TM10	Hidden Power	Normal	—	100	15
TM13	Ice Beam	Ice	95	100	10
TM14	Blizzard	Ice	120	70	5
TM17	Protect	Normal	—	—	10
TM18	Rain Dance	Water	—	—	5
TM21	Frustration	Normal	—	100	20
TM23	Iron Tail	Steel	100	75	15
TM26	Earthquake	Ground	100	100	10
TM27	Return	Normal	—	100	20
TM32	Double Team	Normal	—	—	15
TM39	Rock Tomb	Rock	50	80	10
TM42	Façade	Normal	70	100	20
TM43	Secret Power	Normal	70	100	20
TM44	Rest	Psychic	—	—	10
TM45	Attract	Normal	—	100	15

EGG MOVES
Move Name	Type	ST	ACC	PP
Water Sport	Water	—	100	15
Stockpile	Normal	—	—	10
Swallow	Normal	—	—	10
Spit Up	Normal	100	100	10
Yawn	Normal	—	100	10
Rock Slide	Rock	75	90	10
Curse	—	—	—	10
Fissure	Ground	—	30	5

MOVE TUTOR LIST
Move Name	Type	ST	ACC	PP
Body Slam*	Normal	85	100	15
Defense Curl*	Normal	—	—	40
Double-Edge	Normal	120	100	15
Endure*	Normal	—	—	10
Icy Wind*	Ice	55	95	15
Mimic	Normal	—	100	10
Mud-Slap*	Ground	20	100	10
Rock Slide*	Rock	75	90	10
Rollout	Rock	30	90	20
Sleep Talk	Normal	—	—	10
Snore*	Normal	40	100	15
Substitute	Normal	—	—	10
Swagger	Normal	—	90	15

*Battle Frontier tutor move

174 Sealeo™

ICE
WATER

GENERAL INFO
SPECIES: Ball Roll Pokémon
HEIGHT: 3'7"
WEIGHT: 193 lbs.
ABILITY: *Thick Fat* — Fire- and Ice-type Moves inflict only 50 percent of the damage.

STATS
Stat	Value
HP	50
ATTACK	50
DEFENSE	50
SP. ATTACK	75
SP. DEFENSE	50
SPEED	50

EVOLUTIONS

LV32, LV44

WHERE/HOW TO CATCH
Evolve from Spheal

STRONG AGAINST:
WATER
ICE
FIRE

WEAK AGAINST:
ELECTRIC
GRASS
FIGHTING
ROCK

MOVES LIST
LV	Move Name	Type	ST	ACC	PP
S	Powder Snow	Ice	40	100	25
S	Growl	Normal	—	100	40
S	Water Gun	Water	40	100	25
07	Encore	Normal	—	100	5
13	Ice Ball	Ice	30	90	20
19	Body Slam	Normal	85	100	15
25	Aurora Beam	Ice	65	100	20
31	Hail	Ice	—	—	10
39	Rest	Psychic	—	—	10
39	Snore	Normal	40	100	15
47	Blizzard	Ice	120	70	5
55	Sheer Cold	Ice	—	30	5

TM/HM LIST
TM/HM #	Move Name	Type	ST	ACC	PP
HM03	Surf	Water	95	100	15
HM04	Strength	Normal	80	100	15
HM06	Rock Smash	Fighting	20	100	15
HM07	Waterfall	Water	80	100	15
HM08	Dive	Water	60	100	10
TM03	Water Pulse	Water	60	100	20
TM05	Roar	Normal	—	100	20
TM06	Toxic	Poison	—	85	10
TM07	Hail	Ice	—	—	10
TM10	Hidden Power	Normal	—	100	15
TM13	Ice Beam	Ice	95	100	10
TM14	Blizzard	Ice	120	70	5
TM17	Protect	Normal	—	—	10
TM18	Rain Dance	Water	—	—	5
TM21	Frustration	Normal	—	100	20
TM23	Iron Tail	Steel	100	75	15
TM26	Earthquake	Ground	100	100	10
TM27	Return	Normal	—	100	20
TM32	Double Team	Normal	—	—	15
TM39	Rock Tomb	Rock	50	80	10
TM42	Façade	Normal	70	100	20
TM43	Secret Power	Normal	70	100	20
TM44	Rest	Psychic	—	—	10
TM45	Attract	Normal	—	100	15

MOVE TUTOR LIST
Move Name	Type	ST	ACC	PP
Body Slam*	Normal	85	100	15
Defense Curl*	Normal	—	—	40
Double-Edge	Normal	120	100	15
Endure*	Normal	—	—	10
Icy Wind*	Ice	55	95	15
Mimic	Normal	—	100	10
Mud-Slap*	Ground	20	100	10
Rock Slide*	Rock	75	90	10
Rollout	Rock	30	90	20
Sleep Talk	Normal	—	—	10
Snore*	Normal	40	100	15
Substitute	Normal	—	—	10
Swagger	Normal	—	90	15

*Battle Frontier tutor move

175

Walrein

ICE
WATER

GENERAL INFO
SPECIES: Ice Break Pokémon
HEIGHT: 4'7"
WEIGHT: 332 lbs.
ABILITY: *Thick Fat*—Fire- and Ice-type Moves inflict only 50 percent of the damage.

STATS

HP	50
ATTACK	75
DEFENSE	50
SP. ATTACK	75
SP. DEFENSE	50
SPEED	50

EVOLUTIONS

LV32 → LV44 →

WHERE/HOW TO CATCH
Evolve from Sealeo

STRONG AGAINST:
WATER
ICE
FIRE

WEAK AGAINST:
ELECTRIC
GRASS
FIGHTING
ROCK

MOVES LIST

LV	Move Name	Type	ST	ACC	PP
S	Powder Snow	Ice	40	100	25
S	Growl	Normal	—	100	40
S	Water Gun	Water	40	100	25
07	Encore	Normal	—	100	5
13	Ice Ball	Ice	30	90	20
19	Body Slam	Normal	85	100	15

LV	Move Name	Type	ST	ACC	PP
25	Aurora Beam	Ice	65	100	20
31	Hail	Ice	—	—	10
39	Rest	Psychic	—	—	10
39	Snore	Normal	40	100	15
50	Blizzard	Ice	120	70	5
61	Sheer Cold	Ice	—	30	5

TM/HM LIST

TM/HM #	Move Name	Type	ST	ACC	PP
HM03	Surf	Water	95	100	15
HM04	Strength	Normal	80	100	15
HM06	Rock Smash	Fighting	20	100	15
HM07	Waterfall	Water	80	100	15
HM08	Dive	Water	60	100	10
TM03	Water Pulse	Water	60	100	20
TM05	Roar	Normal	—	100	20
TM06	Toxic	Poison	—	85	10
TM07	Hail	Ice	—	—	10
TM10	Hidden Power	Normal	—	100	15
TM13	Ice Beam	Ice	95	100	10
TM14	Blizzard	Ice	120	70	5
TM15	Hyper Beam	Normal	150	90	5

TM/HM #	Move Name	Type	ST	ACC	PP
TM17	Protect	Normal	—	—	10
TM18	Rain Dance	Water	—	—	5
TM21	Frustration	Normal	—	100	20
TM23	Iron Tail	Steel	100	75	15
TM26	Earthquake	Ground	100	100	10
TM27	Return	Normal	—	100	20
TM32	Double Team	Normal	—	—	15
TM39	Rock Tomb	Rock	50	80	10
TM42	Façade	Normal	70	100	20
TM43	Secret Power	Normal	70	100	20
TM44	Rest	Psychic	—	—	10
TM45	Attract	Normal	—	100	15

MOVE TUTOR LIST

Move Name	Type	ST	ACC	PP
Body Slam*	Normal	85	100	15
Defense Curl*	Normal	—	—	40
Double-Edge	Normal	120	100	15
Endure*	Normal	—	—	10
Icy Wind*	Ice	55	95	15
Mimic	Normal	—	100	10
Mud-Slap*	Ground	20	100	10
Rock Slide*	Rock	75	90	10
Rollout	Rock	30	90	20
Sleep Talk	Normal	—	—	10
Snore*	Normal	40	100	15
Substitute	Normal	—	—	10
Swagger	Normal	—	90	15

*Battle Frontier tutor move

176

Clamperl

WATER

GENERAL INFO
SPECIES: Bivalve Pokémon
HEIGHT: 1'4"
WEIGHT: 116 lbs.
ABILITY: *Shell Armor*—Prevents the opponent Pokémon from scoring a Critical Hit. .

STATS

HP	25
ATTACK	50
DEFENSE	50
SP. ATTACK	75
SP. DEFENSE	50
SPEED	25

EVOLUTIONS

TRADE + DEEPSEATOOTH →

TRADE + DEEPSEASCALE →

WHERE/HOW TO CATCH
Routes 124 and 126

STRONG AGAINST:
FIRE
WATER
ICE
STEEL

WEAK AGAINST:
ELECTRIC
GRASS

MOVES LIST

LV	Move Name	Type	ST	ACC	PP
S	Clamp	Water	35	75	10
S	Water Gun	Water	40	100	25

LV	Move Name	Type	ST	ACC	PP
S	Whirlpool	Water	15	70	15
S	Iron Defense	Steel	—	—	15

TM/HM LIST

TM/HM #	Move Name	Type	ST	ACC	PP
HM03	Surf	Water	95	100	15
HM07	Waterfall	Water	80	100	15
HM08	Dive	Water	60	100	10
TM03	Water Pulse	Water	60	100	20
TM06	Toxic	Poison	—	85	10
TM07	Hail	Ice	—	—	10
TM10	Hidden Power	Normal	—	100	15
TM13	Ice Beam	Ice	95	100	10
TM14	Blizzard	Ice	120	70	5

TM/HM #	Move Name	Type	ST	ACC	PP
TM17	Protect	Normal	—	—	10
TM18	Rain Dance	Water	—	—	5
TM21	Frustration	Normal	—	100	20
TM27	Return	Normal	—	100	20
TM32	Double Team	Normal	—	—	15
TM42	Façade	Normal	70	100	20
TM43	Secret Power	Normal	70	100	20
TM44	Rest	Psychic	—	—	10
TM45	Attract	Normal	—	100	15

EGG MOVES

Move Name	Type	ST	ACC	PP
Refresh	Normal	—	100	20
Mud Sport	Ground	—	100	15
Body Slam	Normal	85	100	15
Supersonic	Normal	—	55	20
Barrier	Psychic	—	—	30
Confuse Ray	Ghost	—	100	10

MOVE TUTOR LIST

Move Name	Type	ST	ACC	PP
Body Slam*	Normal	85	100	15
Double-Edge	Normal	120	100	15
Endure*	Normal	—	—	10
Icy Wind*	Ice	55	95	15
Mimic	Normal	—	100	10
Sleep Talk	Normal	—	—	10
Snore*	Normal	40	100	15
Substitute	Normal	—	—	10
Swagger	Normal	—	90	15

*Battle Frontier tutor move

177 Huntail™
WATER

GENERAL INFO
SPECIES: Deep Sea Pokémon
HEIGHT: 5'7"
WEIGHT: 60 lbs.
ABILITY: *Swift Swim—Doubles the Pokémon's Speed when it rains.*

STATS
HP	50
ATTACK	75
DEFENSE	75
SP. ATTACK	75
SP. DEFENSE	50
SPEED	50

EVOLUTIONS
TRADE + DEEPSEATOOTH
TRADE + DEEPSEASCALE

WHERE/HOW TO CATCH
Evolve Clamperl with Deepseatooth and trade

STRONG AGAINST:
FIRE
WATER
ICE
STEEL

WEAK AGAINST:
ELECTRIC
GRASS

MOVES LIST
LV	Move Name	Type	ST	ACC	PP		LV	Move Name	Type	ST	ACC	PP
S	Whirlpool	Water	15	70	15		29	Scary Face	Normal	—	90	10
08	Bite	Dark	60	100	25		36	Crunch	Dark	80	100	15
15	Screech	Normal	—	85	40		43	Baton Pass	Normal	—	—	40
22	Water Pulse	Water	60	100	20		50	Hydro Pump	Water	120	80	5

TM/HM LIST
TM/HM #	Move Name	Type	ST	ACC	PP		TM/HM #	Move Name	Type	ST	ACC	PP
HM03	Surf	Water	95	100	15		TM18	Rain Dance	Water	—	—	5
HM07	Waterfall	Water	80	100	15		TM21	Frustration	Normal	—	100	20
HM08	Dive	Water	60	100	10		TM27	Return	Normal	—	100	20
TM03	Water Pulse	Water	60	100	20		TM32	Double Team	Normal	—	—	15
TM06	Toxic	Poison	—	85	10		TM39	Rock Tomb	Rock	50	80	10
TM07	Hail	Ice	—	—	10		TM42	Façade	Normal	70	100	20
TM10	Hidden Power	Normal	—	100	15		TM43	Secret Power	Normal	70	100	20
TM13	Ice Beam	Ice	95	100	10		TM44	Rest	Psychic	—	—	10
TM14	Blizzard	Ice	120	70	5		TM45	Attract	Normal	—	100	15
TM15	Hyper Beam	Normal	150	90	5		TM49	Snatch	Dark	—	100	10
TM17	Protect	Normal	—	—	10							

MOVE TUTOR LIST
Move Name	Type	ST	ACC	PP
Body Slam*	Normal	85	100	15
Double-Edge	Normal	120	100	15
Endure*	Normal	—	—	10
Icy Wind*	Ice	55	95	15
Mimic	Normal	—	100	10
Mud-Slap*	Ground	20	100	10
Sleep Talk	Normal	—	—	10
Snore*	Normal	40	100	15
Substitute	Normal	—	—	10
Swagger	Normal	—	90	15
Swift*	Normal	60	—	20

*Battle Frontier tutor move

178 Gorebyss™
WATER

GENERAL INFO
SPECIES: South Sea Pokémon
HEIGHT: 5'11"
WEIGHT: 50 lbs.
ABILITY: *Swift Swim—Doubles the Pokémon's Speed when it rains.*

STATS
HP	50
ATTACK	75
DEFENSE	75
SP. ATTACK	100
SP. DEFENSE	50
SPEED	50

EVOLUTIONS
TRADE + DEEPSEATOOTH
TRADE + DEEPSEASCALE

WHERE/HOW TO CATCH
Evolve from Clamperl with Deepseascale and trade

STRONG AGAINST:
FIRE
WATER
ICE
STEEL

WEAK AGAINST:
ELECTRIC
GRASS

MOVES LIST
LV	Move Name	Type	ST	ACC	PP		LV	Move Name	Type	ST	ACC	PP
S	Whirlpool	Water	15	70	15		29	Amnesia	Psychic	—	—	20
08	Confusion	Psychic	50	100	25		36	Psychic	Psychic	90	100	10
15	Agility	Psychic	—	—	30		43	Baton Pass	Normal	—	—	40
22	Water Pulse	Water	60	100	20		50	Hydro Pump	Water	120	80	5

TM/HM LIST
TM/HM #	Move Name	Type	ST	ACC	PP		TM/HM #	Move Name	Type	ST	ACC	PP
HM03	Surf	Water	95	100	15		TM18	Rain Dance	Water	—	—	5
HM07	Waterfall	Water	80	100	15		TM20	Safeguard	Normal	—	—	25
HM08	Dive	Water	60	100	10		TM21	Frustration	Normal	—	100	20
TM03	Water Pulse	Water	60	100	20		TM27	Return	Normal	—	100	20
TM06	Toxic	Poison	—	85	10		TM29	Psychic	Psychic	90	100	10
TM07	Hail	Ice	—	—	10		TM30	Shadow Ball	Ghost	60	—	20
TM10	Hidden Power	Normal	—	100	15		TM32	Double Team	Normal	—	—	15
TM13	Ice Beam	Ice	95	100	10		TM42	Façade	Normal	70	100	20
TM14	Blizzard	Ice	120	70	5		TM43	Secret Power	Normal	70	100	20
TM15	Hyper Beam	Normal	150	90	5		TM44	Rest	Psychic	—	—	10
TM17	Protect	Normal	—	—	10		TM45	Attract	Normal	—	100	15

MOVE TUTOR LIST
Move Name	Type	ST	ACC	PP
Body Slam*	Normal	85	100	15
Double-Edge	Normal	120	100	15
Endure*	Normal	—	—	10
Icy Wind*	Ice	55	95	15
Mimic	Normal	—	100	10
Mud-Slap*	Ground	20	100	10
Sleep Talk	Normal	—	—	10
Snore*	Normal	40	100	15
Substitute	Normal	—	—	10
Swagger	Normal	—	90	15
Swift*	Normal	60	—	20

*Battle Frontier tutor move

179

Relicanth™
WATER
ROCK

GENERAL INFO
SPECIES: Longevity Pokémon
HEIGHT: 3'3"
WEIGHT: 52 lbs.
ABILITIES: *Swift Swim*—Doubles the Pokémon's Speed when it rains.
Rock Head—Pokémon does not receive recoil damage from moves such as Double-Edge and Body Slam.

STATS
HP	50
ATTACK	75
DEFENSE	75
SP. ATTACK	50
SP. DEFENSE	50
SPEED	50

EVOLUTIONS

RELICANTH DOES NOT EVOLVE

WHERE/HOW TO CATCH
Routes 124 and 126

STRONG AGAINST:
NORMAL
FIRE
ICE
POISON
FLYING

WEAK AGAINST:
ELECTRIC
GRASS
FIGHTING
GROUND

MOVES LIST

LV	Move Name	Type	ST	ACC	PP	LV	Move Name	Type	ST	ACC	PP
S	Tackle	Normal	35	95	35	36	Mud Sport	Ground	—	100	15
S	Harden	Normal	—	—	30	43	Ancientpower	Rock	60	100	5
08	Water Gun	Water	40	100	25	50	Rest	Psychic	—	—	10
15	Rock Tomb	Rock	50	80	10	57	Double-Edge	Normal	120	100	15
22	Yawn	Normal	—	100	10	64	Hydro Pump	Water	120	80	5
29	Take Down	Normal	90	85	20						

TM/HM LIST

TM/HM #	Move Name	Type	ST	ACC	PP	TM/HM #	Move Name	Type	ST	ACC	PP
HM03	Surf	Water	95	100	15	TM18	Rain Dance	Water	—	—	5
HM06	Rock Smash	Fighting	20	100	15	TM20	Safeguard	Normal	—	—	25
HM07	Waterfall	Water	80	100	15	TM21	Frustration	Normal	—	100	20
HM08	Dive	Water	60	100	10	TM26	Earthquake	Ground	100	100	10
TM03	Water Pulse	Water	60	100	20	TM27	Return	Normal	—	100	20
TM04	Calm Mind	Psychic	—	—	20	TM32	Double Team	Normal	—	—	15
TM06	Toxic	Poison	—	85	10	TM37	Sandstorm	Rock	—	—	10
TM07	Hail	Ice	—	—	10	TM39	Rock Tomb	Rock	50	80	10
TM10	Hidden Power	Normal	—	100	15	TM42	Façade	Normal	70	100	20
TM13	Ice Beam	Ice	95	100	10	TM43	Secret Power	Normal	70	100	20
TM14	Blizzard	Ice	120	70	5	TM44	Rest	Psychic	—	—	10
TM15	Hyper Beam	Normal	150	90	5	TM45	Attract	Normal	—	100	15
TM17	Protect	Normal	—	—	10						

EGG MOVES

Move Name	Type	ST	ACC	PP
Magnitude	Ground	—	100	30
Skull Bash	Normal	100	100	15
Water Sport	Water	—	100	15
Amnesia	Psychic	—	—	20
Sleep Talk	Normal	—	—	10
Rock Slide	Rock	75	90	10

MOVE TUTOR LIST

Move Name	Type	ST	ACC	PP
Body Slam*	Normal	85	100	15
Double-Edge	Normal	120	100	15
Endure*	Normal	—	—	10
Icy Wind*	Ice	55	95	15
Mimic	Normal	—	100	10
Mud-Slap*	Ground	20	100	10
Psych Up*	Normal	—	—	10
Rock Slide*	Rock	75	90	10
Sleep Talk	Normal	—	—	10
Snore*	Normal	40	100	15
Substitute	Normal	—	—	10
Swagger	Normal	—	90	15

*Battle Frontier tutor move

180

Corsola™
WATER
ROCK

GENERAL INFO
SPECIES: Coral Pokémon
HEIGHT: 2'0"
WEIGHT: 11 lbs.
ABILITIES: *Hustle*—Increases a move's Attack Power 1.5x, but the Attack's average accuracy is only 80 percent.
Natural Cure—Any negative Status conditions are healed when the Pokémon is removed from battle.

STATS
HP	33
ATTACK	66
DEFENSE	66
SP. ATTACK	66
SP. DEFENSE	66
SPEED	33

EVOLUTIONS

CORSOLA DOES NOT EVOLVE

WHERE/HOW TO CATCH
Route 128 and Ever Grande City

STRONG AGAINST:
NORMAL
FIRE
ICE
POISON
FLYING

WEAK AGAINST:
ELECTRIC
GRASS
FIGHTING
GROUND

MOVES LIST

LV	Move Name	Type	ST	ACC	PP	LV	Move Name	Type	ST	ACC	PP
S	Tackle	Normal	35	95	35	23	Bubblebeam	Water	65	100	20
06	Harden	Normal	—	—	30	28	Spike Cannon	Normal	20	100	15
12	Bubble	Water	20	100	30	34	Rock Blast	Rock	25	80	10
17	Recover	Normal	—	—	20	39	Mirror Coat	Psychic	—	100	20
17	Refresh	Normal	—	100	20	45	Ancientpower	Rock	60	100	5

TM/HM LIST

TM/HM #	Move Name	Type	ST	ACC	PP	TM/HM #	Move Name	Type	ST	ACC	PP
HM03	Surf	Water	95	100	15	TM21	Frustration	Normal	—	100	20
HM04	Strength	Normal	80	100	15	TM26	Earthquake	Ground	100	100	10
HM06	Rock Smash	Fighting	20	100	15	TM27	Return	Normal	—	100	20
TM03	Water Pulse	Water	60	100	20	TM28	Dig	Ground	60	100	10
TM04	Calm Mind	Psychic	—	—	20	TM29	Psychic	Psychic	90	100	10
TM06	Toxic	Poison	—	85	10	TM30	Shadow Ball	Ghost	60	—	10
TM07	Hail	Ice	—	—	10	TM32	Double Team	Normal	—	—	15
TM10	Hidden Power	Normal	—	100	15	TM33	Reflect	Psychic	—	—	20
TM11	Sunny Day	Fire	—	—	5	TM37	Sandstorm	Rock	—	—	10
TM13	Ice Beam	Ice	95	100	10	TM39	Rock Tomb	Rock	50	80	10
TM14	Blizzard	Ice	120	70	5	TM42	Façade	Normal	70	100	20
TM16	Light Screen	Psychic	—	—	30	TM43	Secret Power	Normal	70	100	20
TM17	Protect	Normal	—	—	10	TM44	Rest	Psychic	—	—	10
TM18	Rain Dance	Water	—	—	5	TM45	Attract	Normal	—	100	15
TM20	Safeguard	Normal	—	—	25						

EGG MOVES

Move Name	Type	ST	ACC	PP
Rock Slide	Rock	75	90	10
Screech	Normal	—	85	40
Mist	Ice	—	—	30
Icicle Spear	Ice	10	100	30
Amnesia	Psychic	—	—	20
Ingrain	Grass	—	100	20
Barrier	Psychic	—	—	30
Confuse Ray	Ghost	—	100	10

MOVE TUTOR LIST

Move Name	Type	ST	ACC	PP
Body Slam*	Normal	85	100	15
Defense Curl*	Normal	—	—	40
Double-Edge	Normal	120	100	15
Endure*	Normal	—	—	10
Explosion	Normal	250	100	5
Mimic	Normal	—	100	10
Mud-Slap*	Ground	20	100	10
Rock Slide*	Rock	75	90	10
Rollout	Rock	30	90	20
Sleep Talk	Normal	—	—	10
Snore*	Normal	40	100	15
Substitute	Normal	—	—	10
Swagger	Normal	—	90	15

*Battle Frontier tutor move

PRIMA OFFICIAL GAME GUIDE

181 Chinchou

WATER
ELECTRIC

GENERAL INFO
SPECIES: Angler Pokémon
HEIGHT: 1'8"
WEIGHT: 26 lbs.

ABILITIES: *Volt Absorb* — Restores Pokémon's HP when it is hit with Electric-type Moves.
Illuminate — Increases the chance of encountering wild Pokémon.

STATS

Stat	Value
HP	66
ATTACK	33
DEFENSE	30
SP. ATTACK	66
SP. DEFENSE	33
SPEED	66

EVOLUTIONS

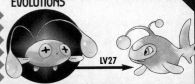

LV27

WHERE/HOW TO CATCH
Routes 124 and 126

STRONG AGAINST:
FIRE
WATER
ICE
FLYING
STEEL

WEAK AGAINST:
GRASS
GROUND

MOVES LIST

LV	Move Name	Type	ST	ACC	PP
S	Bubble	Water	20	100	30
S	Thunder Wave	Electric	—	100	20
05	Supersonic	Normal	—	55	20
13	Flail	Normal	—	100	15
17	Water Gun	Water	40	100	25
25	Spark	Electric	65	100	20
29	Confuse Ray	Ghost	—	100	10
37	Take Down	Normal	90	85	20
41	Hydro Pump	Water	120	80	5
49	Charge	Electric	—	100	20

TM/HM LIST

TM/HM #	Move Name	Type	ST	ACC	PP
HM03	Surf	Water	95	100	15
HM05	Flash	Normal	—	70	20
HM07	Waterfall	Water	80	100	15
HM08	Dive	Water	60	100	10
TM03	Water Pulse	Water	60	100	20
TM06	Toxic	Poison	—	85	10
TM07	Hail	Ice	—	—	10
TM10	Hidden Power	Normal	—	100	15
TM13	Ice Beam	Ice	95	100	10
TM14	Blizzard	Ice	120	70	5
TM17	Protect	Normal	—	—	10
TM18	Rain Dance	Water	—	—	5
TM21	Frustration	Normal	—	100	20
TM24	Thunderbolt	Electric	95	100	15
TM25	Thunder	Electric	120	70	10
TM27	Return	Normal	—	100	20
TM32	Double Team	Normal	—	—	15
TM34	Shock Wave	Electric	60	—	20
TM42	Façade	Normal	70	100	20
TM43	Secret Power	Normal	70	100	20
TM44	Rest	Psychic	—	—	10
TM45	Attract	Normal	—	100	15

EGG MOVES

Move Name	Type	ST	ACC	PP
Screech	Normal	—	85	40
Amnesia	Psychic	—	—	20

MOVE TUTOR LIST

Move Name	Type	ST	ACC	PP
Double-Edge	Normal	120	100	15
Endure*	Normal	—	—	10
Mimic	Normal	—	100	10
Sleep Talk	Normal	—	—	10
Snore*	Normal	40	100	15
Substitute	Normal	—	—	10
Swagger	Normal	—	90	15
Thunder Wave*	Electric	—	100	20

*Battle Frontier tutor move

182 Lanturn

WATER
ELECTRIC

GENERAL INFO
SPECIES: Light Pokémon
HEIGHT: 3'11"
WEIGHT: 50 lbs.

ABILITIES: *Volt Absorb* — Restores Pokémon's HP when it is hit with Electric-type Moves.
Illuminate — Increases the chance of encountering wild Pokémon.

STATS

Stat	Value
HP	100
ATTACK	66
DEFENSE	33
SP. ATTACK	60
SP. DEFENSE	66
SPEED	66

EVOLUTIONS

LV27

WHERE/HOW TO CATCH
Evolve from Chinchou

STRONG AGAINST:
FIRE
WATER
ICE
FLYING
STEEL

WEAK AGAINST:
GRASS
GROUND

MOVES LIST

LV	Move Name	Type	ST	ACC	PP
S	Bubble	Water	20	100	30
S	Thunder Wave	Electric	—	100	20
S	Supersonic	Normal	—	55	20
05	Supersonic	Normal	—	55	20
13	Flail	Normal	—	100	15
17	Water Gun	Water	40	100	25
25	Spark	Electric	65	100	20
32	Confuse Ray	Ghost	—	100	10
43	Take Down	Normal	90	85	20
50	Hydro Pump	Water	120	80	5
61	Charge	Electric	—	100	20

TM/HM LIST

TM/HM #	Move Name	Type	ST	ACC	PP
HM03	Surf	Water	95	100	15
HM05	Flash	Normal	—	70	20
HM07	Waterfall	Water	80	100	15
HM08	Dive	Water	60	100	10
TM03	Water Pulse	Water	60	100	20
TM06	Toxic	Poison	—	85	10
TM07	Hail	Ice	—	—	10
TM10	Hidden Power	Normal	—	100	15
TM13	Ice Beam	Ice	95	100	10
TM14	Blizzard	Ice	120	70	5
TM15	Hyper Beam	Normal	150	90	5
TM17	Protect	Normal	—	—	10
TM18	Rain Dance	Water	—	—	5
TM21	Frustration	Normal	—	100	20
TM24	Thunderbolt	Electric	95	100	15
TM25	Thunder	Electric	120	70	10
TM27	Return	Normal	—	100	20
TM32	Double Team	Normal	—	—	15
TM34	Shock Wave	Electric	60	—	20
TM42	Façade	Normal	70	100	20
TM43	Secret Power	Normal	70	100	20
TM44	Rest	Psychic	—	—	10
TM45	Attract	Normal	—	100	15

MOVE TUTOR LIST

Move Name	Type	ST	ACC	PP
Double-Edge	Normal	120	100	15
Endure*	Normal	—	—	10
Mimic	Normal	—	100	10
Sleep Talk	Normal	—	—	10
Snore*	Normal	40	100	15
Substitute	Normal	—	—	10
Swagger	Normal	—	90	15
Thunder Wave*	Electric	—	100	20

*Battle Frontier tutor move

183 Luvdisc™
WATER

GENERAL INFO
SPECIES: Rendevous Pokémon
HEIGHT: 2'0"
WEIGHT: 19 lbs.
ABILITY: *Swift Swim*—Doubles the Pokémon's Speed when it rains.

STATS
HP	25
ATTACK	25
DEFENSE	50
SP. ATTACK	50
SP. DEFENSE	50
SPEED	75

EVOLUTIONS

LUVDISC DOES NOT EVOLVE

WHERE/HOW TO CATCH
Route 128 and Ever Grande City

STRONG AGAINST:
FIRE
WATER
ICE
STEEL

WEAK AGAINST:
ELECTRIC
GRASS

MOVES LIST
LV	Move Name	Type	ST	ACC	PP
S	Tackle	Normal	35	95	35
04	Charm	Normal	—	100	20
12	Water Gun	Water	40	100	25
16	Agility	Psychic	—	—	30
24	Take Down	Normal	90	85	20
28	Attract	Normal	—	100	15
36	Sweet Kiss	Normal	—	75	10
40	Flail	Normal	—	100	15
48	Safeguard	Normal	—	—	25

TM/HM LIST
TM/HM #	Move Name	Type	ST	ACC	PP
HM03	Surf	Water	95	100	15
HM07	Waterfall	Water	80	100	15
HM08	Dive	Water	60	100	10
TM03	Water Pulse	Water	60	100	20
TM06	Toxic	Poison	—	85	10
TM07	Hail	Ice	—	—	10
TM10	Hidden Power	Normal	—	100	15
TM13	Ice Beam	Ice	95	100	10
TM14	Blizzard	Ice	120	70	5
TM17	Protect	Normal	—	—	10
TM18	Rain Dance	Water	—	—	5
TM20	Safeguard	Normal	—	—	25
TM21	Frustration	Normal	—	100	20
TM27	Return	Normal	—	100	20
TM32	Double Team	Normal	—	—	15
TM42	Façade	Normal	70	100	20
TM43	Secret Power	Normal	70	100	20
TM44	Rest	Psychic	—	—	10
TM45	Attract	Normal	—	100	15

EGG MOVES
Move Name	Type	ST	ACC	PP
Supersonic	Normal	—	55	20
Water Sport	Water	—	100	15
Mud Sport	Ground	—	100	15

MOVE TUTOR LIST
Move Name	Type	ST	ACC	PP
Double-Edge	Normal	120	100	15
Endure*	Normal	—	—	10
Icy Wind*	Ice	55	95	15
Mimic	Normal	—	100	10
Psych Up*	Normal	—	—	10
Sleep Talk	Normal	—	—	10
Snore*	Normal	40	100	15
Substitute	Normal	—	—	10
Swagger	Normal	—	90	15
Swift*	Normal	60	—	20

*Battle Frontier tutor move

184 Horsea™
WATER

GENERAL INFO
SPECIES: Dragon Pokémon
HEIGHT: 1'4"
WEIGHT: 18 lbs.
ABILITY: *Swift Swim*—Doubles the Pokémon's Speed when it rains.

STATS
HP	33
ATTACK	33
DEFENSE	66
SP. ATTACK	66
SP. DEFENSE	33
SPEED	66

EVOLUTIONS

 LV32
TRADE + DRAGON SCALE

WHERE/HOW TO CATCH
Routes 132, 133, and 134

STRONG AGAINST:
FIRE
WATER
ICE
STEEL

WEAK AGAINST:
ELECTRIC
GRASS

MOVES LIST
LV	Move Name	Type	ST	ACC	PP
S	Bubble	Water	20	100	30
08	Smokescreen	Normal	—	100	20
15	Leer	Normal	—	100	30
22	Water Gun	Water	40	100	25
29	Twister	Dragon	40	100	20
36	Agility	Psychic	—	—	30
43	Hydro Pump	Water	120	80	5
50	Dragon Dance	Dragon	—	—	20

TM/HM LIST
TM/HM #	Move Name	Type	ST	ACC	PP
HM03	Surf	Water	95	100	15
HM07	Waterfall	Water	80	100	15
HM08	Dive	Water	60	100	10
TM03	Water Pulse	Water	60	100	20
TM06	Toxic	Poison	—	85	10
TM07	Hail	Ice	—	—	10
TM10	Hidden Power	Normal	—	100	15
TM13	Ice Beam	Ice	95	100	10
TM14	Blizzard	Ice	120	70	5
TM17	Protect	Normal	—	—	10
TM18	Rain Dance	Water	—	—	5
TM21	Frustration	Normal	—	100	20
TM27	Return	Normal	—	100	20
TM32	Double Team	Normal	—	—	15
TM42	Façade	Normal	70	100	20
TM43	Secret Power	Normal	70	100	20
TM44	Rest	Psychic	—	—	10
TM45	Attract	Normal	—	100	15

EGG MOVES
Move Name	Type	ST	ACC	PP
Flail	Normal	—	100	15
Aurora Beam	Ice	65	100	20
Disable	Normal	—	55	20
Splash	Normal	—	—	40
Dragon Rage	Dragon	—	100	10
Dragonbreath	Dragon	60	100	20
Octazooka	Water	65	85	10

MOVE TUTOR LIST
Move Name	Type	ST	ACC	PP
Double-Edge	Normal	120	100	15
Endure*	Normal	—	—	10
Icy Wind*	Ice	55	95	15
Mimic	Normal	—	100	10
Sleep Talk	Normal	—	—	10
Snore*	Normal	40	100	15
Substitute	Normal	—	—	10
Swagger	Normal	—	90	15
Swift*	Normal	60	—	20

*Battle Frontier tutor move

185

Seadra™

WATER

GENERAL INFO
SPECIES: Dragon Pokémon
HEIGHT: 3'11"
WEIGHT: 55 lbs.
ABILITY: *Poison Point* — *Gives the Pokémon's Physical Attacks a 30 percent chance of Poisoning the opponent.*

STATS

HP	33
ATTACK	66
DEFENSE	66
SP. ATTACK	100
SP. DEFENSE	33
SPEED	66

EVOLUTIONS

LV32

TRADE + DRAGON SCALE

WHERE/HOW TO CATCH
Evolve from Horsea

STRONG AGAINST:
FIRE
WATER
ICE
STEEL

WEAK AGAINST:
ELECTRIC
GRASS

MOVES LIST

LV	Move Name	Type	ST	ACC	PP	LV	Move Name	Type	ST	ACC	PP
S	Bubble	Water	20	100	30	22	Water Gun	Water	40	100	25
S	Smokescreen	Normal	—	100	20	29	Twister	Dragon	40	100	20
S	Leer	Normal	—	100	30	40	Agility	Psychic	—	—	30
S	Water Gun	Water	40	100	25	51	Hydro Pump	Water	120	80	5
08	Smokescreen	Normal	—	100	20	62	Dragon Dance	Dragon	—	—	20
15	Leer	Normal	—	100	30						

TM/HM LIST

TM/HM #	Move Name	Type	ST	ACC	PP	TM/HM #	Move Name	Type	ST	ACC	PP
HM03	Surf	Water	95	100	15	TM17	Protect	Normal	—	—	10
HM07	Waterfall	Water	80	100	15	TM18	Rain Dance	Water	—	—	5
HM08	Dive	Water	60	100	10	TM21	Frustration	Normal	—	100	20
TM03	Water Pulse	Water	60	100	20	TM27	Return	Normal	—	100	20
TM06	Toxic	Poison	—	85	10	TM32	Double Team	Normal	—	—	15
TM07	Hail	Ice	—	—	10	TM42	Façade	Normal	70	100	20
TM10	Hidden Power	Normal	—	100	15	TM43	Secret Power	Normal	70	100	20
TM13	Ice Beam	Ice	95	100	10	TM44	Rest	Psychic	—	—	10
TM14	Blizzard	Ice	120	70	5	TM45	Attract	Normal	—	100	15
TM15	Hyper Beam	Normal	150	90	5						

MOVE TUTOR LIST

Move Name	Type	ST	ACC	PP
Double-Edge	Normal	120	100	15
Endure*	Normal	—	—	10
Icy Wind*	Ice	55	95	15
Mimic	Normal	—	100	10
Sleep Talk	Normal	—	—	10
Snore*	Normal	40	100	15
Substitute	Normal	—	—	10
Swagger	Normal	—	90	15
Swift*	Normal	60	—	20

*Battle Frontier tutor move

186

Kingdra™

WATER
DRAGON

GENERAL INFO
SPECIES: Dragon Pokémon
HEIGHT: 5'11"
WEIGHT: 335 lbs.
ABILITY: *Swift Swim* — *Doubles the Pokémon's Speed when it rains.*

STATS

HP	66
ATTACK	100
DEFENSE	66
SP. ATTACK	100
SP. DEFENSE	66
SPEED	66

EVOLUTIONS

 LV32

TRADE + DRAGON SCALE

WHERE/HOW TO CATCH
Evolve from Seadra with Dragon Scale and trade

STRONG AGAINST:
FIRE
WATER
STEEL

WEAK AGAINST:
DRAGON

MOVES LIST

LV	Move Name	Type	ST	ACC	PP	LV	Move Name	Type	ST	ACC	PP
S	Bubble	Water	20	100	30	22	Water Gun	Water	40	100	25
S	Smokescreen	Normal	—	100	20	29	Twister	Dragon	40	100	20
S	Leer	Normal	—	100	30	40	Agility	Psychic	—	—	30
S	Water Gun	Water	40	100	25	51	Hydro Pump	Water	120	80	5
08	Smokescreen	Normal	—	100	20	62	Dragon Dance	Dragon	—	—	20
15	Leer	Normal	—	100	30						

TM/HM LIST

TM/HM #	Move Name	Type	ST	ACC	PP	TM/HM #	Move Name	Type	ST	ACC	PP
HM03	Surf	Water	95	100	15	TM17	Protect	Normal	—	—	10
HM07	Waterfall	Water	80	100	15	TM18	Rain Dance	Water	—	—	5
HM08	Dive	Water	60	100	10	TM21	Frustration	Normal	—	100	20
TM03	Water Pulse	Water	60	100	20	TM27	Return	Normal	—	100	20
TM06	Toxic	Poison	—	85	10	TM32	Double Team	Normal	—	—	15
TM07	Hail	Ice	—	—	10	TM42	Façade	Normal	70	100	20
TM10	Hidden Power	Normal	—	100	15	TM43	Secret Power	Normal	70	100	20
TM13	Ice Beam	Ice	95	100	10	TM44	Rest	Psychic	—	—	10
TM14	Blizzard	Ice	120	70	5	TM45	Attract	Normal	—	100	15
TM15	Hyper Beam	Normal	150	90	5						

MOVE TUTOR LIST

Move Name	Type	ST	ACC	PP
Body Slam*	Normal	85	100	15
Double-Edge	Normal	120	100	15
Endure*	Normal	—	—	10
Icy Wind*	Ice	55	95	15
Mimic	Normal	—	100	10
Sleep Talk	Normal	—	—	10
Snore*	Normal	40	100	15
Substitute	Normal	—	—	10
Swagger	Normal	—	90	15
Swift*	Normal	60	—	20

*Battle Frontier tutor move

187 Bagon™

DRAGON

GENERAL INFO
SPECIES: Rock Head Pokémon
HEIGHT: 2'0"
WEIGHT: 93 lbs.
ABILITY: *Rock Head* — Pokémon does not receive recoil damage from moves such as Double-Edge and Body Slam.

STATS
Stat	Value
HP	25
ATTACK	50
DEFENSE	50
SP. ATTACK	50
SP. DEFENSE	25
SPEED	50

EVOLUTIONS

LV30 → LV50

WHERE/HOW TO CATCH
Meteor Falls

STRONG AGAINST:
FIRE
WATER
ELECTRIC
GRASS

WEAK AGAINST:
ICE
DRAGON

MOVES LIST
LV	Move Name	Type	ST	ACC	PP
S	Rage	Normal	20	100	20
05	Bite	Dark	60	100	25
09	Leer	Normal	—	100	30
17	Headbutt	Normal	70	100	15
21	Focus Energy	Normal	—	—	30
25	Ember	Fire	40	100	25
33	Dragonbreath	Dragon	60	100	20
37	Scary Face	Normal	—	90	10
41	Crunch	Dark	80	100	15
49	Dragon Claw	Dragon	80	100	15
53	Double-Edge	Normal	120	100	15

TM/HM LIST
TM/HM #	Move Name	Type	ST	ACC	PP
HM01	Cut	Normal	50	95	30
HM04	Strength	Normal	80	100	15
HM06	Rock Smash	Fighting	20	100	15
TM02	Dragon Claw	Dragon	80	100	15
TM05	Roar	Normal	—	100	20
TM06	Toxic	Poison	—	85	10
TM10	Hidden Power	Normal	—	100	15
TM11	Sunny Day	Fire	—	—	5
TM17	Protect	Normal	—	—	10
TM18	Rain Dance	Water	—	—	5
TM21	Frustration	Normal	—	100	20
TM27	Return	Normal	—	100	20
TM31	Brick Break	Fighting	75	100	15
TM32	Double Team	Normal	—	—	15
TM35	Flamethrower	Fire	95	100	15
TM38	Fire Blast	Fire	120	85	5
TM39	Rock Tomb	Rock	50	80	10
TM40	Aerial Ace	Flying	60	—	20
TM42	Façade	Normal	70	100	20
TM43	Secret Power	Normal	70	100	20
TM44	Rest	Psychic	—	—	10
TM45	Attract	Normal	—	100	15

EGG MOVES
Move Name	Type	ST	ACC	PP
Hydro Pump	Water	120	80	5
Thrash	Normal	90	100	20
Dragon Rage	Dragon	—	100	10
Twister	Dragon	40	100	20
Dragon Dance	Dragon	—	—	20

MOVE TUTOR LIST
Move Name	Type	ST	ACC	PP
Body Slam*	Normal	85	100	15
Double-Edge	Normal	120	100	15
Endure*	Normal	—	—	10
Fury Cutter	Bug	10	95	20
Mimic	Normal	—	100	10
Mud-Slap*	Ground	20	100	10
Rock Slide*	Rock	75	90	10
Sleep Talk	Normal	—	—	10
Snore*	Normal	40	100	15
Substitute	Normal	—	—	10
Swagger	Normal	—	90	15

*Battle Frontier tutor move

188 Shelgon™

DRAGON

GENERAL INFO
SPECIES: Endurance Pokémon
HEIGHT: 3'7"
WEIGHT: 244 lbs.
ABILITY: *Rock Head* — Pokémon does not receive recoil damage from moves such as Double-Edge and Body Slam.

STATS
Stat	Value
HP	50
ATTACK	75
DEFENSE	75
SP. ATTACK	50
SP. DEFENSE	50
SPEED	50

EVOLUTIONS

LV30 → LV50

WHERE/HOW TO CATCH
Evolve from Bagon

STRONG AGAINST:
FIRE
WATER
ELECTRIC
GRASS

WEAK AGAINST:
ICE
DRAGON

MOVES LIST
LV	Move Name	Type	ST	ACC	PP
S	Rage	Normal	20	100	20
S	Bite	Dark	60	100	25
S	Leer	Normal	—	100	30
S	Headbutt	Normal	70	100	15
05	Bite	Dark	60	100	25
09	Leer	Normal	—	100	30
17	Headbutt	Normal	70	100	15
21	Focus Energy	Normal	—	—	30
25	Ember	Fire	40	100	25
30	Protect	Normal	—	—	10
38	Dragonbreath	Dragon	60	100	20
47	Scary Face	Normal	—	90	10
56	Crunch	Dark	80	100	15
69	Dragon Claw	Dragon	80	100	15
78	Double-Edge	Normal	120	100	15

TM/HM LIST
TM/HM #	Move Name	Type	ST	ACC	PP
HM01	Cut	Normal	50	95	30
HM04	Strength	Normal	80	100	15
HM06	Rock Smash	Fighting	20	100	15
TM02	Dragon Claw	Dragon	80	100	15
TM05	Roar	Normal	—	100	20
TM06	Toxic	Poison	—	85	10
TM10	Hidden Power	Normal	—	100	15
TM11	Sunny Day	Fire	—	—	5
TM17	Protect	Normal	—	—	10
TM18	Rain Dance	Water	—	—	5
TM21	Frustration	Normal	—	100	20
TM27	Return	Normal	—	100	20
TM31	Brick Break	Fighting	75	100	15
TM32	Double Team	Normal	—	—	15
TM35	Flamethrower	Fire	95	100	15
TM38	Fire Blast	Fire	120	85	5
TM39	Rock Tomb	Rock	50	80	10
TM40	Aerial Ace	Flying	60	—	20
TM42	Façade	Normal	70	100	20
TM43	Secret Power	Normal	70	100	20
TM44	Rest	Psychic	—	—	10
TM45	Attract	Normal	—	100	15

MOVE TUTOR LIST
Move Name	Type	ST	ACC	PP
Body Slam*	Normal	85	100	15
Defense Curl*	Normal	—	—	40
Double-Edge	Normal	120	100	15
Endure*	Normal	—	—	10
Fury Cutter	Bug	10	95	20
Mimic	Normal	—	100	10
Mud-Slap*	Ground	20	100	10
Rock Slide*	Rock	75	90	10
Rollout	Rock	30	90	20
Sleep Talk	Normal	—	—	10
Snore*	Normal	40	100	15
Substitute	Normal	—	—	10
Swagger	Normal	—	90	15

*Battle Frontier tutor move

189 Salamence™

DRAGON
FLYING

GENERAL INFO
SPECIES: Dragon Pokémon
HEIGHT: 4'11"
WEIGHT: 266 lbs.
ABILITY: *Intimidate*—Lowers the opponent's Attack by one point at the battle's start.

STATS

HP	50
ATTACK	100
DEFENSE	50
SP. ATTACK	75
SP. DEFENSE	50
SPEED	75

EVOLUTIONS

LV30   LV50

WHERE/HOW TO CATCH
Evolve from Shelgon

STRONG AGAINST:
FIRE
WATER
GRASS
FIGHTING
GROUND
BUG

WEAK AGAINST:
ICE
ROCK
DRAGON

MOVES LIST

LV	Move Name	Type	ST	ACC	PP
S	Rage	Normal	20	100	20
S	Bite	Dark	60	100	25
S	Leer	Normal	—	100	30
S	Headbutt	Normal	70	100	15
05	Bite	Dark	60	100	25
09	Leer	Normal	—	100	30
17	Headbutt	Normal	70	100	15
21	Focus Energy	Normal	—	—	30

LV	Move Name	Type	ST	ACC	PP
25	Ember	Fire	40	100	25
30	Protect	Normal	—	—	10
38	Dragonbreath	Dragon	60	100	20
47	Scary Face	Normal	—	90	10
50	Fly	Flying	70	95	15
61	Crunch	Dark	80	100	15
79	Dragon Claw	Dragon	80	100	15
93	Double-Edge	Normal	120	100	15

TM/HM LIST

TM/HM #	Move Name	Type	ST	ACC	PP
HM01	Cut	Normal	50	95	30
HM02	Fly	Flying	70	95	15
HM04	Strength	Normal	80	100	15
HM06	Rock Smash	Fighting	20	100	15
TM02	Dragon Claw	Dragon	80	100	15
TM05	Roar	Normal	—	100	20
TM06	Toxic	Poison	—	85	10
TM10	Hidden Power	Normal	—	100	15
TM11	Sunny Day	Fire	—	—	5
TM15	Hyper Beam	Normal	150	90	5
TM17	Protect	Normal	—	—	10
TM18	Rain Dance	Water	—	—	5
TM21	Frustration	Normal	—	100	20
TM23	Iron Tail	Steel	100	75	15

TM/HM #	Move Name	Type	ST	ACC	PP
TM26	Earthquake	Ground	100	100	10
TM27	Return	Normal	—	100	20
TM31	Brick Break	Fighting	75	100	15
TM32	Double Team	Normal	—	—	15
TM35	Flamethrower	Fire	95	100	15
TM38	Fire Blast	Fire	120	85	5
TM39	Rock Tomb	Rock	50	80	10
TM40	Aerial Ace	Flying	60	—	20
TM42	Façade	Normal	70	100	20
TM43	Secret Power	Normal	70	100	20
TM44	Rest	Psychic	—	—	10
TM45	Attract	Normal	—	100	15
TM47	Steel Wing	Steel	70	90	25

MOVE TUTOR LIST

Move Name	Type	ST	ACC	PP
Body Slam*	Normal	85	100	15
Defense Curl*	Normal	—	—	40
Double-Edge	Normal	120	100	15
Endure*	Normal	—	—	10
Fury Cutter	Bug	10	95	20
Mimic	Normal	—	100	10
Mud-Slap*	Ground	20	100	10
Rock Slide*	Rock	75	90	10
Rollout	Rock	30	90	20
Sleep Talk	Normal	—	—	10
Snore*	Normal	40	100	15
Substitute	Normal	—	—	10
Swagger	Normal	—	90	15
Swift*	Normal	60	—	20

*Battle Frontier tutor move

---

190 Beldum™

STEEL
PSYCHIC

GENERAL INFO
SPECIES: Iron Ball Pokémon
HEIGHT: 2'0"
WEIGHT: 210 lbs.
ABILITY: *Clear Body*—Moves that lower Ability values don't affect the Pokémon.

STATS

HP	25
ATTACK	50
DEFENSE	50
SP. ATTACK	50
SP. DEFENSE	50
SPEED	25

EVOLUTIONS

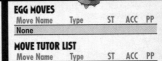

LV20   LV45

WHERE/HOW TO CATCH
Steven's House (after defeating Elite Four)

STRONG AGAINST:
NORMAL
GRASS
ICE
POISON
FLYING
PSYCHIC
ROCK
DRAGON
STEEL

WEAK AGAINST:
FIRE
GROUND

MOVES LIST

LV	Move Name	Type	ST	ACC	PP
S	Take Down	Normal	90	85	20

TM/HM LIST

TM/HM #	Move Name	Type	ST	ACC	PP
None					

EGG MOVES

Move Name	Type	ST	ACC	PP
None					

MOVE TUTOR LIST

Move Name	Type	ST	ACC	PP
None					

191

Metang™

STEEL
PSYCHIC

GENERAL INFO
SPECIES: Iron Claw Pokémon
HEIGHT: 3'11"
WEIGHT: 445 lbs.
ABILITY: *Clear Body*—Moves that lower Ability values don't affect the Pokémon.

STATS

STAT	Value
HP	50
ATTACK	50
DEFENSE	75
SP. ATTACK	50
SP. DEFENSE	50
SPEED	50

EVOLUTIONS

LV20   LV45

WHERE/HOW TO CATCH
Evolve from Beldum

STRONG AGAINST:
NORMAL
GRASS
ICE
POISON
FLYING
PSYCHIC
ROCK
DRAGON
STEEL

WEAK AGAINST:
FIRE
GROUND

MOVES LIST

LV	Move Name	Type	ST	ACC	PP
S	Take Down	Normal	90	85	20
20	Confusion	Psychic	50	100	25
20	Metal Claw	Steel	50	95	35
26	Scary Face	Normal	—	90	10
32	Pursuit	Dark	40	100	20

LV	Move Name	Type	ST	ACC	PP
38	Psychic	Psychic	90	100	10
44	Iron Defense	Steel	—	—	15
50	Meteor Mash	Steel	100	85	10
56	Agility	Psychic	—	—	30
62	Hyper Beam	Normal	150	90	5

TM/HM LIST

TM/HM #	Move Name	Type	ST	ACC	PP
HM01	Cut	Normal	50	95	30
HM04	Strength	Normal	80	100	15
HM05	Flash	Normal	—	70	20
HM06	Rock Smash	Fighting	20	100	15
TM06	Toxic	Poison	—	85	10
TM10	Hidden Power	Normal	—	100	15
TM11	Sunny Day	Fire	—	—	5
TM15	Hyper Beam	Normal	150	90	5
TM16	Light Screen	Psychic	—	—	30
TM17	Protect	Normal	—	—	10
TM18	Rain Dance	Water	—	—	5
TM21	Frustration	Normal	—	100	20
TM26	Earthquake	Ground	100	100	10

TM/HM #	Move Name	Type	ST	ACC	PP
TM27	Return	Normal	—	100	20
TM29	Psychic	Psychic	90	100	10
TM30	Shadow Ball	Ghost	60	—	20
TM31	Brick Break	Fighting	75	100	15
TM32	Double Team	Normal	—	—	15
TM33	Reflect	Psychic	—	—	20
TM36	Sludge Bomb	Poison	90	100	10
TM37	Sandstorm	Rock	—	—	10
TM39	Rock Tomb	Rock	50	80	10
TM40	Aerial Ace	Flying	60	—	20
TM42	Façade	Normal	70	100	20
TM43	Secret Power	Normal	70	100	20
TM44	Rest	Psychic	—	—	10

MOVE TUTOR LIST

Move Name	Type	ST	ACC	PP
Body Slam*	Normal	85	100	15
Defense Curl*	Normal	—	—	40
Double-Edge	Normal	120	100	15
Dynamicpunch	Fighting	100	50	5
Endure*	Normal	—	—	10
Explosion	Normal	250	100	5
Fury Cutter	Bug	10	95	20
Ice Punch*	Ice	75	100	15
Icy Wind*	Ice	55	95	15
Mimic	Normal	—	100	10
Mud-Slap*	Ground	20	100	10
Psych Up*	Normal	—	—	10
Rock Slide*	Rock	75	90	10
Rollout	Rock	30	90	20
Sleep Talk	Normal	—	—	10
Snore*	Normal	40	100	15
Substitute	Normal	—	—	10
Swagger	Normal	—	90	15
Swift*	Normal	60	—	20
Thunderpunch*	Electric	75	100	15

*Battle Frontier tutor move

192

Metagross™

STEEL
PSYCHIC

GENERAL INFO
SPECIES: Iron Leg Pokémon
HEIGHT: 5'3"
WEIGHT: 1,213 lbs.
ABILITY: *Clear Body*—Moves that lower Ability values don't affect the Pokémon.

STATS

STAT	Value
HP	50
ATTACK	100
DEFENSE	75
SP. ATTACK	75
SP. DEFENSE	50
SPEED	50

EVOLUTIONS

LV20   LV45

WHERE/HOW TO CATCH
Evolve from Metang

STRONG AGAINST:
NORMAL
GRASS
ICE
POISON
FLYING
PSYCHIC
ROCK
DRAGON
STEEL

WEAK AGAINST:
FIRE
GROUND

MOVES LIST

LV	Move Name	Type	ST	ACC	PP
S	Take Down	Normal	90	85	20
S	Confusion	Psychic	50	100	25
S	Metal Claw	Steel	50	95	35
S	Scary Face	Normal	—	90	10
20	Confusion	Psychic	50	100	25
20	Metal Claw	Steel	50	95	35
26	Scary Face	Normal	—	90	10

LV	Move Name	Type	ST	ACC	PP
32	Pursuit	Dark	40	100	20
38	Psychic	Psychic	90	100	10
44	Iron Defense	Steel	—	—	15
55	Meteor Mash	Steel	100	85	10
66	Agility	Psychic	—	—	30
77	Hyper Beam	Normal	150	90	5

TM/HM LIST

TM/HM #	Move Name	Type	ST	ACC	PP
HM01	Cut	Normal	50	95	30
HM04	Strength	Normal	80	100	15
HM05	Flash	Normal	—	70	20
HM06	Rock Smash	Fighting	20	100	15
TM06	Toxic	Poison	—	85	10
TM10	Hidden Power	Normal	—	100	15
TM11	Sunny Day	Fire	—	—	5
TM15	Hyper Beam	Normal	150	90	5
TM16	Light Screen	Psychic	—	—	30
TM17	Protect	Normal	—	—	10
TM18	Rain Dance	Water	—	—	5
TM21	Frustration	Normal	—	100	20
TM26	Earthquake	Ground	100	100	10

TM/HM #	Move Name	Type	ST	ACC	PP
TM27	Return	Normal	—	100	20
TM29	Psychic	Psychic	90	100	10
TM30	Shadow Ball	Ghost	60	—	20
TM31	Brick Break	Fighting	75	100	15
TM32	Double Team	Normal	—	—	15
TM33	Reflect	Psychic	—	—	20
TM36	Sludge Bomb	Poison	90	100	10
TM37	Sandstorm	Rock	—	—	10
TM39	Rock Tomb	Rock	50	80	10
TM40	Aerial Ace	Flying	60	—	20
TM42	Façade	Normal	70	100	20
TM43	Secret Power	Normal	70	100	20
TM44	Rest	Psychic	—	—	10

MOVE TUTOR LIST

Move Name	Type	ST	ACC	PP
Body Slam*	Normal	85	100	15
Defense Curl*	Normal	—	—	40
Double-Edge	Normal	120	100	15
Dynamicpunch	Fighting	100	50	5
Endure*	Normal	—	—	10
Explosion	Normal	250	100	5
Fury Cutter	Bug	10	95	20
Ice Punch*	Ice	75	100	15
Icy Wind*	Ice	55	95	15
Mimic	Normal	—	100	10
Mud-Slap*	Ground	20	100	10
Psych Up*	Normal	—	—	10
Rock Slide*	Rock	75	90	10
Rollout	Rock	30	90	20
Sleep Talk	Normal	—	—	10
Snore*	Normal	40	100	15
Substitute	Normal	—	—	10
Swagger	Normal	—	90	15
Swift*	Normal	60	—	20
Thunderpunch*	Electric	75	100	15

*Battle Frontier tutor move

193 Regirock™

ROCK

GENERAL INFO
SPECIES: Rock Peak Pokémon
HEIGHT: 5'7"
WEIGHT: 507 lbs.
ABILITY: *Clear Body*—Moves that lower Ability values don't affect the Pokémon.

STATS

Stat	Value
HP	50
ATTACK	75
DEFENSE	100
SP. ATTACK	50
SP. DEFENSE	75
SPEED	50

EVOLUTIONS

REGIROCK DOES NOT EVOLVE

WHERE/HOW TO CATCH
Desert Ruins

STRONG AGAINST:
NORMAL
FIRE
POISON
FLYING

WEAK AGAINST:
WATER
GRASS
FIGHTING
GROUND
STEEL

MOVES LIST

LV	Move Name	Type	ST	ACC	PP
S	Explosion	Normal	250	100	5
09	Rock Throw	Rock	50	90	15
17	Curse	—	—	—	10
25	Superpower	Fighting	120	100	5
33	Ancientpower	Rock	60	100	5
41	Iron Defense	Steel	—	—	15
49	Zap Cannon	Electric	100	50	5
57	Lock-On	Normal	—	100	5
65	Hyper Beam	Normal	150	90	5

TM/HM LIST

TM/HM #	Move Name	Type	ST	ACC	PP
HM04	Strength	Normal	80	100	15
HM06	Rock Smash	Fighting	20	100	15
TM01	Focus Punch	Fighting	150	100	20
TM06	Toxic	Poison	—	85	10
TM10	Hidden Power	Normal	—	100	15
TM11	Sunny Day	Fire	—	—	5
TM15	Hyper Beam	Normal	150	90	5
TM17	Protect	Normal	—	—	10
TM20	Safeguard	Normal	—	—	25
TM21	Frustration	Normal	—	100	20
TM24	Thunderbolt	Electric	95	100	15
TM25	Thunder	Electric	120	70	10
TM26	Earthquake	Ground	100	100	10
TM27	Return	Normal	—	100	20
TM28	Dig	Ground	60	100	10
TM31	Brick Break	Fighting	75	100	15
TM32	Double Team	Normal	—	—	15
TM34	Shock Wave	Electric	60	—	20
TM37	Sandstorm	Rock	—	—	10
TM39	Rock Tomb	Rock	50	80	10
TM42	Façade	Normal	70	100	20
TM43	Secret Power	Normal	70	100	20
TM44	Rest	Psychic	—	—	10

EGG MOVES

Move Name	Type	ST	ACC	PP
None				

MOVE TUTOR LIST

Move Name	Type	ST	ACC	PP
Body Slam*	Normal	85	100	15
Counter*	Fighting	—	100	20
Defense Curl*	Normal	—	—	40
Double-Edge	Normal	120	100	15
Dynamicpunch	Fighting	100	50	5
Endure*	Normal	—	—	10
Explosion	Normal	250	100	5
Fire Punch*	Fire	75	100	15
Ice Punch*	Ice	75	100	15
Mega Kick*	Normal	120	85	5
Mega Punch*	Normal	80	75	20
Mimic	Normal	—	100	10
Mud-Slap*	Ground	20	100	10
Psych Up*	Normal	—	—	10
Rock Slide*	Rock	75	90	10
Rollout	Rock	30	90	20
Seismic Toss*	Fighting	—	100	20
Sleep Talk	Normal	—	—	10
Snore*	Normal	40	100	15
Substitute	Normal	—	—	10
Swagger	Normal	—	90	15
Thunderpunch*	Electric	75	100	15
Thunder Wave*	Electric	—	100	20

*Battle Frontier tutor move

194 Regice™

ICE

GENERAL INFO
SPECIES: Iceberg Pokémon
HEIGHT: 5'11"
WEIGHT: 386 lbs.
ABILITY: *Clear Body*—Moves that lower Ability values don't affect the Pokémon.

STATS

Stat	Value
HP	50
ATTACK	50
DEFENSE	75
SP. ATTACK	75
SP. DEFENSE	100
SPEED	50

EVOLUTIONS

REGICE DOES NOT EVOLVE

WHERE/HOW TO CATCH
Island Cave

STRONG AGAINST:
ICE

WEAK AGAINST:
FIRE
FIGHTING
ROCK
STEEL

MOVES LIST

LV	Move Name	Type	ST	ACC	PP
S	Explosion	Normal	250	100	5
09	Icy Wind	Ice	55	95	15
17	Curse	—	—	—	10
25	Superpower	Fighting	120	100	5
33	Ancientpower	Rock	60	100	5
41	Amnesia	Psychic	—	—	20
49	Zap Cannon	Electric	100	50	5
57	Lock-On	Normal	—	100	5
65	Hyper Beam	Normal	150	90	5

TM/HM LIST

TM/HM #	Move Name	Type	ST	ACC	PP
HM04	Strength	Normal	80	100	15
HM06	Rock Smash	Fighting	20	100	15
TM01	Focus Punch	Fighting	150	100	20
TM06	Toxic	Poison	—	85	10
TM07	Hail	Ice	—	—	10
TM10	Hidden Power	Normal	—	100	15
TM13	Ice Beam	Ice	95	100	10
TM14	Blizzard	Ice	120	70	5
TM15	Hyper Beam	Normal	150	90	5
TM17	Protect	Normal	—	—	10
TM18	Rain Dance	Water	—	—	5
TM20	Safeguard	Normal	—	—	25
TM21	Frustration	Normal	—	100	20
TM24	Thunderbolt	Electric	95	100	15
TM25	Thunder	Electric	120	70	10
TM26	Earthquake	Ground	100	100	10
TM27	Return	Normal	—	100	20
TM31	Brick Break	Fighting	75	100	15
TM32	Double Team	Normal	—	—	15
TM34	Shock Wave	Electric	60	—	20
TM42	Façade	Normal	70	100	20
TM43	Secret Power	Normal	70	100	20
TM44	Rest	Psychic	—	—	10

EGG MOVES

Move Name	Type	ST	ACC	PP
None				

MOVE TUTOR LIST

Move Name	Type	ST	ACC	PP
Body Slam*	Normal	85	100	15
Counter*	Fighting	—	100	20
Defense Curl*	Normal	—	—	40
Double-Edge	Normal	120	100	15
Dynamicpunch	Fighting	100	50	5
Endure*	Normal	—	—	10
Explosion	Normal	250	100	5
Ice Punch*	Ice	75	100	15
Icy Wind*	Ice	55	95	15
Mega Kick*	Normal	120	85	5
Mega Punch*	Normal	80	75	20
Mimic	Normal	—	100	10
Mud-Slap*	Ground	20	100	10
Psych Up*	Normal	—	—	10
Rock Slide*	Rock	75	90	10
Rollout	Rock	30	90	20
Seismic Toss*	Fighting	—	100	20
Sleep Talk	Normal	—	—	10
Snore*	Normal	40	100	15
Substitute	Normal	—	—	10
Swagger	Normal	—	90	15
Thunderpunch*	Electric	75	100	15
Thunder Wave*	Electric	—	100	20

*Battle Frontier tutor move

195 Registeel™

STEEL

GENERAL INFO
SPECIES: Iron Pokémon
HEIGHT: 6'3"
WEIGHT: 452 lbs.
ABILITY: *Clear Body* — Moves that lower Ability values don't affect the Pokémon.

STATS

Stat	Value
HP	50
ATTACK	50
DEFENSE	100
SP. ATTACK	75
SP. DEFENSE	100
SPEED	50

EVOLUTIONS

REGISTEEL DOES NOT EVOLVE

WHERE/HOW TO CATCH
Ancient Tomb

STRONG AGAINST:
NORMAL
GRASS
ICE
POISON
FLYING
PSYCHIC
BUG
ROCK
GHOST
DRAGON
DARK
STEEL

WEAK AGAINST:
FIRE
FIGHTING
GROUND

MOVES LIST

LV	Move Name	Type	ST	ACC	PP
S	Explosion	Normal	250	100	5
09	Metal Claw	Steel	50	95	35
17	Curse	—	—	—	10
25	Superpower	Fighting	120	100	5
33	Ancientpower	Rock	60	100	5
41	Iron Defense	Steel	—	—	15
41	Amnesia	Psychic	—	—	20
49	Zap Cannon	Electric	100	50	5
57	Lock-On	Normal	—	100	5
65	Hyper Beam	Normal	150	90	5

TM/HM LIST

TM/HM #	Move Name	Type	ST	ACC	PP
HM04	Strength	Normal	80	100	15
HM06	Rock Smash	Fighting	20	100	15
TM01	Focus Punch	Fighting	150	100	20
TM06	Toxic	Poison	—	85	10
TM10	Hidden Power	Normal	—	100	15
TM11	Sunny Day	Fire	—	—	5
TM15	Hyper Beam	Normal	150	90	5
TM17	Protect	Normal	—	—	10
TM18	Rain Dance	Water	—	—	5
TM20	Safeguard	Normal	—	—	25
TM21	Frustration	Normal	—	100	20
TM24	Thunderbolt	Electric	95	100	15
TM25	Thunder	Electric	120	70	10
TM26	Earthquake	Ground	100	100	10
TM27	Return	Normal	—	100	20
TM31	Brick Break	Fighting	75	100	15
TM32	Double Team	Normal	—	—	15
TM34	Shock Wave	Electric	60	—	20
TM37	Sandstorm	Rock	—	—	10
TM39	Rock Tomb	Rock	50	80	10
TM40	Aerial Ace	Flying	60	—	20
TM42	Façade	Normal	70	100	20
TM43	Secret Power	Normal	70	100	20
TM44	Rest	Psychic	—	—	10

EGG MOVES

Move Name	Type	ST	ACC	PP
None				

MOVE TUTOR LIST

Move Name	Type	ST	ACC	PP
Body Slam*	Normal	85	100	15
Counter*	Fighting	—	100	20
Defense Curl*	Normal	—	—	40
Double-Edge	Normal	120	100	15
Dynamicpunch	Fighting	100	50	5
Endure*	Normal	—	—	10
Explosion	Normal	250	100	5
Ice Punch*	Ice	75	100	15
Mega Kick*	Normal	120	85	5
Mega Punch*	Normal	80	75	20
Mimic	Normal	—	100	10
Mud-Slap*	Ground	20	100	10
Psych Up*	Normal	—	—	10
Rock Slide*	Rock	75	90	10
Rollout	Rock	30	90	20
Seismic Toss*	Fighting	—	100	20
Sleep Talk	Normal	—	—	10
Snore*	Normal	40	100	15
Substitute	Normal	—	—	10
Swagger	Normal	—	90	15
Thunderpunch*	Electric	75	100	15
Thunder Wave*	Electric	—	100	20

*Battle Frontier tutor move

196 Latias™

DRAGON
PSYCHIC

GENERAL INFO
SPECIES: Eon Pokémon
HEIGHT: 4'7"
WEIGHT: 88 lbs.
ABILITY: *Levitate* — Pokémon is not affected by Ground-type Moves.

STATS

Stat	Value
HP	50
ATTACK	75
DEFENSE	50
SP. ATTACK	75
SP. DEFENSE	75
SPEED	75

EVOLUTIONS

LATIAS DOES NOT EVOLVE

WHERE/HOW TO CATCH
Random encounter in grass

STRONG AGAINST:
FIRE
WATER
ELECTRIC
GRASS
FIGHTING
PSYCHIC
GROUND

WEAK AGAINST:
ICE
BUG
GHOST
DRAGON
DARK

MOVES LIST

LV	Move Name	Type	ST	ACC	PP
S	Psywave	Psychic	—	80	15
05	Wish	Normal	—	100	10
10	Helping Hand	Normal	—	100	20
15	Safeguard	Normal	—	—	25
20	Dragonbreath	Dragon	60	100	20
25	Water Sport	Water	—	—	15
30	Refresh	Normal	—	100	20
35	Mist Ball	Psychic	70	100	5
40	Psychic	Psychic	90	100	10
45	Recover	Normal	—	—	20
50	Charm	Normal	—	100	20

TM/HM LIST

TM/HM #	Move Name	Type	ST	ACC	PP
HM01	Cut	Normal	50	95	30
HM02	Fly	Flying	70	95	15
HM03	Surf	Water	95	100	15
HM05	Flash	Normal	—	70	20
HM07	Waterfall	Water	80	100	15
HM08	Dive	Water	60	100	10
TM02	Dragon Claw	Dragon	80	100	15
TM03	Water Pulse	Water	60	100	20
TM04	Calm Mind	Psychic	—	—	20
TM05	Roar	Normal	—	100	20
TM06	Toxic	Poison	—	85	10
TM10	Hidden Power	Normal	—	100	15
TM11	Sunny Day	Fire	—	—	5
TM13	Ice Beam	Ice	95	100	10
TM15	Hyper Beam	Normal	150	90	5
TM16	Light Screen	Psychic	—	—	30
TM17	Protect	Normal	—	—	10
TM18	Rain Dance	Water	—	—	5
TM20	Safeguard	Normal	—	—	25
TM21	Frustration	Normal	—	100	20
TM22	Solarbeam	Grass	120	100	10
TM24	Thunderbolt	Electric	95	100	15
TM25	Thunder	Electric	120	70	10
TM26	Earthquake	Ground	100	100	10
TM27	Return	Normal	—	100	20
TM29	Psychic	Psychic	90	100	10
TM30	Shadow Ball	Ghost	60	—	20
TM32	Double Team	Normal	—	—	15
TM33	Reflect	Psychic	—	—	20
TM34	Shock Wave	Electric	60	—	20
TM37	Sandstorm	Rock	—	—	10
TM40	Aerial Ace	Flying	60	—	20
TM42	Façade	Normal	70	100	20
TM43	Secret Power	Normal	70	100	20
TM44	Rest	Psychic	—	—	10
TM45	Attract	Normal	—	100	15
TM47	Steel Wing	Steel	70	90	25

EGG MOVES

Move Name	Type	ST	ACC	PP
None				

MOVE TUTOR LIST

Move Name	Type	ST	ACC	PP
Body Slam*	Normal	85	100	15
Double-Edge	Normal	120	100	15
Dream Eater*	Psychic	100	100	15
Endure*	Normal	—	—	10
Fury Cutter*	Bug	10	95	20
Icy Wind*	Ice	55	95	15
Mimic	Normal	—	100	10
Mud-Slap*	Ground	20	100	10
Psych Up*	Normal	—	—	10
Sleep Talk	Normal	—	—	10
Snore*	Normal	40	100	15
Substitute	Normal	—	—	10
Swagger	Normal	—	90	15
Swift*	Normal	60	—	20
Thunder Wave*	Electric	—	100	20

*Battle Frontier tutor move

197

Latios™
DRAGON
PSYCHIC

GENERAL INFO
SPECIES: Eon Pokémon
HEIGHT: 6'7"
WEIGHT: 132 lbs.
ABILITY: *Levitate*— *Pokémon is not affected by Ground-type Moves.*

STATS

Stat	Value
HP	50
ATTACK	75
DEFENSE	50
SP. ATTACK	100
SP. DEFENSE	75
SPEED	75

EVOLUTIONS

LATIOS DOES NOT EVOLVE

WHERE/HOW TO CATCH
Random encounter in grass

STRONG AGAINST:
FIRE
WATER
ELECTRIC
GRASS
FIGHTING
PSYCHIC
GROUND

WEAK AGAINST:
ICE
BUG
GHOST
DRAGON
DARK

MOVES LIST

LV	Move Name	Type	ST	ACC	PP	LV	Move Name	Type	ST	ACC	PP
S	Psywave	Psychic	—	80	15	30	Refresh	Normal	—	100	20
05	Memento	Dark	—	100	10	35	Luster Purge	Psychic	70	100	5
10	Helping Hand	Normal	—	100	20	40	Psychic	Psychic	90	100	10
15	Safeguard	Normal	—	—	25	45	Recover	Normal	—	—	20
20	Dragonbreath	Dragon	60	100	20	50	Dragon Dance	Dragon	—	—	20
25	Protect	Normal	—	—	10						

TM/HM LIST

TM/HM #	Move Name	Type	ST	ACC	PP	TM/HM #	Move Name	Type	ST	ACC	PP
HM01	Cut	Normal	50	95	30	TM21	Frustration	Normal	—	100	20
HM02	Fly	Flying	70	95	15	TM22	Solarbeam	Grass	120	100	10
HM03	Surf	Water	95	100	15	TM24	Thunderbolt	Electric	95	100	15
HM05	Flash	Normal	—	70	20	TM25	Thunder	Electric	120	70	10
HM07	Waterfall	Water	80	100	15	TM26	Earthquake	Ground	100	100	10
HM08	Dive	Water	60	100	10	TM27	Return	Normal	—	100	20
TM02	Dragon Claw	Dragon	80	100	15	TM29	Psychic	Psychic	90	100	10
TM03	Water Pulse	Water	60	100	20	TM30	Shadow Ball	Ghost	60	—	20
TM04	Calm Mind	Psychic	—	—	20	TM32	Double Team	Normal	—	—	15
TM05	Roar	Normal	—	100	20	TM33	Reflect	Psychic	—	—	20
TM06	Toxic	Poison	—	85	10	TM34	Shock Wave	Electric	60	—	20
TM10	Hidden Power	Normal	—	100	15	TM37	Sandstorm	Rock	—	—	10
TM11	Sunny Day	Fire	—	—	5	TM40	Aerial Ace	Flying	60	—	20
TM13	Ice Beam	Ice	95	100	10	TM42	Façade	Normal	70	100	20
TM15	Hyper Beam	Normal	150	90	5	TM43	Secret Power	Normal	70	100	20
TM16	Light Screen	Psychic	—	—	30	TM44	Rest	Psychic	—	—	10
TM17	Protect	Normal	—	—	10	TM45	Attract	Normal	—	100	15
TM18	Rain Dance	Water	—	—	5	TM47	Steel Wing	Steel	70	90	25
TM20	Safeguard	Normal	—	—	25						

EGG MOVES

Move Name	Type	ST	ACC	PP
None				

MOVE TUTOR LIST

Move Name	Type	ST	ACC	PP
Body Slam*	Normal	85	100	15
Double-Edge	Normal	120	100	15
Dream Eater*	Psychic	100	100	15
Endure*	Normal	—	—	10
Fury Cutter	Bug	10	95	20
Icy Wind*	Ice	55	95	15
Mimic	Normal	—	100	10
Mud-Slap*	Ground	20	100	10
Psych Up*	Normal	—	—	10
Sleep Talk	Normal	—	—	10
Snore*	Normal	40	100	15
Substitute	Normal	—	—	10
Swagger	Normal	—	90	15
Swift*	Normal	60	—	20
Thunder Wave*	Electric	—	100	20

*Battle Frontier tutor move

198

Kyogre™
WATER

GENERAL INFO
SPECIES: Sea Basin Pokémon
HEIGHT: 14'9"
WEIGHT: 776 lbs.
ABILITY: *Drizzle*—*Causes rain to fall when the Pokémon enters battle.*

STATS

Stat	Value
HP	50
ATTACK	75
DEFENSE	50
SP. ATTACK	100
SP. DEFENSE	75
SPEED	75

EVOLUTIONS

KYOGRE DOES NOT EVOLVE

WHERE/HOW TO CATCH
Marine Cave

STRONG AGAINST:
FIRE
WATER
ICE
STEEL

WEAK AGAINST:
ELECTRIC
GRASS

MOVES LIST

LV	Move Name	Type	ST	ACC	PP	LV	Move Name	Type	ST	ACC	PP
S	Water Pulse	Water	60	100	20	45	Hydro Pump	Water	120	80	5
05	Scary Face	Normal	—	90	10	50	Rest	Psychic	—	—	10
15	Ancientpower	Rock	60	100	5	60	Sheer Cold	Ice	—	30	5
20	Body Slam	Normal	85	100	15	65	Double-Edge	Normal	120	100	15
30	Calm Mind	Psychic	—	—	20	75	Water Spout	Water	150	100	5
35	Ice Beam	Ice	95	100	10						

TM/HM LIST

TM/HM #	Move Name	Type	ST	ACC	PP	TM/HM #	Move Name	Type	ST	ACC	PP
HM03	Surf	Water	95	100	15	TM18	Rain Dance	Water	—	—	5
HM04	Strength	Normal	80	100	15	TM20	Safeguard	Normal	—	—	25
HM06	Rock Smash	Fighting	20	100	15	TM21	Frustration	Normal	—	100	20
HM07	Waterfall	Water	80	100	15	TM24	Thunderbolt	Electric	95	100	15
HM08	Dive	Water	60	100	10	TM25	Thunder	Electric	120	70	10
TM03	Water Pulse	Water	60	100	20	TM26	Earthquake	Ground	100	100	10
TM04	Calm Mind	Psychic	—	—	20	TM27	Return	Normal	—	100	20
TM05	Roar	Normal	—	100	20	TM31	Brick Break	Fighting	75	100	15
TM06	Toxic	Poison	—	85	10	TM32	Double Team	Normal	—	—	15
TM07	Hail	Ice	—	—	10	TM34	Shock Wave	Electric	60	—	20
TM10	Hidden Power	Normal	—	100	15	TM39	Rock Tomb	Rock	50	80	10
TM13	Ice Beam	Ice	95	100	10	TM42	Façade	Normal	70	100	20
TM14	Blizzard	Ice	120	70	5	TM43	Secret Power	Normal	70	100	20
TM15	Hyper Beam	Normal	150	90	5	TM44	Rest	Psychic	—	—	10
TM17	Protect	Normal	—	—	10						

EGG MOVES

Move Name	Type	ST	ACC	PP
None				

MOVE TUTOR LIST

Move Name	Type	ST	ACC	PP
Body Slam*	Normal	85	100	15
Defense Curl*	Normal	—	—	40
Double-Edge	Normal	120	100	15
Endure*	Normal	—	—	10
Icy Wind*	Ice	55	95	15
Mimic	Normal	—	100	10
Mud-Slap*	Ground	20	100	10
Psych Up*	Normal	—	—	10
Rock Slide*	Rock	75	90	10
Sleep Talk	Normal	—	—	10
Snore*	Normal	40	100	15
Substitute	Normal	—	—	10
Swagger	Normal	—	90	15
Swift*	Normal	60	—	20
Thunder Wave*	Electric	—	100	20

*Battle Frontier tutor move

199

Groudon™

GROUND

GENERAL INFO
SPECIES: Continent Pokémon
HEIGHT: 11'6"
WEIGHT: 2,095 lbs.
ABILITY: *Drought* — The sun shines when the Pokémon enters battle.

STATS

Stat	Value
HP	50
ATTACK	100
DEFENSE	75
SP. ATTACK	75
SP. DEFENSE	50
SPEED	75

EVOLUTIONS

GROUDON DOES NOT EVOLVE

WHERE/HOW TO CATCH
Terra Cave

STRONG AGAINST:
ELECTRIC
POISON
ROCK

WEAK AGAINST:
WATER
GRASS
ICE

MOVES LIST

LV	Move Name	Type	ST	ACC	PP
S	Mud Shot	Ground	55	95	15
05	Scary Face	Normal	—	90	10
15	Ancientpower	Rock	60	100	5
20	Slash	Normal	70	100	20
30	Bulk Up	Fighting	—	—	20
35	Earthquake	Ground	100	100	10

LV	Move Name	Type	ST	ACC	PP
45	Fire Blast	Fire	120	85	5
50	Rest	Psychic	—	—	10
60	Fissure	Ground	—	30	5
65	Solarbeam	Grass	120	100	10
75	Eruption	Fire	150	100	5

TM/HM LIST

TM/HM #	Move Name	Type	ST	ACC	PP
HM01	Cut	Normal	50	95	30
HM04	Strength	Normal	80	100	15
HM06	Rock Smash	Fighting	20	100	15
TM02	Dragon Claw	Dragon	80	100	15
TM05	Roar	Normal	—	100	20
TM06	Toxic	Poison	—	85	10
TM08	Bulk Up	Fighting	—	—	20
TM10	Hidden Power	Normal	—	100	15
TM11	Sunny Day	Fire	—	—	5
TM15	Hyper Beam	Normal	150	90	5
TM17	Protect	Normal	—	—	10
TM20	Safeguard	Normal	—	—	25
TM21	Frustration	Normal	—	100	20
TM22	Solarbeam	Grass	120	100	10
TM23	Iron Tail	Steel	100	75	15
TM24	Thunderbolt	Electric	95	100	15

TM/HM #	Move Name	Type	ST	ACC	PP
TM25	Thunder	Electric	120	70	10
TM26	Earthquake	Ground	100	100	10
TM27	Return	Normal	—	100	20
TM28	Dig	Ground	60	100	10
TM31	Brick Break	Fighting	75	100	15
TM32	Double Team	Normal	—	—	15
TM34	Shock Wave	Electric	60	—	20
TM35	Flamethrower	Fire	95	100	15
TM37	Sandstorm	Rock	—	—	10
TM38	Fire Blast	Fire	120	85	5
TM39	Rock Tomb	Rock	50	80	10
TM40	Aerial Ace	Flying	60	—	20
TM42	Façade	Normal	70	100	20
TM43	Secret Power	Normal	70	100	20
TM44	Rest	Psychic	—	—	10
TM50	Overheat	Fire	140	90	5

EGG MOVES

Move Name	Type	ST	ACC	PP
None				

MOVE TUTOR LIST

Move Name	Type	ST	ACC	PP
Body Slam*	Normal	85	100	15
Counter*	Fighting	—	100	20
Defense Curl*	Normal	—	—	40
Double-Edge	Normal	120	100	15
Dynamicpunch	Fighting	100	50	5
Endure*	Normal	—	—	10
Fire Punch*	Fire	75	100	15
Fury Cutter*	Bug	10	95	20
Mega Kick*	Normal	120	85	5
Mega Punch*	Normal	80	75	20
Mimic*	Normal	—	100	10
Mud-Slap*	Ground	20	100	10
Psych Up*	Normal	—	—	10
Rock Slide*	Rock	75	90	10
Rollout	Rock	30	90	20
Seismic Toss*	Fighting	—	100	20
Sleep Talk	Normal	—	—	10
Snore*	Normal	40	100	15
Substitute*	Normal	—	—	10
Swagger	Normal	—	90	15
Swift*	Normal	60	—	20
Thunderpunch*	Electric	75	100	15
Thunder Wave*	Electric	—	100	20

*Battle Frontier tutor move

200

Rayquaza™

DRAGON
FLYING

GENERAL INFO
SPECIES: Sky High Pokémon
HEIGHT: 23'0"
WEIGHT: 455 lbs.
ABILITY: *Air Lock* — Makes weather effects disappear.

STATS

Stat	Value
HP	50
ATTACK	100
DEFENSE	50
SP. ATTACK	100
SP. DEFENSE	100
SPEED	75

EVOLUTIONS

RAYQUAZA DOES NOT EVOLVE

WHERE/HOW TO CATCH
Sky Pillar

STRONG AGAINST:
FIRE
WATER
GRASS
FIGHTING
GROUND
BUG

WEAK AGAINST:
ICE
ROCK
DRAGON

MOVES LIST

LV	Move Name	Type	ST	ACC	PP
S	Twister	Dragon	40	100	20
05	Scary Face	Normal	—	90	10
15	Ancientpower	Rock	60	100	5
20	Dragon Claw	Dragon	80	100	15
30	Dragon Dance	Dragon	—	—	20
35	Crunch	Dark	80	100	15

LV	Move Name	Type	ST	ACC	PP
45	Fly	Flying	70	95	15
50	Rest	Psychic	—	—	10
60	Extremespeed	Normal	80	100	5
65	Outrage	Dragon	90	100	15
75	Hyper Beam	Normal	150	90	5

TM/HM LIST

TM/HM #	Move Name	Type	ST	ACC	PP
HM02	Fly	Flying	70	95	15
HM03	Surf	Water	95	100	15
HM04	Strength	Normal	80	100	15
HM06	Rock Smash	Fighting	20	100	15
HM07	Waterfall	Water	80	100	15
HM08	Dive	Water	60	100	10
TM02	Dragon Claw	Dragon	80	100	15
TM03	Water Pulse	Water	60	100	20
TM05	Roar	Normal	—	100	20
TM06	Toxic	Poison	—	85	10
TM08	Bulk Up	Fighting	—	—	20
TM10	Hidden Power	Normal	—	100	15
TM11	Sunny Day	Fire	—	—	5
TM13	Ice Beam	Ice	95	100	10
TM14	Blizzard	Ice	120	70	5
TM15	Hyper Beam	Normal	150	90	5
TM17	Protect	Normal	—	—	10
TM18	Rain Dance	Water	—	—	5

TM/HM #	Move Name	Type	ST	ACC	PP
TM21	Frustration	Normal	—	100	20
TM22	Solarbeam	Grass	120	100	10
TM23	Iron Tail	Steel	100	75	15
TM24	Thunderbolt	Electric	95	100	15
TM25	Thunder	Electric	120	70	10
TM26	Earthquake	Ground	100	100	10
TM27	Return	Normal	—	100	20
TM31	Brick Break	Fighting	75	100	15
TM32	Double Team	Normal	—	—	15
TM34	Shock Wave	Electric	60	—	20
TM35	Flamethrower	Fire	95	100	15
TM37	Sandstorm	Rock	—	—	10
TM38	Fire Blast	Fire	120	85	5
TM40	Aerial Ace	Flying	60	—	20
TM42	Façade	Normal	70	100	20
TM43	Secret Power	Normal	70	100	20
TM44	Rest	Psychic	—	—	10
TM50	Overheat	Fire	140	90	5

EGG MOVES

Move Name	Type	ST	ACC	PP
None				

MOVE TUTOR LIST

Move Name	Type	ST	ACC	PP
Body Slam*	Normal	85	100	15
Double-Edge	Normal	120	100	15
Endure*	Normal	—	—	10
Fury Cutter*	Bug	10	95	20
Icy Wind*	Ice	55	95	15
Mimic*	Normal	—	100	10
Mud-Slap*	Ground	20	100	10
Psych Up*	Normal	—	—	10
Rock Slide*	Rock	75	90	10
Sleep Talk	Normal	—	—	10
Snore*	Normal	40	100	15
Substitute*	Normal	—	—	10
Swagger	Normal	—	90	15
Swift*	Normal	60	—	20
Thunder Wave*	Electric	—	100	20

*Battle Frontier tutor move

201 Jirachi™

STEEL
PSYCHIC

GENERAL INFO
SPECIES: Wish Pokémon
HEIGHT: 0'11"
WEIGHT: 2.42 lbs.
ABILITY: *Serene Grace—Moves that have extra Effects occur more frequently when Pokémon attacks.*

STATS
HP	100
ATTACK	100
DEFENSE	100
SP. ATTACK	100
SP. DEFENSE	100
SPEED	100

EVOLUTIONS

JIRACHI DOES NOT EVOLVE

WHERE/HOW TO CATCH
Trade from *Pokémon Colosseum* bonus pre-order disc

STRONG AGAINST:
NORMAL
GRASS
ICE
POISON
FLYING
ROCK

WEAK AGAINST:
FIRE
FIGHTING
GROUND

MOVES LIST

LV	Move Name	Type	ST	ACC	PP	LV	Move Name	Type	ST	ACC	PP
S	Wish	Normal	—	100	10	25	Refresh	Normal	—	100	20
S	Confusion	Psychic	50	100	25	30	Rest	Psychic	—	—	10
5	Rest	Psychic	—	—	10	35	Double-Edge	Normal	120	100	15
10	Swift	Normal	60	—	20	40	Future Sight	Normal	—	—	15
15	Helping Hand	Normal	—	100	20	45	Cosmic Power	Normal	—	—	20
20	Psychic	Psychic	90	100	10	50	Doom Desire	Steel	120	85	5

TM/HM LIST

TM/HM #	Move Name	Type	ST	ACC	PP	TM/HM #	Move Name	Type	ST	ACC	PP
HM05	Flash	Normal	—	70	20	TM27	Return	Normal	—	100	20
TM03	Water Pulse	Water	60	100	20	TM29	Psychic	Psychic	90	100	10
TM04	Calm Mind	Psychic	—	—	20	TM30	Shadow Ball	Ghost	80	100	15
TM06	Toxic	Poison	—	85	10	TM32	Double Team	Normal	—	—	15
TM10	Hidden Power	Normal	—	100	15	TM33	Reflect	Normal	—	—	20
TM11	Sunny Day	Fire	—	—	5	TM34	Shock Wave	Electric	60	—	20
TM15	Hyper Beam	Normal	150	90	5	TM37	Sandstorm	Ground	—	—	10
TM16	Light Screen	Psychic	—	—	30	TM40	Aerial Ace	Flying	60	—	20
TM17	Protect	Normal	—	—	10	TM42	Facade	Normal	70	100	20
TM18	Rain Dance	Water	—	—	5	TM43	Secret Power	Normal	70	100	20
TM20	Safeguard	Normal	—	—	25	TM44	Rest	Psychic	—	—	10
TM21	Frustration	Normal	—	100	20	TM45	Attract	Normal	—	100	15
TM24	Thunderbolt	Electric	95	100	15	TM48	Skill Swap	Psychic	—	100	10
TM25	Thunder	Electric	120	70	10						

EGG MOVES

Move Name	Type	ST	ACC	PP
None				

MOVE TUTOR LIST

Move Name	Type	ST	ACC	PP
Body Slam*	Normal	85	100	15
Defense Curl*	Normal	—	—	40
Double-Edge	Normal	120	100	15
Dream Eater*	Psychic	100	100	15
Dynamicpunch	Fighting	100	50	5
Endure*	Normal	—	—	10
Fire Punch*	Fire	75	100	15
Ice Punch*	Ice	75	100	15
Icy Wind*	Ice	55	95	15
Mimic	Normal	—	100	10
Mud-Slap*	Ground	20	100	10
Psych Up*	Normal	—	—	10
Sleep Talk	Normal	—	—	10
Snore*	Normal	40	100	15
Substitute	Normal	—	—	10
Swagger	Normal	—	90	15
Swift*	Normal	60	—	20
Thunderpunch*	Electric	75	100	15
Thunder Wave*	Electric	—	100	20

*Battle Frontier tutor move

202 Deoxys™ (Speed Forme)

PSYCHIC

GENERAL INFO
SPECIES: DNA Pokémon
HEIGHT: 5'5"
WEIGHT: 134 lbs.
ABILITY: *Pressure— Opponent Pokémon uses double PP when attacking.*

STATS
HP	50
ATTACK	95
DEFENSE	90
SP. ATTACK	95
SP. DEFENSE	90
SPEED	100

EVOLUTIONS

DEOXYS DOES NOT EVOLVE

WHERE/HOW TO CATCH
Trade from *Pokémon FireRed/LeafGreen*, only caught via special live events

STRONG AGAINST:
FIGHTING
PSYCHIC

WEAK AGAINST:
BUG
GHOST
DARK

MOVES LIST

LV	Move Name	Type	ST	ACC	PP	LV	Move Name	Type	ST	ACC	PP
5	Night Shade	Ghost	—	100	15	35	Agility	Psychic	—	—	30
10	Double Team	Normal	—	—	15	40	Recover	Normal	—	—	20
15	Knock Off	Dark	20	100	20	45	Psycho Boost	Psychic	140	90	5
20	Pursuit	Dark	40	100	20	50	Extremespeed	Normal	80	100	5
25	Psychic	Psychic	90	100	10						
30	Swift	Normal	60	—	20						

TM/HM LIST

TM/HM #	Move Name	Type	ST	ACC	PP	TM/HM #	Move Name	Type	ST	ACC	PP
HM01	Cut	Normal	50	95	30	TM21	Frustration	Normal	—	100	20
HM04	Strength	Normal	80	100	15	TM22	Solarbeam	Grass	120	100	10
HM05	Flash	Normal	—	70	20	TM24	Thunderbolt	Electric	95	100	15
HM06	Rock Smash	Fighting	20	100	15	TM25	Thunder	Electric	120	70	10
TM01	Focus Punch	Fighting	150	100	20	TM27	Return	Normal	—	100	20
TM03	Water Pulse	Water	60	100	20	TM29	Psychic	Psychic	90	100	10
TM04	Calm Mind	Psychic	—	—	20	TM30	Shadow Ball	Ghost	60	—	20
TM06	Toxic	Poison	—	85	10	TM31	Brick Break	Fighting	75	100	15
TM10	Hidden Power	Normal	—	100	15	TM32	Double Team	Normal	—	—	15
TM11	Sunny Day	Fire	—	—	5	TM39	Rock Tomb	Rock	50	80	10
TM12	Taunt	Dark	—	100	20	TM40	Aerial Ace	Flying	60	—	20
TM13	Ice Beam	Ice	95	100	10	TM41	Torment	Dark	—	100	15
TM15	Hyper Beam	Normal	150	90	5	TM42	Facade	Normal	70	100	20
TM16	Light Screen	Psychic	—	—	30	TM43	Secret Power	Normal	70	100	20
TM17	Protect	Normal	—	—	10	TM44	Rest	Psychic	—	—	10
TM18	Rain Dance	Water	—	—	5	TM48	Skill Swap	Psychic	—	100	10
TM20	Safeguard	Normal	—	—	25	TM49	Snatch	Dark	—	100	10

EGG MOVES

Move Name	Type	ST	ACC	PP
None				

MOVE TUTOR LIST

Move Name	Type	ST	ACC	PP
Body Slam*	Normal	85	100	15
Counter*	Fighting	—	100	20
Double-Edge*	Normal	120	100	15
Dream Eater*	Psychic	100	100	15
Dynamicpunch	Fighting	100	50	5
Endure*	Normal	—	—	10
Fire Punch*	Fire	75	100	15
Ice Punch*	Ice	75	100	15
Icy Wind*	Ice	55	95	15
Mimic	Normal	—	100	10
Mega Kick*	Normal	120	85	5
Mega Punch*	Normal	80	75	20
Mud-Slap*	Ground	20	100	10
Rock Slide*	Rock	75	90	10
Seismic Toss*	Fighting	—	100	20
Sleep Talk	Normal	—	—	10
Snore*	Normal	40	100	15
Substitute	Normal	—	—	10
Swagger	Normal	—	90	15
Swift*	Normal	60	—	20
Thunder Wave*	Electric	—	100	20
Thunderpunch*	Electric	75	100	15

*Battle Frontier tutor move

Complete Moves Lists

The Pokémon of the Hoenn region are familiar with many of the moves known by those in Johto and Kanto, but these indigenous Pokémon also know a fair number of exclusive moves. The lists included here detail the moves Pokémon know naturally at inception and those they learn during natural Evolution, as well as those you teach with Hidden Machines (HM) or Technical Machines (TM). There is also a dedicated list that details the moves used in Pokémon Contests and what kind of effects they will have on the attending audience and contest judges.

Field and Battle Moves List

ST = Strength	Range = Whom the move affects in 2-on-2 Battles. The abbreviations used mean: 1E = 1 Enemy; 2E = 2 Enemies; RE = Random Enemy; 1A/2E = 1 Ally and 2 Enemies (i.e., everyone but the caster); S/E = Self and Enemy.
ACC = Accuracy	
PP = Power Points	PA? = Is the move a Physical Attack?
	TM/HM = Does the move have a TM or HM number?

Name	Type	ST	ACC	PP	Range	PA?	TM/HM	Description
Absorb	Grass	20	100	20	S/E	N		The Pokémon recovers half the damage amount that the opponent Pokémon receives from this Attack.
Acid	Poison	40	100	30	2E	N		Has a 10% chance of lowering opponent's Defense by one point.
Acid Armor	Poison	—	—	40	Self	N		Raises the Pokémon's Defense by two points.
Aerial Ace	Flying	60	—	20	1E	Y	TM40	This Attack is always successful.
Aeroblast	Flying	100	95	5	1E	Y		High probability of critical hit.
Agility	Psychic	—	—	30	Self	N		Raises the Pokémon's Speed by two.
Air Cutter	Flying	55	95	25	2E	N		Attack Move with a high Critical Hit ratio.
Amnesia	Psychic	—	—	20	1E	N		Raises the Pokémon's Special Defense by two points.
Ancientpower	Rock	60	100	5	S/E	Y		Has a 10% chance of raising all of the Pokémon's abilities by one point.
Arm Thrust	Fighting	15	100	20	1E	Y		Attacks 2—5 times in one turn.
Aromatherapy	Grass	—	—	5	All Allies	N		Cures the status abnormalities of allied Pokémon.
Assist	Normal	—	100	20	—	N		This move randomly chooses one of the opponent Pokémon's moves.
Astonish	Ghost	30	100	15	1E	Y		30% chance of making the opponent Flinch, nullifying its first move.
Attract	Normal	—	100	15	1E	N	TM45	Affects Pokémon of the opposite sex. Prevents the opponent Pokémon from Attacking with a 50% probability.
Aurora Beam	Ice	65	100	20	1E	N		Has a 10% chance of lowering the opponent's Attack by one point.
Barrage	Normal	15	85	20	1E	Y		Attacks 2—5 times consecutively in one turn.
Barrier	Psychic	—	—	30	Self	N		Increases the Pokémon's Defense by two points.
Baton Pass	Normal	—	—	40	Allies	N		Changes out the casting Pokémon for one of the other allied Pokémon. The substitute Pokémon inherits any beneficial Support Effects gained. The move fails if you don't have any Pokémon with which to alternate.
Beat Up	Dark	10	100	10	1E	N		Attacks opponent a number of times equal to your number of healthy Pokémon.
Belly Drum	Normal	—	—	10	Self	N		Raises Attack to its maximum level, but in return it decreases the Pokémon's max HP by one-half.
Bide	Normal	—	100	10	S/E	Y		Attack continues for 2—3 turns, and the damage received from the opponent during that time is returned doubled.
Bind	Normal	15	75	20	1E	Y		Consecutive Attack for 2—5 turns. Opponent cannot flee until the move has completed.
Bite	Dark	60	100	25	1E	Y		Causes opponent to Flinch with 30% probability.
Blast Burn	Fire	150	90	5	1E	N		A high-level Elemental Attack.
Blaze Kick	Fire	85	90	10	1E	Y		10% chance of Burning the opponent. High Critical Hit ratio. Cures Frozen Pokémon.
Blizzard	Ice	120	70	5	2E	N	TM14	10% additional chance of Freezing the opponent.
Block	Normal	—	100	5	1E	N		Prevents the opponent from fleeing or being switched out of battle.
Body Slam	Normal	85	100	15	1E	Y		30% additional Effect of Paralysis.
Bone Club	Ground	65	85	20	1E	Y		10% chance of making an opponent back off.
Bone Rush	Ground	25	80	10	1E	Y		Attacks 2—5 times consecutively in one turn.
Bonemerang	Ground	50	90	10	1E	Y		Attacks twice in a row in one turn.
Bounce	Flying	85	85	5	S/E	Y		On the first turn, the Pokémon bounces into the air. On the second turn, the Attack takes place. 30% chance of inflicting Paralysis on the opponent.
Brick Break	Fighting	75	100	15	1E	N	TM31	Defeats the Effects of Reflect and Light Screen.
Bubble	Water	20	100	30	2E	N		10% probability of lowering the opponent Pokémon's Speed.
Bubblebeam	Water	65	100	20	1E	N		10% additional chance of lowering the opponent Pokémon's Speed.
Bulk Up	Fighting	—	—	20	Self	N	TM08	Raises your Attack and Defense by two.
Bullet Seed	Grass	10	100	30	1E	N	TM09	Attacks 2—5 times in one turn.
Calm Mind	Psychic	—	—	20	Self	N	TM04	Raises the Pokémon's Special Attack and Special Defense by one.
Camouflage	Normal	—	100	20	Self	N		Pokémon's type is changed to a type that corresponds to the battlefield terrain (e.g., on grasslands, Pokémon becomes a Grass-type; sand = Ground-type; on sea or underwater = Water-type).

215

Name	Type	ST	ACC	PP	Range	PA?	TM/HM	Description
Charge	Electric	—	100	20	Self	N		The turn after using the move, Electric-type Moves are doubled in strength.
Charm	Normal	—	100	20	1E	N		Lowers the opponent Pokémon's Attack by two points.
Clamp	Water	35	75	10	1E	Y		Attacks over 2–5 consecutive turns, during which the opponent can't flee.
Comet Punch	Normal	18	85	15	1E	Y		Attacks 2–5 times consecutively in one turn.
Confuse Ray	Ghost	—	100	10	1E	N		Confuses opponent.
Confusion	Psychic	50	100	25	1E	N		10% additional Effect of Confusion.
Constrict	Normal	10	100	35	1E	Y		Lowers the opponent Pokémon's Speed by one point with a 10% probability.
Conversion	Normal	—	—	30	S/E	Y		Changes your type into one of your Attack types.
Conversion 2	Normal	—	100	30	S/E	Y		Changes your type into one that your opponent's Attack is weak against.
Cosmic Power	Normal	—	—	20	Self	N		Raises the Pokémon's Defense and Special Defense by one.
Cotton Spore	Grass	—	85	40	1E	N		Lowers the opponent Pokémon's Speed by two points.
Counter	Fighting	—	100	20	S/E	Y		Attacks second in battle and inflicts twice as much damage as long as the opponent uses a Physical Attack.
Covet	Normal	40	100	40	S/E	N		Allows you to grab and hold onto the Item the opponent is holding.
Crabhammer	Water	90	85	10	1E	Y		Dousing Move has a high Critical Hit ratio.
Cross Chop	Fighting	100	80	5	1E	Y		Makes it easier to produce a Critical Hit.
Crunch	Dark	80	100	15	1E	Y		Lowers the opponent Pokémon's Special Defense by one point with a 20% probability.
Crush Claw	Normal	75	95	10	1E	Y		50% chance of lowering the opponent's Defense.
Curse	—	—	—	10	S/E	N		Raises the Pokémon's Attack and Defense by one point and lowers the Pokémon's Speed by one point. If cast by a Ghost-type Pokémon, it decreases its own HP by half and Curses the opponent Pokémon. Each turn, a Cursed Pokémon loses up to 25% of its HP.
Cut	Normal	50	95	30	1E	Y	HM01	Normal Attack. Outside of battle, this cuts down thin trees.
Defense Curl	Normal	—	—	40	Self	N		Raises the Pokémon's Defense by one.
Destiny Bond	Ghost	—	—	5	S/E	N		After using this skill, if your Pokémon faints, the opponent Pokémon does, too.
Detect	Fighting	—	—	5	Self	N		Allows you to evade Attack this turn. Success rate decreases with each consecutive use.
Dig	Ground	60	100	10	1E	Y	TM28	Digs a hole during first turn, Attacks on second turn. Outside of battle, use this skill to escape from caves.
Disable	Normal	—	55	20	1E	N		Disables the skill the opponent Pokémon just used for a number of turns.
Dive	Water	60	100	10	1E	Y	HM08	On the first turn, the Pokémon dives underwater, and on the second turn, it Attacks. Outside of battle, use this to dive underwater and re-surface.
Dizzy Punch	Normal	70	100	10	1E	Y		20% additional chance of Confusing the opponent.
Doom Desire	Steel	120	85	5	1E	Y		Waits two turns, then inflicts damage oon foe on the third turn.
Double Kick	Fighting	30	100	30	1E	Y		Pokémon's Attack hits twice in one turn.
Double Team	Normal	—	—	15	Self	N	TM32	Raises the Pokémon's Evasiveness by one point.
Double-Edge	Normal	120	100	15	S/E	Y		Attacks with recoil. The casting Pokémon receives 33% of the damage inflicted on the opponent.
Doubleslap	Normal	15	85	10	1E	Y		Attack 2–5 times in one turn.
Dragon Claw	Dragon	80	100	15	1E	Y	TM02	Normal Attack.
Dragon Dance	Dragon	—	—	20	Self	N		Raises both Speed and Attack.
Dragon Rage	Dragon	—	100	10	1E	N		Does 40 points of damage, regardless of the Pokémon's abilities.
Dragonbreath	Dragon	60	100	20	1E	N		Paralyzes opponent with a 30% probability.
Dream Eater	Psychic	100	100	15	S/E	N		This Effect works only on Sleeping Pokémon. The Pokémon recovers half of the HP damage inflicted.
Drill Peck	Flying	80	100	20	1E	Y		A basic Flying-type Attack.
Dynamicpunch	Fighting	100	50	5	1E	Y		If the skill hits, the opponent becomes Confused.
Earthquake	Ground	100	100	10	1A/2E	N	TM26	Normal Attack. Has no Effect against Flight types, while the strength of the Attack is doubled against Pokémon using the move Dig.
Egg Bomb	Normal	100	75	10	—	Y		Normal Attack.
Ember	Fire	40	100	25	1E	N		10% additional chance of Burning the opponent. Cures Frozen Pokémon.
Encore	Normal	—	100	5	1E	N		Makes the opponent Pokémon repeat the last skill used for 3–6 turns.
Endeavor	Normal	—	100	5	1E	Y		Reduces the opponent's HP to the same level as yours if its total HP are higher than yours.
Endure	Normal	—	—	10	Self	N		Pokémon always survives with 1 HP, regardless of Attack. Repeated use lowers the success rate.
Eruption	Fire	150	100	5	2E	N		The lower your HP, the lesser the move's power becomes.
Explosion	Normal	250	100	5	All	N		The opponent Pokémon faints after the devastating Attack is finished.
Extrasensory	Psychic	80	100	30	1E	Y		10% chance that the opponent will Flinch.
Extremespeed	Normal	80	100	5	1E	Y		Attack always hits first. If both Pokémon use this, it works for the one with the highest Speed.
Façade	Normal	70	100	20	1E	Y	TM42	The strength of this skill is doubled when you are either Poisoned, Paralyzed, or Burned.
Faint Attack	Dark	60	—	20	1E	N		Attack hits opponent without fail.
Fake Out	Normal	40	100	10	1E	N		Pokémon Attacks first and the Attack has a 100% chance of making the opponent Flinch. However, casting Pokémon cannot Attack first on the starting turn.
Fake Tears	Dark	—	100	20	1E	N		Lowers the opponent's Special Defense by 2.
False Swipe	Normal	40	100	40	1E	Y		Leaves the opponent with 1 HP without fail. (You cannot defeat a Pokémon with this skill.)
Featherdance	Flying	—	100	15	1E	N		Lowers the opponent's Attack by two.

Name	Type	ST	ACC	PP	Range	PA?	TM/HM	Description
Fire Blast	Fire	120	85	5	1E	N	TM38	10% additional chance of Burning the opponent Pokémon.
Fire Punch	Fire	75	100	15	1E	Y		10% additional chance of Burning the opponent Pokémon. Cures Frozen Pokémon.
Fire Spin	Fire	15	70	15	1E	N		Pokémon consecutively Attacks for 2–5 turns. Opponent Pokémon cannot flee. Cures Frozen Pokémon.
Fissure	Ground	—	30	5	1E	N		Defeats the opponent with one Attack. Doesn't work against Flying-types.
Flail	Normal	—	100	15	1E	Y		Inflicts more damage the lower the Pokémon's HP.
Flamethrower	Fire	95	100	15	1E	N	TM35	10% chance of burning the opponent. Cures Frozen Pokémon.
Flame Wheel	Fire	60	100	25	IE	Y		10% chance of Burning opponent; ice is melted if opponent is frozen.
Flash	Normal	—	70	20	1E	N	HM05	Lowers opponent's Accuracy by one point. When used outside of battle, this illuminates dark caves.
Flatter	Dark	—	100	15	1E	N		Confuses the opponent but raises its Special Attack by one.
Fly	Flying	70	95	15	1E	Y	HM02	Fly into the air on Turn 1 and Attack on Turn 2. Outside of battle, use this skill to fly to the cities you've visited.
Focus Energy	Normal	—	—	30	Self	N		Raises the possibility that the casting Pokémon's next Attack will make a Critical Hit.
Focus Punch	Fighting	150	100	20	S/E	N	TM01	Attacks from behind without fail. When you take damage from the opponent, you Flinch and cannot Attack.
Follow Me	Normal	—	100	20	Self	N		Casting Pokémon takes over the move the opponent uses in that turn, becoming its teacher.
Foresight	Normal	—	100	40	1E	N		Opponent's Evasiveness returns to normal. Fighting and Normal Attacks become effective against Ghost-type Pokémon.
Frustration	Normal	—	100	20	1E	Y	TM21	The more the Pokémon dislikes you, the higher the move's Attack strength.
Fury Attack	Normal	15	85	20	1E	Y		Attacks 2–5 times consecutively in one turn.
Fury Cutter	Bug	10	95	20	1E	Y		The strength of this skill doubles with each consecutive turn it is successfully used. It returns to normal when you stop using it or a hit misses.
Fury Swipes	Normal	18	80	15	1E	Y		Attacks 2–5 times consecutively in one turn.
Future Sight	Psychic	80	90	15	1E	N		Psychic-type Move Attacks the opponent Pokémon after two turns.
Giga Drain	Grass	60	100	5	S/E	N	TM19	The Pokémon recovers half the amount of damage the opponent Pokémon receives from this Attack.
Glare	Normal	—	75	30	1E	N		Paralyzes opponent Pokémon.
Grasswhistle	Grass	—	55	15	1E	N		Puts opponent Pokémon to Sleep.
Growl	Normal	—	100	40	2E	N		Lowers the opponent's Attack by one point.
Growth	Normal	—	—	40	Self	N		Raises the Pokémon's Special Attack by one.
Grudge	Ghost	—	100	5	S/E	N		Reduces to 0 the number of PP of the move an opponent uses to make your Pokémon faint.
Guillotine	Normal	—	30	5	1E	Y		In one blow, you knock out the opponent. Move has no effect if the opponent's level is higher than casting Pokémon, but it has a higher chance of succeeding if the opponent's level is lower than yours.
Gust	Flying	40	100	35	1E	N		Normal Attack. Damage is doubled when used against a Pokémon using Fly.
Hail	Ice	—	—	10	All	N	TM07	Summons a hailstorm that lasts for five turns. At the end of each turn it causes damage to all non–Ice-type Pokémon active in the battle.
Harden	Normal	—	—	30	Self	N		Raises the Pokémon's Defense by one point.
Haze	Ice	—	—	30	All	N		Returns all status anomalies (the casting Pokémon's and the opponent Pokémon's) to normal.
Headbutt	Normal	70	100	15	1E	Y		30% chance of causing the opponent to Flinch.
Heal Bell	Normal	—	—	5	All Allies	N		Recovers all of an ally's status anomalies.
Heat Wave	Fire	100	90	10	2E	N		10% chance of Burning the opponent. Cures Frozen Pokémon.
Helping Hand	Normal	—	100	20	All Allies	N		Move increases the Attack strength of your ally's move by 1.5.
Hi Jump Kick	Fighting	85	90	20	S/E	Y		If this Attack fails, casting Pokémon receives 25% of the possible damage inflicted.
Hidden Power	Normal	—	100	15	1E	N	TM10	Changes type and power based on the Pokémon using it.
Horn Attack	Normal	65	100	25	1E	Y		Normal Attack.
Horn Drill	Normal	—	30	5	1E	Y		In one blow, the opponent is knocked out. Does not affect Pokémon whose levels are higher than yours, while the chance of success is greater against Pokémon with lower levels.
Howl	Normal	—	—	40	Self	N		Raises your Attack by one point.
Hydro Cannon	Water	150	90	5	1E	N		High-level Water attack, but user cannot move during next turn.
Hydro Pump	Water	120	80	5	1E	N		Normal Water-type Attack.
Hyper Beam	Normal	150	90	5	1E	N	TM15	Inflicts a large amount of damage, but the Pokémon cannot Attack on the next turn.
Hyper Fang	Normal	80	90	15	1E	Y		10% chance of making an opponent back off.
Hyper Voice	Normal	90	100	10	2E	N		Normal Attack.
Hypnosis	Psychic	—	60	20	1E	N		Puts opponent to Sleep.
Ice Ball	Ice	30	90	20	1E	Y		Attack lasts more than five turns or until it misses. Damage increases every turn the Attack succeeds.
Ice Beam	Ice	95	100	10	1E	N	TM13	10% additional Effect of Freezing the Pokémon's opponent.
Ice Punch	Ice	75	100	15	1E	N		10% additional Effect of Freezing the Pokémon's opponent.
Icicle Spear	Ice	10	100	30	1E	N		High-level Ice Attack for Shelder.
Icy Wind	Ice	55	95	15	2E	N		Lowers the opponent Pokémon's Speed by one point.
Imprison	Psychic	—	100	15	S/E	N		If you know one of your opponent Pokémon's moves, it cannot use it in the battle.
Ingrain	Grass	—	100	20	Self	N		Each turn, you recover a few HP, but casting Pokémon cannot switch with a reserve Pokémon.
Iron Defense	Steel	—	—	15	Self	N		Raises casting Pokémon's Defense by two.
Iron Tail	Steel	100	75	15	1E	Y	TM23	30% probability that it will lower the opponent Pokémon's Defense one level.
Jump Kick	Fighting	70	95	25	1E	Y		If an Attack misses, receive 1/8 of the damage that it would have caused.
Karate Chop	Fighting	50	100	25	1E	Y		Makes it easier to produce a Critical Hit.
Kinesis	Psychic	—	80	15	1E	N		Lowers opponent's Accuracy by one point.
Knock Off	Dark	20	100	20	1E	Y		When hit, the opponent drops the Item it is holding, losing its effect. After the battle, the Item is returned.
Leaf Blade	Grass	70	100	15	1E	Y		Makes it easy to produce a Critical Hit.

Name	Type	ST	ACC	PP	Range	PA?	TM/HM	Description
Leech Life	Bug	20	100	15	S/E	Y		The Pokémon recovers half of the amount of damage that the opponent Pokémon receives from this Attack.
Leech Seed	Grass	—	90	10	S/E	N		Absorbs opponent's HP with each turn and recovers part of the HP absorbed. This Effect continues even after the opponent's Pokémon is changed.
Leer	Normal	—	100	30	2E	N		Lowers opponent's Defense by one point.
Lick	Ghost	20	100	30	1E	Y		Additional Effect of Paralysis (30%).
Light Screen	Psychic	—	—	30	Self	N	TM16	Halves the damage from Special Attacks for five turns. The Effect continues after changing Pokémon.
Lock-On	Normal	—	100	5	1E	N		The Pokémon's Attack hits with certainty on its next turn. Best used in tandem with a powerful Attack move.
Lovely Kiss	Normal	—	75	10	1E	Y		Makes an opponent Sleep.
Low Kick	Fighting	—	100	20	1E	Y		The heavier the opponent's Pokémon, the stronger the Attack.
Luster Purge	Psychic	70	100	5	1E	N		Has a 50% chance of lowering the opponent's Special Defense one point.
Mach Punch	Fighting	40	100	30	1E	Y		Move strikes first without fail. (If both Pokémon produce this Attack, the one with the highest Speed rating goes first.)
Magic Coat	Psychic	—	100	15	1E	N		Reflects moves that have Effects such as Poison, Paralyze, Sleep, Confusion, and Leech Seed.
Magical Leaf	Grass	60	—	20	1E	N		Move that hits the opponent 100% of the time.
Magnitude	Ground	—	100	30	1A/2E	N		Strength of the Attack randomly changes (10, 30, 50, 70, 90, 110, or 150). The strength of the Attack is doubled when used against a Pokémon who has used Dig. Attack affects any ally outside of battle as well as opponent Pokémon.
Mean Look	Normal	—	100	5	1E	N		Makes the opponent Pokémon unable to flee from battle or be switched out.
Meditate	Psychic	—	—	40	Self	N		Raises the Pokémon's Attack by one point.
Mega Drain	Grass	40	100	10	S/E	N		The Pokémon absorbs half of the damage inflicted.
Mega Kick	Normal	120	75	5	1E	Y		Normal Attack.
Mega Punch	Normal	80	85	20	1E	Y		Normal Attack.
Megahorn	Bug	120	85	10	1E	Y		Normal Attack.
Memento	Dark	—	100	10	S/E	N		Lowers the opponent's Attack and Special Attack by two, but makes your Pokémon faint.
Metal Claw	Steel	50	95	35	1E	Y		Raises the Pokémon's Defense by one with a 10% probability.
Metal Sound	Steel	—	85	40	1E	N		Lowers opponent's Special Defense by two.
Meteor Mash	Steel	100	85	10	1E	Y		20% chance that it will raise your Attack by one.
Metronome	Normal	—	—	10	S/E	Y		Randomly uses an Attack from entire repertoire.
Milk Drink	Normal	—	—	10	S/E	Y		Restores half of HP; splits 1/5 of HP among your other Pokémon.
Mimic	Normal	—	100	10	S/E	N		Allows the Pokémon to copy and use the opponent Pokémon's last Attack for the duration of the battle.
Mind Reader	Normal	—	100	5	1E	N		The Pokémon's next Attack hits.
Minimize	Normal	—	—	20	Self	N		Increases the caster's Evasiveness by one.
Mirror Coat	Psychic	—	100	20	S/E	N		Pokémon Attacks second in battle (regardless of Pokémon's Speed). Returns double the Special Attacks of the opponent Pokémon.
Mirror Move	Flying	—	—	20	1E	N		Pokémon counters with the same Attack used by the opponent Pokémon.
Mist	Ice	—	—	30	2E	N		Casting Pokémon cannot be affected by skills that lower abilities.
Mist Ball	Psychic	70	100	5	1E	N		50% chance of lowering the opponent's Special Attack.
Moonlight	Normal	—	—	5	Self	N		Recovers 50% of the Pokémon's max HP. The Effectiveness changes based on the time of day.
Morning Sun	Normal	—	—	5	Self	N		Move recovers HP, but the effectiveness changes based on the time of day.
Mud Shot	Ground	55	95	15	1E	N		Always lowers the opponent's Speed by one.
Mud Sport	Ground	—	100	15	All	N		Halves the strength of Electric-type Moves for the Pokémon who uses this move.
Muddy Water	Water	95	85	10	2E	N		30% chance of lowering the opponent's Accuracy.
Mud-Slap	Ground	20	100	10	1E	N		Lowers opponent's Accuracy by one point.
Nature Power	Normal	—	95	20	1E	N		Changes other moves to correspond to the battlefield's terrain (grass = Stun Spore; long grass = Razor Leaf; sand = Earthquake; underwater = Hydro Pump; sea = Surf; pond = Bubblebeam; mountain = Rock Slide; cave = Shadow Ball; other = Swift).
Needle Arm	Grass	60	100	15	1E	Y		30% chance of making the opponent Flinch.
Nightmare	Ghost	—	100	5	1E	Y		Gives an opponent nightmares; works only when opponent is Sleeping.
Night Shade	Ghost	—	100	15	1E	N		Inflicts damage equal to the Pokémon's level, regardless of the Pokémon's or the opponent Pokémon's abilities.
Octazooka	Water	65	85	10	1E	N		50% chance of lowering opponent's Accuracy by one.
Odor Sleuth	Normal	—	100	40	1E	N		Opponent's Evasiveness returns to normal. Fighting and Normal Attacks become effective against Ghost-type opponent Pokémon.
Outrage	Dragon	90	100	15	RE	Y		Consecutive Attacks for 2–3 turns, but casting Pokémon becomes Confused when the Attack is finished.
Overheat	Fire	140	90	5	S/E	Y	TM50	Lowers the opponent's Special Attack by two.
Pain Split	Normal	—	100	20	1E	Y		Combines your HP with your opponent's HP and splits them between both of you.
Pay Day	Normal	40	100	20	1E	Y		After a battle, receive money equal to: (your level) x (number of Attacks) x 2.
Peck	Flying	35	100	35	1E	Y		Normal Attack.
Perish Song	Normal	—	—	5	All	N		Passes a sentence on the Pokémon on outside of battle which makes both Pokémon used in battle faint after three turns.
Petal Dance	Grass	70	100	20	RE	Y		Attacks for 2–3 turns, then when the Effect ends, Confuses the Pokémon.
Pin Missile	Bug	14	85	20	1E	N		Attacks 2–5 times in one turn.
Poison Fang	Poison	50	100	15	1E	Y		30% chance of Poisoning the opponent. Poison damage grows greater with each passing turn.
Poison Gas	Poison	—	55	40	1E	N		Infects opponent with Poison.
Poison Sting	Poison	15	100	35	1E	N		30% additional Effect of Poison.

Name	Type	ST	ACC	PP	Range	PA?	TM/HM	Description
Poison Tail	Poison	50	100	25	1E	Y		Easy to score a Critical Hit. 10% chance of Poisoning the opponent.
Poisonpowder	Poison	—	75	35	1E	N		Infects opponent with Poison.
Pound	Normal	40	100	35	1E	Y		Normal Attack.
Powder Snow	Ice	40	100	25	2E	N		Freezes the opponent Pokémon with a 10% probability.
Present	Normal	—	90	15	1E	Y		May cause damage of 40, 80, or 120, or may restore HP by 80.
Protect	Normal	—	—	10	Self	N	TM17	Defends against the opponent's current Attack. The success ratio is lowered when consecutively used.
Psybeam	Psychic	65	100	20	1E	N		10% additional chance of Confusion.
Psycho Boost	Psychic	140	90	5	1E	N		High-level attack, but lowers user's SP ATK status.
Psych Up	Normal	—	—	10	S/E	N		When the opponent uses moves that have beneficial side effects (such as Leech Seed, etc.), the same Effects benefit your own Pokémon.
Psychic	Psychic	90	100	10	1E	N	TM29	Reduces opponent's Special Defense by one point with a 10% probability.
Psywave	Psychic	—	80	15	1E	N		Randomly inflicts 0.5 to 1.5 points of damage times the Pokémon's level.
Pursuit	Dark	40	100	20	1E	Y		When you use this move, if the opponent changes Pokémon, it inflicts twice the amount of damage as it is changed.
Quick Attack	Normal	40	100	30	1E	T		Get a pre-emptive Attack without fail. (If both Pokémon use this Attack, the one with the highest Speed lands the Attack first.)
Rage	Normal	20	100	20	1E	Y		For one round of battle, the strength of the Attack increases by the amount of damage inflicted by the opponent.
Rain Dance	Water	—	—	5	All	N	TM18	Summons a rain storm that raises the strength of Water-type Attacks for five turns.
Rapid Spin	Normal	20	100	40	S/E	Y		Releases the Pokémon from continuous moves such as Bind, Whirlpool, Clamp, Sand Tomb, Fire Spin, Wrap, Spikes, and Leech Seed.
Razor Leaf	Grass	55	95	25	2E	N		Easy to produce a Critical Hit.
Razor Wind	Normal	80	100	10	2E	N		Gathers strength during Turn 1 and Attacks during Turn 2. Makes it easier to do a Critical Hit.
Recover	Normal	—	—	20	Self	N		Recover HP up to half the maximum points.
Recycle	Normal	—	100	10	Self	N		Makes it possible to reuse a Held Item a second time.
Reflect	Psychic	—	—	20	Self	N	TM33	Halves the damage from Physical Attacks for five turns. Effect continues even if you change Pokémon.
Refresh	Normal	—	100	20	Self	N		Cures the conditions Poison, Paralyze, and Burn.
Rest	Psychic	—	—	10	Self	N	TM44	After the Pokémon recovers all HP, it lies down to Sleep for two turns.
Return	Normal	—	100	20	1E	Y	TM27	The Pokémon you are using becomes stronger the more emotionally attached it is to you.
Revenge	Fighting	60	100	10	1E	Y		The Attack's strength doubles when you take damage from the opponent's Attack on that turn.
Reversal	Fighting	—	100	15	1E	Y		The less HP the casting Pokémon has remaining, the stronger the Attack.
Roar	Normal	—	100	20	1E	N	TM05	Opponent is scared away from battle. In a Trainer's battle, the Pokémon is forcibly changed. Move has no Effect if the opponent doesn't have any Pokémon in waiting.
Rock Blast	Rock	25	80	10	1E	N		Attacks 2—5 times in one turn.
Rock Slide	Rock	75	90	10	2E	N		30% additional chance of causing the opponent to Flinch.
Rock Smash	Fighting	20	100	15	1E	Y	HM06	Lowers the opponent's Defense by one point with a 50% probability. Outside of battle, this crushes rocks, possibly releasing a Pokémon.
Rock Throw	Rock	50	90	15	1E	N		Normal Attack.
Rock Tomb	Rock	50	80	10	1E	N	TM39	Lowers the opponent's Speed by one.
Role Play	Psychic	—	100	10	Self	N		Gives you and the opponent Pokémon the same innate ability. However, it is impossible to copy Wonder Guard.
Rolling Kick	Fighting	60	85	15	1E	Y		30% chance of making an opponent back off.
Rollout	Rock	30	90	20	1E	Y		Consecutive Attacks for up to five turns until it misses. Increases damage with each hit. Strength of the Attack is doubled when you use Defense Curl the turn before.
Sacred Fire	Fire	100	95	5	IE	N		50% chance of Burning opponent.
Safeguard	Normal	—	—	25	Self	N	TM20	Over five turns, this protects against status anomalies. Effect continues when you change Pokémon.
Sand Tomb	Ground	15	70	15	1E	N		Attacks for 2—5 turns. The opponent cannot flee or switch out during the Attack's duration.
Sand-Attack	Ground	—	100	15	1E	N		Lowers opponent's Accuracy by one.
Sandstorm	Rock	—	—	10	All	N	TM37	For five turns a sandstorm rages, damaging both players each turn. Does not affect Rock-, Earth-, or Steel-type Pokémon.
Scary Face	Normal	—	90	10	1E	N		Lowers opponent's Speed by two.
Scratch	Normal	40	100	35	1E	Y		Normal Attack.
Screech	Normal	—	85	40	1E	N		Lowers the opponent Pokémon's Defense by two.
Secret Power	Normal	70	100	20	1E	N	TM43	30% chance of giving the opponent a status condition that corresponds to the battlefield's terrain (grass = Poison; tall grass = Sleep; sand = Lowered Accuracy; underwater = Lowered Defense; sea = Lowered Attack; pond = Lowered Speed; mountain = Confusion; anything else = Paralyze). Outside of battle, use this to open Secret Bases.
Seismic Toss	Fighting	—	100	20	1E	Y		Inflict damage on the opponent equal to the Pokémon's level, regardless of both Pokémon's abilities.
Selfdestruct	Normal	200	100	5	All	N		Devastating Attack. Pokémon faints after using this move.
Shadow Ball	Ghost	80	100	15	1E	N		Lowers opponent's Special Defense by one point with a 20% probability.
Shadow Punch	Ghost	60	—	20	1E	Y	TM30	Attack that hits without fail.
Sharpen	Normal	—	—	30	S/E	Y		Temporarily increases Pokemon's Attack.
Sheer Cold	Ice	—	30	5	1E	N		In one blow, the opponent is knocked out. Does not affect Pokémon whose level is higher than yours, while the chance of success is greater against Pokémon with a lower level.
Shock Wave	Electric	60	—	20	1E	N	TM34	This Attack is always successful.
Signal Beam	Bug	75	100	15	1E	N		10% chance of Confusing the opponent.
Silver Wind	Bug	60	100	5	S/E	N		10% chance of raising your Attack, Defense, Speed, Special Attack, and Special Defense by one.
Sing	Normal	—	55	15	1E	N		Lulls opponent to Sleep.
Sketch	Normal	—	—	10	1E	Y		Replaces itself with the opponent's last Attack, Defense, Sp. Attack, Sp. Defense, and Speed by one level.
Skill Swap	Psychic	—	100	10	S/E	N	TM48	Gives you and the opponent Pokémon the same innate ability. However, it is impossible to copy Wonder Guard.

Name	Type	ST	ACC	PP	Range	PA?	TM/HM	Description
Skull Bash	Normal	100	100	15	S/E	Y		Raises the Pokémon's Defense by one point during Turn 1 and Attacks during Turn 2.
Sky Attack	Flying	140	90	5	1E	N		Gathers strength during Turn 1, Attacks during Turn 2. 30% chance of causing the opponent to Flinch.
Sky Uppercut	Fighting	85	90	15	1E	Y		Also effective against Pokémon using Fly.
Slack Off	Normal	—	100	10	Self	N		Recover 50% of your max HP.
Slam	Normal	80	75	20	1E	Y		Normal Attack.
Slash	Normal	70	100	20	1E	Y		Easy to produce a Critical Hit.
Sleep Powder	Grass	—	75	15	1E	N		Puts opponent to Sleep.
Sleep Talk	Normal	—	—	10	—	N		Randomly uses one of the skills you possess, but only when you are asleep.
Sludge	Poison	65	100	20	1E	N		30% chance of Poisoning the opponent.
Sludge Bomb	Poison	90	100	10	1E	N	TM36	30% chance of Poisoning the opponent.
Smellingsalt	Normal	60	100	10	1E	Y		Inflicts twice the damage if the opponent is Paralyzed, but it cures that Paralysis.
Smog	Poison	20	70	20	1E	N		Infects opponent with Poison with 40% probability.
Smokescreen	Normal	—	100	20	1E	N		Lowers opponent's Accuracy by one.
Snatch	Dark	—	100	10	S/E	N	TM49	On the turn this move is used, if your opponent used a move that recovers HP or increases its abilities, this move steals that Effect and applies it to you.
Snore	Normal	40	100	15	1E	N		This is only effective when the Pokémon is asleep. Makes the opponent Pokémon Flinch with a 30% probability.
Softboiled	Normal	—	100	10	S/E	Y		Restores half of HP; gives 1/5 of Chansey's HP to another one of your Pokémon.
Solarbeam	Grass	120	100	10	1E	N	TM22	Absorb light on Turn 1 and Attack on Turn 2. Move works best during sunny weather, while the Effect is halved when it is raining.
Sonicboom	Normal	—	90	20	1E	N		Does 20 points of damage regardless of the opponent's Attack or Defense strength.
Spark	Electric	65	100	20	1E	Y		Paralyzes opponent with a 30% probability.
Spider Web	Bug	—	100	10	1E	Y		Prevents escape; prevents substitutions in Trainer battles.
Spike Cannon	Normal	20	100	15	1E	N		Attacks 2–5 times in one turn.
Spikes	Ground	—	—	20	AE	N		Inflicts damage whenever the opponent tries to flee or changes Pokémon. You can use this move up to three times in a battle and the strength of the move increases as used.
Spit Up	Normal	100	100	10	1E	N		Move's power becomes greater the more the Pokémon uses Stockpile.
Spite	Ghost	—	100	10	1E	N		Randomly decreases 2–5 PP in the skill that the opponent last used.
Splash	Normal	—	—	40	—	N		The Pokémon splashes about. Nothing else happens.
Spore	Grass	—	100	15	1E	N		Puts the opponent to Sleep.
Steel Wing	Steel	70	90	25	S/E	Y	TM47	Raises the Pokémon's Defense by one point with a 10% probability.
Stockpile	Normal	—	—	10	Self	N		Use up to three times to build up the strength of the moves Swallow and Spit Up.
Stomp	Normal	65	100	20	1E	Y		30% additional chance of causing the opponent to Flinch. Strength of Attack is doubled if opponent used Minimize.
Strength	Normal	80	100	15	1E	Y	HM04	Normal Attack. Outside of battle, use this to move rocks.
String Shot	Bug	—	95	40	2E	N		Lowers opponent's Speed one level.
Struggle	Normal	50	100	1	S/E	Y		You can use this after you use up the PP of the Pokémon's other moves. The Pokémon receives one-quarter recoil damage.
Stun Spore	Grass	—	75	30	1E	N		Paralyzes opponent.
Submission	Fighting	80	80	25	S/E	Y		Recoil hits the Pokémon, causing it to take one-quarter damage inflicted by the opponent.
Substitute	Normal	—	—	10	Self	N		Build the Pokémon's own alter-ego using one-quarter of the Pokémon's max HP. Pokémon takes no damage while the substitute remains.
Sunny Day	Fire	—	—	5	All	N	TM11	Raises the power of Fire-type Moves for five turns.
Super Fang	Normal	—	90	10	1E	Y		Knocks opponent's HP to half.
Superpower	Fighting	120	100	5	S/E	Y		Lowers your Attack and Defense by one.
Supersonic	Normal	—	55	20	1E	N		Confuses opponent.
Surf	Water	95	100	15	2E	N	HM03	Normal Attack. Outside of battle, use this to surf across the water.
Swagger	Normal	—	90	15	1E	N		Makes the opponent Confused, but increases its Attack by two.
Swallow	Normal	—	—	10	Self	N		You recover more HP the more you use Stockpile.
Sweet Kiss	Normal	—	75	10	1E	N		Confuses the opponent Pokémon.
Sweet Scent	Normal	—	100	20	2E	N		Lowers the opponent Pokémon's Evasiveness by one point.
Swift	Normal	60	—	20	2E	N		Attack hits without fail.
Swords Dance	Normal	—	—	30	Self	N		Raises the Pokémon's Defense by two points.
Synthesis	Grass	—	—	5	Self	N		Recovers 50% of the Pokémon's max HP but the effectiveness changes based on the weather.
Tackle	Normal	35	95	35	1E	Y		Normal Attack.
Tail Glow	Bug	—	100	20	Self	N		Raises your Special Attack by two.
Tail Whip	Normal	—	100	30	2E	N		Lowers opponent's Defense by one point.
Take Down	Normal	90	85	20	S/E	Y		Casting Pokémon takes one-quarter of the damage inflicted on the opponent.
Taunt	Dark	—	100	20	1E	N	TM12	On the turn after you use this move, the opponent can no longer use the Attack move it just used.
Teeter Dance	Normal	—	100	20	1A/2E	N		Confuses the opponent. It also affects allies when fighting 2-on-2 Battles.
Teleport	Psychic	—	—	20	Self	N		Ends the battle. Has no effect in Trainer battles. Outside of battle, this teleports you to the last Pokémon Center you visited.
Thief	Dark	40	100	10	S/E	Y	TM46	Allows the Pokémon to steal any Item that a wild Pokémon has attached to it. Becomes a basic Attack if the opponent Pokémon has nothing.

Name	Type	ST	ACC	PP	Range	PA?	TM/HM	Description
Thrash	Normal	90	100	20	RE	Y		Pokémon continues raging for 2–3 turns, then when the Effect ends, the Pokémon suffers Confusion.
Thunder	Electric	120	70	10	1E	N	TM25	30% chance of causing the opponent Paralysis. Accuracy becomes 100% when it is raining, but drops to 50% when sunny. Attack strength is doubled when used against a Pokémon using Fly.
Thunder Wave	Electric	—	100	20	1E	N		Paralyzes the opponent Pokémon.
Thunderbolt	Electric	95	100	15	1E	N	TM24	10% additional Effect of Paralysis.
Thunderpunch	Electric	75	100	15	1E	Y		10% additional Effect of Paralysis.
Thundershock	Electric	40	100	30	1E	Y		10% additional Effect of Paralysis.
Tickle	Normal	—	100	20	1E	Y		Lowers opponent's Attack and Defense by one.
Torment	Dark	—	100	15	1E	N	TM41	Prevents the opponent from using the same move twice in a row.
Toxic	Poison	—	85	10	1E	N	TM06	Infects opponent with Poison. With each turn, the Poison damage increases.
Transform	Normal	80	100	10	1E	Y		Change to same Pokémon as opponent with same Attacks; all PP at 5.
Tri Attack	Normal	80	100	10	1E	Y		20% additional chance of either Paralysis, Burn, or Ice.
Trick	Psychic	—	100	10	S/E	N		The Pokémon and opponent switch the Items they are holding.
Triple Kick	Fighting	10	90	10	1E	Y		Attacks three times in a row; damage increases each time.
Twineedle	Bug	25	100	20	1E	Y		Attacks twice in a row during a turn; 20% chance of Poisoning opponent.
Twister	Dragon	40	100	20	2E	N		20% chance of causing the opponent Pokémon to Flinch. Attack doubles in strength when used against a Pokémon using Fly.
Uproar	Normal	50	100	10	All	N		For 2–5 turns, neither you nor your opponent are affected by Sleep.
Vicegrip	Normal	55	100	30	1E	Y		Normal Attack.
Vine Whip	Grass	35	100	30	1E	Y		Normal Attack.
Vital Throw	Fighting	70	100	10	1E	Y		Attacks second in battle; next Attack hits without fail.
Volt Tackle	Electric	120	100	15	1E	N		A high-level Electric attack.
Water Gun	Water	40	100	25	1E	N		Normal Attack.
Water Pulse	Water	60	100	20	1E	N	TM03	20% chance of causing the opponent Pokémon to become Confused.
Water Sport	Water	—	100	15	All	N		Halves the strength of Fire-type Moves.
Water Spout	Water	150	100	5	2E	N		The strength of the Attack lessens as your HP dwindles.
Waterfall	Water	80	100	15	1E	Y	HM07	Normal Attack. Outside of battle, you can use this to climb waterfalls.
Weather Ball	Normal	50	100	10	1E	N		Changes the type of the move to correspond with the weather and doubles its power (sunny = Fire; rain = Water; hail = Ice; sandstorm = Rock).
Whirlpool	Water	15	70	15	1E	N		Inflicts damage for 2–5 turns. During this time, the opponent Pokémon cannot flee.
Whirlwind	Normal	—	100	20	1E	N		Ends battle by blowing away opponent. In Trainer battles, the opponent's Pokémon is compulsively changed.
Will-O-Wisp	Fire	—	75	15	1E	N		Burns the opponent.
Wing Attack	Flying	60	100	35	1E	Y		Normal Attack.
Wish	Normal	—	100	10	Self	N		At the end of the turn after using this move, you recover 50% of your max HP. Effect continues even if you change Pokémon.
Withdraw	Water	—	—	40	S/E	N		Raises your defensive power by one level.
Wrap	Normal	15	85	20	1E	Y		Attacks for 2–5 consecutive turns. During this time, opponent can't flee.
Yawn	Normal	—	100	10	1E	N		Makes the opponent Pokémon fall asleep at the end of the turn after you use this move.
Zap Cannon	Electric	100	50	5	1E	N		This Attack Paralyzes the opponent Pokémon.

Move Tutors

Pokémon Emerald also introduces Move Tutors who teach the Pokémon of Hoenn moves previously known only by those living in Johto and Kanto. The following lists detail where to find Hoenn's Move Tutors, and describe the moves they teach Pokémon.

Move Tutor Moves

NAME	TYPE	ST	ACC	PP	RANGE	PA?	DESCRIPTION
Mega Kick	Normal	120	75	5	1E	Y	Normal Attack. Damages opponent.
Mega Punch	Normal	80	85	20	1E	Y	Normal Attack. Damages opponent.
Metronome	Normal	—	—	10	1E	N	Casting Pokémon randomly chooses Attack.
Softboiled	Normal	—	100	10	Self	N	Healing move restores one-half of max HP.

Move Tutor Locations

LOCATION	MOVE TAUGHT	LOCATION	MOVE TAUGHT
Battle Frontier	Defense Curl	Battle Frontier	Thunder Wave
Battle Frontier	Fire Punch	Battle Frontier	Thunder Punch
Battle Frontier	Ice Punch	Battle Frontier	Rock Slide
Battle Frontier	Icy Wind	Battle Frontier	Swords Dance
Battle Frontier	Mud-Slap	Battle Frontier	Counter
Battle Frontier	Snore	Fortree City	Sleep Talk
Battle Frontier	Swift	Lavaridge Town	Mimic
Battle Frontier	Endure	Lilycove City	Substitute
Battle Frontier	Softboiled	Mauville City	Fury Cutter
Battle Frontier	Fire Punch	Mossdeep City	Dynamicpunch
Battle Frontier	Psych Up	Pacifidlog Town	Explosion
Battle Frontier	Seismic Toss	Slateport City	Swagger
Battle Frontier	Dream Eater	Sootopolis City	Double-Edge
Battle Frontier	Mega Kick	Verdanturf Town	Metronome
Battle Frontier	Mega Punch	Verdanturf Town	Rollout
Battle Frontier	Body Slam		

Pokémon Contest Moves

The Pokémon Contest may only be in Lilycove City in *Pokémon Emerald*, but that doesn't change the dynamics of the competition. When your Pokémon gets on stage to strut its best moves, check this list to make sure you are putting your best foot forward. The judges and attending audience prefer certain moves over others. Make note, though, that some moves have Effects that go outside appealing to judges. Some moves, for example, affect appeals or the other Pokémon scores.

Unless noted, the Effects of the moves described in this list happen during the current round, when the move is used.

♥ = 10 Appeal Points
♥ = 10 Counter Appeal Points

Move Name	Type	Appeal Points	Counter Points	Description
Absorb	Smart	♥♥	♥♥♥	Subtracts 30 appeal points from the Pokémon who appealed right before you.
Acid	Smart	♥	♥♥♥♥	Subtracts 40 appeal points from the Pokémon who appealed right before you.
Acid Armor	Tough	♥	—	You gain a ★ if your Condition is good, and you receive 10 x the number of ★ in appeal points after the next round. Every ★ you have (up to 3) lessens by 10% the probability of your Pokémon becoming nervous.
Aerial Ace	Cool	♥♥	—	Get triple the appeal points only when you use this as your first appeal.
Aeroblast	Cool	♥♥♥	—	Move is affected by the initial appeal in the round.
Agility	Cool	♥♥♥	—	Turns the next round to the first round of appeals.
Air Cutter	Cool	♥♥	♥	Subtracts 40 appeal points from any Pokémon who appealed before you who used the same type of move. Subtracts 10 points from any who did not use the same type of move.
Amnesia	Cute	♥	—	You gain a ★ if your Condition is good, and you receive 10 x the number of ★ in appeal points after the next round. Every ★ you have (up to 3) lessens by 10% the probability of your Pokémon becoming nervous.
Ancientpower	Tough	♥♥	—	You gain a ★ if your Condition is good, and you receive 10 x the number of ★ in appeal points after the next round. Every ★ you have (up to 3) lessens by 10% the probability of your Pokémon becoming nervous.
Arm Thrust	Tough	♥♥	♥	Subtracts 50 points from any Pokémon in Combo Standby who appealed prior to you. Subtracts 10 points from any Pokémon not in Combo Standby.
Aromatherapy	Smart	♥♥	—	Get triple the appeal points when you use this as your fourth appeal.
Assist	Cute	♥	—	Changes the appeal points to 10, 20, 40, 60, or 80.
Astonish	Smart	♥♥	♥♥♥	Subtracts 30 appeal points from the Pokémon who appealed right before you.
Attract	Cute	♥♥	—	Makes the Pokémon who appeal after your turn nervous.
Aurora Beam	Beauty	♥♥	♥	Subtracts 40 appeal points from any Pokémon who appealed before you who used the same move type. Subtracts 10 points from any who did not use the same move type.
Barrage	Tough	♥♥	—	Effectiveness increased if the previous move is also Tough.
Barrier	Cool	♥	—	Prevents you from receiving any counter appeal points during the current round.
Baton Pass	Cute	♥♥	—	Makes the Pokémon who appeal after your turn nervous.
Beat Up	Smart	♥♥	♥	Keeps all Pokémon that made appeals from receiving Counter Points.
Belly Drum	Cute	♥	—	You gain a ★ if your Condition is good, and you receive 10 x the number of ★ in appeal points after the next round. Every ★ you have (up to 3) lessens by 10% the probability of your Pokémon becoming nervous.
Bide	Tough	♥	—	Prevents you from receiving any counter appeal points during the current round.
Bind	Tough	♥♥♥	—	When you make your appeal, the crowd's excitement continues until the end of the round.
Bite	Tough		♥♥♥	Subtracts 30 appeal points from all of the Pokémon who appealed before you.
Blast Burn	Beauty	♥♥♥♥	♥♥♥♥	Removes appeal points from Pokémon that appealed before you. However, you cannot participate in next round of appeals.
Blaze Kick	Beauty	♥♥♥♥	—	No additional Effect.
Blizzard	Beauty	♥♥♥♥	—	No additional Effect.
Block	Cute	♥♥	—	Makes the Pokémon who appeal after your turn nervous.
Body Slam	Tough	♥	♥♥♥♥	Subtracts 40 appeal points from the Pokémon who appealed right before you.
Bone Club	Tough	♥♥	♥	Removes appeal points from a Pokémon that has the Judge's attention.
Bone Rush	Tough	♥♥♥♥	—	Appealing move with no additional effect.
Bonemerang	Tough	♥♥♥♥	—	Appealing move with no additional effect.
Bounce	Cute	♥	—	Prevents you from receiving any counter appeal points during the current round.
Brick Break	Cool	♥	♥♥♥♥	Subtracts 40 appeal points from the Pokémon who appealed right before you.
Bubble	Cute	♥♥	♥♥	Subtracts 20 appeal points from all Pokémon who appealed before you.
Bubblebeam	Beauty	♥	♥♥♥	Subtracts 30 appeal points from all of the Pokémon who've appealed before you.
Bulk Up	Beauty	♥	—	You gain a ★ if your Condition is good, and you receive 10 x the number of ★ in appeal points after the next round. Every ★ you have (up to 3) lessens by 10% the probability of your Pokémon becoming nervous.
Bullet Seed	Cool	♥♥	♥	Cuts in half the number of appeal points the Pokémon who appealed before you made. (Automatically rounds up from a fraction.)
Calm Mind	Smart	♥♥	—	Prevents you from receiving counter appeal points once during the current round.

Move Name	Type	Appeal Points	Counter Points	Description
Camouflage	Smart	♥♥♥	—	If the appeal points for the Pokémon who appealed right before you were less than 30, you get double the appeal points. (If they were greater than 30, you get 0 points.)
Charge	Smart	♥♥	—	If the Pokémon who appealed right before you used the same type of move, you get triple the appeal points.
Charm	Cute	♥♥	♥	Subtracts 40 appeal points from any Pokémon who appealed before you who used the same type of move. Subtracts 10 points from any who did not use the same type of move.
Clamp	Tough	♥♥♥	—	When you make your appeal, the crowd's excitement continues until the end of the round.
Comet Punch	Tough	♥♥	—	Effective move if used after another Tough-type Move.
Confuse Ray	Smart	♥♥♥	—	Appeals happen in random order in the next round.
Confusion	Smart	♥♥	♥♥♥	Subtracts 30 appeal points from the Pokémon who appealed right before you.
Constrict	Tough	♥♥	♥♥♥	Subtracts 30 appeal points from the Pokémon who appealed right before you.
Cosmic Power	Cool	♥	—	You gain a ★ if your Condition is good, and you receive 10 x the number of ★ in appeal points after the next round. Every ★ you have (up to 3) lessens by 10% the probability of your Pokémon becoming nervous.
Cotton Spore	Beauty	♥♥	♥	Subtracts 50 points from any Pokémon in Combo Standby who appealed prior to you. Subtracts 10 points from any Pokémon not in Combo Standby.
Counter	Tough	♥♥	—	Prevents you from receiving counter appeal points once during the current round.
Covet	Cute	♥	—	Half the number of appeal points given to the Pokémon who appealed right before you are added to your score. (If the total is a negative number of points, they are not added to your score.)
Crabhammer	Tough	♥♥♥	—	If the appeal points for the Pokémon who appealed right before you were less than 30, you get double the appeal points. (If they were greater than 30, you get 0 points.)
Cross Chop	Cool	♥♥♥	—	If the appeal points for the Pokémon who appealed right before you were less than 30, you get double the appeal points. (If they were greater than 30, you get 0 points.)
Crunch	Tough	♥	♥♥♥♥	Subtracts 40 appeal points from the Pokémon who appealed right before you.
Crush Claw	Cool	♥	♥♥♥♥	Subtracts 40 appeal points from the Pokémon who appealed right before you.
Curse	Tough	♥	—	Turns the next round to the fourth round of appeals.
Cut	Cool	♥♥	♥	Cuts in half the number of appeal points the Pokémon who appealed before you made. (Automatically rounds up from a fraction.)
Defense Curl	Cute	♥♥	—	Prevents you from receiving counter appeal points once during the current round.
Destiny Bond	Smart	♥♥♥♥♥♥♥	—	On the turn after next, you cannot participate in the appeals. During that time, counter appeals cannot influence you.
Detect	Cool	♥♥	—	Prevents you from receiving counter appeal points once during the current round.
Dig	Smart	♥	—	Prevents you from receiving counter appeal points during the current round.
Disable	Smart	♥♥	—	Makes the Pokémon who appeal after your turn nervous.
Dive	Beauty	♥♥	—	Prevents you from receiving counter appeal points once during the current round.
Dizzy Punch	Cool	♥	♥♥♥♥	Subtracts 40 appeal points from the Pokémon who appealed right before you.
Doom Desire	Cool	♥♥♥	—	Move temporarily prevents the audience from getting excited.
Double Kick	Cool	♥♥	—	If the Pokémon who appealed right before you used the same type of move, you get triple the number of appeal points.
Double Team	Cool	♥♥	—	Prevents you from receiving counter appeal points once during the current round.
Double-Edge	Tough	♥♥♥♥♥♥	—	When you are countered by another Pokémon, twice the usual number of counter appeal points are subtracted.
Doubleslap	Tough	♥♥	♥	Subtracts 50 points from any Pokémon in Combo Standby who appealed prior to you. Subtracts 10 points from any Pokémon not in Combo Standby.
Dragon Claw	Cool	♥♥	♥	Subtracts 40 appeal points from any Pokémon who appealed before you who used the same type of move. Subtracts 10 points from any who did not use the same type of move.
Dragon Dance	Cool	♥	—	You gain a ★ if your Condition is good, and you receive 10 x the number of ★ in appeal points after the next round. Every ★ you have (up to 3) lessens by 10% the probability of your Pokémon becoming nervous.
Dragon Rage	Cool	♥	—	On this turn you exchange the number of times you appealed for appeal points (1 appeal = 10 points, 2 = 20 points, 3 = 40 points, 4 = 80 points).
Dragonbreath	Cool	♥♥	♥♥♥	Subtracts 30 appeal points from the Pokémon who appealed before you.
Dream Eater	Smart	♥♥	♥♥	Subtracts 20 appeal points from all Pokémon who appealed before you.
Drill Peck	Cool	♥♥♥♥	—	No additional Effect.
Dynamicpunch	Cool	♥♥	♥	Subtracts 50 points from any Pokémon in Combo Standby who appealed prior to you. Subtracts 10 points from any Pokémon not in Combo Standby.
Earthquake	Tough	♥	♥♥♥	Subtracts 30 appeal points from the Pokémon who appealed before you.
Egg Bomb	Tough	♥♥♥♥	—	Appealing move with no additional effect.
Ember	Beauty	♥♥♥♥	—	No additional Effect.
Encore	Cute	♥♥	—	Makes the Pokémon who appeal after your turn nervous.
Endeavor	Tough	♥♥	—	Get triple the appeal points only when you use this as your fourth appeal.
Endure	Tough	♥♥	—	Prevents you from receiving counter appeal points once during the current round.
Eruption	Beauty	♥	—	On this turn, you exchange the number of times you appealed for appeal points (1 appeal = 10 points, 2 = 20 points, 3 = 40 points, 4 = 80 points).
Explosion	Beauty	♥♥♥♥♥♥♥♥	—	On the turn after next, you cannot participate in the appeals. During that time, counter appeals cannot influence you.
Extrasensory	Cool	♥	♥♥♥♥	Subtracts 40 appeal points from the Pokémon who appealed right before you.
Extremespeed	Cool	♥♥♥	—	Turns the next round to the first round of appeals.
Façade	Cute	♥♥	—	Get triple the appeal points only when you use this as your fourth appeal.
Faint Attack	Smart	♥♥	—	Get triple the appeal points only when you use this as your first appeal.

Move Name	Type	Appeal Points	Counter Points	Description
Fake Out	Cute	♥♥	♥	Subtracts 40 appeal points from any Pokémon who appealed before you who used the same type of move. Subtracts 10 points from any wh o did not use the same type of move.
Fake Tears	Smart	♥♥	—	Get triple the appeal points only when you use this as your fourth appeal.
False Swipe	Cool	♥	♥♥♥	Subtracts 30 appeal points from the Pokémon who appealed before you.
Featherdance	Beauty	♥♥	—	Get triple the appeal points only when you use this as your fourth appeal.
Fire Blast	Beauty	♥♥♥♥	—	No additional Effect.
Fire Punch	Beauty	♥♥♥♥	—	No additional Effect.
Fire Spin	Beauty	♥♥♥	—	When you make your appeal, the crowd's excitement continues until the end of the round.
Fissure	Tough	♥♥	♥	Cuts in half the number of appeal points the Pokémon who appealed before you made. (Automatically rounds up from a fraction.)
Flail	Cute	♥	—	On this turn, you exchange the number of times you appealed for appeal points (1 appeal = 10 points, 2 = 20 points, 3 = 40 points, 4 = 80 points).
Flamethrower	Beauty	♥♥♥♥	—	No additional Effect.
Flame Wheel	Beauty	♥♥♥	—	Appealing move with no additional effect.
Flash	Beauty	♥♥♥	—	Cancels Combo Standby for any Pokémon who has appealed before you.
Flatter	Smart	♥♥	—	Makes the Pokémon who appeal after your turn nervous.
Fly	Smart	♥	—	Prevents you from receiving any counter appeal points during the current round.
Focus Energy	Cool	♥	♥♥♥	Subtracts 30 appeal points from the Pokémon who appealed before you.
Focus Punch	Tough	♥♥	—	Turns the next round to the fourth round of appeals.
Follow Me	Cute	♥♥	—	When you make your appeal, the crowd's excitement continues until the end of the round.
Foresight	Smart	♥♥	—	Makes the Pokémon who appeal after your turn nervous.
Frenzy Plant	Cool	♥♥♥♥	♥♥♥♥	Removes appeal points from Pokémon that appealed before you. However, you cannot participate in next round of appeals.
Frustration	Cute	♥	—	When the move does not match the contest type, this adds 1 to the crowd excitement figure.
Fury Attack	Cool	♥♥	♥	Subtracts 50 points from any Pokémon in Combo Standby who appealed prior to you. Subtracts 10 points from any Pokémon not in Combo Standby.
Fury Cutter	Cool	♥♥♥	—	Prevents you from receiving penalties for two consecutive rounds.
Fury Swipes	Tough	♥♥	♥	Subtracts 50 points from any Pokémon in Combo Standby who appealed prior to you. Subtracts 10 points from any Pokémon not in Combo Standby.
Future Sight	Smart	♥♥♥	—	When you make your appeal, the crowd's excitement continues until the round's end.
Giga Drain	Smart	♥♥	♥	Subtracts 50 points from any Pokémon in Combo Standby who appealed prior to you. Subtracts 10 points from any Pokémon not in Combo Standby.
Glare	Tough	♥	♥♥♥	Subtracts 30 appeal points from the Pokémon who appealed before you.
Grasswhistle	Smart	♥	♥♥♥	Subtracts 30 appeal points from the Pokémon who appealed before you.
Growl	Cute	♥♥	—	Get triple the appeal points only when you use this as your fourth appeal.
Growth	Beauty	♥	—	You gain a ★ if your Condition is good, and you receive 10 x the number of ★ in appeal points after the next round. Every ★ you have (up to 3) lessens by 10% the probability of your Pokémon becoming nervous.
Grudge	Tough	♥	—	On this turn, you exchange the number of times you appealed for appeal points (1 appeal = 10 points, 2 = 20 points, 3 = 40 points, 4 = 80 points).
Guillotine	Cool	♥♥	♥	Cuts in half the number of appeal points the Pokémon who appealed before you made. (Automatically rounds up from a fraction.)
Gust	Smart	♥♥♥	—	Appeals happen in random order in the next round.
Hail	Beauty	♥	♥♥♥	Subtracts 30 appeal points from the Pokémon who appealed before you.
Harden	Tough	♥♥	—	Prevents you from receiving counter appeal points once during the current round.
Haze	Beauty	♥♥♥	—	Cancels the good Condition rating of the Pokémon who appealed before you in this round.
Headbutt	Tough	♥♥	♥♥♥	Subtracts 30 appeal points from the Pokémon who appealed right before you.
Heal Bell	Beauty	♥♥	—	Get triple the appeal points only when you use this as your fourth appeal.
Heat Wave	Beauty	♥♥♥♥	—	No additional Effect.
Helping Hand	Smart	♥♥	—	Makes the Pokémon who appeal after your turn nervous.
Hi Jump Kick	Cool	♥♥♥ ♥♥♥	—	When another Pokémon counters you, twice the usual number of counter appeal points are subtracted.
Hidden Power	Smart	♥♥♥	—	Prevents you from receiving penalties for two consecutive rounds.
Horn Attack	Cool	♥♥	—	No additional Effect.
Horn Drill	Cool	♥♥	♥	Cuts in half the number of appeal points the Pokémon who appealed before you made. (Automatically rounds up from a fraction.)
Howl	Cool	♥	—	You gain a ☆ if your Condition is good, and you receive 10 x the number of ☆ in appeal points after the next round. Every ☆ you have (up to 3) lessens by 10% the probability of your Pokémon becoming nervous.
Hydro Cannon	Beauty	♥♥♥♥	♥♥♥♥	Removes appeal points from Pokémon that appealed before you. However, you cannot participate in next round of appeals.
Hydro Pump	Beauty	♥♥♥♥	—	No additional Effect.
Hyper Beam	Cool	♥♥♥♥	♥♥♥♥	Subtracts 40 appeal points from the Pokémon who appealed before you. However, in the next round, you cannot participate in the appeals.
Hyper Fang	Cool	♥	♥♥♥♥	Removes appeal points from Pokémon in the first position.
Hyper Voice	Cool	♥	♥♥♥	Subtracts 30 appeal points from the Pokémon who appealed before you.

Move Name	Type	Appeal Points	Counter Points	Description
Hypnosis	Smart	♥	♥ ♥ ♥	Subtracts 30 appeal points from the Pokémon who appealed before you.
Ice Ball	Beauty	♥ ♥ ♥	—	When you make your appeal, the crowd's excitement continues until the end of the round.
Ice Beam	Beauty	♥ ♥	♥	Subtracts 40 appeal points from any Pokémon who appealed before you who used the same type of move. Subtracts 10 points from any who did not use the same type of move.
Ice Punch	Beauty	♥ ♥ ♥ ♥	—	No additional Effect.
Icicle Spear	Beauty	♥ ♥	♥	Removes appeal points from Pokémon that used the same type of move before you.
Icy Wind	Beauty	♥	♥ ♥ ♥	Subtracts 30 appeal points from all of the Pokémon who've appealed before you.
Imprison	Smart	♥ ♥ ♥	—	Makes the Pokémon who appeal after your turn nervous.
Ingrain	Smart	♥	—	Prevents you from receiving any counter appeal points during the current round.
Iron Defense	Tough	♥	—	Prevents you from receiving any counter appeal points during the current round.
Iron Tail	Cool	♥	♥ ♥ ♥ ♥	Subtracts 40 appeal points from the Pokémon who appealed right before you.
Jump Kick	Coo	♥ ♥ ♥ ♥ ♥		Appealing move, but leaves the Pokémon vulnerable to losing appeal points in later round.
Karate Chop	Tough	♥ ♥ ♥	—	If the appeal points for the Pokémon who appealed right before you were less than 30, you get double the appeal points. (If they were greater than 30, you get 0 points.)
Kinesis	Smart	♥ ♥ ♥	—	When you make your appeal, the crowd's excitement continues until the end of the round.
Knock Off	Smart	♥	♥ ♥ ♥ ♥	Subtracts 40 appeal points from the Pokémon who appealed right before you.
Leaf Blade	Cool	♥ ♥ ♥	—	If the appeal points for the Pokémon who appealed right before you were less than 30, you get double the appeal points. (If they were greater than 30, you get 0 points.)
Leech Life	Smart	♥	♥ ♥ ♥	Subtracts 30 appeal points from the Pokémon who appealed right before you.
Leech Seed	Smart	♥ ♥	♥ ♥	Subtracts 20 appeal points from all Pokémon who appealed before you.
Leer	Cool	♥ ♥ ♥	—	When you make your appeal, the crowd's excitement continues until the end of the round.
Lick	Tough	♥	♥ ♥ ♥ ♥	Subtracts 40 appeal points from the Pokémon who appealed right before you.
Light Screen	Beauty	♥	—	Prevents you from receiving any counter appeal points during the current round.
Lock-On	Smart	♥ ♥ ♥	—	When you make your appeal, the crowd's excitement continues until the end of the round.
Lovely Kiss	Beauty	♥	♥ ♥ ♥	Removes appeal points from Pokémon that appealed before you.
Low Kick	Tough	♥	♥ ♥ ♥ ♥	Subtracts 40 appeal points from the Pokémon who appealed right before you.
Luster Purge	Smart	♥ ♥	♥ ♥ ♥	Subtracts 30 appeal points from the Pokémon who appealed right before you.
Mach Punch	Cool	♥ ♥ ♥	—	Turns the next round to the first round of appeals.
Magic Coat	Beauty	♥	—	Prevents you from receiving any counter appeal points during the current round.
Magical Leaf	Beauty	♥ ♥	—	Get triple the appeal points when you use this as your first appeal.
Magnitude	Tough	♥	—	The appeal points awarded change depending upon the level of the crowd's excitement (Level 0 = 10 points, Level 1 = 20, Level 2 = 30, Level 3 = 50, Level 4 = 60).
Mean Look	Beauty	♥ ♥	—	Makes the Pokémon who appeal after your turn nervous.
Meditate	Beauty	♥	—	You gain a ☆ if your Condition is good, and you receive 10 x the number of ☆ in appeal points after the next round. Every ☆ you have (up to 3) lessens by 10% the probability of your Pokémon becoming nervous.
Mega Drain	Smart	♥	♥ ♥ ♥ ♥	Subtracts 40 appeal points from the Pokémon who appealed right before you.
Megahorn	Cool	♥ ♥	—	If the Pokémon who appealed right before you used the same type of move, you get triple the number of appeal points.
Mega Kick	Cool	♥ ♥ ♥ ♥	—	Appealing move with no additional effect.
Mega Punch	Tough	♥ ♥ ♥ ♥	—	Appealing move with no additional effect.
Memento	Tough	♥ ♥ ♥ ♥ ♥ ♥ ♥ ♥	—	On the turn after the next, you cannot participate in the appeals. During that time, you cannot be influenced by counter appeals.
Metal Claw	Cool	♥ ♥ ♥	—	No additional Effect.
Metal Sound	Smart	♥	♥ ♥ ♥	Subtracts 30 appeal points from the Pokémon who appealed before you.
Meteor Mash	Cool	♥ ♥	—	If the Pokémon who appealed right before you used the same type of move, you get triple the number of appeal points.
Metronome	Cute	♥ ♥ ♥	—	Move can be used repeatedly without Judge losing interest.
Milk Drink	Cute	♥ ♥	—	Effectiveness increased if the previous move is also Cute.
Mimic	Cute	♥	—	The same number of appeal points given to the Pokémon who appealed right before you are added to your score. (If that Pokémon received a negative number of points, they are not added to your score.)
Mind Reader	Smart	♥ ♥ ♥	—	When you make your appeal, the crowd's excitement continues until the end of the round.
Minimize	Smart	♥ ♥	—	Prevents you from receiving counter appeal points once during the current round.
Mirror Coat	Beauty	♥ ♥	—	Prevents you from receiving counter appeal points once during the current round.
Mirror Move	Smart	♥	—	The same number of appeal points given to the Pokémon who appealed right before you are added to your score. (If that Pokémon received a negative number of points, they are not added to your score.)
Mist	Beauty	♥	—	Prevents you from receiving any counter appeal points during the current round.
Mist Ball	Smart	♥	♥ ♥ ♥ ♥	Subtracts 40 appeal points from the Pokémon who appealed right before you.
Moonlight	Beauty	♥	—	Changes the appeal points to 10, 20, 40, 60, or 80.
Morning Sun	Beauty	♥	—	Changes the appeal points to 10, 20, 40, 60, or 80.
Mud Shot	Tough	♥	♥ ♥ ♥	Subtracts 30 appeal points from the Pokémon who appealed before you.
Mud Sport	Cute	♥ ♥ ♥ ♥	—	No additional Effect.
Muddy Water	Tough	♥ ♥	♥	Subtracts 50 points from any Pokémon in Combo Standby who appealed prior to you. Subtracts 10 points from any Pokémon not in Combo Standby.
Mud-Slap	Cute	♥ ♥	♥	Subtracts 50 points from any Pokémon in Combo Standby who appealed prior to you. Subtracts 10 points from any Pokémon not in Combo Standby.

Move Name	Type	Appeal Points	Counter Points	Description
Nature Power	Beauty	♥	—	The appeal points awarded change depending upon the level of the crowd's excitement (Level 0 = 10 points, Level 1 = 20, Level 2 = 30, Level 3 = 50, Level 4 = 60).
Needle Arm	Smart	♥	♥♥♥♥	Subtracts 40 appeal points from the Pokémon who appealed right before you.
Nightmare	Smart	♥	♥♥♥	Removes appeal points from Pokémon that appealed before you.
Night Shade	Smart	♥♥	♥	Subtracts 40 appeal points from any Pokémon who appealed before you who used the same type of move. Subtracts 10 points from any who did not use the same type of move.
Octazooka	Tough	♥♥	♥	Removes appeal points from a Pokémon that has the Judge's attention.
Odor Sleuth	Smart	♥♥♥	—	Cancels the good Condition rating of the Pokémon who appealed before you in this round.
Outrage	Cool	♥♥♥♥	♥♥♥♥	Subtracts 40 appeal points from the Pokémon who appealed before you. However, in the next round, you cannot participate in the appeals.
Overheat	Beauty	♥♥♥ ♥♥♥	—	When another Pokémon counters you, twice the usual number of counter appeal points are subtracted.
Pain Split	Smart	♥	♥♥♥♥	Removes appeal points from Pokémon in the first position.
Pay Day	Smart	♥	—	Appealing move with added effects when audience is excited.
Peck	Cool	♥♥♥♥	—	No additional Effect.
Perish Song	Beauty	♥♥♥	♥	Cuts in half the number of appeal points the Pokémon who appealed before you made. (Automatically rounds up from a fraction.)
Petal Dance	Beauty	♥♥♥♥	♥♥♥♥	Subtracts 40 appeal points from the Pokémon who appealed before you. However, in the next round, you cannot participate in the appeals.
Pin Missile	Cool	♥♥	♥	Subtracts 50 points from any Pokémon in Combo Standby who appealed prior to you. Subtracts 10 points from any Pokémon not in Combo Standby.
Poison Fang	Smart	♥♥♥	—	Makes the Pokémon who appeal after your turn nervous.
Poison Gas	Smart	♥♥♥	—	Makes the Pokémon who appeal after your turn nervous.
Poison Sting	Smart	♥♥	♥♥♥	Subtracts 30 appeal points from the Pokémon who appealed right before you.
Poison Tail	Smart	♥♥♥	—	Makes the Pokémon who appeal after your turn nervous.
Poisonpowder	Smart	♥♥♥	—	Makes the Pokémon who appeal after your turn nervous.
Pound	Tough	♥♥♥♥	—	No additional Effect.
Powder Snow	Beauty	♥♥♥♥	—	No additional Effect.
Present	Cute	♥♥♥	—	Move can be used repeatedly without Judge losing interest.
Protect	Cute	♥	—	Prevents you from receiving any counter appeal points during the current round.
Psybeam	Beauty	♥♥♥	—	Appeals happen in random order in the next round.
Psych Up	Smart	♥♥	—	If the Pokémon who appealed right before you used the same type of move, you get triple the number of appeal points.
Psychic	Smart	♥	♥♥♥	Subtracts 30 appeal points from the Pokémon who appealed before you.
Psycho Boost	Smart	♥♥♥ ♥♥♥	—	Appealing move, but leaves the Pokémon vulnerable to losing appeal points in later round.
Psywave	Smart	♥♥	♥	Cuts in half the number of appeal points the Pokémon who appealed before you made. (Automatically rounds up from a fraction.)
Pursuit	Smart	♥♥	♥	Cuts in half the number of appeal points the Pokémon who appealed before you made. (Automatically rounds up from a fraction.)
Quick Attack	Cool	♥♥♥	—	Turns the next round to the first round of appeals.
Rage	Cool	♥♥♥	—	Prevents you from receiving penalties for two consecutive rounds.
Rain Dance	Tough	♥	—	The appeal points awarded change depending upon the level of the crowd's excitement (Level 0 = 10 points, Level 1 = 20, Level 2 = 30, Level 3 = 50, Level 4 = 60).
Rapid Spin	Cool	♥♥	—	Prevents you from receiving counter appeal points once during the current round.
Razor Leaf	Cool	♥♥	—	If the appeal points for the Pokémon who appealed right before you were less than 30, you get double the appeal points. (If they were greater than 30, you get 0 points.)
Razor Wind	Cool	♥♥♥	—	If the appeal points for the Pokémon who appealed right before you were less than 30, you get double the appeal points. (If they were greater than 30, you get 0 points.)
Recover	Smart	♥♥	♥	Subtracts 40 appeal points from any Pokémon who appealed before you who used the same type of move. Subtracts 10 points from any who did not use the same type of move.
Recycle	Smart	♥♥♥	—	Prevents you from receiving penalties for two consecutive rounds.
Reflect	Smart	♥♥♥	—	Prevents you from receiving any counter appeal points during the current round.
Refresh	Cute	♥	—	You gain a ⭐ if your Condition is good, and you receive 10 x the number of ⭐ in appeal points after the next round. Every ⭐ you have (up to 3) lessens by 10% the probability of your Pokémon becoming nervous.
Rest	Cute	♥♥	—	Prevents you from receiving counter appeal points once during the current round.
Return	Cute	♥	—	When the move does not match the contest type, this adds 1 to the crowd excitement figure.
Revenge	Tough	♥♥♥	—	Turns the next round to the fourth round of appeals.
Reversal	Cool	♥♥	—	Get triple the appeal points when you use this as your fourth appeal.
Roar	Cool	♥♥♥	—	Appeals happen in random order in the next round.
Rock Blast	Tough	♥♥	—	If the Pokémon who appealed right before you used the same type of move, you get triple the number of appeal points.
Rock Slide	Tough	♥	♥♥♥	Subtracts 30 appeal points from the Pokémon who appealed before you.
Rock Smash	Tough	♥	—	Get three times the usual points given for being in good Condition.

Move Name	Type	Appeal Points	Counter Points	Description
Rock Throw	Tough	♥ ♥	—	If the Pokémon who appealed right before you used the same type of move, you get triple the number of appeal points.
Rock Tomb	Smart	♥ ♥ ♥	—	When you make your appeal, the crowd's excitement continues until the round's end.
Role Play	Cute	♥	—	Half the number of appeal points given to the Pokémon who appealed right before you are added to your score. (If the total is a negative number of points, they are not added to your score.)
Rolling Kick	Cool	♥	♥ ♥ ♥	Removes appeal points from Pokémon that appealed before you.
Rollout	Tough	♥ ♥ ♥	—	When you make your appeal, the crowd's excitement continues until the round's end.
Sacred Fire	Beauty	♥ ♥ ♥ ♥	—	Appealing move with no additional effect.
Safeguard	Beauty	♥	—	Prevents you from receiving any counter appeal points during the current round.
Sand Tomb	Smart	♥ ♥ ♥	—	When you make your appeal, the crowd's excitement continues until the round's end.
Sand-Attack	Cute	♥ ♥	♥	Subtracts 50 points from any Pokémon in Combo Standby who appealed prior to you. Subtracts 10 points from any Pokémon not in Combo Standby.
Sandstorm	Tough	♥ ♥	—	Appeals happen in random order in the next round.
Scary Face	Tough	♥ ♥	♥	Subtracts 50 points from any Pokémon in Combo Standby who appealed prior to you. Subtracts 10 points from any Pokémon not in Combo Standby.
Scratch	Tough	♥ ♥ ♥	—	No additional Effect.
Screech	Smart	♥	♥ ♥ ♥	Subtracts 30 appeal points from the Pokémon who appealed before you.
Secret Power	Smart	♥	—	Get three times the usual points given for being in good Condition.
Seismic Toss	Tough	♥ ♥	♥	Subtracts 40 appeal points from any Pokémon who appealed before you who used the same move type. Subtracts 10 points from any who did not use the same move type.
Selfdestruct	Beauty	♥ ♥ ♥ ♥ ♥ ♥ ♥ ♥	—	On the turn after the next, you cannot participate in the appeals. During that time, counter appeals cannot influence you.
Shadow Ball	Smart	♥ ♥ ♥	—	Cancels the good Condition rating of the Pokémon who appealed before you in this round.
Shadow Punch	Smart	♥ ♥	—	Get triple the appeal points only when you use this as your first appeal.
Sharpen	Cute	♥	—	Pokémon gains a ★ if condition is good. Every ★ you have (up to three) lessens the chance of Pokémon becoming nervous.
Sheer Cold	Beauty	♥ ♥	♥	Cuts in half the number of appeal points the Pokémon who appealed before you made. (Automatically rounds up from a fraction.)
Shock Wave	Cool	♥ ♥	—	Get triple the appeal points when you use this as your first appeal.
Signal Beam	Beauty	♥ ♥ ♥	—	Appeals happen in random order in the next round.
Silver Wind	Beauty	♥	—	You gain a ★ if your Condition is good, and you receive 10 x the number of ★ in appeal points after the next round. Every ★ you have (up to 3) lessens by 10% the probability of your Pokémon becoming nervous.
Sing	Cute	♥ ♥	—	Makes the Pokémon who appeal after your turn nervous.
Skill Swap	Smart	♥	—	Half the number of appeal points given to the Pokémon who appealed right before you are added to your score. (If the total is a negative number of points, they are not added to your score.)
Skull Bash	Tough	♥	♥ ♥ ♥ ♥	Subtracts 40 appeal points from the Pokémon who appealed right before you.
Sky Attack	Cool	♥ ♥ ♥	—	If the appeal points for the Pokémon who appealed right before you were less than 30, you get double the appeal points. (If they were greater than 30, you get 0 points.)
Sky Uppercut	Cool	♥ ♥	♥	Subtracts 40 appeal points from any Pokémon who appealed before you who used the same move type. Subtracts 10 points from any who did not use the same move type.
Slack Off	Cute	♥	—	On this turn, you exchange the number of times you appealed for appeal points (1 appeal = 10 points, 2 = 20 points, 3 = 40 points, 4 = 80 points).
Slam	Tough	♥ ♥	♥	Subtracts 40 appeal points from any Pokémon who appealed before you who used the same move type. Subtracts 10 points from any who did not use the same move type.
Slash	Cool	♥ ♥ ♥	—	If the appeal points for the Pokémon who appealed right before you were less than 30, you get double the appeal points. (If they were greater than 30, you get 0 points.)
Sleep Powder	Smart	♥	♥ ♥ ♥	Subtracts 30 appeal points from the Pokémon who appealed before you.
Sleep Talk	Cute	♥ ♥ ♥	—	Prevents you from receiving penalties for two consecutive rounds.
Sludge	Tough	♥	♥ ♥ ♥ ♥	Subtracts 40 appeal points from the Pokémon who appealed right before you.
Sludge Bomb	Tough	♥ ♥	♥	Subtracts 50 points from any Pokémon in Combo Standby who appealed prior to you. Subtracts 10 points from any Pokémon not in Combo Standby.
Smellingsalt	Smart	♥ ♥	♥ ♥ ♥	Subtracts 30 appeal points from the Pokémon who appealed right before you.
Smog	Tough	♥	♥ ♥ ♥	Subtracts 30 appeal points from the Pokémon who appealed before you.
Smokescreen	Smart	♥ ♥ ♥	—	Cancels Combo Standby for any Pokémon who has appealed before you.
Snatch	Smart	♥ ♥	♥	Cuts in half the number of appeal points the Pokémon who appealed before you made. (Automatically rounds up from a fraction.)
Snore	Cute	♥ ♥ ♥ ♥	—	No additional Effect.
Softboiled	Beauty	♥ ♥ ♥ ♥	—	Appealing move with no additional effect.
Solarbeam	Cool	♥ ♥ ♥ ♥	—	No additional Effect.
Sonicboom	Cool	♥ ♥	—	If the Pokémon who appealed right before you used the same move type, you get triple the number of appeal points.
Spark	Cool	♥	♥ ♥ ♥ ♥	Subtracts 40 appeal points from the Pokémon who appealed right before you.
Spider Web	Smart	♥ ♥	—	Move makes all Pokémon following the user more nervous.
Spike Cannon	Cool	♥ ♥	♥	Subtracts 50 points from any Pokémon in Combo Standby who appealed prior to you. Subtracts 10 points from any Pokémon not in Combo Standby.
Spikes	Smart	♥ ♥	—	Makes the Pokémon who appeal after your turn nervous.
Spit Up	Tough	♥ ♥ ♥ ♥	—	No additional Effect.
Spite	Tough	♥	—	On this turn, you exchange the number of times you appeal for appeal points (1 appeal = 10 points, 2 = 20 points, 3 = 40 points, 4 = 80 points).
Splash	Cute	♥ ♥	—	Get triple the appeal points only when you use this as your fourth appeal.

Move Name	Type	Appeal Points	Counter Points	Description
Spore	Beauty	♥	♥ ♥ ♥	Subtracts 30 appeal points from the Pokémon who appealed before you.
Steel Wing	Cool	♥ ♥	—	If the Pokémon who appealed right before you used the same type of move, you get triple the number of appeal points.
Stockpile	Tough	♥ ♥	—	Prevents you from receiving counter appeal points once during the current round.
Stomp	Tough	♥	♥ ♥ ♥ ♥	Subtracts 40 appeal points from the Pokémon who appealed right before you.
Strength	Tough	♥ ♥	♥	Subtracts 40 appeal points from any Pokémon who appealed before you who used the same type of move. Subtracts 10 points from any who did not use the same type of move.
String Shot	Smart	♥ ♥	♥ ♥ ♥	Subtracts 30 appeal points from the Pokémon who appealed right before you.
Struggle	Cool	♥ ♥ ♥ ♥	—	Appealing move with no additional effect.
Stun Spore	Smart	♥ ♥	♥	Cuts in half the number of appeal points the Pokémon who appealed before you made. (Automatically rounds up from a fraction.)
Submission	Cool	♥ ♥ ♥ ♥ ♥ ♥	—	When another Pokémon counters you, twice the usual number of counter appeal points are subtracted.
Substitute	Smart	♥ ♥	—	Prevents you from receiving counter appeal points once during the current round.
Sunny Day	Beauty	♥	—	The appeal points awarded change depending upon the level of the crowd's excitement (Level 0 = 10 points, Level 1 = 20, Level 2 = 30, Level 3 = 50, Level 4 = 60).
Super Fang	Tough	♥ ♥	♥	Removes appeal points from Pokémon that successfully appealed before you.
Superpower	Tough	♥ ♥ ♥ ♥	—	When you are countered by another Pokémon, twice the usual number of counter appeal points are subtracted.
Supersonic	Smart	♥ ♥ ♥	—	Appeals happen in random order in the next round.
Surf	Beauty	♥ ♥ ♥	—	If the appeal points for the Pokémon who appealed right before you were less than 30, you get double the appeal points. (If they were greater than 30, you get 0 points.)
Swagger	Cute	♥ ♥	—	Get triple the appeal points only when you use this as your first appeal.
Swallow	Tough	♥	—	You gain a ☆ if your Condition is good, and you receive 10 x the number of ☆ in appeal points after the next round. Every ☆ you have (up to 3) lessens by 10% the probability of your Pokémon becoming nervous.
Sweet Kiss	Cute	♥ ♥	—	Makes the Pokémon who appeal after your turn nervous.
Sweet Scent	Cute	♥	♥ ♥ ♥	Subtracts 30 appeal points from the Pokémon who appealed right before you.
Swift	Cool	♥ ♥	—	Get triple the appeal points only when you use this as your first appeal.
Swords Dance	Beauty	♥	—	You gain a ☆ if your Condition is good, and you receive 10 x the number of ☆ in appeal points after the next round. Every ☆ you have (up to 3) lessens by 10% the probability of your Pokémon becoming nervous.
Synthesis	Smart	♥	—	Changes the appeal points to 10, 20, 40, 60, or 80.
Tackle	Tough	♥ ♥ ♥ ♥	—	No additional Effect.
Tail Glow	Beauty	♥	—	You gain a ☆ if your Condition is good, and you receive 10 x the number of ☆ in appeal points after the next round. Every ☆ you have (up to 3) lessens by 10% the probability of your Pokémon becoming nervous.
Tail Whip	Cute	♥ ♥	—	Get triple the appeal points only when you use this as your fourth appeal.
Take Down	Tough	♥ ♥ ♥ ♥ ♥ ♥	—	When you are countered by another Pokémon, twice the usual number of counter appeal points are subtracted.
Taunt	Smart	♥ ♥	—	Makes the Pokémon who appeal after your turn nervous.
Teeter Dance	Cute	♥ ♥ ♥ ♥	♥ ♥ ♥ ♥	Subtracts 40 appeal points from the Pokémon who appealed before you. However, in the next round, you cannot participate in the appeals.
Teleport	Cool	♥	—	Prevents you from receiving any counter appeal points during the current round.
Thief	Tough	♥	—	Half the number of appeal points given to the Pokémon who appealed right before you are added to your score. (If the total is a negative number of points, they are not added to your score.)
Thrash	Tough	♥ ♥ ♥ ♥	♥ ♥ ♥ ♥	Subtracts 40 appeal points from the Pokémon who appealed before you. However, in the next round, you cannot participate in the appeals.
Thunder	Cool	♥ ♥	♥ ♥	Subtracts 20 appeal points from all Pokémon who appealed before you.
Thunder Wave	Cool	♥ ♥	♥	Cuts in half the number of appeal points the Pokémon who appealed before you made. (Automatically rounds up from a fraction.)
Thunderbolt	Cool	♥ ♥ ♥ ♥	—	No additional Effect.
Thunderpunch	Cool	♥ ♥ ♥ ♥	—	No additional Effect.
Thundershock	Cool	♥ ♥ ♥ ♥	—	No additional Effect.
Tickle	Cute	♥ ♥ ♥	—	Cancels the good Condition rating of the Pokémon who appealed before you in this round.
Torment	Tough	♥ ♥	—	Makes the Pokémon who appeal after your turn nervous.
Toxic	Smart	♥ ♥ ♥	—	Makes the Pokémon who appeal after your turn nervous.
Transform	Smart	♥ ♥	—	Move can be used repeatedly without Judge losing interest.
Tri Attack	Beauty	♥ ♥	♥ ♥	Subtracts 20 appeal points from all Pokémon who appealed before you.
Trick	Smart	♥ ♥	—	If the Pokémon who appealed right before you used the same type of move, you get triple the number of appeal points.
Triple Kick	Cool	♥ ♥ ♥ ♥	—	Appealing move with no additional effect.
Twineedle	Cool	♥ ♥	♥ ♥ ♥	Removes appeal points from Pokémon that appealed before you.
Twister	Cool	♥ ♥ ♥	—	Appeals happen in random order in the next round.
Uproar	Cute	♥ ♥ ♥	—	Appeals happen in random order in the next round.
Vicegrip	Tough	♥ ♥ ♥ ♥	—	No additional Effect.
Vital Throw	Cool	♥ ♥ ♥	—	Turns the next round to the fourth round of appeals.

Move Name	Type	Appeal Points	Counter Points	Description
Vine Whip	Cool	♥♥♥♥	—	Appealing move with no additional effect.
Volt Tackle	Cool	♥♥♥ ♥♥♥	—	Appealing move, but leaves the Pokémon vulnerable to losing appeal points in later round.
Water Gun	Cute	♥♥♥♥	—	No additional Effect.
Water Pulse	Beauty	♥♥♥	—	Appeals happen in random order in the next round.
Water Sport	Cute	♥♥♥♥	—	No additional Effect.
Water Spout	Beauty	♥	—	On this turn you exchange the number of times you've appealed for appeal points (1 appeal = 10 points, 2 = 20 points, 3 = 40 points, 4 = 80 points).
Waterfall	Tough	♥♥	—	Get triple the appeal points only when you use this as your fourth appeal.
Weather Ball	Smart	♥♥♥♥	—	No additional Effect.
Whirlpool	Beauty	♥♥♥	—	When you make your appeal, the crowd's excitement continues until the end of the round.
Whirlwind	Smart	♥♥♥	—	Appeals happen in random order in the next round.
Will-O-Wisp	Beauty	♥	♥♥♥♥	Subtracts 40 appeal points from the Pokémon who appealed right before you.
Wing Attack	Cool	♥	—	If the Pokémon who appealed right before you used the same type of move, you get triple the number of appeal points.
Wish	Cute	♥♥♥	—	When you make your appeal, the crowd's excitement continues until the end of the round.
Withdraw	Cute	♥	—	Prevents Pokémon from losing appeal points, but cannot participate in next round.
Wrap	Tough	♥♥♥	—	When you make your appeal, the crowd's excitement continues until the end of the round.
Yawn	Cute	♥♥	—	Makes the Pokémon who appeal after your turn nervous.
Zap Cannon	Cool	♥♥♥♥	—	No additional Effect.

Possible Combos

There are situations in a Pokémon Contest where you can pull off spectacular combinations that earn extra appeal points. The first move used is called the Combo Standby Move. Selecting one of these moves indicates that you may be gearing up for a Combo. The move selected after the Combo Standby Move is the Target Move—it completes the Combo in the following round of the Pokémon Contest. If you can pull off a successful Combo, the audience and judges will go wild, giving you twice the number of appeal points!

COMBO STANDBY MOVE	POSSIBLE TARGET MOVES
Belly Drum	Rest (TM44)
Bone Club	Bone Rush, Bonemerang
Bone Rush	Bone Club, Bonemerang
Bonemerang	Bone Club, Bone Rush
Calm Mind (TM04)	Confusion, Dream Eater, Future Sight, Light Screen (TM16), Luster Purge, Meditate, Mist Ball, Psybeam, Psychic (TM29), Psycho Boost, Psywave, Reflect (TM33)
Charge	Shockwave, Spark, Thunder (TM25), Thunderbolt (TM24), Thunderpunch, Thundershock, Thunder Wave, Volt Tackle
Charm	Flatter, Growl, Rest (TM44), Sweet Kiss, Tail Whip
Confusion	Future Sight, Kinesis, Psychic (TM29), Teleport
Curse	Destiny Bond, Grudge, Mean Look, Spite
Defense Curl	Rollout, Tackle
Dive (HM08)	Surf (HM03)
Double Team	Agility, Quick Attack, Teleport
Dragon Dance	Dragonbreath, Dragon Claw (TM02), Dragon Rage
Dragon Rage	Dragonbreath, Dragon Claw (TM02), Dragon Dance
Dragonbreath	Dragon Claw (TM02), Dragon Dance, Dragon Rage
Earthquake (TM26)	Eruption, Fissure
Endure	Destiny Bond, Endeavor, Eruption, Flail, Pain Split, Reversal
Fake Out	Arm Thrust, Faint Attack, Knock Off, Seismic Toss, Vital Throw
Fire Punch	Ice Punch, Thunderpunch
Focus Energy	Arm Thrust, Bone Rush, Brick Break (TM31), Cross Chop, Double-Edge, Dynamicpunch, Focus Punch (TM01), Headbutt, Karate Chop, Mega Kick, Mega Punch, Sky Uppercut, Take Down, Triple Kick

COMBO STANDBY MOVE	POSSIBLE TARGET MOVES
Growth	Absorb, Bullet Seed, Frenzy Plant, Giga Drain (TM19), Magical Leaf, Mega Drain, Petal Dance, Razor Leaf, Solarbeam (TM22), Vine Whip
Hail (TM07)	Blizzard (TM14), Powder Snow, Weather Ball
Harden	Double-Edge, Protect (TM17), Rollout, Tackle, Take Down
Horn Attack	Fury Attack, Horn Drill
Hypnosis	Dream Eater, Nightmare
Ice Punch	Fire Punch, Thunderpunch
Kinesis	Confusion, Future Sight, Psychic (TM29), Teleport
Leer	Bite, Faint Attack, Glare, Horn Attack, Scary Face, Scratch, Stomp, Tackle
Lock-On	Octazooka, Superpower, Thunder (TM25), Tri-Attack, Zap Cannon
Mean Look	Destiny Bond, Perish Song
Metal Sound	Metal Claw
Mind Reader	Dynamicpunch, Hi Jump Kick, Jump Kick, Mega Kick, Mega Punch, Submission, Superpower
Mud Sport	Mud-Slap, Water Gun, Water Sport
Mud-Slap	Mud Sport, Sand-Attack
Peck	Drill Peck, Fury Attack
Pound	Doubleslap, Faint Attack, Slam
Powder Snow	Blizzard (TM14)
Psychic (TM29)	Confusion, Future Sight, Kinesis, Teleport
Rage	Leer, Scary Face, Thrash
Rain Dance (TM18)	Bubble, Bubblebeam, Clamp, Crabhammer, Dive (HM08), Hydro Cannon, Hydro Pump, Muddy Water, Octazooka, Surf (HM03), Thunder (TM25), Water Gun, Water Pulse (TM03), Water Spout, Water Sport, Waterfall (HM07), Weather Ball, Whirlpool, Withdraw

COMBO STANDBY MOVE	POSSIBLE TARGET MOVES	COMBO STANDBY MOVE	POSSIBLE TARGET MOVES
Rest (TM44)	Sleep Talk, Snore	Sunny Day (TM11)	Blast Burn, Blaze Kick, Ember, Eruption, Fire Blast (TM38), Fire Punch, Fire Spin, Flamethrower (TM35), Flame Wheel, Heat Wave, Moonlight, Morning Sun, Overheat, Sacred Fire, Solarbeam (TM22), Synthesis, Weather Ball, Will-O-Wisp
Rock Throw	Rock Slide, Rock Tomb (TM39)		
Sand-Attack	Mud-Slap		
Sandstorm (TM37)	Mud-Slap, Sand-Attack, Sand Tomb, Weather Ball		
Scary Face	Bite, Crunch, Leer, Super Fang	Surf (HM03)	Dive (HM08)
Scratch	Fury Swipes, Slash	Sweet Scent	Poison Powder, Sleep Powder, Stun Spore
Sing	Perish Song, Refresh	Swords Dance	Crabhammer, Crush Claw, Cut (HM01), False Swipe, Fury Cutter, Slash
Sludge	Sludge Bomb (TM36)		
Sludge Bomb (TM36)	Sludge	Taunt (TM12)	Counter, Detect, Mirror Coat
Smog	Smokescreen	Thunderpunch	Fire Punch, Ice Punch
Softboiled	Egg Bomb	Vicegrip	Bind, Guillotine
String Shot	Spider Web	Water Sport	Mud Sport, Refresh, Water Gun
Stockpile	Spit Up, Swallow	Yawn	Rest (TM44), Slack Off

Complete Item Lists

You can find and collect hundreds of Items in *Pokémon Emerald*, from a variety of Poké Balls to precious stones that can be sold for extra P at Pokémarts. The following lists details their names and uses, as well as where you can find all of these Items. The lists have been sorted into eight different categories: TMs and HMs, Items, berries, Held Items, Key Items, Mail, Poké Balls, and Secret Base Decorations.

Technical Machines (TM) and Hidden Machines (HM)

Technical Machines and Hidden Machines are used to teach new moves to Pokémon. Not all moves can be taught to every Pokémon. See the Pokédex to find out what TMs and HMs are compatible with which Pokémon.

TMs AND HMs

TM/HM #	NAME	LOCATION	PRICE	TM/HM #	NAME	LOCATION	PRICE
HM01	Cut	Cutter's House in Rustboro City	—	TM10	Hidden Power	Slateport Market, Fortree City	P3,000
HM02	Fly	Route 119	—	TM11	Sunny Day	Scorched Slab—Route 120	—
HM03	Surf	Wally's House in Petalburg City	—	TM12	Taunt	Trick House	—
HM04	Strength	Rusturf Tunnel	—	TM13	Ice Beam	Mauville Game Corner (4,000 Coins)	—
HM05	Flash	Hiker inside the entrance to Granite Cave	—	TM14	Blizzard	Lilycove Dept. Store	P5,500
HM06	Rock Smash	Mauville City	—	TM15	Hyper Beam	Lilycove Dept. Store	P7,500
HM07	Waterfall	Cave of Origin	—	TM16	Light Screen	Lilycove Dept. Store	P3,000
HM08	Dive	Mossdeep City	—	TM17	Protect	Lilycove Dept. Store	P3,000
TM01	Focus Punch	Route 115	—	TM18	Rain Dance	Abandoned Ship	—
TM02	Dragon Claw	Meteor Falls	—	TM19	Giga Drain	Route 123	—
TM03	Water Pulse	Sootopolis City (Gym Leader battle)	—	TM20	Safeguard	Lilycove Dept. Store	P3,000
TM04	Calm Mind	Mossdeep City (Gym Leader battle)	—	TM21	Frustration	Pacifidlog Town	—
TM05	Roar	Route 114	—	TM22	Solarbeam	Safari Park	—
TM06	Toxic	Fiery Path	—	TM23	Iron Tail	Meteor Falls	—
TM07	Hail	Shoal Cave	—	TM24	Thunderbolt	Mauville Game Corner (4,000 Coins)	—
TM08	Bulk Up	Dewford Town (Gym Leader battle)	—	TM25	Thunder	Lilycove Dept. Store	P5,500
TM09	Bullet Seed	Route 104	—	TM26	Earthquake	Seafloor Cavern	—

TMs AND HMs CONTINUED

TM/HM #	NAME	LOCATION	PRICE		TM/HM #	NAME	LOCATION	PRICE
TM27	Return	Fallarbor Town, Pacifidlog Town	—		TM39	Rock Tomb	Rustboro City (Gym Leader battle)	—
TM28	Dig	Route 114	—		TM40	Aerial Ace	Fortree City (Gym Leader battle)	—
TM29	Psychic	Mauville Game Corner (3,500 Coins)	—		TM41	Torment	Slateport City	—
TM30	Shadow Ball	Mt. Pyre	—		TM42	Façade	Petalburg City (Gym Leader battle)	—
TM31	Brick Break	Sootopolis City	—		TM43	Secret Power	Route 111, Slateport Market	₽3,000
TM32	Double Team	Mauville Game Corner (1,500 Coins)	—		TM44	Rest	Lilycove City	—
TM33	Reflect	Lilycove Dept. Store	₽3,000		TM45	Attract	Verdanturf Town	—
TM34	Shock Wave	Mauville City (Gym Leader battle)	—		TM46	Thief	Slateport City	—
TM35	Flamethrower	Mauville Game Corner (4,000 Coins)	—		TM47	Steel Wing	Granite Cave	—
TM36	Sludge Bomb	Dewford Town	—		TM48	Skill Swap	Mt. Pyre	—
TM37	Sandstorm	Desert (Route 111)	—		TM49	Snatch	S.S. *Tidal* (after end of game)	—
TM38	Fire Blast	Lilycove Dept. Store	₽5,500		TM50	Overheat	Lavaridge Town (Gym Leader battle)	—

Items

Items are objects you pick up while adventuring across Hoenn. These include recovery Items that restore HP, Items you can sell for ₽, and Items that affect Pokémon evolution.

ITEM NAME	DESCRIPTION	LOCATION	PRICE
Antidote	Cures a Pokémon of the Poison status.	Pokémarts in towns and cities except Mossdeep City, Ever Grande City, and Sootopolis City	₽100
Awakening	Cures a Pokémon of the Sleep status.	Pokémarts in towns and cities except Sootopolis City, Ever Grande City, and Mossdeep City	₽250
Big Pearl	Sell this in a shop to make lots of money!	Sell at any shop	—
Black Flute	Flute made of glass. Repels wild Pokémon.	Route 113 (Glass Workshop)	—
Blue Flute	Flute made of glass. Awakens Sleeping Pokémon.	Route 113 (Glass Workshop)	—
Blue Shard	Piece of an ancient tool. Give to the Treasure Diver on Route 124.	Route 124 and wild Pokémon	—
Burn Heal	Heals the Burn condition.	Pokémarts in Lavaridge Town, Verdanturf Town, and Lilycove City	₽250
Calcium	Raises your Pokémon's Special Attack stat.	Select shops, Slateport City Open Market, and found outside of battle	₽9,800
Carbos	Raises your Pokémon's Speed stat.	Select shops, Slateport City Open Market, and found outside of battle	₽9,800
Dire Hit	Makes it easier to perform a Critical Hit. Can be used only in battle.	Pokémarts in Mauville City, Fallarbor Town, and Lilycove City	₽650
Elixir	Recovers up to 10 PP of all skills.	Route 119 and Route 123	—
Energy Root	Recovers up to 200 HP, but is bitter. Pokémon dislike this medication.	Herb Shop in Lavaridge Town	₽800
Energypowder	Recovers up to 50 HP, but is bitter. Pokémon dislike this medication.	Herb Shop in Lavaridge Town	₽500
Escape Rope	Lets you escape from caves and other dungeon-like areas. Returns you to the dungeon's entrance.	Pokémarts in towns and cities except Fortree City, Sootopolis City, and Ever Grande City	₽550
Ether	Recovers up to 10 PP of one skill.	Petalburg Woods, Petalburg City, and Route 116	—
Fire Stone	Use to evolve certain Pokémon.	Fiery Path	—
Fluffy Tail	Lets you escape from any battle with a wild Pokémon.	Pokémarts in Verdanturf Town and Lilycove City	₽1,000
Fresh Water	Recovers up to 50 HP.	Lilycove City Department Store	₽200
Full Heal	Recovers all status abnormalities.	Pokémarts in Lilycove City, Mossdeep City, Sootopolis City, and Ever Grande City	₽600
Full Restore	Fully restores HP and all status abnormalities.	Pokémarts in Ever Grande City, Team Magma Hideout, and Victory Road	₽3,000
Green Shard	Piece of an ancient tool. Give to the Treasure Diver on Route 124.	Route 126 and wild Relicanth	—
Guard Spec.	Can be used only during battle. Makes it so your Pokémon's abilities cannot be lowered.	Pokémarts in Mauville City, Fallarbor Town, and Lilycove City	₽700
Heal Powder	Recovers all status abnormalities, but it is bitter. Pokémon dislike this medication.	Herb Shop in Lavaridge Town	₽450
Heart Scale	A popular treasure. Give to the Move Tutor in Fallarbor Town for his services.	Route 124, Route 126, and wild Pokémon	—
HP Up	Raises the base figure of your Pokémon's Hit Points.	Available at Lilycove City, Slateport City Open Market, and found outside of battle	₽9,800
Hyper Potion	Recovers up to 200 HP.	Pokémarts in Fortree City, Lilycove City, Mossdeep City, and Sootopolis City	₽1,200

ITEM NAME	DESCRIPTION	LOCATION	PRICE
Ice Heal	Cures the Frozen status.	Pokémarts in Verdanturf Town and Lilycove City	₽250
Iron	Raises your Pokémon's Defense stat.	Lilycove City, Slateport City Open Market, and found outside of battle	₽9,800
Lava Cookie	Cures a Pokémon of all status abnormalities.	Mt. Chimney	₽200
Leaf Stone	Used to evolve certain Pokémon.	Route 119	—
Lemonade	Recovers up to 80 HP.	Lilycove City Department Store	₽350
Max Elixir	Recovers the PP of all skills.	Team Magma Hideout, Route 123, and Victory Road	—
Max Ether	Recovers the PP of one skill.	Rusturf Tunnel, Route 113, and Mt. Pyre	—
Max Potion	Recovers a Pokémon's HP entirely.	Pokémart in Ever Grande City	₽2,500
Max Repel	This repels weaker Pokémon for up to 250 steps.	Pokémarts in Lilycove City, Mossdeep City, Sootopolis City, and Ever Grande City	₽700
Max Revive	Recovers the Pokémon from the Fainted status; recovers all HP.	Petalburg City, Team Magma Hideout, Route 133, and Safari Park	—
Moon Stone	Used to evolve certain Pokémon.	Meteor Falls and wild Pokémon	—
Nugget	Sell this in a shop to make lots of money!	Route 112, Route 120, and Team Magma Hideout	—
Paralyz Heal	Heals the Paralyze condition.	Pokémarts in Oldale Town, Petalburg City, Rustboro City, Slateport City, and Lilycove City	₽200
Pearl	Sell at a store.	All routes	—
Potion	Recovers up to 20 HP.	Pokémarts in towns and cities except Fortree City, Mossdeep City, Sootopolis City, and Ever Grande City	₽300
PP Max	Raises the base amount of a skill's PP to the max.	Trick House	—
PP Up	Raises the base amount of a skill's PP.	Lilycove City, Slateport City Open Market, and found outside of battle	—
Protein	Raises your Pokémon's Attack stat.	Lilycove City, Slateport City Open Market, and found outside of battle.	₽9,800
Rare Candy	Raises your Pokémon's Level by one	Granite Cave, Route 110, Team Magma Hideout, Trick House, and hidden outside of battle	—
Red Flute	Flute made of glass. Heals Pokémon of the Attract status.	Route 113 (Glass Workshop)	—
Red Shard	Piece of an ancient tool. Give to the Treasure Diver on Route 124.	Route 124 and wild Pokémon	—
Repel	Repels weaker Pokémon for about 100 steps.	Pokémarts in towns and cities except Fortree City, Mossdeep City, Sootopolis City, and Ever Grande City	₽350
Revival Herb	Recovers a Pokémon from the Fainted status. Pokémon dislike this medication.	Herb Shop in Lavaridge Town	₽2,800
Revive	Recovers the Pokémon from the Fainted status and recovers half of its HP.	Pokémarts in Lavaridge Town, Fortree City, Lilycove City, Mossdeep City, Sootopolis City, and Ever Grande City	₽1,500
Shoal Salt	Special ingredient used for making a Shell Bell that is found only in the Shoal Cave.	Shoal Cave	—
Shoal Shell	Special ingredient used for making a Shell Bell that is found only in the Shoal Cave.	Shoal Cave	—
Soda Pop	Recovers up to 60 HP.	Lilycove City Department Store and Route 109	₽300
Star Piece	Sell in a store.	Route 133 and wild Pokémon	—
Stardust	Sell in a store.	Outside of battle and wild Pokémon	—
Sun Stone	Used to evolve certain Pokémon.	Mossdeep City and wild Pokémon	—
Super Potion	Recovers up to 50 HP.	Pokémarts in Rustboro City, Slateport City, Mauville City, and Lilycove City	₽700
Super Repel	This repels weaker Pokémon for up to 200 steps.	Pokémarts in Fallarbor Town, Lavaridge Town, Fortree City, and Lilycove City	₽500
Thunderstone	Used to evolve certain Pokémon.	New Mauville	—
Tinymushroom	Sell in a store.	Petalburg Woods	—
Water Stone	Used to evolve certain Pokémon.	Abandoned Ship	—
White Flute	Flute made of glass. Attracts wild Pokémon.	Route 113 (Glass Workshop)	—
X Accuracy	Raises the accuracy of skills. Can be used only in battle.	Pokémarts in Mauville City and Lilycove City	₽950
X Attack	Raises the Pokémon's Attack. Can be used only in battle.	Pokémarts in Petalburg City, Rustboro City, Mauville City, Fallarbor Town, Sootopolis City, and Lilycove City	₽500
X Defend	Raises a Pokémon's Defense. Can be used only during battles.	Pokémarts in Petalburg City, Rustboro City, Mauville City, Fallarbor Town, Sootopolis City, and Lilycove City	₽550
X Special	Increases a Pokémon's Special Attack. Can be used only during battle.	Pokémarts in Lilycove City, Verdanturf Town, and Fallarbor Town	₽350
X Speed	Increases a Pokémon's Speed. Can be used only during battle.	Pokémarts in Rustoboro City, Mauville City, Fallarbor Town, Lavaridge Town, and Lilycove City	₽350
Yellow Flute	Flute made of glass. Heals Confused Pokémon.	Route 113 (Glass Workshop)	—
Yellow Shard	Piece of an ancient tool. Give to the Treasure Diver on Route 124.	Route 126 and wild Pokémon	—
Zinc	Raises your Pokémon's Special Defense stat.	Lilycove City, Slateport City Open Market, and found outside of battle	₽9,800

Berries

Berries grow all over Hoenn. Many can be used as recovery Items for your Pokémon, curing condition abnormalities or restoring HP. You can also use them to create PokéBlocks.

NO.	NAME	DESCRIPTION	LOCATION
1	Cheri Berry	Cures Paralysis.	Berry Master's House; several routes, including Route 103 and Route 104
2	Chesto Berry	Awakens Sleeping Pokémon.	Berry Master's House; several routes, including Route 116 and Route 121
3	Pecha Berry	Cures Poisoned Pokémon.	Several routes, including Route 102, Route 104, Route 112, and Route 120
4	Rawst Berry	Cures Burned Pokémon.	Berry Master's House; several routes, including Route 112 and Route 121
5	Aspear Berry	Cures Frozen Pokémon.	Berry Master's House; several routes, including Route 120 and Route 121
6	Leppa Berry	Restores PP to a move when it reaches 0.	Several routes, including Route 103, Route 104, Route 119, and Route 123
7	Oran Berry	Recovers 10 HP. When held by a Pokémon, this Item is used when the Pokémon's HP reaches the halfway mark.	Berry Master's House; several routes, including Route 102 and Route 104
8	Persim Berry	Cures Confused Pokémon.	Berry Master's House; several routes, including Route 114 and Route 121
9	Lum Berry	Cures a Pokémon of any status abnormality.	Berry Master's House
10	Sitrus Berry	Recovers 30 HP. When held by a Pokémon, this Item is used when the Pokémon's HP reaches the halfway mark.	Berry Master's House; several routes, including Route 118, Route 119
11	Figy Berry	When held by a Pokémon, this Item is used to recover HP when the Pokémon's HP reaches the halfway mark. Pokémon dislike the spicy taste and become Confused.	Several routes, including Route 120 and Sootopolis City
12	Wiki Berry	When held by a Pokémon, this Item is used to recover HP when the Pokémon's HP reaches the halfway mark. Pokémon dislike the dry taste and become Confused.	Route 120
13	Mago Berry	When held by a Pokémon, this Item is used to recover HP when the Pokémon's HP reaches the halfway mark. Pokémon dislike the sweet taste and become Confused.	Route 120
14	Aguav Berry	When held by a Pokémon, this Item is used to recover HP when the Pokémon's HP reaches the halfway mark. Pokémon dislike the bitter taste and become Confused. Cures Sleep state.	Route 120
15	Iapapa Berry	When held by a Pokémon, this Item is used to recover HP when the Pokémon's HP reaches the halfway mark. Pokémon dislike the sour taste and become Confused.	Route 120 and Sootopolis City
16	Razz Berry	Used for planting and PokéBlocks. Does not have any special Effects.	Several routes, including Route 111 and Route 120
17	Bluk Berry	Used for planting and PokéBlocks. Does not have any special Effects.	Route 115
18	Nanab Berry	Used for planting and PokéBlocks. Does not have any special Effects.	Several routes, including Route 110, Route 120, and Route 121
19	Wepear Berry	Used for planting and PokéBlocks. Does not have any special Effects.	Several routes, including Route 117 and Route 120
20	Pinap Berry	Used for planting and PokéBlocks. Does not have any special Effects.	Several routes, including Route 116 and Route 120
21	Pomeg Berry	Used for planting and PokéBlocks. Does not have any special Effects.	Berry Master's House; several routes, including Route 119 and Route 123
22	Kelpsy Berry	Used for planting and PokéBlocks. Does not have any special Effects.	Berry Master's House; several routes, including Route 115
23	Qualot Berry	Used for planting and PokéBlocks. Does not have any special Effects.	Berry Master's House; several routes, including Route 123
24	Hondew Berry	Used for planting and PokéBlocks. Does not have any special Effects.	Berry Master's House; several routes, including Route 119
25	Grepa Berry	Used for planting and PokéBlocks. Does not have any special Effects.	Berry Master's House; several routes, including Route 123
26	Tamato Berry	Used for planting and PokéBlocks. Does not have any special Effects.	Berry Master's House
27	Cornn Berry	Used for planting and PokéBlocks. Does not have any special Effects.	Berry Master's House
28	Magost Berry	Used for planting and PokéBlocks. Does not have any special Effects.	Berry Master's House
29	Rabuta Berry	Used for planting and PokéBlocks. Does not have any special Effects.	Berry Master's House
30	Nomel Berry	Used for planting and PokéBlocks. Does not have any special Effects.	Berry Master's House
31	Spelon Berry	Used for planting and PokéBlocks. Does not have any special Effects.	Berry Master's House
32	Pamtre Berry	Used for planting and PokéBlocks. Does not have any special Effects.	Berry Master's House
33	Watmel Berry	Used for planting and PokéBlocks. Does not have any special Effects.	Berry Master's House
34	Durin Berry	Used for planting and PokéBlocks. Does not have any special Effects.	Berry Master's House
35	Belue Berry	Used for planting and PokéBlocks. Does not have any special Effects.	Berry Master's House
36	Liechi Berry	When held by a Pokémon, it raises its Attack by one when the Pokémon's HP are low.	Mirage Island
37	Lansat Berry	When HP is low, it raises Accuracy.	Battle Frontier
38	Snarf Berry	Ability to raise multiple stats, including Attack or Defense.	Battle Frontier

Held Items

Held Items are given to Pokémon. They often have an effect on battle performance, but some recover HP or increase the amount of ₽ earned from a battle.

ITEM NAME	DESCRIPTION	LOCATION
Amulet Coin	When the Pokémon to whom it is attached is used in a Trainer battle, you win twice the amount of money.	Littleroot Town
Black Belt	When held by a Pokémon, it increases the strength of Fighting-type Moves.	Route 115
Blackglasses	When held by a Pokémon, it increases the strength of Dark-type Moves.	Route 116
Blue Scarf	When held by a Pokémon, this Item raises its Beauty.	Slateport City (Pokémon Fan Club)
Bright Powder	When held by a Pokémon, it Confuses the enemy with light and lowers its Accuracy.	Battle Tower Prize
Charcoal	When held by a Pokémon, this increases the strength of Fire-type Moves.	Lavaridge Town
Choice Band	When you first use a move, its strength is increased 1.5x, but you can use only that move until the Pokémon is replaced with another.	Battle Tower Prize
Cleanse Tag	When held by a Pokémon, this decreases the chance of encountering Wild Pokémon.	Mt. Pyre
Deepseascale	When held by Clamperl, this doubles its Special Defense. Also necessary for evolving that Pokémon through trading.	Slateport City
Deepseatooth	When held by Clamperl, this doubles its Special Attack. Also necessary for evolving that Pokémon through trading.	Slateport City
Dragon Fang	When held by a Pokémon that can learn and use Dragon-type Moves, this increases the Dragon-type Moves' strength.	Meteor Falls
Dragon Scale	When attached to certain Pokémon, this Item causes them to evolve when traded.	Wild Pokémon
Everstone	A rare stone used to keep the Pokémon it's attached to from evolving.	Found attached to wild Geodude and Graveler
Exp. Share	When held by a Pokémon, it earns half of the experience points given out in battle, even if the Pokémon does not participate.	Rustboro City (Devon Corporation)
Focus Band	When held by a Pokémon, this occasionally prevents the Pokémon from fainting by giving it 1 HP.	Shoal Cave
Green Scarf	When held by a Pokémon, this Item raises its Smartness.	Slateport City (Pokémon Fan Club)
Hard Stone	When held by a Pokémon, this increases the strength of Rock-type Moves.	Trick House; wild Aron and Lairon
King's Rock	When held by a Pokémon, it causes the opponent Pokémon to Flinch when you use a damage-inflicting attack.	Mossdeep City and wild Hariyama
Lax Incense	When held by a Pokémon, this Item lowers the accuracy of the opponent's moves. Wobbuffet can produce an Egg when in Pokémon Day Care	Mt. Pyre
Leftovers	When held by a Pokémon, this recovers HP during battle.	Battle Tower Prize
Light Ball	When held by Pikachu, it doubles the strength of its Special Attacks.	Wild Pokémon
Macho Brace	Makes it easier to raise your Pokémon's stats, but it halves the Pokémon's Speed.	Route 111 (the Winstrate House)
Magnet	When held by a Pokémon, this increases the strength of Electric-type Moves.	Trick House
Mental Herb	When held by a Pokémon, this prevents it from becoming Attracted to its opponent.	Fortree City
Metal Coat	When held by a Pokémon, this raises the strength of Steel-type Moves.	Wild Pokémon
Metal Power	Increases Defense by half.	Wild Ditto
Miracle Seed	When held by a Pokémon, this strengthens Grass-type Skills.	Petalburg Woods
Mystic Water	When held by a Pokémon, this increases the strength of Water-type Moves.	Held by the Castform you get at the Weather Institute
Nevermeltice	When held by a Pokémon, this increases the strength of Ice-type Moves.	Shoal Cave
Pink Scarf	When held by a Pokémon, this Item raises its Cuteness.	Slateport City (Pokémon Fan Club)
Poison Barb	When held by a Pokémon, this increases the strength of Poison-type Moves.	Attached to wild Pokémon such as wild Cacnea
Quick Claw	When held by a Pokémon, it allows the Pokémon an occasional pre-emptive Attack.	Rustboro City and wild Pokémon
Red Scarf	When held by a Pokémon, this Item raises its Coolness.	Slateport City (Pokémon Fan Club)
Scope Lens	When held by a Pokémon, this makes it easier to perform a Critical Hit.	Battle Tower Prize
Sea Incense	When held by a Pokémon, this Item raises the strength of Water-type Moves.	Mt. Pyre
Sharp Beak	When held by a Pokémon, this increases the strength of Flying-type Moves.	Wild Pokémon
Shell Bell	When held by a Pokémon, the Pokémon recovers HP equal to 1/8 of the damage its moves deal.	Shoal Cave
Silk Scarf	When held by a Pokémon, this increases the strength of Normal-type Moves.	Dewford Town
Silverpowder	When held by a Pokémon, it increases the strength of Bug-type Moves.	Route 120
Smoke Ball	When held by a Pokémon, it allows you to flee from wild Pokémon.	Trick House and wild Pokémon
Soft Sand	When held by a Pokémon, this raises the strength of Ground-type Moves.	Route 109 and wild Pokémon
Soothe Bell	When held by a Pokémon, this Item makes it become attached to you more easily.	Slateport City (Pokémon Fan Club)

ITEM NAME	DESCRIPTION	LOCATION
Soul Dew	Ability to Raise Special Attack and Special Defense to certain Pokémon.	Southern Island
Spell Tag	When held by a Pokémon, this increases the strength of Ghost-type Moves.	Attached to wild Pokémon such as wild Duskull and Dusclops.
Twistedspoon	When held by a Pokémon, this increases the strength of Psychic-type Moves.	Attached to wild Pokémon
White Herb	When held by a Pokémon, this Item returns lowered stats to their original level.	Route 104
Yellow Scarf	When held by a Pokémon, this Item raises its Toughness.	Slateport City (Pokémon Fan Club)

Key Items

Key Items directly affect the story in *Pokémon Emerald*, such as the Basement Key, which is required to open the New Mauville power plant, or the Super Rod, which catches super-elusive Water-type Pokémon.

ITEM NAME	DESCRIPTION	LOCATION
Acro Bike	A bike built for doing tricks.	Rydel's Cycles in Mauville City
Basement Key	A key that opens the door to the underground electrical plant called New Mauville.	Mauville City
Claw Fossil	A mysterious fossil of an ancient Pokémon hidden in the desert; turns into Anorith.	Desert on Route 111
Coin Case	Holds up to 9,999 Coins.	Trade a piece of Harbor Mail to a woman in Mauville City
Contest Pass	A card that allows you to enter your Pokémon in Pokémon Contests.	Contest Hall in Verdanturf Town
Devon Goods	A package of miscellaneous parts from the Devon Corporation that needs to be delivered to Capt. Stern in Slateport City.	Rescue from Team Aqua grunt in Rusturf Tunnel
Devon Scope	A new gadget that allows you to uncover invisible Pokémon.	Get from Steven on Route 120
Go-Goggles	Goggles that allow the wearer to see clearly in a sandstorm.	Get from Brendan/May in Lavaridge Town
Good Rod	Use this to fish for Pokémon. Allows you to capture a higher level of Pokémon than the Old Rod.	Route 118
Itemfinder	Points out fallen Items in the area with an alarming sound.	Get from Brendan/May on Route 110
Letter	A letter from the president of the Devon Corporation to Steven.	Devon Corporation in Rustboro City
Mach Bike	A bike built for speed.	Rydel's Cycles in Mauville City
Magma Emblem	Token held by Team Magma members.	Mt. Pyre
Meteorite	Meteorite that fell from the sky.	Meteor Falls
Mystery Egg	A mysterious egg holding the baby Wynaut.	Lavaridge Town
Old Rod	Tool for catching some Water-type Pokémon.	Dewford Town
PokéBlock Case	A case used for holding PokéBlocks.	Contest Hall in Slateport City
Pokédex	A PDA in which the secrets of the Pokémon you've seen and captured are recorded.	Prof. Birch in Oldale Town
PokéNav	A new type of PDA that records meetings with Pokémon Trainers and keeps track of your Pokémon's Condition. Also contains a map of the Hoenn region.	Devon Corporation in Rustboro City
Powder Bag	A bag used to keep berry powder.	Stateport City
Rm. 1 Key	Key used to unlock a locked stateroom on the Abandoned Ship.	Abandoned Ship
Rm. 2 Key	Key used to unlock a locked stateroom on the Abandoned Ship.	Abandoned Ship
Rm. 4 Key	Key used to unlock a locked stateroom on the Abandoned Ship.	Abandoned Ship
Rm. 6 Key	Key used to unlock a locked stateroom on the Abandoned Ship.	Abandoned Ship
Root Fossil	A mysterious fossil of an ancient Pokémon hidden in the desert; turns into Lileep.	Desert on Route 111
Running Shoes	Special sneakers that allow you to run fast when you press Ⓑ.	Get from Mom in Oldale Town
S.S. Ticket	Use this ticket to ride the S.S. *Tidal* to the Battle Tower.	Get from Dad in Oldale Town
Scanner	A scanner that Capt. Stern needs salvaged from the Abandoned Ship.	Abandoned Ship
Soot Sack	A large sack that holds the ash covering the ground and long grass on Route 113. When it is full, take the ashes to the Glass Workshop to be turned into glass Items.	Glass Workshop on Route 113
Storage Key	A key to the locked storage room on the Abandoned Ship.	Abandoned Ship
Super Rod	A Fishing Rod that allows you to capture stronger Water-type Pokémon.	Mossdeep City
Wailmer Pail	A watering pail used to water recently planted berries and seedlings. Holds an infinite supply of water.	Pretty Petal Flower Shop on Route 104

Mail

Many towns have unique stationery that is desired by people all over Hoenn. You never know who will want special paper from a faraway town.

NAME	DESCRIPTION	LOCATION	PRICE
Bead Mail	Stationery printed with an image of the Pokémon you are holding.	Trick House	—
Glitter Mail	Stationery with a Pikachu design.	Trick House	—
Harbor Mail	Stationery with a Wingull design.	Pokémart in Slateport City, Trick House	₽50
Mech Mail	Stationery with a Magnemite design.	Lilycove City Department Store, Trick House	₽50
Orange Mail	Stationery with a Zigzagoon design.	Pokémart in Petalburg City, Trick House	₽50
Retro Mail	Stationery with three Pokémon designs on it.	Battle Frontier	—
Shadow Mail	Stationery with a Duskull design.	Pokémart in Sootopolis City, Trick House	₽50
Tropic Mail	Stationery with a Bellossom design.	Trick House	—
Wave Mail	Stationery with a Wailmer design.	Lilycove City Department Store, Trick House	₽50
Wood Mail	Stationery with a Slakoth design.	Pokémart in Fortree City, Trick House	₽50

Poké Balls

The are essential tools for Pokémon Trainers. Different Poké Balls have different capture success rates. Chances are, the more expensive the Poké Ball, the greater your chances of catching a Pokémon with it.

NAME	DESCRIPTION	LOCATION	PRICE
Poké Ball	A tool for catching Pokémon.	Pokémarts in several towns and cities, including Oldale Town, Petalburg City, Rustboro City, and Slateport City	₽200
Great Ball	Makes it easier to capture Pokémon than a Poké Ball.	Pokémarts in several towns and cities, including Slateport City, Mauville City, Verdanturf Town, and Fallarbor Town	₽600
Ultra Ball	Makes it easier to capture Pokémon than a Great Ball.	Pokémarts in several towns and cities, including Fortree City, Lilycove City, Mossdeep City, and Sootopolis City	₽1,200
Master Ball	The ultimate Poké Ball. It allows you to catch a Pokémon regardless of strength, level, or power.	Pokémon Lottery at the Lilycove Dept. Store and Team Magma Hideout	—
Dive Ball	A special Poké Ball that makes it easier to catch a Pokémon underwater.	Pokémarts in Mossdeep City and the Abandoned Ship	₽1,000
Luxury Ball	A luxurious Poké Ball that makes the Pokémon caught with it like you more.	Abandoned Ship	—
Nest Ball	A special Poké Ball that makes it easier to capture weaker Pokémon.	Pokémarts in Verdanturf Town, Route 120, and Team Magma Hideout	₽1,000
Net Ball	A special Poké Ball that makes it easier to capture Bug- and Water-type Pokémon.	Pokémart in Mossdeep City	₽1,000
Premier Ball	A special Poké Ball commemorating an event at the Devon Corporation.	After purchase of 10th Poké Ball; Rustboro City	—
Repeat Ball	A special Poké Ball that makes it easier to capture Pokémon you've caught before.	Rustboro City, Route 116	₽1,000
Safari Ball	A special Poké Ball used to capture Pokémon in the Safari Park on Route 121.	Safari Park (30 for ₽500)	—
Timer Ball	A special Poké Ball that makes it easier to capture a Pokémon the longer your battle with it lasts.	Rustboro City and Trick House	₽1,000

Secret Base Decorations

After you decide on a little pocket of Hoenn to call your own, personalize it with these colorful Items. The only limit to interior decorating is your imagination, so arrange your personal space to your own liking. Besides, you never know who may drop by.

ITEM NAME	LOCATION	PRICE (BP)	ITEM NAME	LOCATION	PRICE (BP)
A Note Mat	Slateport City Market (Secret Power Club Store)	500	Marill Doll	Lilycove City Department Store, Slateport City Market	3,000
Attract Mat	Lilycove City Department Store	4,000	Meowth Doll	Battle Frontier	48
Azurill Doll	Lilycove City Department Store, Slateport City Market	3,000	Mud Ball	Lilycove City Department Store (Clear-Out Sale)	200
B Note Mat	Slateport City Market (Secret Power Club Store)	500	Mudkip Doll	Mauville Game Corner (1,000 Coins)	—
Ball Cushion	Lilycove City Department Store	2,000	Pichu Doll	Lilycove City Department Store	3,000
Ball Poster	Lilycove City Department Store	1,000	Pika Cushion	Lilycove City Department Store	2,000
Baltoy Doll	Lilycove City Department Store	3,000	Pika Poster	Lilycove City Department Store	1,500
Big Plant	Pretty Petal Flower Shop on Route 104	5,000	Pikachu Doll	Lilycove City Department Store	3,000
Blastoise Doll	Battle Frontier	256	Pokémon Chair	Fortree City Shop	2,000
Blue Balloon	Slateport City Market (Secret Power Club Store)	500	Pokémon Desk	Fortree City Shop	3,000
Blue Brick	Slateport City Market (Secret Power Club Store)	500	Powder Snow Mat	Lilycove City Department Store	4,000
Blue Poster	Lilycove City Department Store	1,000	Pretty Chair	Glass Workshop on Route 113	—
Blue Tent	Trick House	—	Pretty Desk	Glass Workshop on Route 113	—
Breakable Door	Lilycove City Department Store (Clear-Out Sale)	3,000	Pretty Plant	Pretty Petal Flower Shop on Route 104	3,000
Brick Chair	Fortree City Shop	2,000	Ragged Chair	Fortree City Shop	2,000
Brick Desk	Fortree City Shop	9,000	Ragged Desk	Fortree City Shop	6,000
C High Note Mat	Slateport City Market (Secret Power Club Store)	500	Red Balloon	Slateport City Market (Secret Power Club Store)	500
C Low Note Mat	Slateport City Market (Secret Power Club Store)	500	Red Brick	Slateport City Market (Secret Power Club Store)	500
Camp Chair	Fortree City Shop	2,000	Red Plant	Pretty Petal Flower Shop on Route 104	3,000
Camp Desk	Fortree City Shop	9,000	Red Poster	Lilycove City Department Store	1,000
Charizard Doll	Battle Frontier	256	Red Tent	Trick House	—
Chikorita Doll	Battle Frontier	80	Rhydon Doll	Lilycove City Department Store (Clear-Out Sale)	10,000
Clefable Doll	Battle Frontier	48	Round Cushion	Lilycove City Department Store	2,000
Colorful Plant	Pretty Petal Flower Shop on Route 104	5,000	Round TV	Lilycove City Department Store (Clear-Out Sale)	15,000
Comfort Chair	Fortree City Shop	2,000	Sand Ornament	Lilycove City Department Store (Clear-Out Sale)	3,000
Comfort Desk	Fortree City Shop	6,000	Sea Poster	Lilycove City Department Store	1,500
Cute Poster	Lilycove City Department Store	1,000	Seedot Doll	Lanette's House on Route 114	—
Cute TV	Lilycove City Department Store (Clear-Out Sale)	15,000	Silver Shield	Battle Tower	—
Cyndaquil Doll	Battle Frontier	80	Skitty Doll	Lilycove City Department Store, Slateport City Market	3,000
D Note Mat	Slateport City Market (Secret Power Club Store)	500	Sky Poster	Lilycove City Department Store	1,500
Diamond Cushion	Lilycove City Department Store	2,000	Slide	Lilycove City Department Store (Clear-Out Sale)	8,000
Ditto Doll	Battle Frontier	48	Small Chair	Fortree City Shop	2,000
Duskull Doll	Lilycove City Department Store	3,000	Small Desk	Fortree City Shop	3,000
E Note Mat	Slateport City Market (Secret Power Club Store)	500	Smoochum Doll	Battle Frontier	32
F Note Mat	Slateport City Market (Secret Power Club Store)	500	Snorlax Doll	Battle Frontier	128
Fence Length	Lilycove City Department Store (Clear-Out Sale)	500	Solid Board	Lilycove City Department Store (Clear-Out Sale)	3,000
Fence Width	Lilycove City Department Store (Clear-Out Sale)	500	Spikes Mat	Lilycove City Department Store	4,000
Fire Blast Mat	Lilycove City Department Store	4,000	Spin Cushion	Lilycove City Department Store	2,000
Fire Cushion	Lilycove City Department Store	2,000	Spin Mat	Lilycove City Department Store	2,000
Fissure Mat	Lilycove City Department Store	4,000	Stand	Lilycove City Department Store (Clear-Out Sale)	7,000
G Note Mat	Slateport City Market (Secret Power Club Store)	500	Surf Mat	Lilycove City Department Store	4,000
Glass Ornament	Lilycove Museum	—	Swablu Doll	Lilycove City Department Store	3,000
Glitter Mat	Lilycove City Department Store	2,000	Thunder Mat	Lilycove City Department Store	4,000
Gold Shield	Battle Frontier	—	Tire	Lilycove City Department Store (Clear-Out Sale)	800
Gorgeous Plant	Pretty Petal Flower Shop on Route 104	5,000	Togepi Doll	Battle Frontier	48
Grass Cushion	Lilycove City Department Store	2,000	Torchic Doll	Mauville Game Corner (1,000 Coins)	—
Green Poster	Lilycove City Department Store	1,000	Totodile Doll	Battle Frontier	80
Gulpin Doll	Lilycove City Department Store	3,000	Treecko Doll	Mauville Game Corner (1,000 Coins)	—
Hard Chair	Fortree City Shop	2,000	Tropical Plant	Pretty Petal Flower Shop on Route 104	3,000
Hard Desk	Fortree City Shop	9,000	TV	Lilycove City Department Store (Clear-Out Sale)	12,000
Heavy Chair	Fortree City Shop	2,000	Venusaur Doll	Battle Frontier	256
Heavy Desk	Fortree City Shop	6,000	Wailmer Doll	Lilycove City Department Store (Clear-Out Sale) and Sootopolis City	10,000
Jigglypuff Doll	Lilycove City Department Store	3,000			
Jump Mat	Lilycove City Department Store	2,000	Water Cushion	Lilycove City Department Store	2,000
Kecleon Doll	Lilycove City Department Store	3,000	Wynaut Doll	Lilycove City Department Store	3,000
Kiss Poster	Battle Frontier	16	Yellow Balloon	Slateport City Market (Secret Power Club Store)	500
Long Poster	Lilycove City Department Store	1,500	Yellow Brick	Slateport City Market (Secret Power Club Store)	500
Lotad Doll	Lanette's House on Route 114	—	Zigzag Cushion	Lilycove City Department Store	2,000

POKéMON

Pokédex Collector's Edition

NOW AVAILABLE

- Exclusive Poster Inside

- Gigantic Pokédex with complete, up-to-date stats for all 380 + 6 Pokémon

- Interview with Pokémon Director Junichi Masuda

- Huge appendix featuring detailed info on moves, HMs, TMs, Berries, and more

- Mini-walkthroughs for *Pokémon Ruby* and *Pokémon Sapphire*, *Pokémon FireRed* and *Pokémon LeafGreen*, and *Pokémon Colosseum*

PRIMA
GAMES